Connected Lives

Ozodi Thomas Osuji, Ph.D.

ISBN 978-1-955156-94-3 (paperback)
ISBN 978-1-955156-95-0 (hardcover)
ISBN 978-1-955156-96-7 (digital)

Copyright © 2021 by Ozodi Thomas Osuji, Ph.D.

All rights reserved. No part of this publication may be reproduced, distributed, or transmitted in any form or by any means, including photocopying, recording, or other electronic or mechanical methods without the prior written permission of the publisher. For permission requests, solicit the publisher via the address below.

Rushmore Press LLC
1 800 460 9188
www.rushmorepress.com

Printed in the United States of America

INTRODUCTION

WHERE AM I LEADING ME AND PEOPLE TO?

I AM LEADING ME AND PEOPLE TO KNOW THAT THE ONLY PROBLEM THEY HAVE IS THEIR PATTERN OF THINKING AND THAT THEY MAKE SURE TO HAVE LOVE-BASED THINKING, WHICH MEANS REMOVING THE EGO AND COMPLETELY SEPARATING FROM IT TO EXPERIENCE THE LOVE AND UNION THAT IS ALREADY IN THEM.

CHANGE YOUR PATTERN OF THINKING AND YOU WILL CHANGE YOUR PERSONALITY AND BEHAVIOR.

Personality, self-concept, self-image, and mindset are not things; they are patterns of thinking and behaving. One can think fearfully, angrily, and manically in pursuit of the desire for a false grandiose self to cover a falsely believed inferior self.

The most important thing to do then is to change one's pattern of thinking.

One's pattern of thinking, mind, and personality is obviously influenced by one's inherited body, social experience, and culture.

My desire to change all people and make them behave in a beautiful manner is rooted in my perception of myself as not good. I desire to change and make me beautiful and the projection of that desire is the desire to change all people who I see are not good enough.

Ozodi Thomas Osuji, Ph.D.

What I need to do is change my pattern of thinking toward me. I must now think of myself as having an inner perfect self. The son of God in all of us is perfect, but our egos, our personalities, and behaviors are limited by the bodies we live in.

LIFE IN BODY MADE YOU FEEL SMALL AND DEGRADED AND YOU DEVELOPED A PATTERN OF THINKING THAT DEGRADES YOUR FAMILY MEMBERS AND ALL PEOPLE.

THIS IS A SICK PROJECTION AND MUST BE CHANGED FOR NO ONE LIKES TO BE DEGRADED.

If you perceive people objectively, you do not judge them as good or bad but just a mass of body doing what they have to do to survive. People try to survive in ego-separated selves (ego-separated selves are not things but ideas) and that is what you can say objectively about people. You may not like what they are doing to survive.

Not liking something is a judgment which is infused by your own desires and value system.

THE TERM EGO IS NOT A THING BUT A THOUGHT. THE ENTIRE UNIVERSE IS NOT THINGS BUT THOUGHTS. EVEN GALAXIES, STARS, PLANETS, COUNTRIES, PLANTS, ANIMALS, AND PEOPLE ARE IDEAS OR CONCEPTS, NOT THINGS

There is nothing real out there. Whatever we see, be they galaxies, stars, planets, plants, animals, people, and everything are not verifiable external things but representations of our ideas. The world is our ideas (our thinking made manifest as things).

Since everything is our ideas, it can be asked whether anything, including people, exist outside our thinking.

Nothing exists outside our thinking. All things are our ideas—outward projections of our past and present thinking. If we change our thinking about what we had thought are independent things, we change our perception of them.

Perception is truly a projection of our thinking.

Everything we see in the universe is the permutation of our thinking.

ONLY THINKING EXISTS.

Only thinking exists in the universe. The universe thinks through us and everything in it. The universe is not outside us. We are the universe thinking about itself. We are the universe.

God, son of God, and ego are products of our thinking. Only thinking exists.

The universe is thinking through everything, and for our present purposes, is thinking through us. The universe is not outside us. The universe is our thinking made to seem external and solid when in fact it is our thoughts projected out.

FROM COGNITIVE THERAPY TO MENTATION THERAPY

If you understand what I wrote here, you are on your way to changing your life for your life reflects the sum of your past, present, and future thinking.

What we call mental and personality disorders are patterns of thinking influenced by the individuals' biological and social experiences. People can understand their patterns of thinking, hence behaviors, and become the idea called mental health.

What we need is not cognitive therapy but mentation therapy, changing our patterns of thinking.

WHAT IS THE BENEFIT OF THE PHILOSOPHY OF CONNECTED LIVES?

This book is propounding an abstract metaphysics in which the immediate benefit is certainly not on how to make money, so why would a person buy it? Of what use is this to the reader?

The book conveys a philosophy of life—a philosophy based on my considerable studies of Western philosophy, science, oriental religions, and my understanding of the largely unwritten African religions.

It is a synthesis of the various philosophies that I have read. It is not syncretic in the sense that it does not bastardize a particular philosophy so that people would accept it. It is a standalone philosophy.

Every once in a while, usually thousands of years, a person gives the world a new philosophy that helps people cope with their sorrowful existence. This is one of those books.

I am a bringer of knowledge, bringer of light to the world of darkness. Gautama Buddha, Jesus Christ, and a few others are also bringers of light to a people that live in darkness (separation from God is darkness; union with God is light).

The philosophy of the book, if followed, gives me peace of mind and happiness; therefore, I dare say that it would also give the reader peace and joy.

It does not give the reader money or show him how to make money. If money is what you desire, well, go make it in an old-fashioned way. Work for it.

Figure out what your aptitude is. Train it. If you have not already done so, train it in a profession and use that profession to make a living.

Not all aptitudes and vocations will make you a billionaire. If you have computer skills in today's world and can come up with an app, you could become rich really quickly, but not all of us have computer skills. All I know about computers (despite taking classes on the damn things) is how to use them to type manuscripts on.

And before you become cocky, be advised that the era of computers making folk overnight millionaires is coming to pass. In a few more years, you probably would be unemployed if you studied computer science.

Nevertheless, do what you are good at and are interested in. Be yourself regardless of whether you make money from it or not (I am very good at philosophy and psychology and passable in physics. None of those would make me rich but I love them).

My book, if its philosophy is adhered to, gives people peace of mind. Peace is a desirable quality in this world of conflicts.

It contains profound psychological insights. Following its guideline helps one to understand one's personality and how one came to be so.

If one has neurosis (anxiety), it helps one to overcome it. If one has depression, it would help one deal with it. If one has personality disorders (paranoid, schizoid, schizotypal, narcissistic, histrionic, antisocial, borderline, avoidant, dependent, obsessive-compulsive, or passive-aggressive), it would help one to understand those dysfunctional lifestyles and work on changing them. If one has mental disorders such as mania and schizophrenia, well, I do not know if it can help one. Psychotics seldom have the mindfulness to read books. If they do, I dare say that they, too, can benefit from my book.

The book helps you to understand who you are. In the empirical universe, you are a human personality housed in a body. In metaphysical language, you are a separated ego-self. It asks you to figure out who your real self is.

It says that your real self is a part of the whole self. The whole self is God. The part of the whole self is the son of God.

God and his sons are formless unified spirit.

To regain awareness of your true self as part of unified spirit, you have to love yourself, other people, and God and forgive those who harmed you on earth.

It does not define forgiveness in a moral sense. It defines forgiveness as overlooking this world for it sees the world as a dream—the dream of the sons of God who, while still in God, dream that they are in a separated world that is the opposite of God's unified state.

In God, we are a formless spirit. We dream of its opposite and now see ourselves as in forms made of bodies (in light if we are of a higher attainment). We live in space, time, and matter. All these are illusions that seem real to us just as dreams seem real to sleepers.

On earth, in the dream of separation from God, one has two options: to let the ego, the separated self, guide one or to let the Holy Spirit guide one.

If the ego guides your thinking, you think of what is good for you at the expense of other people. If the Holy Spirit guides your thinking, you think of what is good for all of us on earth and work toward them.

Ultimately, if the Holy Spirit guides your thinking, you learn that the world is a chimera, tinsel town, transitory, and ephemeral. It is here today and gone tomorrow.

The life in a body lasts maybe for one hundred and twenty years and in dying, the body rots, decays, and is eaten by worms. Worms are then eaten by bacteria. Our bodies are nothing. Therefore, a rational person affirms that which has worth in his life, his soul.

He affirms his soul—the spirit of God in him. He stops identifying with the ego and identifies with Christ.

The Christ is a person like Jesus who let go of his identification with ego-separated self and identified with his real self being the unified son of God and loved all his brothers.

Let go of your ego, love all people, and see what happens.

I am not a religious person. I am a scientist. Despite my cynicism and skepticism, when I am in a total loving and forgiving state, I often see other people in pure light forms. I mean this literally. All the people, animals, trees, and everything you see on earth has light forms. You see them in light forms if you have purified your thinking and now have thinking infused with love and forgiveness. Try loving yourself and all people and see if you would not see the world of light forms.

From seeing the world of light forms, you will one day experience the formless world of God. The world of God is beyond words. When you experience it, you will know for you feel at home (heaven and its God is our real home. We are currently prodigal sons of God dreaming that we are away from our home and father).

In heaven, God, which I call a formless unified spirit, you know that there are infinite souls. However, all of them are unified as one soul—one son of God who is one with their creator, God. You feel blissful, eternal, permanent, and changeless.

All these seem magical thinking, right? Just try loving and forgiving yourself and all people and then see what happens. Igbos say:

"Owu ala dindu ana eshi agugo."

Roughly translated into English, this proverb says, "If where you are going to is nearby, you do not argue about what is in it. You go there and find out."

Do what awakens you from the dream of self-denial and you awaken and experience your real self as part of God's unified self. After that experience, you live in peace and joy and see our present world as a dream.

Like Gautama Buddha, you no longer seek this world in a way that you value it and get frustrated when its transitory things go.

In the words of our elder brother, Jesus Christ, now you live in the world but are not of the world; you live with total detachment, not attached to any ego-based thing.

As a result of your detachment to the things of this world, you live in peace, doing things with aptitude and interest and using it to serve our earthly needs. If you are a medical doctor, you heal our sick bodies realizing that we have spiritual selves; hence, you respect your patients.

My book gives you a path to peace and emotional stability. It helps you become a stable adult (you are not like the narcissistic child in the American White House who calls himself a stable genius while behaving like a foolish child).

I live in peace; I give you my peace; I live in light; I give you my light (knowledge of our oneness is what the metaphor light symbolizes); I live in unified state and give you a path to return to God, our creator.

Dr. Helen Schucman, a professor of clinical psychology at Columbia University, New York, in her book *A Course in Miracles*, said what I said here. She was a spiritual poet and wrote in lovely poetic forms. I am a rationalist and write in simple prose. You can awaken to your real self by reading my books or from reading Dr. Schucman's book. You can also do so from Buddhism, Hinduism, Gnosticism, and other higher religions of mankind.

THE EGO AND BODY ARE MEANS OF SEPARATION.
THE SEPARATOR IS THE SON OF GOD.

The ego sense of I and its body are mere means of separation. They are not the separator. They are neutral. The separator is the son of God who is now sleeping and dreaming through the ego and body, both of whom do not actually exist.

So, do not blame the ego or body. Blame the son of God who dreams through them. It is the son of God who needs to change his mind and stop using the ego and body to do his wishes in separation. But as long as he sleeps, the Holy Spirit remembers his real self for him.

The ego cannot change; the body cannot change; only the son of God can change his dreams.

MY SALVATION COMES FROM MY REAL SELF,
THE SON OF GOD WHO IS ONE WITH GOD.

My salvation comes from my real self, the son of God, not from the ego or body, for those are mere means of dreaming.

Ozodi Thomas Osuji, Ph.D.

GOD AND HIS SON THINK AND USE MIND TO EXPRESS THEMSELVES IN CREATIONS.

My real self, the son of God, thinks with God to express himself when awake. God thinks to express himself.

When the son of God wishes for the impossible, in separation he uses his thinking, the mind to dream the impossible, the existence of ego and body, space, time, matter, and all illusions.

In the dream, the Holy Spirit remembers union for the seemingly separated son of God, now called the ego in body until he is willing to awaken from the dream of self-forgetfulness and know that he is one with God and continue expressing himself through his unified thinking, unified mind.

IT IS THE SON OF GOD WHO DREAMS OUR DAY WORLD AND ALSO OUR NIGHTLY DREAMS. THE EGO DOES NOT KNOW HOW OUR DAY OR NIGHTLY DREAMS TAKE PLACE.

THE HOLY SPIRIT ENABLES US TO AWAKEN FROM THE DREAM, BUT IN AS MUCH AS THE DREAM IS A DREAM OF SPECIALNESS, EACH OF US HAS A SPECIAL ROLE TO PLAY. THE ULTIMATE ROLE IS TO OVERLOOK THE DREAM, BUT HOW WE GET TO DO IT IS DONE BY EACH OF US WITH HIS SPECIAL SKILLS. QUANTUM PHYSICISTS HELP US TO KNOW THAT THE WORLD IS NOT REAL. SPIRITUAL PSYCHOLOGISTS HELP US TO KNOW THAT THE DREAM IS NOT REAL. ONE'S SPECIAL FUNCTION IS NOT THE SAME AS OTHER PEOPLE'S SPECIAL FUNCTIONS.

1

CREATION OF UNIVERSES ARE DONE BY GOD AND HIS SONS THROUGH THEIR THINKING

God is a creator. He creates by thinking. He thinks of something and it comes into being. He thinks about having sons and sons come into being.

God gave his creative, thinking ability to his sons. God's sons are like God. They, too, create or invent by thinking.

In eternity, heaven, the sons of God created by thinking. They used their thinking to decide to have a separated self and world and that produced our present universe of space, time, matter, and separated states. It is the wishes, which is thinking, that produced our universe of stars, galaxies, planets, animals, people, and plants.

On earth, we think. Our individual thinking produces the world we see in our nightly dreams. Our collective thinking produces the world we see during the daytime.

This is why one must be careful what one thinks for one's thinking produced the world one lives in. The world one sees is the outward picturing of one's thoughts for one to see them.

Our wills in heaven create. Our wishes on earth produce the world of illusions (space, time, and matter) we see.

Think loving thoughts and see a loving world; think hateful thoughts and see a hateful world. Think fearful thoughts and see you live in a world persecuted by people. Your mind produced your persecutory world.

In a dream, your mind takes from the world and people who have the desire to hate and persecute you and draws (attracts) them to you so that you experience persecution.

During the daytime, our collective thinking produces the world we experience as members of the human race (whatever subgroup we belong to, our thinking produced it and placed us in it).

Black peoples' thinking draws racists who want to enslave and discriminate against them so they experience the hate they want to experience. If they change their minds and now wish love, all they will see is a world that loves them.

Thinking (in the form of wishes and beliefs) produced the world we see and live in. Therefore, one must monitor and discipline one's thinking or mind so that one thinks only loving thoughts if one wants to live in a loving and abundant world (one's thinking produces one's level of wealth and poverty).

ARE YOU RESPONDING TO REAL THREAT OR TO YOUR IMAGINATION OF THREAT?

I do not know about other people but I do know about me. My mind responds to things that are objectively threatening to our lives and to mere thought that things are threatening with fear. It does not make a difference to my mind whether the threat is real or imaginary. It simply reacts with fear. I feel all the symptoms of fear—rapid heartbeat, rapid central and peripheral nervous system movements (as messages are sent from all parts of my body to my brain and my brain interprets them and sends feedback to all parts of my body to stay and fight the source of threat or flee from it), tort muscles, rapid thinking and talking, and so on.

The mind does not distinguish between reality and imaginary reality. An example is this. I am in this old house. It is creaky. In the middle of the night, I am walking around in the dark, perhaps, going to the bathroom. I hear some weird noise and my mind reacts with fear. Then, I think about the source of the sound and it is perhaps hot water running through the pipes in the wall.

One must ask oneself—am I reacting to an actual fear-making stimulus or am I reacting to my imagination of what my mind perceives as fear-making? It is crucial that one ascertains the difference because the human mind can respond with fear, anger, depression, and paranoia to perfectly innocuous stimuli.

People often misperceive the intentions of other people and respond to them with fear, anger, or paranoia (suspiciousness, distrust).

You must not allow your mind to deceive you by making you respond inappropriately to environmental stimuli.

Much of human interpersonal conflicts are rooted in peoples' misperception of each other's intentions; therefore, to have harmonious social relationships, folks must make sure that they are reading each other's behaviors correctly. Nations have gone to war because of misperception of each other's intentions.

Make sure that what you think that you see is actually there before you respond to what you think that you see for your mind is programmed to respond with fear or anger to what you interpret to be fear- and anger-making regardless of whether it is in fact fear- or anger-making—true or not.

Our minds can enslave us and can also liberate us.

GOD IS LOVE

That love is to be experienced when one overlooks the world of ego and separation; union is love.

Our nature in God, in heaven, and in unified spirit is love. God is love and as his parts, his sons, we are love.

We decided to experience the opposite of love (love is union with all selves) and attacked ourselves and separated from love.

Upon birth on earth, we forget the nature of love—our true self. We attack and punish ourselves from the minute that we are born on earth with experiences of lack of love and fancy that they give us ego power and such nonsense.

From the moment I was born on earth, I have never known love for myself or shown love to other people for I did not know what love is and so did you.

The Holy Spirit now teaches us how to return to love but does not give us love. It teaches us to remove the obstacles we placed to love (God) by relinquishing the pursuit of the ego and special self. When we give up our desired separated self-concept, the ego, and its identification with the body, we have met the conditions for love and we experience love but not until we have done so. As long as we cling to a bit of the ego, we have clung to all of it and will not experience love.

The Holy Spirit does not give us love. It shows us how to return to love. It is us who give us love when we remove what we made to prevent us from experiencing love (our true self is love; that is, unified).

From now and onward, remove your ego-self-concept and forgive all people. When you do so, you would experience love, your true nature.

This experience of unspeakable love is what Hindus call Samadhi, Buddhists call Nirvana, and Zen calls Satori, and Christian Mysticism calls the mystical union of God and his sons.

MY POLITICS IS CHRIST-BASED POLITICS

In politics, my politics is based on Christ politics which is politics based on love. There is Christ realism, which is the politics of love for all humanity. This is my politics, Christ politics or Holy Spirit-directed politics.

This is not naïve, idealistic politics—the seeking of the fantasy of love. No, it is how the Holy Spirit, part of our minds, construe politics, politics from our right minds, politics from Christ and from love, and politics that overlook ego politics and corrects it with love-based politics.

For example, I know that American Republicans are stark insane. Their minds are sold to hate, to the devil. They tell lies very easily. See, Donald Trump is a pathological liar. Every word that comes out of that man's mouth is a lie. I see these folk's lies and hatred and still do what I know is right, which is treating all people with love.

LIVING FROM EGO IS LIVING FROM FEAR. LIVING FROM HOLY SPIRIT BRINGS ONE NEAR LOVE. LIVING FROM LOVE IS LIVING FEARLESSLY.

If you live from your ego, you live in fear. The ego points out to you what could harm or kill you and ask you to take defensive measures.

Your ego imagines all kinds of things that could harm you, such as ghosts killing you (and since there are no ghosts in the day world, your ego in your nightly dreams presents to you ghosts trying to harm you).

In fear, one populates the world with fearful things, avoids them, and lives in isolation from other people.

In fear, you imagine what other people would say or do and respond to them. You are not responding to actual people but to your imaginations of what real people would say or do. You are responding to your projections to other people.

In obedience to your ego, you mostly relate to your ego, not to other people. You avoid other people and not relate to them realistically and do what you need to do to succeed in the ego world. Then, you fail.

To have an extreme ego is to fail in life.

IN LOVE, GOD, YOU ARE SAFE.

God is love. In love, God, you are safe and do not feel fear. God is fearlessness.

If your thinking and behavior are directed by the Holy Spirit, you are not in God, for if you are in God, you would not need the help of the Holy Spirit.

Christ is your real self. He is formless and unified with God. He is in love and does not feel fear. Right now, you live in ego and body and do feel fear. To live as an ego in body is to live in fear. The ego is the prisoner of fear. Christ is fearless.

Return to Christ to return to living fearlessly; hence, peacefully and happily.

TO HAVE EVEN A LITTLE EGO IS TO BE
IN PRISON OF ONE'S MAKING.

If you have even a little bit of ego, you will defend it; you will be conscious of how other people treat it. When you feel that your ego is slighted, albeit it slightly, you feel disrespected and angry. The level of your anger from this minuscular slight is as much as when you are physically attacked.

The ego feels angry at those who slight it or attack it. In anger, the ego defends itself and can attack to kill the person it feels humiliated it. From this situation, you can see that the ego is madness itself. To live in ego is to be insane.

Consider. Yesterday, I was at a grocery store. I did not have my store card to get the savings on what I bought. The cashier asked me for my card. I know that I had it so I looked in my wallet and it is not there. She asked for my phone number to look it up. I signed up for that card over ten years ago and have changed phone numbers. I gave her my present phone number and it is not the number the card is registered under. She asked me to go to the customer service section of the store to fill out a form for another card. I was irritated that I had to do so but went and got another card. With the card, I saved over five dollars on my groceries.

The point here is that the cashier was doing her job, as she is supposed to do it, but I felt, given the runaround, and my ego felt slighted, disrespected, and angry. Of course, I did not show that irritation outwardly but felt it inside me.

This means that I still have an ego. I am still in ego prison. As long as I have an ego, such things as been kept waiting by cashiers would irritate me.

If I do not want to be irritated by other people, I must let go of the ego in its entirety. To have ego, even a tiny little bit of it, is to be in prison, in hell.

Folks want to seem like important egos (this is more so with Nigerians; many Nigerians have swollen egos; they pretend to be very important persons) without realizing that to have an ego, small or big, is to be in prison and hell of their own making.

The most liberating moment of one's life is when one relinquishes one's ego. To have no ego is to be in heaven, literally, not figuratively. To have no ego is to be freed from jail and hell. To have no ego is to live in peace and happiness. What is heaven, God, but peace and joy, bliss!

Teachers of God are folks who show people how to live in love, joy, and peace. What else can one ask for from life but love, joy, and peace?

THE DREAMER IS NOT HIS DREAM

In a dreaming situation, you are on your bed and project another self that looks like your day self into a dream to interact with other people in the world of space, time, and matter. You make all the people in the dream do what they do. But when you wake up from the dream, the dream world and its people disappear.

THE FORMLESS SONS OF GOD DREAM OUR WORLD

There is another you, the son of God, that while in God, sleeps and projects out you and your world on earth. It is not the dream you and the world it sees on earth. It is a formless son of God and other formless sons of God that along with you, project them into our world of forms, a dream world.

You are not your earthly ego-self and earthly body. This means that you can deny that you are your earthly dream self and deny that you are your earthly body and wake up in dreamless unified self in God, heaven.

Or you can die on earth. The earthly dream is a drama, a play that requires you to enter it through birth in body and forgetting your spirit self upon entering it and leaving it through the death of your dream ego and body.

This is illusion. The dream world and people do not exist so nobody is born on earth or dies on earth. You might as well change your mind and wake up without dying.

LIGHT FORM IS WHAT CHRISTIANS CALL CHRIST'S GLORIFIED SELF.

Enlightened folks like Jesus, while on earth, remembered their formless self and simply changed from body to light self (light form is what Christians call Christ's glorified body; it is in this light form that I interact with the old boy—two of us in light bodies) and ultimately, to formless self. They did not have to die.

If while on earth and you had died not remembering your real self and are not being fully illuminated to your formless self, you will reincarnate in body and reenter the drama of life with it until you learn to give up your ego-self-concept and how to transform your body to light body and ultimately to formlessness.

When you attain the awareness of formlessness while on earth, you do not come back to the earth anymore. You are now a world teacher of God, such as Jesus, who, while in unified spirit, guides those people who are still on earth. You help them to remember their true selves.

IF YOU HAVE NO EGO, YOU ARE NO LONGER A HUMAN BEING IN BODY. YOU ARE NOW A HUMAN BEING WHO HAS RECOGNIZED THAT HE IS THE SON OF GOD. YOU ARE NOW CALLED CHRIST.

If you remember that you are the son of God, hence Christ, you do not need the Holy Spirit to guide you anymore (you are now the same as the Holy Spirit, a teacher of how to return to God).

But as long as you see yourself as the dream-separated self, ego, you need the dream-Holy Spirit to guide your thinking.

Holy Spirit is not a person apart from you. It is a pattern of thinking that overlooks; that is, forgiveness, the egos' world to wake from it.

The Christ is a person who while on earth remembers that he is the son of God. He is now capable of taking form, say, light form, to help guide those still in matter form; that is, he takes the illusion of having light form to help those in the illusion of living in dense body.

YOU CHOSE THE TYPE OF BODY YOU ARE BORN IN.

Before birth on earth, a son of God is part of unified spirit. He then closes his unified spirit eyes and goes to sleep.

He chose the type of body, parents, and society he is born in. He sometimes chooses a pained body so as to use it to form an extreme ego.

This is what I did. I was born into an incredibly pained body; hence, rejected my body and ego and sought ways to return to the awareness of my true self, Christ, son of God.

To be in extreme ego causes one loads of problems and struggles until one realizes that one is not one's body and the ego. One realizes that making efforts to heal one's body with medications and taking good care of one's body with good food and exercise would not heal one. Those assume the reality of ego and body and keep one in the world of dreams.

What heals one is to completely deny that one is ego and body. When one does so, one has overcome the ego and its world of separation; one returns one's mind to Holy Spirit, and thereafter, wakes up as the son of God and becomes the Christ (or as Buddhists call it, Buddha self).

I REACQUAINT WITH ANOTHER SON OF GOD WHO HAS REMEMBERED HIS REAL SELF, CHRIST.

This afternoon, I picked up one of my phones that I had not taken a look at for almost a week. In it was a call from a dear friend, Dr. Kofi Agyapong, a Ghanaian attorney who lives in Washington DC. He had called to tell me that an old friend of mine called Dr. O had asked him to tell me that he wanted to talk to me.

I talked to Kofi briefly and then called Dr. O (he lives in DC). As in the past, we spent over an hour talking. He, as usual, talked to me about God. He talked about how we all have an indwelling God in us and that we forget that spiritual self while living as human beings.

He said that we are like larvae, a caterpillar that forgets that he could become a butterfly and fly. He is a man steeped in traditional Christianity and knows the Bible upside down. He quotes from the Bible to make his points.

He must have referred to twenty quotations from the Bible as we talk. I am kind of good with the references to the Bible. I even got out my old Bible and looked up some of his quotations and he was always on the mark!

In the final analysis, the man is saying the same thing that I say in my spirituality. He comes at it from the Bible whereas I come at it from spiritual psychology.

Dr. O is a son of God who is enlightened to his real self, Christ. It is nice to know that another African is also illuminated to his true self.

We agreed to resume our talks every evening or something like that. Since he is much older than I am, I consider him my mentor.

Like me, he was a professor at an American university before the call came to him—the call to find out his true self—and he quit college teaching, delved into spirituality, and eventually experienced what Hindus call Samadhi, oneness with God.

This year has begun auspiciously by reconnecting me to my lost guru, my teacher of God. I told him that I am going to build a college in Arizona, to teach leadership and business studies. He supported the idea and asked that spirituality be part of the curriculum.

As he sees it, the white man is lost in his pursuit of science. Science is useful but it deals with the superficial and peripheral aspects of people—matter, space, and time but does not ask serious questions about who we are.

Most people, for example, do not know that they can close their eyes in meditation, tune out our empirical world, and enter the world of light forms where they could talk with enlightened people, such as Jesus. This is said.

Anyway, I am glad that I reconnected with my old teacher, Dr. O. I also have Hindu gurus. This weekend, I will talk to my Swami Bhaskrananda who lives in Seattle, Washington. He is the head of the Vedanta Center of Western Washington. I learned much about Hinduism and Buddhism by talking to my Hindu guru, weekly.

USING MENTAL DISORDERS TO RATIONALIZE AND JUSTIFY EVIL BEHAVIOR IS INAPPROPRIATE.

In my view, Donald Trump and Republicans are evil human beings. They are evil because they do unloving things, such as locking up Latino children at the US-Mexican border. Trump clearly has a personality disorder—narcissistic personality disorder.

Adolf Hitler and his fellow Nazis killed millions of people. Hitler had personality disorders—paranoia and anti-social personality disorders.

African leaders do evil things, such as killing their people and stealing their peoples' wealth. They have personality disorders.

We now diagnose these evil people and give them neat psychiatric diagnoses. We use mental disorders to rationalize their evil behaviors.

The question is this: does having a mental illness justify one's evil behaviors?

I do not think so. I think that even mental illness itself is chosen by the mentally ill. Their choice is mediated by inherited biological and sociological factors.

People have mental disorders or personality disorders in pursuit of big and powerful egos (see my metaphysical writing for explanation).

As I see it, people are responsible for their mental illnesses and evil behaviors. If they harm other people because of their alleged mental disorders, they chose their evil behaviors. They are responsible for their evil acts. They must be judged and punished, sent to jail, or shot to death.

I make no excuses for mental illness and evil behavior. This is where I stand and will not move. I refuse to take moral responsibility away from human beings and have them be mere animals that their supposed mental disorders and environment make them do what they do.

As I see it, people choose to do whatever they do and must be held responsible for their actions. I initiate the process of reclaiming human responsibility from the so-called mental health professionals.

Psychology and psychiatry reduced people to mere animal status by taking away responsibility for their actions from them, rationalizing and justifying people's anti-social hence evil behaviors with the bugaboo of mental disorder (and biology).

I agree with Thomas Szasz that mental illness is a self-chosen behavior pattern.

A COURSE IN MIRACLE TEACHES ONE TO GIVE UP ONE'S SELF-CONCEPT AND RETURN TO ONE'S UNIFIED SPIRIT SELF.

A course in miracles can be summarized thus. We have unified self in God. We opposed that unified self and want to have separated selves. In unified self, aka heaven, we are equal and know that God created us and we did not create ourselves.

We wanted to seem unequal, see ourselves as special, indeed, and we wanted to see ourselves as the creator of God and ourselves.

To make our desired special, separated selves seem possible, we invented space, time, and matter and now seem to be living in body, space, and time.

In body, space, and time, each of us constructs a special separated self that makes him seem very important and powerful (more powerful than the whole, God). The separated, special self is a false self but that is what we currently know about and walk around as having it.

We incarnate on earth in several lifetimes. During each incarnation, we struggle to improve the ego separated self-concept or regress to more primitive self-concepts.

Ultimately, we have to learn that the separated special self, no matter how much we improve it, is false. At that point, we let it go and remember our true self—the unified spirit self.

When we remember our unified spirit self, the world of separation, space, and time is now over for us. We can take on the light form and use it to teach those still in dense body form that our true nature is a formless unified spirit self.

Now, one is one with the Holy Spirit (one is now the Christ; the Christ is the son of God who while in the dream, on earth, is living as a separated ego-self in body, remembers his true self as part of God; hence, is enlightened to his shared God-self) in teaching us to overlook the separated, special self and return to unified self.

The lesson for me this year of 2020 is to no longer think and behave from the ego separated self but live from the Holy Spirit self, the Christ self, and occasionally experience Holy instant, the unified spirit self.

THE CHOICE TO LIVE FROM EGO OR HOLY SPIRIT/CHRIST: TO SERVE ONLY ONE'S SELF OR THE COMMUNITY?

When you wake up in the morning, you do not know what life is going to throw at you today. You have no way of predicting what today and the future will bring.

The only thing you have control over is how you choose to respond to the present and future events in your life.

You have two choices—to respond from ego (selfish thinking and behavior) or from the Holy Spirit/Christ (thinking and behavior that serves social interests).

At any point in your life, you are choosing ego or Christ, selfish interests, or social interests. If you choose ego, you receive conflict and lack of peace and joy in your life. If you choose to have the Holy Spirit, your right mind, the part of your mind that thinks about what serves our collective good to guide you, you experience peace and happiness. The choice is for you to make.

EGO, HOLY SPIRIT, CHRIST, AND GOD ARE METAPHORS, NOT PERSONS.

Ego, Holy Spirit, Christ, and God are metaphors. They are not literal persons. They are not outside you. They are patterns of thinking and behavior.

You, a part of the whole, anthropomorphized as the son of God, is the one making ego or Christ choices as you choose to live—in peace or at war with the whole and war with yourself.

Choose ego and you are at war with your real self and live in conflict. Choose Holy Spirit and Christ and you are at peace with your whole self and all people.

MAKING CAREER CHOICES: GOOD CAREER CHOICE IS DOING WHAT IS IN ALIGNMENT WITH YOUR NATURE.

If you choose to work in a line of work that is congruent with your nature, the you that you know yourself to be, you live in peace and joy and perhaps make a little money while you are at it, although money is not guaranteed from living the right life. What is guaranteed is peace and joy.

In childhood, I rejected my real self and pursued the ego ideal self—how to make me, other people, social institutions, and the world ideal. I pursued careers that promised me the opportunity to change myself and the people and make the world ideal.

For example, as a psychotherapist, I had the erroneous belief that I could change people and make them behave better. I later learned that I do not have such grandiose power to change people. Only the individual can change himself. Other people cannot change him. To believe that you can change other people is to be deluded, insane.

Later, I realized that I was pursuing illusions since it is not possible to change my nature, other people, and social institutions (social institutions reflect people's psychological status). I gave up desiring ego ideals.

I replaced ego ideals with seeking spiritual ideals. That, too, is a chimera and unrealistic, for who defines what spiritual ideal is but me? There is no ideal in anything in an imperfect world.

The only realistic profession/vocation is for me to live from my real self, which is the son of God and since that is not known in this temporal world, it is for me to be guided by the Holy Spirit/Christ.

Ego, Holy Spirit, Christ, and God, as already noted, are metaphors, not real states. To be guided by the Holy Spirit and Christ is for me to think and behave from my right mind, the part of me that loves myself and all people in bodies. It means for me to see our mistakes and work to correct those that can be corrected and live with those that cannot be corrected.

I am interested in leadership matters. The first book I wrote right after graduate school is on leadership. I keep thinking and writing about leadership. What this means is teaching me and all people to think and behave from our right minds, to do what serves social interest.

Good leadership is positing goals that serve social interests, such as developing and modernizing Africa and improving people's interpersonal relationships.

Healed relationships are situations where one sees oneself as one with all people and work for all people's good. It means doing what enables one to get along with all people.

THE DELUDED PERSON IS TRYING TO LIVE FROM A FALSE POWERFUL SELF. WHEN HE LETS GO OF THAT EFFORT, HE LIVES FROM HIS REAL SELF, WHICH IS PART OF GOD

In paranoia and delusion disorder, the person sees himself as inferior and powerless, denies it, and tries to live as the magically powerful self that his imagination created.

When he stops trying to be the false and imaginary powerful self, he is healed of his delusion; he now lives peacefully and happily. He reclaims his place as a son of God, as a part of the whole who works for the good of the whole, not just for his false, grandiose ego.

This is why most seasoned psychotherapists know that healed paranoid persons become sane sons of God.

Therapists also know that they cannot heal paranoid persons for paranoia or delusion disorder results from the individual's self-rejection and choice to live "as if he is an imaginary powerful self." He made that choice and only he can choose to let it go. You cannot choose for him.

All that you, a therapist, can do is showing him the alternative to his paranoid choices. Initially, he would see you as the paranoid one (deluded persons call their therapists the deluded ones), but when he decides to let go of his choice to be a false, grandiose self, a son of God who lives in peace and happiness is born in him.

IF I KNEW THAT THIS WORLD IS A DREAM, WOULD I RESPOND TO DREAM DANGERS AS IF THEY ARE DANGEROUS? NO.

At night, I dream. Dangers confront me and I respond with fear. If I knew beforehand that it was only a dream danger, would I respond with fear? No.

By the same token, if our day world is a dream and I know it for sure, would I respond with fear to the things of this world? No. Would I respond with fear to white racism? No.

I must see the world as real to respond to its events as real and for fear to be justified, but if I know for sure that the world is a dream, then fear, anger, and other emotions are not warranted. I must then cancel my body and all its responses to danger for they are now superfluous.

How come Jesus is the only one who knew that this world is a dream, hence did not respond with fear to what makes those of us who see the world as real do?

HELEN SCHUCMAN COMBINED ADLER, HORNEY, KELLY, FREUD, BEHAVIORISTS, PLATO, HINDUISM, AND BUDDHISM IN HER SPIRITUAL PSYCHOLOGY.

As a psychologist, Helen Schucman studied Freud, Adler, Horney, Kelly, and behaviorists, and as a student of comparative religions, she studied Gnosticism, Hinduism, and Buddhism. She also studied western philosophy, such as Plato and Aristotle (Plato figured in a lot of places in *A Course in Miracles*).

Apparently, her unconscious mind mixed this disparate information to construct her spiritual psychology, a poem.

How her mind did it, she did not know (You may say that a part of her mind talked to her in telling her to write *A Course in Miracles*. True, parts of our minds do talk to us. When we say that God or Holy Spirit said something to us, it is our mind that said something to us).

One must give her kudos for taking all that she studied and used them to write her wonderful spiritual poems.

One must, however, not take her poems and their metaphors as literal truth, for then, one would be making a mistake. To write in regular rational prose, one must be conscious, not unconscious as poets do.

Helen did make some useful contributions to psychology. She asked us to let go of our egos and think from the Holy Spirit; that is, from collective interest perspective. As Adler also advocated, let go of your ego (self-interested thinking) if you want peace and joy. As long as you think and behave from the ego, you are attacking reality, you, and other people and must be at war with you.

I take what is true from ACIM and throw the rest away.

AFRICANS ARE BACKWARD BECAUSE THEY LIVE FROM EGO-SELF-INTEREST, NOT FROM HOLY SPIRIT AND CHRIST'S SOCIAL INTEREST.

Africans think and behave from their egos; hence, are self-centered, and out of their self-centeredness, they sold their people into slavery. Even in the present their leaders only work for their self-interests, not for the public good.

Until Africans learn to think and behave from the Holy Spirit, that is, work for social interest, Africa will continue to remain a primitive and shiftless place.

Africans may blame white men all they like for their backwardness. The real reason why Africa is backward is that they live from ego, not Christ—from self-interest not from social interest.

WHY DID I STUDY A COURSE IN MIRACLES AND SPIRITUALITY IN GENERAL?

One would expect a hyper-rational philosopher like me not to pay attention to so-called spirituality, so, why did I get attracted by religions and spirituality?

It is because I have always sought idealistic goals. Idealism is a chimera. Nevertheless, I sought ideals. I studied *A Course in Miracles* in my quest to have a magic wand with which I transformed myself, people, and the world to their ideal forms. That is, I studied it and spirituality in general for magical reasons. I wanted something to make my life better. I wanted to have spiritual powers.

In time, I learned that the course and spirituality, in general, does not change people, did not change Helen and her crew, have not changed me, and have not given me magical powers to change myself and the world. I have not become powerful and rich.

Yet, I did learn something useful from this spirituality stuff. I take what is real in them and use them to live my life. I throw away the overly spiritual for those are merely wishful thinking—poetry, not scientific facts.

The ideas on God, Holy Spirit, Jesus Christ, and ego are patterns of thinking. One can choose to think from each and get the results.

DREAM
6 AM
JANUARY 5, 2020

In this dream, I was at a restaurant and ordered food. The food was kind of like Mexican food, such as tacos and burritos. The food preparers went to the kitchen, prepared the food, and brought it close to the cash registrar counter, and for some reasons, placed it behind the counter, behind the cashiers, and ran away. I waited for them to come back and give me the food. For over ten minutes, they were not back. I went about looking for them and asked folks where they ran to. I then complained to those sitting and eating their food in the restaurant that that is how white folks treat black folks and that this event is how racism works. No one listened to me, so it seemed, anyway. These days, folks dismiss black folks' perpetual complaint of racism because they have heard about it too much and do not believe that it is true anymore. Thereafter, the food preparers came to the counter and I asked for my food and they looked for it and found it, but before they brought it to the counter, I woke up.

What does this dream mean? It dramatizes the story of my life. I desire something. I almost get it but before I get it, something intervenes and I do not get it and have to worry about getting it.

The lesson is for me to do things for myself and not rely on other people to do things for me. If I rely on other people to do things for me, there are always setbacks.

For example, beginning next week, I go to Arizona to build a college dedicated to teaching leadership. This is because Africans and black folks in general lack leadership abilities and I construe it as one of my tasks to teach them how to become leaders.

I have written tons of literature on leadership. I must now be a leader and use my leadership skills (I ran mental health and social agencies as their executive director for over fifteen years) to run the school and not just talk about leadership.

I am no longer a schoolboy talking about how to do something. It is now time for me to do something with my whole heart and energy and do it well.

Talk is easy; action is what counts. I must not rely on other people to help me do what I got to do. If I rely on other people, especially Africans, they cannot help me. They will rip me off for they are mostly thieves lacking conscience. They lack desire to do something right. They are always looking for a way to gratify their little egos. They work only for their little self-centered minds but cannot devote their lives to serving the public interest.

I will give to Africans but I do not expect to get anything from them for they are not givers. They are takers—stealers, actually.

My view of Africans is totally negative. This is based on my interaction with them. Nothing good comes from them. I hate people who steal and are too quick to be corrupt. They lack courage. They are little freaking cowards who are always serving their self-interests and when the kitchen gets hot, they run away.

If you listen to them talk about how to help Africa, you would be misled into thinking that they can serve the public. If you believe them, you are a fool and do not know who these freaking African slave sellers are.

My job is to civilize them but not to think that they are already civilized. I am totally realistic when I deal with Africans. I have no illusion about them.

I make no apology for seeing them as self-centered primitives. I do not engage in political correctness that sees thieves as good people so as to not offend their idiot proud egos. I call them thieves. If they do not want to be so-called, then they should stop stealing too much.

Ozodi Thomas Osuji, Ph.D.

DO YOU DO DREAM INTERPRETATION? THERAPISTS ENCOURAGE YOU TO DO SO.

DREAM
JANUARY 6, 2020
8:20 AM

I stayed up late typing a paper on leadership and management. I typed ten pages and got to bed around 4 AM. I went to sleep right away. I woke up four hours later with the following dream fresh in my mind so I went and typed it to figure out what it means.

In this dream, I was in Eugene, Oregon (I did my undergraduate studies at the University of Oregon in Eugene, Oregon). I parked my present car, Ford Windstar, on the street and went into a neighborhood store to buy something. When I came out a few minutes later, my car was gone. I saw a guy directing traffic and asked him what happened to my car. He told me that cars are towed to a couple of blocks, that my car is packed on 13th Avenue, and that I should go pick it up there. I got to Thirteenth Avenue and the car wasn't there. I kept looking for it and got frustrated. I began walking back to the store to talk to the guy directing traffic, but saw a different guy directing traffic. I told him that I could not find my car. He pointed to where my car is parked—on the store's parking lot. I saw the car and began walking toward it but before I got to it, I woke up.

INTERPRETATION

In this dream, someone took what belongs to me, my car, and placed it elsewhere. I was looking for what already belongs to me that someone else placed where I had not placed it and was having difficulty finding where he placed it.

The dream means that God (my car) is already inside me but someone, Christianity, placed it outside of me where I could not easily see it. I was looking for it until someone, Helen Schucman and her *A Course in Miracles* re-interpreting Christianity, pointed out where it is at but did not take me to it.

It is for me to go to where my soul and God is. No one else can give me my real self; only I can do so. Other people, such as Helen and her book can point in the direction to find what I am looking for, salvation, but only I can find it and save me.

This is my first interpretation of this interesting dream. Every dream has many interpretations. Each interpretation suits your present needs. As your needs change, the same dream can be interpreted differently.

YOU HAVE TO KNOW WHERE YOU ARE GOING TO BE ABLE TO GET THERE.

A different interpretation of the dream is—if you do not have clarity of what your goal is, what your destination is, you will not get to it. You have to have a purpose before you can accomplish it.

Your goal must be congruent with your aptitudes and interests. It must be what you can do, not just what you want to do. For example, I am no good at computers so if my goal is to be a computer wizard, I am living in la-la land.

I am good at psychology and philosophy. If my goal is in those realms, I will do well at them. You have to know what you are looking for to be able to find it.

My thinking is that Igbos, Nigerians, Africans, and black folks, in general, do not understand leadership. They tend to pursue their self-interests in lieu of social interests. They are full of their egos and do not work for social interests. When they venture into the leadership arena, they want leadership positions to make them seem important and prestigious in people's eyes but not to work their asses off for the good of their people.

I have written books and tons of articles on leadership. I doubt that there is an African who has written on leadership as much as I have. I am considered the authority on leadership studies.

I want to establish an institute where we train Africans and Black Americans on leadership matters. I want to teach them to transcend to their ego-self-interests and pursue social interests, serve the public good, and if need be, die trying to serve the public.

In a way, the car in the above dream that I am looking for means that I am searching for an appropriate vocation for me.

Car is a means of transportation. I am looking for a means of transportation to take me from point A to point B—from where I am to where I need to be next.

The question is whether teaching leadership and management (I have taught most MBA courses, including micro and macro-economics, finance, accounting, marketing, human resources, labor relations, contracts, general management, production management, and e-commerce and been the chair of a business department at a college) is what I should be doing.

Since I have explored spirituality in detail, shouldn't I be writing and teaching spirituality? Good question.

Spirituality is my avocation, not my primary vocation. I am by nature a philosopher. Running a school where we teach good leadership and management is congruent with my philosophical desire for beauty (in leadership). I love beautiful things; ugliness depresses me.

In Abraham Maslow's terms, I will be actualizing my real self by being a good leader and teaching it by example—role modeling it, not just talking about it.

EVERY PERSON YOU SEE ON EARTH IS A SEPARATED EGO-SELF, A DREAM FIGURE, NOT REAL.

Take a good look at you and all the people around you—all the people on planet earth. They are not real people. They are separated ego selves housed in bodies that you projected into your dream. They, too, do the same thing. They projected themselves and other people as separated egos in bodies into their dreams.

In the dream, that separation is possible. We house ourselves in bodies and see us in space and time. We are zombies walking around as if we are real.

Our real selves are spirit, a part of the unified spirit. We are sons of God. In unified spirit, we are eternal, immortal, happy, and peaceful, but in our replacement selves, in egos and bodies, we are mortal. In egos, we can live up to 120 years and then die.

Our dream selves die but our real selves that were not born in body do not die.

The world is a place where egos are in bodies. Here, they dance their ego dances of "I am separated from you and have different self-interests." They work for their self-interests and in the process, hurt one another.

You, for example, serve your perceived self-interests. You see other people serve their perceived self-interests. In the process, you hurt other people and they hurt you.

When they hurt you, you feel fear and anger and want to defend your self-interests. You conveniently forget when you hurt other people or rationalize it by saying that they did something for you to hurt them.

You defend your ego and its interests and they, too, do the same thing and the result is the perpetual conflict we live in.

The Holy Spirit, the God in the temporal universe, in our right minds, see what we are doing as egos in bodies. It knows that it is just a dream and is not bothered by our apparent hurtful behaviors.

Whether you live a day or 120 years and die does not matter for the person in the body is not you. Nevertheless, since you want to live in the body, be a dream figure the Holy Spirit tells you to—forgive the wrongs other people did to you in the dream.

This is not because you are a coward and fear them killing you. If you are a black man, you must forgive the wrongs white folks did to black folks. It is not because you are a coward as we all know black folks are physically stronger than white folks and in physical war, would even defeat white folks.

No, you forgive what is done in dreams for as Brother Jesus said on the cross: Father, forgive them for they do not know what they are doing. They think that they are egos in bodies that can die and hence, can kill each other. If they know the truth of who they are, they would know that they are eternal spirits playing in ego and body and love each other.

Forgive those who harmed your ego and body to be forgiven by your real self and your own harm to other people. White abuse of black people is actually only five hundred years (1400–1900). Before that, there was no such thing as white people abusing black folks; in fact, it was Africans and Egyptians that took civilization to Europe. Only God knows how they behaved toward white folks then. You see the present world where white folks screw black people. In the past, black people screwed white people.

If you forgive all, you have a happy dream on earth. The earth is still not real but you seem to enjoy it.

In ego state, we perceive those who attacked us as real and want to attack them in response.

Here is an example. There is this deluded, paranoid, criminal Igbo man called Nebu (that is not his real name; he uses many names to engage in his criminal activities). Apparently, he did not like my writings and gave himself the permission behind my back to talk to the members of my family to dig up dirt on me and flash it on the internet. Above all, he tried to do a 419 on my daughter (he asked her to give him her bank account saying he would put money in it; if she did, he would have taken all her money plus do identity thieving on her).

When I heard about it, I contacted an internet address search company and paid them a few dollars and in less than one hour, they gave me his address. If you have an email, they can locate your address in a few hours.

I got his address and managed to take a look at him. He is an old man with a fat tummy; he is a living dead man. My original intention was to shoot him to death. Oh, yes, I do not hesitate from killing in the cause of justice.

But the Holy Spirit reinterpreted my intention for me. He told me that the garbage I am looking at represents the garbage called Igbos, Nigerians, and Africans. These people are self-centered beyond belief. They work mostly for their egos. To make profit, they sold their people into slavery and at present, steal their people's money.

He told me to learn from them. He said that I am also an ego and have similar self-centered proclivities. He asked me to learn from them and know what egos are and overlook their ego dances but teach them the right behavior, working for our mutual good so as to have a happy dream while we are dreaming that we are separated egos in bodies.

That is to say, the person who wronged me was seen with the eyes of forgiveness. The Holy Spirit and I learned from him about Africans' idiocy and my own idiocy.

If I had killed the motherfucking scumbag as my ego wanted to do, I would have changed nothing in Africa.

Africans are criminals that need to get taught social interest behaviors so as to produce a modern Africa.

If you understand other people, you understand yourself. If you forgive other people, you forgive yourself. That is the gospel of the Holy Spirit which Jesus embraced and lived and in the process, is the first son of God to completely awaken from the sleep and dream of specialness and separation (Buddha, Bahaullah, and others had partial awakening).

DISCUSSION

See people as clearly as your ego eyes show you what they are like. Now, do not respond to them with how your ego asks you to do. Punish them when they wrong you.

Do as the Holy Spirit asks you to do. Forgive them and teach them how to the serve the public good. If we all serve the public good, we are still in egos and bodies but now we are having happy dreams.

To live in ego and body is to be insane but when we use our egos and bodies to love one another, we are having mild insanity, not the psychosis of ego.

From the mild insanity of life guided by the Holy Spirit, we see ourselves in light forms and in the world of light forms. From there, we give up all desire for forms and regain our awareness of a formless, unified spirit self and the universe ends in a few trillion years.

The universe exists for each of us to make this realization that we are unified in God and forgive and love all people.

CONCLUSION

To be a human being is to have the illusion that one has the choice to love or not to love—the choice to be ego or Christ. We seem to have that choice in the dream.

If you are enlightened and illuminated to your real self as the son of God, Christ, you give up the illusion of making choices, you accept yourself as God created us—as part of him. You overlook the world; you correct what your ego and other egos do.

In effect, while still sleeping and dreaming, you allow the Holy Spirit to guide your thinking and behavior.

The Holy Spirit is not a person outside you. It is your right mind's thinking. It is the part of you that asks you to love and forgive the wrongs of yourself and all people.

I no longer have the choice to love or not love. I love myself and all people. I have given up the illusion that the son of love (God is love) can be anything but love.

I am not an ego; I am Christ. Christ is perfect love. I am perfect love for me and for all people. I dream with the Holy Spirit with forgiveness.

Forgiveness is not an end but a means to awaken to the perfect love of God that is already in us. Forgive and know the love already in you.

I am now love. As love, I do not need to eat too much food as I used to do. As love, I do not need addiction to food, alcohol, smoking, and drugs. I live a simple life. Maybe I eat a bowl of salad in a day, if at all. I do not need too much food or anything to stimulate my nonexistent body, as I used to overeat to stimulate my body and make it real for me (other folks use alcohol and drugs to make their bodies real and in the process forget the spirit).

EGO-LESSNESS MEANS PEACE AND JOY.
EGOFULNESS MEANS CONFLICT AND WAR.

If it were possible to attain no ego in you and you think and behave from a non-ego, that is, non-self-centered, from no desire to do things that serve only your self-interest at the expense of other people and if it were possible to do only what serves the public good, you would know only peace and joy in you.

But as long as you are on planet earth, you are in ego state. As long as you can see yourself in body and see other people in bodies, you are in ego state. The most you can now do is think and behave from the right part of your mind. Metaphorically, this means that you think from the Holy Spirit and the Christ part of your mind. That part of your mind thinks as God thinks; that is, it does what serves the whole instead of the part.

This is the wisdom of Gautama Buddha's no self-approach to people and Alfred Adler's injunction to think and behave from what serves social interest.

If one wants to heal one's neurosis (Adler defines neurosis as self-centeredness and pursuit of a false superior self to mask a false inferior self), one becomes happy and peaceful.

TO HAVE EGO IS TO BE PRONE TO ADDICTIONS.
YOU CANNOT QUIT ADDICTIVE BEHAVIORS
FROM EGO THINKING AND BEHAVING.

The *Alcoholics Anonymous: Big Book* has what it calls the twelve steps to quit addictions. The first step is that one understands that all of one's behaviors were from the ego and that one has now quit doing so and given one's life to a higher power to guide one.

When I first came in contact with that philosophy, I dismissed it as religious razzmatazz for I did not see how a human being who by nature is a separated ego-self can behave as if he is not an ego.

Well, over time, I tried to quit my only addiction, eating too much food. I found that as long as I approached the problem from my ego thinking, I could not quit overeating. I would always rationalize with thoughts like this—we have to eat to live; our bodies need food; if we did not eat, we would not live; starving people die; food tastes good; in heaven, we live in bliss so our nature is to seek bliss, now in body called pleasure.

But when I resolved to not think from the ego but to see things from my right mind, that is, to allow me to be guided by what had hitherto seemed to me an irrational way of thinking, asking God to help me, I found me able to resist addiction.

THINKING FROM THE HOLY SPIRIT HELPS ONE NOT TO GIVE IN TO EGO DEFENSES OF FEAR AND ANGER.

Consider. I see a person do something. I can approach him from my ego. That means looking at what he did from my ego rational mind. Here, I evaluate what he did and ascertain whether it is good or not for me. If it is good for me, I relax and let it be. If it is not good for me, I defend myself.

Ego defense could mean doing something bad to that person or avoiding him; either way, I am trying to retain my ego.

The alternative is to see what that person did and affirm that it is in the egos' world, which is harmful, and then ask how the Holy Spirit would have you relate to it.

The Holy Spirit would ask me to forgive it. The other person reflects me. He is a mirror of my thinking projected out for me to see me well. If I forgive him, I forgive me. If I do not forgive him, I do not forgive me.

My ego rallies around and tells me that it seems irrational to ask me to forgive the person who harmed me in the egos' world.

Over time, I learned that there is logic to the Holy Spirit's way of behaving. If someone slapped me, I feel pain. If I do not give in to the urge to slap him back and give him pain, I have said that he did nothing to me. Despite the pain he gave me, I have said that his action to me is done in our mutual dream of separating from our unified spirit self.

Not defending one's self means that one says that one is not ego and body. It means that one sees the world as a dream, as non-existent.

If one continues not defending one's ego and body one day, one sees one's ego and body literally disappear. One experiences a reality that is formless, pure spirit in which one feels one with all and one is peaceful and happy beyond words (this experience is called Holy Instant, Samadhi, Nirvana, or Satori of mystical union of God and his son).

From that Holy Instant experience, one begins to see one's self and people every once in while in light forms (there is a world of light forms where we are all in light form and everything is in light form). It is the purified world remade from our world.

IF YOU ALLOW THE HOLY SPIRIT TO GUIDE YOU, YOU WOULD NOT GIVE IN TO ADDICTIONS.

If you allow the Holy Spirit to guide you, you would not be prone to addictions; you will overcome addictions.

As long as you are in ego, you will be prone to addictions. Addictions stimulate your ego and body and make your ego and body seem real in your awareness. They make you feel separated from your real self, the holy son of God, and separated from other people.

Addictions, be they to food, sex, smoking, alcohol, and drugs, are means of maintaining the ego separated self and feel apart from other people and define you as only in our ego and body.

THE LOGIC OF THE HOLY SPIRIT CANNOT MAKE SENSE TO THE EGO'S LOGIC.

If you allowed the Holy Spirit to guide you, you have denied that you are only ego and body. The logic of the Holy Spirit does not make sense to the logic of the body and ego.

To the ego, that person slapped you and you feel pain and it seems only natural for you to defend yourself by counter-slapping him. If you do, you and he remain in ego for you have reinforced the ego in both of you.

The Holy Spirit's logic, the logic of God, does not make sense to the ego's logic. The Holy Spirit's logic presumes that you are not ego and body and that what is done to your ego and body is not done to you. The Holy

Spirit's logic says, in effect, you have a spiritual self that is not the body and ego you see with your physical eyes.

These days, I always ask the Holy Spirit, God, to guide me and give him thanks for the good and bad that happens to me (we learn from the bad that happens to us as much as the good that happens to us).

Try it. Allow your right mind, the Holy Spirit/Christ, to guide your thinking and behavior and see if you would not live a more peaceful and happy life.

NOTHING CAN HAPPEN TO ONE IF ONE DOES NOT WISH TO EXPERIENCE IT TO LEARN SOMETHING FROM IT.

Given that nothing can happen to one that one does not desire to experience, I chose my crummy body. Through it, I wanted to experience that body poses a problem for people. It makes them believe that they are bodies; hence, are egos.

Body and illnesses of body accentuate one's identification with ego and body. It is difficult to see you as spirit if you are in bodily pain.

I used my weak and pained body to learn how body makes me and people deny spirit and identify with body and ego; I used my body issues to learn about the role of body in human separation from God. Without the illusions of body (matter), space, and time people would not feel separated from God and from each other.

Now that I have learned all these, it is time for me to deny that I am body despite the problems it causes me and for me to affirm that I am the son of God. The son of God is not body; he is spirit.

The body is nothing. It will die and decay and return to the elements that compose it. Those elements will decay into particles. The particles (electrons, protons, and neutrons) will decay to light. Light returns to nothingness from whence we conjured it out and used it to create the physical universe.

The body is nothing. It has no worth and value, so I must deny it as who I am. I am not body. I am spirit. That is my affirmation of the day.

My negative experience with body led me to validate my spirit nature. In that sense, I chose a crummy body to enable me to learn and eventually return to a unified spirit self, my real self.

Ego and body have served the usefulness of enabling me to learn that they are nothing and that what is important is the affirmation of my spiritual nature.

I do not need to defend body and ego anymore; I now transcend them and return to my real self, son of God. That real self is spirit, a part of unified spirit.

In unified spirit, I am eternal, peaceful, and happy.

IT IS OUR MINDS THAT TELL US THAT SOMETHING IS SCARY AND WE FEEL FEAR OF THAT THING.

There are no accidents in our lives. We enter into every situation we are in to learn something about ourselves from it. I once moved into an apartment and there was sound like some folks were running around the place. My girlfriend who moved in with me said that they belong to ghosts. I had dreams in which unseen things were attacking me and I would be scared but struggle with them and wake up.

Those dreams and what stimulated them and the weird sound in the apartment were there to teach me something about myself. They taught me that deep down, I am a very fearful person.

Fear of this or that held me down. No external thing held me down. It was my fear of things that held me down.

I chose the apartment and the ghost idea to learn about myself and to learn about my fearfulness. It was me who made the sound and supposed ghosts fearful. If you do not attribute fear-making to anything, it would not scare you. My girlfriend did not react with fear to the constant feet like stuff running around the apartment.

It is our interpretations of the meaning of things that scare us. Perception of things as scary does not mean that they are scary to other people. You must believe that something can harm you for it to elicit fear in you.

As for the apartment, I made up my mind that it is my mind that made unknown sounds scare me and I stopped allowing myself to be scared. You know what?

The moment I stopped allowing myself to be scared by the unexplainable sound, the sound went away. The sound was there to teach me a lesson and when that lesson was learned, it was no longer useful to me.

Metaphysics tells us that everything we see in our world are dream events projected out by our dreaming minds. In that sense, it was my mind that projected out the weird sound in the apartment as well as projected out the apartment and everything else in my world.

I live in Alaska and go on extended four-hour walks in the bush. There are bears all over the place. As I walk on the hiking trail, sometimes I would see folks stand a few yards away from a bear by the side of the path, waiting for it to leave before they walk on. So, I said to myself: these folks believe that the bear would kill them; hence, they are afraid of it.

But suppose they do not believe that the bears could harm or kill them; suppose they see the bear as a friend, would it hurt them? Find out.

I would see such bears on my path and I would say a silent prayer inside me. I would say: you bear and I are the sons of God; I love you and you love me. And I would mean that love angle. If you do not love the bear, do not dare it for your fear would be picked up by it and it would attack you.

Love is the absence of fear and fear is the absence of love. If you have love for people and things in your mind, they would have love for you and would not harm you. If you fear things, meaning that you do not love them, they would attack, harm, or kill you.

With love for the bear in my mind, I would walk-on past the people scared out of their wits thinking that the bear would kill them.

The point is that it is us who project fear arousing nature to whatever we are afraid of. Believe that something cannot harm you, provided that you love it, and it will not harm you.

EVERY CHOICE THE INDIVIDUAL MAKES, HE MAKES FOR THE ENTIRE PEOPLE AND THE UNIVERSE

Everything that I choose to do affects those immediately close to me and ultimately affects all people. By the same token, every choice another person makes affects not only him and those close to him but all humanity and the universe. This includes choices made by non-human beings. A butterfly flying affects everything in the universe.

If one inherited certain biological issues, one asks: when did I make the choice to have those issues? The fact is that all people who lived in the past, all animals, and all things made that choice for one's own choice affects the birth of every child, animal, and thing on earth.

The universe is a system—what one part of it does affect all parts of it. There is no such thing as an individual's choice that does not affect other people and the universe. The universe is one organic whole and what any part of it does affects all parts of it. What one person chooses, he has chosen for all people and the universe.

Within the universal system are individual systems. One's body, for example, is a system. Disease in any part of one's body makes all parts of one's body to respond to it with disease.

So, you ask: when did I choose to be prone to fear? You chose it when you were born in a specific body that is prone to fear excitation. All people and the universe worked together to make that body possible so all people and the entire universe chose it for you and you chose it for you.

If you prefer to put it in religious metaphors, you can say that you, a son of God, and all other sons of God chose it for you and you chose whatever happens to other sons of God (sons of God include animals, trees, and everything in the universe; galaxies, stars, and planets are included for they all work in concert, as one whole, affecting each other).

The entirety of the sons of God, the entire universe, dreams through each individual. There is no such thing as one dreaming alone.

The choice one son of God made, all sons of God, animals, and things are affected. So, if you say that you do not know when you made the choice to be who you are, the answer is that all people and yourself made it for you in the past, as you participated in making choices for all people in the past, present, and future.

What you need to do in the present is to accept that your choices affect all people and things and therefore make sure that your choices are well-intentioned—good for all people and all things.

In physics, what I said above is called systems thinking. We live in a general system where everything affects everything else. You affect all people and they affect you.

Why are you poor or rich? It is because of the actions of all people and your own actions. Your parents' or society's action contributed to your poverty or wealth.

If that is the case, then we must all work for every child's welfare by giving him publicly paid education in the university and giving all people publicly paid health insurance. It is stupid to work only for your self-interest and ignore other people's self-interest.

In Igbo land, folks work only for their self-interests and ignore other people's welfare. Those born poor grow up to hate the rich, kidnap them, and hold them hostage for financial ransom. And the supposed victims are kidnapped by the poor for they must work for every person's welfare and give up the egoistic nonsense that Igbos are Republican and that each person should only care for himself and not bother with other's welfare.

The moral density of Igbos truly amazes me; it is as if they are born stupid. They always manage to do the wrong things. Instead of learning from those who know the right things, they come out swinging with their ignorance that they think is knowledge. In Nigeria, Igbos are those championing support for Donald Trump. When you try to correct them, they come up with the most stupid arguments why they must support a racist who sees them as dogs and would not hire them for even janitorial jobs. I do not know what else to do to give Igbos some sense. I have tried my best. Maybe the above cogitation on systems thinking might help these lost people called Igbos.

THE ENTIRE UNIVERSE THINKS THROUGH ONE. THE ENTIRE SONSHIP THINKS THROUGH THE INDIVIDUAL.

The entire universe thinks through each of us: human beings, animals, trees, and everything. Whatever a person does is done by the entire universe. If one is rational, the universe is rational through one. If one is irrational, the universe is irrational through one. If one is sane, the universe is sane through one. If one is insane, the universe is insane through one. If you are healed, the universe is healed through you.

The universe acts through me and you. I am, therefore, the universe and you are the universe. If the universe is the collective sons of God, then we are the collective sons of God acting through one.

If the universe is God, then one is God. I am God and you are God and all of us are God.

The idea of individuality by one's doing something without other's involvement in it is balderdash. Lift your hands; wind state permits you to do so. If the wind is strong, you cannot lift your hand. Whatever one does, the entire universe allows one to do it. Therefore, it is fantasy to say that the individual by himself can do anything.

In religious language, Jesus said: by myself, I cannot do anything but by the power of my father in me (meaning the whole universe), I can do anything. True.

WHAT WOULD HAPPEN IF A PERSON DID NOT SEEK THE DELUSION OF IMPORTANCE?

I have looked at human beings in every way one could. What I see are people who suspect that they have no intrinsic worth and are seeking worth. People are right from the beginning of their lives on earth seeking existential significance.

If they have healthy bodies, they appear to get affirmed social worth by doing well at sports, school, and work.

In some instances, they do not get worth from socially approved ways. Neurosis is seeking of worth from false ways, such as trying to seem superior to other people when there is no evidence that one is superior to people in any activities.

Psychosis is belief that one has worth that there is no evidence for, hence is delusional worth. Personality disorders are rooted in seeking worth and value in one's eyes and in other people's eyes.

People seek worth from religion and belief in God. They posit an imaginary powerful figure that they call God and attach their insignificant self to him. As long as they identify with that imaginary, powerful God that allegedly created them and the universe, they derive a sense of false worth.

Women pursue spirituality and psychic phenomenon because in doing so, they give their egos and bodies worth. They mask their underlying sense of worthlessness, insignificance, and nothingness.

The belief in God is delusional. This is because there is no evidence that God exists. God is a figment of the human imagination that belief in it gives people false worth.

Belief in God makes one feel important, significant, and special. If people did not attach themselves to God, they would feel their underlying sense of nothingness, worthlessness, and valuelessness. Without the delusion of God, people know that they are nothing. They are just part of nature. They live and die like animals do. They have no worth, except the imaginary worth they give to themselves.

The term ego means seeking importance, pride, arrogance, or specialness. People's desire for ego is their desire for importance.

What it means to be a human being is to feel worthless and seek worth. Those born with medical issues tend to have accentuated sense of worthlessness and seek it more intensely. They try to use their minds to give themselves sense of worth by pursuing mind-constructed, imaginary, important, and powerful self.

The psychologically powerful self thereafter gives them secondary disease—psychological pain, anger, fear, depression, and paranoia.

So, what would happen if one did not seek any delusion of worth? If one accepted one's self as unimportant, insignificant, worthless, valueless, and as nothing, one would know peace and happiness.

It is the pursuit of imaginary worth that gives people loads of physical and psychological stress, fear, anger, depression, paranoia, mania, schizophrenia, and personality disorders.

IS BELIEF IN GOD DELUSIONAL?

Richard Dawkins wrote a book called *The God Delusion*. He made an argument that there is no such thing as God. Therefore, to believe in him is to believe in that which does not exist. Those who believe in what does not exist are deluded. Religious people are, therefore, deluded.

Sigmund Freud, in his book, *The Future of an Illusion*, pretty much said the same thing as Dawkins. God is an illusion that seems real but is not real, so to believe in it is to believe in an illusion. To Freud, the condition of human existence is precarious. We are born and suffer all kinds of diseases and poverty and want a caring father figure to protect and provide for us.

No one on earth protects and provides for us so we came up with an imaginary father figure and call him God and hope that if we flagellate ourselves by worshipping him that he would protect and provide for us, but he does not protect and provide for us because he does not exist.

I agree with the two gentlemen. But does that mean that there is nothing besides human beings that is intelligent in the universe?

IMPERSONAL INTELLIGENCE IN THE UNIVERSE

My experience tells me that the entire universe itself is intelligent. If you understood what goes on inside an atom, the dance of electrons, protons, and neutrons, or inside the cells of animals and plants, or what goes on inside stars as hydrogen is fused to helium, you must reach the conclusion that there is a kind of intelligence at work in the universe. But that intelligence is impersonal and does not care for human beings.

If there is an earthquake, tornado, tsunami, hurricane, volcano, flood, drought, disease, or epidemic, it kills people as it kills animals and trees. There is simply no evidence of a benevolent figure in the universe taking care of people's needs.

Nevertheless, there is intelligence operating in everything in the universe—in galaxies, stars, planets, people, animals, and plants. The mistake that religious people make is to project their needs to that intelligence and worship it as if it is a caring force.

Actually, when one gives up the desire for an important self and accepts no-self, one tends to experience a different reality, what Hindus call Samadhi, Buddhists call Nirvana, Zen calls Satori, and Christian Mysticism calls the mystical union of one and the universe.

I am not writing metaphysics here and will not explore this subject here; I have done so elsewhere.

PEOPLE WHO SEEK BIG MAN STATUS ARE PRONE TO TENSION, STRESS, AND TELLING LIES

People who are motivated to seem important and powerful or who want to seem like they are very important persons are big men and women generally living in physical and psychological tension and are stressed out.

They are generally immature; they tell lies that make them seem important, powerful, rich, and intelligent. A prime example is the US President, Donald Trump. Practically, every word that comes out of that man's mouth is a lie calculated to make him seem important. The man is a pathological narcissist.

A narcissist exists to seem special and seek attention from people who make him seem important. He is also anti-social in that he pursues criminal activities and uses people to attain his goals and discards them when they are no longer useful to him. He marries women not because he loves them but because of their beauty. He wants to use them as parlor trophies and throw them away when they begin to age for they no longer make him seem youthful and powerful. He must have young beautiful women around him to enhance his machismo.

As children, those seeking importance in people's eyes tell tall tales that make them seem important kids. Even in their old age, they live to tell lies.

An old Igbo Nigerian called Nebu lives to make up stories that make him seem important, powerful, wealthy, and knowledgeable in other people's eyes, except that those around him see him as a pathological liar and a thief. At best, they see him as entertaining (he has a peculiar style of writing English).

Many Igbo Nigerians are driven to seem important and work hard to seem like it seldom caring for other people's needs. They seem to live to seem important in their eyes and as long as they seem individually successful, they are fine. Their narcissism gives them that immature quality people see in them.

This morning news reached me that a popular Nigerian novelist called Chukwuemeka Ike (1932-2020) has died. I read some of his novels, including *Toads for Supper*. I looked in the newspapers to read about the circumstances of his death. They had a picture of him bedecked in Igbo regalia, including red cap and beads around his neck. They appended his numerous titles to him. As I beheld the numerous titles, I asked: what are they for? Why call him Professor Dr. Chief Emeka Ike? Why not just call him Mr. Emeka Ike? The numerous titles are of course meant to show how important and accomplished he was. But he is now food for worms, yes or no?

These people are yet to learn that what makes a person mature is for him to love and care for other people and to serve social interests, not just for one's ego needs. It is not the title one's ego and body is adorned that makes one important. The many titles they adorned the man with kind of made me feel sorry for him—sorry because it occurred to me that he must have felt unimportant and inferior to log around those titles that seem to give him vicarious importance, kind of wipe off his nothingness. Titles cannot make that which has no worth, our egos and bodies, worthwhile.

(Although I have a basket full of academic degrees, I prefer to be referred to without titles. Mr. Ozodi Osuji is fine with me, thank you.)

THE CURE FOR ALL MENTAL, PERSONALITY, AND ADDICTION DISORDERS IS TO STOP SEEKING FALSE WORTH AND ACCEPT ONE'S WORTHLESSNESS.

If you accept your worthlessness and accept other people as also worthless, they merely amuse you when they try to get you to dance their delusional dance of seeming worthwhile. You smile and leave them alone, for to dance that dance is to reinforce their madness. You refuse to make people mad by agreeing to see them as having worth when you know that they have no worth.

In Nigeria, most of the men and women feel like they are shit and mask it with phony worth. They give themselves worthless titles, such as Doctor, Professor, or Chief this or that (Alhaji, Alhaja, and Emir are Nigerian Muslim titles for seeking sham worth).

They call themselves by their profession, such as say engineer this, architect that, lawyer this, teacher that, or professor this. Their professions give them false worth.

They adorn flowery robes to make them seem like lords of the feudal manor. As long as they are attired in these discarded middle ages Arab robes, they seem important in their eyes; as long as they wear those fanciful robes, they are unproductive. They just have to wear the same clothes folks in the industrial west wear to become productive in the workplace.

The women dress in fancy robes and paint their bodies up (they are painted sepulcher) and masquerade around as very important women.

In the USA, having millions or billions of dollars and important political positions, such as Senator, Governor, and President is the way of seeming to have worth in one's and society's eyes. Actors and sportspeople make tons of money and that gives them sense of phony worth.

I, too, danced this dance of seeking false worth. In time, however, I realized that worth is a mere act, that I am not really worthwhile but seeking it and feeling angry when other people did not respect me.

If you want to be killed by people, do not respect them; when you do not respect people, you return them to the awareness of their underlying sense of unimportance and since they want to seem important, they will attack to kill you. In killing you, they have removed the source of their sense of unimportance and return to the delusion of seeming important in their society's eyes.

I decided to see myself as mister nothing, mister unimportance, mister insignificance, mister powerlessness, mister unintelligence, and mister any other negative adjective that makes people feel like they are garbage.

Since I accepted that I am nothing in my eyes and in other people's eyes, what people think or say about me no longer bothers me. I am already nothing so if you call me nothing, you said something new to me.

Since I know that you are also nothing, I know that you are merely pretending to have worth when, in fact, your body is flesh waiting to die and rot and smell worse than feces.

The human body smells worse than shit when it dies. People hide that fact by dressing the dead up, placing them in fancy caskets, and building monument (mausoleum) for them.

Ancient Egyptians built pyramids not to live in them while alive but to store their mummified dead bodies and have the delusion that they are not going to rot and get eaten by worms. It is human vanity that built those Egyptian pyramids.

So, let go of that vanity and pride that you have worth and value and accept that you are nothing, I told me. Thus, I gave up my ego and its desire for false worth.

What happens is that I now know peace—the type of peace that the slaves pursuing the delusion of worth cannot know.

There are thousands of psychiatrists and psychologists out there. They babysit their patients and clients (I used to be one of these so-called mental health professionals). I suppose that they have to do so to be in business and make a living. But if they wanted to heal their clients, they would tell them to accept the simple truth that they have no existential worth, value, and importance. (Some infantile psychologist would probably say that I am depressed because I accept my worthlessness. The childishness of the average psychologist and psychiatrist makes me puke. I have supervised many of them so I know what I am talking about.)

Here is the unadorned truth: people are one giant nothing. Do not seek worth in your eyes and in other people's eyes. Do so and your brain, mind, and thinking are corrected and you live a peaceful life.

You do not have to be the neurotic telling folks that he is superior to people, the manic person who believes that he is the richest and most famous person on earth, the paranoid and deluded person believing that he is god in importance, the schizophrenic believing that he is God himself in importance, or the depressed person who feels like nothing just because she does not see herself as important anymore; hitherto, she had the illusion that she was important until some disappointment made her now feel unimportant, hence her depression. If she could accept her existential unimportance and still determine to live fully, she would no longer be depressed.

All mental disorders are rooted in the desire for importance, desire for big ego-self. Let go of the desire for the special, big ego, accept your existential nothingness, and your mental illnesses are gone.

Indeed, if you can manage to give up the desire for the ego itself, the separated special self, and know you as having no self, you would live in peace and joy despite the nothingness of our lives on planet earth.

RACISTS ARE THE MOST INFANTILE HUMAN BEINGS ON PLANET EARTH.

Have you lived in the USA? I live in the USA. I see many white racists. What do you think that they are doing?

Deep down, racists know that their bodies are food for worms. They know that they will die and rot and smell like shit. They know that they are slaves working hard to make a living for bodies that will die and rot. Refusing to accept this existential reality, they deny it and hide it from their immediate consciousness.

Instead, they look around and find African-Americans, who are obviously at a lower stage of scientific and technological development. They then fancy themselves superior to black folks.

They look down on black folks. To be like black folks in their minds is to be worthless and they do not want that status. Thus, they discriminate against black folks and pretend to be superior people.

I look at them and they amuse me for I know that they are not different from my dog, Ivory; they are going to die and rot. They are nothing, just as I am nothing. The difference between us is that I accept my existential nothingness whereas they hide theirs, hence do the irrational things they do from pretending nonexistent worth.

In Africa, certain tribes pretend to be superior to other tribes and in so doing, mask their existential nothingness.

Igbos pretend that they are superior to other Nigerians and look down on them. They masquerade around as superior people and then die and smell like shit.

If only all people would become realistic and accept their existential worthlessness as I have done and know peace.

SEEK A PROFESSION THAT INTERESTS YOU AND DO IT.

When it is said that one should not desire a big self, it does not mean that one should not have a job. One must have a job to make a living.

Given the reality of human existence, living in a world where no other person or thing cares for one, if you choose to not have a job, which is your right, then you have chosen to starve and die and you are entitled to that choice.

What one needs to do is figure out what line of work one is interested and has aptitude in, goes train for it, and do it because one enjoys doing it.

If you are doing what you like doing, our meaningless and pointless existence becomes a kind of joy; existentialist thinkers like Albert Camus, Jean-Paul Sartre, and Karl Jasper (I am an existentialist) think so, anyway.

I HAVE ONE PROBLEM: THE PURSUIT OF A BIG SELF.
I HAVE ONE SOLUTION TO IT; NOT SEEKING A BIG SELF.
I ALWAYS HAVE A SELF FOR IF I HAVE NO SELF,
THE UNIVERSE DOES NOT EXIST FOR ME.

My one problem is my desire for a big self; my one solution is to not pursue a big self; I always have a self for without the self, the universe would not be known by me or other people.

In not seeking a big self, I relax and have less or no fear, anger, depression, and paranoia; I have a whole world to gain from not seeking a big self.

This is what *A Course in Miracles* is teaching. I came to the same conclusion on my own, actually from reading Alfred Adler and Karen Horney. I am grateful to Sister Helen Schucman for reinforcing the truth I discovered by myself.

THE ONLY PERSON YOU NEED TO CHANGE
IS YOU, NOT OTHER PEOPLE.

The only person I have to change is me; it is not for me to change other people; it is not for me to change the world.

The ego knows that you cannot change other people and the world urges you to change them. It points to others and asks you to change them because it knows that is a doomed enterprise.

THE ONLY THING THAT NEEDS TO CHANGE IS THE EGO ITSELF.

The only thing that needs to be changed is the ego itself. What needs to be done is to remove the ego from one. Just remove the ego in you; do not think or behave from your ego. Do that and do not bother with other people's egos.

It is your ego that needs to end its reign of tyranny over your life. What do you need to change in other people, anyway? Make their egos better, ideal?

Have you made your ego better and ideal?

The world's problem is the ego; the solution to that problem is to get rid of your ego. When you end your ego, you no longer see yourself as your body and as such, would no longer defend your body.

With no attachment to the foreigner (foreigner because he is not your real self, your real self is the son of God) in your life, ego, you would thereafter know only peace, joy, and no fear, anger, depression, and paranoia.

BLAMING YOURSELF FOR YOUR PAST MISTAKES IS SILLY.

I say to myself, if I did not engage in the pursuit of the big ego as I did in the past, I would have done all the right things. True.

WE DO NOT HAVE BIG EGOS. WE MERELY PURSUE THEM.

You do not have a big ego; you pursue a big ego. In heaven, the son of God has a self that is the same and equal with other selves but he pursues a big ego, hence comes to this world to do so.

TO PURSUE A BIG EGO IS TO LIVE IN HELL.

To pursue a big ego is to live in hell; I have lived in hell all my life.

TO NOT PURSUE A BIG EGO IS TO BE IN HEAVEN.

To have no pursuit of big ego is to live in heaven. In heaven, there is still a self but not a proud one. It is one used to love all sons of God.

The word ego is the I, the son of God now seeking pride, specialness, and separation, hence in hell. In pursuit of big ego, the son of God inflicts pain on himself.

It is only a mad man that inflicts pain and suffering on himself. So, you must have been mad to seek a big ego, hence inflict pain and suffering on you. You do not blame a mad man but heal him.

You heal him by showing him how to let go of his pursuit of the big ego so that he lives happily with less self-punishment.

It is therefore a waste of time and silliness to blame one's self for being in pursuit of a big ego, for being mad, and for giving oneself pain.

ON EARTH, EACH PERSON HAS A DIFFERENT EGO BUT NOT NO EGO. NO EGO IS BEING IN HEAVEN.

Each person has an ego. If you had a different ego, you would be a different person. Folks with less rigid pursuit of big ego tend to make friends easily, hence live happily. They have many girlfriends and if girls, many boyfriends.

Men with rigid ego tend to fear social rejection, hence limit themselves to one girlfriend and fear her leaving them. This means that they are in hell. Let go of the ego and you are in heaven.

HOW DID DOCTOR OLUMBA KNOW WHAT HE KNOWS? HE TALKS LIKE AN ORACLE.

When my friend, Dr. O, talks about the spiritual world, he talks like an oracle with certitude and confidence that is out of this world. He knows a lot about spiritual matters. He said that he has visited the spiritual realm, heaven and hell, and knows how they operate.

He sees our world as an illusion, a dream—that when we die, we awaken from the dream and do not remember those in the dream. He said that we even do not remember our wives and children because they are illusions we attracted to our dream but in spirit, are not our wives or children; hence, we do not remember them over there.

The man knows as much as what is written in *A Course in Miracles*. He has not heard about the book and certainly has not read it. Yet, he was not told what he knows by Jesus, as Helen Schucman claimed that Jesus told her.

The only thing that I can say is that some people are highly spiritually evolved. Dr. O says that on earth, some people are in hell, some are soulless, and many are sleeping and dreaming; the dreaming ones are the ones that can be awakened.

He says that what we call our conscious mind is dream mind; he said that we have other types of mind, including the one we have in universal mind, what he calls God's mind. I am very glad that I have this man as my mentor. I just talked to him this morning and he nourished my spirit.

ON THE SELF, REAL AND FALSE SELF AND OTHER MATTERS: NO EGO MEANS NO SELF IN FORM.

If you completely let go of the ego, you return to formless existence in God; you bypass existence in light form for that requires ego, albeit purified ego. Without ego in body, you would not respond to anything in our world and exist only as matter.

Dead bodies do not respond to anything in their environment except in so far as they respond as other matter does—change forms. You can burn, cremate the dead human body, and it would have no motivation to feel fear and anger or run away.

THE FORMLESS SELF IS IN GOD.

The formless self is the son of God, the part of God, the Christ who is one with God, is in God, and God is in him; he does not talk of being apart from God and other parts of God and does not feel superior to other parts of God for to do so is to be unrealistic, to be insane.

Christ is sane hence knows that he is the same, equal, and one with God and all things.

BIOLOGICAL ORGANISMS RESPOND TO THEIR ENVIRONMENT.

The human body and biological organisms in general are always responding to changes in their environment and to things inside and outside them. Their bodies respond and their minds respond, all designed to keep them alive. If there is no body, then there is no response to changes to the environment.

If there is no body and no environment, as metaphysics says, then nothing is responding to anything. In this light, our world and body are dreams projected out by our mind.

Whose mind? Mind of the sleeping sons of God.

HUMAN MOTIVATION IS DRIVEN BY DESIRE TO STAY ALIVE IN BODY AND OBTAIN EGO IMPORTANCE.

If one is hungry, one is motivated to get food. If one is cold, one is motivated to get shelter and clothes and warmth. If one is in pain, one is motivated to eliminate the pain. If one is lonely, one is motivated to find friends. If one is afraid, one is motivated to find no fear.

As egos, we give ourselves pain and all of the above to make us feel like we exist in bodies, and existing in bodies makes us feel like we have powerful separated selves even though a separated self is impossible in the universe where everything is connected.

Folks feel delusional superiority to other folks and things which also are impossible for if one is one with all things, how can one be superior to other things except in madness?

Most Africans are poor and can hardly afford food. They are motivated to go to school, and if possible, university, obtain good education, and go get jobs. With jobs, they hope to be able to feed themselves, their siblings, and parents.

They produce children rather mindlessly as if food will drop from heaven to feed them; hence, they struggle all their lives to feed the many unnecessary mouths they created.

If told to have two children per family, they cry out saying that one wants to reduce Africa's population. They will keep multiplying until eventually, there is no food in Africa and they try to smuggle themselves to Europe and elsewhere, and when those close their doors, they starve and die.

FROM MY CONVERSATIONS WITH DR. O:

Dr. O recognizes that if he is God and God is all-powerful, then he must have power to do works and wonders; a God that created this world must also have the power to do with the world as it pleases. If he does not have such powers and claim to be God, as he says, he ought to be locked up as a lunatic or seen as the greatest fake and fraudulent person that has ever existed.

Dr. O says God told him that he created black folks superior and that they are the chosen race. He will be proclaimed as the replacement of Jesus Christ and that event will be marked by him performing works of wonder and miracles unheard of by man. That would then prove to the world that he is the God-man.

He said that Jesus was God sent to the world to save it whereas he is man chosen to be God and makes a big deal between the two. It seems to make him feel superior to Jesus yet he said that Jesus would be the one to announce his coming.

He said that he has done 90% of the work he needs to do to become God-realized but still has 10% of work left. That ten percent is Adam still clinging to him. That adamic stuff is his seeing himself as body not spirit and he is working on seeing himself as spirit and not body and he will soon accomplish that goal.

Christ is the son of God who knows that all he does is derived from God's power whereas the ego is the son of God who believes that all he does is derived from his own power, hence is proud and arrogant.

This man is very sensitive, feels white supremacy to his core, and wants to overcome it by proclaiming that he is God. If God is made a black man, that would wipe out all white supremacy.

(My observations.)

Alas, Africans are unable to govern themselves well and are so corrupt that they could be seen as subhuman beings; hence, folks will still see them as subhuman beings despite Dr. O's wishes.

I have come to the conclusion that he has not eliminated his ego, hence is not Christ, is still ego, and will not accomplish what he wants to accomplish. If he eliminates his ego and stop saying that he is the chosen one, then he can accomplish what he wants to accomplish.

He is invested in being the chosen one and has stories of how in visions when he was nineteen-years-old, God told him that he is to save the world; how in 1981, 1995, 2007, and 2010, the angel Raphael told him that he is God's chosen one.

He appears deluded but talks as if he is sane. I will just listen to him and desist from giving him western psychiatric diagnosis.

THERE ARE NO ACCIDENTS. PEOPLE MEET FOR A PURPOSE, TO LEARN FROM EACH OTHER AND TEACH EACH OTHER.

As I see it, Dr. O is here to teach me some lessons that I need to learn. There are no accidents. He is me projected out; he mirrors my thoughts;

his egoism is my egoism; what he is teaching me is that if I let go of my egoism, I will be God-realized. He volunteered to show me how a very bright man who wants to be God-realized but keeps the ego cannot achieve it, meaning that if I want God-realization, I must let go of my ego—all of it. Keep some ego and you are in the world of space, time, and matter and see you as body and you will die.

As the man said, if he is God, why would he die? He would simply pass to glory; transform his body to light form. He said that death is suicide and I agree.

The four levels of being are:

our world of dense matter;
the world of light forms, which is our world purified with forgiveness and love;
the world of pure thought, aka gate of heaven; folks here guide those on earth;
heaven; heaven is formless thinking; those in heaven do not understand the physical universe for to them, the physical universe does not exist.

THE EGO IS THE PROUD SON OF GOD.

To live from ego means to live from a proud self, hence to be deluded, to be insane. One avoids other people so as to go retain a false proud self (example is avoidant personalities) or if one is the active type, one joins other people and try to get them to see one as superior to them, such as narcissistic egos. An example is Donald Trump.

TO LIVE FROM THE REAL SELF IS TO LIVE FROM OUR SHARED UNIFIED SELF.

To live from the real self is to live from our shared selves, same and equal. One always has a self in heaven and on earth; in heaven, the self is equal to other selves; on earth, the self is separated and arrogant hence hellish.

The Buddhist idea of having no ego means that one still has a self but the self of heaven, not the proud ego-self of our world. The Buddha self is the same as the Christ self—the son of God who is one with God but is not God. He is also one with other selves but is not other selves.

If one is truly a psychologist, one would understand the madness of folks and ignore them since they cannot be corrected. You do what is right and overlook a mad world. For example, the Republican-controlled US Senate is currently engaged in a charade of trying Donald Trump. It is not a real trial; how can you have a trial without witnesses? I know that the Republicans are egos, mad egos, so I overlook them and do not pay attention to their brand of ego madness.

CHRISTIAN BELIEF ACCORDING TO DR. O:

God created us in glory; Adam and Eve sinned; Jesus allowed his body and ego to be crucified so that he regained his glorious self that God created, so his crucifixion was a coronation. He reunited with God; you, too, have to do the same: crucify your ego and body and reunite with God, be reborn in God as Jesus did and become a God-self once more.

In the filthy cradle of Bethlehem, God became man so that man in the clothes of calvary may become God.

I need do nothing to return to awareness of God. It is in trying to do something that I developed the proud ego-self hence punish me. Remove the ego, do nothing, and know that you are already a son of God and obtain his glory (*A Course in Miracles*).

Adam and Eve left the power and glory of God to seek separation in flesh, space, and time. They did so with the delusion that it gives them power—the power of science and technology. They sacrificed the power of God, the union in them, for the power of the individuated self.

Jesus came and sacrificed the ego's individuated power, sacrificed nothing, and returned to real power, the power of the totality, the whole, God. Now that he has regained God's power, he can do miracles—resurrect the dead from ego state to God and Christ state, walk on water, change water to wine, and heal the sick.

So, what benefit do ordinary people who now say that they have given up their attachment to the ego and its false power derive from saying so?

Are they empowered and do miracles, give themselves wealth, and overcome death and diseases? This is the realistic me asking mystics a basic question: what do you get if you let go of ego and embrace God?

You go about telling people to give up their ego power and accept God's power but they are still poor, weak, diseased, and would die; why should they listen to you? Indeed, if they do and see themselves as God and are still poor, folks will see them as psychotic.

Hindus ran around calling themselves God but remained poor and diseased; their mystics were supported by their followers so they had only manipulative power, not real power.

Ego power is power based on separated self and is powerless.

Ego-lessness is returning to Christ state, to Holy Spirit, and to God and its power is derived from union, not individuated power.

ELIXIR

Dr. O's book is to be called *Elixir*, meaning eternal life, eternal youth, never aging, or from return to God state. His religion, he says, is called Christism instead of Christianity.

So, we remove our egos and return to ego-lessness, which is Christ self, son of God, and God power, and never taking personal responsibility for what one does but realizing that everything is done with God's power in one, hence humility and real power going together for one does not take credit for the power. This is because one knows that power comes from the whole and is real.

Technically, if you let go of your ego, you are in Christ, son of God, and since God is all power and his son is all power, you now have all power. You can now have all power over the universe as Jesus did. You could perform miracles.

According to ACIM advanced teachers of God who now live from Holy Spirit and live in peace, in their presence you experience only peace; they do not plan their day but do as Holy Spirit asks them to do; their bodies are healed and they can heal people.

POSITIVE EGO AFFIRMATION LEADS TO WEALTH.

Rich Americans have good egos and affirm their egos in doing something that contributes wealth to them and society; they are outgoing.

My ego withdraws to go seek idle power and is not affirming itself in anything positive in the egos' world other than criticizing people for not being perfect. My personality has been this way from childhood and is a product of my weak body.

BODY, PERSONALITY, SPACE, AND TIME ARE REAL IN THE DREAM.

We invented body and matter. We used light to form matter and used matter to form different bodies for us. Our bodies are then used to differentiate us physically and personality-wise. Each of us is made different from others because of our body and personality. In the dream, our body and personality are real to us just as matter, space, and time are real to us and he must live in them.

Without body, personality, society, matter, space, and time we all revert to oneness, sameness, or equality. In the long run, all body is made from matter and matter is made from light which is made from nothing, so the body while seeming determinant of ego and personality, really does not exist. You can use your mind and belief to will the body, space, and time away and experience yourself as part of God's unified spirit.

On earth, body is real; if a heavy stone falls on your body, it will crush it to death; the sun will burn you to death; you need cars and other means of transportation to travel from point A to B.

POETS WRITE RELIGION AND SPIRITUALITY AND PUT WHAT CAN BE EXPLAINED SCIENTIFICALLY IN EMOTIONAL AND EVOCATIVE LANGUAGE.

God is. This means that God is the whole and only the whole exists; each of us is a part of the whole; the whole is in us and we are in the whole but the whole is in me and other people and whereas it is the same everywhere, in the dream giving the body, space, and time it manifests. In each of us, the whole seems different. This is because each of us seeks specialness.

The same chemicals are in your body and in other people's bodies but are arranged a bit differently in you and other people to give you different personalities, specialness. If you melt down the chemicals in the human body, you reduce them to light and to nothingness, meaning that the different personalities given to people are in dreams, not in reality. In reality, we remain the same, equal, and unified, although in our present awareness, we do not see those.

The ego and its differentiated world as articulated by science are what we see, so science and technology appear to have won over God as it is supposed to do on earth.

There are infinite egos; they all act in concert to invent this world and they all must act to end this world; when one son of God is enlightened, he has to continue doing something to help end the universe, waiting for all the other children of God to do their bit for the universe to end.

One Christ cannot end the world; all of them must do so. Let go of your ego and let Christ, son of God, and Holy Spirit think and behave through you.

Your ego gave you all your suffering and your Christ gives you all your liberation from suffering.

DREAM
JANUARY 17, 2020
2:42 AM

In this dream, I looked into a culvert and saw writing pads in a box but I could not enter the culvert to get the box out since there was a barbed wire on my side of the road; so, I walked along the road until I found a place to enter into a field that would take me to the culvert. I saw a bunch of high school kids and initially felt fear that they might mug me but asked them to come help me get the box and they agreed to do but the road became extended and we had to cross pools of water and most of them turned back. Only a couple were now with me as we approached the culvert and I woke up.

The meaning of this dream is that I have one more book to write to complete my writing on metaphysics. I still have not put my metaphysics in a coherent form. The dream also means that only a few persons will help me complete the task.

MY EXISTENCE FORCED ME TO BE BODY-CONSCIOUS.

My existence and its body issues forced me to be body-conscious. In being body-conscious, I forget consciousness of God. To be body-conscious is to be not God-conscious. That is, the body problems I have forced me to be body-conscious; they were designed for me to forget God and my higher self.

CONSCIOUSNESS IS REALLY OF BODY, MATTER, SPACE, AND TIME; IT IS FORGETTING GOD.

Self-consciousness is body consciousness and an attempt to forget spirit consciousness. When we fell from the Garden of Eden, what happened is that we became body, time, and space-conscious and forgot being spirit-conscious. The fall into darkness is the decision to forget our real self, souls, spirit, God and become aware of this world, hence live in darkness.

Salvation from the sin of Adam and Eve is to return to spirit consciousness. Jesus came to get people to leave their Adam and Eve body consciousness and return to God, spirit consciousness.

IF YOU LIVE FROM HOLY SPIRIT THAT IS FROM GOD, YOU HAVE OMNIPOTENT POWER.

If you live from God and God is all-powerful, then you have all the power of the universe in you and can use your mind to give you whatever you want.

If your god mind, the mind of the son of God, can invent this world, then your mind parked in the Holy Spirit can reinvent this world and give you all the wealth and power in this world. You do not have to wait to win lotto and become rich.

Dr. O uses the gospel of John, Chapter fourteen, where Jesus talked about himself and God as one. To say that he and God are one, Jesus did not use another person's saying to make his God-self real. He experienced God and knew that it is true and does not use external references to make his point. Dr. O needing external reference points means that he has not experienced oneness with God and is just talking intellectual stuff on God. He lacks power that can only be derived from experience of oneness. He changes the date when he would do this or that, from January 17 to January 27 to the end of the month; he is merely expressing his ego power wishes and not speaking from the authority of God. He is an egotistical Igbo who has read spirituality and claims powers he does not have. His blindness means that he is not seeing well; he has not corrected his perception to vision yet; as such, he cannot help anyone else to correct his perception, to vision.

IN DELUSION, DISORDER IS CERTITUDE OF BELIEF.

Dr. O has total certitude that he is the God-man, that he is God-self, a part of God who is one with God and has God's power. If that is true, how come he is poor and is seeking the keys on how to win the lotto so that he wins and gives folks money? If he is truly God, he would have real power to manifest money or get the wealth to give folks millions. He is a study in religious delusion disorder, the God delusion.

Hang around him and use him to understand the God delusion. There is God alright but he is an impersonal intelligence operating in all of us.

The soul of man is restless until he knows that he is part of God. Ephemerality is an illusion.

Humanity lives in lies if it believes that it is flesh, not spirit. Humanity is derived from humus, that is, earth; that is the notion that people are of the earth, dust. These are lies; the truth is that people are spirit.

Dr. O has certitude in his belief that he is part of God, is son of God, and wants to act as if he has the power of God's son, as Jesus allegedly had. This certitude could be real or could be deluded. Who knows?

Dr. O is really smart. If he used mere intellectual thinking to reach his conclusions, which are as good as what Helen Schucman reached and attributed to Jesus, then he is very smart. He probably had a 4 GPA. I suspect that he has genius level IQ, at least 160. He is one of those unique Africans with IQ that is outside this world. If he eliminates his ego, he would be the God-self he wants to be. He is already it but his ego covers it, as it does in deluded persons.

He talked about three possible lines of action: one by man that helps other men as much as possible; hence, he wants to give ten thousand dollars to Igbo traders whose shades were burned down; the line of action of government that builds infrastructure; the line of action by God that has omnipotent power to change things.

Using laxative or coffee to bring about bowel movement is artificial and dangerous; what needs to be done is to change one's eating habits and eat only what gives one regular bowel movements.

Spirit is restless until it returns to God. Upon entering body, spirit forgets its spirit nature and identifies with body and in body, sees itself as body and experience the illusion that it is separate from God and other spirits. Spiritual light projected out physical light.

Christianity is supposed to teach people that they are the sons of God hence spirit, but instead, it teaches them that they are body. Christianity is institutionalized hypocrisy—it turned Christianity into a self-centered institution.

WE SEEK ATTENTION FOR OUR BODIES TO FORGET THAT WE ARE SPIRITS.

We compulsively seek attention for our bodies and in so doing, forget that we are spirits. Yet, body will die and decay hence is nothing, so we are seeking attention for nothing. Body and ego are the same and both die; our thinking and its output die with our death; spirit is not in body and lives forever; spirit has unified thinking which we in ego separated thinking cannot understand.

MAYBE THE REASON WHY NO ONE HAS PRACTICED CHRISTIANITY IS THAT CHRISTIANITY IS A HOAX.

Dr. O talked about how no one has yet practiced Christianity. Christianity is the teaching that we are not bodies but spirits. To be a Christian is to know that one is the son of God and is spirit. Instead, the Christian church teaches people to believe that they are bodies, a falsehood.

Dr. O said that he traveled 7 billion miles to reach God and that God looks like a person but is made of diamond, glittering; thus, he created us to look like him, in his self-image; he made us of sand, nothingness, but sand is crystal which ultimately is diamond and light.

IN DREAMS, WE SEE A SEEMINGLY SOLID WORLD SO OUR DAY WORLD COULD ALSO BE A DREAM AND ULTIMATELY, THERE ARE INFINITE UNIVERSES EACH A DREAM AND DOES NOT EXIST BUT SEEM TO EXIST FOR THOSE IN IT/THEM.

In effect, only self and its thinking apparatus, mind exists.

LIVING FROM THE REAL SELF

Living from the real self means living from the son of God; the son of God is spirit so it means living from spirit; it means living from Christ; Christ is the son of God who knows that he is one with God; it means living from a self beyond body and ego and living from love.

The payoff of living from God's spirit is that one lives in peace and joy whereas living from body and ego means that one lives in fear, anger, depression, and paranoia; those who live from ego and body devote most of their time to protecting their egos and bodies.

Since the ego and body are affected by a myriad of dangers, such persons devote most of their energies to defending their bodies and egos; when they die, both their bodies and ego thoughts die; only spirit lives on; spirit is not in body.

One now uses one's body to communicate love, to teach union, and return to the awareness of spirit in people.

The mindset of man is that he is Adam; this means that I am one with my body and will die; the mindset of the son of God is that he is spirit and is eternal; one goes from human consciousness, that is, ego conscious to divine consciousness to Christ consciousness—the awareness that one is one with God.

Dr. O agrees with me on these conclusions; the only difference is that he sees himself as a person chosen by God to represent him in the extant world. I know that some persons are spiritually more aware than others; the average person has only human, that is, animal consciousness.

He also believes that black people are created superior to white folks and says that black people are the chosen race by God. He says that white folks have laid claim to science and technology and that there is no way that black folks can compete with them in those fields; he says that white folks are lacking in spiritual matters and that it is only in spiritual matters that black folks will shine more than white folks.

DREAM
JANUARY 23, 2020
8:40 AM

THE MIND THINKS IN SYMBOLS.

In this dream, I was sitting by a university, maybe UCLA (When I was a student there, I was once sitting at a bus stop at Westwood Boulevard, the bus stop before you enter the campus, and Wilt Chamberlain came by, wearing shorts and in general basketball player outfit and stood at the bus stop; he was over seven feet tall and dwarfed me. Neil De Grasse Tyson dwarfed me in this dream). I saw a tall, lanky black man, over ten feet tall and asked him: are you Neil De Grasse Tyson, the black astrophysicist who does TV shows on the origin and nature of the universe? He looked at me and I stood up to shake his outstretched hand and my head was right around his waist. We talked and he asked me what I do and I told him that I am a professor. We walked around the campus, talking tête-à-tête. We saw some oriental students walking around (Orientals are taking over America's top universities); I invited him to my house and pointed at it, and then I woke up.

Here, my mind in a dream took a black man who is an astrophysicist and made him very tall when in real life, he is right around my height, medium. Why did my mind make him tall?

He studies astronomy, the heavens, and my mind placed his head into the sky symbolizing that he studies the heavens above my head. His tall height also symbolizes my admiration of him for I'm proud that a black man has Ph. D. in astrophysics and is nationally known in that line of work to the point of doing a television series on it. He has also written books on it.

In dreams, our minds do things in symbols. Poets, religionists, and spiritualists also talk in symbols. If my mind could create a dream in symbols that look real, how do I know that the day world is also not a dream world in symbols, this time in symbols that seem solid?

We know that the material universe is made from light so the entire world could be light used to make solid symbols to have us experience limited existence in a world where we see solid things, like our bodies and walls limiting what we do.

If we correct our thinking, we could transcend the world of apparent solidity and experience the spiritual world.

FATHER DIVINE AND DR. O

Last night, I talked to Dr. O. He talked about his belief that he is God, and that God chose him to represent him in this world at this time; he sees himself as the person Jesus promised to come after him to do greater works than him.

His firm belief that he is God kind of makes me see him as deluded yet he does not talk like a deluded man. So, after talking to him, I remembered another black man who claimed to be God, Father Divine (1876–1965), and read up on him before going to bed.

I asked myself: what makes these people claim to be God? Father Divine had claimed to be God and folks believed that he was insane, so he was given psychiatric examination but was not deemed psychotic. He preached his stuff and many gathered around him; he apparently had many followers until he died in 1965. So, what makes some people claim to be God? I do not know.

DR. O DEPOWERS HIMSELF BY CLAIMING TO BE GOD.

Dr. O calling himself God, son of God, Christ, and so on is actually depowering himself. He is assuming that God is so powerful that he needs to be as powerful as God. One should not call oneself by another person's name.

The psychotic denies his apparent powerless self and claims to be God or Jesus Christ because that claim makes him seem powerful since those are deemed powerful in our world.

What one needs to do is live what makes sense to one without saying that one is God, Jesus, or whatever other so-called spiritual being one deems powerful.

I am not God (God is the whole, I am a part of that whole, not all of it) nor Jesus nor Krishna nor Rama nor any other name deemed powerful. I am a part of a universal life force that folks call God and you too are part of it. Some of us seem more aware of that reality but nevertheless, all of us are parts of God.

WHEN YOU ARE CALLED TO DO SPIRITUAL WORK, YOU CANNOT RETURN TO SECULAR WORK.

Years ago, I found college teaching the most nonsensical work there is and cast for something else to do. I did mental health work. Clinical work for a while seemed satisfactory. A few years later, it was humdrum so I cast for something else to do. Since I am a trained college teacher, why not go back to teaching at colleges? I tried but found doors closed to me.

I found that if one is called to doing spiritual work, teaching oneself and mankind that we are spirit is what satisfies one; pretending to be bodies and devoting all one's energies to protecting one's body can no longer suffice. One must now affirm our spirit self and cannot find any other type of work satisfactory.

I must talk about spiritual, psychological, and physical matters to be me and find living satisfactory. I cannot go back to being a mere secular scholar.

LIVE WHAT YOU KNOW TO BE TRUE.

I do know that there is a life force that we can call God but it is actually nameless; for to give him a name is to limit him with whatever that name connotes in our mind.

That life force is like spiritual light and each of us is a particle of that wave of spiritual light. That life force is eternal and is love. I know this to be true. Therefore, I must live it, that is, love me, love other people, and love the entirety of being. I live it and teach it.

I know that our bodies and matter, in general, is made from physical light projected out by spiritual light. Our bodies are vulnerable and feel harmed by all sorts of things, we feel weak and are preoccupied with defending our bodies, hence see us as bodies.

We are not bodies. We must overlook our bodies and live as we are, spirit beings. In living as loving spirit beings, we know peace and joy. This much I know to be true and must live it for in doing so, I live my truth.

THERE IS NO US AND WORLD. OUR MINDS MADE THEM UP.

In dreams, one's mind takes from one's experience during the day events or persons and uses them to make a point it wants made; it does so symbolically, not factually.

In the dream, my mind made Neil De Grasse over ten feet tall to symbolize his interest in astronomy, a person who studies the skies above our heads.

In my vision/dream where Jesus appeared to me as a white man in papal clothes, the dream used Jesus in a manner that my Catholic upbringing would believe—see him as a pope, a holy man.

In both dreams, the characters were distorted. Neil Grasse is about five feet ten inches tall and Jesus was probably an Arab-looking guy.

In the dream in which my mind used weird sounds in my apartment to invent ghosts attacking me in my dream world, my mind used mere sound to produce faceless attackers.

The point to all these is that the dreaming mind takes actual events or mere ideas accepted by one's mind as true or possible to create a dream event.

Jesus may or may not have existed as an actual person; if he existed, he was brown, not Nordic; De Grasse is not ten feet tall; there are no ghosts.

The lesson of these three instances where my mind distorted what my day life would call reality to make a point for me is that the day world itself is the invention of my mind.

There is no world, day, or night; all worlds are made up by my mind and your mind. We invent worlds to experience whatever we want to experience.

There is no me in body, no you in body, no matter, space, and time; my mind, your mind, and our minds conjointly made us up and made up the world we seem to live in.

Therefore, we can reject our egos and bodies and the world of space, time, and matter and regain awareness of our real selves, unified spirit selves.

Even that is conceptual and thus, not true. What is true is the conceptualizer. What the conceptualizer is, none of us on this side of heaven knows.

That is to say that we do not know what our real self is; we merely have conjectures of what it is and accept our concepts and ideas as true when they are not true.

And do not talk to me about physics, chemistry, and biology for I can teach you those; I know that matter is apparent, not real. All matter can be reduced to light but where did that light come from?

We do not know. Physics ends at singularity before the Big Bang, the explosion that began the world. What lay beyond singularity, the Big Bang, matter, space, and time we do not know?

IT IS A FALLACY TO CLAIM TO BE ALL OF GOD.

The problem with Father Divine and my friend, Dr. O, who claim to be God is that they are overstating the truth. They are not God. There is God.

All of us are parts of God, in anthropomorphic language; we are the sons of God. One God extended himself to each of us. Collectively, we can be said to be God but even that is not true for the whole is greater than the sum of its parts.

God is in me, you, and all things. God is in us and outside us; God is therefore larger than each of us and all of us added together.

Hindu mystics made a similar mistake when they claimed God-realization; what is true is for them to claim to have realized Atman, their real self, a part of God but not all of God.

What Father Divine or Dr. O should say is that he is part of God or that he is a son of God, which is the same thing as saying that he is the Christ also called the Buddha, Atman, or Chi.

People go off the deep end when they call themselves all of God. If father Divine is God, and since God is eternal, why did he die at age 89? He should have lived eternally.

My friend, Dr. O, is blind. If he is God and has the power of God, he would not be blind or could heal his blindness.

In the future, God working through all of us, that is, as scientists, would figure out a way to heal blindness and indeed, science would figure out a way to remove our bodies and show us that our true selves are eternal spirit selves.

Poor education is behind Father Divine and Dr. O's claim to be God. If they had studied physics and also understood metaphysics, they would have known that all of us are parts of God and that one person alone cannot be all of God.

Their claim is motivated by pride and hubris, the egos desire to create the entire world and not have God be the creator of the world, hence wrong.

There is delusional quality to their claims. However, they are not clinically deluded; they are just mistaken. Education in physics would have corrected their overly poetic statements about reality.

Richard Dawkins talked about the God delusion. He too is wrong but it is delusion to claim to be God. God exists alright but what he is we still do not know. We merely project our limited understanding of God to him.

DETERMINISM VERSUS ACCIDENTS

IF EVERYTHING IS OF GOD, IT FOLLOWS THAT WHATEVER HAPPENS TO YOU IS DONE TO YOU BY GOD AND SINCE YOU ARE PART OF GOD, YOU AND ALL PEOPLE DID TO YOU WHATEVER HAPPENS TO YOU.

If everything is God and something happens to you, it follows that God did to you whatever happens to you. Since you are part of God, you and everything that happens to you was done to you by you. So, you cannot blame other persons, yourself, or God for what happens to you in your life.

You attracted everything that happens to you in your life to experience it; you attracted the person who seemed to harm you in your life or did bad things to you, so as to experience what he did to you, and learn whatever lesson you want to learn in this lifetime.

There are no accidents; there is no way something can happen to a son of God that he did not want to experience and learn from it.

For example, black folks attract racists to their lives to learn about discrimination or putdowns and despite it, have positive self-esteem and not hate the racists calling for hatred.

You decided what family you are born into to learn from their configuration of characters. You decided on the people you meet to learn from them.

For example, I am Igbo. I chose to be born Igbo so as to learn about Igbos. The Igbos and their njakiri can destroy folk's self-confidence but can also enable folks to learn not to pay attention to what other people say about them. I attracted specific Igbos such as Nebu into my life to learn from their crazy characters. From Nebu, for example, I learned that one can be insane—the man is deluded and still seem to be sane. I learned that many people on earth are lunatics while seeming to be rational.

You have to have confidence that God, meaning all people, will do the right thing for you. You must not have fear and doubt in your mind for God protects his son, you. Even if bad things happen to you, they are for your long-term good. Thus, you must be grateful for everything that happens to you. In this, you know that there are no accidents and you are in peace. Love all and leave it at that.

People come to this world in groups. You came with your parents, siblings, and people around you in general. Each of you agreed to play a role in each other's lives. You play a role for me and I play a role for you. You may play the role of my father, mother, or sibling and I play the role of your child or sibling. When that role is done, we move on.

In the world of after death, people may momentarily recognize those that they had played roles for but may not (the roles were done in dreams; the earth is a dream hence easily forgotten). They move on to play other roles for other people on earth. There are infinite roles and people requiring roles for them.

The point is that those who are related to you on earth are not related to you in eternity except in so far that they are all sons of God.

An atheist may dismiss all of the above as gibberish; to him, everything that happens in this world is accidental. Accidents determine our birth, those around us, and what happens to us. Science seems to agree with the atheist that accidents determine our lives. I have no plan to argue with atheists and scientists' belief in randomness, chance, and accidents. I have done that elsewhere.

Believe what you like. Whatever makes you feel good, accept it into your life. As for me, I know that there are no accidents in my life.

However, for logical consistency, even when folks attract events into their lives, those events are accidental for they did not have to happen, could be changed, and are not written in stone.

ARTISTS ARE IN DREAM STATE.

Artists are generally in a dream state; they are dreaming and in a dream, do their painting, sculpturing, writing novels, plays, and poems, and composing their music but do not know how to explain them nor do they want to explain them for to explain them is to spoil their beautiful works of arts.

Philosophers are beginning to awaken from the dream called life in body and want to explain it. Scientists explain physical phenomenon but not life itself.

Founders of religion such as Buddha, Jesus, and Krishna are like artists; they are in dream states and write poems that they call religion. Those religious poems are explicated by philosophers, aka theologians.

I love classical music. One of the greatest surprises of my life is to learn that the great musicians such as Bach, Mozart, and Beethoven could not explain what their beautiful music means. No painter can explain what he paints. It is left to critical thinkers to attempt to explain art and merely project their own understanding of what the immortal artists worked on.

DEATH IS THE FINAL DELUSION.

Death is the final delusion. Death is an effort to make ego and body real. One must have first believed in ego and body for one to die. If one had not believed in ego and body, one cannot die. We do not live in ego and body and ego and body do not exist, hence do not die. But in the dream, we make ego and body seem real and death-like sickness is another means of making what does not exist seem to exist.

AN IDEALISM, DELUSION IS AN ATTEMPT TO MAKE A WORLD, SELF, AND BODY THAT DOES NOT EXIST SEEM TO EXIST.

In delusion disorder, one wishes for a big, powerful self. It does not exist but one posits it and defends it and defense makes it seem to exist for one. If other people do not acknowledge it, one feels fear of its death or anger at them for not acknowledging one's wishes for big self.

If you wish for no big ego, let go of the big ego. You would not have a need to defend the big ego and would not be deluded.

In delusion disorder, one defends a false, nonexistent bogus self.

DREAM
JANUARY 27, 2020
2:30 AM

In this dream, I stood in front of a man in a cage, the type government clerks are in; he was answering questions for folks. When it got to me, he would not let me ask my question. He ignored me. When someone else came up and asked a question, he answered it. Finally, I got frustrated and asked him why he is ignoring me. He still ignored me. Over time, he came out of his cage, grabbed my head, and turned it to those standing around and said, "Look at this man, he is a well-read man and yet he is here asking me questions and has no project he is working on." I woke up.

The meaning is that I have had my questions about God answered and I keep wasting my time asking the same questions without working on any project to put what I already know into practice. The lesson is for me to stop asking God, Jesus, and the Holy Spirit questions because they have already given me all the answers to my questions but for me, like Jesus' story of talents to go use the talents, answers were given to me to make a living and increase wealth for all humanity.

Interestingly, before I went to sleep, Dr. O talked about his realization that God had given him all the answers he needs to do his work but for some reason, he has not begun his work and is still waiting for God to give him his omnipotent power by giving him the key to win lotteries, get into billionaires' heads and make them give him millions of dollars, and sundry other ways to make money with which he does his work.

MY RELATIONSHIP WITH L

She is here to enable me to correct my perception of women and people in general and my self-perception. I see her dancing around with many people on social media and that annoys me. She is seeking attention from many folks because she feels alone just as I seek attention from people because I feel lonely. The goal is for me to overlook her ego and body behaviors and join the Christ in her and in doing so, become one with her, heal myself, and heal her and know love and security. It is not for me to judge her behavior as good or bad or talk about it with other people to desecrate her name.

PSYCHOTHERAPY: PURPOSE, PROCESS, AND PRACTICE
According to *A Course in Miracles:*

A Course in Miracles was written by Professor Helen Schucman. She was a clinical psychologist who taught at Columbia University, New York City. Later on, she wrote a 24-page pamphlet called *Psychotherapy: Purpose, Process, and Practice*. That pamphlet is now added as an appendage to the main text, *A Course in Miracles*. It is an extension of the principles of the course to psychotherapy.

In this write-up, I will try as much as possible to translate Dr. Schucman's verse to prose. She was a poet and wrote in poetic language. I am a philosopher and find it difficult to grasp poems. I made a valiant effort to understand what Dr. Schucman wrote from what I call a poet's stream of consciousness.

She said that Jesus Christ dictated the materials she wrote to her. However, she was a trained psychologist and psychoanalyst and only a psychologist would have written what she wrote. I prefer to see her writings as from her subconscious mind.

There is a higher part of us that we do not understand. Some call that higher part of us our right mind, the Holy Spirit, and ultimately, God. I tend to see merit in that belief but, in this writing, I am going to proceed on the assumption that Dr. Schucman wrote her book.

She begins by asserting that all therapy is psychotherapy. This is because, according to her, all illness is of the mind. Mind is sick when it seeks what she calls specialness, essentially, when it desires to create itself, create God, and create other creations of God.

In heaven, it is impossible for a son of God to be special. He was created as an extension of God and cannot become the creator of his creator. Unable to create God, himself, and his brothers, the son of God, as it were, cast a magical spell on his self and went to sleep. In his sleep, he dreams that he is now separated from his father. Our phenomenal world of space, time, and matter is the dream in the mind of the sleeping son of God.

That world seems real but is not real. It is mere thoughts projected into a dream and made to seem to be real. On earth, we sleep and project out a world that seems real and while we are sleeping, that world seems real to us but upon waking up in the morning, we realize that that dream world had never existed.

Our present world is a dream; when we wake up from it, we realize that at no point has it existed. Not for a second has the world existed.

Look at yourself, a self in body, walking around in space and time and interacting with other people in bodies but none of you are real. You are all dream figures.

In the dream, we take the dream world as real. If we know that it is not real, we would no longer be asleep and dreaming. We must forget that it is a dream for its dream events to not seem real to us.

Dr. Schucman says that the world is an illusion, not real. Space, time, and matter are all illusions. You in body, other people, animals, trees, planet earth, stars, galaxies, and the physical universe do not exist; they are all illusions that to us seem real.

They are real to us because we want them to seem real. They are our handiwork, our idols, we made them and we are proud of them. Their seeming reality makes us seem powerful, like the creator of the universe.

When we seem to have separated from God and began inventing this world, God could no longer commune with us as he did in heaven. He did not want to wake us up. Instead, he created the Holy Spirit and placed him in our right minds.

The Holy Spirit is in heaven and knows heavenly unified reality but is also in our temporal minds and sees our world. It does not prevent us from seeing and dreaming but reinterprets our dreams. It gives a different meaning to our dreams.

When in our dreams we see other people attack and hurt us, the ego-mind asks us to defend ourselves by counterattacking the attackers. If we counterattack our attackers, they too will defend themselves and counterattack us, hence, the unending attacks and counterattacks of this world. The Holy Spirit tells us that the attacker wants to push us away from him, to separate from him. He asks us not to attack him in return for to attack him is to push him away, hence maintain separation between us. It asks us to forgive the attack on us.

Whereas the ego and the logic of the world ask us to defend ourselves, the Holy Spirit has its own logic. It asks us to forgive attackers. In forgiving attackers, we overlook their attacks and the attacking world.

The logic of defenselessness is that the world we see attacked in is a dream world. Defense makes the dream world seem real. But if we do not defend ourselves when we are attacked, that is, if we are forgiving, we have judged the attack and the world of attacks as not real and overlooked it. We have, in effect, overcome the ego and the egos' world, for now, we see the world as a dream world and what is done in dreams has not been done.

If we judge the world as nonexistent, the Holy Spirit says that we have made the right judgment and we wake up from the dream, for that means that we no longer value what the dream world offers us—life in bodies and in space, time, and matter.

Since we may still value life in form, the Holy Spirit remade the world of forms into forms of light. Thus, when we forgive people and the world, we see ourselves and the world in light forms. Our entire world, people in bodies, now look in light forms; animals, trees, planets, stars, and galaxies are now in light forms. This is a beautiful world to look at but it is still an illusion. It is a delightful illusion to look at for a while before we transit to formless heaven.

God and his sons live in the world of formlessness. Heaven is formless. We can see heaven as spiritual light. God is the wave of that light and each of his infinite sons is particle of that light.

The purpose of spiritual psychotherapy is to help both the therapist and patient to give up their illusions and belief that their egos, bodies, and the world are real.

The physical universe does not exist; it has not existed for a second and cannot exist. To us, it seems to exist. So, we first change our perception from seeing it in dense forms to seeing it in light forms and thereafter, not seeing it at all as it disappears into the nothingness from where we conjured it out.

The purpose of psychotherapy is to enable us to change our self-concepts from special, separated selves living in matter to forgiving and loving separated selves living in light forms.

The Holy Spirit does not take us back into heaven. We are always already in heaven but while in it, sleeping, dreaming, and seeing the world of matter, space, and time. When we have decided to give up belief in specialness and forms, we simply awaken and know that even when we saw ourselves as on earth, we were always in heaven.

Psychotherapy brings us to the gate of heaven but does not take us into heaven.

People go to therapists in pain. They see their minds and bodies in pain. But they do not know that the source of their pain is their self-concepts. As long as they have separated self-concepts, they have attacked themselves and attacked reality.

They want therapists to make their egos stronger so that they are able to deal with their pain. But their self-concepts and egos are the problems.

Healing is not making the ego stronger; healing is in giving up the ego and its body altogether and not desiring and defending them.

People go to therapists and tell them what their parents, siblings, and people, in general, did to harm them. Ego therapists see them as victims and talk to them on how to better defend their egos and bodies. They do so expecting relief but merely making their pain either masked or exacerbated.

Secular therapy enhances the ego and this enhances the problem and does not heal anyone. Spiritual therapy heals people by asking them to jettison the ego, to not retain any bit of it.

Let go of all ego. To let go of the ego, one must see what other people did to one as what one asked them to do to one.

God has only one son. That one son of God divided himself into infinite sons of God. Each of us is the one son of God with infinite sons of God in us. When other people do things to us, we, in effect, did them to us through what seems like other people. Therefore, we must forgive those who did harmful things to us and in doing so, forgive ourselves for the harms we did to other persons.

The initial goal of psychotherapy is to enable us to change our self-concepts—from unforgiving self-concepts to forgiving self-concepts.

When the self-concept is retained but made a forgiving one, one now is capable of forming what the course calls a holy relationship. Here, one sees oneself and other selves as one shared self, hence no longer blame other people or oneself for the seeming wrongs that happen to one. One knows that the world is an illusion, a dream where bad things seem to happen but have not happened for what is done in dreams have not been done. One is now having a happy dream and is at the gate of heaven, but not in heaven for heaven itself is formless.

A forgiving person is a peaceful and happy person whereas an unforgiving person is an unhappy person.

What needs to be done to become healed is for us to use our purified self-concepts to join other people in our interpersonal relationships.

Our ego and its defenses are designed to separate us from other people. Therapy enables us to let go of those defenses so that we now become aware of our eternally joined, unified nature.

What is healing? Healing is the awareness of one's joined state with other people. When one knows that one is joined with other people, one is healed.

Here are quotations from the pamphlet that make the points I made above:

"The world he sees does therefore not exist. Until this is at least in part accepted, the patient cannot see himself as really capable of making decisions. And he will fight against his freedom because he thinks that it is slavery."

"All psychotherapy leads to God in the end."

"Psychotherapy is a process that changes the view of the self. At best this 'new' self is a more beneficent self-concept, but psychotherapy can hardly be expected to establish reality. That is not its function. If it can make way for reality, it has achieved its ultimate success. Its whole function, in the end, is to help the patient deal with one fundamental error..."

"The therapist as well as the patient may cherish false self-concepts, but their respective perceptions of 'improvement' still must differ. The patient hopes to learn how to get the changes he wants without changing his self-concept to any significant extent. He hopes, in fact, to stabilize it."

"No one who learns to forgive can fail to remember God. Forgiveness, then, is all that need be taught, because it is all that need be learned. All blocks to the remembrance of God are forms of unforgiveness, and nothing else. This is never apparent to the patient, and only rarely so to the therapist. The world has marshaled all its forces against this one awareness, for in it lies the ending of the world and all it stands for."

"One wholly egoless therapist could heal the world without a word, merely by being there. No one need see him or talk to him or even know of his existence. His simple presence is enough to heal."

"Hear a brother call for help and answer him. It will be God to whom you answer, for you called on him. There is no other way to hear his voice. There is no other way to seek his son. There is no other way to find yourself. Holy is healing, for the Son of God returns to heaven through its kind embrace. For healing tells him, in the voice of God, that all his sins have been forgiven him."

"Only Christ forgives, knowing His sinlessness. His vision heals perception and sickness disappears. Nor will it return again once its cause has been removed. This, however, needs the help of a very advanced therapist, capable of joining with the patient in a holy relationship in which all sense of separation finally is overcome."

"Strictly speaking, the answer is no. How could a separate profession be one in which everyone is engaged? And how could any limits be laid on an interaction in which everyone is both patient and therapist in every relationship in which he enters?"

"There are some in this world who have come very close, but they have not accepted the gift entirely in order to stay and let their understanding remain on earth until the closing of time. They could hardly be called professional therapists. They are the saints of God. They are the saviors of the world. Their image remains because they have chosen that it be so. They take the place of other images, and help with kindly dreams."

"Only an unhealed healer would try to heal for money, and he will not succeed to the extent to which he values it. Nor will he find his healing in the process. There will be those of whom the Holy Spirit asks some payment for his purpose. There will be those from whom he does not ask. It should not be the therapist who makes these decisions. There is a difference between payment and cost. To give money where God's plan allots it has no cost. To withhold it from where it rightfully belongs has enormous cost. The therapist who would do this loses the name of a healer, for he could never understand what healing is. He cannot give it, and so he does not have it."

DISCUSSION

Every person in your life you attracted into your life and are there for you to choose differently, to choose once again, and see him as part of you. To be in this world, you had chosen to see him as separate from you; now you must choose that you are joined to him. Now, choose to see him or her as a brother, as joined with you.

Your wife, husband, child, girlfriends, and any human being in your world is there to help heal you. They do bad things to you and normally, your ego defends against them by doing bad things to them. You judge them as evil and push them away.

The Holy Spirit asks you to forgive them. In forgiving them, you love them. In forgiving, hence loving people, you join them, hence heal your relationship with them.

The therapist removes his sense of specialness and separation from the patient and sees him as one with him and sees his issues as his issues. He forgives the patient's issues and joins him and in so doing, heals himself. He has now seen the patient as innocent, guiltless, sinless, and holy.

Each of us believes that he separated from God and heaven and feels guilty. It is that sense of sinfulness that makes us sick. We have not separated from God and therefore, have not sinned.

Nevertheless, we cherish separation, hence feel sinful. We are to see people as not separated from us and from God. We are to see what they did in the world of separation, on earth as done in dreams, hence not done.

Thus, despite what they did that seem evil, they remain as God created them, innocent. We are always innocent and holy despite what we did to each other and our seeming separation from God.

All psychotherapy lies in seeing oneself and other people as innocent, sinless, guiltless, and holy. When a person sees himself as joined to God and all people, he feels innocent, and in that feeling, has changed his mind and returned it to unified state. His mind is no longer separated from God and is healed.

When his mind is healed, whatever illness he had projected to his body is now healed. Body sickness reflects our sick minds—our beliefs that we are special and separated from God.

Heal your mind by seeing other people as one with you and your physical issues are automatically healed.

All these entail letting go of one's ego, separated self-concept. If one becomes egoless, that is, no longer believes oneself to be special and separated from God and all people, one is healed.

As a healed person, one is now a healer. One can literally heal all people. One heals all people by seeing them as innocent and knowing that they are one with one.

It does not mean that removing one's sense of separated self would make other people's bodies healed. They must themselves also believe that they are one with God and all people for them to be healed. They add their sense of union with the therapist's sense of joining with them to be healed.

An egoless person is now the son of God who is as God created him, unified with God and all people. He is now the Christ. He works with the Holy Spirit in healing the world; that is, in teaching people that they are unified and should forgive each other, overlook each other's ills.

Unfortunately, most therapists, like most pastors, are unhealed healers. They retain their sense of specialness and separation and are thus sick. With their sick minds, they want to heal other's sick minds.

An unhealed healer cannot heal other persons. Let go of your belief that you are body and is separated from other people and you have removed the veil that covers the face of Christ in you. You have changed your self-concept; from ego separated self to Christ unified self, corrected your perception, and now see holistically.

You see other people in light forms, that is, Christ vision. You are now a healed healer and are a savior of the world. You join the other healers of the world and heal God's sick sons.

We are all sick if we believe that we are bodies in space, time, and matter. We are healed when we know ourselves to be one with God and all people and are not in bodies; not for a second have we lived in bodies.

Body is an illusion. Ego is an illusion. Do not defend them for they are not who you are; they are false aspects of you, your dream self that you defend to make them seem real.

Defense does not make the unreal real. The real does not need defense to make it real; it is always real.

Who is a psychotherapist? All of us are therapists but there are professional therapists who may be useful if they know that they are not the healer and accept that the right part of their minds, the Holy Spirit and forgiveness, is the healer. If they assert their ego expertise, they are not healers; they are like religious ministers who are unhealed healers making the situation worse.

Should therapists be paid for their services? In our world, we all have financial needs; we have to pay our bills. Therefore, whereas therapy should not be charged for, patients should pay what they can pay the therapist.

The therapist will be given the money he needs to do his work. The Holy Spirit somehow will make sure that those with money give the therapist the money he needs to do his work but under no circumstances should a therapist be in the business of healing people because of the money he charges them.

CONCLUSION

Has anyone seen any of these ideas work in our world? Jesus Christ is said to have been led by the Holy Spirit and healed people.

In my world, I have not seen anyone do what Helen Schucman said is done when the Holy Spirit guides one. Nevertheless, somehow, I believe that what she said is true. I am supposing that I am just going to have to remove my ego and join people and God and see if what the lady said is true in my life.

Until I know it to be true, all I can say is that it is an interesting idea.

Essentially, Helen Schucman's spiritual psychotherapy is a version of what secular therapists call cognitive behavior therapy. It aims at changing people's minds, their cognition, and patterns of thinking from seeing themselves as separated from God and all people to see themselves as unified with God and all people.

It is in return to unified thinking that one feels unified with all people and in that state of union, one is healed in one's mind.

A healed mind, that is, a joined mind, heals one's apparent sick body. All sickness inheres in separated minds; return your mind to eternal union with God and you are healed—your mind and body are healed.

Forgiveness and love are the primary means of returning to the awareness of our eternal union hence to health, mental and physical.

- Schucman, Helen (1976). *A Course in Miracles*. Mills Valley, California: Foundation for inner peace.
  See section called *Psychotherapy: Purpose, Process and Practice*.

A COURSE IN MIRACLES IN PSYCHOTHERAPY:
PURPOSE, PROCESS AND PRACTICE SAYS THAT:

"One wholly egoless therapist could heal the world without a word, merely by being there. No one need see him or talk to him or even know of his existence. His simple presence is enough to heal."

Beginning today, my birthday, January 28, 2020, I, Ozodi Thomas Osuji, undertake to be egoless. I do so because I have experienced the stressful gifts of the ego, first hand.

The ego, especially the wish for a big ego, is responsible for all my anger and fear episodes. Wishing for a big self, I am acutely aware of when other people did not treat me as if I am very important and powerful. I erupt in anger at them saying, in effect, how you dare treat me as if I am not important. My fear is also rooted in my ego's wish not to fail.

At school, I was so afraid of not doing well in my classes that I nearly dropped out of elementary school to go maintain my wished-for big self.

The pursuit of the big ego is responsible for my anger, fear, depression, and paranoia. If I do not pursue big ego, I would be at peace. I would be calm all the time.

It is the wish for big ego that led me to withdraw from other kids and society and in social isolation, nursed a false big ego (this is what shy, avoidant personalities do).

If I let go of the ego, all of it, big or small, I am then empty inside me and the Holy Spirit, love, takes over. I love me and all people and all people love me. The universe of God gives me all I need to survive and teach ego-lessness.

5

EACH PERSON'S BODY HAS BEEN EVOLVING SINCE THE BEGINNING OF THE UNIVERSE 13.8 BILLION YEARS AGO AND SO IS HIS EGO-SELF

According to contemporary physics, the universe came into being 13.8 billion years ago. It has been evolving since then. It evolved into each person's present body. Each person's present body is the product of 14 billion years of evolution. The mind that operates through the individual's body has also evolved for fourteen billion years.

Maybe the individual is produced by accident or design; it makes no difference which is true; what is objective is that the universe evolved to who he is now in body and mind.

Thus, religious folks are correct in saying that each person has been planned from the foundation of the universe.

Dr. O is correct in saying that who he is today is planned from the inception of the universe. His absolute egotism that sees him as God's representative on earth evolved to what it is today from the beginning of the universe, fourteen billion years ago.

He can change it by giving up his ego and becoming egoless, hence becomes the savior of the universe he is craving for. If only he lets go of his ego and loves and forgives all people, that is, allow the Holy Spirit to take over and make him a changer of people, a savior of the world; but if he keeps his grandiose ego, he is going nowhere.

He is however useful to me; he enabled me to learn from his egoism the pitfalls of pursuing big ego. What I learn from him is to give up my wish for big ego. I am not the big ego I wish for.

Evolution, which I am a part of, made my body weak (so as to my father, grandfather, siblings, and children). I evolved a big self and planned to use it as a magic wand, a powerful god with which I overcome my ego and body weakness.

I inherited a mitochondria disorder, Cytochrome C oxidase deficiency, as well as spondylolysis and Mitral valve prolapse. Those combined to make my body traumatized and hellish to live in. I live in bodily trauma that translates to psychological trauma.

But that desired big ego becomes the source of all my present problems; it gave me fear, anger, depression, paranoia, and other emotional disturbances and inability to settle on a career.

Each career I tried did not seem to have enough power for me, did not give me the opportunity to change me and the world, hence not satisfactory, and I give it up. This is meant to be. It was inevitable.

I am meant to learn from this situation and then give up the wish for passive big ego that withdraws to nurse big ego or wish for big ego that enters society and struggle to act as the big ego.

Now I wish for no ego. The ego is not who one is. It is a big self one wishes that one ought to become and evolve toward it.

It is the special self—the pursuit of which led one to separate from God and his creation to go become it.

Who one is, in fact, is the egoless self, the son of God, the Christ. If the big ego is not pursued and one accepts egoless self, one then returns to the awareness of one's true self, the son of God, the Christ, a part of God, and in it has all power. However, it would not be ego-given power but power given by the whole universe, aka God, hence is now able to change the entire world.

In pursuit of big ego, I have not done a job with one hundred percent mental presence for I was always aware that no job is good enough to give me the type of total power I wish; moreover, extant jobs were hard on my fragile body.

Now, I live egolessly and teach ego-lessness (that is, teach people how to live in peace and joy). What is my vocation, my job, my career? It is to live egolessly and model it to all people, and live in the peace and joy it gives me.

Living egolessly, which means living as the Christ, the son of God who depends on his father to provide for him, the entire universe gives me all that I need to live and do my work, a work that only I, the egoless self, can do.

I am an advanced teacher of God; the universe and its God gives me all I need to teach about God, which is to teach about living egolessly, lovingly, forgivingly, and living as Christ.

DR. O IS SELF-DECEIVED.

Dr. O is playing an elaborate game on himself. He said that he has finally been given the keys to the wealth of this world. This is supposed to have occurred on January 17, 2020. From January 27, he would start picking up billions of dollars and on February 1, 2020, he will give me a million dollars to do some of his work. Of course, this is wishful thinking and is not going to happen.

This is because he is still in ego and is not an enlightened man. Everything he says is self-referential, meaning that his ego is grandiose and delusional.

Only the egoless can actually conjure money out of nowhere for they are now in God. And the egoless is not in human forms, body or light form.

This man deceives himself. He will not call me for a while and thereafter, will call and give a reason why he is not now a billionaire or even thinks that I had forgotten it and talk about other egoistic nonsense about how he is a God-man.

He is a study in idealism becoming religious delusion disorder.

NORMAL PEOPLE ARE IN DEEP SLEEP AND VALUE THEIR EGOS AND BODIES. THEY VALUE NOTHINGNESS.

Normalcy is taking the ego and body as important and worth working to provide for. Normal people have deep acceptance of the human ego and body as worthwhile; normal folks work hard to preserve their egos and bodies; they serve them as slaves serve their masters.

All of human civilization is meant to protect the ego and body. Food, clothes, medications, houses, and governments are all meant to protect the human body and ego.

Normal people set up governments to protect their egos and bodies. Governments are given the authority to kill those who threaten or harm what folks value—their egos and bodies.

Society is an agreement by egos to protect the human body and ego. The desire to protect the ego indeed led to inventing matter to house egos; space, time, and matter were invented to house special ego selves.

Normal people wish for specialness and separation; they are deep asleep; they are not yet beginning to awaken to their true spirit selves.

Normal people are totally deluded in seeing the nonexistent. Ego and body are not only existent but worthy of desire and protection.

Neurotics devalue their egos and bodies and other people's egos and bodies and seek an exaggerated ego and body to replace them in themselves and people.

Not valuing people's egos and bodies set them up to be hated by other persons.

Igbo neurotics want to seem great egos and bodies and devalue other people's egos and bodies, hence other people hate and kill them and will continue doing so until they become normal and value and respect all people's egos and bodies or grow out of neurosis, value the spirit in people, and keep quiet about the value of their egos and bodies.

The entire universe exists to value egos and bodies so you must not negate it in people and expect them to like you.

The sons of God have God's powerful minds and with those powerful minds, wish for specialness and separation. They invented the universe of space, time, and matter.

Minds that invented this universe are powerful and you must respect them.

Even if you know that the universe is illusory, you must still respect ego-minds that invented and adapt to this universe.

You can understand that normal folks have group delusion disorder in valuing the valueless and worthless, ego and body, and leave them alone without telling them that they ought to not value their worthless egos and bodies and the things of this world.

In the here and now world, people engage in scientific and engineering feats to construct the wonderful buildings and structures of this world to make their living in it pleasant, make their egos and bodies, make nothing, and live well. Leave them to do what they value and do not tell them that they are psychotic for valuing nothing.

Not every person is ready to transcend ego and body. No more than a person or two in every century is ready to leave the world of space, time, and matter.

EGOLESS PEOPLE LEAVE THIS WORLD AND ARE NOW SAINTS.

The world exists to make people who live in ego and body live well. If one is not in ego and body, one will leave this world. Dr. Schucman, in *Psychotherapy: Purpose, Process, and Practice*, said that folks who have completely let go of their self-concept egos do not stay in this world but leave it, and people in this world remember them as saints and pray to their images for help.

Without ego, what is one to do on earth? It is ego that learns so without ego, there is nothing to learn. One returns to knowledge, which is of formless heaven.

If you see anyone on earth and he is in body, he is still in ego and still learns ego-lessness and forgiveness; when he is done, he returns to egoless heaven. On earth there are, however, degrees in people's state of ego, some more so than others.

"There are some in this world who have come very close, but they have not accepted the gift entirely in order to stay and let their understanding remain on earth until the closing of time. They could hardly be called professional therapists. They are the saints of God. They are the saviors of the world. Their image remains because they have chosen that it be so. They take the place of other images, and help with kindly dreams."

Forgiveness requires learning. Having learned forgiveness, one returns to love, knowledge, and heaven.

Learning ends with forgiveness. Forgiveness begins on earth and continues through the world of light forms and ends there and folks return to love, knowledge, and heaven.

Love does not require forms, body or light forms. Egoless people are the sons of God, Christ, but because they had lived in forms before, they can show themselves in light forms to those on earth but do not return to earth, for they have nothing to do on earth; the earth is for egos and learning and is no longer useful for forgiving and egoless people.

Egoless persons cannot live in body for living in body entails living in ignorance, dreaming, but they are now awake and live in knowledge, not in body.

WE LIVE IN A WORLD WHERE OPPOSITES MUST EXIST FOR IT TO EXIST.

Inside atoms are negative electrons and positive protons (and neutral neutrons). Our bodies are composed of atoms.

Atoms are differentiated into elements by the number of electrons, protons, and neutrons in them. For example, hydrogen has one electron and one proton (its isotopes have neutrons). Helium has two electrons, two protons, and two neutrons. Carbon has six electrons, six protons, and six neutrons. Oxygen has eight electrons, eight protons, and eight neutrons. You go down the periodic table until you get to the heaviest element—uranium with ninety-two electrons, ninety-two protons, and one hundred and forty-six neutrons.

The point is that all atoms have negative and positive parts to them. Our bodies are composed of atoms and elements and have positive and negative parts in them. Without these positive and negative parts to our bodies, our bodies would not exist.

At the macrolevel, we have opposites, such as day and night, good and bad, man and woman, adult and child. Without these dualities, these opposites, nothing moves in our universe. Your car and all other locomotive equipment require opposites to spark for them to move.

Planets, stars, galaxies, and the entire universe need the presence of opposites for them to exist and work.

In social life, we have competition and cooperation. We must compete and must also cooperate. If we only compete, there would be no human society, so we must also cooperate. If we only cooperate and do not compete, there would be no new things and society would die from stagnation.

Paradoxes and contradictions must exist in our world. There must be good and evil for our world to exist. If you want only good and not evil, you must be outside our world.

Here is my metaphysics and ontology. Our world came into being in opposition to God. Because it came into being in opposition to God, everything in it must oppose each other.

What is God? No one has seen God so whatever one says about God seems speculative. Be that as it may, my conception of God is that he is one self that is simultaneously infinite selves.

God is one wave of spiritual light that contains infinite particles of spiritual light. The wave and particles are one. In effect, God is one self that acts from all of its infinite parts and they all act in tandem, in concert. God is one self and one mind that thinks through its infinite parts to that one mind.

Each of us is a part of God. I am thinking. This means that God is thinking through me. He also thinks through you.

In heaven, all the infinite sons of God and God are one; they share one self and one mind. They are formless energy that can be transformed into infinite things (matter).

We desired specialness, superiority, and inferiority, power and powerlessness. In heaven and in God, we are the same and equal, so we cannot gratify our wish for specialness in God and his heaven.

We closed our spiritual eyes and dream of a world that is the opposite of God, heaven. We dream of a world of opposites, a world where people are separated from each other and live in space, time, and matter (space, time, and matter enable us to seem to live separated from each other).

In our world, everything opposes everything. That opposition is the condition for the existence of our physical world.

RETURN TO ETERNITY, GOD, AND HEAVEN

If we give up opposing each other, having different political ideologies, and so on, we return to unified state, to God and his heaven where only the same and equal selves exist. It is only in God and his heaven that we can eliminate living in opposition to each other.

As long as we are on earth in matter, space, and time, we must oppose each other. There will be men and women, capitalism and socialism, competition and cooperation, rich and poor people, and so on. This is the nature of our being on planet earth. You cannot change it.

If you want to change it, then tune out the world of opposites and reawaken to the world of sameness and union. We are actually always in the world of sameness and union while dreaming that we are in the world of opposites. We live in eternity and dream that we are in the world of time, life, and death.

If you think about it, there can be no life and death; it is either one exists or both do not exist; if there is life, there is no death; if there is death, there is no life; if there is light, there is no darkness, etc.

DISCUSSION

What I said above is not exactly new. The Chinese and Korean concept of yin and yang pretty much says the same thing. Hindus talk about us living in the world of opposites and multiplicity. *A Course in Miracles* talked about how our world came into seeming being from opposition to the unified will of God, hence in it is divided wills.

I said nothing new but have said it in my own way. You say it in your own way. There is nothing new under the sun.

I was what folks call a dilettante. I was very good at psychology, philosophy, and physics. I could not make up my mind to channel all my energy to one of those fields. I did not understand why. Now I know why.

I needed insights from all three fields to provide Africans with a reasonable philosophy, one based on up-to-date psychology and physics. Africans lived in primitive societies and had primitive religions and philosophies. They are therefore lost in the modern world of science and technology. They need a new philosophy to enable them to adapt to the exigencies of this world. I am here to provide them with that philosophy.

When they talk about African religions, they talk arrant nonsense, such as those who want to return to what they call Egyptian religion, Kemet. Egyptians embalmed their dead bodies to prevent them from rotting and being eaten by worms and to live forever in body. This is based on their primitive religion. If they had the equivalence of modern physics, they would know that their bodies are composed of matter, which is made of atoms made of particles and which is made of nothing. Thus, they would not have had the elaborate nonsense of embalming their bodies. Their religion is primitive and we do not have to return to it.

We do not have to return to any African religion for they are all primitive, and I have studied them and known that they are simply primitive attempts to cope with the phenomena. Africans need science, a reasonable religion, and philosophy. I provide it to them.

NOTHINGNESS DOES NOT EXIST; SOMETHING EXISTS.

All matter and energy during the Big Bang, 13.8 billion years ago, came from nothingness. Nothingness does not exist. Something exists. That something is spirit. God existed before the Big Bang.

The physical universe of space, time, and matter does not exist. Physical phenomenon seems to exist when it is wished for and believed in. If the desire and belief are withdrawn, they do not exist.

For example, when you die, the physical universe does not exist for you. You do not see the world. However, if you still have a desire for separated self, you will see yourself in a world of separation, perhaps the world of light forms.

At night, you sleep and do not know about the existence of the day world. Your desire to still live in a separated self in body wakens you to that day world; if your desire for separation is not there, you will not wake up from your nightly sleep.

Spirit and matter cannot coexist; it is either one exists or the other does not exist. We have spirit in us; otherwise, we would not think and matter cannot produce thinking. Therefore, only spirit exists.

DR. O AND ADOLF HITLER HAVE SIMILAR PSYCHOLOGY.

Dr. O is pretty much like Adolf Hitler. He talks about how black people are superior to other races; Hitler talked about how Germans are superior to other people (this is, of course, nonsense for in truth, all human beings are the same and coequal). He talks about how his Igbo people are a special people, chosen by God to lead the world (this is self-serving rubbish, a neurosis that seeks superiority and see other people as inferior to him and his people); he talks about how he is the representative of God on earth and the most gifted spiritual leader. Hitler talked about himself as the best political leader on earth.

These two gentlemen suffer from delusion disorder, one political and the other religious. Psychologically, we can say that racism made Dr. O feel totally inferior and he compensates with desire for false, neurotic superiority and reverses racism and makes his Igbo and black people superior to those who see them as inferior, white people, and sees his inferior-feeling self as superior to all people, at least, in the world of religion.

Psychology is useful but there is also spirituality. He has spiritual pride—the same pride that led us, the sons of God, to separate from our father, God, and dream a world where we seem different from each other and pursue different interests.

This man presented himself to me to study the nature of man; man is inherently deluded and hallucinates. Our physical world does not exist except as a dream in which we see what is not there and hear those not there talking.

Dr. O is playing an elaborate game on himself. He said that he has finally been given the keys to the wealth of this world. This is supposed to have occurred on January 17, 2020. From January 27, he would start picking up billions of dollars and on February 1, 2020, he will give me a million dollars to do some of his work. Of course, this is wishful thinking and is not going to happen.

This is because he is still in ego and is not an enlightened man. Everything he says is self-referent, meaning that his ego is grandiose and delusional.

Everything he says is self-referent, meaning that his ego is grandiose and delusional. (If you are a clinician, see David Swanson et al (1970). *Paranoia*. New York: Norton.)

Only the egoless can actually conjure money out of nowhere for they are now in God. And the egoless is not in human forms, body or light form.

This man deceives himself. He will not call me for a while and thereafter, will call and give a reason why he is not now a billionaire or even thinks that I had forgotten it and talk about other egoistic nonsense about how he is a God-man.

He is a study in idealism becoming religious delusion disorder; he is what psychologists call the paranoid prophet.

Ozodi Thomas Osuji, Ph.D.

EVENTS IN OTHER UNIVERSES FILTER INTO OUR DREAMING MINDS.

I had the television on and fell asleep. In my sleep, I dreamed of US military movements in Africa. I saw US troops in West Africa, East Africa, and elsewhere in Africa. I woke up and looked at the still on television and General Carter who had been appointed the commander of US military presence in Africa talking to an interviewer about US military activities in Africa. He was not on the tube when I was awake and must have come on while I was asleep.

What he was saying apparently filtered into my dreaming mind. My body, brain, and nervous system picked up what was going on the television and incorporated it into my dream, albeit in a distorted manner.

I am very visual; my mind visualizes whatever it hears. If I am in a lecture hall and the lecturer is talking about, say, events in Europe, my mind would visualize what he is saying in pictures of it taking place in Europe. In this situation, the general was merely talking about US military formations in several parts of Africa without showing pictures of those military formations but my mind visualized the military formations as he talked about them, albeit in a distorted manner in my dream.

The lesson here is that when we are sleeping, our bodies and minds pick up what is going on in the external world and incorporate them into our dreams. We respond to events in our day world while we are dreaming and supposedly have tuned out that world and are not aware of what is going on in it.

I am positing a hypothesis that our day world is also a dream. In this dream, we do not know what is going on in other dimensions of being. Our brains somehow pick up what is going on in some dimensions of being. Events in other dimensions, other universes, filter into our minds and we do not see or know about them as accurately as they are but distort them.

I have had what folks call near death and out of body experience. I have been in what folks call the world outside this world. I am not here arguing the veracity or lack of it of the world NDEs see. Knock yourself out arguing its real or not. All I know is that I have seen myself go outside my body, go through a dark space, see a point of light, pursue it, and enter a world of light forms. That world still looks like our world except that everything in it is in light forms. People, animals, trees, houses, planets, stars, galaxies, and everything in our world is in it but they are in light forms and are incredibly beautiful.

Tell me that I was dreaming and I say yes provided that you also tell me that what you call our world is a dream. In that light, there are many dream worlds where each of them seem real for those in it, just as when you are in our world, you take it as real even though it is not real.

Well, I have had out of body experiences and been to the world of light forms. I also know that that world is a dream world; it is not real just as our current world is not real.

I know that there is another world that is what folks call heaven. Heaven is formless. In it, people are mere ideas—ideas of parts in an idea of a whole. The idea of the whole is what people call God and the idea of parts is what people call sons of God. There is God and there are his infinite sons.

God and his sons are in each other. There is no space or gap between them. Where one ends and another begins is nowhere; they have one self and one mind. They are in eternal union.

In their eternal union, they are incredibly happy and peaceful. You cannot understand what I said unless you have had union experience.

To have union experience, you must be a loving and forgiving person. Heaven and God are love. If you want to come to heaven, to God, to love, you must be a loving and forgiving person. Hate one son of God and heaven closes its doors to you.

Those who hate each other are sentenced to the prison house called planet earth. Yes, planet earth is a literal jailhouse for unloving persons.

Imperfectly loving persons are in the world of light forms and perfectly loving persons are in the formless world of God.

The point I am making here is that events in the world of light forms and in heaven do filter into our minds on earth. They do so in a distorted manner just as when we sleep and dream and our minds pick up events outside our bodies and distort them.

Some of us have extraordinarily sensitive bodies and minds. It is people like me who pick up events in other worlds whereas dense people, people closer to animals than to human beings, the unloving brutes that constitute the majority of mankind, do not tune in to what is going on in other worlds.

Before you show your little learning, may I remind you that in 1958 Hugh Everett, at Princeton University, someone wrote a doctoral dissertation, supervised by the great Nobel Prize Quantum physicist, John Wheeler, in which he argued that the Big Bang produced many worlds?

David Deutch of Oxford University has devoted his academic life to arguing for what he calls multiverse, the idea that there are many universes, and that although we do not know about them, they somehow affect us and we affect them.

I believe that the idea of multiverse is true. By the end of this century, physics would have proved the existence of many universes. For now, let us see the idea as heuristic. Let us see my contention that ideas from other universes filter into our minds, albeit in a distorted manner, as a hypothesis. Let us just think about it and stop running around with the less than one percent understanding of known phenomena that we call knowledge.

Dark energy constitutes 73% of our universe and we know nothing about it; dark matter constitutes 23% of our universe and we know nothing about it. We have only begun understanding the 4% of our universe that is visible. We live in near-total ignorance of our world and masquerade around as experts on things in our world.

And if you are one of those psychologists who say that NDE and OBE are the product of certain neurochemicals released in our brains when we are dying, may I ask you to prove your hypothesis with experiment? Real science accepts only what we can observe and experimentally prove.

In the early 1950s, two professors at the University of Chicago, Urey and Miller, tried to prove the hypothesis that life originated in a pool of water where accidentally, the sixty-four elements in the human body (carbon, hydrogen, oxygen, nitrogen, iron, copper, calcium, zinc, magnesium, potassium, phosphor, sodium, chlorine, and so on) accumulated and heat from lighting made the elements to combine to form biological cells, flesh. We know that on earth, bacteria formed about 3.5 billion years ago.

They placed those elements in a test tube and heated them up. They obtained a kind of jelly but certainly not animal flesh.

I wonder why other biochemists and biophysicists have not tried to improve on Urey and Miller's experiment, and go on to figure out a way to speed up the jelly's life for 3.5 billion years to see if human cells would form? And if human body is formed, would it have consciousness?

If you believe that consciousness is produced by the permutation of elements in our brains, especially by electrochemical behavior in our brains, please perform an experiment and prove it. Demonstrate that matter produced consciousness.

Until you do so, I choose to believe that consciousness is not the product of matter. I believe that consciousness uses our human bodies to play with. Our bodies are like cars and consciousness is like drivers. Drivers use cars, our bodies, to drive around. The nature of cars, our bodies, affect the driver's ability to drive around. Sick bodies impair our thinking.

And while you are at it, let me tell you that I see God as a positive force and see hell as a negative force. I see God as a kind of energy and matter and see hell as kind of like anti-matter and anti-energy. Those two forces are attacking each other trying to annihilate each other, as matter and anti-matter do.

After you have thought about my hypothesis, then write about your finding and let me know about it; perform this thought experiment and let us read your result.

This afterthought is mostly what occurred to me yesterday after I had posted an essay on how opposing forces make our world work. The thought is that I needed to have pointed out that the belief in solids is an illusion. Why so?

During the Big Bang, a point of light not larger than a pin's head came out of nowhere. It exploded into photons and sped off and the photons of that light formed electrons and quarks. Quarks formed protons and neutrons. Protons and neutrons combined to form nuclei. 400, 000 years later, nuclei captured electrons and atoms; mostly hydrogen and helium were formed. The resulting cloud of hydrogen was separated into clumps. Each clump was acted on by gravity to form a star (in stars, hydrogen atoms fuse into helium).

Exploded massive stars, supernova, produced elements beyond iron. The resultant 92 elements formed planets, comets, asteroids, and medium-sized stars such as our star as well as our bodies and everything else.

If you heat your body, animals, plants, land, mountains, planets, or stars with enormous heat, you would reduce them back to light.

That is to say that everything in the universe is light in a congealed form. If you had the right equipment, you would see your body and all bodies as swirling light energy. The table and solid things around you are light in disguised forms.

Folks with purified eyes, that is, loving persons, do see things in light forms (love is light). This means that the idea of the world of light forms is very scientific but it may not be as obvious to dense minds as it is to sharp minds.

Only light exists.

Where did the physical light that formed our material universe come from? It came from what we do not know. I call the originator of the universe Spirit, not spirit as is understood by traditional religions, for those are primitive conceptions of reality.

In time, science will prove that only formless spirit, aka consciousness, exists. Hang around and keep learning from science and meta-science.

6

NOT MY WILL BUT MY FATHER'S WILL, JESUS SAID AND ACCEPTED CRUCIFIXION; WHAT DOES THAT MEAN?

> [39] Jesus went out as usual to the Mount of Olives, and his disciples followed him. [40] On reaching the place, he said to them, "Pray that you will not fall into temptation." [41] He withdrew about a stone's throw beyond them, knelt down and prayed, [42] "Father, if you are willing, take this cup from me; yet not my will, but yours be done."
>
> —Luke 22: 39-42 (New International Version)

This talk by Jesus implies that he would like this cup to be taken away from him but that if it is his father's will, his will be done not his, Jesus, will. He accepted his father's will and then willingly allowed himself to be arrested and crucified without struggling to live in body. This situation would seem to suggest that his father's will is that he die to ego and body and return to him, that he be reborn in God's will which is not that he lives in ego and body.

So, what exactly is God's will for his sons, us? Does he want us to die to our egos and bodies and reawaken in him in spirit? Does it mean that when a person does God's will, he no longer lives in ego and body but henceforth live in spirit?

This prayer by Jesus also implies that we currently do not live in accordance with God's will; it suggests that to live on earth, to be a human being, is to oppose God and not live according to his will and that we must return to living according to God's will.

We must return to living in the kingdom of God, spirit, not in our own kingdom, ego, and body. God's will must be done on earth as it is done in heaven. And when God's will is done on earth, the earth becomes heaven, for the earth is just a mask we use to cover the heaven we always live in.

At present, we are the sons of man (sons of man are Jesus' name for what I call egos) and must do what Jesus did: return to being the sons of God.

The sons of God live according to God's will. The sons of man live according to their own human will. In effect, we must die to our human nature and be born again—be born in Christ; we must die to man and become reborn in spirit, as God created us, his sons.

In spirit, the will of the sons of God is the same as the will of God. As it were, we are currently dead to our true spirit self and must resurrect to it. We must no longer live according to our will but according to the will of God.

The son of God is one with his father; both of them have the same will, to be unified; to do his father's will is to do his own real will; therefore, he must do his father's will to do his own real will.

When he does his father's will, he is one with his father and is spiritually alive; in ego, he is dead and needs to be resurrected from death.

To live is to do God's will.

This means that if I accept that I am the son of God, I must be dead to be the son of man. I must be dead to human nature.

All these are confusing metaphors, so let me present a story of creation and use it to help us understand what they mean.

A STORY OF CREATION

There is God. God is life. God, aka life, extends himself to his son. He gives all of himself to his son. That means that he gave his creative power to his son. His son can and do extend his own self to his own sons. This way, creation begins in God and extends to his sons and from his sons to other sons, ad infinitum.

Creation has no beginning and no end; it is always taking place. In eternity, heaven, we are always creating our sons. Heaven is composed of God and his infinite sons.

Where is heaven? Heaven is not a place; heaven is in you; you are heaven. God and his infinite sons are in you and are you.

The infinite sons of God are in God and he is in them and they are in each other. Where God ends and his sons begin is nowhere. Where one son of God ends and another begins is nowhere. God and his creation are in each other; there is no space and gap between them. There is no matter, space, and time in eternity.

God and his sons share one self and one mind; in their shared state, they are eternal, immortal; in their oneness, they live in perfect peace, joy, and bliss.

At a point, since there is no time in eternity that point has not occurred (please remember that we are merely talking about a myth of creation, not actual creation), the sons of God wished that they created themselves and created God. They have already been created and cannot create themselves or create God.

The wish for self-creation was so powerful that, as it were, while still in God, they cast a magical spell (Hinduism calls it Maya) on themselves and went to sleep and in their sleep, dream that they are now in a new universe, one that they invented. They invented a universe of space, time, and matter and those give them the means to become special and feel separated from each other.

Our universe is the dream in which the sons of God now seem special and separated from their creator and from each other.

THE PHYSICAL UNIVERSE AND OUR EGOS AND BODIES ARE OUR OPPOSITION TO GOD'S WILL.

Our universe came into being in opposition to the will of God. The will of God is that he and his sons are eternally one. We willed that we become separated and special and since we cannot accomplish that goal in God, we sleep and seem to accomplish it in a dream state.

In truth, no one can disobey the will of God. Right now, we are still in God but while in God, we seem to be sleeping and see darkness (darkness is another means of opposing God who is light).

In darkness (the physical universe, the earth), we use the light of God in us that we bring to the darkness of the physical universe to invent galaxies, stars, planets, trees, animals, and our bodies. In darkness, we now seem to live in separated egos and bodies. We are, as it were, now dead to our true selves.

As God created us, we are spirit selves; we are all parts of one unified spirit self; we are one shared self and one shared mind. But in our dream world, we now see ourselves as separated ego selves in bodies, living and walking around in space and time.

TO RETURN TO THE WILL OF GOD IS TO GIVE UP THE PHYSICAL UNIVERSE AND EGO WE INVENTED.

To be on earth, to live in body, to be a separated self, is to live in opposition to the will of God. To return to the will of God is to give up the wish or desire that led to the existence of our material universe. To do the will of God, which is what Jesus did, is to allow oneself to voluntarily die to the desire to live in body and ego.

Like all of us on earth, Jesus wanted to live as a body and ego, hence came to this world, but realized that that is not the will of God. The will of God is that he lives as spirit. Thus, as it were, the drama of him being arrested, crucified, and resurrected to his real self, the Christ, the son of God who is one with God, was enacted.

Each of us must repeat the drama. Each of us must voluntarily allow his ego separated self-concept and the body that houses it to be crucified so that he is reborn again in his true self, as God created him, in spirit.

The prospect of allowing oneself to be crucified is scary. Fortunately, there is no such thing as egos in bodies so there is nothing to be crucified. Therefore, relax and fear nothing.

Ego-self-concept, the self in a human body, a universe of space, time, and matter do not exist; they are make-belief; they exist in a dream state but, in fact, do not exist.

To allow oneself to be crucified means to voluntarily decide not to live as a special separated self in body and on earth and in a physical universe and tune the physical universe out. If you do so, give up the desire to live as a separated self. You no longer defend your ego and body, you will see our physical universe disappear, and you know that you have always been in God, in union with creation and its creator and while in it, seem to be on earth.

There are no such things as birth, death, and earth. Those are illusions—fictions of the imagination that we made to seem real in our awareness.

Jesus recognized that there is no ego-self-concept, body, space, time, and matter and stopped wishing for them. He, in our earthly terms, gave up his will that produced those illusions and woke up in his true self as Christ, the eternal son of God who is one with God. He merely gave up what he never had for he was not ego and body.

He was arrested, tried, and crucified. If he did not live in ego and body, how can he be physically arrested and crucified?

Okay, he once believed that he lived in body and was the son of man. That was his dream state. In his dream state, he was arrested and killed but since he was never in the dream, he was not arrested and crucified. No one crucified him. It was all a dream drama.

Because it was a dream drama, nothing happened. Therefore, he does not accuse his brothers of killing him. He loves all his brothers for playing roles in the elaborate play they enacted.

Jesus now plays the role of a savior for you trying to get you to awaken from your dream that you are a body and ego.

Simply believe that you are not ego and body, do not defend them, and see them disappear as you experience yourself first as a self in light form and later as a formless self in formless heaven, in God, in all of us.

BUDDHISM SUMMARIZED

This sounds magical, does it not? Don't argue with yourself. Do what I am asking you to do. Do what Buddha asked you to do.

Buddha said that the temporal world exists as a result of desire. We desire to live as special, separated selves. That desire produced our universe of space, time, and matter and made us live in body. In body, we suffer and seem to die. To stop suffering, simply give up the desire to live as a special separated self. Let the root cause that brought the world and suffering go and your suffering ends and you are resurrected and become the Buddha, the Christ, the son of God who is one with God.

HINDUISM SUMMARIZED

The son of God who is one with God is God. There is only one self in God, so the son of God (who Hindus call Atman) is God (Brahman) hence Hindus talk about God-realization in Samadhi.

In meditation, Hindus tune out their egos to experience their real self—Atman who is Brahman. If attained, they say that they are God-realized. Buddhists call the experience of oneness, nirvana, illumination, and enlightenment to our real self, unified spirit self.

Give up your desire for ego separated self, love all people's true selves, that is, love the spirit in them, not their false ego selves in bodies, meditate, and see yourself in oneness with Brahman, with God.

DISCUSSION

At the moment, we are in a dream (Hinduism calls it Maya). In that dream, we see ourselves in a seemingly solid world that seems real. We seem to live in space, time, and matter. We seem to live in bodies. Bodies are born, grow old, weaken, and die. We bury dead bodies and see them rot, decay, and eaten by worms. All these seem real to us.

The universe seems to have been around for 13.8 billion years (since the Big Bang). The sun and earth seem to have been around for 4.5 billion years and will continue being around for another five billion years until hydrogen is exhausted in the sun and it swells up and explodes.

We know from physics that the universe will be around for trillions of years in the future. Physics teaches that the galaxies are expanding. As they speed away from each other, they lose heat. In a few trillion years, the universe will be very cold. The stars will explode in supernovas. All stars and planets will decompose to the 92 elements that compose them. The elements will decompose to electrons, protons, and neutrons. Those would decay to quarks which ultimately will decay to light.

The universe has a story of origin and end, ontology, and scatology. Thus, a universe that came into being in light ends in light. Is that not interesting?

(By the way, the story of Big bang is a story, not factual; what does not exist did not come into existence and will not die. In the dream, however, the universe seems to have come into being fourteen billion years ago, but what took place in dreams has not taken place.)

We are always light while pretending to live in bodies. (Bodies were made from light ... study physics to understand what I am talking about.)

To us, the universe seems real. It seems solid. You can see your body, walls, animals, trees, land, mountains, stars, galaxies; if you bump into a wall, your body would feel pain. The universe seems real to you. But energy and matter are merely congealed light and with sufficient heat, can be reduced to the light from which they were made.

Mystics know that we are light. When they see you in body, they see you in light form. They see animals, trees, everything in light forms. To them, the universe is light. But you would not know this to be true as long as you wish for a special, separated self.

If you do what mystics do, see you as the son of God, not son of man, love yourself, all people, and God, no longer desire to have a special, separated self, and not defend your present ego and body (ego and body are one phenomenon ... if you have a weak and pained body, like I do, see Alfred Adler's ideas of inferiority and superiority, neurosis ... you have an ego that seeks superiority; I used to feel superior to all human beings, black and white), well, if you give up your ego and stop defending it, you begin occasionally having spiritual experiences.

WHAT A COURSE IN MIRACLES CALLS HOLY INSTANTS

You would suddenly see our physical universe disappear and you know yourself to be in a formless, unified self where there are God and his infinite sons and you are one of the sons; you would not see space, time, and matter there. There is no ego-you and others. There is no subject and object, seer and seen. All of us share one unified self. You would feel eternal, peaceful, and incredibly happy.

This probably sounds magical to you. To prove its reality, do what mystics ask us to do: love all people, meditate, and tell yourself neti, neti, not this not that, you are not ego and what ego thinks of; keep quiet and then see what happens.

You can choose to behave like primitive Nigerians who deny God and the sons of God, fancy themselves egos, and pursue important egos (they try to kill the son of God and try to replace him with a substitute ego-self).

Igbos are all over the place wanting to seem very important egos. They sell drugs, steal, and engage in incredible criminal activities to make money—money with which they make their nonexistent egos and bodies seem important. Then they die and their bodies are eaten by worms. What fools they are! They ignore what matters in life, the spirit, and seek nothingness, egos, and bodies.

The job, from the beginning of time, that I accepted to perform for them and for all mankind, is to tell them who their real selves are, spirit selves.

It may be in this lifetime or in future lifetimes (reincarnation is real provided that you understand that they all take place in dreams for the sons of God do not get born or die but seem to do so in dreams of specialness and separation). Well, in time (that does not exist, everything happens in the present and now), you will do what you have to do to crucify your ego and body and return to the awareness of your real self, Christ; Christ is one with God and all his creation.

CONCLUSION

Think about the points made in this essay. If they make sense to you, try to live them. But if they do not make sense to you, you are sound asleep and see you as an animal. Keep on sleeping.

When you are ready to awaken from that sleep of self-forgetfulness, you would gravitate to information that would enable you to do what you have to do to awaken.

Salvation, redemption, and deliverance are very simple. All it requires that you do is for you to stop seeing yourself as a special, separated self in body and living on earth, space, and time. Do nothing else.

Do not protect your ego and body. That is all you have to do—do not desire and protect your ego and body.

The ego and body are not you; the ego is a stranger in your mind. Let go of the alien in you, the ego, keep quiet, and know that you are a son of God who is one with God.

It is the ego that requires you to do the elaborate things we do on earth, all intended to make our fragile bodies feel protected. Yet, our bodies do not exist. What fools we are. We protect bodies that do not exist.

If you believe that you are ego and body, then use your ego and body to love other people who believe that they are egos and bodies. If you do so, you would obtain relative peace and joy, not the perfect peace and joy of heaven.

Forgive what other people do to hurt your ego and body, love them, and obtain some joy. You will have a happy dream if you use your body and ego to love all the sons of God in egos and bodies.

When you are tired of dreaming that you are ego in body, you would simply give them up as Jesus did and resurrect in unified spirit.

And when you do, you join Jesus, the Holy Spirit, and enlightened sons of God to teach our brothers still living in the darkness of the ego and body that they are light.

We are the light of the world but some of us know it and others do not.

Jesus was a son of man, an ego who defended his ego and body. At age thirty, he learned that he is not ego and body. He taught people that they are the sons of God, spirit selves.

They said that he committed blasphemy by claiming to be one with God and arrested and crucified him.

He resurrected from ego death as the Christ and showed his Christ self, which is in light form, to his apostles (you can see him in his light body if you love and forgive all).

Jesus then disappeared into formless God and is on the righthand side of God; this metaphor means that he now thinks rightly and sees himself as one with God.

In conclusion, to obey the will of God is to stop trying to be ego in body. The desire to be ego and body is your will which you juxtapose to God's unified spirit's will.

Now, stop wishing to be ego in body and be who God created you as, who you always are, son of God, Christ, a spirit being pretending to be in body in space and time.

A COURSE IN MIRACLES' PHILOSOPHY AND ME

A Course in Miracles teaches that there is no physical universe and there is no me in ego and body in a nonexistent universe. There are no other people in that non-existent universe, either.

The universe that I and other people see is a dream in our collective minds. We are always in unified spirit state, in heaven; while there, we sleep and dream the seeming universe of space, time, and matter and see us in it and it seems real to us. It is not there and we are not in it.

This is total denial of our physical universe and the people and activities done in it. The physical universe denies heaven's spiritual reality and *A Course in Miracles* reverses that denial, denies the universe, and affirms heaven's reality as the only reality there is.

It says that right now, I am in spirit and while there, dream and see myself in body. My dreaming mind made my body problematic so that my dream self, the ego, may use the dream frustrations of the body to feel angry at the dream universe that gave me such a pained body. I use my dreaming mind to have dream persons frustrate my dream ego by not doing good things for me from childhood to feel angry and justify my anger at people and my fear.

Other dream selves are doing what I am doing to make them feel that their dream egos and bodies are real for them.

Our goal, my goal, is to forget our real self, the son of God Christ, and see our dream self, ego, and body as real. That is what the universe is for—to make the dream self and body seem real and determine what we do. Pained, we defend the dream self and body and in doing so, make the dream self and body real in our awareness and perpetuate the dream and our sense of specialness and separation from spirit, God.

DECIDE THAT THE DREAM IS NOT REAL. THE DREAM SELF AND BODY ARE NOT REAL AND DO NOT WISH OR DEFEND THEM.

The book says that I can decide to see myself as not my dream ego and body and see the dream selves and egos I see as not real (realizing that each self I see on earth has a son of God dreaming through it and he, like me, does not know that he is a dream self and deceive himself to believing that he is his dream self and body and like me, defends his dream self and body, believing that if they are attacked, killed, and die, he would die).

No one can attack people without their wish and they do not die even when they seem to die in the dream for it is dream death.

The people I see on earth die have not died; they seem to have died in dream death but have not done so for they were never born in body, did not live in body, and do not die.

If I decide that I am not my ego and body, since the objective of the dream is to make me seem the ego and body and if I stop being aware of body and ego, then my ego and body would disappear from my awareness and I would become aware of myself as the idea of part, son of God in the idea of whole-self called God, a formless self.

THE DREAM DENSE BODY AND THE DREAM LIGHT BODY

When I have experienced myself as a formless self, I can reenter the dream as either a dream dense body or a dream light self; I do so not to live in the dream for I have transcended it but to interact with dream selves and help them.

If I still wish to be in the dream, then I reenter it as an enlightened self in it, now no longer seeing me as the dream self in body; dense body or light body are not me; I am a formless spirit self that can take on a dream body or a dream light body to help those still attached to dream bodies and egos. Now, I have the power of God via the Holy Spirit, the part of God that is in the dream but has the power of God. I can use that power to give me whatever I need to help people in the dream, including unlimited money and ability to perform miracles.

> PEOPLE CAME TO THE WORLD TO BELIEVE THAT IN EGOS AND BODIES, THEY HAVE WORTH. LEAVE THEM ALONE. THEY CANNOT CHANGE IT AND IF THEY DO, THEY AWAKEN FROM THE DREAM.

The sons of God came to earth—to the dream to make their dream selves and bodies seem real—to make their ego and bodies. Nothingness seems to have worth. That is what they are doing.

Knowing that that is what they are doing would not make them stop doing it for if they stop seeing themselves as egos and bodies and stop valuing their egos and bodies, they would not be on earth.

Telling people to stop valuing their egos and bodies and asking them not to seek ego importance, prestige, and power would not make them stop doing so; they would not even listen to me for they do not want to hear that; they came here to make their egos and bodies seem important.

Perhaps, in every millennium, one thousand years, one person gives up valuing his ego and body and stop seeking body-based worth.

THE PURPOSE OF THE WORLD IS TO MAKE EGO AND BODY SEEM TO HAVE WORTH—TO MAKE THE WORTHLESS AND WHAT DOES NOT EXIST SEEM TO HAVE WORTH.

The whole purpose of the world and the universe is to make the ego and body seem important and powerful so as to oppose God and seem powerful.

Human civilization and society exist to make ego and body seem worthwhile. We work for food, medications, clothing, and houses to maintain our egos and bodies in existence; everything we do on earth is all designed to make our egos and bodies seem worthwhile.

All we do is protect our egos and bodies yet those will die. That which needs negative protection with fear anger, depression, paranoia, and mania and eventually dies has no worth and is better off dead. Except that as non-existent things, they do not die. Stop valuing and seeking them and see them disappear, not die.

Leave people to dance their dream dance. Stop dancing the dream dance by not seeing me as ego and body, by not valuing ego and body, and by disappearing from the ego and body world. Leave people to dream ego body worth for that is the nature of human existence and civilization; that is what people came to earth to do.

Do not moralize about people valuing anything; do not berate people for valuing nothing but get you out of the nothing dreams and know peace and joy.

Each person lives in his private hell by seeking ego and body, this world. If anything, as Buddha said, have compassion for them while understanding that they are where they chose to be and are doing what they came to do and even if you stand on your head upside down and preach, letting go of their attachment to the ego, body, and the world they would not do so, for they are too deep in sleep to even know what you are talking about.

DO NOT FEEL HUMILIATED FROM RECEIVING GIFTS FROM PEOPLE FOR THAT IS EGO AND PRIDE.

When you live from ego-lessness, people would be giving you things; if you are in ego, you would feel ego pride injury and feel humiliated.

You are not ego and cannot be humiliated. Those who do God's work are supported by those in a deeper dream who work and give them the money to live on so as to be on earth and teach ego-lessness, which they vaguely listen to but do not yet want to practice to awaken from the dream.

THERE ARE INEVITABILITIES IN LIFE.

What happens in the world has to happen. This is true at the larger, macrolevel as well as at the smaller, microlevel. Every society is where it needs to be for the people are having those dreams.

Every individual is where he needs to be, for he is the one dreaming his life. There is nothing that you can do to change the world for the world reflects our present ego thinking.

We can change the individual's dream but changing the dream at the collective level takes thousands of years. The universe will last trillions of years; thus, be giving all God's children the opportunity to come and dream that they are special, separated selves. You cannot end the collective dream today.

Everything that happens to me or to you is your dream and mine and it is the way it is until each of us has different dreams and has different life experiences.

Collectively, Africans are having their primitive dreams, Europeans are having their narcissistic dreams, and Americans are having their racist dreams. They have to have those dreams despite your wishes. Instead of worrying about the collective stupidity of mankind awaken from the dream, let go of your desire to be in ego, body, and the world, awaken, and become the teacher for those in the dream telling them what to do to awaken.

Until you awaken, you are an unhealed healer and cannot heal those in dreams, that is, awaken them.

HAVE FAITH IN YOUR BELIEF AND GIVE UP FEAR
AND DOUBT (FEAR AND DOUBT IS OF THE EGO).

Fear and doubt are the teachings of the ego telling one that one does not know the truth but should live in the tentative world of the ego and its science where there is no truth.

First, believe in your truth, then live it, act on it, and you see the fruits of your belief. But as long as you do not believe and act on it and is fence-sitting, merely talking about the truth, is wishy-washy, or vacillating, you are not going to see the results you wish.

THE WORLD CAME INTO BEING BECAUSE WE WISHED IT AND ACTED ON OUR BELIEFS. IT WILL END WHEN WE WISH AND ACT ON ITS OPPOSITE.

You believed in the reality of the ego special, separated self and its world to see you in it; now, reverse the belief, believe in unified spirit self, let go of the ego, and act on that belief, then you see your ego, body, and world disappear.

Until you first believe and act accordingly, you will not see the world you are wishing for—the world of light forms and ultimately, the formless world of God.

DR. O STILL VALUES THE EGO AND ITS WORLD.

Dr. O still values his ego and body; he values his Igbo society, values black people, and sees attacks on them by white dream figures as real. He wants to punish the racists for what they did to the blacks. That is, he takes dream attacks as real. He does not forgive what is done in dreams. He does not yet know that the world is a dream that can be overlooked.

Therefore, he is not an enlightened, illuminated person. He is in his private ego hell. It will take a long time to heal him. Instead of wasting my time trying to heal him, I must heal myself by seeing the world as a dream, not valuing it, letting it go, having Holy Instant, and returning to the dream as a light self or dense self but all along, living in the formless world of God.

Like Adolf Hitler, he wants to establish a one-thousand-year new world order that he rules, his millennium of God's glorious kingdom.

The man is an egotist, hence does not know that God means not valuing things of the ego. Leave him alone.

7

JESUS CHRIST SAID THAT HIS KINGDOM IS NOT OF THIS WORLD BUT OF GOD. WHAT DOES THIS MEAN?

³⁶ Jesus said, "My kingdom is not of this world. If it were, my servants would fight to prevent my arrest by the Jewish leaders. But now, my kingdom is from another place."

³⁷ "You are a king, then!" said Pilate.

Jesus answered, "You say that I am a king. In fact, the reason I was born and came into the world is to testify to the truth. Everyone on the side of truth listens to me."

³⁸ "What is truth?" retorted Pilate. With this he went out again to the Jews gathered there and said, "I find no basis for a charge against him. ³⁹ But it is your custom for me to release to you one prisoner at the time of the Passover. Do you want me to release 'the king of the Jews'?

—John 18:36-38 (New International Version)

In many places in the four gospels that described the teaching of Jesus Christ, he said that this world is not his kingdom and that his kingdom is in God.

The Jews had expected a messiah, a war leader, in the mode of David to come and liberate them from the yoke of Rome but apparently, Jesus had other plans. He wanted to return Jews to God, not form an army, go fight and defeat the Romans, and chase them out of Palestine.

Jesus wanted people to turn toward God for, according to him, they came from God. This world, in his view, is not their home; this world is a place of exile. We are aliens in this ego and body world of space, time, and matter.

Our real home is in the kingdom of God, which is spirit. We have to let go of this world and return to God. The egos' world is a mistake and we correct that mistake by returning to God, to Spirit.

There are people who all they want is to improve this world and make the most of it. They want to live in this world. Indeed, there are people who do not believe that there is God, much more his kingdom. Atheists do not believe in God. To them, we are the product of matter and when we die, that is the end of it. Their kingdom is this world. As such, they want to make the most of this world, live well, and die.

Study science and technology and use those to improve this world, live well, and die. Science says that the human body can live to be one hundred and twenty years, so strive to live until those years and die. When you die, your body rots and are eaten by worms that in turn, are eaten by bacteria.

We came from sand and return to sand, so do not cry for us. Atheists say and make the most of their lives and buzz off. They have what is called a realistic perspective on life whereas Jesus has what is called an idealistic view of life. Idealistic because most of us have not seen God and his kingdom and can only believe in it.

What do I believe in? I do not know that what Jesus said is true or not. I am agnostic. I currently see myself in this world. I want to use science and technology to improve this world. I want to live well in this world and then buzz off. Does this mean that the old boy was wrong and there is no kingdom of God that we should strive after? Are atheists, right?

What exactly are God and his kingdom? To me, God is love. God's kingdom is love. Striving after the kingdom of God is transforming our world into a loving place. God is love; therefore, returning to God means returning to love. Spirit is love; therefore, returning to spirit means making this world a loving place. Perhaps, I believe in what Jesus was talking about. I do, if you know what I mean.

To me, the universe and people are mystery and I devote myself to trying to understand that mystery. I believe that by the time we are done unraveling the mystery of the world, we would see that life is eternal, permanent, and changeless. But until we get there, it is sufficient to accept who we are and love us in an unconditionally positive manner.

I believe in love for all people. There is absolutely no need to hate any human being, man or woman, adult or child, black or white. There must be no exception from love. Love makes our world a pleasant happy dream.

In as much as people do evil things, we must build jails and prisons, incarcerate them, and while they are there, attempt to teach them prosocial behavior.

WHAT IS THE REAL SELF? LIVING FROM THE LOVING SELF

The real self is a loving self;
the real self is a unified self;
the real self is a spirit self;
the real self is God;
the real self is the son of God.

So, which is true? All of them are true. Love is, however, my preferred view of the real self, for love is the glue that joins all sons of God and God together; love is what makes them one. It is love that unifies the many into one self. Therefore, we must live from the loving self to live from the real self.

CHRIST CONSCIOUSNESS VERSUS EGO CONSCIOUSNESS

In Christ consciousness, you see yourself as spirit, as part of God's spirit; in ego consciousness, you see yourself as separated self and as body. In ego, you accentuate body and self-interests. In Christ, you accentuate spirit, God, and love. In Christ consciousness, you can perform miracles because you have the power of God in you; in ego and body, you are weak.

AS A RESULT OF MY CHILDHOOD BODY TRAUMA, I WANTED OTHER PEOPLE TO RESCUE ME AND THEY DID NOT AND I FELT ANGRY AT THEM; I ASK THEM, HOW DARE YOU ASK ME TO DO SOMETHING FOR YOU WHEN YOU DID NOT RESCUE ME FROM PAIN?

Body, space, and time must be desired and defended to be real for one. If one does not desire them and do not defend them, they disappear for one. If you do not desire your ego and body and do not defend them, they die and go out of existence. Animals and trees must desire to be alive to gather the nutrients they have to live.

This stomach issue that I am now having is my final effort to tell me that I am ego and body. After it, I aim to affirm that I am spirit and that is all there is to it. No food for food is a defense of body.

Dr. O read John's gospel chapter fourteen and interpreted it to mean that Jesus said that only he is the one to come and do more wonders than he, meaning that he is totally egotistical; Jesus was talking to all his apostles, all people, not to just one person. The man is lost in egoism, delusion disorder. There is no cure for him; he is too far gone.

THERE IS NO SPIRITUAL TEACHER IN THE CONTEMPORARY WORLD.

To be a true spiritual teacher, one must be egoless; that is, one must not identify with ego and body; one must see oneself as spirit and as in God.

One such person is now like the Holy Spirit; he is in unified spirit, God, heaven, but sees the people in the egos' world of bodies, space, and time but does not identify with them and does not take what they do seriously and does not interfere with them but when asked, he asks folks to overlook the world of egos.

One such egoless person is healed for he has joined the entire world, has a healed body, and can heal all people in body. That was what Jesus did: while still in body, he gave up identification with body and ego and lived as the Holy Spirit, the Christ, and as such, could heal any person with physical illness.

For the past week, I have been sick; I had serious stomach issues. During that week, I simply laid on my bed not afraid to die for long ago,

I accepted death as my reality. What preoccupied my mind is how much I saw myself as a body and all my thoughts were how to make my body healthy. That is, I identified with body. Finally, I told me that I am not body, and as such, should not be sick. Body as well as space, time, and matter are illusions; they do not exist and what do not exist do not die or feel sick.

This lesson was the goal of this one-week illness, to finally accept that I am spirit not body and give up any and all identification with body. Lesson learned and sickness is gone.

My girlfriend, Lady Jewells, is truly a loving woman. She did everything in her power to facilitate my recovery, not in an intrusive manner but by her loving and caring presence. She introduced me to alternative medicine such as a hydrotherapist who flushes the stomach with water and removes all fecal matter in it; that helped get rid of the sense of bloating I had.

I gave up on Western medicine a long time ago; medical doctors are essentially drug pushers hooking folks on unnecessary drugs that make money for the pharmaceutical industry and then kill the people.

ONE'S SIGNIFICANT OTHER VOLUNTEERED TO PLAY ROLES FOR ONE IN ONE'S DRAMA THAT ONE IS BODY IN SPACE AND TIME.

Your parents, spouse, children, siblings, and all the significant people in your life volunteered to play close roles for you in your drama that you are a separated ego-self in body, space, time, and matter. When the roles are over, they move on and you may not know who they are in the afterlife or vaguely remember them from the manner they walked or behaved.

In a recent dream, I saw my daughter walking into a mall and vaguely remembered her to be related to me; she and her friends simply walked by and did not pause to say hi to me. She played the role of an oppositional defiant child for me to see and learn about myself. That role is now over and we move on.

DEATH AND RESURRECTION OF IGBOS

Igbos are literally unborn, yet they are not yet born into human status. They need to be reborn and learn to become human beings, people who work for social good, not just for individual ego importance. Right now, they cannot form and mount a human civilization for each of them is too bent on seeking personal prestige to work with other people and engage in organizational work, pay taxes, and run governments with the money they generate.

Igbos' idea of government is to go share the money they childishly believe that the government pluck from thin air and give to people, not the people giving the government money to do work with. Stealing from the government is their understanding of government work. This is truly said.

They need to be re-socialized to internalize the fact that the government is set up by the people and paid for by the people with the goal of providing social services. You do not get from the government but give money to it.

THE EDUCATION OF A SPIRITUAL TEACHER/ THE TRAINING OF A TEACHER OF GOD

The education of a teacher of God is for him to come to the realization that the individual is spirit, that I and God are one shared self and with one shared mind. The knowledge that one is not body but is spirit is the sole goal of training to become a teacher of God.

At present, we denied our true identity as spirit and identify as body; we must now deny that we are body and return to our true self, spirit self. Acceptance that one is part of God's unified spirit is also called Christ consciousness.

This entails the awareness that God acts through one and that there is nothing that one can do without the power of God in one. By oneself, one has no power; only the whole has power; the part has no power.

One always obeys the will of God for God's will is the will of his son; the son is deluded if he believes that he has a separated and special will; he merely dreams when he sees himself as apart from his father.

TO SEE ONESELF AS BODY IS TO ATTACK ONESELF.

To see oneself as body is to attack oneself, to try to murder one's spirit self, literally, except that spirit is eternal and cannot be destroyed but stays in the background as the murderous and mad ego tries to seem a body in space and time, does so for many lifetimes, and exhaust itself.

I am one with God and all spirits and cannot live apart from God and all people, I cannot live in anybody. Body does not exist.

WHAT DOES NOT EXIST DOES NOT SICKEN AND DIE.

What does not exist does not become sick or die, so one does not feel sick or die, although in the dream those seem real to one by one's wishes.

A son of God who while on earth accepts that he is one with God will simply see his body transform to light form and he continues living in the world of light forms (remember the trans-figurative experience of Jesus in the Bible where he was in light form with two other prophets) and from there, enter the formless world of God where we all share one self (heaven is formless).

To God, the world is a dream but to the ego, the dream is the reality.

THE UNIVERSE IS THINKING AND GIVING
SOLIDITY TO ITS THOUGHTS.

There is nothing in the universe until the sense of I, separated existence, disturbed eternal harmony and peace. Say I, self, and you unleash disturbance of the universe. If you withdraw the I, you stop disturbing peace, and that is what meditation is all about, to remove I and return to peace, joy, and nothingness.

EACH OF US IS A POINT OF LIGHT. IN POLITICS, EACH
POINT OF LIGHT, LIFE, AND PEOPLE IS TRYING TO MAKE
ITS I PREVAIL AND STRUGGLE FOR COMPROMISE.

Nothing solid exists; our thinking gives ideas, thoughts, flesh, solidity, space, and time and makes them seem to exist and they exist for us (in a dream state).

ONLY MATHEMATICS, IDEAS, AND NUMBERS EXIST
AND OUR THINKING CLOTHES THEM IN SOLIDITY.

FEAR, ANXIETY, AND ANGER RELEASE ADRENALINE
AND OTHER HORMONES INTO THE BLOODSTREAM
AND GUT AND THOSE CHEMICALS TEMPORARILY STOP
DIGESTION, HENCE AFFECT DIGESTIVE HEALTH.

My digestion issues are related to or caused by the constant state of fear and anger I was in.

GOD VERSUS SATAN; GOOD VERSUS EVIL; SATAN IS THE OPPOSITE OF GOD; THIS WORLD IS THE KINGDOM OF SATAN FOR SATAN RULES IT AS THE OPPOSITE OF GOD'S LOVE.

I am not body.
I am light.
I am spirit.
I am holy.
I am eternal, permanent, and changeless.
I am perfect, innocent, guiltless, and sinless.

All these are my status in spirit but in time, I am their opposite. So, how do I regain the knowledge of who I am in spirit? That is what existence on earth is all about—first, we deny our real self, spirit, and clothe ourselves in body and then struggle to return to the awareness of our eternal spirit nature. In spirit, we are in God and he is in us and we are in each other as one unified and Holy Spirit.

MODERN SCIENTIFIC MAN LIVES IN QUIET DESPERATION.

The modern scientific man accepted the scientific methodology that tells him that only the observable and verifiable should be accepted as true. So, he operates on the scientific method.

He dares not accept anything that he cannot prove to be true. But many things are not observable and thus, he lives with limited knowledge. He lives a life of quiet desperation, all induced by the success of the scientific method.

He believes that there is no consciousness outside body and matter and if that is so, then he is a mere animal and is no better than mosquitos. But something in people would like to believe that they have something eternal in them; that desire for eternity is the only thing that gives their lives worth; the rest is the false worth of scientists.

WHY DOCTOR O WANTS WEALTH

Dr. O, like other Igbos, desire independence; that means that he must have independent means of money to avoid dependence on other people. Hence, he seeks the key to becoming rich and from wealth, is able to do his religious work.

The man has always had a desire for the big—desire to be president of Nigeria; that desire is now transmuted to becoming the world's greatest teacher of God. He is a great idealist.

Is he deluded and grandiose? Maybe, but what is that?

Believe that you are spirit not body, act accordingly, and see results.

Dr. O's feedback to me is for me to believe that I am a son of God, that I am spirit, eternal, and act on it. What is believed and acted on works for one.

If I do not believe that I am spirit and keep desiring to be body, I would act as body, hence get accompanying results. The ego and body are weak and gives one weak power; it is spirit, Christ consciousness, that gives one real power.

POSITIVE BELIEF VERSUS NEGATIVE BELIEF

I have negative beliefs. My negative belief has as much power as positive belief. It is a negative belief that desires to separate from God and go become powerful in body. That negative belief produced this world for me.

THE CONTRADICTORY DESIRE TO BE BODY AND MAKE IT STRONG

The desire to be body and desire for a strong body is contradictory. Body is inherently weak and cannot be strong. The desire to make body become strong so that it is able to cope with the demands of living on earth, is ego's self-defeating belief for body cannot become strong.

Positive belief lies in seeing one as spirit and eternal and acting on that. Positive belief has more power than the power of negative belief; it returns one to God, spirit, to bliss.

TO LIVE IN FEAR IS TO LIVE WITHOUT LOVE. TO
LIVE WITHOUT LOVE IS TO LIVE OUTSIDE GOD.
TO LIVE OUTSIDE GOD IS TO LIVE IN FEAR.

GOD IS LIFE SO WE ALWAYS ARE PART OF LIFE BUT
WHILE IN IT, DREAM THAT WE ARE OUTSIDE IT.

TO LIVE IN DOUBT IS TO SUSPECT THAT GOD
DOES NOT EXIST. SINCE GOD, LIFE EXISTS TO
LIVE IN DOUBT AND IS AN EGO GAME.

I AM EGO MEANS THAT I AM A BOY WHICH MEANS
THAT I AM WEAK. I AM CHRIST; A PART OF GOD IS
TO BE STRONG. THEN ONE TRIES TO MAKE ONE'S
EGO AND BODY STRONG WHICH IS IMPOSSIBLE OF
ACCOMPLISHMENT. STRENGTH LIES ONLY IN GOD, CHRIST.

Much of human culture is designed to make nothingness, ego, and body seem to have worth and is something, hence to live in it. Yet, body is nothing that would die and rot away. Indeed, body does not exist.

There is no use trying to make ego and body strong; let them go or play with them without seeing them as important. There is no body, no food, no ego-eating food, no virus and bacteria, no birth and death, no diseases—they are all dream events. You can wake up from the dream and see the physical universe disappear from your awareness.

Notes from a hospital:

I was hospitalized for four days (February 22–26) and had a gastrointestinal surgery to remove an issue that probably has been there all my life. As I was in my hospital room, a room that is as good as the best hotel suites I have ever stayed in and I have been in them all: Hilton, Sheraton, etc., well, as I lay on that bed, occasionally got up, and looked outside the window at the city beyond, my mind cogitated on certain things.

The ego is totally powerless. I could not predict the intestinal issue that brought me to the hospital or prevent it. The ego cannot predict our present and future; it is a make-belief powerful agent we employ in deluding ourselves.

Anger is the ego pretending to be powerful. In anger, something happened to you to make you feel frustrated and powerless and you feel angry at whatever made you frustrated. But your anger is pointless for it cannot fix the problem. My *anger* could not fix my GI issues. However, anger is very destructive for you could use it to lash out at a person you falsely believe is the source of your problem. Anger is not creative. Give it up.

Our thinking produces our dreams. Nigeria is literally the empire of thieves. The politicians are the master criminals of them all. I lie in my palatial hospital room wondering where we can have hotel rooms and talk less about hospital rooms that look this comfortable in the shithole called Nigeria. Why cannot the thieves that rule Nigeria provide the people with hospitals like this? When they are sick, they run to the West for the best medical treatment like the one that I am getting. Press a button, a nurse is there; doctors of all specialties parade through my room—cardiologists, GIs, surgeons, and so on. So, why don't Africans pay attention to their people? I got angry and imagined gathering all Nigerian politicians in a house, pouring gasoline on them, and burning them to death; they are useless and might as well be dead. I thereafter dozed off to sleep. In the sleep, I dreamed. In the dream, a bully attacked me. Generally, even though I look gentle, if you dared touch me, you are dead. I will pursue you into your mother's vagina. I do not forgive bullies. I grabbed the bully's head and tried to pull his head off his neck. I woke up. The dream says that if you think violence, you will see violence in your life. Think love and you see love in your life.

In traditional Igbo villages, when a young man becomes an adult, he marries and builds his house and compound and walls it off. He and his wife and children live in it. They do whatever they can to survive and occasionally request their neighbors' help in cutting their farms or constructing new houses but other than that, each Igbo man lived by his own resources. Igbos are extremely individualistic and self-reliant. This is good but they must be trained to care for other people ala Alfred Adler's serving social interests. They must be trained to pay at least 30% of their annual incomes in taxes—money with which we serve social needs.

There was the desire to see nude women. When I was at secondary school, Anglican Grammar School, Port Harcourt, a boarding school, some of the boys would go to town and come back with playboy magazines.

We would all gather around to see the picture of the nude women in them. We particularly wanted to see the vagina. Why do men want to see naked women, especially to look into their vagina? I think that it is because the female body is beautiful. It represents the human body at its best. We came to this world to be bodies. We want to be bodies. It is the attraction of bodies that made us want to see female bodies. The desire to be body is the desire to be in the world of bodies, space, and time. We are spirit but currently want to be bodies. We must now seek ways to give up the desire for body and return to the awareness of spirit.

With nothing to do in the hospital, I read the gospel according to John, the Acts of Apostles, and Paul's letter to the Romans. What struck me is how different the teaching of Jesus is from the teaching of the Torah, the Jewish Holy Book that began with Moses. Jesus, Peter, Paul, and the other apostles kept trying to fit their radical religion to Moses' religion, the law. Why didn't they just make a clean break from Judaism and build a new religion? They ought to have left Jews to their religion and that way, would not have been persecuted by Jews as Jesus and Paul were. Did they lack the courage to establish their own religion?

There is no space, time, and matter. All three are illusions. Sooner or later, my body will die. It will decay to the sixty-four elements that compose it (carbon, hydrogen, oxygen, nitrogen, potassium, magnesium, calcium, copper, and so on). Each of those is composed of electrons, protons, and neutrons. Those particles of the atom are composed of quarks and ultimately of light. Light is composed of nothing. My body will decay to elements and atoms that will decay to particles. Those particles will decay to light and light will decay to nothingness from which it came during the Big Bang, 13.8 billion years ago. The entire universe of galaxies, stars, and planets will all die and decay to nothingness. In trillions of years, nothingness will exist in the universe.

If there is no matter, there can be no space and time, so in effect, the universe itself would not exist in trillions of years to come.

Nothing exists but our minds make things seem to exist. I see this hospital room's walls. They limit me. But those walls actually are congealed light, nothingness hence does not exist. It is my mind wishing to experience limitations that made nothingness seem solid walls, hence limits me. I can also choose to not believe in solids, hence stop limiting my mind.

It is either the universe exists or it does not exist. It cannot be both. You cannot see both at the same time. You see the one you want to see and experience. You cannot eat your cake and have it. The universe does not exist, QED.

There are protocols that make the body seem important. Lying on this hospital bed, I am conscious that at any moment, especially during surgery, I could die. Upon death, my body would decay to the elements that compose it. In effect, my body is nothing; it has no value except the imaginary one that I give to it.

This same body, nothingness, we have elevated to high heaven. If a person touched my body disrespectfully, I would be angry at him. Women would literally put you in prison if you disrespect their bodies. Touch their bodies without their permission, and killing you is not ruled out. Men would literally kill you if you attempt to sexually abuse their children. The point is that we all overvalue our bodies—bodies that intrinsically are nothing and ultimately do not exist. This is weird, is it not? We came to earth to experience body, hence our protocols to make body seem important.

In his epistle to the Romans, Paul talked about the laws of Moses: laws requiring circumcision, not eating certain food, and so on (all those seem silly to me). This emphasis on laws that protect the human body makes body important, yet he kept on devaluing flesh as nothing and asking to return to spirit; what a contradictory man, that Paul. Modern psychoanalysis would say that Paul was an obsessive-compulsive neurotic; in psychiatric terms, he had obsessive-compulsive personality disorder. He was motivated by perfection, hence moralized; he posited perfect ideal standards of behavior and perpetually judged people's actual behaviors with those imaginary ideal standards. The man must have been a pain in the ass to live with. He reminded me of my father who was always judging me and finding me not good enough relative to his mentally constructed ideal standards. Both Paul and my father were geniuses; each had an IQ of at least 160. They were unusual men.

I was a spoilt child. When sick, I wanted a mother to be there serving me twenty-four seven and if she was not, I felt angry and threw giant temper tantrums. Once I was in a hospital and she missed coming to see me for a day and the next day when she came, I told her what a rotten mother she is. My trajectory in life is to have a weak body and seem about to die and have my significant others (my parents, spouse, siblings, children, etc.) take care of me. I grew up expecting the world to take good care of me. I wanted people and the world to take care of me. So, here I lay on a hospital bed and folks are taking good care of me. I realized that I had to be childlike, weak, for them to take care of me. If I am an adult, I should take care of myself and should not feel angry if others do not help me. My mother and all people did their best for me. They do not owe me more. Thus, I should thank them and not feel angry at them for not taking care of me. I must help those in need as these white folks in this hospital are taking care of me.

We are spirit having body experience. The goal now is to give up identification with body and return to identification with spirit. My true identity is the son of God, who is spirit. The son of God, you and I, are one with God. God is in his son and his son is in God. God and his sons are not separate from each other.

As the old boy, Jesus said in John 14:12 in response to Philip—where you see the son, you see the father for the father is in the son. To love God is to love his son. That is, love the people around you if you want to love God.

For my present purpose, my real self is spirit, the son of God who is one with God and his creation. I must live according to this insight. If I do so, I would be God-realized and live in peace and joy.

I am not body. I am spirit. Spirit is light. I am light. I am the light of the world. I give the world the light of God in me, the love of God in me. In doing so, I help to make the world a loving, hence peaceful place.

Spirit is eternal, permanent, and changeless. My real self is eternal, immortal, permanent, and changeless.

My body is the opposite of spirit, is mortal, and indeed does not exist, except as a dream existent thing.

My girlfriend, Lady Jewells, came to the hospital to visit me every day. I am blessed to have such a loving woman as my friend. No man can ask for a more loving woman. I am blessed to have her in my life. I love you, Lady Jewells.

ADDICTIONS

Addiction is rooted in belief that we are bodies; we use food, alcohol, and drugs to stimulate our bodies and thus, affirm bodies as who we are.

Adam and Eve lost belief that we are spirit; Jesus returned to belief that we are spirit by dying to body.

If God is your father, then you are like him, spirit, and have all his powers.

Don't rely on the five senses to know God for those adapt to body and ego. You must transcend to the five senses and body to return to God.

WHAT IS KNOWLEDGE?

Knowledge is the certainty that you and God are one self, that you are his son; hence, you have Christ consciousness.

PHONY LIVING

Being a phony big self. All my life, I lived as if I am the wished big ego-self. The pursuit of the big self made me a mask, a phony, ever-living a lie.

My bloated stomach that took me to the hospital is rooted in my bloated self-concept. My ego was puffed up and my body, especially my tummy, became puffed up.

Now, let go of the wish for a big self and live from the real self, spirit. You will relax, calm, and heal your body.

Igbo live from the phony big self, hence their madness and delusion disorder and their heated, anxious, and angry behaviors.

They are trying to prove to the world and to themselves that they are their imaginary big selves. They are trying to change the reality of our equality to a reality they created where they are special and superior and get the people to accept it. It's impossible to attain. They are madmen.

They have to let go of the pursuit of big self, relax their bodies and souls, and return to God.

DREAM
5:30 AM
FEBRUARY 28, 2020

I was the only person on a plane. I am doing some kind of test, apparently. I was sitting in front of the door and was supposed to press a number of buttons. One of which opens the door where the wind would suck me out of the plane and I die so I was supposed to be very careful. I went along and eventually pressed a button that said select it. The door opened and I was hanging outside the plane, gripping the bars. I looked down and thought of instant death and said I am the only son of God and was back in the plane and woke up.

Before going to sleep, I was reading the gospel of John. He emphasized that we are the sons of God. I guess that remembering to say that I am the son of God is affirmation of my true identity and I was saved. The meaning of the dream is to test my remembrance of my true self; thus, I had to do something for the door to open for me to remember God or die.

The fear and doubt. I went into the bathroom and changed my wound. I washed the cup. I returned to bed. Then I wondered whether I washed the cup or not. This is doubt. Doubt is rooted in a lack of certainty in God; doubt is of the ego. When one returns to accepting that one is the son of God and changes one's life to loving God, all his sons would no longer have doubt.

PSYCHOANALYSIS INSISTS THAT OUR DREAMS BE ANALYZED

In psychoanalysis, folks are told to have a pad of paper on their beds. If they wake up from dreams, they are told to write the dreams down and later, try to understand the importance of the dreams (by themselves, with the help of friends, or through their psychoanalyst). You can understand yourself by trying to understand your dream.

Sigmund Freud, Alfred Adler, and Carl Jung, the founders of psychoanalysis, urged their clients to do dream analysis. You will understand yourself better if you understand your dreams for dreams are the royal road to the unconscious mind. Our day behaviors are shaped by unresolved irrational issues in our unconscious minds, not by our rational thinking in our ego-conscious minds.

A man may consciously see himself as powerful. Unbeknown to him, he has belief that he is powerless. That sense of powerlessness is hidden in his ego-unconscious mind. Thus, at the conscious level, he acts as the insane man who goes about fancying himself as superior to other people when in fact, folks see him as a clown.

It is when you are humble and sees yourself as equal to all that people see you as mature and rational. Bluster superiority and even fools will see you as deluded and not respect you. See Donald Trump. He at the conscious level wants to seem powerful. In his ego-unconscious mind, he is a coward who did not join the army to go fight in Vietnam. We all know that he is a coward masquerading as a powerful man. Raise your voice and the freaking coward would run away. Yesterday, while giving a speech at a right-wing gathering with his supporters, there was a loud sound and he immediately dodged behind the podium.

If he had the courage, he would have jumped to the front, taken charge to try figure out the source of the sound, and tackle it. That is, he would have behaved like a leader. Instead, his true character, a coward pretending to be courageous, showed itself for even his supporters to see.

DREAM
MARCH 1, 2020
9:00 AM

In this dream, we took some kind of test. I passed it. I was sent to go collect my certificate from a different part of the building. I got there and saw two lines formed to go get their certificate. Instead of finding which line I should queue in, I left the room to find out what line to queue in. When I got back, there was no more line. I saw an Igbo man and asked him where to get my certificate. He told me to return on Monday to get it as they are closed for the day. I suspected that he wanted me to give him bribe before he gives me my certificate. I left him and saw another Nigerian, a non- Igbo, and told him why I am there and he went into an office and got my certificate. As he was handing it to me, I woke up.

The meaning of this dream is that I had stereotyped Igbos as bribe-takers and corrupt (in an essay, I wrote yesterday on the Igbo character in Nigerian politics) and in my dream, saw an Igbo as a corrupt person. The lesson is that the world is your dream and what you think of people, you see them as and they present themselves as. See people as loving, and they will present themselves as loving. See Igbos as decent persons, and you begin seeing decent Igbos.

THE WORLD IS OUR INDIVIDUAL AND COLLECTIVE DREAM.

The world is the dream of the collective and individual sons of God. Our nightly dreams are our individual dreams. Our day world is our collective dream. We all collectively dream our day world while individually dream our nightly dreams. Because our day world is collective, it lasts long—trillions of years—and because our night dreams are not shared, they last for as long as we sleep and disappear when we wake up. Our day world, our collective dream, will end when we all wake up.

We wished for specialness and separation from the whole life, aka God, and dream a world of separated selves and things—a world of space, time, and matter and a world we see each person housed in body and walk around in space and time.

Heaven is unified, hence love; we dream a world that is the opposite of heaven, a world of separated selves, hence hates. The world is a place we see the opposite of God. We made the world.

We now have to have different wishes and desires; we must now see ourselves as unified, hence as love, dream love, and see loving people.

The world and people we see are projections of our wishes, beliefs, and our thoughts. Each of us made his world by his thinking. The people and things you see are your thoughts mirrored for you to see. You want to see attack and see an attacking world.

Now, desire to see love and project out loving people around you. You invented the world you see. You have no one to blame for your life for it is your dream, your projection, and your thoughts pictured for you to see and experience.

Change your thinking from hate to love and you see a different world.

DREAM
MARCH 2, 2020
3:30 AM

In this dream, I was at Augusta's Golf Tournament in Georgia, USA. Thereafter, I was on a train. We were heading north. I was admiring the landscape as the train sped along; I compared it to Alaska, my home state. The train blew a whistle indicating that it would soon stop. People began getting ready to get off the train. I looked at my feet and my shoes were not on them. I found the shoes and two pairs of white socks and put one of them on; one foot already had socks on. I was in a state of fear wondering whether I would be able to have my shoes on by the time the train stops and I get off or whether I would not be able to do so in time to get off in time and the train carries me beyond the station that I am supposed to get off. I woke up in this undecided and unsettled state of mind.

The dream shows my habitual tendency to have self-doubt. Obviously, I had to have my shoes on to be on the train but I forgot that fact and panicked looking for the shoes before the train stopped.

The root cause of my doubt is my uncertainty as to whether I am the son of God or the ego.

If I accept that I am the son of God, I end my lifelong self-doubt, but as long as I waver between ego and Christ, I will always have self-doubt.

DREAM
MARCH 1, 2020

Someone said something that I believed humiliated me. I looked for two guns with the intention of giving him one gun and having one gun and we shoot at each other and may the best shot win. Dueling and killing the other guy were a way to rehabilitate my injured vanity.

But dueling is not fair if one person is a better shot than the other. Therefore, one must seek a different way to overcome humiliation.

To start with, one cannot be humiliated by other people. One humiliated self by being born as a separated self in body.

Human beings, my parents, Igbos, Africans, and white people did not humiliate me; I humiliated myself by identifying with ego and body.

Ego and body do not exist. I return to my true self—Christ—and he cannot be humiliated for he always has eternal worth in God.

DREAM
MARCH 2, 2020

In this dream, I sent my family, including my parents to a different town, to a place where it is cold, Alaska. I was planning to join them the next day. I stayed to clean the apartment. Then I was filled with guilt for not consulting my family before sending them away. I made a decision for them, which seemed unfair. Some folks came by, made fun of me, and I woke up.

This dream shows that I have guilt in me—guilt that I wronged folks. I did not wrong anyone on earth. If anything, my folks abandoned me when I was a child.

The guilt is existential. It came from the belief that I separated from God and his other sons. But since I cannot separate from them and have not separated from them, except as in dreams, I have no business feeling guilty.

I remain as God created me, in him.

Make these affirmations daily:

I AM THE SON OF GOD, I AM SPIRIT, I AM NOT BODY,
I AM LOVE, I AM LIGHT, I AM ETERNAL, PERMANENT,
AND CHANGELESS, AND I AM ALWAYS AS GOD CREATED
ME, PART OF HIM, NOT SEPARATED FROM HIM.

At some point in our lives, each of us must make a declaration of which is his identity. One must state who one's real self is.

To be in this world, to begin with, one had said that one is a separated ego-self housed in a body. In eternity, all is spirit and all spirits are the same, equal, and unified. Each of us on earth decided to seem special and to seem that he created himself. He cannot be so in unified spirit. So, he separated from God and his brothers and manifested in the world of space, time, and matter (space, time, and matter are three illusions; they seem to exist but do not exist).

Like most people, I separated from God. Like all people, I invented a self-concept, a separated self that says that I am body and is apart from God and all other people, a self that mostly looks after its interests at the expense of other people's interests or perhaps cooperates with other people.

It does not take rocket science to realize that if all I am is body, I am an animal and is nothing. My body is composed of the various elements and atoms held together by chemical bonds. Those elements and atoms will decompose—decay into particles of electrons, protons, and neutrons. Those will decay to quarks and light. Light will decay to the nothingness it came from during the Big Bang 13.8 billion years ago.

If all I am body and flesh, I am nothing. I have no worth and value. Try as I do to give me value and worth in body, the fact is that as body, I have no worth.

Vaguely, I remember that I have a different self, a spirit self. Spirit self, something tells me is non-material, is eternal, permanent, and changeless, and as such, has worth.

But ego reasoning tells me that the desire for spirit self is magical thinking, that there is no evidence of spirit's existence.

Thus, I end up in uncertainty, in doubt as to who my identity is—ego and its body or spirit and its formlessness. I live in doubt and uncertainty.

So, who am I? To find out, I studied religious books. Hinduism, Buddhism, *A Course in Miracles* and the Christian Bible. These books say that I am the son of God and that the son of God is spirit. My ego says that I am body and live for a hundred years and die off.

So, who is correct? Am I spirit or body? If I am spirit, how come I have no awareness of it?

Last week, I had a two-hour surgery. I was under anesthesia during those two hours. I did not remember anything that took place during the two hours. But when the anesthetizing medication wore off, I regained consciousness of being me, an ego in body who lives in space, time, and matter. I did not know anything about the previous two hours. Was I dead during those two hours, or what?

Thinking about it, I came to realize that we have different selves and different homes—awareness of them we currently do not know. To be in ego and body, we had to forget the real self and its home in God. You cannot be on earth and know about your spirit real self and God. It is either you know about spirit or you know about ego but not both of them at the same time.

To be on earth, in ego, body, space, and time, we are, as it were, dead to the knowledge of our unified spirit self.

God created us as his sons. We are the sons of God. As it were, the eternal sons of God died to the awareness of their spirit state and replaced it with the awareness of their selves in bodies.

Our current self, the ego, must now be allowed to die and we become reborn in the knowledge of our true self, unified son of God.

Rebirth means dying to the old ego-self and being reborn in God as God's son. This means regaining Christ consciousness.

Christ is the son of God who knows himself to be as God created him—part of God and God's creation.

I must now voluntarily let my ego-self and body die for me to be reborn in Christ. When I do so, Christ has come into my life the second time. The first time was when God created me as his son, then in pursuit of ego, I died to Christ but now have returned to the knowledge of Christ.

As the son of God, I regain the power that God gave his son to his creation. I do not understand that power. My ego cannot understand God's power.

What is true is that every time I say to myself that I am the son of God, the Christ, and shut up, things do happen in my life that reason cannot understand. Our ego conceptual reasoning cannot understand God and his powers. All we have to do is accept our identity as the sons of God and let God do the rest.

What to the ego seems impossible, to God, it's not difficult!

WHAT IS TEMPTATION?

Temptation is the wish to see me as ego and body and deny that I am Christ spirit and is formless. I am always tempted to see myself as ego in body instead of my real self, unified Christ.

A LESSON UNLEARNED IS REPEATED UNTIL IT IS LEARNED.

I have not learned the lesson that I am spirit and not ego. Life will continue giving me trials—lessons to decide whether I am ego and body or formless unified Christ.

When I finally accept that I am Christ, son of God, there will no longer be temptations and lessons to learn.

Our true identity is the son of God, Christ. Upon birth on earth, we forget that identity and take on false identity as separated ego selves in bodies. We forget God and gradually learn a new self-concept, the separated self-concept; the ego is learned on earth, it is not given to us by God. By adulthood, each of us has learned a self-concept, a personality, and behaves accordingly.

The self-concept is conceptual. We live in the conceptual world. Concepts adapt to the world of perception, to the world of space, time, and matter.

Concepts cannot understand the unified world of God. Concepts cannot understand the truth—the truth is beyond concepts for concepts are of the ego separated self.

Truth inheres in unified state which only unified mind can understand; separated minds cannot understand unified self and truth, aka God.

To regain the knowledge of the world of God, we must now give up all self-concepts, concepts of who people are and what the world is, and remain silent.

In a mind cleaned of concepts the truth of who one is, the holy son of God, the unified self, dawns on its own. But as long as one has concepts of who one is, other people and things are one and cannot know who one's true self is.

Overlook the world of concepts, forgive the world, and what is done in it. Do not engage in ego thinking, do not apply ego rationality to anything, and simply be a mind emptied of all wishes and have no ego and body wishes.

SEE PEOPLE AS SPIRITS, NOT BODIES.

Seeing people as spirit and not as body means that one has developed divine consciousness that overlooks body to see the Christ in people.

When you *overlook* people's bodies and affirm the spirit in them, they know it and feel recognized as spirit, feel good, will smile a lot, be at peace, do stuff to help the person who overlooks their ego plays, and affirm their spirit selves. If you see people only as body, they feel angry at you for to see people as body is to attack them, to abuse them, to deny their divinity, and to affirm that they are dust for the body is dust.

THE DEATH OF YOUR EGO IS NECESSARY FOR YOU TO RETURN TO GOD.

Jesus, that is ego, died on the cross; we must die to the ego-self we made to replace the self that God created us as. This is a law that must be obeyed for no one who is ego comes to God, returns to his real self, and knows peace.

You must replace the separated self in body that you made and used to replace the unified self that God created you as—with your true self, Christ, son of God. This is a law and there is no getting around it. You cannot retain ego separated self and come to unified spirit self, God.

YOUR CRUCIFIER IS YOUR SAVIOR!

What is salvation? Salvation is the elimination of your self-concept, your ego, your self-definition that you are a separated self housed in a body. It is your idea that you are a self that you made but not the self that God created you as.

God created you as an extension of himself. God is a formless spirit and extends that formless spirit to you and all people. All of you are the same, coequal, and unified.

You rejected that unified self and invented an ego-self housed in a body living in space, time, and matter. When you kill the ego-self and its body and become aware that you are a formless, unified self, Christ, you experience peace, joy, eternity, permanency, and changelessness, hence are saved from the ego you made.

YOUR EGO PUTS YOU WHERE YOU ARE HATED.

Your ego-self puts you into every situation you find yourself in on earth. The earth is your dream and those around you are those your ego-mind projected out to interact with you. If you are attacked and crucified by those around you, you made them do it. You want them to crucify your ego so that your Christ self may shine through.

Black people project out white racists who crucify their pride, ego-self, hence develop sense of humility and egolessness and in the process, regain awareness of Christ and are saved.

· White people save themselves if they also let their egos be crucified. They regain awareness of Christ. Your supposed enemy enables you to let go of your ego, hence is not your enemy but your savior.

Be grateful to your enemy for killing your ego and returning you to Christ consciousness.

Life is very simple but we complicate it through our ego pride. Take whatever happens to you without pride and flow with it, and life is very simple. We take life too seriously and should not do so. Be light and play with life.

It would be better if one projected out only loving persons, as we do in heaven. But on earth, one hates one's real self, the son of God, and projects out those who would hate one. To be in ego is to hate oneself. One must hate oneself to be in body, deny it, and project out people who hate one and that justifies anger at them. Then one attacks them to attack oneself.

You can transform the hatred from others to forgiveness of them, hence forgiveness for yourself for hating yourself.

Ego hates the sons of God and places them in bodies that give them pain to make them hate themselves and feel like they must have sinned for God to cause them such pain.

Now forgive your self-hatred and choice to be born in body, relax in peace, and your peace will heal your body

A COURSE IN MIRACLES RENDERS A PSYCHOANALYTIC AND PSYCHOLOGICAL INTERPRETATION OF THE STORY OF JESUS.

A Course in Miracles provides a psychological cum psychoanalytic interpretation of the Bible, especially the Jesus story (Jesus represents man, ego; Christ represents son of God, the real self). Here, we separated from God and each other and helped each other to form separated selves, egos, and personalities and use those to replace our original self, the unified self that God created us as. We suffer until we let go of the selves we made and with which we replace the self that God created us as, holy self. Is this true?

There is no proof that it is true as there is no proof for any psychological theory; it is rational but not scientific in the sense that there is no proof for it while it seems philosophically right.

What heals people is to love their real selves, love all people, and work for social interests.

I PROVIDE FOLKS WITH A CONSISTENT PHILOSOPHY.

As you can see, the philosophy I teach in my various writings is very consistent; it teaches a world view that is consistent in its parameters, although to science, it may be gibberish. If you accept it, as I do, it will give you a consistent way of approaching your life and its issues.

There are no accidents in our lives. You chose to be born when you were born in body and the family you are born in—in the society and historical epoch you are born in and chose the problems that confront you. You did so to initially feel oppressed by those you see do bad things to you. You did those bad things to you. Your goal is to learn that the bad things you see done to you have not been done by either you or other people. It was all a nightmarish dream in your mind.

You have not done the awful things you believe that you did, deny your real self, unified spirit self, and become born in body that lives and dies.

You remain in God all the time you dream yourself on earth. Laugh at the ugly world you see for it is a dream that merely passed through your mind.

Awaken to your real self by not desiring our world and by giving up your ego. Do so and while still on earth and live in relative peace and joy.

THE WORLD OF LIGHT FORMS

Upon death, you live in the world of light forms. You do not have to die to live in the world of light forms. If you really desire it, you can let go of our world of gross matter and continue living in the world of light forms. In the world of light forms, it's everything in our present world but in light forms.

FORMLESS UNIFIED HEAVEN

Ultimately, you can give up even the world of light forms and experience yourself living in the formless, unified world of God, heaven, our real home. We are aliens in our present world.

YOU CHOSE TO LIVE IN TODAY'S WORLD.

We live in the world of space, time, and matter and past present, and future (those do not exist in the unified world of God where only now exists). In our world, there was the past, a present, and a future. People lived in the past and dealt with their issues and will live in the future and deal with their issues.

You chose to live in the present world, a world with its unique issues, issues that did not exist in the past nor will exist in the future. You chose this present world to solve its problems and find your peace of mind, salvation.

You solve your issues by giving up your desire for separation from God and by giving up the separated self you made to make you seem separated from God.

WHAT IS SALVATION?

Salvation means giving up the separated self you made to substitute for the unified self that God created you as; as long as you identify with a separated ego-self, you feel like you disobeyed God and your real self by living as a replacement self. When you give up identification with the false ego-self, you no longer feel guilty, sinful; you now live as God created you.

FEELING OF INNOCENCE FROM GIVING UP THE SEPARATED EGO-SELF

As long as you identify with the ego separated self, you will feel guilty, sinful, and bad; you will feel innocent and holy when you have returned to your holy self, Christ self, egoless self.

The point is that your salvation is to be put to effect now, today, not in the past or future. Decide today to give up your ego and regain sense of oneness with God and feel innocent, guiltless, and sinless hence, saved.

THE WORLD IS A DREAM AND WHAT IS DONE IN IT HAS NOT BEEN DONE SO WE REMAIN INNOCENT DESPITE THE SEEMING EVIL WE DO ON EARTH.

The world of space, time, and matter and past, present, and future you see and seem to live in and what is done in it does not exist so you have not separated from God, have not sinned, and are not guilty. You and all people despite what you see people do on earth have not done those things, hence remain innocent for they are not in the world of time but always are in the unified world of God.

Accept ego-lessness and guiltlessness and live innocently, hence peacefully and happily now.

YOU NEED TO PRAY AND MEDITATE DAILY.

In praying, you talk to God and tell him about your needs (which he knows before you ask). In meditation, you listen to God for the answers he has given to your prayers.

God hears all our prayers and answers all of them. However, to receive the answers he has already given to our requests, we must do what he asked us to do: Forgive and love ourselves and each other.

To forgive and love is to let go of the ego we made to replace the holy son of God when we separated and in our separated state, do awful things to each other, in the dream. We must now forgive each other our evils because they were done in dreams and what is done in dreams has not been done.

Forgive and you have loved the person you forgave, you and other people. If you do not forgive, you say that what is done in the dream of separation is real, hence not to be forgiven. You must forgive to come to God.

How many times must we forgive? One of his apostles asked Jesus and he said seventy times seventy times, meaning, always. There is no exception to this rule.

Regardless of the enormity of the evil, we are to forgive it if we want to receive God's answers to our prayers.

Jesus taught his disciples only one prayer:

The Lord's Prayer

"Our Father who art in heaven, hallowed be thy name. Thy kingdom comes. Thy will be done on earth as it is in heaven. Give us this day our daily bread, and forgive us our trespasses, as we forgive those who trespass against us, and lead us not into temptation, but deliver us from evil. For thine is the kingdom and the power, and the glory, forever and ever. Amen."

In this prayer, Jesus told his disciples that their father is in heaven and that his name is to be praised and glorified. They are to ask God for their daily bread, their daily needs, while they are on earth. They ask him to forgive them their trespass because they have forgiven those who trespassed against them. That is, they must forgive those who offended them if they want God to forgive them. Forgiveness is a contract we made with God to forgive each other before God forgives us; there is no exception to this rule.

Pray in the morning and in the evening. Meditate, at least, once a day. In meditation, you let go of your ego and become a mind without ego. When you let go of your ego, God will talk to you. In a mind without ego, chattering knowledge of your real self dawns.

Normally, we fill our minds with ego concepts, ego ideas of what the truth is. Those may be true in the world of separation but are not true in the world of union.

Concepts and ideas are useful in our world but cannot take us to heaven for heaven has its own logic. We must therefore let go of all our ego concepts and say: I do not know who I am, I do not know who other people are, I do not understand what anything is, and then ask God to tell us. We keep quiet and refuse to answer our questions.

If one can keep one's mind silent for one hour without ego chattering, one will begin to experience other worlds. Keep quiet every evening for one hour before you go to sleep. For one thing, you will feel relaxed. If you have also forgiven all their trespasses, you will begin experiencing the Holy Spirit respond to your requests if they are in accord with love (God answers only prayers motivated by love, not hate for your so-called enemies for you have no enemies; only egos have enemies; Christ, your real self has no enemy).

From a psychological perspective, praying and meditating are useful for your mental health. In praying, you recognize a higher power above your ego and humble yourself before him. The ego, the false self, wants to seem big, grandiose, and important. The ego does not exist; it is a mere puff of smoke that pretends to be powerful. You silence the ego and keep quiet and ask a really powerful self, God, to guide you and keep quiet and hear his guidance in meditation. People with swollen egos need to pray and humble themselves to become mentally healthy.

Note, here is my daily prayer:

> I AM THE SON OF GOD, I AM SPIRIT, I AM NOT BODY, I AM LOVE, I AM LIGHT, I AM ETERNAL, PERMANENT, AND CHANGELESS, AND I AM ALWAYS AS GOD CREATED ME, PART OF HIM, NOT SEPARATED FROM HIM. AS PART OF GOD'S UNIFIED, HOLY SELF, I AM GUILTLESS, SINLESS, AND INNOCENT. IN SEPARATION, I FEEL GUILTY AND SINFUL BUT SEPARATION IS IMPOSSIBLE, SO I AM ALWAYS INNOCENT AND SO IS EVERY SON OF GOD. GOD ENABLES ME TO LOVE ME AND ALL YOUR SONS. GIVE ME WHAT IS GOOD FOR ME, NOT WHAT MY EGO DESIRES.

DR. O IS AN IDEALISTIC MIND.

Dr. O is a hopeless idealist. His mind comes up with all that he talks about and pictures ideal people—Africans as superior people, heaven, and so on. But he lacks the ability to practicalize his wishes and dreams in pictures. He plans to get money to carry out his idealistic projects and they are not going to come to fruition. Don't criticize him; just listen to him to learn about the nature of an idealistic mind.

We did not meet by accident. I projected him out and he projected me out. He was projected out by my mind to teach me about my own idealistic manner of thinking that produces ideal worlds that are not going to come into being. Learn from him and make my thinking realistic.

ONLY ONE MIND OR THINKING EXISTS IN THE UNIVERSE.

Only one mind exists. It is one mind that is simultaneously infinite minds and infinite units of thinking, all of them coordinated into one mind thinking in tandem. Folks call it God's mind. Each of us is a unit of that God's mind. We think with God's mind.

THREE LEVELS OF MIND OR THINKING
THE EGO-MIND

There are three levels of thinking. At the lowest level of mind or thinking is the separated ego-mind. Here, we think in images and project out the seemingly solid world we see and live in. That world is in our minds. The ego-mind, aka left mind, is responsible for inventing the world of perception we see.

It is my ego-mind and its thinking that produced the world I am living in; the same goes for you. The ego-mind also has visions. When you have visions of Jesus Christ, it is your mind that produced it just as it is your mind that produced your day world.

THE HOLY SPIRIT-DIRECTED MIND

The second level of mind is what Christians call Holy Spirit. Here, mind sees the world that the ego-mind invented but forgives it, loves it, and in so doing, purifies it and it becomes a beautiful dream, a world where all things are in light forms.

This is the world we see when on earth we die; it is the world near-death experiences see. It is also a dream world, a fiction not real. It is kind of a happy dream, happy fiction, happy insanity (our current world is a nightmarish dream, insanity).

GOD'S ONE MIND

The final level of mind is the one mind that God and his sons share. It is literally one mind that has infinite units in it. Each of us is a unit of that mind. The whole mind, God, is in each unit of mind and the unit of mind is in the whole mind; this is the mind we have in heaven. It is very creative whereas the ego-mind is inventive and the Holy Spirit mind is corrective—corrects what the ego-mind made.

All three levels of mind are levels of one mind; they are in you and me; they are not separate from us. We do think from all three levels of our minds but on earth are not aware of our thinking done at the level of one mind, unified mind, and God's shared mind.

One's mind ultimately produced unified mind, heaven, where it is at rest, peace, eternal, permanent, and changeless; that is, mind at home.

It is your entire mind. You deny it and attribute it to God, Holy Spirit, or ego. It is your mind thinking at several levels. It is your mind that thinks at ego level, at Holy Spirit level, and at God's level. Each level of your mind produces a world for you to experience.

Mind is very powerful for the thinking that produced this entire universe and more is very powerful, so you have to be mindful of your thinking for it produces everything that happens to you. There is no use blaming other people for your fate.

If you are poor, your mind produced it; if you are a suffering African, your mind produced it; if you are rich, your mind produced it.

You can change the pattern of your thinking, that is, change your mind and produce a different life for you. Love and forgive all and see your life peaceful, joyful, and rich. Hate, and you live in misery and poverty.

How mind produced our egos' world we do not know, how it produces dreams and visions we do not know, how it produces the world of light forms we do not know, and how it produces heaven's unified, holy state we do not know.

The take away from all these is that it is my mind that produces everything in my life. How it does it I have no clue. I take ownership and responsibility for everything that happens in my life.

This is my present level of understanding.

9

UNDERSTAND YOUR SHY CHILD

Each of us has a personality. Personality is the individual's habitual pattern of responding to other people and to his environment.

About 90% of the people have normal personalities. About eight percent have personality disorders. About two percent have psychosis, that is, mental disorders, and about two percent have mental retardation—IQ under 70. About 90% of the people have an average IQ (85–115).

About two percent of the people have superior IQ—anything above 132; about 8% of the people have above-average IQ—118–130. Above average IQs are the professors and professionals of this world, medical doctors, engineers, architects, and so on. Those with superior IQ tend to go into research and discover new things; IQ over 140 is genius which is very rare.

Try to figure out your personality type. Clinical psychologists do give folks personality tests, such as the MMPI and figure out their personalities (they also give IQ tests, such as WAIS, WISC, and Stanford-Binet to figure out folks' IQs).

As noted, most people are normal. If you are psychotic, mentally ill, you would not be reading this piece. However, many folks with superior IQ tend to have personality disorders.

As a child, I was extremely shy. Psychologists see shy children as having avoidant personality disorder. Such children feel that as they are, they are not good. Even though they make it first in their classes at school, they feel that they are no good. They feel that if other people get close to them, they would see that they are no good and reject them. To avoid being seen as no good and rejected, they withdraw from other kids and keep to themselves. In social isolation, they wish that they have good selves—powerful selves.

You can understand your personality type and work on changing it. Below is a snippet on avoidant personality disorder. Elsewhere, I wrote on all the known personality disorders: paranoid, schizoid, schizotypal, narcissistic, histrionic, borderline, antisocial, dependent, obsessive-compulsive, and avoidant. I have also written on the psychoses, schizophrenia, bipolar affective disorder, delusion disorder, etc.

Nigeria and most African countries are ruled by antisocial personality disordered persons, aka sociopaths and psychopaths. As long as Africa is ruled by criminals, obviously, Africa is not going to be well-governed and will remain the chaotic place it is—a place where politicians come to steal from public offices, not to serve the public good.

SO, I, OZODI, HID FROM OTHER PEOPLE TO PROTECT MY BIG EGO; NOW THAT I HAVE NO BIG OR SMALL EGO, I STOP HIDING, YES!

In childhood, I posited a wish for big ego and since it is not real, hide from other people to protect it. I avoided people to protect the wished-for big ego.

Put in metaphysical language, while in heaven, eternal state of union, I separated from God and his son, my real self, unified self with God; I invented a separated ego-self that I gave desire for power and grandiosity.

The ego and its wish for power do not exist; they are just mere wishes in my mind, the mind of the son of God. I have given the wish for separated ego up.

Now that I have no wish for big or small ego, do I still have a need to hide to protect the ego? No. I hide from no one for I am protecting nothing.

If you have no ego, you must revert to the knowledge of your real self, son of God, Christ, for you always have a self. It is either the ego you made to replace your real self that God created or the son of God that God created, Christ, aka unified self.

I am now aware that I am the son of God, Christ; in Christ, I am calm, peaceful, and happy.

A CASE OF GOD DELUSION
DELUSION DISORDER, AKA PARANOIA BRIEFLY DEFINED

This paper makes the assumption that the reader has some understanding of delusion disorder hence is not going to systematically describe the phenomenon. However, briefly, in delusion disorder, aka paranoia, the individual feels inordinately powerless and inadequate.

Many biological, social, and existential factors play roles in human sense of worthlessness and powerlessness. The individual tries to compensate with desire for power and over adequacy. He posits a self-concept and self-image that sees him as the most powerful and important person on earth.

Since that self-assessment is false, he is at all times trying to prove it as real and true; he is very defensive, guarded, and generally does whatever he does to seem important. He scans his environment looking for anyone who demeans him, humiliates him, degrades him, and belittles him, and generally makes him feel small and he quarrels with that person and tries to establish in his eyes that he is very important.

He looks for danger and finds it and defends against it. He is always defensive hence tight and rigid and looks guarded; that is, paranoid.

In society, he argues with most people; he is argumentative. His goal is to win and have those he argues with lose. If you lose and he wins, then he has power and you are powerless. He does not want to lose in anything for that would make him feel powerless and inadequate, a situation he would rather not be in.

He is playing the role of a powerful God, the most powerful being in the universe, the creator of the universe. His idea of God is generally derived from the God of the Old Testament, a pathologically narcissistic God who feels insecure and seeks all people to pay attention to him and to admire him, a God that asks his creation to perpetually praise and glorify his name and if not, he punishes them.

The Old Testament god is obviously crazy and cannot possibly be the real God, if God exists. The paranoid person wants to feel as powerful as the Old Testament god. He seeks other folks' attention and admiration hence is a lunatic.

The real God, if he exists, is in all people, as all people's real selves hence feel the same and coequal in all people.

Gnosticism calls the Old Testament god, Yahweh and Lucifer the false God, the Demiurge, the crazy God who out of pride separated from the real loving God to go create our unloving and egoistic world.

I often ask: how did RO, an attorney, come to believe in the Old Testament God in a literal manner? It seems to me that the best a Christian could do is see the Christian idea of God as a metaphorical rendition of God, a kind of allegory and simile but not a literal God. How did an educated man come to believe in the primitive God of Christians?

Wonders never cease in our world. Even the teaching of Jesus, useful as they are, is not without faults. Jesus in the Syrophoenician woman had Jews eat at the table and the woman, non-Jew, begged for the crumbs that fall from the table. What kind of God-realized man would utter such arrant rubbish?

Jesus in the temple was angry and flogged folks for transforming his father's house into a merchants' house. Anger and flogging people is a sign of immaturity, presence of pride.

The Jesus of the Bible was by no means a mature person. Simply put, pure reason cannot accept the Bible, Old and New Testament as literal truth.

How RO managed to accept the old book of fables as true beats my understanding. Anyway, the issue here is delusion, not God.

The deluded person denies his real self which he believes is not good and wears a false self—a mask that he feels makes him seem good. He perpetually defends the persona, mask of a perfect and powerful person he wears hence is almost always anxious and tense; he does not know relaxation and joy. He does not behave spontaneously and authentically because he is trying to become a false powerful self; he wants to become but is not and cannot become. He must relax and smell the roses. There is nothing in this world that is worth the level of tension the paranoid person lives in.

THE CASE

A Ghanaian friend, Kofi Ayanpong, asked me to talk to his friend, RO. I asked why he wanted me to talk to him. He said that he does not know what to make of the man, that both of them went to Howard University at

Washington DC, and that at school, he was brilliant but lately, is something else. Kofi is not a mental health professional. He is an attorney. While I was pondering whether to talk to a complete stranger or not, he connected RO on the phone and introduced him to me. Thus, I began talking to the man.

We talked over a period of three months. I am generally free in the evenings and either called him or he called me. I would allow him to talk and asked leading questions. Sometimes, he talked for three hours, non-stop. If I tried to get a word in, he would find an excuse to terminate the talk so I learned to simply allow him talk. Boy, can he talk!

It did not take me more than an hour to know that he has delusion disorder, grandiose type, and that he also has delusion disorder of the religious type (see the vignette on delusion disorder below from psych central).

He is what psychoanalysts call the paranoid prophet. He talks with absolute certainty when he talks about God. And don't make mistake about it, he has given God quite a bit of thinking and has interesting thoughts on him. His thoughts on God are set, rigid, and inflexible. You cannot get him to reconsider them. If you tried to provide a different take on God, he would hang up on you. He hung up on me several times and a few days later, he would call back and say something about why he should not have done that.

I knew that he hung up on me because whatever I said attacked his set view, his pride, and made him seem imperfect. The paranoid, deluded person wants to seem perfect and powerful and if you say or do what makes him seem imperfect and weak, he feels angry at you for you have de-exalted him, so you must collude with his ego and tell him that he is perfect, powerful, and is God.

The man is proud beyond belief; he takes his vain opinions on God as the absolute truth. If you doubt him, he feels angry and yells at you and if that would not make you change your mind, he hangs up on you.

He is an extraordinarily bright man; his ideas are quite fascinating except that they are mostly not true. He is an idealist. He used his imagination to imagine ideal states and came to believe that his imaginary states are true.

Normal folks test their imaginations on the external world and if they do not comport with environmental reality, they discard them. No, this man dismisses social reality and sees his mentally reached views as the only reality there is. He does not deal with empiricism and observation of social and physical phenomena. Only his subjective views, he believes, are true.

First, he imagined how the ideal human politics ought to be and as a nineteen-year-old boy, resolved to go into politics and become the president of his country. He left for higher studies in the USA and as his contemporaries said, he was a brilliant student.

Upon completing his studies, he returned to Nigeria and tried to get into politics. Apparently, he had some setbacks, and while in Nigeria, in 1981, he had some unusual experiences and took them to mean that God wanted him to turn his attention to religion.

He returned to the USA and did some study of the Bible and other religious books and thereafter formed ideas on God.

As an idealist, he imagined what God is like; to him, God is like a human being with a body made of diamond-like material that he calls Azerbaijan. God, he said, is eternal, and God's creation is also eternal.

He said that he had gone to heaven and to hell and gives fanciful pictures of heaven and hell, both the product of his imaginations that his mind visualized in pictures for him to experience as if they are real.

He said that he and God have written a book called Elixir, a book that would help people recognize their eternity.

(Where is the book so that I might read it? But he said that it is not yet time for him to share the book with the world. Of course, there is no such book.)

He talked about when he went to heaven, saw God seated on his throne, and that he entered God and God entered him and both of them became one. He said that God told him that he is the one that Jesus said would come to make his teaching clear to mankind. He likes quoting the Gospel of John chapter fourteen, verses 8–14:

> 8Philip said, "Lord, show us the Father and that will be enough for us."
>
> 9Jesus answered: "Don't you know me, Philip, even after I have been among you such a long time? Anyone who has seen me has seen the Father. How can you say, 'Show us the Father'? 10Don't you believe that I am in the Father, and that the Father is in me? The words I say to you I do not speak on my own authority. Rather, it is the Father, living in me,

who is doing his work. 11Believe me when I say that I am in the Father and the Father is in me; or at least believe on the evidence of the works themselves. 12Very truly I tell you, whoever believes in me will do the works I have been doing, and they will do even greater things than these, because I am going to the Father. 13And I will do whatever you ask in my name, so that the Father may be glorified in the Son. 14You may ask me for anything in my name, and I will do it."

His picture of God and his heaven are clearly the product of his imagination. If you imagine something and go to sleep, you can see what you imagined in your dream. Thus, his dream or vision of God is the projection, his phantasmagoria.

I tried to tell him that God cannot possibly be in an image of a person and still be in all people. He reminded me that somewhere, God said:

"Let us create man in our image." (Genesis)

Therefore, God must have an image and a form (I said that it could be said that man created God in his human image, and he would not hear that).

The man is firm in his belief that he and God are one, as Jesus said in John 14:10–12 (see attached excerpt of John's gospel below). I tried telling him that the same chapter can be interpreted to say that God and all his creations are one. He would not listen to that.

He said that in a private audience, God told him that he, RO, is the only one who is one with God. He is the one to replace Jesus and teach the world what God is teaching.

His new religion is called Christism, not Christianity. It is to usher in a new millennium where the word of God prevailed in the world.

He uses everything in the Bible and elsewhere to give himself grandiosity and grandiose power.

He talked about how God is omniscient, omnipresent, and omnipotent and that he has those powers, except that he has not yet perfected the omnipotent attribute of God. When he does so, he would be able to manifest money at will, will be picking up millions every day, would be able to resurrect the dead, and the world would marvel at the signs, wonders, and miracles he performs.

Every once in a while, he calls me and tells me that he now has the key to the wealth of the world. I ask how he would manifest the money he talked about. He said that he would win the lotto that weekend. Occasionally, he would give me the number he picked and say that it is going to win the lotto. Of course, his numbers do not win and will not win any lotto for he does not have the power to transcend the statistical parameters on which lottos are predicated.

I observed that if, in fact, he is able to tune into God and use his powers to pick lotto numbers that would win every week hence make him rich, he could also use that power of God to manifest money in different ways. He could ask the rich to put millions into his bank account and they would do it.

Of course, he does not have access to God's so-called omnipotent power, whatever that is. The idea of God's omnipotent power is a human invention, not a reality. People think that God has such power and there is no evidence for it.

He is deceiving himself in believing that he is going to become wealthy and have the omnipotent power of God. That belief makes him feel powerful when in fact, he is not.

He is blind. If he is that powerful, how come he has not given himself sight. I was tempted to ask him and decided not to go there.

His blindness could be interpreted to represent his willful desire not to see the truth, his desire to take his views as the truth. The blind does not see the truth, the truth of our equality and oneness. The blind like him wants to believe in the mirage that he is superior to other people and is God's only special son. God does not have special sons; we are all the same.

The current coronavirus pandemic is another instrument in his hands to make himself seem powerful. He said that God has shown him how to cure the viral pandemic. I asked him why he has not healed a fear-stricken mankind yet. He said that God wants many people to die off.

Thereafter, another virus which he called Rafaela (made up from his first name, Rufus, shows his wish for power and grandiosity) will sweep through the globe and kill millions, and thereafter, humanity will be prepared to listen to his new teaching on God. I almost laughed out loud when he said this but decided that I must not offend him.

I know that in talking to him, it is either his way or the highway so I must not say anything contrary to his set views, and so I kept quiet and allowed him to ramble on and on with religious gibberish.

Connected Lives

He is a religious idealist, a religious utopian. He began as a political idealist and gravitated to religious idealist; he projects his ideas on how God and heaven should look like to what he says is God and heaven.

We do not know for sure whether God and heaven exist. Whatever the individual says about God and heaven is his conjecture, not fact.

In childhood, he used his imagination to construct alternatives to what is. He then imagined an ideal world which he wanted to actualize hence he studied political science and law. When that desired El Dorado was not realized, he transferred his desires to religion and became a religious idealist.

He used imagination to imagine what God and his heaven are like and came to believe in his imaginations. He no longer lives in our imperfect earthly reality and escaped into the imaginary ideal world of God.

He postponed living in our imperfect world and gave up all efforts to adapt to our imperfect world. He dropped out of our world and lives in his imaginary world.

He abandoned his wife and seven children and his wife essentially raised his children. The wife kicked him out since he was no longer contributing to paying for the family's upkeep; he sat around talking about God. The Ghanaian friend mentioned above took him in. When he remarried, he said that the new wife got tired of having him around and not contributing to the cost of food and house needs, and asked him to leave.

He lived at homeless shelters for a while until a white woman took him in and gave him a room in her house. She essentially feeds him. He is currently living in a room in the woman's house.

It does not bother him that a woman supports him; he said that it is the will of God, that God has her support him so that he has the freedom to do his work.

In my view, no one should support him; he either works for his daily bread or he knows what to do: Commit suicide rather than have other people carry you on their backs and you break their backs. I am totally opposed to welfare doles for men; for women with children, I can understand.

He began his escape from work in 1981, that is, 39 years ago. One would think that after almost forty years of waiting on God to do something and he has not done it that he would give up. He is 83-years-old. His voice is already the feeble voice of an old man. He said that he would not die and that eventually, he would transit to God and not experience corruption of his body. This is delusional denial of death and decay of the human body, a wish, a part of the magical thinking of a deluded man.

(The man is Igbo; as I pointed out elsewhere, for whatever reasons, many Igbos have delusion disorder; grandiose and persecutory types; they live in a fantasy land where their wishes are reality. They wish to be special and superior to other people, believe it, and act as if they are superior. Of course, they are not superior to even dogs. I do not know why many Igbos are deluded, believe in the fantasy of their superiority; many of them also have delusion, persecutory type, and believe that other people want to kill them. They look down on people and people feel angry at them for doing so and attack them. This is part of paranoid's self-fulfilling prophecy; they believe that other people are hostile to them. They do what makes people hate them and people hate them and they say: didn't I tell you that people and the world are hostile to us? They forget that they stimulated people's hatred to them by their boasting of their superiority, looking down on folks, and calling them derogatory names. This is clinically called group delusion disorder, folie à deux. See my writings on Igbos.)

EGO-LESSNESS IS CONDITION FOR PEACE, JOY, AND RETURN TO GOD.

I studied Hinduism, Buddhism, and Taoism. Those religions say that to know God, one must totally give up one's ego. No one who retains the ego, that is, having separated self, and its pride can come to God, for God is unified state.

RO has grandiose ego. As noted, if you said what he does not agree with, he feels angry and hangs up on you. This shows the presence of egoism, pride, and vanity. His proud ego is easily pricked and hurt.

Because he is still in ego, he is not living from his real self, which Hinduism calls Atman, aka son of God, a spirit self that is one with Brahman, God. He is not living in the peace and joy of God.

Hindus say that when the ego is given up, one lives in peace and joy, bliss. To live as ego, called Ahankara by Hinduism, is to have rejected one's real self, Atman. To have attacked one's real self and God is to be at war with one's real self and with God. One must give up attachment to the ego to know peace and joy, and to come to God.

This man is at war with his real self and with God and as such, is not in peace and therefore, not God-realized. I do not even think that he knows what God is beyond his fantasies about what his ego intellect tells him that God is.

Hinduism says go ahead and use your ego to conjecture about God, Jnani Yogis do so, but at some point, you must realize that God is beyond ego conceptualization and human intellect. You are to keep quiet, and in a mind without any ideas on God and ego, God dawns on his own.

As long as you have ideas on what God is, you do not know God for God is beyond our definitions and understanding.

God extended himself to his infinite sons. God is in his infinite sons and they are in him, they are one, according to what *A Course in Miracles* teaches.

Thereafter, the sons of God, out of opposition to God, decided to separate from God. They could not do so in reality. While still in God, they sleep and dream that they are separated from God.

Our empirical world is the dream world of the sons of God. As long as we are in ego, we are not in God.

Ego limits us to space and time and to the body we are in. If you let go of your ego, then your empirical I, self, dies.

When your ego, the human personality, dies, you return to the awareness that you are part of one unified self, aka God. As part of God, you are everywhere that God is.

God is formless. In God, you are formless, not in body of matter or light.

I shared with RO what *A Course in Miracles*, Hinduism, and Buddhism teach and he said that those are no good, that God talks to him personally, and that the information he has transcends whatever other writers on God have.

He is Igbo. Like most Igbos, he is firmly convinced that Igbos are the most superior people on earth. He said that Igbos are God's chosen people and that he is at the head of those God-chosen people. I reminded him that Adolf Hitler had a similar view, that Germans are a superior people, and that he is the most superior German of them all hence the need for all to listen to him, the fuhrer prince.

RO wants all people to listen to him and his Igbos. He believes that God allowed black Americans, who are mostly Igbos, to be enslaved because God wants to use them for a special purpose, to save mankind.

Any talk that sees oneself and one's people as special and superior to other people is delusional for, in reality, we are all the same and equal.

I tried to inject science into what he is saying and he tells me that science is intellectual fantasy, not true. He said that the truth is only what comes out of his mouth for it comes from God. But what he says is poor intellectual masturbations. He is not trained in physics, chemistry, and biology and therefore, does not know much about science and his opinions on it are silly.

At the moment, we have coronavirus. Folks all over the world are looking to scientists for an answer to save them from death. They are not looking to religious folks for answers. This is because religion is mere wishful thinking, not reality.

Religion does not solve our human problems. This does not mean that there is no God. Whatever God is, he is not part of this world and does not solve our problems for us. For all his talk about having omnipotent power, RO cannot solve our virus problem!

The man is stuck in his delusions.

I HAD TO MEET AND STUDY THIS MAN.

There are no accidents. RO was presented to me to learn about a man who is smart but is stuck. He is stuck because he misinterpreted the Bible to mean that he is special, the one coming to save the world. As long as he retains that sense of superiority, he is going nowhere

In true spirituality, one knows that we are all members of God's one family hence equal. God does not make one of his sons superior to others.

His being stuck shows me my own stuck status. I am egotistical; until I transcend the ego, I am going nowhere.

Like RO, I am an idealist. I have a weak, sensitive body, used my imagination to invent ideal self and world, and want to bring them into being.

I escaped into my ideal self and world that is not realistic to this world hence had to fail. Yet, I had to escape to idealism given my sensitive body. The idealist had to be so, hence failed.

The realist is closer to animals in body and had to be realistic and cannot be idealistic. Every person is where he or she is at by the dictates of his body.

However, regardless of whether one is idealistic or realistic, one has an ego and must let one's ego go to know God.

RO came into my life to be my teacher. I am also his teacher but he is so convinced of his superiority to me that he would not listen to me.

He does not know that we are each other's teachers and students. If God is in all of us and all of us teach us about God, we are all teachers and students of each other, but this arrogant prick would not listen to me or to other people and instead wallows in his infantile ideas—ideas that make me want to spank him, grow up, face reality, and quit escaping into his never-never land of God.

DISCUSSION

Can this man be healed of his delusion disorder? No therapist has ever healed a deluded, paranoid person. This is because delusion is a mask over a sense of inferiority and inadequacy.

The deluded person feels inferior and latches unto whatever makes him feel superior hence compensates for his underlying sense of inferiority.

To give up his delusions is to revert to feeling inferior. He does not want to feel inferior. For example, in our extant world, black folks feel inferior to white folks. This is because white science-based civilization is in fact superior to primitive African religions and civilization; Africans worship trees and folks die from assorted diseases that medical science could heal.

Therefore, a deluded black feels superior to whites to compensate for his underlying sense of inferiority. That is fantasy. If he were to give up that fantasy, he would revert to feeling inferior to whites.

There is a solution to delusion disorder: it lies in accepting reality as it is, accepting temporary superiority of scientific civilization, and striving to attain it.

Ultimately, what cures delusion disorder is giving up the wish to seem superior and accepting human inadequacy and our sameness and equality.

As to whether God and heaven exists or not, we do not know. I am agnostic with a wish that God and heaven ought to exist to make our existence worthwhile.

Arthur Schopenhauer said that the universe makes a mistake in producing people. We live and fancy ourselves important, having value and worth, then we die and decay and return to elements that return to particles of electrons, protons, and neutrons that return to photons that return to nothing. It was better we did not exist for we are nothing. Or are we something important? I do not know.

CONCLUSION

My three-month relationship with RO has taught me how difficult it is to heal delusion disorder, aka paranoia. Here you have a man who is rational in most other areas of his life but in one area, believes what is not true as true and uses that false belief to organize his thinking and behavior.

RO feels inadequate and inferior, as most Africans and black Americans do. He restituted with magical wish for adequacy. Now he feels special and superior. That feeling makes him feel good.

Alas, he is just like all of us, nothing. We have no worth and importance. We are food being prepared for worms.

All of us, in varying degrees, have fantasies of our worth when in fact, we have no worth. If your neighbor wishes to, he can kill you and you can kill him. If you are important, would he be able to kill you, and would you be able to kill him?

We have no existential worth. But we can make our lives pleasant by accepting and loving ourselves.

Delusion disorder emanates from our efforts to make us seem important. Religious delusion, as Richard Dawkins pointed out in his book *The God Delusion,* originates in our efforts to posit a God that gives us a sense of worth and eternal life.

We have no worth for we will die. What happens after we die? I do not know and leave it at that. RO has been a God sent to me. He enabled me to study delusion disorder up close and understand it more intimately.

I wished that I could help him to let go of his swollen ego and his fantasies of being God. I do not have the power to change anyone's mind.

In the meantime, I have total sense of gratitude for RO for volunteering to teach me about mental disorders.

I hope that this writing helps folks to understand delusion disorder and try to get rid of their own delusions, for all of us have aspects of delusions.

THE GOSPEL OF JOHN, CHAPTER FOURTEEN

Jesus Comforts His Disciples

1 "Do not let your hearts be troubled. You believe in God; believe also in me. 2My Father's house has many rooms; if that were not so, would I have told you that I am going there to prepare a place for you? 3And if I go and prepare a place for you, I will come back and take you to be with me that you also may be where I am. 4You know the way to the place where I am going."

Jesus The Way to the Father

5Thomas said to him, "Lord, we don't know where you are going, so how can we know the way?"

6Jesus answered, "I am the way and the truth and the life. No one comes to the Father except through me. 7If you really know me; you will know my Father as well. From now on, you do know him and have seen him."

8Philip said, "Lord, show us the Father and that will be enough for us."

9Jesus answered: "Don't you know me, Philip, even after I have been among you such a long time? Anyone who has seen me has seen the Father. How can you say, 'Show us the Father'? 10Don't you believe that I am in the Father, and that the Father is in me? The words I say to you I do not speak on my own authority. Rather, it is the Father, living in me, who is doing his work. 11Believe me when I say that I am in the Father and the Father is in me; or at least believe on the evidence of the works themselves. 12Very truly I tell you, whoever believes in me will do the works I have been doing, and they will do even greater things than these, because I am going to the Father. 13And I will do whatever you ask in my name, so that the Father may be glorified in the Son. 14You may ask me for anything in my name, and I will do it.

Jesus Promises the Holy Spirit

15 "If you love me, keep my commands. 16And I will ask the Father, and he will give you another advocate to help you and be with you forever—17the Spirit of truth. The world cannot accept him, because it neither sees

him nor knows him. But you know him, for he lives with you and will be in you. 18I will not leave you as orphans; I will come to you. 19Before long, the world will not see me anymore, but you will see me. Because I live, you also will live. 20On that day you will realize that I am in my Father, and you are in me, and I am in you. 21Whoever has my commands and keeps them is the one who loves me. The one who loves me will be loved by my Father, and I too will love them and show myself to them."

22Then Judas (not Judas Iscariot) said, "But, Lord, why do you intend to show yourself to us and not to the world?"

23Jesus replied, "Anyone who loves me will obey my teaching. My Father will love them, and we will come to them and make our home with them. 24Anyone who does not love me will not obey my teaching. These words you hear are not my own; they belong to the Father who sent me.

25 "All this I have spoken while still with you. 26But the Advocate, the Holy Spirit, whom the Father will send in my name, will teach you all things and will remind you of everything I have said to you. 27Peace I leave with you; my peace I give you. I do not give to you as the world gives. Do not let your hearts be troubled and do not be afraid.

28 "You heard me say, 'I am going away and I am coming back to you.' If you loved me, you would be glad that I am going to the Father, for the Father is greater than I. 29I have told you now before it happens, so that when it does happen you will believe. 30I will not say much more to you, for the prince of this world is coming. He has no hold over me, 31but he comes so that the world may learn that I love the Father and do exactly what my Father has commanded me.

"Come now; let us leave."

EGO-BASED POWER IS POWERLESSNESS. LOVE AND CHRIST-BASED POWER IS REAL POWER.

For whatever reasons, Igbos, like Jews, believe themselves to be the chosen children of God. It has always been that way.

I have always tried to disabuse them of that belief in their specialness because from it, they look down on other Nigerians. My personal view is that all people are the same and coequal.

I undertook to teach Igbos to let go of their ego arrogance and come to see themselves as like everyone else, but they refuse to do so; they cling to their sense of specialness.

I believe that what makes Igbos feel the way they feel is ego, arrogance, and pride. Out of ego pride, they seek power. But ego power is powerlessness; ego power is weakness; hence, Igbos have no power. However, if they can let go of their egoism and believe in their real selves, who the sons of God are, Christ, they would actually acquire real power.

The sons of God are powerful in God, not in ego.

God is love. The power of God is love-based power. Ego is the opposite of Christ and God, the opposite of love. If Igbos let go of their attachment to the ego and return to Christ, they would acquire power based on love, power based on God, which is the real power, the type of power that changes the world.

What people ask for is not always what they get. Igbos ask for power based on ego arrogance. But I want them to get power based on Christ's humility.

Africans are arrogant empty vessels that lack humility. They pretend to be important but cannot even rule themselves well. If Igbos return to love and acquire love-based power, they would acquire real power and help to properly govern Africa.

I want Igbos to return to living from love, living from ego-lessness, living from Christ, living from God, and living from the Holy Spirit, which means living in peace and joy and having real power, not the powerlessness of the ego that masquerades as power.

Nigerian big men have ego power which means that they have no power; they are weak. In God's power, one is quiet, peaceful, and happy. One knows that one is part of the eternity of God and does not feel fear, anxiety, depression, paranoia, and other mental disorders.

Ego power is the empty power that the ego gives its slaves.

Igbos are said to love money, so we can ask: does one make money from living from Christ and love?

The perennial wisdom of mankind teaches that when you do what you love, love, all people, and money will find its way to you.

Goethe, the premier German poet, said that when one is committed to doing what one loves, the entire universe, all people, open doors for one, but if one is merely trying to do what other people do but not what one believes to be true, the universe closes doors to one.

Hinduism, Buddhism, Taoism, Zen, *A Course in Miracles,* and Gnosticism all teach us to give up our egos, to die to the egos, give up our self-concepts, self-images, egos, and identification with body.

Jesus asked his followers to die to their old ego selves and be reborn in Christ. To be born again is to let the ego separated self we made replace the unified spirit self that God created us as, go.

God created us his extensions, his sons, Christ. We rebelled against God and invented ego separated selves hidden in bodies so that we do not see that we still remain as God created us—one with all people and with God.

Now, we voluntarily give up the ego separated self and return to the awareness of Christ unified self, to love. If we do so, we live in peace and do what we enjoy doing.

If one does what one enjoys doing that benefits other people, they will buy it and one would make a living from doing so.

God-realized persons, that is, those who have given up their egos and identified with God, Christ and love have their needs met; how, they do not know; money seeks them out.

Egotist has to struggle for money, as egoistic Africans do.

Loving sons of God love all people and do what actualizes their loving nature and people buy their goods and services and they live decently.

I do what I love doing, understanding people and sharing my findings on human nature. I serve people and a grateful people generally buy my services so that I do not lack for money.

The lesson for today is for me to strive to live egolessly; that is, to give up my identification with the separated self and return to living as God created me, to live from the unified self, aka living from the Christ, from God.

I want other people to live egolessly that are from the sons of God in them, from the Christ in them, which means to love all people, themselves included.

In doing so, we have peace and joy in this conflict-ridden world.

To have internal conflict is to identify with the ego; the ego false self conflicts with one's real self, the Christ; to be ego is to be at war with one's real self. Whoever is at war with his real self knows no peace.

Accepting and loving your real self, the Christ, returns you to peace, joy, bliss, the state of eternity.

10

THIS ENTIRE UNIVERSE OF SPACE, TIME, AND MATTER DO NOT EXIST, IS AN ILLUSION, A MIRAGE

If you see you and people in bodies walking around in space and time, you are in ego. The universe of space, time, and matter is the ego, the dream self, and its world projected out by the sons of God, to replace the unified universe without space, time, and matter created by God.

In God and his universe, everything is in one self, one place; in our universe of opposites, people and things are separated from each other—all illusions.

In the dream, each of us, with the aid of other people, invented a separated ego-self (the self-concept, the self-image, the human personality). Thus, as long as one is on earth, one has an illusory ego-self.

God through his Holy Spirit made another perceptual self for one, the Christ in light body, who also is illusory but purified hence approximates one's real self but is not it for the real self; one's real self is the son of God who is one with God; the son of God is not in forms, dense, or light.

In the world of light forms, you see yourself in light form still in space and time (light is not matter but forms matter). You are still in ego albeit purified ego; you are now a happy mad self.

In God, there is no space, time, and body; all share one self. There is no past, present, and future in God, as we normally construe them. In God, there is only now, the eternal present of God.

The point to all these is that one always has a self, be it in heaven where the self is unified with God and all other selves, or in our world of dense matter, ego, and light forms.

Use your Holy Spirit to counter your ego for in this world, you always think from ego first before you think from Holy Spirit.

The ego and its universe have apparent existence but do not exist; the ego's universe exists when it is desired and defended; if not desired and defended, it disappears.

Only the unified universe of God exists.

While I am wishing for all people to give up their egos and become God-realized, history shows that only a few persons have accomplished that task throughout history, such as Rama, Krishna, Buddha, Jesus, and so on.

A Course in Miracles says that only one such person changes the world and urges one to become such a person. One of them comes every thousand years, or so. So, one should strive to lose one's ego, first become guided by the Holy Spirit, and eventually live from one's real self, the son of God, that is, speak and behave from God, hence save the world and give the world peace.

I strive to become the egoless son of God who has removed the self he made to replace the self that God created him as.

In discarding the ego, one becomes the light of the world and the Christ who has come to the world a second time is reborn and is no longer ego but reborn as the Christ, unified self God created us as.

The masses are not ready for mass transformation. So, do it and do not ask others to do it. Asking other people to do it means that one is not yet ready to save oneself.

Save yourself by removing your ego and living from Christ.

I AM PERFECT AND NEED DO NOTHING TO BE PERFECT.

You probably have heard the saying that you are already perfect and need do nothing else to make you perfect. I have heard it several times and did not know what it means until I read *A Course in Miracles* (ACIM is probably the only complete book on spirituality in the extant world).

According to *A Course in Miracles,* God extended himself to each of us. We are parts of God. God is perfect, therefore, his extensions, his creations, are perfect.

However, they can only remain perfect if they remain as he created them. He created them as parts of him, as parts of his formless unified spirit, and as unified with him and with each other. If we remain formless parts of God's unified spirit, we are perfect.

God created us perfect, holy, guiltless, sinless, and innocent; as long as we remain as he created us, we retain those qualities. But we entered a competition with God.

The sons of God wanted to create God and create ourselves. Unable to do so in eternity, we went to sleep and, in our sleep, seem separated from God and from each other and in our seeming separated state, invented different selves for us.

We invented separated selves and placed them in space, time, and matter (in God, everything is in one self and one place; there is no separation, space and time in God; in God, there is no past, present, and future as we understand them).

We invented our phenomenal world of space, time, and matter, housed ourselves in bodies, and now walk around in seeming separated selves. Each of us, with the aid of all people, invented separated self-concepts and self-images, that is, human personalities.

In our new replacement and substitute selves, we seem imperfect. Body is imperfect. Space and time buffet bodies and make them sick needing help. In body, we feel weak and will die and so feel imperfect.

In body and its ego, we feel imperfect and struggle to seem perfect. All egos, people on earth, struggle to seem perfect. The earth is a place where we come to struggle to seem perfect, for to be on earth is to feel imperfect and inadequate.

In egos and bodies, we feel guilty and sinful because we separated from our real selves and whoever separated from his real self must feel sinful and guilty.

In ego, we literally attacked our real selves, attacked the sons of God and their father, and want them to die so that the selves we invented, egos in bodies, may live.

On earth, in body, in ego, we feel imperfect and struggle to seem perfect. If you identify with ego and body, which you must do to be on earth, you must feel imperfect. You feel imperfect from the day you were born on earth and you have struggled to seem perfect from day one of your life on earth. Those in egos must struggle to seem perfect; that is the nature of the ego; life in ego is struggled to seem perfect. It is a futile struggle, for to be in ego is to be imperfect.

But we are always perfect, holy, guiltless, sinless, and innocent in God, in the state of union with God, and in formless state.

All you need to do to know that you are already perfect is stop wishing to be ego separated self in body, go inward, and experience your already perfect state, the Christ you, the son of God you.

In God, you do not need to do anything to become perfect, you do not have to do anything to change and improve yourself, for what God created is already perfect.

Any person who is in how his God created him needs to do nothing to be better, to improve himself. What God created needs no improvement, for it is perfect.

It is the ego that needs improvement, change, and perfection. One seeks it and never gets it for the ego and body cannot ever become perfect. Ego in body is imperfect so you are condemned to seeking perfection and not getting it, for as long as you identify with ego.

Tell yourself that you need do nothing to be perfect for you are already perfect. For this to be true, you must mean the self that God created you as not the ego and body self that you made for you to replace the real self that God created you as.

I found it necessary to type this response for I just listened to Donald Neal Walsh in a video talking about how we are born perfect. He said that the newborn baby is perfect in everything, including body, but society makes him feel imperfect and he now struggles to be perfect. Mr. Walsh wrote the conversation with God series.

Listen, some newly born children have body sickness and are not perfect in body.

What Walsh needed to say is what I said above, that in unified spirit, that is, in God, we are perfect but in ego and body, we are imperfect. I have explained why above.

WHAT EXACTLY IS LOVE?

We band the term love about but what exactly does it mean? For many years, I defined love from the perspective of my favorite psychoanalyst, Erich Fromm (see his 1956 book, *The Art of Love*).

Fromm defined love as caring for people; to him, love is kind of like the Christian concept of agape; that is, giving to people without asking for what is in it for you.

That definition is moralistic and not satisfactory. Moralization is of the ego, and therefore, love must transcend the ego and its moralism.

So, what exactly is love? I said that I do not know. Just help people and don't worry about the clarity of definitions, I told me.

This afternoon, at Bookman's bookstore at Mesa, Arizona, I had one of those insights that come to people only a few times in their lives. What is love, I asked as I was browsing through books.

It dawned on me that love is anything done from ego-lessness. In love, you have removed identification with your ego separated self and has no ego (you still have ego but minimized it) and behave from ego-lessness.

When you do not see yourself as the separated ego-self and do not defend your perceived self-interests, you are in God, in selfless self, in unified self.

Whatever you do from ego-lessness, from selflessness, from Christ, from the son of God, and from God, is done from love.

Without identification with the ego separated self and defense of the ego, you are now one with all selves and one with God. Whatever you do to other people, good or bad, you do to yourself literally, for all people are parts of your one shared self.

If you love other people, you love yourself; if you hate other people, you hate yourself. Since pure reason tells us that to love oneself is better than to hate oneself, therefore, a rational person loves all selves to love his real self, his whole self.

Love is a giving thing. What you give to seeming other people, you give to yourself. Giving is receiving. There is only one self on earth, God's one son, and what you give to him, you effectively give to you.

And since God's son is part of God, what you give to God's son, you have given to God. Loving people means loving you and loving God; hating people means hating you and hating God.

The problem with us, egos, is that we see seeming other people as not us and believe that what we do to other persons, we have not done to us.

All of us share one unified self and what you do to seeming other people, you do to yourself. You may not see it right away, but that remains the truth.

Africans see people as different and separated from them and either sell people or exploit them and not work for them. To their myopic eyes, the evil they did to others, they did not do to themselves. Now look at Africa, what do you see?

You see people living inside gutters and people wallowing in their vomits for they give evil to each other, hence to themselves. (I use Africans to illustrate my points; the points apply to all people.)

Africans and all people need to realize that what they do to other people, they do to themselves, for all of us share one unified self in eternity and in time.

To have a peaceful and happy world, we must work for all people's welfare. Alfred Adler, the famous Viennese psychoanalyst, recognized this fact hence said that neurosis inheres in serving only one's interests whereas health lies in serving our collective self-interests. That is, some socialism is good for us.

Capitalism is a necessary evil but it has to be mitigated by caring for other people, for all people are part of the capitalist's self-grasping self.

In conclusion, love is any thinking and behavior done from ego-lessness.

What is ego-lessness? If the ego is what Carl Jung called the individuated self, ego-lessness means the unified self, all of us as one shared self.

Try to understand what ego-lessness is, for ego-lessness is the true meaning of God and heaven.

Ego-lessness gives us peace and joy—bliss, really.

EGOISM GIVES US FEAR, ANXIETY, DEPRESSION, PARANOIA, AND OTHER DISTURBANCES OF OUR EMOTIONS.

I do not need your gratitude to be in peace. Nevertheless, you must learn to be grateful to every person who cares enough for your well-being to give you information that serves you well. If you said thank you to the writer of this essay, you will feel good with you, but if not, you will continue experiencing the conflict and madness that is the fare of most human beings. We, teachers of love, give mankind peace. To love is to be in peace.

PLEASING OTHER PEOPLE IS MOTIVATED BY DESIRE FOR IMPORTANCE.

The desire to please is the desire to have importance and power. My father had desire to please his parents, siblings, and people in general. He gave these people most of his money. In pleasing them, he felt important and powerful in their eyes.

His siblings that he spent a lot of money on did not see him as important and did not give him any material things. When he felt that despite pleasing them, doing things for them, yet they did not see him as important, he felt angry at them.

If he did not have ego desire for importance, he would not seek to please anyone and would not feel fear and anger.

Like my father, I used to be a pleaser, giving folks all my money but they were not respecting me, so I stopped doing it and let each person fend for himself. Now, I could care less whether people see me as important or not. I am not important. My ego is nothing; my body is not important and is food for worms.

Without ego entirely, one has no fear, anxiety, depression, and paranoia. Without ego, one's body is calm and peaceful. If one's body is calm, one's body is healed and healthy.

With total ego-lessness, you will not be in this world; if already in this world and you develop ego-lessness you will be out of this world, you will be in the world of light forms and later in the formless world of God, heaven.

Jesus transcended his ego and was out of this world. This world is a place folks come to be ego separated selves and when they transcend the ego they stay for a while teaching ego-lessness, as I am currently doing, and then leave the world, not by death but by transfiguration.

ANGER IS ROOTED IN DESIRE FOR IMPORTANCE IN PEOPLES' EYES AND PERCEIVED TREATMENT OF NO IMPORTANCE BY PEOPLE

If you have no desire for importance, you will not have the perception of other people treating you as not important, and you will not feel angry from what seems other people's insult of you.

Igbos have a primitive society where most people run around seeking others' positive approval; each of them wants to be seen as important by others. They work hard to get money so that folks see them as important. Many of them even steal to obtain money so that other people see them as rich, hence important. They fear not been seen as socially important. In their world, they try to shame folks and make them seem unimportant if they are not socially achieving much.

When I began pointing out their faults, they believed that I am one of them, a primitive who is motivated by a desire to obtain the approval of his fellow primitives.

I could care less what you say of me. Call me poor (although most of them are poorer than me yet they call me poor). Well, the rustics tried to shame me but it was water off my skin. Some of them began calling me shameless.

And those who did that name-calling are 419 scam artists, wire frauds, parting Americans from their money. These people are lacking in conscience; they are criminal beyond belief. They steal as if stealing is in their DNA.

And when they try to steal from you and you catch them, they will turn around and say that you did what they did. I tried to put a few of these criminals into jail when they tried to steal from my school.

You cannot control me by calling me putdown names. I already know that I am not important; I am worthless, and also know that despite your grandstanding, you are even more worthless than I am. We are all food for worms and our pretense of importance is childish.

Ego and body are worthless and do not even exist. You are not ego and body but act as ego body; you can also act as spirit and Christ and see it happen in your life.

Am I deceiving myself in making these statements? Are they magical thinking? No, they represent the truth as I know it. That truth is articulated poetically in *A Course in Miracles*. It is there stated metaphorically but I know it to be true and state it in simple prose.

LEARNING ABOUT YOUR PERSONALITY AND CHANGING IT BY UNDERSTANDING YOUR DREAMS

DREAM
MARCH 18, 2020
3:45 AM

In this dream, I was looking for a place to park my car in a huge parking lot. I found one and for some reason, instead of driving to it, I simply used my fingers to drag the car to the parking space. I got out and saw another guy parking beside me and began bragging about my car, which is now a convertible. Then I thought that it might rain, so I decided to put up the cover in case it rains. I pressed a button and an umbrella came up. An umbrella was now hoisted in the middle of the roofless car and it occurred to me that if it rained, water would still enter the car and I wondered what kind of cover this is. I walked away thinking that I should not have talked to the driver who parked beside me. He could steal my car, I thought. I walked on and turned a corner and a huge, six foot six inches tall black man grabbed one of my fingers. I told him to let go and he kept holding me. I felt angry and jerked my hand to get away from him and woke up from the dream.

MEANING

First, it is my mind that produced the dream; how it did so, I do not understand; I do not believe that any human being understands how our minds produce dreams. One's mind produced everything in one's dream. It uses what is in one's world to produce the dream. I used a convertible car that obviously exists in our world but that I did not make. I transformed it to what my dream wants and had an umbrella in place of the rooftop cover for the convertible car, and since the umbrella was not going to cover the entire inside of the car, the rainwater would still enter the car, drench it, and possibly destroy my expensive car.

My plan for protection of the car is not good enough. This translates to my ego's plan for my protection is not good enough; only God's plan for one's protection is good.

It is my mind that suspected that the guy I talked to could steal my car, and that shows fear in my mind. That fear produced the big burly black man to pose as danger to me (here, my mind stereotyped big black men, the footballer type as empty brains who casually hurt people).

I wished that I had a pocketknife to stab the guy or a gun to kill him. That is the normal ego's response to danger, to defend itself. Because we all attack our attackers, we live in a world of offense and defense, and there seem to have no exit from it.

There is another pattern of dealing with attack, forgiveness. That manner of response leads to peace in the world.

If I defended me by stabbing him or killing him, the problem is not solved in my mind and would produce other sources of danger for me to feel endangered. What would solve the problem is to have love, not fear, in my mind.

I always have fear in my mind and it produces danger for me. I walked around a corner and saw the humongous black man and he posed danger to me, threatening me, grabbing my finger. My mind produced danger for me.

I wished that I had a knife to stab him or a gun to shoot him to death. But I jerked my hand to free it from his grip and woke up.

Even in my dreams, my mind produces fear episodes for me to gratify my wish to see the world as a dangerous, threatening place.

The question is this, why is my mind always producing fear and danger but not love? This is because there is no love in my mind. I do not feel secure in my mind. I feel insecure.

Some people have love in their minds and feel secure and that produces a loving dream for them both at night and during the daytime.

The entire world does not exist, is delusional, make-belief, and is whatever you want it to be for you. We try to make a world that does not exist seem to exist and important for we want what we invented to seem important.

We now have to let go of the wish for the world, see it disappear, and revert to the awareness of where we always are, formless heaven, our true home. But we forget it and dream of this world. The world is non-existent and all our efforts cannot make it exist. We may make it a happy dream by overlooking it, not taking it seriously and in so doing, return to love.

DREAM
MARCH 18, 2020
10:20 AM

In this dream, at a family gathering, Lawrence attacked and pushed me, so I pushed him back, he fell down on his back and I jumped on top of him and pinned him down. He was begging me to get off him. I did not want to do so until I tried to leave him and could not also do so. I asked Kinsley to lend me a hand, I took it, and got up.

In this dream, there was danger. In my dreams, there are always dangers. Someone did something bad to me and I fought back but could not get up and leave that it took another man to pull me up.

The lesson is that it is better to help, forgive the attacker, and love than to fight back when attacked.

When I remove the ego, the block to the awareness of love, remove all desire for vengeance, stop bearing grievances, and forgive all, then my mind returns to love and my dreams will be loving, happy dreams, things, still dreaming, not real; in God, love, there is no dreaming.

LOVE IS EGO-LESSNESS. IT TRANSCENDS SPACE, TIME, AND MATTER AND CANNOT BE EXPLAINED WITH EGO LANGUAGE.

A Course in Miracles, in its introduction, says that you cannot understand love, for love cannot be understood with ego intellect or defined.

All we have to do is remove the obstacles to the awareness of love and we experience the love that we always live in. We are always in love, God, eternity, but wish separation to mask love; remove the ego and defenses of space, time, and matter and you experience the love that you are already in.

The ego and its world of space, time, and matter are the blocks to the knowledge of union, love, God.

Even after experiencing love, you cannot explain it in the language of separated self, for love is union of all selves in one self, God; ego language explains only separated things, not unified things.

Post Script:

People all over the world are gripped by the fear of Covid-19 and I am here talking about dreams. Is this not idle, shouldn't I be talking about the bigger virus?

Is it not self-preoccupation and narcissistic to be talking about oneself when mankind is afraid of death? I could be talking about Covid-19.

But what are folks talking about but fear?

People have fear of harm and death and perceive threat to their valued lives in bodies and are in fear. Fear rules people's behaviors.

In fear, folks revert to pure animal status and live self-centered existence. See, out of fear, the nations of the world are shutting their borders, not allowing outsiders to come in; they do not want folks with diseases coming to infect and killing their people. People are fearful and selfish creatures. I get that.

What I am trying to do is to overcome fear in me and then show the world how to overcome their fears. One overcomes fear if one does not identify with ego and body and instead, identify with Christ, the son of God who is eternal and is always safe in his father, in unified self, heaven.

You actually might learn a thing or two by looking at your dreams instead of always looking outside you and talking about things that you have no control over, such as Covid-19.

If diseases come, they come; if one dies, one dies—big deal. What matters is to live fearlessly and then die (move on to other dimensions of being).

ON AFRICANS' NEED FOR CHRISTIANITY

You try to show your sophistication by making fun of the Christian religion; you present it as a foreign religion imposed on you and your people by Europeans. You give yourself the permission not to behave from the moral strictures of Christianity.

You must also have noticed what has happened in Alaigbo where Christianity did not take deep roots before folks ditched it. It has reverted to anarchy and chaos, the jungle where criminals and kidnappers are all over the place kidnapping folks for a monetary ransom.

Our people have essentially reverted to the jungle where they lived before Christianity met them a hundred years ago and tried to transform them from savages to human beings. They had no respect for human dignity, hence captured and sold their people to all buyers; inter alia, among other things, Christianity gives respect for human dignity; our people have lost respect for human dignity hence now kidnap people for money.

We did not allow the saving gospel of Christ to take root in us and cavalierly question it. Now see where we are.

Fyodor Dostoyevsky in his famous novel, *Brothers Karamazov*, said that without belief in God, all behaviors are permissible. Our people have removed belief in God and now, all behaviors are permissible and they live in Thomas Hobbes' (Leviathan) state of nature without laws, all are at war with all, and life is nasty, brutish, and short.

Keep making fun of Christianity. What is left of it gives you folks the little civilization you have. With absence of total Christianity, you folks will become jungle dwellers, kidnapping and selling your people to no one since Europe and North America now no longer needs Africans.

Have you noticed that they used the fear of coronavirus to ask folks not to come to their lands and they are not going to open their doors when the virus is cured to Africans? They have learned that Africans are mostly lawless and gravitate to criminal activities at an alarming rate, and as such, are transforming Europe and North America into a lawless criminal place and they do not want African criminals in their lands.

Africans would have to stay in Africa and steal and kill each other and the Western press would not cover it. The racist would say, let the bastards kill off each other that care?

Nicollo Machiavelli, in *The Prince*, said that if there is no God, the prince, meaning the ruler, must invent one and impose it on the people if he wants them to obey the laws. Without God, there is no basis for morality. You have to learn that fact.

Perhaps, you are too unintelligent to learn that fact. Some of us are agnostic but choose to agree with religion because we know that without it, there is no human civilization.

Africans need to be forced to become Christians if they are to be civilized. Very few of them are intellectually developed enough to self-monitor and supervise, as expected in atheistic scientists.

Ponder these points and stop being a cavalier in your approach to all things; nature gave you brains; use it and stop being a foolish African.

PURSUIT OF IDEALISM IS THE DESIRE FOR ABSOLUTE
POWER TO RECREATE THE WORLD IN ONE'S IMAGE.

The idealist rejected his body, other people's bodies, and the world and wants to remake them to suit his image—what they should be according to his desire. He was born to behave exactly that way for there are no accidents in our lives, we experience only what we want to experience.

He chose a weak body that gives him loads of problems so that he rejects it, rejects all bodies, the world, and social institutions, and desire different ones. By age one, all these desires are already in place. In fact, he was born to do so from day one of his life.

His desires seem to make sense—education for all at all levels, health care for all, make the poor wealthy—all these are desirable goals.

However, tomorrow, what was ideal yesterday is no longer ideal and different ideals are posited, desired, and pursued. There is no end to idealism.

Realistic normal people without drive for crazy power accept people and the world as they are. They let things be as they are.

SAVING SOCIAL FACE IS ROOTED IN DESIRE FOR POWER AND IMPORTANCE.

Saving social face is also motivated by desire to have an important ego and fear of it becoming socially unimportant; avoidance is meant to make the ego seem important.

The ego does not exist and is not important, so let it go. You cannot make you and people better; each person is living as he wants to live and the world is as it is meant to be at any point in time. Live with people and the world as they are.

THE HOLY SPIRITS REINVENTED THE WORLD OF LIGHT FORMS.

The Holy Spirit has already changed the egos' world to a world of light forms. In the world of light forms, people and things are still as they are on earth except that they are now purified, made in light forms, and do not die. From light forms, people transit to the world of God, our real home.

God and heaven are formless.

In God, where we always are, there is perfection and no need for change to suit our egos. The world of God is formless—all are ideas in the mind of God and all are unified as one mind and one self.

RO IS AN EXAMPLE OF A POLITICAL AND RELIGIOUS IDEALIST ON POWER QUEST.

RO is an idealist, a political and religious idealist; he wants to change the world to fit his mental construction of how the world should be.

RO is totally egotistical and on a power quest. He wants to be the most powerful person on earth. It is either his way or the highway. He wants to be the number one in everything—the boss whose ideas are not challenged. He roots his half-baked ideas in God and said that God gave them to him and therefore, one should accept them and not question them.

RO said that by doubting him, I make him doubt his belief in his God. This means that he does not have knowledge but mere belief. He is not God-realized but a man who has visions, ego-based visions but has not transcended the ego to reach God, hence has no certainty.

If he has certainty, he would not feel that I could dissuade him from his god or make him doubt winning the lotto and become rich.

He is still in ego for he blames folks for his issues; only the ego blames other egos for its issues; Christ, that is, son of God that has realized his oneness with God, does not blame anyone for his mistakes and imperfection; he is perfect for he behaves from perfect God.

11

PHYSIOLOGY PRECEDES PSYCHOLOGY. PSYCHOLOGICAL PROCESSES ARE SECONDARY RESPONSES TO UNDERLYING BIOLOGICAL PROCESSES

Psychological processes are responses to the individual's underlying physiological processes; in other words, biology precedes psychology, and in many ways, determines psychology. Psychology is a secondary human behavior, not primary; biology is.

You have to first live as a biological organism before your brain can respond to what is going on in your body and external environment with thinking and behaviors.

Consider a child born with peripheral neuropathy (damaged nerves: variations are Grierson-Gopalan Syndrome and many other types of damaged nerves). His body is almost always in a state of burning sensations; the littlest effort, such as standing on his feet for, say, two hours, or walking or exercising, and his legs feel on fire. He literally feels like his body is burning. He responds to this pain and burning sensation with his mind, thinking and trying to understand it unaided by medical science.

He wishes that the pain and burning sensation would go away. Of course, it would not go away. He wishes for a magic wand that would make it go away but that is not going to happen.

In pursuit of a solution, he posits a powerful, ideal self that saves him from his state of pain. The wished-for ideal, powerful self, of course, is not going to come into being to solve the problem.

He withdraws from whatever physical environment that causes him pain and from social activities where he is likely to feel pained and keeps to himself to reduce the pain in his legs and body.

In behavior and personality, he develops an avoidant personality, feels that as he is, he is not good, and that if other people come close to him, they would see that he is not good and reject him; to avoid social rejection, he withdraws from society and keeps to himself. In social isolation, he wishes for a big, powerful self.

He sometimes behaves as if he is the wished-for grandiose self; he feels angry when other people treat him as if he is not the powerful big self.

Most personality and mental disorders are psychological responses to underlying medical, physiological processes. Biology determines psychology.

MIND CAN UNDERSTAND BODY AND HEAL IT.

However, regardless of the biological causation of psychological processes, the individual has the ability to understand his body and psychology. He can use his mind to stop wishing for the big self he had wished for while in pain. Indeed, he can decide and stop having any kind of ego separated self.

The ego-self is a concept, an idea, a thought. One can give up one's self-concept and self-image. You can get up one day and tell yourself that you are not your self-concept and self-image; indeed, that you are not your body. You can follow that up by not defending your self-concept (say, with avoidance and anger).

If you give up all ego, small or big, and have no ego separated self-concept, instead of dying as you think that you would, all that happens is that you live in peace.

The desire for the ego separated self-concept is the greatest source of human psychological suffering. Hindus realized that the ego, which they call ahankara, is a mere wished-for self. We do not have ego self-concepts. Whatever self-concept we developed in childhood is a chimera that can be let go and one has no ego-self. When the ego-self-concept is let go, what remains is the life in one and in all people.

Hindus believe that we have a real self, a unified self that they call Brahmin; there is one Brahman, God, and we are all parts of that one unified self. The goal of Hinduism is for people to give up their false separated self and become aware of their real self, Atman, who is one with Brahman, God. In God-realization, people are said to feel peaceful and happy.

Life is probably what folks call spirit and God. Let us not here debate what is life and spirit, but for now, accept that life is always in one despite one giving up all attempts to restrict it to one's ego parameters.

DISCUSSION

Whatever affliction one has, there is a silver lining in it. It is from those who have serious biological issues that sometimes, the wisest human beings emerge.

Philosophers are usually human beings who suffered a lot and from their suffering, learned the limits of what human beings can do.

Religionists say that there is a divine purpose in every problem regardless of how bad it is. New thought patterns are often generated by folks who have had serious issues that normal patterns of thinking have no answer for.

Alfred Adler, a Viennese psychiatrist, from his biologically induced sense of physical weakness and sense of inferiority and how he responded to it with false desire for superiority and power, he gave the world psychology that to the present, remains one of the best in the world.

Some people's life exigencies make them feel inferior and they use their minds to posit superior selves, pursue those false selves, and act as if they are them and thus, have personality disorders. They heal themselves when they stop seeking to become superior selves and have no wish for a self other than have life that is the same and equal in all people.

People often masquerade around as if they have worth and significance when in fact, they have absolutely no worth in body. Life in body has no purpose or meaning but the false ones we give to it and use it to make a mess of our lives.

CONCLUSION

My observation shows me that children born with loads of physiological problems, especially pains due to damages in their peripheral nerves, generally feel powerless because they are unable to make the excruciating pains go away. They develop secondary psychological issues, such as wishing to be ideal, powerful selves who have magic wands with which they can wish away their pain.

There is no such thing as a magic wand, so that avenue is frustrated. They end up developing neurosis, personality disorders, or even serious mental disorders.

The thesis of this paper is that psychological disorders are secondary responses to underlying biological and/or medical disorders.

One has not observed all children and people to make this conclusion true in all cases. Nevertheless, one holds it as true. If you can disprove it, one would like to see how you did it.

RO'S PHILOSOPHY AND HIS MISTAKE

RO's philosophy is that God created us and that as his creations, we share his attribute of eternity. To him, we are the sons of God and since God is eternal, we are eternal.

To see us as human beings is to see us as hummus, dust, and dust people. To see us as human beings is to see us as dead people, as nothing. We commit suicide when we separate from God. We are dead if apart from God.

Resurrection or the second coming of Christ into our lives is when we discard the identity of ego and accept our true self as Christ, the sons of God. So far, he is correct.

One would think that he is aware that all of us is the Christ, but no, he sees himself as the person Jesus talked about as coming to teach the world about his gospel; that is, he is the second coming of Christ, not all of us. It is true that each of us is at a different stage of spiritual development. He is wrong in seeing only himself as the Christ and the second coming of Christ referring only to him.

That shows that he has not yet transcended the ego, hence is confused. He would seem to be deluded but actually understands what delusion disorder is, belief in what is not true to be true; he sees his beliefs as true, hence does not see himself as deluded or egotistical.

His only problem is to see himself as the only Christ. The truth is that all of us are the sons of God, Christ. Christ was created when God created us. Christ died when we separated from God, and Christ resurrected when we discard belief that we are egos and accept that we are the sons of God.

Christ comes to our world and lives a second time when we accept and live as the sons of God, love each other as God loves us, and forgive and correct each other's mistakes without punishment.

The Holy Spirit corrects our mistakes; he is a part of our right minds, not apart from us. Since we live in the world of separation, ego, our instinct is to see the world as real, not a dream, and see the evil done to us as real; hence, we bear grievances and seek vengeance for them. The Holy Spirit, our right minds, know that the world is a dream and that it must be overlooked and forgiven for us to return to God, to love. Thus, the Holy Spirit asks us to overlook others' evils for they were done in dreams and are not real and asks us to forgive all to forgive us. When we forgive those who wronged us, we are acting as the Holy Spirit for he is not apart from us, just as the ego is not apart from us.

Ego and Holy Spirit are parts of our mind while we are on earth and time; our true mind is the mind of the Son of God, unified mind. On earth, we can choose to live from ego-mind or from Holy Spirit mind—left mind or right mind.

Finally, RO does not forgive those who wronged him. He wants to punish Nigerians for abusing Igbos, and he wants to punish white people for abusing black people. He is still operating in ego, for it is the ego that keeps grievances and seeks revenge for the evil done to him.

If he is the Christ, he would know that all Nigerians are parts of Igbos and that white people are parts of black people, just parts of them that they deny, project out, and have done the evil he sees them done to blacks, hence to be forgiven, blacks need to know peace and return to God.

RO is not yet God, Christ-realized; he is still in the world of ego. It is my duty and function to teach him what God and Christ realization is, as I have done here. Would he accept it, would he let go of his desire to be the only Christ? I suspect not in this lifetime.

The psychotic says that only he is God, not other people; the mystic knows that all of us are parts of one God. Seeing himself as the only God and Christ makes the psychotic ego feel superior to other people.

In God, we are the same and coequal; we are all parts of God, all sons of God, and all are Christ. Christ is the son of God; any of us who knows that he is a son of God and since God is love, loves himself and all selves and in doing so, live in peace and joy.

CONCLUSION

RO is correct in most of his views on God. I learned a lot from him. He is wrong in seeing himself as the only Christ. That view of himself is egoistic and antichrist, actually. He is here to serve a function for me. He helped me to appreciate my own arrogance.

I am also here to serve a function for him. We are each of us teachers and students of each other. He wants to be the teacher of all and does not see himself as anyone's student. Here, he is wrong.

Since I have tremendous spiritual insights, I tended to see myself as superior to all other human beings. I am not kidding. I tended to look at people as children with no understanding of spirituality. RO has similar view of himself.

Seeing him in that view enabled me to see the error of one seeing oneself as better than all other people. He enabled me to correct my self-assessment to now seeing all of us as the sons of God, Christ, although in space, time, and matter, some people do not know that and accept it.

It is for you, the reader, to know that you are a son of God and Christ and reclaim your Christ state by being loving and forgiving of all people.

As for me, I know that I am one of God's infinite sons. I follow that up by forgiving those who wronged me to forgive me my wrongs against other people. In forgiveness, I transcend my ego's desire for bearing grievance and vengeance. In forgiveness, I become egoless.

In ego-lessness, I return to love. Love cannot be described in the ego's language, for the ego language presumes separated selves—you and not you, me and other people, subject and object, seeing and not seeing.

In God, all are one shared self with one shared mind and in that world, language is not like we have it on earth. Love exists in unified state, not in our separated world, but while here, we can approximate love by forgiving each other, overlooking the dream so as to return to unified state, which is love.

Ozodi Thomas Osuji, Ph.D.

DREAM
MARCH 22, 2020
8:30 AM

In this dream, I visited a black woman big cheese in her office to say hi to her. A young black woman entered the office and was touching my ass. I wondered why and checked it out and there was a tear, a hole there, and my body showed through. I got out of the office and decided to go change my pants. I was walking home, then stopped and got a handful of my dried laundry, and was taking them to my house. As I walked on, some of the clothes fell down and I stooped to pick them up and ended up picking up old laundry on the ground that had been rained on. I got them all and walked on and when I got to my home, it now seemed like an office and Norman Johnson was sitting outside talking to folks, and I woke up.

This is a potpourri of scenes from my stay in Seattle. It does not mean anything in particular; certainly, nothing came to my mind as its meaning.

Before going to sleep, I was thinking about writing a paper for IPOB and Biafrans in which I carefully delineated what constitutes leadership and what they ought to be doing to extricate themselves from Fulani rule. I was going to do it in a detached manner without insulting Igbos, putting them down as I normally do. I began putting Igbos down when some of them started insulting me and I decided to tell them what I think of them—primitive folks.

Why haven't I used my understanding of leadership to start an organization, pursue a goal, and be useful to people?

RO has no realistic solutions; he wants divine intervention to save Igbo from Fulani rule, save the black race from white rule, save the world, and be the God-realized leader who does all these. He is not going to do it; his are childish wishes; they prevent him from actually solving problems in the here and now world. He is childish.

He reminds me of my own childish temper tantrums and not loving me and people, which has caused problems for my children and women around me. It is now time to grow up and love all people. People are crying out for love, not those who merely talk about love.

Black Americans have been useful to me. In Portland, Edna Pittman helped make me the executive director of my mental health agency; Dr. Leslie Gunn hired me. Professor Derick Milner, a house nigger, mullato, played nigger games with me at Portland State University and Dr. little was a talker, not a doer.

At Seattle, Norman Johnson gave me a good administrative job and due to my talking to him as if he is beneath me, feared that I wanted to take over his job and essentially asked me to leave.

In Alaska, Dr. Washington Brown, a psychologist, helped me a lot; he gave me an office in his office suites, which I did not have to pay for. Mini and Tyron Charles (fellow psychotherapists) were all helpful black folks.

In Washington DC, Professor Robert Cummings, he and I went to UCLA, the same department, tried to help me at Howard University (he was intimidated by my awesome mind).

The point is that black Americans have always tried to help me. I was, however, not invested in blacks. Deep down, I do not respect black folks because they do not seem civilized. If you do not respect people, you cannot get along with them. I am around blacks but do not feel one with them. I am an outsider in the black world.

I do not respect Africans because they sold their people, and in the present, instead of developing their people, steal from them. I have never had any desire to live in Africa for it seems like living with savages.

As for white folks, I admire their civilization, their science, and technology but see them as evil hence ambivalent toward them.

I do not care for Asians for they do not have what I want—science and technology.

In the end, I am man alone, the penultimate social outsider. This is not all bad though for being outside the group, I think outside the box, hence I am probably the best philosopher and psychologist in the extant world.

I AM A PARADOXICAL FELLOW.

After typing Leadership Training for Igbos, a 32 pages paper, in the first rough draft, a thought entered my mind. I am trained on the subject I typed. In my youth, I was preoccupied with how to produce good leaders in Africa and wrote books and countless articles on the subject.

In my late thirties, my mind shifted to spiritual matters. Over time, I ignored what folks call the real world for it had no meaning for me.

Leadership deals with the world of the here and now. Leaders try to improve their peoples' living in the extant world.

Since I am no longer involved in the empirical world, is it not a contradiction for me to write on leadership training for Igbos?

Leaders lead, manage, and supervise people doing to adapt and cope with the exigencies of the phenomenal world. Over the years, I came to see the phenomenal world as Maya, an illusion, a dream, an unreal world, and I devoted my attention to seeking otherworldly living, spiritual living.

I worked hard to understand the human ego separated self and try to drop it and live from my real self, which I believe is a spiritual self.

I came to believe that each of us can think and behave from one of three parts of our mind—from our Holy or unified mind, the mind we use in unified state, aka heaven, and the ego separated mind, the mind we employ in the separated world of space, time, and matter on earth, or improve the ego-mind, think, and behave from what serves the collective good and emphasizes spiritual matters.

Ego and spiritual idealism

In childhood, I saw my body, self, and the empirical world as not good enough and rejected them. I used my thinking to construct an idealized self, world, and standards of behavior. I rejected my bodily self and pursued the idealized self.

I used the ideal self to judge my bodily self and other people's bodily selves, find them not good, and reject them.

I rejected all people and everything earthly and sought the El Dorado of idealism. I used my mind to recreate an ideal world and seek to attain it.

Naturally, the imaginary cannot be attained in the world of matter, space, and time so I did not attain my ideals.

I made a mess of my life by wishing to attain the imaginary ideal. Over time, I learned that I must not judge myself and people with my ideal self-concept and its ideal standards. I learned to just accept the bodily self and see it as a dream self, a worthless and meaningless self, but the only self we have on earth.

I saw our real self as the unified spirit self, aka the Christ self. I believe that there is a spirit self, an invisible self that manifests in all of us, animals, and trees. What it is I do not know.

For our present purposes, over the past three days, I put my mind in an academic mood and wrote a twenty-eight pages paper with seven pages of it for references and bibliography. I literally vomited this stuff without looking at any book, yet if submitted to an academic journal, there is no doubt that it would be accepted and published.

I thought that I had left the world but apparently, my mind can still recall the real world. Am I then not a contradictory fellow, a man of paradox, a man with one foot in the spiritual world and another in the empirical world?

Interesting this creature called human beings!

Post Script:

I will sleep on the paper I wrote, chew on it for a while, redraft it, and next week, share it on social media.

I talked to my friend, Dr. O, about the paper and he told me not to bother sharing it in the social media crowd; as he sees it, his fellow Igbos seem incapable of thinking at the academic level and would, instead of appreciating my effort to help them understand leadership, call me unprintable names; as he sees it, they are mostly interested in imanjakiri and putting Nigerians down so as to feel falsely superior to them, and getting Nigerians to hate them and make life difficult for them. I did not know that this man understands his people that much.

Three years ago, I related to another Igbo professor with Ph. D. from Harvard; he had sent to me a book he wrote to review for publication and I did. I do book reviews. He then pipped up and told me that he is aware that the Igbo yahoo crowd has an animus toward me. He recommended that I desist from responding to that crowd. He said that they are functioning at a very low level and do not appreciate critical thinking.

It is amazing that the Igbo intelligentsia understands their people's socially untoward behaviors rather well but keeps quiet over it!

Anyway, I may make additional corrections to my paper and submit it to an academic journal for publication.

Finally, Charles, Chidi Achodo, since you are an international civil servant and understand leadership, management, and supervision matters, can I send the draft paper to you for your feedback? Thanks.

BODY, EGO, SPACE, AND TIME ARE MEANS OF SEPARATING FROM LOVE, GOD.

The purpose of body and ego is to separate from God, the whole, that is, to separate from love. Ego, body, space, and time were designed to mask God, love, to make us not love ourselves, other people, and God.

Love inheres only in unified state, God, heaven, and we chose to experience the opposite of love, God, hence invented space, time, matter, our bodies, and separated ego selves. In doing so, we are no longer aware that we are part of unified spirit self, God, our real self.

Yet, body, ego, space, time, and the physical universe do not exist. Race and gender, black and white, and man and woman are all means of making sure that we do not know about love, means of hatred of love, and means of opposing love.

Fear is a means of not loving oneself and not loving other people. In fear, one fears that other people could reject one or destroy one and one avoids them, hence not go to them and not join them in love.

The Holy Spirit, who is not a person, is our right minds, right thinking, thinking that approximate love, union with all, God, transforms what we made to hate to love with. When we forgive those who harmed us, we approximate love for them while we are still in body, ego, space, and time. That is to say, that body, ego, space, and time can be used to love you, me, and all of us and used to approach love, God.

THE REAL REASON WE FEEL ANGER IS TO PUSH FOLKS WHO INJURED OUR EGOS AWAY AND NOT LOVE THEM.

There is a deeper real reason why we feel angry when our ego is injured but not the reason given by the ego. The real reason is to separate from the source of injury to the ego, not to love him, hence not to love oneself.

To love is to join all people including the person your ego made to injure your ego and body, hence to separate from him and not love you and God.

EGO-LESSNESS MEANS TO RETURN TO UNIFIED SPIRIT, LOVE, AND NOT SEEING THIS WORLD.

If you have no ego and are egoless, you would not see yourself in body, space, and time and would not have desire for food and sex; you would be back in unified spirit, God, love, and you would be in bliss and not desire the paltry pleasures of body and ego.

I MUST FROM NOW ON LIVE AS THE SON OF GOD, CHRIST, LOVE, AND FORGIVENESS.

People believe in what they are doing, in fact, they are doing what they are here to do and what they can do best at this time given their body and psychology. If they are teaching politics or doing politics that they are, they believe in the world and want to organize their society well; they cannot be talking and doing metaphysics. Scientists are people of this world and they are doing what understands and adapts to the world and will eventually overcome the world through scientific breakthroughs. They are totally sleeping and dreaming, but they are the sons of God and have used their minds to miscreate the world and will use that mind to understand and rise above the world. Leave them to do their thing.

Ego and spiritual idealism are escapes.

I tried to escape from this world through an idealistic fantasy of ideal self, ideal society, and ideal everything. That failed. Then I tried idealistic religion and that too is of the ego and cannot help solve the world's problems. What is called for is for me to live love and forgiveness, correct errors, mine and other peoples', so as to live peacefully and joyously.

ANOTHER DREAM OF ATTACK

My brain in sleep produces people attacking me. Today, March 28, 2020, at 2:30 PM, daytime, while sleeping, I felt a force trying to engulf me and I fought it and woke up. This is in Arizona. Yesterday, I heard noises coming from the board rest on my bed and wondered whether I was going to start having the same attacks and nightmares I had in Alaska when I heard a noise in the wall in my bedroom and viola. I had this nightmare. Is this produced by fear or an oversensitive body that sees attacks at it that are not real?

I will get to a point where I have no fear in me and sound would not generate a sense of attack on me in dreams.

OLUMBA'S TALK OF SPIRITUAL WARFARE

O talks of spiritual warfare that began in heaven when Lucifer fought God and was chased out of heaven, and on earth where Adam and Eve disobeyed God and were chased out of the Garden of Eden and we continue that warfare by not living as the sons of God but instead as egos. We must die to the ego and body, become born again in spirit, and live from son of God status, he said.

The whole world, he said, is groaning in pain, awaiting the sons of God to be reborn in people and for he and me so that we help the world. We must, he said, have access to money to be able to do that.

He said that if we come by chance to have millions of dollars and help Igbos and stop helping them, they would begin verbally abusing us. The Igbos, he said, are a devilish people; yet we must help them, he said.

The man makes loads of sense, I say.

HEAVEN FORGOTTEN AND HEAVEN REMEMBERED

Here is the deal. To be on earth, which we enter through human birth and exit through death, one must totally forget one's real self, part of unified spirit self, and unified mind. We deliberately chose to forget unified spirit state and learn to see ourselves as living in a separated state in space, time, and matter. We chose to be born in bodies and now see our identity as body and ego.

The ego-self-concept is not the self that God created us as; therefore, it is not real for only what God created is real. The ego is a learned phenomenon; it is a concept, an idea of who we think that we now are. It is influenced by the nature of our bodies, society, space, and time, by culture.

The ego lives in the world of perception; no perception is ever real; perception is socially constructed reality; something in our perceptual world is real because we all agree that it is real, consensual reality, but apart from our agreement, it does not exist. What is real is the world of knowledge, which inheres only in the world of God.

In God, everything is permanent, eternal, and changeless, hence is real. The changeable is not real. Our phenomenal world is changeable, hence not real.

FORGET THE WORLD TO REMEMBER THE FORGOTTEN WORLD OF UNIFIED HEAVEN, GOD.

Now, we must deliberately forget the earth, forget the physical universe, forget space, time, and matter, and forget science, technology, and the other pursuits that enable us to adapt to earth, to the dream.

This is what Jesus meant by overlooking the world, forgiving the world, and dying to the world for a new you, the Christ you to be reborn in you.

As it were, to be in body is to be dead to our real selves and we must now metaphorically die to body to resurrect in spirit. One must not do anything to adapt to the reality of the world of space, time, and matter—no eating food, having sex, or doing anything that accentuates body and egos reality.

Jesus did that by fasting for forty days in the desert; Gautama Buddha did it by sitting in one spot for thirty days without getting up, meditating, trying to rise above the world, and reaching his real self and its world, heaven, what is better called unified spirit state. Mohammed gleaned that world by going to the cave to pray and meditate for months before he began hearing voices by angels (messengers of God).

The world of space, time, and matter are illusions, masks with which we cover our spirit self and its home in heaven. We must deliberately remove the veil preventing us from the awareness of Christ, our true self as the son of God.

The ego tries to tell us that the earth is real and its world is real. It tells us that those living as slaves are in pain and we must struggle to free them, true, but by struggling to free them, we make the earth real for us. If one overlooks slavery and slave masters, both one's projections, then one rises above the world of egos.

One literally does not have to die physically for physical death is a trick to make life in body real. Death is the last illusion that seems real.

Consider that in our dreams, when we sleep at night, we also see people die, are buried, and would decay, but when we get up in the morning, we know that the whole thing only happened in our dreams. Our death happens only in a dream state which we call our day world.

One can literally change one's mind and is now in body of light and from there, change one's mind and is in formless heaven where all are unified as one shared self and one shared mind.

In heaven, there is no space and gap between us and God; we are in each other and in God; we share one formless spirit self that begins nowhere and ends nowhere.

Those who believe in the reality of ego must seem to die and rot in body. All games and dreams for body do not exist so no one actually sickens and dies.

HOW DID GOD CREATE HIS SONS?

Consider biology and cell-division, mitosis and meiosis. Here, an existing cell in the body divides and produces new cells. Are the new cells new or part of the old one? They are not new; they are part of the old cell but now seem new.

Consider what happens in sex. The man injects sperm into a vagina and it unites with an ovum to form a cell. That cell begins dividing. DNA from a man and a woman in the chromosomes unite to form a new cell, divide, and seem to produce new cells, new DNA and RNA, but in fact, carry the old DNA, carry the parents in them, so one is not a new creation.

God is one as he was dividing himself and produces new selves out of his old self. The new selves, you and I, are part of his old self. The new selves, the sons of God, seem born new but are actually part of God, hence as old as God, which is eternal.

The Gospel of John puts it poetically. It said that in the beginning is God. God was with the word, the son of God; the word created the earth. What is said here figuratively is that God is always with his sons and that the sons invented our physical universe. You and I, human beings, invented the physical universe. God did not create our world. Our world is ephemeral and transitory; God does not create the temporal; what God created is always permanent and eternal. Our souls are eternal so God created them.

What God created is our real selves; in opposition to God, we wanted to separate from God and invented the world of space, time, and matter and now seem to live in bodies.

Moreover, God is joy so he could not have created our pained world; only those who desire to experience pain could have invented our sorrowful world.

Because we seem to have opposed God, separated from him to live in body, we feel guilty. But we did not separate from God and as such, are not guilty. We remain as God created us, innocent, guiltless, sinless; we remain holy, unified. But to experience innocence and holiness, we must stop seeking separated ego selves.

The earth is meant to be in opposition to unified state, God. But no one can oppose God; no one can separate from God so we remain as God created us, in him and in one another; while in spiritual union with God, we dream that we are separated from him and from one another.

The new sons of God then divide and produce new sons who are also part of them and parts of God. That way, creation seems ongoing but each new self-contains old selves and God and is as old as God, which is eternal.

You probably would not understand what I am talking about. But try forgetting the world, forget that you are ego and body, forget the reality of ego, body, space, and time, and keep quiet. Do not think with your ego separated mind. This is called emptying your mind of all ego and its categories.

If you can attain a mind without ego thoughts in it for one hour, you would see our world disappear, literally, and first, you see yourself in another world, a world of light forms. Everything in it would be like on earth except that they are made of light.

That world of light forms is called astral world by Hinduism, paradise by Islam, purgatory by Catholicism, and gate of heaven by metaphysics. It seems real but is still an illusion for there is still space and time in it.

If you understand that the world of light forms is not heaven although it is an improvement of our world, you forget it, too, and keep quiet. Finally, you experience yourself in heaven.

Heaven is formless, it is unified, joined, there is no you, seer and seen, subject and object, no space, time, and matter—all selves share one God-self and share one God mind. In it, you are eternal and experience perfect joy and peace that your ego-mind cannot understand.

Try to overlook our world, forget our world, forgive our world, do not take anything done in it as real, overcome the world, die to the awareness of ego, body, space, and time, meditate, and see if you would not see the world of light forms, and later experience formless eternity in heaven.

Post Script:

Yesterday, if you tried to read my three-part 32-page write-up on Training Igbo leaders, you probably encountered many typographical errors. Unfortunately, I cannot see my errors if I go read the stuff in less than two weeks. So, in two weeks when the material is off my mind, I will go and correct whatever grammatical mistakes and typographical errors are in it and then send it to my editor for formal editing before publication.

Yesterday, I talked about the phenomenal and phenomenological world of the here and now; today, I talk about the metaphysical world. You can switch your mind from esoteric stuff to physical stuff. Some shallow folks do not realize that some of the greatest scientists were also metaphysics buffs.

Isaac Newton established physics as science but wrote more on esoterica, God, than he did on physics. Quantum physicists like Schrodinger spent more time writing on Hinduism, Buddhism, and Taoism than they wrote on the new physics.

Some of us have minds that can shift from science to meta-science. Man, in his present form, as Rene Descartes, Ludwig Leibnitz, Immanuel Kant, and George Hegel said, is dual, spirit, and matter. I can relate to the best scientists and go toe to toe with them on any aspect of science and yet when I feel like it, I talk about the nature of God (God is beyond science), as I did today.

WHAT IS THE CAUSE OF MY EXCESSIVE FEAR, EXCESSIVE DESIRED BIG EGO, AND EXCITABLE BODY?

I am prone to excessive fear. That fear leads me to develop an avoidant personality. An avoidant personality anticipates harm and rejection from other people and fears rejection and harm, and to prevent those, avoids relating to people and keeps to himself most of the time. In social isolation, he nurses a big ego that is out of this world.

I have a big ego, a big ego that easily feels slighted and angry at the person it perceives slighted it. My excessive fear is also present in my dreams. In my dreams, I experience things trying to harm me and respond with fear.

It seems that my mind constructed things that seem to scare me in dreams and in the day world. This fearfulness could be due to my desired big ego and my hypersensitive body.

But could it also be due to my separation from my real self, the son of God who is one with God? The big ego is now a sword preventing me from returning to God, for to return to God, one must not have an ego at all and must be humble, not a proud ego as I am.

There seems to be a correlation between my hypersensitive body, my fear, and big ego. Could it be that before birth on earth, the son of God in me chose my hypersensitive body hence grandiose ego and associated excessive fear? It is probably so. I will investigate this matter further. This is because it might be superficial to attribute the excessive fear to only biological and social factors as I did from the study of psychology. It may well be due to spiritual issues, my separation from God, unified self, my real self, and desire to live as an ego in body, in space, time, and matter.

A VERY DUMB POINTLESS UNIVERSE

It was better the physical universe of space, time, and matter, people, animals, and trees did not exist; it exists as a dumb universe; it has no purpose other than existing and then dying. People are cursed with the desire to live at all costs, hence they tolerate pain and suffering and posit a god that they think can help them and he does not help them for he does not exist. The universe exists and all that can be done is to see it humorously and not take it seriously; one must pass through it without much ado about nothing, for it is nothing.

There is intelligence in the universe but it is impersonal. My writings try to explicate the nature of that intelligence.

THE EGO IS AN EFFORT TO MAKE THE HUMAN BODY SEEMS TO HAVE WORTH AND VALUE.

THE WORTH DERIVED FROM THE EGO AND BODY IS A SUBSTITUTE WORTH. REAL WORTH LIES IN GOD.

That which seeks worth does not have worth and value; the ego is constantly seeking worth; this is because it intrinsically does not have worth; its worth is make-belief; because it is not real, it easily feels slighted when its worth is not acknowledged by other people. If it has worth, it would not mind whether other folks see it as having worth or not, for opinions do not matter to reality.

Yet, human beings must seek worth, value, and significance; this is because without seeking worth, albeit false, the human being is a mere piece of meat that will die, rot, and smell awfully. It is the worth that people confer on their bodies—their egos that make them tolerate their pointless existence in bodies.

The pursuit of worth, which is what life on earth is all about, and is the nature of human society and civilization, is a maneuver for importance; apart from ego and body, people are sons of God, people are extensions of God and in God, are eternal and have total worth.

Let go of your effort to value the ego and body and you realize your total worth in the whole, unified spirit self. As brother Jesus said, one must die for a new self to be born in one. The old self, ego in body, must die for the new self, Christ, the real son of God, to be resurrected in one's awareness.

Jesus overcame the world, which means that he overlooked the ego and body to know that he has another self, the son of God who is eternal, not the temporary ego and body.

We seek separation from the whole, unified spirit self, aka God and in our false new state in body, space, and time, seek to give the worthless, the nonexistent worth.

The false worth given to the ego makes people tolerate giving in body. If they did not seek worth in ego and body, they would realize that they are nothing and at that point, would awaken to where real worth is, in God.

In the meantime, leave people to dance their dance of having worth in ego and body for that is what they came to earth to do. When they realize and accept the total worthlessness of ego and body, they would then return, awaken to their real selves, the eternal sons of God who are one with God, and in God, have total worth.

ON YOUR FACE IS WRITTEN WHO YOU ARE.

What is in a person's mind is reflected on his face. The faces of the south Eastern Nigerian governors reflect emptiness and tendency to petty thievery. None of them indicates a serious thinker or a person with useful public policy agenda for his state.

The governor of Anambra looks like a ghetto gangster or a pimp; his manner of dressing is classic pimp attire; the governors of Abia and Enugu look like overfed nonentities; the governor of Imo looks like a fat puppy; the governor of Ebony is almost serious in his demeanor but difficult to figure out.

On the whole, what we have as leaders in the southeast are really not serious leaders with the intention of modernizing their people.

The people who elect these clowns are, of course, to be faulted as well as the clowns. People get the government they deserve.

YOU ARE ALWAYS IN HEAVEN DREAMING THAT YOU ARE APART FROM IT.

A while ago, I woke up from sleep feeling totally calm and happy; I did not feel like I have a body. Thoughts went through my mind. They are as follows.

You and all people are innocent. All of you, human beings and every biological organism, are innocent, holy, guiltless, and sinless. I know that you believe that you have committed a lot of sins but you and people have not. The sins you and people seem to have committed were committed in a dream setting; the world is a dream setting; what is done in dreams has not been done, in fact. You and people have done nothing, in fact, neither good nor not good; you have done nothing, period.

God's will is union—that he and his creations are unified. No power can separate from eternal union, although they can dream that they have separated from it. If it were possible for the sons of God, us, to separate from God and from each other, then we are more powerful than God; we would have destroyed God, usurped his power, and are now the creator of the world of separation. We would have succeeded in our desire to be more powerful than God, to leave God, and go invent our own world apart from the unified world that God created. We cannot do so although we can dream separation.

The world of separated ego selves walking around in space and time is the world of illusion; it seems to exist but does not exist, literally. You, me in body, seemingly separated selves, do not exist; we are a chimera, seemingly separated beings, our bodies as boundaries from each other, but in fact, do not exist (we exist as the formless sons of God who are always in God and in each other).

In the universe, people suffer pain and die. If that were possible, then God is not love. If pain and suffering exist, God is cruel, wicked, and does not exist.

The universe of pain and suffering seems to exist as in a dream and the pain and suffering in it have not happened.

There is no coronavirus going on; no one is dying from that virus or other diseases for no one had lived in bodies that could be afflicted with diseases and die. God is thus still love for nothing bad has happened to his sons.

What happened is that the sons of God, while still in God, peace, and joy, wished to experience the opposite of God, which is separation, closed their spiritual eyes to experience the opposite of God, union, joy, and love. They seem to have experienced it on earth.

None of them can experience anything on earth that he and all of them did not individually and collectively wish to experience in a dream. If it were possible for a person to experience what he does not want, what only other people want him to experience, then there is no justice in the universe and a universe without justice is a universe without God, for God is justice.

You should not bear grievances and grudges against anyone who did something bad to you, as the ego judges it to be; this is because he has done nothing to you, and to the extent that you see him do something to you, you wanted to experience it and projected him into your dream. He projected himself into your dream for you to experience what you experienced from him and for him to experience what he experienced from you.

(The slave projected out the slave master and the slave master projected out the slave for both to experience what they experienced; both share one mind and the wish of each is gratified by the other's wish.)

Bearing grievances and seeking vengeance is a way of making the dream and what is done in it seemed real. Overlook the dream; overlook what you see people do to you, good or bad; overlook racism, slavery, and everything people do; overlook people in bodies of black and white; deny the reality of the world and do not make it real for you by not forgiving it.

If you do not forgive the world, you make it real for you and suffer in it but if you forgive it, it is not real for you and you do not suffer—you are in peace and joy.

Forgiveness gives you peace and joy for it returns you to the truth where nothing bad can ever happen to a son of God without his wishing to dream it.

You are always safe in God and from there, dream that you are in a world where enemies are attacking and harming your nonexistent body and ego.

You and people are in heaven right now while dreaming that you have gone on a journey without distances, a journey to nowhere for everywhere, you and people are in God (in peace and joy, in bliss; in eternity while dreaming mortality).

You do not have to do anything good to merit heaven, to attain heaven. You are already and always in heaven and cannot leave heaven and so is every person.

You are in heaven and dream a dream where you placed yourself in body and made it feel pain, weakness, sickness, and death to make body and your substitute self, ego, seem real in your awareness.

If you deny your ego and body, deny space, time, and matter, deny the physical universe, and see yourself and all people as innocent, you will awaken right now in heaven and know that you are always innocent and that all people are always innocent and have never been in body of white or black for a second.

Of course, you can dream that you are on earth in body, and play with your body, but not see it as real. In which case, your body is light and sickness-free and when you are tired of playing the game of pretending to be ego and body, you transform your body to light body and live in the light world, and thereafter, give up body and awaken in formless unified spirit, aka God, heaven, our real self and home.

These thoughts went through my mind in a split second, and then I remembered that they are what are written in *A Course in Miracles*. That book's world view is now my world view.

The thing now is for me to live its truth, to see me and all people as innocent, forgive our seeming earthly mistakes, and relapse into the love, unified state that is our nature and home.

Post Script:

What is the utility of this manner of thinking and behaving? It is because it returns one to one's real self, the eternal son of God. Those who think along these lines, forgive all, know that all are unified literally, and have their needs met for them by people who they forgive and who also forgive them. If you forgive, you give yourself and the person you forgive peace and joy. Feeling peaceful, those people literally give you what you need to live on earth without you asking for it.

Africans are the most unforgiving human beings on earth. They are egotists and bear grievances. Say something that slights their humongous and ginormous egos, and they would not forgive you. Because they do not forgive, they live apart from God even as they go to phony Pentecostal churches and yell the name of Jesus all the time. Because they are egotists and are not forgiving persons, they are like Adam and Eve and must live apart from God's grace.

Those who live in God's grace have their needs met for them as Adam and Eve's needs were met in the Garden of Eden until they disobeyed God by separating from him. Africans disobey God by separating from him and accentuating their self-made replacement selves, egos, and by not forgiving one another. As a result, they live in poverty and have to struggle to eke out a miserable living in their godforsaken condiment.

They do not realize that forgiveness and ego-lessness would change their dreadful lives and give them what they need to live this life pleasantly; they do not have to be the satanic people they currently are, folks who know only selling their people and exploiting them and not working for them.

It is because of their dreadful state that I feel an urge to help them with the true interpretation of the teachings of Jesus, the son of God, the Christ, who is one with us.

But would they listen? It does not matter whether they listen and do what they are told to do or not; my job is to articulate the truth for them; a part of them, their right minds, the Holy Spirit in them, have heard what I said, received it, and kept it until they are ready to listen and they would remember what the Holy Spirit in me told them, live it, find peace and joy, and return to God, not go on futile and fruitless journeys apart from love, apart from God.

MY MIND AND ALL OTHER MINDS IN CONCERT PRODUCE ALL THAT HAPPENS TO ME IN MY LIFE.

My mind produces all that I see in the world; my mind thinks and converts its thinking to images and projects them to seemingly outside world and I experience it as if I am a victim thrown about by a seemingly outside world.

My past and recent experience are used by my mind to produce my dreams at night and during the day world. I do not experience anything at night or daytime that my mind did not produce.

I produced the corrupt African governments, along with all Africans, to experience the eyesore that is Africa, just as I produced Africa's backwardness to experience it and feel small and then use that sense of inferiority vis a vis the developed Western world to seek ego bigness and give me pain and suffering; my mind also produced my weak body and used it to justify seeking big ego to give me psychological pain. There is nothing in my world that my thinking, mind, did not produce nor bear any.

That same mind can produce a different body, a healthy one, and a beautiful Africa.

If my mind in conjunction with other minds produced my experience and world, how can my mind produce a different world and experiences for me? It is by thinking and living from the Holy Spirit, that means by overlooking the wrong I and others did and correcting them with forgiveness.

Love is already there and when I remove the obstacles to love, union, and abundance, I experience it. Believe it, live it, and you see the results. In doing it, you gain confidence in the power of the Holy Spirit to give you happy dream, which includes material abundance. You will be living in grace where God, meaning all things on earth and in heaven, give me what I need to live effortlessly. Do not just talk about it.

THE CORONAVIRUS AND COVID-19 FEAR HAVE DEMONSTRATED THAT PEOPLE ARE PRIMARILY MOTIVATED BY FEAR ROOTED IN THEIR DESIRE TO LIVE AS EGOS AND BODIES.

Given the coronavirus scare, individuals are doing whatever they can to protect themselves so that they may survive and live to see another day; the governments they set up is doing what they are set up to do, protect them, and if they fail in doing so, would be removed.

Fear is what primarily motivates egos in bodies for it shows them how to survive when danger threatens their egos' and bodies' survival. This means that ultimately, each human being, each ego, is self-centered for he must survive before he helps other egos to survive.

If you did not know this fact in the past, now know it. It is the nature of human existence on planet earth; the alternative is to jettison the ego and live in the world of light forms and ultimately to return to spiritual living in unified spirit, aka God and his heaven.

GOD IS NOT OUTSIDE US FOR YOU TO WORSHIP HIM.

God is not outside us; it is our real self. You do not talk about God, Brahman, Atman, and Christ as if they are not you; they are your real self, our collective real self. Thus, God-realized persons do not say that they realized Atman, Christ, son of God, but God-realized for the son of God is God and God is his son.

WOMEN ARE EGOS AND SEEK SPECIAL RELATIONSHIPS WHERE YOU AFFIRM THEIR EGOS AND BODIES AS IMPORTANT; DO NOT DO SO AND THEY END THEIR RELATIONSHIP WITH YOU NOW, NOT TOMORROW.

Do you want your woman to kick you out today, this very minute? Then do not positively affirm her beautiful body and ego; do not gratify her vanity. Women seem only capable of special love relationships where they are seen as important egos and beautiful bodies and worshipped. Do not do so and your relationship with them ends. If you do not respect your woman's body and ego, you are asking her to ask you to leave her. You do not have to fear her asking you to leave for she is going to ask you to leave. If you want her around you, then gratify her ego's vanity.

Very few women are capable of holy relationships where folks overlook each other's behaviors, egos, and bodies and affirm their oneness in spirit. Holy relationship is the ideal, not the reality on earth.

THAT WHICH NEEDS CONSTANT PROTECTION TO EXIST DOES NOT EXIST.

Children under age twelve must be protected by their parents and adults or they would not survive. In adulthood, people must constantly protect themselves from nature and from other people's attacks. They must eat and defend their bodies, or else they would not survive. Our bodies need constant protection and therefore, do not have permanent existence; upon death, the body dissolves to matter, carbon, hydrogen, oxygen, nitrogen, and other elements that decay to electrons, protons, and neutrons that decay to light. In effect, only light exists. And light decays to nothingness. People's bodies are nothing.

It is the spirit in people, wishing separation from unified spirit, aka God, that urges them to defend their bodies for the spirit wants to live in body, space, and time, for those illusions enable spirit to seem to have separated existence when in fact, it is always part of one unified spirit and one unified mind.

TO JUDGE DREAMS AS GOOD OR BAD IS FOOLISHNESS.

The world is a mutual, collective dream within which each person has his own brand of the dream. Dreams mean nothing. To judge dreams as good or bad is a waste of time, is ultimate foolishness. Leave each person and groups of persons to have their dreams. Some groups, such as Igbos, dream of their group importance; they are neither good nor bad, just dreams that have not happened; they are all ego quests and since the ego does not exist, they do not exist.

HOW TO ATTAIN INNER PEACE IN A WORLD AT WAR WITH ITSELF

It is apparent that people are at war with their neighbors. We are at war with each other because each of us has self-interests and pursues them and they sometimes conflict with other people's interests. We live in social conflict.

Because we are at war with each other, we set up governments to protect us from each other. We have police to make sure that our neighbors do not harm us and for them to arrest those who harm us; we have courts and judges to send to jails and prison those who harm us. We have prisons to incarcerate those who harm us. Simply put, we live in a state of war and conflict and prepare for it by doing what we do with the government.

Thomas Hobbes said all these in his seminal book, *Leviathan*, published in 1651. That book along with Plato's *Republic*, Aristotle's *Politics*, Machiavelli's *The Prince*, John Locke's *Second Treaty on Government*, Jean Jacque Rousseau's *Social Contract*, Charles Montesquieu's *Spirit of Laws*, Jeremy Bentham's *Morals*, and John Stuart Mill's *On Representative Government* are must-read in political science; in fact, they constitute western political science; the rest are detail (when I taught at universities, I had my students read those books; without a thorough grasp of them, you cannot understand Western social organization and government).

As long as we live on earth, this mutual state of war is probably always going to be the case. The reason why it is going to be the case is that we came to earth to live as the opposite of where we came from. In eternity, we lived in union with each other. There is no space, time, and matter in eternity. We are literally in each other and where each of us ends and another begins is nowhere.

While in eternity, aka heaven, we decided to go live as the opposite of our unified state. We decided to live as separated selves. We collectively invented space, time, and matter (the three illusions in that they do not exist but seem to exist) and use matter to construct bodies for each of us and now seem to be living in bodies.

Bodies give us a sense of separation from each other. Space, time, and matter also give us a sense of separation from each other.

Since we came to live as separated selves, we helped each other to invent a separated self-concept, the ego. The ego is not our real self, it is our substitute and replacement self.

Our real self is unified spirit self. But we now live as false separated ego selves housed in bodies. Each of us sees distance between him and other egos. He believes that he has different self-interests, protects them, and defends his interests if you detract from them.

This is the nature of our lives on earth. Our lives on earth are literally a state of war; we fight each other, protecting our separated interests, and generally inflicting pain and suffering on each other.

If you want to reduce your level of the war we declared on ourselves, you begin by understanding that you have a different self called the unified spirit self (Christians call it the sons of God or the Christ; I am not a religious person; I am a thinker, a philosopher). The unified spirit self is our real self.

The pursuit of the ego separated self is the desire to live as the opposite of the unified spirit self. The desire for ego is declaration of war on our real self, unified spirit self. The ego is literally attacked by our real selves. The sons of God, members of unified spirit self who are eternally unified with each other and with God, literally wanted to kill themselves, kill their father, and invent different, separated selves, and go live as them.

Those who attack their real selves want to experience pain, so in ego, we do feel pain. The more we desire a grandiose ego, the more pain we inflict on ourselves.

Now what one needs to do is understand one's ego type, one's personality. Psychologists and their personality testing can help one to understand one's ego type; that is, one's self-concept and personality, one's behavior pattern.

Regardless of what is the type of one's personality, ego, all you need to do is decide that you no longer desire it and let it go. Do not think or behave from it. Overlook your ego, transcend your ego, let go of your ego, and do not think or do anything that your ego asks you to do.

What you now need to do is forgive whatever you did from your ego and forgive what other people did and do from their egos.

You now practice thinking and behaving from what you understand serves our collective interests. Since the ego asks you to do what serves your personal interests, now do what serves public interests. This is not a moral issue but a realistic one.

Doing what serves our collective social interests, Alfred Adler in his individual psychology correctly observed, cures one's neurosis, for neurosis inheres in trying to serve only one's interests.

Do not see yourself as your ego and its body. Do not argue with your ego or other egos. I say so because your ego will counter all I said above. Other egos, argumentative people, the neurotics out there, will point out the silliness of trying to forgive all people. They will say, should we forgive murderers, thieves, and rapists? No, arrest them, put them in prisons, and try to teach them to serve our collective good, not kill or steal from people. We need to correct the behavior of criminals. Forgiveness includes trying to correct one's and other people's antisocial behaviors.

Thereafter, engage in meditation. By that, it meant to not think from ego. Jettison the ego and try to attain inner silence, a situation where there are no ego thoughts in your mind (mind does not exist as a thing; it is synonym for thinking). Be silent and go about doing what serves our mutual good. Do so and you attain relative peace in your life.

In this piece, I am not interested in talking about elaborate metaphysics. But let me say that if you live your life serving collective good, forgiving and correcting antisocial behaviors in you and other people, you occasionally escape from our world and enter the world of light forms, a world that still looks like our world, but everything in it is made of light, it is our world purified with love. From that world, it is also a fictional, dream world, you finally disappear into the unified spirit world where all are one shared self, one shared thinking, one shared mind—the world where our shared thinking, shared mind produced our present universe and what takes place in it.

Before this century runs out, science would have demonstrated that our physical universe is a matrix of sorts. By that, it meant that we have a different self, the unified spirit self that wrote a script, a play, and assigned to each of us a role to play in and we on earth are those playing roles assigned to us by our real selves, the unified spirit self.

On earth, we are like people in a dream; someone else dreams through dream figures. That someone else is our real self. So, it is not like another person does to us what we do on earth; we do to us what we do on earth. Our unified self does through us what we do on earth.

Since what we do on earth is not real, is a movie, or a dream, we can understand it and make the dream a happy one, the movie a pleasant one, and ultimately get out of the movie by overlooking it, by not desiring it.

Mystics and God-realized people check out of the movie and first return to the world of light forms and from there, teach those still in the world of dense forms and ultimately return to formless heaven.

THE CORONAVIRUS PANDEMIC TEACHES US THE PRIMACY OF BIOLOGY OVER PSYCHOLOGY.

With the coronavirus thing going on, I have noticed that most people are now doing whatever they have to do to physically survive—engaging in social distancing, wearing mouth and nose masks when outside their houses, and generally keeping to themselves. People are engaged in the struggle for biological survival. When the struggle is for survival at the biological level, all other issues take the back seat.

I do not hear anyone talking about his psychological issues. Of course, people have psychological issues, such as personality disorders, anxiety disorders, drug addictions, addictions to food and sex, mental disorders, and so on but those are now secondary to the primary issue of physical survival. You must first survive at the physical level before you talk about your psycho-social issues.

Also, very few persons are talking about religion. Apparently, people know that religion is just a talk and that what enables them to survive is medical science, biological science, and science in general, not some escape into wooly ideas on God. They do not expect God to make them overcome the Covid-19 issue but expect science to do so for them.

In Abraham Maslow's schema, when folk's physiological health is taken for granted, they revert to their favorite past time, creating God in the human image, saying that God created them in his image and writing elaborate theologies on the nature of God.

Listen, we, the parts of the whole, in religious terms, the sons of God, wrote a drama and are enacting it out in our lives on earth. We are responsible for what we do on earth for the earth is our play.

If you want to make your life on earth pleasant, love yourself and all people, and correct your and our antisocial behaviors.

PSYCHOLOGY VERSUS RELIGION AND SPIRITUALITY

Believe it or not, the formal study of how human beings think and behave psychology is rather recent. In the old, folks studied human nature and wrote tons of stuff on it. It was only in the late nineteenth century that some Germans, led by Wilhelm Wundt, decided to study how human beings think and behave.

Wundt (1897), Freud (2006), Adler (1938), Kraepelin (2008), Jung (1980), and others began the formal study of the human mind (mind is not a thing; mind is a name we give to our thinking). These scientists decided to limit their studies of human thinking processes to what they can actually verify, and not merely write philosophical dissertations on mind.

The English, given their logical positivism, their culture, and beginning with Francis Bacon, decision not to entertain any idea that cannot be observed and verified, took the Germans' intentions to a whole new level. They injected what is now called behaviorism into psychology.

Behaviorism only talks about what we all can see about people and eschews any speculation about people that cannot be observed. John Watson and B.F. Skinner completely ignored German psychoanalysis for it is speculative and emphasized behaviors.

In the present, neuroscientists accept only what the study of the brain, biochemistry of the brain, suggests is the nature of thinking.

Thus, we can say that psychology limits its inquiry to what we can observe and verify in people; it embraces the scientific method that says that knowledge is only what we all can independently ascertain to be true in our world.

Religion and spirituality go beyond the observable universe and speculates on what is behind the universe. People ask such questions as: who am I, where did I come from, and where do we go to when we die? These questions are given individual answers; one person's answer is different from another person's answers; the answers are mere conjectures and speculations and cannot be demonstrated to be true by all of us.

Religious people accept some of the answers provided by those human beings who claim to speak from the authority of what they call God. The supposed credibility of the religious person, such as Moses, Jesus Christ, Mohammed, Krishna, Buddha, and others give people the feeling that what they believe is true.

Yet, there is no way that all of us can ascertain the truth of what the founders of religions said is true. They say that there is God, that heaven and hell exist. Where are God, heaven, and hell? We cannot see them.

We can only believe in God, have faith that he exists, but cannot observe him and verify him. Obviously, we cannot have a school where all the various ideas on God are taught. Therefore, we rationally remove the teaching of religion and spirituality from our public elementary and secondary schools and universities.

Religions and spirituality should not be taught at public schools for what they teach cannot be verified. Only what all of us can verify should be taught at public schools.

Be that as it may, there is probably something beyond matter; metaphysics probably has some truth in it, if only we can understand its truth.

In the meantime, psychology limits itself to the scientific method and does not indulge in speculating on why questions.

But as we all know, until the individual comes to terms with where he believes that he came from, who created him, and where he goes when he dies, he tends not to be happy and peaceful. So, it is up to the individual to try to figure out the answers to those questions but not for anyone else to tell him what they are.

If in his opinion there is no God and everything is the product of the permutation of matter, atheism, he must cling to that belief to be honest to himself. However, like religion, atheism must not be taught at schools for it is a belief, not proven fact; physics tells us that we have not understood 96% of the universe, dark energy and dark matter, and indeed, the 4% of the visible universe we began understanding we have not understood one percent of, so making categorical statements about the existence of God or lack of it is statement of belief is not science.

If, on the other hand, one believes in God, one must accept that to have personal integrity. If one is like me, an agnostic who speculates on the nature of reality, one must do so to respect oneself.

I cannot accept what other people tell me about reality based on their supposed authority on such matters. I do not accept what any scientist tells me is true until I perform experiments and verify his claims; I do not accept what any religionist or theologian tells me about God until my experience tells me that it is possibly true.

My public psychology therefore limits itself to empiricism but my personal psychology embraces speculation on spirit. In my life, I find that I need both scientific psychology and spirituality. Even though I know that religion and spirituality are a bunch of speculations, I find that I need them to complete my being; the empirical sciences alone are not enough for me. I love physics and allied sciences but it deals with matter, space, and time; I happen to believe that people are more than physics.

PEOPLE MUST HAVE GOALS, EVEN DELUDED GOALS TO LIVE FOR OR THEY DIE.

It is really true that people must have goals that they are living for or they die. The goals may not be crystal clear in folk's minds but they nevertheless are there if folks are living fully.

In childhood (up to age twelve), children are fascinated by the world they find themselves in. Exploring their world is their goal. Just trying to understand their world, playing with trees and roses, are good enough goals to be alive for.

During their teenage years (age thirteen to nineteen), kids begin making serious friends that are satisfactory and setting conscious goals of what they want to do and be when they grow up. Some say they want to be a medical doctor, engineer, teacher, firefighter, policeman, or soldier. These goals give young people direction in their lives.

At secondary school, they find out what their vocational goals required for them to actualize them and go do them. By adulthood (twenties), they are beginning to actualize their goals, are in school to become doctors, engineers, are in the military, are policemen, teachers, and so on. They learn their vocations and by their late twenties, are sufficiently skilled to make good income from their jobs and marry.

In their thirties, they have children. They provide for their children through their forties. By age fifty, most of them have children who are now adult and have left home so they are alone (with their spouses or are divorced). They enter midlife and have to figure out how to live the rest of their lives.

There are idealists. When I was a teenager and college student, my goal was to do whatever I could to develop Africa. I had an all or nothing desire to develop Africa and that informed my studies at college. I used to lie on my bed visualizing what a modernized Africa is like, with people going to universities and technical schools, with modern cities everywhere, with factories and industries everywhere. I imagined Africa that looked like Western Europe and North America. I rejected Africa as it was for it seemed to be primitive and unacceptable (this means that I rejected me as I was for, I seemed to be primitive). That was my overarching wish, dream, fantasy, vision.

By my mid-thirties, I realized that it was a delusion to wish to modernize Africa. Africa has no basis for modernization. She is too backward to be dragged into the modern era in a generation. The people live in primitive cultures. Cultures take time to change. You cannot change cultures with a magic wand. Africans themselves have little or nothing worthwhile in their heads. You cannot take such persons and teach those physics, chemistry, biology, medicine, engineering, and modern business practices, the types of learning that modernized people should have. It dawned on me that Africa will gradually develop but not as rapidly as I had wanted it to do.

All things being constant, in about two hundred years (2200s), Africans would have joined the rest of the world and begin operating at the same level as the rest of the world but they could not do it quicker. When you actually talk to Africans, you appreciate how backward they are; their frame of reference is what exists in the primitive world, not what you find in those trained in the scientific method—those found in the USA and Western Europe.

I must say that I find it difficult to talk to a typical African because his reference group is not mine. I am operating in a world way ahead of his that there is no basis for communication between us. I may condescend and patronize the African and pretend to be bantering with him but the fact is that he can seldom say what makes sense to me.

You first have to learn to walk before you can walk and run. Africa has to learn to walk before it can run. It simply does not have the enabling environment to operate as a modern scientific and technological society. Thus, my wishes for a modernized Africa were dashed.

If your goals are delusional, that is, not realistic, you tend to feel bad when you realize that they cannot be immediately realized. If, for example, you wish to be the most powerful man in your world, the president of your country, and fancy all the things you could do, well that wish can keep you going for a while but by your mid-fifties, you would know if you are going to realize your goals or not. Delusions and delusional goals can keep you going in youth, through age forty, but not much longer.

When your wishes are dashed because they are delusional, now what? It is here that people have nothing more to live for. They become sick and without awareness that they wish to die, wish to die.

All death is suicide. People who have no more wishes, desires, and goals that they are living for; people in their late fifties and early sixties generally become living dead persons. Soon they overeat, grow fat, have heart attacks, strokes, or diabetes, and die.

I had one such friend. He got out of college in California and got a job with the city of Los Angeles, Parks and Recreation Department. He worked for over thirty years and retired. I asked him what he is now going to do with the rest of his life. He had no answer for me. I discovered that for over twenty years, he had no interest in his job and was just going through the motions to make a living and pay his bills. Upon retirement, in quick order, he had a stroke and died a couple of years later. I actually expected him to die. Yes, I told him that much. I said to him that if he does not find a goal to live for, he is going to die. He did not find a goal to live for and died.

People who have no abiding goals are living for nothing, so a deeper part of their minds have them die and get it over with.

One must change one's goals from illusions and delusions to more realistic goals. One must figure out a goal that speaks to one's essence and live for it. You cannot have delusional and illusory goals after age sixty. You must now do what is realistic and contribute to society in a meaningful way or you are a living dead person and soon die off.

You do not need to live in despair; folks live in despair when their illusory goals are not met. Each person has a useful thing he can contribute to society. If a person truly has a useful goal, he could live to be over a hundred years, depending on his inherited body, for genetics plays a role in how long a person lives.

As for me, I find a mixture of scientific psychology and spirituality to be my calling and literally live it every minute of my life. As long as I am doing this kind of stuff, I feel like I am useful to evolution. That keeps me going until my inherited body runs its cause (biological science says that people can live up to 120 years).

In conclusion, you must discover a goal that makes sense to you, that speaks to your essence, and pursue it. Devote your time and energy to it twenty-four seven. In Abraham Maslow's categories and Alfred Adler's individual psychological categories, you must be actualizing a goal that represents what life means for you. You must go for it with all you have. Even if it does not yield money for you, just do it, for it is in doing it that at a deeper level of your mind, you have reason to live on planet earth and tolerate its pains and sorrows.

WHY DID THIS AND NOT THAT HAPPEN TO ME?

We often ask: why did this happen to me? Why didn't that happen to me? Why didn't I get the job that I applied for? Why did I not get into the school that I wanted to go to? Why was I rejected for that promotion? Why did many employment doors close to me and only crummy jobs open to me? Why didn't I pursue a different career that I could have easily done and improved my life? Why was I born where I was born? Why did I have my parents instead of others? Why did I inherit this body instead of another one?

There are no accidents; everything that happened to you or did not happen to you was supposed to be so. Everything to you, to other people, and to the world, happened when it was supposed to happen. Nothing happens in this world that did not happen when it was not supposed to happen.

You were born when you were supposed to be born, born where you were supposed to be born, and experienced whatever you have experienced.

All that happened to you was supposed to give you the experience you had. Your experience gave you the training to do whatever you are now doing. Your past prepared you for your present.

The world is a Metrix, a play that we, in spirit, collectively wrote and things happen to you and all people at exactly the time they are supposed to happen, not before or after. There are no accidents; you are where you are supposed to be and doing what you are supposed to be doing.

You are doing the work that you are supposed to be doing that the script, the play called for you to do and that only you actually can do.

The coronavirus that is going around the world today is supposed to be going around the world; those that are supposed to die from it (by their choice and by our collective choice), will die from it. The scientists who are eventually going to come up with a vaccine for it will do so and could only have done so because it occurred.

All the evils that happened in the past, such as slavery, discrimination, and colonialism were supposed to happen; the play asked for them to happen.

The universe is our collective play, all of us, unified spirit self, wrote the play and enact it out, and it unfolds whenever and however it unfolds.

You are doing the work that only you can do; that is why it is silly envying other people for their work or their political position or for their wealth.

What I do only me can do for only my body and experience prepared me to do it and envying me is a waste of your time. What you do only you can do and I cannot do it as well as you do it, so I do not envy you.

Decide on something that you want to do, go do it, do it with your entire mind, and do it twenty-four seven; if you do so, the script called for you to do so. That is what life is all about.

Asking why this or that happened to you is a waste of your time and if you insist on doing so, you will learn that whatever happened to you, to other people, and in the world, was designed by you and all people to happen as they did. The world is our individual and collective dream; we dream it together.

Our minds are joined as one mind—the one mind of God's one son, one son that is all of us, and whatever happens in the world, we collectively did it and dream it.

On earth, we shall soon design a computer that is joined to all computers and they all do something collectively, in concert; that is how our minds work; there are infinite minds and all of them are joined into one mind and do things together, each mind playing a role for other minds to do what they want to do and they playing a role for him to do what he wants to do, each doing so freely.

For example, you chose your parents, siblings, and the ethnic and racial group that you are born in and they chose you. All of you experience whatever you want to experience in that association. Thereafter, you move to other associations, groups in the several dreams, roles we play in space, time, and matter (so-called reincarnations are better called dream times).

When the individual has had enough dreams, he does what he has to do to get out of the dream-play; he awakens to the awareness of his real self, son of God, part of unified spirit self. Buddha and Jesus Christ have awakened from the dream of self-forgetfulness and now know themselves as not egos but as the son of God who is one with God.

What is the utility of this type of thinking? It prevents you from blaming other people for your fate; you chose your fate and then turn around to seeing you as a victim and blaming those that seem to victimize you. The victimizer merely played a role for you in your nightmarish dream and you played a role for him.

You can choose to have a happy dream by forgiving and loving yourself and all people. The ultimate use of this type of thinking is that it enables you to be at peace in this world in the dream you and all of us chose to have at this time.

Finally, this type of thinking will not make sense to your ego intellect. Your ego intellect will dismiss it as bullshit, encourage you to blame your seeming victimizers, and you do so and live in misery.

Africans blame white folks for their absurd poverty but despite all their blaming of whites, they still live in poverty and suffer their incredible poverty in a world of abundance. They have to learn to accept responsibility for their fate and now choose love for one another instead of their crazy hate for their fellow Africans.

Fulanis kill other Nigerians and think that it is powerful to do so. They cause problems for other Nigerians and soon, other Nigerians will be killing them. This shows you how stupid African egos are. If they are rational, they would love each other and stop screwing each other.

TO SCIENCE, EVERYTHING HAPPENED BECAUSE OF ACCIDENT, CHANCE, AND RANDOMNESS.

This is a postscript to my yesterday's essay that says that everything happens for a reason and that there are no accidents.

Science has one answer to the question: why did this or that happen? Is it an accident, chance, and randomness? To science, we are accidents; I am an accident, you are an accident. To science, the universe is a dumb thing whose pointless, purposeless, and meaningless workings produced everything in it, including human beings, animals, trees, mountains, stars, galaxies, everything. There is no reason why it produced anything; it just did.

Science's story of creation says that the universe began in a Big Bang. 13.8 billion years ago, a point of light came out of nowhere, became hot, and exploded into particles. The particles joined to form protons, neutrons, and electrons. Immediately, protons and neutrons joined to form nuclei. 400, 000 years later, nuclei captured electrons, and atoms of hydrogen were formed.

Millions of years later, clouds of hydrogen separated into clumps. Gravity acted on clumps of hydrogen and in their core heat and pressure, led to ignition, fusion. Hydrogen formed helium and stars are born. The initial stars were very massive in size.

In time, these huge stars exhausted their hydrogen, formed other elements, and when the forming process, called nucleosynthesis, reached iron, they exploded in supernova and that explosion formed all the other elements beyond iron. The elements were spilled into space as nebula.

In time, those 92 elements aggregated into medium-sized stars and planets and in time, to plants and animals, human beings included. That is, the accidental workings of the universe produced all things in it, people included.

The stars and galaxies are expanding away from each other and in trillions of years, the universe would be cold and stars and planets would die. The universe would end in cold death, big chill.

I know all these but choose to believe that I am not the product of accidents. However, my body appears to be the product of accidents, even that seems designed by an intelligent being, but I am willing to accept that my body is the product of accident. However, I choose to believe that my thinking, my mind, is the working of an intelligent being. That intelligent being I call the son of God, the part of the whole.

The son of God is one and extends to infinite us and through us, experiences the world as we do. You are free to believe in science's belief in accident. I am not fighting with you and your beliefs; I merely state what makes sense to me.

As I look at my life, it seems to me that what made me who I am began with my inherited biological issues, my struggles to overcome them, the subsequent development of idealistic pursuits, and the wish for ideal self, ideal people, ideal world, and ideal everything. My body made it difficult for me to adapt to the world as it is, and thus, I developed thinking and used it to understand my body, people, and things and in the process, developed a very powerful mind.

At an age where most kids are not even giving anything serious thought, I was already reading Western philosophy. At age fourteen, I could discuss with the best of scholars' folks like Plato, Aristotle, Descartes, Leibnitz, Kant, Hegel, Schopenhauer, Nietzsche, Feuerbach, David Hume, George Berkeley, Jean Jacque Rousseau, Voltaire, Blaise Pascal, Henri Bergson, William James, and other Western philosophers. At college, I gravitated to psychology and could teach it by my third year at college.

Through pure thinking, I formulated a new philosophy, one that I know is useful to the world and indeed what the coming world needs, for the old philosophies are now useless and do not help folks cope with the exigencies of their lives.

Let me reiterate that I believe I am not the product of my body and environment and that there is something in me trying to articulate new thoughts and that there's something in me and you folks call spirit, but I do not quarrel with what names folks call it. For now, it is enough for me to restate my belief that people are not products of accidents.

If you choose to believe in accidents, you have large company, contemporary science that teaches us that we are the products of accidents. To science, a dumb universe produced us; we are dumb playthings of that dumb universe.

Make your choice; I made mine, as written in my essay, why things happen to us. As I see it, the universe and people in it are a kind of matrix; we, the sons of God, have a joined mind, have one unified mind, and use that mind to write a script, play, and drama, assign parts to each other, and enact the play out as our lives on earth. We do so in a dream setting; the universe and people in it are dream things; the dreamer is our real self, the spiritual us. We remain eternal parts of an eternal unified spirit while seeing ourselves as persons in bodies in a dumb universe that seem to begin in a hot point of light and would end in cold chill.

If you negate the ego, your body, and the universe, you can transcend the pointless dream universe and awaken to your real self, the eternal son of God.

LIVING FROM LOVE AND LIGHT

God is a unified spirit self. God is love. God is light. God is love and light. We are parts of love and light; therefore, we are love and light.

In God are infinite spirits but all of them are one spirit. God is infinite spirits that are one spirit. Love is what glues all the infinite spirits into one spirit. Thus, God is love.

God is formless light, not physical light as we see on earth, but spiritual light. Thus, God is love and spiritual light.

On earth, to say that one lives from love is to say that one lives from God. However, our idea of love is attenuated love for it is not love as it exists in heaven.

In heaven, people are ideas of parts in the idea of a whole called God. In heaven, people are not in body, space, and time and are in formless spirit. Because they are in formless spirit, they are in each other. Where one spirit ends and another begins is nowhere.

In that unified state, love is at its most perfect state. On earth, we live in separated states in bodies; there is space, time, and matter between us and other people. We therefore cannot live as in heavenly love. Our earthly love is attenuated, is imperfect, whereas love in God is perfect.

In heaven, what we do to ourselves, we have done to others and what we do to others, we did to ourselves. In heaven, we experience the effects of our thoughts and actions immediately. This is because we are unified as one shared self and one shared mind.

On earth, we have the illusion of having separated ego selves housed in bodies, and believe that we live in space and time. Because other people seem distant from us, what we do to them, we do not seem to have done to us and what we do to us, we do not seem to have done to them.

In truth, what we do to seeming other people is what we do to us and what we do to us is what we do to seeming other people, but given the logic of space and time, it takes time for us to experience what we did to seeming other people.

If you enslave other people, you seem not to have enslaved you. But you have enslaved you. White folks in the USA enslaved black folks and seem not to have enslaved themselves but they actually did to themselves what they did to black folks. Today, white Americans are literally slaves; their social policies assume hate for themselves. If they had love for themselves, they would engage in providing education for all and health insurance and doing what serves all peoples' interests.

THINK AND BEHAVE FROM LOVE.

On earth, do whatever you do from love. This means doing whatever you do from egoless state. In egoless state, you park your mind in that part of your mind that thinks in terms of what is good for all human beings. You think and work for social good, not just for your personal good.

In religious terms, you do not do anything from ego but from the Holy Spirit. The Holy Spirit is the part of our minds that remember God, remember heaven's eternal union, while we are on earth. When you think and behave from the Holy Spirit, you do whatever you do with the understanding that it serves the good of all people on earth; you serve all peoples' interests. If you do so, you experience relative peace, not the perfect peace and joy, bliss of perfect union in heaven.

On earth, you cannot experience perfect union and perfect peace except momentarily when you transcend ego and body and are in God while still on earth (what *A Course in Miracles* call the state of Holy Instant, Hinduism calls Samadhi, and Christian mystics call mystical union of the son with his father).

On earth, you can think and behave from one of three parts of your mind—from the ego separated mind, our usual thinking and behavior, or from the Holy Spirit, aka Christ/Buddha mind; that part of our mind that does what serves all people, hence approximate heaven's love, and forgive those who harmed our egos and bodies for we are not egos and bodies, and what they did to us have not been done; and momentarily, we can also think and behave from God, from unified state, from the one mind God and his sons share in heaven.

While on earth, you cannot be aware of one mind, unified mind, for if you are aware of it, you would not see yourself as ego and body and would not see other people on earth; in unified mind, you are formless and all people are formless; you are part of our formless self and its formless mind.

We are actually always in formless self and formless mind, in heaven, that is, but while in it, think and behave as if we are outside it; we dream as if we are separated from God and each other.

We cannot separate from God for no power can separate from God. God wills his eternal union with all his sons. They cannot separate from God but they can believe that they are separated from him and see themselves on earth, the dream of separation.

God is perfect freedom and gave his sons perfect freedom. In our freedom, we can dream of separation from God and from each other. God will not prevent us from that dream because he knows that it is mere dream and that in reality, we remain as he created us, formless unified parts of him. We are him, so how can we separate from him, from ourselves?

We remain as God created us and cannot have substitute and replacement ego selves. We remain the unified sons of God.

SALVATION, REDEMPTION, AND DELIVERANCE

Salvation means to deliberately allow your ego-self and its body to metaphorically die so that you resurrect to the awareness of your real self, formless unified self. It means dying to the ego and being reborn in Christ.

Christ is the son of God who, while in space and time, remembers that he is the formless son of God and loves all other sons of God for he sees them as formless parts of his one infinite but unified self. The words salvation, redemption, and deliverance mean the same thing.

DEATH AND REBIRTH, BEING A BORN-AGAIN CHRISTIAN

Death and rebirth mean dying to your identification with the ego and body and remembering and living from your real self, the Christ, the unified son of God.

If you call yourself a born-again Christian, what that means is that you have received Christ into your life, you have died to ego, and is now reborn in the self God created you as, the son of God. This means that you have remembered that love is your nature, you love all, and forgive those who wronged you.

If you still live as the ego, you have not died to the ego and are not reborn in Christ. Your old self, ego, is still part of you; you have not begun living from the new self in you, the new man in you.

The new man, Christ, lives in the light-formed world, the gate of heaven (what Christians metaphorically call New Jerusalem or New Israel).

To live in heaven itself, one must not be in form, dense, or light.

HAPPY AND NIGHTMARISH DREAMS

Life on earth is a dream; it can be made a happy dream or a nightmarish dream. It is a nightmarish dream when you hate yourself and other people, and do not love and forgive yourself and other people. It becomes a happy dream when you love yourself and other people and forgive your past mistakes and all peoples' past mistakes, and in the present, emphasize correction of mistakes, talk about loving, and work for our mutual good.

THE NEW WORLD ORDER, THE KINGDOM OF GOD, A WORLD IN WHICH PEOPLE LIVE FROM LOVE

The new world order, NWO, that people expect and talk about is what brother Jesus called the kingdom of God coming to earth; the kingdom of God, aka heaven and unified spirit self, is inside us; we seem to have separated from it and are not currently aware of it; we live on earth but when we live from love and light, we are in the kingdom of God on earth, the new world order.

My vocation, what I came to this world to do, is to live from a unified spirit self, love, and light; I write books and articles on living from love; I give public lectures on living from love and light.

On earth, what we call love is the only part of us that approximates God. If I am doing the right thing, I am in relative peace and make an abundant living.

LIVING FROM LOVE # 1

I NEED DO NOTHING TO KNOW LOVE/GOD.

When folks hear that they need to live from love, they believe that they would start doing something that is called love. Here is the deal.

You are already love. Love is who you are. Love is inside you. You need to do nothing to live from the love you already are.

It is your effort to do something, loving or not, that covered the love you are. Now you need to do nothing and you would know that you are already love.

You can be nothing else but love. You are already and always love. You are a part of God and since God is love, you are a part of love.

God is permanent, eternal, and changeless. You are permanent, eternal, and changeless. Love is permanent, eternal, and changeless in you. It is what you did that covers your awareness of the love that you are. You now need to do nothing to know the love that you are. Actually, this means that you need to undo what you did to block your awareness of the love already in you.

SEPARATION ATTACKS AND THINKS THAT IT DESTROYED UNION, THAT IS, LOVE.

The desire to separate from the whole self, from God and all his extensions, sons of God as one unified self, is what prevents you from awareness of the love you already are. Love inheres in the awareness of being a part of unified self. Love is the awareness that one is in union with God and his creations.

The ego is the desire to be a separated self. The desire for the ego is the desire to be the opposite of eternal union; ego is the opposite of heaven, opposite of God and his real sons.

As long as you desire to be an ego, a separated self, and work for your ego's self-interest at the expense of other egos or people, you are not aware that you are part of unified self and you feel that you are not a part of love.

So, stop trying to be ego separated self, stop seeking self-interests at the expense of collective interests, and you know the love you already and always are.

Your real self is always unified spirit self, hence love. Ego separated self prevents your awareness of unified self, love. So, stop desiring ego, and you relapse into the love you already are.

You will of course still see the world of egos, the world of separated selves, the world of space, time, and matter but know that they are illusions, not real, and do not take them seriously. For now, play with the world of matter, space, and time and people in bodies. They actually do not exist except as in a dream but pretend that they exist, play with them, and do not take them seriously.

The ego tells you that love is caring for other people and is self-sacrificing in the sense of dying for other egos' good. Why should you die for other egos to live? What are those egos living for that is better than what you are living for? Do nothing for doing something is chasing the egos' idea of love such as chasing wealth to care for your dependents. Becoming rich is in the egos' world; you do not need egos wealth although if you stop chasing the ego, you already have material abundance, wealth beyond your belief.

GOD, HIS SONS, AND THE PHYSICAL UNIVERSE ARE INSIDE YOU.

Everything is inside one. The entire universe is inside one. Heaven, hell, and all people are inside one. Inside one are several parts including God. Yes, God is inside one.

The physical universe and the things in it are inside one; as we do at night when we sleep, dream, project out a world, and see ourselves in it, our day world is also in our minds, we sleep and project it out, and now see ourselves in it. The universe that seems external and solid is the mirror of our thinking; it represents our collective thinking, our thinking projected into pictures for us to experience them as if they are outside us.

God's mind called universal mind is already inside one. God is the whole and each of us is a part of God; the whole is inside each part.

The part is an extension of God and is like God but we can call it the son of God or soul. Inside, you are universal mind, God's mind, and your souls' mind.

God has two sides to it, God and his son, and two minds to it, universal mind and your soul's mind; inside you is also the ego.

The ego has two parts to it—the ego conscious mind and the part that we are aware of. The ego also has what Carl Jung called the collective unconscious mind. The collective unconscious mind can also be called the psychic mind; it contains the memory of all your experience from the moment you were born on earth, the memory of all people on earth, and the memory of all existence on earth. It is the repository of all human experiences.

The ego unconscious mind does not think logically. It goes from one topic to another. It is the part of mind that we see at night when we sleep and dream. As you know, in a dream, you easily go from one scene to another—at one moment are in the USA and in the next moment are in England. There is no logical sequence in dreams at night; that is because your mind is retrieving things from the ego unconscious mind and the collective unconscious mind and using them to construct its yarns, its poetry of dreams (you can actually interpret your dreams and see the meaning behind the seeming illogical yarns of the ego unconscious mind; Sigmund Freud said that dreams are teaching us stuff about us, albeit disguised; according to him, in dreams, wishes we could not gratify during daytimes, we gratify; there are also prophetic dreams where you can see something happen to people and it happens to them in day life).

The ego conscious mind and the ego unconscious mind, the psychic mind, die with your ego and the death of your body. What lives on when you physically die, the universal mind in you and your soul's mind?

God has mind and your real self, the son of God, has mind. Mind is the means of thinking by God and his sons.

God's self and your real self are eternal; God's mind, universal mind, and your real self's mind, the mind of the son of God, is eternal.

God's mind and your soul's mind are in you; they are not apart from you; you contain everything.

Whereas your ego and body will die and go out of existence and your ego conscious mind and ego unconscious mind will die and go out of existence, your real self does not die and its mind does not die.

Actually, you do not even have to die at the ego and body level. If you understand reality clearly and if you understand that you are the son of God, a part of God, and know that at that level, your soul is eternal, then you do not have to die.

You simply do what you came to earth to do and when you are done doing it, you use your soul's mind to make your body disappear. This means that you use your soul's mind to make the 64 elements in your body (carbon, hydrogen, oxygen, nitrogen, calcium, iron, magnesium, potassium, zinc, copper, etc.) and the trillions of electrons, protons, and neutrons in them to transform themselves to light.

Atoms (there are 92 types of atoms called elements) and their particles were made from light. You then see your body in light form. This is a fact, not mere conjecture. I have seen myself in light form and seen the world of light forms.

It is what Jesus did instead of dying. He used his mind to transfigure (transfiguration) his body, matter, to light. Enlightened and illuminated persons do it (en-light-ened; illu-mi-nated, means folks who know that they are light).

Remember the transfiguration scene in the bible where Jesus was with Moses and Elijah and all three of them were in light forms; that is what I am talking about; all three of them are enlightened to the fact that they are made of light, hence can appear in light forms.

You can use your soul's mind to transfigure your body to light form (your body is light transmuted to matter) and see you in the world of light forms, a world that still looks like our world except that everything in it is in light forms. That world is not heaven for it still has forms and there is space, time, and purified matter, light in it.

The world of light forms, like our world, is still illusory, except that it is an illusion where some love has entered, hence is better than our world of dense forms; in it is relative peace and joy. It is still not real; it is still insane but can be called happy insanity.

THE PURPOSE OF OUR LIVES ON EARTH IS FIRST TO FORGET OUR REAL SELVES AND LATER TO REMEMBER THOSE REAL SELVES.

The purpose of our lives on earth is first to see us as in body and matter, living in space and time. Here, we have forgotten our real selves, unified spirit self. We came here to forget our true selves. We live in this self-forgetfulness for a lifetime and or for many lifetimes.

The next purpose is to remember our true self as part of unified spirit self. Here, we die to identification with ego separated self and body and remember our deliberately forgotten real self.

THE WORLD OF LIGHT FORMS IS NOT HEAVEN.

Before we disappear from the earth, we have another dream, the dream of light forms. In this dream, we are still in form that looks like our bodies on earth but they are now in light forms. This is still dreaming and unreal, but it is our world purified, made forgiving, approaching, loving; it is at the gate of heaven, is paradise, purgatory, and so on.

Finally, we decide to fully awaken from the dream of self-forgetfulness and let go of the desire for separated existence, in dense or light form, and simply relapse to the awareness of ourselves as part of one unified spirit self with one unified mind.

You do not have to literally die in body to awaken, for, as noted above, you can use your purified mind to make the matter in your body transform into light forms and then disappear into formless God.

DEATH IS THE FINAL ILLUSION.

Death is the final illusion. Death is a trick we employ in convincing ourselves that we are in fact body and that body is real. If body and death are real, then we are separated from God and our real selves, God is dead, and his son's illusions prevail.

Sickness, sex, food, birth, and death are all means of making our bodies seem real to us—means of making us seem separated from God (this is a topic for another essay).

IT IS ABSOLUTELY CRUCIAL THAT WE STUDY SCIENCE.

In the meantime, you are on earth. While on earth, please do study science. Whereas science makes matter, space and time seem real, but through science, you can also understand that matter, space, and time do not exist, you banish them, and awaken from the sleep of self-forgetfulness.

I came to God-realization from playing with science, especially quantum mechanics. So, study science; it is fun. The physical universe is the plaything of the sons of God.

We wrote the play, the drama, and the script, and enact our mutually assigned roles in it; we made the dream seem real. The world is a matrix; a play.

We want to understand the laws of the universe we made at the physical level. So, study science to understand the laws of nothingness—the laws that make what does not exist, and the physical universe seem to exist.

When you have understood the laws of nothingness, science, then you choose, when you like, to let them go and remember that you are the dreamer, the playwright who made the physical universe and gave it its laws; you overlook them and wake up in unified spirit.

DISCUSSION

Let me reiterate that my approach to awakening from the dream of self-forgetfulness is not for all people. Most people still want to dream of self-forgetfulness and pretend that they are bodies in space and time. Let them dream on. When they have had enough dreaming, they will begin trying to awaken. Until they have the desire to awaken, what I write would not make sense to them.

Let me also state that there are many ways of awakening. Some are less cerebral. My path to awakening requires you to be a philosopher, psychologist, and a person with superior intelligence. I do not see how a person whose IQ is less than 130 can follow my writing. If you are of average (IQ of 85-115) or above-average (IQ of 116-130), my writing is not for you, look elsewhere and do not disturb your peace trying to understand what your mind cannot yet understand. My writing is for the two percent of mankind that has IQ of over 132, those with superior minds, and the geniuses of this world (to be a genius, your IQ must be over 140).

When you choose to become enlightened, you will manifest on earth as a smart child and set things up for you to inevitably start thinking about God and reality; you will do so from a very early age.

When you let go of your ego, you feel like you have no separated self; you feel empty of ego; you feel like your body is not real, is not there. You are now at peace. In that peace, you become an astonishing quick learner. What those with rigid egos take years to learn, you learn in a short time.

Our world of dense matter and the world of light forms are worlds of learning. In God, we know everything, but we deliberately choose to forget what we already know, place ourselves in a dream of not knowing, and start struggling to know.

You do learn things on earth, and when you enter the world of light forms, you continue learning. In the world of light forms, folks like Jesus, Buddha, and those who while on earth realized their real self as parts of God, still continue teaching those who have not understood what I am teaching here.

Topnotch scientists in the world of light forms continue teaching less gifted scientists. Folks like Albert Einstein and Isaac Newton keep teaching physics in the world of light forms (folks like me in the world of light forms keep teaching what I am teaching here).

From the world of light forms, we enter the formless world of God, the world of knowledge where there is no learning but knowing.

In God, everything I wrote here you already know, but you chose to forget them when you chose to leave heaven, manifest it on earth, and while on earth, relearn them.

CONCLUSION

You need do nothing to love. In your real self, the son of God, you know that you are joined to God and his other sons and that love is what glues all creation and its creator together. In heaven, you are always love.

You chose to forget love and now seem to be relearning what love is and folks like me undertake to teach you what love is.

Love is awareness of your eternal and changeless union with all creation and its creator.

However, in as much as you are currently on earth and see space and distance between you and other people, you are tempted to think that you can harm other people and not harm you and do what serves your self-interest at the expense of other people's interests. Do not follow that advice of the ego.

In the egos' world, only do what you believe serves your and our collective interests. This is actually what the Viennese psychiatrist, Alfred Adler, Sigmund Freud's second-in-command, taught when he said that to be neurotic is to seek to be superior to other persons and serve only your self-interest and to be healthy is to accept our mutual equality and serve social interests.

We, teachers of love, teachers of our union, and teachers of God, do not teach new things but teach the perennial wisdom of mankind in our specific languages. Everything that I said here, you can glean from Gnosticism, Hinduism, Buddhism, Taoism, Zen, and *A Course in Miracles*. I merely restated the truth in my prose but did not say anything that other persons have not said before me or will say after me. There is therefore no need for me to feel proud. Humility, the mark of God, enlightened persons, emanate from their awareness that everything they do is from God and that by their selves alone, they can do nothing.

The truth, concretized as the Holy Spirit in God's separated children, say the same things through each of us who decided to awaken to the knowledge that we are one and can be nothing else but one shared self.

Love is awareness of our one shared self and one shared mind. Remove your identification with the ego separated self and you know that you are already love and are living from love.

YOU SAID THAT YOU WILL NOT FORGIVE THE EXPERIMENTERS AT TUSKEGEE.

The teaching of Jesus Christ can be summarized as forgiveness; he asked his followers to forgive those who harmed them. He walked his talk by forgiving those who crucified him: "Father, forgive them for they do not know what they are doing." And you who call yourselves Christians will not forgive those who wronged you at Tuskegee while in Nigeria, you allow a few thieves to steal most of the country's money and you sing their praises. Are you not a thing of laughter? Jesus literally stood on his head and told people what to do to be saved, that forgiveness brings you back to love, which is to God, and no one understood him or does what he asked them to do. I came along and stand on my head trying in every way possible to say what Jesus told you but you refused to learn and indeed, you take pride in your refusal to learn the man's simple message that to forgive is to love. God, what shall we do with Africans? They have bastardized Christianity to mean tithing for pastors instead of working for those they forgive, hence love? These people make me throw up but something in me does not want to give up on them and move on with my life.

DO NOT ATTACK ANYONE UNLESS YOU EXPECT TO BE ATTACKED.

If you slap a person, what do you expect him to do? He will slap you in return. If he feels that you have more power, he will endure it waiting for a future time when he has the power to slap you. That is, he has not forgiven your slap.

The ego does not forgive anyone who slighted or harmed it and you ought to know that if you are an adult.

FORGIVENESS

The person you slapped may forgive you. He can only forgive you if he thinks that you are foolish and did what you did out of stupidity given that you ought to know about the human beings' tendency to seek vengeance. If the person you hurt believes that he is not his ego and body and that you slapped him in a dream and since what is done in dreams have not been done, you have not slapped him, so he overlooks your slapping him, then you're wrong.

The lesson is to not slap anyone unless you desire to be slapped or forgiven. Do not call anyone a put-down name unless you want to be called a put-down name, or worse, killed.

EGO-LESSNESS LEADS TO FORGIVENESS.

If you have ego pride and someone insults you, you do not forgive him, you seek revenge and pursue that person until you take him down, or he takes you down. The result is a world at war. If you have no ego pride, you shine off the evil people do to you and move on living peacefully and happily.

THE EGO SAYS FORGIVE AND DIE AND IT DOES NOT WANT TO DIE.

The ego says that you cannot forgive insult and attack on you unless you want to die. You are attacked, enslaved, and if you do not fight back, you are enslaved or die. Therefore, telling the world of egos to forgive people is a waste of time. The world is composed of egos and they are here to defend themselves, not forgive anyone.

Jesus forgave those who killed him, died, and left this world. If you did what Jesus did, forgive, you die and leave this world. The ego, not realizing that Jesus did not die but resurrected from death that to live as ego in body is to be metaphorically dead, preaches bearing grievances and seeking vengeance.

DO YOU FORGIVE THOSE WHO WRONGED YOU?

Telling other people to forgive is easy, but do you, the talker forgive those who wronged you, or are you very vindictive? The message is for me to forgive, let my ego and body die, and my spirit to live in peace and joy.

IN GOD, WE ARE ALL INNOCENT BUT ON EARTH, WE ARE NOT.

IN GOD, BECAUSE WE ARE IN THE STATE OF UNION, WE CANNOT HURT ANYONE ELSE FOR WE KNOW THAT WHAT WE DO TO PEOPLE WE DO TO OURSELVES BUT ON EARTH, IF YOU ATTACK FOLKS, THEY WILL FEEL HURT AND DEFEND THEMSELVES BY ATTACKING YOU.

IF YOU STEAL FROM FOLKS, YOU EXPECT TO BE CAUGHT AND PUNISHED

IF YOU ENGAGE IN HURTFUL ACTIVITIES SUCH AS RAPING WOMEN AND ABUSING CHILDREN, YOU EXPECT TO BE CAUGHT AND PUNISHED, EVEN KILLED.

DELUSION CAN BE SHOWN BY THE DESIRE TO MODERNIZE OTHER PEOPLE WHILE RETAINING YOUR GRANDIOSE EGO.

I have a grandiose ego. That big ego feels belittled by the presence of developed and powerful Westerners. I feel furious having a white man tell me what to do. I ask, who the hell you think that you are telling me what to do? That is my pride speaking.

To make me and Africans powerful, I want to modernize Africans in a hurry. I was willing to kill many Africans to develop them. Developing them makes my ego feel powerful and important, superior, and compensates for its feeling of inferiority.

In reality, Africans are so backward that it would take, at least, two hundred years before they reach the level other people are at. Getting them to give up their tendency to seeking shortcuts and taking and giving bribery will take, at least, a century to stop.

Leave Africans alone and deal with your big ego, shrink it, and leave Africans to shrink their egos when they want to. Salvation is for me now.

I am saved when I let go of my ego. Salvation is to deliberately let one's ego and body die so that one resurrects to Christ, the son of God who is as God created him. To be saved is to be born again.

God created us his unified sons, but we separated from him and from each other, to go seek grandiose egos and miscreate the world to fit our egos. Now, one must voluntarily die to the ego and be reborn in Christ.

Christ is love. This means that one must love at all times. On earth, folks do wrongs to another; to love them is to forgive them.

Salvation then means forgiving those who wronged one. If you forgive, you feel peaceful and happy; you are brought to the gate of heaven. Heaven is perfect love.

Perfect love can only exist in a unified spiritual state. On earth, we are separated and cannot have perfect love even if we forgive, but we can attain attenuated, imperfect love through forgiveness; forgiveness brings us to the gate of heaven, and thereafter, heaven opens its door and welcomes us into its perfect love, peace, and happiness.

WHAT WAS WAS WHAT WAS. WHAT IS IS WHAT IS. WHAT WILL BE WILL BE IF YOU FIGHT FOR IT.

We devote enormous time and energy to fretting over what took place in the past. Despite our crying over spilled milk, we really cannot recoup the milk (in thermodynamics, this is called the law of entropy—you cannot retrieve all the heat or energy that is spilled into the environment); we cannot change the past. But we can learn from the past to improve the present.

What is in the present is generally the product of what was in the past. What is in the present is what is in the present. We may not like many things that are in the present. All that we really can do is work to improve the present and especially the future.

Describe the future you want and work for it and that is just about all that you can do. I desire publicly paid health insurance for all and publicly paid education, at all levels, for all; they do not exist at the present; I fight for them, and hopefully, they will come into being in the future. That is all that I can do. I cannot change the past but I can help shape the future.

Some people dwell on a past that they know they cannot change; they dwell on the ills of the present and describe it in detail but do not work for a better future. They are escapists wasting their time.

Don't talk to me about such past issues as slavery and discrimination; talk to me about how to prevent them in the present and future; I cannot change them in the past.

What do you call this type of philosophy? I call it idealistic-realism, not capitalism, socialism, democratic socialism (in Scandinavia), or market socialism (China), but plain idealism mixed with realism.

Human beings are both idealistic and realistic; to say that they are one or the other is not true; however, people tend to have proclivity to either idealism or to realism.

GOOD FRIDAY, DEATH, AND RESURRECTION ARE METAPHORS OF TRANSCENDING THE EGO TO LIVE FROM LOVE.

Ozodi Thomas Osuji, Ph.D.

THE MEANING OF EASTER, SALVATION, REDEMPTION, AND DELIVERANCE

I enjoyed reading your write-up called Bad Friday (below). I was tempted to respond to it point by point but instead, decided to provide an alternative to the Christian story of Good Friday and Easter.

Over time, I found that it does not help fighting with any one's theology but instead, it merely posits a view of spirituality that makes sense to me and leave it to other people to think about it and if it makes sense to them for them to accept it and if not, to reject it.

Christianity's central teaching probably inheres in the story of a Jewish man called Joshua Ben Joseph, who the Greeks called Jesus Christ, dying on Good Friday and resurrecting on Easter Sunday. He was supposedly crucified on Good Friday and on Easter Sunday, resurrected from death (that is to say he was dead for two days, not three days, for Friday to Sunday is two days). His feat of resurrecting from death apparently gives Christians the consolation that they, too, would die and resurrect from death.

Mankind is afraid of death and if Jesus could die and resurrect from death, then his followers too would die and resurrect from death. Jesus gave his followers the faith that they too would do what he did, die, overcome death, and resurrect from it, if not in three days, then in the fullness of time.

Many Christians believe that although Jesus is currently in heaven, that in the future, he would return to earth, have all dead persons resurrect from death, and would sit in (last) judgment over mankind, judge the good and the bad and the bad would be cast away (to hell?) and the good would live with him in a new world called New Jerusalem or New Israel.

The people selected to live with Jesus in his new Israel are called new men. Their old self is dead and now they live through their new self, the self that obeys the will of God. The old self is dead and a new self is reborn in them. This is the story of death and rebirth that Christians talk about.

A Christian says that he is dead to his old self and is rebirthed in a new self, the Christ self; Christ has come to his life and world a second time.

Christ was born when God created him as his son; Christ died when the son of God forgot his oneness with God and like the prodigal son, went on a journey to go live separated from God.

Christ is reborn in the Christian's awareness when the prodigal son realizes that he cannot separate from his father and brothers and returns. To return to his father, he must acknowledge his mistake and error in going away from his father, God. Mistakes must be acknowledged for the truth to be accepted.

Jesus leads his newborn people in his new world for a thousand years and thereafter, they would be raptured into heaven. Heaven is deemed to be above the earth, up in the sky.

Christians believe that after they die, they would resurrect from death, as their savior and Lord Jesus supposedly did. Let us examine why they have this belief.

FEAR OF DEATH, FINITUDE, OBLIVION, AND DESIRE FOR RESURRECTION FROM DEATH

On earth, we are born and do die. We all would rather not die. But the fact is that we do die. The next best thing to not dying is to resurrect from death. Since Jesus promised that eventually, we would resurrect from death, we can understand why those who live in fear of death, finitude, and oblivion, flock to his religion.

THE CHRISTIAN STORY OF CREATION; ADAM AND EVE IN THE GARDEN OF EDEN

Jews, Christians, and Muslims, the three Abrahamic religions, accept the story of creation found in the Jewish Tora, Christian's Old Testament, in the section called Genesis. Here, it is reported that God created Adam and Eve and placed them in a Garden of Eden. He asked them to eat all fruits in the garden but not to eat the fruits of a particular tree.

They were tempted by Satan in the guise of a snake (snake denotes deceiver in Christian world view). The Snake, Satan, told Eve to eat the forbidden fruit. She did and got her husband to also eat it. In so doing, both of them had disobeyed God as they had done what God asked them not to do.

As a result of disobeying God, they were cast out of the Garden of Eden, out of paradise where all their needs were met by God. Subsequently, they had to work for their food and eventually die. The wages of sin, disobedience to God, is death.

ORIGINAL SIN, FALL FROM GOD'S GRACE: DESCENT INTO DARKNESS AND THE NEED FOR REDEMPTION

By eating the apple, doing what God told them not to do, human beings' ancestors are said to have committed the original sin of disobeying God, and as a result, they were cast out of paradise and have to suffer and die.

Original sin is now inherited by all the children of Adam, us. We are now said to be born in sin and live in sin.

We must be saved from sin, redeemed from sin, and delivered from sin. When we are saved from sins, we would no longer suffer and die. We would return to our original state in paradise where God provided for us.

JESUS THE REDEEMER OF MANKIND FROM ADAM'S SIN

Adam and Eve sinned by disobeying God. Jesus is said to have paid for our sins by coming to the earth and voluntarily agreeing to completely obey the will of God. As a result of obeying the will of God, since God requires him to die for our sins, Jesus had to die on the cross. Now that he has fully obeyed God and died, he was rewarded by God with resurrection from death.

On the third day, God raised him from death, and forty days later, he ascended to heaven in the sky where he now stays at the righthand side of God waiting for the day of judgment when he would return to judge the good and the bad and live with the good in New Jerusalem, new earth, and thereafter, they would be raptured to heaven.

Jesus' death has washed out Adam's and our subsequent sins. If we believe in him, we are reborn in God and our sins are washed away.

The meaning of Good Friday is that Jesus completely obeyed the will of God and died for the sins of man since Adam and Eve.

On Easter Sunday, he is rewarded with resurrection and returned to living in paradise where his father provides for all his needs. If we believe in him, we shall also resurrect from death and return to living in the Garden of Eden, paradise, where God's grace gives us all we need to live on.

PURE REASON CANNOT ACCEPT ORIGINAL SIN, DEATH, AND RESURRECTION.

From the perspective of pure reason, this story does not add up and at best, is a metaphor. It is a metaphor representing mankind's fate of dying and hopes for resurrection from death.

Apparently, mankind believed that they must have offended an angry, vindictive God and he relegated them to suffering and death and that if they do something to please him, die, that he would forgive them and give them eternal life with him.

Did mankind do something bad, disobey the will of an angry, vengeful, and vindictive God? That is what Jews, Christians, and Muslims apparently believe.

I am not a Jew, Christian, or Muslim. I am an Igbo. For our present purpose, I do not feel guilty for any alleged sin I must have committed to making our lives full of suffering and death.

I know that we are born, grow up, age, get weak, and die. It seems unfair to me that this would be our fate. Be that as it may, I do not attribute it to some alleged sin I and my ancestors must have committed in the past.

The Christian notion of original sin and the need for redemption does not make sense to me. I see it as a metaphor teaching a useful lesson about our living on earth. However, if reinterpreted, it may even help us to understand our lives.

MY STORY OF CREATION

Without beating around the bush, let me share with you my story of how this world came into being, my story of creation, and my creation myth. I call it a myth because while it approximates the truth, it is not the entire truth.

Scientists' Big Bang story of the origin of the universe of space, time, and matter resembles the truth of material things but is not the entire truth for it leaves out the spiritual aspect of people. People have a spiritual and material aspect.

In my mythology, there is God. God is not a person. God is life itself. There is one God; that is, there is one life. That one life is creative. It is always creating other lives all of who are like it and are it.

God, life, created you and I. You and I are now parts of God. We are parts of God but not the entirety of God for life includes you, me, animals, and other living things; life is inside us and also outside us.

We, the parts of life, the sons of God decided to experience life in a physical universe of space, time, and matter. Why not?

We are eternal and can experience whatever type of life we want to experience. In this particular mode, we made us live in body that we know will age and die. We also know that in spirit, we are eternal, so there is no need to fear death, for death is ephemeral and transitory.

We, the sons of God, the parts of God, the parts of life, as it were, went to sleep, and in our sleep, dream this present universe. We invented this universe as scientists tell us that the universe evolved.

SCIENCE'S STORY OF CREATION

According to science's story of creation, it is a story, a myth, for it has not been conclusively proved that 13.8 billion years ago, a point of light, not larger than the period at the end of this sentence, came out of nowhere. It grew hot and exploded.

The particles of light, photons, from the explosion joined to form electrons, quarks, and quarks formed protons and neutrons. Within a minute, protons and neutrons joined to form nuclei of the simplest atoms, hydrogen, lithium, and helium.

The universe expanded at an inflationary rate at a speed greater than the speed of light, 186, 282 miles per second. The inflationary speed apparently prevented the universe from collapsing back to itself.

400, 000 years later, nuclei captured electrons and atoms of hydrogen were formed. For millions of years, the universe remained a sea of hydrogen.

Thereafter, an asymmetric thing occurred (one of several events called anthropic accidents that made the existence of the universe possible); space occurred in the cloud of hydrogen.

Gravity acted on each clump of hydrogen; heat and pressure forced hydrogen to fuse into helium. The fusion led to giving up light and heat.

Light and heat traveled out of the core of the stars and escaped as the light we call starlight. The original stars were massive in size and a few million years later, exhausted their hydrogen and began synthesizing other elements, such as carbon and oxygen; when nucleosynthesis reached iron, the star became very hot, expanded, and exploded in supernova.

The tremendous heat accompanying the supernova created all elements beyond iron; there are 92 naturally occurring elements in the universe.

These elements, aka stardust, were spilled into space and gather as nebula. In time, the nebula collapses into medium-sized stars, planets, comets, and asteroids.

Our star, the sun, and its nine planets, were formed from exploded large stars. Our sun, nine planets, asteroids, and comets have been around for 4.5 billion years. The sun has enough hydrogen to keep fusing helium for another five billion years.

In about a billion years, our star will start fusing other elements, feel hotter, and expand. In three billion years, all water on earth would have been dried up by the hot sun. In five billion years, the sun explodes and its inner core collapses to white dwarf star (when huge stars explode, their cores collapse to either black holes or neutron stars; in black holes, not even light can escape from its events horizons; in neutron stars, the star rotate at the mind-dizzying rate).

Stars aggregate into groups called galaxies. There are over 200 billion galaxies, each having over 200 billion stars. Our Milky Way galaxy has over 200 billion stars and it takes light over 100, 000 years to travel across our galaxy.

The galaxies are expanding away from each other. In about two trillion years, they would be so separated from each other that the universe would be too cold and stars explode into elements, the elements decay to electrons, protons, and neutrons, and those eventually decay to cold radiation, photons, light. The universe that began in hot light ends in cold light.

In the meantime, on planet earth, in a pool of water heat from light, combined the 64 elements that formed cells into cells, and this formed biological life forms like animals, human beings, and plants. So far, we know that biological life forms exist on planet earth but have not discovered life on exoplanets.

Although science's story of creation has many holes in it, I do not plan to point them out here. Let me just say that science revises its story of creation and will no doubt revise the present one. For now, it seems to help scientists to do their work.

SELF-FORGETTING AND THE EGO

On earth, we forgot our real selves which are parts of God, sons of God, in Christian terminology, Christ. I call our real self the unified self, the self that knows that it is joined to all creation and its creator, life. All parts of life, God, share one life, one self, and one mind.

In God, we share one self and one mind; we are unified and are one. But on earth, we have separated selves, egos that identify with our bodies and look after our self-interests.

The earthly self, the separated self, the ego, the human personality, the self-concept, sees itself as apart from other selves and does what serves its self-interests, occasionally serving other people's interests, but when push comes to shove, serve one's interests at the expense of other people's interests. We are all self-centered, selfish.

The self that serves its interests at the expense of other selves' interests is the human ego. That self is at war with other ego selves; hence, our world is a place of war.

Inside us, the ego is also at war with our real selves, hence we live in internal conflict. There are, as it were, two selves in us, the false ego-self and the real spirit self, and both are at war. Eventually, we must resolve this war for one or the other.

We resolve the war by allowing the false ego-self to metaphorically die in us (metaphorically because it is a dream self, is not real, and the unreal cannot die). When we voluntarily let the ego in us to die so that we live from the real self, the son of God, the Christ, the part of life in us, we tend to have recovered our true selves, and then we live in peace and joy.

GOOD FRIDAY IS SYMBOLIC OF THE DEATH OF THE EGO; EASTER SUNDAY IS SYMBOLIC OF RESURRECTION OF THE CHRIST IN US.

Good Friday is the symbol of a human being allowing his ego, false self to metaphorically die. On Easter Sunday, his real self was resurrected, reborn in him. Christ, his real self, came to his life a second time.

Christ is the self that God created, a self we allowed to die when we denied it and identified with the false ego-self housed in body. When we allow the ego and its body to be crucified and die, then the Christ in us, the real self, is reborn in our awareness.

This does not mean literal physical death for the physical self does not exist and what does not exist does not die. It means consciously deciding to be a loving and forgiving self and not be the old self that is unforgiving that bears grievances and seeks revenge to die. We are talking transformation of character here.

Good Friday does not have to be taken literally but as symbolic, as metaphor of a man choosing to die to his ego-self and be reborn, on Easter day (which is any day one chooses to be reborn) in him. Seen in this metaphoric light, Jesus died on the cross and resurrected to his real self. He did not literally die and resurrect from death.

Why should he literally die when our lives in bodies and egos are not real and are dream things? While we see ourselves as on earth, in ego and body, we are in unified spirit as part of God, part of one unified life.

If you see the drama of Jesus Christ in this light, you might accept the story as meaningful for you. It means that you have to willingly let your ego false self to die and you live from your real self, the loving and forgiving part of you.

If you do so, you would actually occasionally see yourself disappear from physical state and experience yourself first in light form and finally in formless unified life, aka God.

DISCUSSION

I share your skepticism about the story of Jesus told in the Bible and as propagated by the Christian church. It cannot be true.

As you hinted at, a loving God could not have planned for his son to die to assuage his apparent blood-thirsty self. Jesus was not crucified on the cross.

The idea of Jesus being crucified on the cross is metaphoric. Living in ego is being crucified. We who identify with ego are crucified and live in pain.

Actually, to live in ego and body is to be metaphorically dead. We on earth in ego and body are metaphorically dead. That is, we have forgotten our true self, unified spirit self, aka the son of God, the Christ.

We resurrect from the death that is our earthly living by returning to the awareness of our real selves, spirit selves, souls who are one with God.

You talked about how Jesus was hated by the religious establishment of his time. If one speaks the truth, one will be hated by the sham, phony religionists that call themselves pastors and ministers of God.

You concluded by saying that God does not accept human sacrifices. You are correct. The idea of animal blood sacrifices was part of old Middle Eastern beliefs. Abraham wanted to sacrifice his son, Isaac, to God to please God. Terrorists today kill and sacrifice people to please their blood-thirsty Allah.

In my religious philosophy, God is absolute love; love does not harm anyone or wish anyone harm.

We reach God by forgiving and loving all human beings, ourselves included, not by sacrificing human beings for their alleged sin of separating from God.

God's will is that he and his sons are one unified self. We are one with God. We cannot separate from God for to separate from him is to have a will that is more powerful than God's will.

All we did is be in God, in eternal union, sleep, and dream that we are separated from God.

CONCLUSION

Good Friday is the symbol of the day human beings allow their old selves, their egos, to die. Easter Sunday is the symbol of human beings allowing their real selves, the sons of God, Christ, to be reborn in them.

Good Friday and Easter are symbols of death and resurrection, not actual events in the world of space, time, and matter. In our world, there is no evidence that an actual Jew called Emmanuel Ben Joseph lived in the first century AD.

Romans kept meticulous records of their governmental activities and they did not record crucifying a Jew in Palestine in 33 AD.

During the third century, a Jewish historian called Josephus wrote that he heard that the Romans did once crucify a rabbi giving them trouble but he did not tell us who he was and when the rabbi was crucified.

Therefore, it is necessary to assume that the story of Jesus is not literal but metaphoric rendition of man's need to die to his ego and be reborn in his real self as a part of life, the Christ, a loving person.

The ego, old self in us, hates, bears grievances, and seeks revenge for the wrong done to him. The new self, the Christ in us, the Buddha in us, the son of God in us, forgives those who wronged him for he knows that the wrongs they did to him was done in dreams and what was done in dreams have not been done in reality.

In reality, all of us remain as God created us, sinless, for we have not separated from him; to sin is to separate from God.

We are guiltless, holy, and innocent. Treat all people as innocent, holy, and guiltless and see them feel happy and peaceful; treat people as guilty and punish them and they shrivel up.

As you, Ufuoma Bernard, can see, what I wrote in response to your piece is my own theology; it does not in any way refute or disprove what you wrote. What I summarized here is written at length in my many essays, articles, and books. Check out some of my books. Buy them from Amazon.com.

Good Friday means the day we allow our ego separated selves to die; Easter means the day we allow our real selves, unified selves, to replace our ego separated selves; Easter is when we live through our forgiving, hence loving self.

Ordinarily, we live in the world of illusions, the make-belief world, when we see ego and its body, space, and time as real. When we break through the various illusions, see them as unreal, and live as forgiving and loving unified selves, we are now born again, reborn in Christ. This is the message of Easter, not a gory story of a man being crucified on Friday and dying for our sins; we do not have sins for we did not separate from God; however, we do sleep, dream, and do bad things to each other in the dream on earth. When we do only loving things to one another, we are resurrected from ego death and live Christ love.

WITHOUT LOVE, PEOPLE ARE ANIMALS. WITHOUT LOVE, YOU CAN DO WHATEVER YOU WANT TO PEOPLE, INCLUDING KILLING THEM.

Mass murderers, such as Adolf Hitler, had no love for themselves and for people and therefore, could kill people without qualms or conscience. Conscience arises if you see people as more than animals.

Love makes you see people as more than animals. Ultimately, love is rooted in spirit; to love, you must see people as rooted in spirits.

The ultimate spirit is God. If you see people as the children of God, you will love them and not desire to harm them.

Loveless people, especially atheists, easily harm people and rationalize their antisocial actions (and you do the same to them and treat them lovelessly, as animals and discard them; after all, they do not have a lack of reasoning).

Parents must love their children for unloved children tend to grow up, more or less, like robots, impersonal in their thinking and can harm other people given their lack of love, attachment, and bonding with people. Love your children and neighbors if you want to prevent mass murderers and other anti-social persons.

HAPPY EASTER TO ALL PEOPLE.

EASTER MEANS THAT YOUR OLD, HATEFUL EGO-SELF DIED ON GOOD FRIDAY AND YOUR NEW CHRIST, LOVING SELF, WAS REBORN ON EASTER SUNDAY. ARE YOU NOW A NEW PERSON?

Easter means that your old, hateful ego separated self died on Good Friday and your new self, the unified, forgiving, and loving self is reborn in you on Easter Sunday, today.

Are you now a new person, a forgiving and loving person, or are you still the same old, fear-driven, unforgiving, and unloving self?

THE AGNOSTIC DOES NOT KNOW THAT THERE IS GOD OR NO GOD BUT HE THINKS ALONG THE LINES BELOW.

If we assume there is no God, then the concatenation of the physical universe of space, time, and matter produced intelligent animals that ask questions about the universe and want to understand the universe. If that is the case, then the universe is magical and miraculous.

It is a miracle for a dumb universe to produce intelligent persons. Therefore, the odds of the universe having intelligence, aka God, in it are very high. This is the agnostic's credo:

WOMEN'S GENITAL ORGANS SMELL AWFUL BUT MEN DESIRE THEM AND IN SO DOING, GIVE THEM VALUE. THIS IS SYMBOLIC.

HUMAN EXISTENCE IS NOTHING BUT WE GIVE IT VALUE BY DESIRING IT; AND WHO ARE THE PERSONS DOING THE DESIRING AND VALUING OF NOTHINGNESS? IT IS GOD'S SONS, SO YOU STILL MUST VALUE PEOPLE DESPITE THE NOTHINGNESS OF THEIR EGOS AND BODIES.

HEREIN LIES THE SO-CALLED MYSTERY OF BEING; PEOPLE AND THEIR WORLD ARE NOTHING AND DO NOT EXIST EXCEPT AS A DREAM YET YOU MUST VALUE THE SPIRIT IN THEM. IF YOU CHOOSE TO NOT VALUE THEM, THEN

YOU DO NOT VALUE YOURSELF. IF YOU CHOOSE TO KILL THEM, WHICH YOU CAN DO, YOU HAVE CHOSEN TO KILL YOU IN THE DREAM BUT IN REALITY, YOU CANNOT KILL PEOPLE OR KILL YOU FOR ALL CREATION AND ITS CREATOR ARE ETERNAL; HITLER AND THOSE HE KILLED ARE RIGHT NOW IN GOD AS PART OF HIS ETERNAL SELF. OF COURSE, IT IS BETTER NOT TO GIVE ANYONE PAIN AND HURT BY KILLING ANYONE EVEN IN THE DREAM. IT IS BETTER TO GIVE FOLKS HAPPY DREAMS AND GIVE YOU HAPPY DREAM VIA THE HOLY SPIRIT PART OF YOU INSTEAD OF GIVING YOU NIGHTMARISH DREAM VIA THE EGO PART OF YOU.

YOU ARE ALWAYS CONNECTED WITH ALL THINGS AND CANNOT SEPARATE FROM THEM SO SEPARATION IS IMPOSSIBLE ON EARTH AND IN HEAVEN. ON EARTH, YOU HAVE THE ILLUSION THAT YOU ARE SEPARATED FROM OTHER THINGS.

YOU ARE ALWAYS IN LOVE WITH ALL THINGS BUT THINK THAT YOU ARE NOT.

GOD IS IN EVERYTHING; THEREFORE, EVERYTHING THAT HAPPENS TO YOU IS BY GOD.

SEPARATION FROM OTHER EGOS AND FROM GOD IS IMPOSSIBLE SO YOUR EGO DEFENSES ARE FOOLISH.

On earth, we are dreaming and see ourselves as separated ego selves in the world of space, time, and matter and see other people seem to do hurtful things to us and we defend ourselves; the earth is ego and body defense.

In defending your ego and body, you attack union, love, and seemingly separate from them and form special love relationships that maintain your ego and body. The defense and protection are what make you feel like you are in ego.

If you stop defending your ego and body, you know that the ego and body, space, and time, do not exist except as in a dream and you experience union, love.

That is, whereas defense makes you feel separated, you are at no point separated from God and all his creations; you just deceived yourself into believing that you are separated from them and separation seems real to you.

When you stop ego defenses, you do not die; you simply experience union, love, peace, joy, and formlessness and thereafter, make another choice to be in light forms and then in dense forms. All your choices are dreams, but they seem like things that happen to you, not your choice.

Since God is everywhere, what happens to you by other people, animals, trees, or diseases were done to you by God and since you are God, were done to you by you. It is all a matter of interpretation.

See someone do bad to you and know that you did that bad to you. Why? It is to experience separation from that person hence separation from your real self, and anger at that person, hence anger at you.

Solution: do not do any bad to you through other people. Reinterpret what other people did to you and see them as what you did to you; if rejected by others, you did not want their acceptance, hence you rejected you through them; if not given a job by other persons, you did not want that job and made it seem like other persons denied you a job that you can do with your eyes closed.

Now go do the job that you can do and give it to you by you, either through other persons or directly by you. Create your own job.

LOVE THE SPIRIT IN WOMEN AND OVERLOOK THEIR BODIES.

The average woman is narcissistic and loves her ego and body; women generally want men to love their egos and bodies and form special love relationships with them; in such a relationship, the men perpetually tell them how lovely and beautiful their egos and bodies are and value them. If men do not value their bodies, they believe that such men could destroy them and since men destroy what they do not value, women fear that if men do not like them, they could destroy them. They call such men misogynists.

If you do not value the human body, especially sexual organs, the trick is to love women's spirits and overlook their egos and bodies, for if one focuses on their egos and bodies, one is focusing on one's ego and body, hence is away from one's spirit where one needs to be.

You must remember that despite the nothingness, worthlessness, and valuelessness of the human ego and body in men and women, those people are no other but the sons of God and must be loved. At root, people are love and you must love them.

In God, spirit, people have total worth, so you must value their spirit while overlooking their bodies.

THE SON OF GOD SLEEPS AND PROJECTS OUT THE PHYSICAL UNIVERSE AND HIMSELF AS THE EGO IN IT.

The son of God sleeps and dreams, and in his dream, projects out the physical universe of space, time, and matter; he projects a substitute, replacement self that adapts to the world of space, time, and matter he made, the ego into that dream universe. The ego then interacts with the world.

The ego and the physical universe are the same in that both are false, do not exist, and will die. Both ego and the universe must be transcended for they are dreams and do not last longer than the dream.

What exists eternally is the son of God. While in the dream, if the son of God remembers that he made the dream and the ego, he can change his mind and know that he is one with God and all creation and overlook the ego and its world and is now the Christ.

THE REALIST ACCEPTS OTHER EGOS. THE IDEALIST WANTS TO ANNIHILATE OTHER EGOS.

The idealist wants to annihilate other egos and superimpose his ego on them; the realist accepts his ego and other ego's quest for power, works with them, with people and political systems, and seeks a way to have some influence on people but not change them or make them obey him.

The realist adapts and succeeds in the world for he acknowledges the other egos. The idealist fails in the world for he negates other egos. He then lives in his own world as a deluded person, such as Dr. O, the ultimate religious idealist.

The realist wants shared ego power whereas the idealist wants total absolute ego power which he hides and calls power from God.

LIVING FROM LOVE # 2

THREE LEVELS OF BEING: ONE REAL AND TWO FICTIONAL

There are three levels of being, one real and two fictional; they are:
Living from God, unified spirit self (real);
Living from the ego separated self (unreal);
Living from the Holy Spirit's approximate unified self (unreal but approximate reality).

GOD IS ALSO CALLED UNIFIED SPIRIT SELF.

God is the union of all things as one thing. God is one thing that is simultaneously all things. God is one self that gave rise to infinite selves. One God extended himself to all of us; all of us are parts of one God; there is no space, time, and matter between us and God and us and each other.

God is not a person or thing. God is spirit. That means that he is not this or that thing but all things. One God extends to infinite selves and is all of them and they are him but not all of him; where God ends and each of his extensions, creations begin nowhere.

We are always in God and cannot be outside God for he is our real self. How can we leave God if he is in us? And how can he leave us if we are in him?

Our real self is in unified spirit self. Each of us is a part of God, in Christian language, a son of God. God is in each of us and we are in God and in each other; separation is impossible; if separation occurred, both God and his sons would die and nothing would exist.

THE EGO SEPARATED SELF, THE ILLUSION

While we are in God and are eternal, permanent, and changeless, we are free to do whatever we want to do. Every manner of thinking goes through our minds. Thoughts emanate from nowhere and pass through our minds. We do not originate most of our thoughts and can pursue those we want to pursue.

A thought flashed through our minds—the thought of becoming greater than God, the thought of creating God instead of him creating us, the thought of living as the opposite of God when God is unified with all his creations, and the thought encouraging us to separate from God.

We cannot separate from God for we are eternal parts of God and each other but we can pretend to have separated from him. Knowing that we cannot separate from God, we thought, why not seem separated from God for the experience? How, we cast a sort of magical spell on our minds, Maya, and went to sleep and in our sleep, dream that we are now separated from God. That dream is our present existence in the universe of space, time, and matter.

(We do have all kinds of thoughts and all kinds of dreams and experiences in infinite universes; heaven is not boring.)

We on earth, in space, time, and matter, now seem to have separated from God and from each other. We see each other housed in bodies and do not see God.

God is not perceptual and cannot be seen; he is invisible, formless spirit that is everywhere and is everywhere.

While still in God, we now see ourselves in bodies and develop substitute and replacement selves called egos. Egos are the sense of separated selves housed in bodies.

Egos are not real; they are mere ideas or self-concepts we have of ourselves. Ego self-concepts are not given to us by God; we conjointly made self-concepts or egos for each other; we learn our egos in the dream of separation and of real self-forgetfulness on earth. Because they were not created by God, they are transitory, ephemeral, and can be let go at any time we wish to do so.

Egos adapt to the exigencies of the world of separation—space, time, and matter. Each ego identifies with a specific body and sees other bodies as not part of it; it defines its interests as separate and different from other people's interests. It does what harms other selves and they do what harms it.

All egos are at war with each other; they attack each other and defend against others' attacks and expected attacks. The ego is always defended and believes that if it is not defended, it will die.

Each ego does what the logic of its body disposes it to do—to survive in body and as a separated self. This is not a moral issue but existential. If one inherited a weak and pained body, one must do what that body disposes one to do; conversely, if one inherited a robust, healthy body, one must do what that body disposes one to do.

In as much as it is one and all of us that chose separation, we chose the type of body, parents, and society we are born in; there are no accidents in our lives.

The ego is always looking out for itself. It does not know love for love is that state of being where one knows that one is one with all beings and does what serves everyone's interests.

HOLY SPIRIT

On earth, egos are at war because they define their interests as different from each other. In the same person, a different level of being that Christians call the Holy Spirit can dawn on his mind and he realizes that logically, he cannot really separate from the whole, aka God, and from other selves.

Whether you know it or not, you are always a part of the whole; you are always part of all people; separation, space, time, and matter are illusions.

When you realize that you and all people are one, you realize that whatever you do, other people played a role in it for you and whatever other people do, you played roles for them to do it.

You are literally one with other people and did what they did and they did what you did. Thus, there is no use blaming you or other people for our mutual attacks. You develop the capacity to forgive.

Forgiveness means that you ignore what other people did to harm your ego and body; you overlook their harms, still love them, and work to correct their and your wrongs.

On earth, forgiveness does not mean allowing other people to harm folks. If a man is running around murdering, stealing from, or raping people, you do not overlook it and say that he is doing so in dreams; on earth, he is inflicting dream pain on dream people, so you arrest him and jail him, and hopefully, teach him love. If he does not want to love, kill him, for there is no one killed. You merely removed him from the present dream and he will have other dream states to experience.

To live from the Holy Spirit is to while in the world of separation, know that you are one with God and all people, and do only what serves all peoples' mutual interests, as you understand them. When you work for social good, you live in relative peace with your neighbors. This is not the absolute peace of God.

In God, we are all unified as one formless spirit self. On earth, we are in seeming separation and therefore, cannot have perfect peace.

Living from the Holy Spirit will give you relative peace, not perfect peace. You can only have perfect peace and joy when you completely let go of the desire for a separated self, give up identification with body, and become aware that you are part of unified spirit self.

LACK OF LOVE

God, heaven, unified spirit, is perfect love. Love glues all the infinite sons of God to each other and to God so that where one ends and another begins is nowhere; they are in each other and yet having selves.

In heaven is perfect love. When we decided to separate from each other, even though we cannot separate from each other, what we wish is powerful for it produced the world we now seem to live in; desire, as Gautama Buddha correctly surmised, produced our egos and world; a desire that produced a universe of galaxies, stars, planets, human beings, animals, and trees is not powerless.

We currently seem separated from each other and see ourselves as separated selves living in space and time.

As Buddha also correctly assessed, our desires produced our world and suffering and we end our suffering and world when we give up the desire for separated existence and return to unified living in God.

The desire to separate from God, the whole, is the desire to separate from love. On earth, each of us is separated from God and separated from love. In truth, we cannot separate from God and love; we are always in love, always in God, but in the present, have awareness of lack of love.

Separation is attack on union, attack on love, attack on God, and attack on one's real self and on other sons of God. On earth, we have attacked love and live lovelessly (not really for love is life and if we have no love, we would not be alive; we merely cover our ever-present life in love and in God).

You have to accept this fact that at present, you do not live from love—that you live from hate of God, hate for your real self, and hate for other people's real selves. Once you have accepted our earthly reality, you then decide to change your mind and start thinking and behaving from the Holy Spirit part of your mind.

Now you see you and other people as one shared self and know that whereas you may seem able to harm other people and get away from them that since they are parts of you, what you do to them, you do to you.

If we enslave other people, we have enslaved ourselves for the jailer is in the jailhouse with his inmates. If we destroy the environment, people will die, including you, maybe years later.

In Holy Spirit living, you regain awareness of some love but not the perfect love of God. On earth, you are still in the world of perception where you see other people as not you, and therefore, you cannot have perfect love for people; for when push comes to shove, you will probably do what serves your interests and rationalize why you did what harmed other people.

Consider. When I got divorced, I watched as my ex-wife, a woman who hitherto seemed a loving woman, saw me as another person and used the judicial system to get from me whatever she could. She literally tried to enslave me so that I lived to work for her; to her, it did not matter whether I starved and was homeless provided that I gave the money to her.

I realized that she reverted to pure ego state and is doing what egos do—serve their self-interests at the expense of other interests. I wrote and explained to her what I am explaining here, asked her to live from the Holy Spirit, and she ignored me. Apparently, her ego told her to screw me and that I can do nothing about it; as long as the judicial system was on her side, she felt like a god, very powerful.

I am a black man and am acutely aware of racism. I do not like any white man making decisions that affect me. Of course, they are currently making decisions that affect me but I try to avoid being in situations where a white man decides for me what to do.

When I came to court to decide who has custody of our children, I wanted joint custody; the judge was a white man. My impulse was to walk right out of the courtroom for I did not recognize the jurisdiction of a white man to tell me what to do to decide the fate of my children. I was so furious that I told the ugly, fat pompous judge that he is a bloody racist pretending to be looking after the interests of my three children, that he is trying to destroy them, and when they commit crimes, would gladly put them into prisons. Most prison inmates in the USA are blacks put in there by white judges and this woman brought me before a freaking, motherfucking white judge.

(She made me realize who is in charge in America; she made me aware of my total powerlessness in America; she and her judicial system humiliated me and for that, I could not forgive her and left the courtroom with a decision never to talk to her for as long as she lived. I kept to my resolution unless it was absolutely necessary to talk to her over the phone. I did not see her in person for to me, she was disgusting and is better not seen.)

One day, I woke up in the morning without knowing why I wrote to her telling her that she is going to lose her mind, as in Alzheimer's disease, and that it is because she decided to not use her mind to understand what is right or wrong. Indeed, I told her at what age this would happen. Please do not ask me how I got this thought; it just entered my mind.

There is a part of our minds that tunes into higher parts of our minds and know what would happen in the future; we generally do not understand that higher part of our minds and cannot explain it.

Thereafter, I dropped out of the capitalist economic system for I did not want to work and have thousands of my money given to her on a monthly basis. I did whatever I liked doing regardless of whether I made money or not. I have the intelligence, education (Ph. D.), and ability to make millions, even billions, but money was no longer of interest to me. I read up on Hinduism, Buddhism, Taoism, Gnosticism, Zen, and other religions.

I moved on and forgot her existence, for to me, she was no longer a human being, and if we did not have children, I would not care whether she existed or not.

One day, I got a phone call from our son telling me that his mother has lost most of her memory. A year later, our son called to tell me that she is dead. I did not like her death for it was better she was around for her children.

I know that I, too, will someday die, but I prefer death than treat a human being as a slave, as the woman treated me.

As for the racist judicial and concomitant political system that permits some people to treat others as slaves, well, what can I say? Its days are numbered. The fall of America will not be eventful; she would pass from history, and thereafter, is perhaps remembered as an evil empire that called itself Christian but chose hate and slavery instead of love as the Jewish mystic called Jesus Christ asked his followers to do.

I am not saying that I am perfect. I have my issues. I did not know what love is. Objectively, I did not really love my ex-wife although I was not cruel or abusive. I simply coexisted with her and did not evince love toward her. In that regard, I did something wrong, for a human being deserves total love. My excuse was that I did not know what love was.

I totally identified with the ego. Whoever lives from the ego has chosen to not live from love, for the ego is the opposite of love. I chased after a grandiose ego. My wish for a grand ego was such that I did not recognize other human beings as my equal. I felt totally superior to all people, black and white.

As a college student, I visited the White House. Ronald Reagan was the president. I said to me, this is a magnificent building but how I wish that monkey, Reagan, did not dirty it by living in it. To me, Reagan was a monkey, period. I did not see him as even close to being a subhuman being.

I see most members of the Republican Party as subhuman beings. Donald Trump, the present narcissistic creature in the white house, to me, is so evil that he is not even worth thinking about; the man is going down with his house of evil.

You get the idea; I have a big ego. That big ego means that I fled from love. I do not love myself and do not love other people. The ego is absence of love.

THE ETIOLOGY OF A GRANDIOSE EGO

Whereas the ultimate origin of our egos is in our decision to separate from God and go invent a universe we rule, on earth, some people inherited certain bodies that made them have big egos.

I inherited a problematic mitochondria disorder that makes me feel weak and inferior; in Alfred Adler's categories, I compensated with desire for total sense of superiority to all people. I do not have the Nobel Prize in anything but while I respect the Nobel Prize winners, I do not consider any of them as good as I am. I am arrogant and proud beyond belief. When I taught at colleges, the other professors to me seemed unintelligent.

I totally lacked love for me and for all people, and certainly, had no love for God. If you said God, I would ask you, what God? Get out of here. I have been agnostic from the moment I became self-aware.

One's problem is also one's opportunity. My big ego that gave me lovelessness also gave me an opportunity to search for love.

Since I know firsthand the problems caused by my having a big ego—absence of peace and joy—I have no business liking the ego. I can therefore choose to let go of the ego. If I let go of my big ego, given the problems it caused me, I would become aware of my true self as one with God and all his creation.

Those with small egos, the so-called normal folks, may not even know that they have egos; they are those who go to church and worship God. Me, I could not worship God and could not pray to God, for my ego was in competition with God; my ego wanted to be number one and did not like God having power and authority over it.

As a child, I used to ask, who the hell is God?

The ego is a block to the awareness of love, God; if I let the ego go, I would regain awareness of love, God. The ego gave me war and lack of peace and joy; if I let the ego go, I would experience peace and joy. The ego gives me nothing of value other than make me pretend to be an important person, an important person that would die and worms eat his body.

DISCUSSION

Being an ego is not something to be moralized about. We are all egotists. If you are not an egotist, you would not be in this world for the world is a dream in which the sons of God forgot their real selves and take on false, separated ego selves.

Most human beings live in fear. If you live in fear, you live in ego for fear is a mechanism of the ego that alerts it to what could harm its body or denigrate its pride. If you transcend your ego, you simultaneously transcend fear, anger, depression, paranoia, and pride.

All that one can do is have what we might call refined egos. White folks, for example, are egotists but seemed civilized egotists; Africans are egotists but seem primitive egotists. The point is that all people, black, white, and Orientals are egoists, for being an ego is the condition for being on earth.

When you transcend the ego, let your ego die from your awareness. A new self, the Christ self, is reborn in your awareness.

The human being who while on earth recognizes that he is one with all selves and loves all selves is called the Christ self or Buddha self. The payoff of living as a Christ self is attaining relative peace and joy, not the perfect peace and joy, bliss of God. As it were, while one is still on earth, in the place of separation, one is now at the gate of heaven, close to heaven. People in heaven do not live as egos in bodies; they are parts of unified self, aka God. If you decide to let go of your ego and attachment to body, you do not die out as the ego tells you would happen; instead, you experience yourself as a unified self, in a field of spiritual, invisible light and love.

On earth, if you live a forgiving and loving life, occasionally, you would see your entire ego and the world of space, time, and matter disappear and you are aware of being in God, in unified state, where there is just oneself with infinite selves in it and you are one of those infinite selves in God's unified self; in God, you feel eternal, permanent, and changeless.

CONCLUSION

Understand your ego, do not attack it; do not blame it for it is not an accident; it is, given the totality of your being on earth, your biological constitution and social experience; your ego is who you had to be. The ego you have is not an accident. You could not have been a different ego given your body and social experience so it is pointless wishing to be another human being, another ego. All egos are unique; you are different from all other egos, they are different from you, and so it is. Deal with who you are, not who you could have been.

Now, thank your ego and gently let it go. Tell it that it is a pretended self and that your real self is formless, unified spirit self.

Let your ego die. It is like a reed floating in the wind and temporarily attached itself to you, a son of God; gently blow on it and it is carried away by the wind, leaving you the awareness of your real self, a son of God.

In reclaiming your status as a part of God, you experience relative peace and joy, and ultimately, in completely letting go of ego, body, space, time, and matter, you return to heaven and know perfect peace and joy, what Hinduism calls bliss.

Post Script:

I do not belong to any religion. I take from each of them whatever contributes to me living from love.

ATTRIBUTION OF DANGER TO SOUNDS AND HAVING NIGHTMARISH DREAMS

I heard weird sounds in my room. I attributed them to ghosts. I had dreams where unknown things or ghosts attacked me. My brain or mind used the attributed, not real ghosts, to produce ghostly attacks for me. Mind then can take anything, including false attributions, and use them to have dreams.

ONE CAN USE FALSE INFORMATION ONE PICKED UP FROM SOCIETY TO CONSTRUCT SELF-LIMITING LIFESTYLE; SOCIAL PROGRAMMING CAN MAKE ONE LIMIT ONE'S LIFE.

One's mind can use false information one picked up during the daytime, from other people, and the culture to construct false day life for one—a fearful life or paranoid life.

THE DESIRE TO LIVE AS SEPARATED EGO IN BODY LEADS TO FEAR. WITH NO SUCH DESIRE OR DESIRE FOR LOVE, THERE ARE NO FEARS, FOR LOVE IS THE OPPOSITE OF FEAR.

Love protects the child and us. If you have love, you feel safe; if you do not have love, you feel unprotected.

If you have no love, you feel fear.

To cure your fears, then have love in your life. God is love; God as love is what protects people. Ego is separation from love, all, whole, hence, there is fear in ego for ego is alone, separated from the whole, man and God.

PSYCHOSIS IS PEGGING YOUR WORTH TO OTHER PEOPLE AND GOD.

In delusion disorder, you say that God is powerful so you see you as God to be powerful; the power is derived from attachment to a false powerful self. It could also be attachment to another person that society deems powerful, such as Napoleon.

Dr. O feels weak and derives power from attaching himself to God, whom he deems omnipotent, very powerful. He ought to feel limited, not total power only from himself, not God. God is an excuse for him to seek grandiose false total power that he is not going to get.

Mankind is deluded because it feels weak and derives false power from what it calls God. It needs to resign itself to the little power that the individual can get by his own humble efforts.

THE STUPIDITY OF BUILDING SOLOMON'S TEMPLE IN HIS VILLAGE.

Dr. O wants to rebuild the Temple of Solomon that was at Jerusalem in his African village. That would not make it the Temple of Solomon for his temple would not have the historical connotations that Solomon's temple has for Jews—Jewish history and events in it.

A church built a replica of Solomon's temple at Sao Paulo, Brazil and yet, it is not Solomon's temple. Dr. O's temple in his village is part of his effort to derive power from attaching himself to Christian and Jewish things. He needs to derive real power from his own self.

However, one can see the whole as God, see oneself as part of the whole, and derive some power from the whole, and that is healthy.

THE IMPLICATION OF GOD BEING THE ONLY ONE WHO CAN LET ONE ENTER HEAVEN OR HAVE GOD EXPERIENCE.

A Course in Miracles says that the Holy Spirit can guide one to the gate of heaven but cannot get one inside it. Only God can open heaven's gate and let one in. What does this metaphor mean?

It means that one can try, via the Holy Spirit, right thinking, to get one to living as purified ego, gate of heaven, world of light forms, but it takes only God to give one God experience. This suggests that God is apart from the son, from the Holy Spirit, and the ego. After all, God created his son so he is more powerful than his son.

REVELATION AND GOD EXPERIENCE IS GIVEN TO US BY GOD.

In our experience, you can live a good life, but only a higher power can give you God-realization; you cannot give it to you.

Only God chooses when he reveals himself to you, not you telling him when to reveal himself to you. This implies that God does judge; he judges your dreaming self, knows when it has let go of the ego entirely, and lets you become part of him again.

You can also say that you and God make the decision to reveal God to you, for you to have God experience.

At the God-level, God and his sons think together; in the dream, the son thinks that he can think and behave separately, hence the dream of separation.

EGO THINKING BUILT OUR WORLD AND IS VERY POWERFUL.

A Course in Miracles said that the son of God via his wishes invented the dream world, our physical universe. The son of God invented the world and the ego as his replacement self while he is in the dream. It is a self and world that seeks separation, bears grievances, seeks revenge, and punishes people who harm its body that can be harmed and destroyed.

Our world is based on crime and punishment; we judge people guilty and punish or kill them. Grievances built and maintained our world. Governments, courts, judges, prisons, and people desire punishment and our world is based on punishment for the ego and body can be hurt so it punishes those who hurt it or could hurt it.

FORGIVENESS WILL BUILD A CORRECTIVE CIVILIZATION, ONE THAT CORRECTS THE CIVILIZATION BUILT BY CRIME AND PUNISHMENT.

The world of forgiveness builds a forgiven world, a civilization based on light forms.

POLITICIANS AND MILITARY LEADERS BUILD CIVILIZATIONS; RELIGIONS AND THEIR MINISTERS MAKE PEOPLE OBEY THE CIVILIZATIONS BUILT BY EGO POLITICIANS; SPIRITUAL LEADERS TRANSFORM EGO CIVILIZATIONS TO PURIFIED CIVILIZATIONS BUT DO NOT BUILD THEM FROM THE SCRATCH.

It is egotists, politicians, crime, and punishment that build human civilizations; religions maintain those civilizations; religions' priests get people to obey the laws that maintain those civilizations; spiritual leaders do not build new civilizations but purify and take them to the gate of heaven for God to open his gate and let people in.

Political leaders, priests, and spiritual leaders are very important in society. Politicians, military leaders, and religion ministers maintain society. They need to do so for present and future generations, sons of God who are on earth and who will come to earth to experience life in bodies and egos, and they will be coming for thousands, if not millions of years into the future, and eventually remember their true selves as the sons of God. They come forgetting their true selves and while here, through the help of teachers of God, spiritual scientists, learn that they are the sons of God and they hesitantly let go of their attachment to egos, trust that they are spirits, begin trying to behave like spirits, Christ, awaken, return to God, and end their stay in ego land.

The point is that political leaders and the other masters of the dream state that make living on earth pleasant are useful to the sons of God who came, and will come, to experience self-forgetfulness and then rediscover their real selves. Each person, those who maintain the egos' world and those who teach ways to leave the egos' world, are performing appropriate functions for the sons of God in the dream state.

EGOLESS VERSUS NO EGO

Being egoless means that one has an ego separated self but less of it. No ego means that one has no ego separated self. If one has no ego, one is not in the world of egos and is back to awareness of being in unified self, in God, in heaven.

If you have no ego, you are not in this world but you can have less ego and be in this world. It is kind of like fearlessness which means less fear but not absence of fear.

This is a world of egos; egos compete for positions in society and some egos lead other egos in society. They, egos, are all dream figures, things that do not, in fact, exist. There are no human beings and their leaders in reality, but in the dream, they obviously exist.

IF YOU FORGIVE, YOU CANNOT BE IN THIS WORLD.

If you forgive those who wronged you, you would have no ego and body, would leave this world, and return to a place of no ego, heaven; this is what Jesus did.

Lack of forgiveness, crime, and punishment is what maintains this world, what keeps the world going.

AMERICAN WHITE MALES ARE THE WORLD'S MOST FEARFUL COWARDS.

They are used to obeying their kings in Europe and in America, their governments. They will literally go to wars and kill strangers who did nothing to them if their king or government ask them to do so. But standing up and fighting for social justice, they would not do so.

A HUMAN BEING IS ALWAYS IN LOVE, IN GOD, AND HEAVEN AND CANNOT SEPARATE FROM THEM BUT WHILE IN THEM, PRETENDS TO BE IN EGO AND BODY AND GIVE HIMSELF SUFFERING.

A human being is always in love, God and in heaven; he cannot separate from them. While in them, he pretends to be separated from them and is now an ego separated self instead of being the self God created him as—the son of God. He merely covers his eyes so that he does not see the love he is always living in.

What he now needs to do is remove the veil he himself placed over love and the experience love he is always in.

His real question is how he is going to find happiness, peace, and love. The answer is very simple—stop attacking love, peace, and happiness by desiring separation.

Remove the desire for the ego and its world of seeming separation, do nothing else, and he relapses into the love, heaven, union, God he always is in. In other words, stop sleeping and dreaming that he is separated from his real self, part of unified spirit self, and he wakes up.

How simple is salvation?

CORONAVIRUS TELLS US THAT WE ARE BODIES.

Coronavirus shows us that we are bodies, biological organisms; we are now afraid of death and have set everything aside as we struggle to stay alive, via social distancing, wearing face masks and staying locked down. We must be alive before we talk about all the things that normally preoccupy our thoughts, such as doing science and religion.

EVIDENCE THAT MIND IS OUTSIDE BODY

When you are sleeping and dreaming and someone jerks you up, you feel pounding in your head; this is probably because your mind was outside your brain and body and had to return to it fast and that led to the pounding in your head. This seems to prove that our minds are outside our bodies.

Moreover, out of body and near-death experience shows one's mind leaving one's body and going to another place, now in a different body, body in light form, and one eventually returns to one's body.

OBE and NDE prove that reincarnation is probably true. If I could leave my body and re-enter it, I can also enter different bodies, as in birth.

TOTAL IDENTIFICATION WITH BODY AND FEAR OF THE DEATH OF BODIES

People have total identification with their bodies and believe that if their bodies die, they would die. This is probably not true; if their bodies die, they enter different bodies and keep living until they are tired of life in bodies and they return to life in formless state.

YOU MUST HAVE A SENSE OF DOING SOMETHING IMPORTANT TO BE ALIVE.

At the deep level, you must have a sense of doing something important with your life to be alive. When you no longer feel that what you are doing is important for you and people, you have no desire to live and with a little disease, you succumb to it and die.

What is important is individually defined. It could be taking care of your children, training them through college, going to school, getting a degree, working on a book, exploring what life means, or doing a certain kind of job.

The individual must ascertain what he believes is important and contributes to life and keep doing it no matter what. You know that you are doing what you deem important when making money is not part of your reason for doing it even though you could make money from it if you want.

I write and give away information on psychological matters that very few psychologists even understand and I could certainly write books on them and make loads of money from them.

Ask yourself: what am I doing that I believe is important? Have clarity on it and do it twenty-four seven.

I am trying to understand whether there is life after we die or not and understand our real selves, for the opposite is people as I see them living as mere animals which is not good enough for me, and if there is God, self, I am seeking God-realization also called self-realization; I write on politics when the mood moves me but not regularly; I write on psychological and spiritual matters for I believe that people ought to know who they are and try to improve their lives.

I believe that each of us came to this world to do certain things; they have done it over several lifetimes and have improved on it. For example, even before I went to college, I knew more psychology than Freud himself; this is because I had been a psychologist in past lifetimes. In this lifetime, I came to understand spirituality based on science; my knowledge of physics is formidable.

I came to establish spirituality on scientific bases, what I call spiritual science or science of spirituality, using the scientific method to understand spiritual matters and thus, take them out of the realm of speculation and superstition.

WHAT IS IT IN US THAT DREAMS WHEN WE SLEEP?

The universe implanted something into us, human beings and animals, that dreams through our brains. That thing takes from our day experiences, recent and past, and uses them to formulate dreams. The dreams may be sensible or nonsensical, just as some aspects of our day lives are sensible and others nonsensical. Some books of fiction and movies based on them are sensible and others are senseless.

Whatever dreams through us is the same thing that enables us to navigate our daily living. What is it that dreams through us?

Is it just electrons, protons, and neutrons in the atoms in our brains? I do not think so. Then what is it? I do not know. I call it unknown intelligence.

HIDING TO PROTECT A GRANDIOSE EGO LEADS TO POVERTY.

Poverty is sometimes brought about when a person has a big ego and withdraws from society to go protect his big ego instead of working in the social world. Protecting his big ego, pride, and dignity is now more important to such a person for he does not want it to make a mistake in the public, fail in society, be laughed at, or seen as nobody so he must hide his ego-self to avoid losing social face; he must protect his ego's vanity and sense of importance.

If you give up your desire for a big ego, simply do the type of job you like, do it among people, and not thinking about what people think about you, you will succeed and make a decent living.

It is desire to protect a big ego that leads to hiding to protect it that makes one poor. A friend, a man with JD (juris prudence doctor) and Ph. D. (doctor of philosophy), hides in his room thinking about becoming the omnipotent God; that is, being a big ego, before he does anything in the world, for if he is not god himself in power (having omnipotent power means having all power), he could fail, and the world and its people would laugh at him.

He wants to be a grandiose ego that uses magic wands to transform the world to whatever he likes it to be; he hides to protect his false, grandiose ego.

This man has seven children. His withdrawal from the work world meant that only his wife raised his children. He would tell me that his pursuit of God is so important that he did not fulfil his family obligations.

It is as if that is an excuse for not meeting his family obligation and kind of makes him important. Over and over, he tells me that for thirty-nine years, 1981–2020, he has not worked but only thought about God.

I believe that he is on an ego trip. Pursuit of the ego can disguise itself as pursuit of God. The ego is very clever and deceives the sons of God. The man is deceived by his clever ego.

By the way, who is the ego? The ego is the son of God who in rebellion to his real self, the son of God, wants to live as a replacement and substitute self, a separated self.

The real son of God is unified with God and is not separated from God. The real son of God is rational and knows that as an eternal part of God, he cannot do anything by himself but always with the power of God in him; he can misuse that power to be destructive on earth, in the dream.

If you call my friend's attention to his egoism, as I did, he feels angry and drops the phone on you. He has done this to me three times and a few days later, he would call and apologize for being socially inappropriate in hanging up the phone on me.

Clearly, he has delusion disorder, grandiose type; this type of deluded person is rational in all other aspects of his life; for example, he was a good lawyer and teacher of law, but has systematic delusion in one area of his life. In this case, his wish to be the most important person on earth (he is unable to accept that we are all equal and the same, he actually sees me as his student, his disciple, for that is the only way he can accept me; he will call me and talk for two or more hours on God and if I try to say a word, he feels irritated; who am I to tell him something about God that he does not already know?).

The man exhibits childish temper tantrums; he cuts off from talking to you to go protect his oversized egoism.

He ends up poor and is maintained, kept alive by other people. He is an example of what pursuit of godlike ego does to people—make them poor.

Yet, everything in his life disposed him to feel inferior and pursue superiority. As a black man, he realistically saw white racism for what it is, attempt to make black folks feel inferior, and accept white folks as superior to them. He felt inferior and compensated with desire to seem superior to white folks and later, to all people.

He wants to seem superior to all people by giving the world what he calls a new and improved Christianity, kind of like what Father Divine did in yesteryears America.

He is the paranoid prophet of God, the deluded prophet. Yet, ninety-nine percent of what he says about the Bible makes sense; it is the one percent, where he wants to be God, and no other people, that makes him deluded (delusion disorder is a weird form of psychosis for such a person can be successful in the world; there are deluded mathematicians, scientists, medical doctors, engineers, and so on).

Recently, I had a disagreement with him. He read for me what is said in the gospel of John, chapter fourteen, verses ten to twenty-eight. In it, Jesus responded to Philips' question—where is God—by telling Philip that where you see the son of God, him, Jesus, you see God, for the father is in the son.

I told him that the passage means that God is in all of us since all of us are sons of God. He said that we are all sons of God alright but that God is not in all of us but only in him. He said that he is the only representative of God on earth and is to teach the rest of us about God.

I told him that that is not the general interpretation of the said passage. He felt angry at my audacity to contradict him and dropped the phone on me.

He is the supreme egotist and has to let go of his ego before he can regain awareness of God; he must not retain even a little bit of ego for him to become healthy and now go to the world and relate to people, work, and make a living that his obvious good intelligence would generate for him.

But he is not willing to do that, so I told him that he is stuck, is deluded, and at that point, he hung up on me.

I said to me: good riddance, except that something in me wants to help him to understand that all people and animals are the creations of God and that we are all the same and coequal before God. That is to say that the mental health professional in me wants to help heal his delusion disorder.

However, the seasoned clinician in me knows that a human being cannot heal another human being; all that you can do is explain the process of healing, which means explaining the nature of the ego and asking people to drop the ego and live from love, love for God and all his creation, and leave them to make that choice or not.

You can only choose for you but cannot choose for other persons, for each of us have the freedom to choose when to let go of the ego and return to God or stay in ego land.

Salvation is nothing more than letting go of one's ego, separated self-concept; all of the ego must be let go; keep a bit of it and you have kept all of it and as such, is still on earth, in hell of your making.

On earth, you can only attain agelessness; that is, have minimal ego; not having ego at all means that you will not be on earth (in meditation, you may occasionally attain no ego and at that moment is in God, what Hinduism calls Samadhi, Buddhism calls Nirvana, Zen calls Satori, and Christian mysticism calls the union of the son with his father; you cannot be in that God-realization state for long; otherwise, you exit from this world; you must return to the ego, now a purified ego, a kind of loving and forgiving ego); the earth is the place of egos, for those in separation, space, time, and all illusions; the earth is the place of illusions.

In sum, if you desire a grandiose ego, you may avoid other people and keep to yourself to nourish your ego and in the process, will not be in the world of people to do what you have to do to make a decent living. Having a big ego gives people poverty.

Ego-lessness gives folks relative peace of mind (not the perfect peace from no ego, the peace of God) as well as material abundance; you choose what you want—pain from ego or peace and abundance from ego-lessness.

The information in this essay is what you would get from reading God-realized persons, such as Ramana Maharshi. How much should you pay for it? I give it to you for free. Would you acknowledge the gift? Do what it suggests and return to no ego state, hence to unified state, to God; refuse to do so and live in hell, in the prison called planet earth.

You do not return back to God by dying physically but by jettisoning the false, separated self you made and with which you replaced your real self, the unified son of God that God created you as.

You are always in God but while in him, dream that you are separated from him, is in a place of space, time, and matter and punish yourself. Have pity on you by letting go of the ego and return to peace and joy.

THE WORLD IS A PLACE OF PERPETUAL WAR BECAUSE TO BE IN EGO IS TO BE AT WAR WITH ALL.

In his seminal book, *Leviathan*, Thomas Hobbes (1651) wrote about how in the state of nature, people are self-centered. Each person look after his self-interests, and if necessary, use other people to gratify his interests that led to war between all individuals, and life was nasty, brutish, and short. To reduce their personal insecurities, they selected a king and gave him the power to make laws that protected all of them and the power to arrest and send to prison anyone who negatively affected others' interests. Hobbes advocated capital punishment for psychopaths who derive sadistic pleasure from harming or killing other people.

Clearly, Hobbes described human beings as we see them on earth; hence, we say that he was a political scientist for he impersonally described an aspect of phenomena as it is, not as we hope that it is. Empirical observation shows us that people are predatory animals and if you look away, your neighbor will take you to the cleaners, kill you, and pee on your grave. People's talk of God and religion is a smokescreen.

I agreed with Hobbes the moment I read him during my college years (I took a course on Western political philosophy and he and Machiavelli were central to that philosophy). But could what he said also have roots in metaphysics? Yes.

My metaphysics posits that in eternity, also called heaven, all are one, all share one self. While in this state of oneness, some of them decided to separate from oneness, to go do their different things. How do they separate? They had to attack each other. That mutual attack led to the sons of God separating from each other.

That mutual attack is what is called the Big Bang. The physical universe began with a mutual attack by all against all.

God, the father of the warring sons, immediately reestablished oneness and stopped the mutual attack in heaven so that in heaven, they remained as one shared self, but in their dream, the effect of God's attempt to stop the mutual attack was the recombination of the particles of light (they are light) into electrons and quarks and quarks into protons and neutrons and those into nuclei and eventually nuclei capturing electrons to form hydrogen atoms.

The early universe was one sea of hydrogen atoms; the cloud of hydrogen separated into clumps and each clump was acted on by gravity, heat, and pressures to form other elements beginning with helium. Massive stars were formed, lived for millions of years, and exploded. New stars and planets were formed from their debris and on planet earth, plants and animals were formed.

The salient point is that people on earth, egos, came here as a result of the war they declared on each other while they were still in heaven. As long as they live in egos and bodies, they are at war. The earth is a place of war. War is the nature of human existence on earth. Even animals and plants are fighting with each other. Trees fight with each other to get access to light so as to survive.

The earth is a house of war and will always be so. That is why everywhere you look, you see people at war with each other; people separate into tribes and nations and those are at war with each other.

(Some religions postulate that the earth began in war. Gnosticism, for example, talked about how a proud self, the Demiurge, rebelled against God, was chased out of heaven, and came to earth to start the kingdom of darkness, our earthly human existence; Gnosticism wants to return people to the kingdom of light, which is how they describe heaven. Aspects of Catholicism talked about how Lucifer, a proud angel, challenged God and some angels led by the Archangel Michael organized to fight him on behalf of God and how eventually, Lucifer was chased out of heaven and came to earth to establish his kingdom, a kingdom based on ego pride and vanity. Of course, all these stories of creation of the earth are not true but they are metaphors trying to capture the idea that our world came into being as a rebellion against heaven and its God. That which began in rebellion began in war and is characterized by war. To be a human being, a separated ego living in body, is to be at war with other separated egos and war with the whole, aka God.)

There is nothing that you can do to stop people from fighting each other; they came to earth to be at war with each other, to live as the opposite of heaven's peace and joy. Heaven is love and they came to hate each other. They will find every possible reason to hate each other and be at war (whites against blacks, now Americans against Chinese, and so on.)

The best that they can do is set up political and social institutions to catch and punish those who fight unfairly. Governments (military, police, judicial systems, and prisons) must exist in human society for the egregious in hurting people must be punished. The earth is a place of crime and punishment.

If you do not like the nature of the earth, you can seek spirituality, find your way to relinquish your ego of war, and return to Christ of peace, the self that is as God created him. But as long as you opt to live as an ego, you are at war with Christ, the sons of God, and God and all people. This war starts the moment that you are born a human being. It is not learned; it is who people are.

African political idealists, such as Dr. Patrick Lumumba (is that really his name or did he change his name to the name of the first prime minister of Congo, Patrice Lumumba? He tries very hard to speak like Martin Luther King indicating that he is insecure and a phony), well, these African idealists seem to think that if you take away western neocolonialism, all will be hunky-dory with Africa, that African nation-states would combine into one African country and govern Africa right. I sympathize with them for I, too, used to think along that line, and still wish for a united Africa except that now as a political realist, I know that only exercise of brutal military force can unify Africa, not by merely appealing to Africans' good nature.

Look away and Africans will sell you into slavery and use the money they got to buy the accoutrements that make their egos and bodies seem important and like apes, laugh as if they did nothing wrong and blame those they sold their people to; look away and Arabs and Europeans would buy Africans and use them to do their work and thus live easier lives and justify their devilish behavior with phony religions of Christianity and Islam. We need laws to catch and punish evil people. Without laws and governments that enforce, those people would revert to anarchy and chaos. Despite what political correctness liberals tell us, human beings by nature are evil. Be prepared for their evil behaviors or live to regret them.

The relevant point is that people are by nature evil and will always be evil for they came to earth to be evil; it is not their environment that makes them evil; they came here to be evil. Evilness, separation, is written into their genes; it is in their DNA.

You cannot change people for that would mean changing their DNA, rewriting it. That is not going to happen. However, every once in a while, a human being awakens from the house of war and returns to the house of peace in God, but that behavior is so rare that you should not count on it happening everywhere. There is no mass awakening from the dream of war.

To separate from other people is to be at war with them. We came here to separate from each other and to be different from each other.

Our home, unified spirit state, is unified, love, and we decided to experience the opposite of union and love and declared war on ourselves. War we must have for it is what we came to have and experience.

Let people have their wars, as individuals and as nations. That is their game. If you do not like it, then seek a spirituality that takes you out of this world, but as long as you choose to be in ego, separated state, to be in this world, you must be at war with God, be at war with your real self, the son of God, be at war with other sons of God, and on earth, be at war with other egos.

The earth, the physical universe, is a dream in which we are at perpetual wars. Don't cry for people who are at war. They can choose to relinquish their egos and return to peace and joy.

CONCLUSION

This essay assumes that you have studied Western political philosophy and understand the major writers in it, such as Plato, Aristotle, Nicolo Machiavelli, Thomas Hobbes, John Locke, Charles Montesquieu, Jean Jacque Rousseau, Jeremy Bentham, John Stuart Mill, Karl Marx, and others. If you have not studied those folks, please go. Do so before you even pretend to have understood what I said and what more, pretend to have a useful opinion on my thesis. Proffering uneducated opinions does not alter reality.

The earth's reality is that people are separated egos and that egos must always be at war with each other, for ego is a declaration of war on one's real self, the son of God, and declaration of war on God and all creations of God.

Finally, please do not make the mistake of seeing those who talk religion and spirituality as naïve. They are often the most realistic thinkers there are. For example, I know that you are an ego, and as such, is out looking for your interests and if you could, you would take advantage of me. As such, I look out to see you try it and if you do, I would not hesitate for a second in using the law to punish you and if that fails, send you back to the world of darkness you came from.

I am a total realist; I eschewed sentimentalism long ago and take people as they are, evil egos. In eternity, people are good, but on earth, they are evil; we must not hesitate in punishing evildoers. If I have my way, I would punish Africans to teach them to love instead of always harming each other, selling each other while pretending to be good people, and blaming other people for their evil behaviors to avoid taking responsibility for their evil behaviors. If they do not take responsibility for their antisocial behaviors, they are not going to correct them.

13

THE PARADOX OF HUMAN LIFE

Human beings come into the world through sexual intercourse. Sexual intercourse is an animal behavior. Human beings may like their sexual activities because of the pleasure they say that they derive from them yet what they really think of their sexuality is shown by the fact that they generally hide it.

People engage in sexual activity behind closed doors. They do not want other people to see them engaged in their sexual activity. It as if they feel that the activity is so degraded that it would lower their self and social esteem should other people see them engage in it.

Indeed, they also hide their genitals. Even in cultures where people are almost naked, they use either piece of clothes or leaves to cover their genitals; it is as if they do not want other people to see their genitals.

People hide their sexual organs probably because those parts of their bodies make them feel like they are mere animals and they would rather not be animals; people also hide the process of defecating; apparently, they would rather stress the activity of their minds for their intellectual outputs make them feel like what they call the gods.

Clearly, the human mind is awesome. Our minds can study nature and apparently understand certain parts of it. Anyone looking at what humanity has accomplished in science and engineering must marvel at the creature called human beings. Humanity certainly does not seem like a mere animal.

A creature that can understand its body, animals, plants, planets, stars, galaxies, and the universe seems more than an animal being.

Yet, he is an animal. He came into the world through ridiculous sexual intercourse; he lives, ages, weakens, and dies and decays like animals.

The ridiculousness of the human manner of birth and death denotes that people are animals and no more than that. It is difficult to see them as anything more than dumb animals.

Indeed, when you look at the totality of their behaviors, their chasing after power and fame knowing that they are going to die and become food for worms, makes you conclude that they are even stupider than animals.

What are our lives all about? Our lives seem like an exercise in futility and vanity. We are born, grow up, feel weak, and feel like we are not important.

Nature (earthquakes, hurricanes, volcanos, floods, droughts, tsunamis, etc.) and diseases sweep us to death as they sweep animals and plants to death, indicating that we are not special to nature.

We seem to have no inherent worth but we confer worth to us. Worth, significance, and importance are social constructs. People consider themselves important and those who did certain things more important than others.

Generally, outstanding political leaders, wealthy people, and accomplishing scientists like Isaac Newton and Albert Einstein are socially considered more important than ordinary people; yet those great achievers, too, die and are eaten by worms.

Apparently, one of the ways human beings give themselves worth is to posit gods. Gods are said to be eternal, permanent, and changeless; they are deemed all-powerful. We have not seen gods. Apparently, our God is made in human image but we turn around to say that human beings are created in God's image.

None of us has seen God, and as such, do not know what his image is like. The image of him that we have is our self-images.

We say that God is omnipotent, omnipresent, and omniscient, qualities we see in us, project to a God we have not seen, exaggerate those qualities in him, and expect him to act as such and he does not do so for he probably does not exist.

If God exists, it is certainly not as we construe him to be; he probably exists as formless intelligence that is everywhere.

What exactly are human beings? He seems very intelligent yet he is an animal, lives a ridiculous life, and dies. Who are we?

We remain a mystery to ourselves, Erich Fromm said and I agree. I certainly do not know who I am and who other people are beyond the superficial ramblings of psychology and philosophy. I do not know who our real selves are.

I understand the human personality; personality is derived from the term persona, mask. Who is behind the mask of personality? Who is our real self?

Do you know who you are and who other people are? You would be deluded to say that you know who you are. You may not even understand the constituents of a hair on your body!

Here is a reason why we have not understood who we are. Everywhere you see people, they seek a sense of grandeur; they want to seem important in their eyes and in other people's eyes. Some of them do so excessively and we call them neurotics and indeed, some of them, despite apparent nothingness, see themselves as very important and we call them deluded (grandiose). But why do people seek grandeur?

Alfred Adler says that it is because their existence in body and society makes them feel inferior and they react with a compensatory effort to seem superior. But is that an acceptable answer?

We see the US President Donald Trump seeking social importance. He is like a nine-year-old child who feels that he lacks worth and insists on getting it through appearing socially important, through narcissistic means.

The man wants to make his country great, and what is wrong with that? Is it better to settle for littleness and poverty? Surely, the mind, intelligence that can understand this universe, deserves great abundance, not poverty!

Looking at the human body and what we do with it, sex, defecation, and its end, death and decay, one can conclude that people have no worth.

Just about all that people do in society and human civilization is actually predicated on seeking worth. People do mostly what they do in an attempt to give themselves worth.

That which is sought and defended probably is not real. The real does not need to be sought and defended.

Could it not be that people seek grandeur because they came from a place, God, heaven, where they have total grandeur and worth but now in body, on earth, feel its absence hence seek it in an obsessive-compulsive manner and will not stop seeking it until they return to God where they have absolute importance?

If God exists, surely his children deserve total abundance, wealth; is powerlessness and poverty a virtue? And why should they be?

I do not have the answer to the philosophical questions that exercise my mind. Do you have the answers beyond dogmatically asserting what your religion told you? If you have verifiable answers, please share them with me and us.

- See Hamlet's soliloquies, in Shakespeare's great play, Hamlet, the scene in the graveyard where he asked the type of questions I asked here.

RELIGIONS' SACRED BOOKS ARE WRITTEN IN METAPHORS, NOT LITERAL TRUTH.

Most religions' sacred books are written in poetic and metaphoric forms. This is the case with Hinduism (Vedas Ramayana, Mahabharata, and Bhagavad Gita), Buddhism (Sutras), Judaism (Torah, Bible's Old Testament), Christianity (New Testament part of the Bible), Islam (Koran, Hadith, and Sharia) and *A Course in Miracles* (which is a legitimate message from the Holy Spirit in the guise of Jesus Christ).

Metaphors are mostly employed in poetic writing; writers of religious sacred books tend to be poets. Metaphors attempt to express in language that which is not easily expressed in words.

God and spiritual matters transcend speech and language so we cannot really write them in words. Words were devised by the separated ones as a medium of speaking and relating to each other.

God is unified, God is one self; that is, simultaneously infinite selves; the various selves in God do not need the words we employ on earth to communicate/commune. They are each other, know what each other are thinking about, and respond to each other as they think their thoughts.

Poets and those who have had some God experience try to write about what they experienced in human-separated language and cannot succeed but try to do so nevertheless. They use the language of metaphors and poetry in their efforts to make the inexplicable explicable.

If you read *A Course in Miracles* and take it literally, you would think that the separation from God happened in a second. What happened in less than a second is the pursuit of the wish for separation (Big Bang) but the actual separation by the sons of God did not happen immediately. They went to sleep, and in their sleep, worked on what we now call the universe. It took them thirteen billion years before they could make the creatures they invented (animals) capable of becoming the conduit for their dreaming. They are at no time in animal state, not in bodies, but while still in unified spirit, aka God, identify with bodies and seem to live in the world of matter, space, and time, our world.

They will be having this dream of self-forgetfulness for more billions of years; in their dreams, they will see stars exploding in supernovas, planets dying, and eventually, the entire universe dying as galaxies separate from each other and the universe is very cold to sustain massive objects in it. Only photons of light would survive and those eventually disappear and the sons of God awaken to their real selves as the sons of God.

The point is to not take *A Course in Miracles,* the Bible, or any religion's holy book literally. The story of Adam and Eve, for example, is a metaphor talking about how initially people lived in union with God, then lived in an early world situation where they still retained knowledge of God hence were in a kind of paradise, finally forgot God, and now live as pure egos and suffer in our world. The story is not a literal truth.

The Charles Darwin story of human evolution, more or less, captured the journey of human beings from single-celled organisms to multi-celled organisms and to where they are today.

THOSE PEOPLE WHO CLAIM RESPONSIBILITY FOR ALL THAT IS GOOD IN LIFE ARE ON AN EGO TRIP AND ARE COWARDS.

There are people in Alaigbo today who write that everything good in life is introduced to the world by Igbos. To them, Igbos are responsible for all that is good in the world (they want to personally feel responsible for all that is good in life and project their desire to Igbos; they suffer from the desire for absolute power, hence are deluded). In the meantime, they do nothing to improve Nigeria; they allow Fulanis to rule Nigeria and screw

Nigerians. They are cowards obtaining a false sense of power from making psychotic claims to being the best people in the world.

DR. O IS A COWARDLY DELUDED MAN ON A QUEST FOR TOTAL POWER OVER PEOPLE.

Dr. O is a coward; he will not lift a finger to do the little that human beings with little power can do on earth but is waiting for the day he would have total power like he imagines that God has and use magical commands to change the world to his liking. In the meantime, he tolerates the current imperfect world doing nothing to improve it a little bit as normal people with little but no absolute power do. He is waiting for the day God would give him absolute power to bring into being whatever he wants magically.

He wants to be the most powerful person on earth via his conception of an omnipotent God. He has not seen omnipotent God; it is man that defines omnipotent God.

The man takes the stories in the bible, such as the story of Adam and Eve literally instead of seeing them as the metaphors they are—metaphors the ancients used to explain the origin of the world but not facts.

He truly has delusion disorder, grandiose type; he seeks total power but is realistic enough to know that if he goes out there and claims it without the ability to back it up with action, he would be laughed at and locked up as the madman he is.

The lesson for us is that if you are waiting for the day God would give you total power and with it, you change the world, you have always wanted to change the world and become the most powerful person on earth. You feel powerless and inferior and compensate with desire for absolute power, which now you associate with God giving it to you, a God of your imagination, hence is not going to give it to you.

Go do the little that human beings can do in this world and make incremental changes in the world, not total change, for you do not have total power to totally change the world.

EJ IS LIKE DR. O; SHE TOO DESIRES TOTAL ABSOLUTE POWER AND CANNOT GET IT IN THE REAL WORLD SO HAS TO HIDE IN NOTHINGNESS WHILE CRITICIZING THOSE TRYING TO DO THEIR BEST IN THE REAL WORLD. SHE HAS TO LET GO OF HER EGO'S DESIRE FOR ABSOLUTE PERFECT POWER

AND GO FOR MINIMAL POWER, THE TYPE ALLOWED
FOR REAL HUMAN BEINGS. IF SHE DOES SO, SHE WOULD
RELAX AND NO LONGER BE TENSE; HER INTENSITY IS
ROOTED IN HER QUEST FOR ABSOLUTE POWER, PARANOID
POWER, TO MASK HER SENSE OF POWERLESSNESS.

Yet, folks like Dr. O and EJ had to be who they are; they saw the world as not good enough, are seeking an ideal world, and used their imagination to invent an ideal world that they want to use in replacing the present ugly world. They did what they had to do, and in the process, had to have a big ego and withdraw from the ugly world to go nourish their egos. Because they are recreating the world to a different world, even if it is a better world, they are on a power trip, being more powerful than God, hence had to feel fear and develop paranoia from the sense of false power that they feel God and other people do not like in them.

What they now need to do is let go of their egos and relax to a non-egoistic self, the Christ self, the real son of God as God created him.

GO ACQUIRE SOME LEADERSHIP SKILLS TO DO THE
LITTLE THAT PEOPLE CAN DO TO IMPROVE THE WORLD.
DO NOT WAIT TO HAVE TOTAL POWER TO COMPLETELY
CHANGE THE WORLD FOR NO PERSON HAS TOTAL POWER
TO CHANGE THE WORLD. IF YOU WANT TO COMPLETELY
CHANGE PEOPLE AND THE WORLD, YOU ARE DELUDED
AND NOT GOING TO DO A THING, NOT EVEN THE LITTLE
THAT ORDINARY FOLKS DO. YOU ARE WAITING FOR
PERFECT POWER WHICH NO HUMAN BEING HAS.

A realistic leadership institute teaches people to go do the little human beings can do to improve their world and does not encourage people to have paranoid, deluded wishes to completely change people and society to a perfect people and world.

Each person deals with the environment he inherits and cannot have a magical power to wave and change the world.

There are other people aspiring power who will fight you tooth and nail for their own version of how society should be, so you are not going to get your version into being.

The desire for perfection is the enemy of the good in people and in public policies.

RELIGION IS PRIMITIVE PSYCHOLOGY; PRIESTS WERE PRIMITIVE PSYCHOLOGISTS AND PSYCHOTHERAPISTS; SCIENTIFIC PSYCHOLOGISTS ARE PRIESTS OF THE NEW RELIGION CALLED PSYCHOLOGY AND PSYCHIATRY.

The human mind wants to understand what exists after people die; the answer it has to that question determines the individual's peace of mind or a mind filled with fear, anxiety, anger, paranoia, and depression, so both religion and psychology deal with the same subject, the human mind (mind is the name for human thinking; mind does not exist as a tangible thing apart from our thinking).

Scientific psychology in rejecting religion pretends that it can get people to be mentally healthy without addressing spiritual issues; it cannot. Therefore, we have to return to spirituality and this time, study it scientifically with the scientific method. That is what we do at the center for spiritual science.

THERE IS A GOD-SELF; HE IS IN EACH PERSON, ANIMALS, AND THINGS; GOD AND HIS SONS SHARE ONE SELF; WHERE GOD IS, HIS SONS ARE; THEY CANNOT BE APART FROM EACH OTHER.

The entire universe is God. God is the whole universe; the whole universe is in units of the whole universe. God has consciousness and intelligence that is akin to what human beings have; therefore, we can call him God the Father and call his part God the Son.

God the Father and God the Son shares one self and one mind; God the Father extended himself to each God the Son and both share one self and mind.

The universe is filled with God the Father and God the Son in infinite units. Where you, God the Son, are is where God the Father is; God is part of yourself but you are not God and God is not outside you although he is also in other people.

IN EVERY DECISION TIME, THE EGO SPEAKS FIRST AND THE HOLY SPIRIT SPEAKS SECOND.

Whenever you open your mouth to speak, the first ideas that come to your mind and mouth are ego thoughts; they are rational, adapt to this world, and tell you to do what is in your self-interest.

In ego speaking, you feel fear, anger, anxiety, paranoia, and depression for you are speaking as the son of God without his father (the ego is the son of God who pretends to be separated from his father and siblings, impossibility).

Before you think, speak, or do anything, if you pause and ask God what to say, the Holy Spirit part of your mind, God in the temporal universe, speaks through you. Here, your thoughts and actions serve collective social interests and are not characterized by fear, anxiety, anger, paranoia, and depression.

In speaking with the Holy Spirit, you are realistic, for you have spoken with your father God in you. What you thought and spoke through the Holy Spirit, your higher self (the ego is your lower self), is still not real because you are still in the unreal world of separation, space, and time but because you thought and spoke with God in you in the temporal universe, you are calm and not afraid.

Whenever the son of God thinks and acts without consulting his father, God, he is in fear, anxiety, paranoia, and depression for he is unrealistic. You are only realistic when you consult God.

In heaven, that is, outside the physical universe, we still consult God in everything we think and do; on earth, we consult the Holy Spirit or the ego (Holy Spirit and ego are not independent persons; they are manners of thinking and behaving in the temporal universe—one speaking and behaving that has God as its frame of reference; the other speaking and behaving that sees itself as apart from God).

THE HOLY SPIRIT REINTERPRETS EVENTS TO SERVE SOCIAL INTEREST.

The Holy Spirit always reinterprets the situation that you find yourself in. Say, you feel discriminated by other people and your ego feels fear and anger and asks you to be defensive, attack, or get away from the situation, if you consult the Holy Spirit, God in the temporal universe, he will tell you that that job or thing is not good for you; it would not do you any good, so you do not respond with anger, but with peace.

Behaving only from the ego is immature and unrealistic; behaving from the Holy Spirit is realistic and mature for you consulted the God in you, not the ego, in what you think or do.

Both ego and Holy Spirit thinking and actions are false, fictional, and insane for they respond to an insane world that is not there but the Holy Spirit's response is kind of like a peaceful madness, happy insanity in an insane world. *A Course in Miracles* calls it a happy dream, for the world is a dream and you can choose to dream it with the ego and be unhappy or with the Holy Spirit and have a happy dream.

WHAT ARE GOD, THE SON OF GOD, THE HOLY SPIRIT, AND THE EGO?

It will take me a lot of space to explain what is meant by God the Father, God the Son, God the Holy Spirit, and the ego, but since an understanding of those terms is necessary to follow my writeups, briefly, they are as follows:

In eternity, aka heaven, is God. God is creative and extends himself to his son. God created infinite sons. Each of us, you and me, is a son of God.

Thoughts and ideas are always passing through the mind of God and his sons. God knows that he is one with his sons.

A thought that it is possible to separate from God and their siblings entered the minds of the sons of God. They said, why not pursue it, and how?

Since they are always unified with God, the only way to pursue it is to forget their eternal union with God and each other. Thus, as it were, while still in God, they cast a magical spell on their minds and went to sleep and in their sleep, dream that they are now separated from God and from each other.

To make separation seem possible and real, they invented the universe of space, time, and matter. They now seem to be in bodies and see space between them.

They are now in a dream of self-forgetfulness, the dream of separation from their eternal union with God and each other. To them, the dream is real.

God could no longer conjointly think with his sons for they now seem separated from him. He realized that they are engaged in a play, a game where they pretend that separation from their father and siblings is possible. It is only a play, so why disturb it? Thus, God did not end the idea of separation. He allowed us to dream that we are separated from him.

God created another aspect of himself, the Holy Spirit, and placed him in our sleeping right minds. The ego is in our sleeping left minds. The ego is the means of dreaming separation. The ego first dreams and then the Holy Spirit reinterpret the ego's dreams.

Thus, now there seems three ways of thinking: holistic thinking, our thinking with God, is how we think in heaven; separated thinking, our ego thinking on earth; and Holy Spirit-directed thinking in the world of separation that urges us to love and forgive each other for the evils we do to each other are done in dreams and are not real.

There are now four seeming persons: God the Father, God the Son, and God the Holy Spirit; these three shares one self; the Catholic Church calls them the Holy Trinity, three persons in one God (and the ego).

In heaven, we think with God; on earth, we can choose to think with the Holy Spirit or with the ego. If you are on earth, you are already thinking and behaving from the ego hence live in fear, anxiety, anger, paranoia, and depression. You can choose to think from the Holy Spirit part of your mind and know relative peace, not the perfect peace of heaven but the imperfect peace we can have on earth.

The three patterns of thinking and behaving produced three worlds. Unified thinking produced heaven; here, all are formless joined light; where one ends and another begins is nowhere.

On earth, we are in separated states in space and time and live in fleshy bodies.

In the world of light forms, aka paradise, gate of heaven, we still have forms but our forms are now in light forms; there is still space and time in paradise, the gate of heaven.

We on earth attain the world of light forms if we consistently love and forgive all people; if we do, we transit to the world of light forms. If we keep hating and attacking each other, we are on earth.

Occasionally, a human being decides to think and behave from the Holy Spirit part of his mind and regains awareness of his joined nature with God and all his sons. Such a person lives in peace and joy. He may experience life in the world of light forms and then the world of formless light (called Samadhi, Nirvana, and Satori, Mystical union of the son and his father or Holy Instant).

Such an awakened son of God is called the Christ or Buddha self. Jesus and Gautama Buddha were such sons of God who while on earth, regained the awareness of their being a part or a son in God; they forgive and love all people.

The above descriptions are metaphoric, not literal facts, but they so approximate reality that you might as well consider predicating your thinking and behavior on them and know relative peace and joy, not the perfect peace and joy of God that words cannot express. God is ineffable.

- The instructors at the center for spiritual science have, at least, master's level education in psychology, philosophy, physics, comparative religions (Hinduism, Buddhism, Gnosticism, Zen, Taoism, etc.); they use a combination of all those in helping people to cope with the reality of being spiritual and secular creatures.

WHY EXACTLY DID I CHOOSE TO STAY IN THE USA?

I did not want my children to be raised in Nigeria for Nigeria seemed to me a madhouse, which it is. I wanted them raised in a scientific environment, not a primitive environment.

What did I hope to accomplish in the USA beyond providing my children with a civilized environment? What did I hope to be doing on a daily basis in America?

Writing about how to develop Africa from America, would it not be better to write about developing Africa in Africa?

I search to understand myself, to become an ideal self; one needs not to desire a better self but needs to return to who one already is, the perfect son of God in one, not the idealized ego that is outside one.

It seems to me that there was no real reason why I stayed in America. America treated me as it treats black folks, as nothing.

I first treated me as nothing for America to treat me as nothing.

If one does not have clarity of where one is going, one would get nowhere.

I did not have a realistic goal of what I wanted to accomplish other than an idealistic desire to improve Africa, and therefore, could not accomplish anything.

All these questions are retrospective introspection. Where do I want to go today so as to get there?

MY TODAY'S GOAL

To write about the interface of spiritual and secular psychology, I need to go inward and recognize the already holy, sinless, guiltless, innocent self that I am; as the son of God, I am already perfect; I must give up seeking an ego that in the present, tells me that I am imperfect and urges me to seek future perfection in other ego's eyes.

I am already perfect and need do nothing else to become perfect. God created me his perfect son. I cannot add or subtract how God created me, perfect.

It is a lie by the ego to say that as I am now, that I am imperfect, and for me to seek future perfection that is never attained.

The ego asks me to seek future perfection based on ego standards knowing that it is unattainable so as to make me frustrated and unhappy.

Every person needs to stop seeking the ego for the ego is a lie, a pretended self, and instead, acknowledge his real self, the already perfect son of God in him.

RELIGIONS' SACRED BOOKS ARE WRITTEN IN METAPHORS, NOT LITERAL TRUTH.

Most religions' sacred books are written in poetic and metaphoric forms. This is the case with Hinduism (Vedas Ramayana, Mahabharata, and Bhagavad Gita), Buddhism (Sutras), Judaism (Torah, Bible's Old Testament), Christianity (New Testament part of the Bible), Islam (Koran, Hadith, and Sharia) and *A Course in Miracles* (which is a legitimate message from the Holy Spirit in the guise of Jesus Christ).

Metaphors are mostly employed in poetic writing; writers of religious sacred books tend to be poets. Metaphors attempt to express in language that which is not easily expressed in words.

God and spiritual matters transcend speech and language so we cannot really write them in words. Words were devised by the separated ones as a medium of speaking and relating to each other.

God is unified, God is one self; that is, simultaneously infinite selves; the various selves in God do not need the words we employ on earth to communicate/commune. They are each other, know what each other are thinking about, and respond to each other as they think their thoughts.

Poets and those who have had some God experience try to write what they experienced in human-separated language and cannot succeed but try to do so nevertheless. They use the language of metaphors and poetry in their efforts to make the inexplicable explicable.

If you read *A Course in Miracles* and take it literally, you would think that the separation from God happened in a second. What happened in less than a second is the pursuit of the wish for separation (Big Bang) but the actual separation by the sons of God did not happen immediately. They went to sleep, and in their sleep, worked on what we now call the universe. It took them thirteen billion years before they could make the creatures they invented (animals) capable of becoming the conduit for their dreaming. They are at no time in animal state, not in bodies, but while still in unified spirit, aka God, identify with bodies and seem to live in the world of matter, space, and time, our world.

They will be having this dream of self-forgetfulness for more billions of years; in their dreams, they will see stars exploding in supernovas, planets dying, and eventually, the entire universe dying as galaxies separate from each other and the universe is very cold to sustain massive objects in it. Only photons of light would survive and those eventually disappear and the sons of God awaken to their real selves as the sons of God.

The point is to not take *A Course in Miracles,* the Bible, or any religion's holy book literally. The story of Adam and Eve, for example, is a metaphor talking about how initially people lived in union with God, then lived in an early world situation where they still retained knowledge of God hence were in a kind of paradise, finally forgot God, and now live as pure egos and suffer in our world. The story is not literal truth.

The Charles Darwin story of human evolution, more or less, captured the journey of human beings from single-celled organisms to multi-celled organisms and to where they are today.

THOSE PEOPLE WHO CLAIM RESPONSIBILITY FOR ALL THAT IS GOOD IN LIFE ARE ON AN EGO TRIP AND ARE COWARDS.

There are people in Alaigbo today who write that everything good in life is introduced to the world by Igbos. To them, Igbos are responsible for all that is good in the world (they want to personally feel responsible for all that is good in life and project their desire to Igbos; they suffer from the desire for absolute power, hence are deluded). In the meantime, they do nothing to improve Nigeria; they allow Fulanis to rule Nigeria and screw Nigerians. They are cowards obtaining a false sense of power from making psychotic claims to being the best people in the world.

DR. O IS A COWARDLY DELUDED MAN ON A QUEST FOR TOTAL POWER OVER PEOPLE.

Dr. O is a coward; he will not lift a finger to do the little that human beings with little power can do on earth but is waiting for the day he would have total power like he imagines that God has and use magical commands to change the world to his liking. In the meantime, he tolerates the current imperfect world doing nothing to improve it a little bit as normal people with little but no absolute power do. He is waiting for the day God would give him absolute power to bring into being whatever he wants magically.

He wants to be the most powerful person on earth via his conception of an omnipotent God. He has not seen omnipotent God; it is man that defines omnipotent God.

The man takes the stories in the bible, such as the story of Adam and Eve literally instead of seeing them as the metaphors they are—metaphors the ancients used to explain the origin of the world but not facts.

He truly has delusion disorder, grandiose type; he seeks total power but is realistic enough to know that if he goes out there and claims it without the ability to back it up with action, he would be laughed at and locked up as the madman he is.

The lesson for us is that if you are waiting for the day God would give you total power and with it, you change the world, you have always wanted to change the world and become the most powerful person on earth. You feel powerless and inferior and compensate with desire for absolute power, which now you associate with God giving it to you, a God of your imagination, hence is not going to give it to you.

Go do the little that human beings can do in this world and make incremental changes in the world, not total change, for you do not have total power to totally change the world.

EJ IS LIKE DR. O; SHE TOO DESIRES TOTAL ABSOLUTE POWER AND CANNOT GET IT IN THE REAL WORLD SO HAS TO HIDE IN NOTHINGNESS WHILE CRITICIZING THOSE TRYING TO DO THEIR BEST IN THE REAL WORLD. SHE HAS TO LET GO OF HER EGO'S DESIRE FOR ABSOLUTE PERFECT POWER AND GO FOR MINIMAL POWER, THE TYPE ALLOWED FOR REAL HUMAN BEINGS. IF SHE DOES SO, SHE WOULD RELAX AND NO LONGER BE TENSE; HER INTENSITY IS ROOTED IN HER QUEST FOR ABSOLUTE POWER, PARANOID POWER, TO MASK HER SENSE OF POWERLESSNESS.

Yet, folks like Dr. O and EJ had to be who they are; they saw the world as not good enough, are seeking ideal world, and used their imagination to invent ideal world that they want to use in replacing the present ugly world. They did what they had to do, and in the process, had to have big ego and withdraw from the ugly world to go nourish their egos. Because they are recreating the world to a different world, even if it is a better world, they are on a power trip, being more powerful than God, hence had to feel fear and develop paranoia from the sense of false power that they feel God and other people do not like in them.

What they now need to do is let go of their egos and relax to a non-egoistic self, the Christ self, the real son of God as God created him.

GO ACQUIRE SOME LEADERSHIP SKILLS TO DO THE LITTLE THAT PEOPLE CAN DO TO IMPROVE THE WORLD. DO NOT WAIT TO HAVE TOTAL POWER TO COMPLETELY CHANGE THE WORLD FOR NO PERSON HAS TOTAL POWER TO CHANGE THE WORLD. IF YOU WANT TO COMPLETELY CHANGE PEOPLE AND THE WORLD, YOU ARE DELUDED AND NOT GOING TO DO A THING, NOT EVEN THE LITTLE THAT ORDINARY FOLKS DO. YOU ARE WAITING FOR PERFECT POWER WHICH NO HUMAN BEING HAS.

A realistic leadership institute teaches people to go do the little human beings can do to improve the world and does not encourage people to have paranoid, deluded wishes to completely change people and society to a perfect people and world.

Each person deals with the environment he inherits and cannot have a magical power to wave and change the world.

There are other people aspiring power who will fight you tooth and nail for their own version of how society should be, so you are not going to get your version into being.

The desire for perfection is the enemy of the good in people and in public policies.

YOU CANNOT SEE GOD, THE HOLY SPIRIT, OR THE EGO FOR THEY ARE IN EVERYTHING.

God is in his sons, in his parts, and is also outside them as pure energy, pure intelligence, and pure love. The Holy Spirit being part of God is also in everything and not apart from them. The ego is the idea of separation, is not apart from people, and is in people, animals, plants, and all things.

Thus, you cannot see God, Holy Spirit, and ego; all three are in you.

Each of the three, however, has a world, those three worlds are in you, and you choose which one you want to experience at any time.

God is in you. If you jettison the ego and live pure love, you experience yourself outside our world and are in a formless, unified spirit world, the world with those who have had God-realization or self-realization experience; it is in them and outside them; they projected that world out and experienced it as if it is outside them.

While on earth, if you live a forgiving and loving life, you are on earth and eventually in the world of light forms.

If you desire separated ego-self and are hateful and unforgiving, you are on our earth; that is, while in God, you projected out our earth and seem to live in it.

All the three worlds, heaven, light world, and our dense world are in the individual and he projects out the one his mental state wants to live in—pure love, ameliorated love, or hate.

A COURSE IN MIRACLES IS SPIRITUAL PSYCHOLOGY WRITTEN BY THE HOLY SPIRIT, JESUS, AND HELEN SCHUCMAN; THE THREE AT THE SPIRITUAL LEVEL AGREED TO WORK ON THAT BOOK AND USED HELEN'S EARTHLY PERSONALITY AND HER TRAINING IN PSYCHOLOGY AS A MEDIUM TO WRITE IT.

MY GRANDFATHER AND FATHER WERE NOT LEADERS; TO BE A LEADER, YOU MUST HAVE A COMMUNITY THAT YOU IDENTIFY WITH AND LEAD; THEY WERE EGOTISTICAL OUTSIDERS; I AM A LEADER OF A WORLDWIDE COMMUNITY OF BELIEVERS IN A NEW PHILOSOPHY.

A leader must have a group, a community, whose values he agrees with, and he identifies with the group and works to improve it.

Grandfather Osuji was an egotistical outsider trying to impose his grandiose ego on people and thus, was not looking after folks' interests and was not a leader.

My father, Johnson, more or less, avoided people to go preserve his big ego.

I avoided people to preserve my idealistic ego that rejected the extant world as not good enough and was seeking perfection in people.

I understand what leaders do, so I establish a new worldwide spiritual community (centers for spiritual science), identify with it, and work for its good, hence is its leader. Whatever is left of my ego is channeled to working for the good of the philosophy's propagation and the people who embrace it; it appeals to about one percent of mankind, the thinkers (my audience is one percent of people worldwide, the Jnana yogis, and not every person for most people do not think).

The coronavirus lockdown gave me time to rethink the purpose of psychology and turn secular psychology into spiritual psychology and thus, give mankind truly useful psychology, one that truly heals them first by healing me to give up my ego.

The ego speaks first; the ego first makes the world and makes ego psychology, philosophy, and science, and the Holy Spirit does not destroy what the ego made to separate from his real self but uses them to help him return to his eternal union with God; when the ego is given up, the son of God pretending to be an ego returns to unified state and know bliss.

Generally, I have little or nothing to do with western medicine. This year, February, I had stomach issues, an exaggeration of an issue that has always been there all my life. Beginning in childhood when I eat, I feel exhausted, lacking energy, and have to go lie down for a while. I assumed that I will eventually die from complications from this stomach problem, whatever it is. Medical doctors did not tell me what it is.

This year, the problem was so exacerbated that I went to a hospital where I stayed for a week. The problem is remedied. While going to surgery, I told myself that I might die, and that was welcome to me, for I did not want to live as a vegetable. But I did not die.

I told me that the illness and surgery represented the death of my attachment to my body and ego. From now on, I live as a resurrected son of God that lives as the Christ; that is, lovingly, forgivingly, and in peace and then do my work of teaching spiritual psychology.

I have always known that my vocation, why I came to this world, is to teach spiritual psychology and establish centers for spiritual science, psychology all over the world. Secular psychology seemed superficial to me and I wanted to improve it. I now embark on doing so.

In childhood, I had a big ego. The grandiose ego is made in an inferior feeling ego attempt to solve his biological and social problems, but that is a magical solution and does not work; the big self magnifies the problems of the ego; the big ego gives one anxiety, fear, anger, paranoia, and depression.

What works is the Holy Spirit's insistence of reinterpreting the ego, making it loving and forgiving, and eventually letting it go.

14

I DO NOT KNOW WHAT GOD IS. I DO NOT KNOW WHAT LOVE IS. I DO NOT KNOW WHO PEOPLE ARE. I DO NOT KNOW WHY PEOPLE DO WHAT THEY DO. I DO NOT KNOW WHO I AM. I DO NOT KNOW WHY I DO WHAT I DO. WHATEVER I SAY ON THESE ISSUES ARE MERE SPECULATIONS AND CONJECTURES

Since one asks questions about who one is and others are and why people do what they do, and does not know the answers and merely speculate and take one's speculations as the truth and behave toward oneself and other people as if what one thinks of them is true, which is not right, one, therefore, should just keep quiet and not make any assumptions about people and their behaviors.

Only the Holy Spirit, God in the temporal universe, knows why people do what they do; since one is not God, one, therefore, ought to keep quiet instead of talking on subjects that one does not know anything about. I guess that is why wise people generally talk less and keep quiet whereas shallow people talk too much, mostly making noise.

ON SEXUAL DESIRE

I do not know why sex is such a big deal in our lives. Based on pure ratiocination, sexual activity is an animal behavior. I am supposing that sex has such a hold on people because it is the means of procreation and since people feel a compulsion to procreate, they feel a compulsion to engage in sex.

I do know something about my sexual behavior. I desire sex when my body is excited. If my body is calm and peaceful, I do not desire sex.

Meditation calms down the human body, hence those who meditate daily and calm their bodies, spiritualized people, do not engage in much sex; in fact, many of them do not engage in sex at all.

Buddha and Jesus probably did not engage in sex from the moment they quieted their bodies after their God-realization. Sex is, thus, mostly for those who are not yet God-realized hence peaceful and happy; God-realized persons do not have children; Buddha had a son before his God-realization after which he had no more children; Jesus had no children.

THE PURPOSE OF PSYCHOTHERAPY IS NOT TO CHANGE PEOPLE BUT TO GET THEM TO ACCEPT THEIR REAL SELVES.

The purpose of psychotherapy is not to change people but to ask them to stop seeking a wished-for ego ideal for that is the root of their problem. They have to accept their real selves which are already in them and transcend ego and body; the real self is spirit and they need to do nothing to be it.

DIAGNOSING AND ANALYZING PEOPLE DO NOT CHANGE THEM.

Diagnosing and psychoanalyzing people does not change them. A hundred years of psychoanalysis does not change people. If a person is intemperate, such as Yaya Fanusi, he would still react angrily and can kill folks out of his childish anger. It is because he is behaving from the ego-self-concept. Can he change it? Yes, with loads of efforts, efforts that you cannot make for him. I myself have not changed despite years of self-analysis.

Deal with people as you see them to be, imperfect, but do not ever wish to change them to become your ego's idea of good persons. If you cannot live with them, then move away from them and toward those whose level of imperfection your level of imperfection can deal with.

BE WHO YOU ARE AND DO THE WORK THAT FITS WHO YOU ARE.

Be who you are, son of God; who you are determine what line of work that you are suited for. I am suited for spiritual and secular psychology, philosophy, and physics.

THE EGO DOES THINGS AND THE HOLY SPIRIT REDOES THEM.

THE EGO INVENTS SCIENTIFIC PSYCHOLOGY AND THE HOLY SPIRIT INVENTS IT.

EGO INVENTS TO MAINTAIN THE EGO; HOLY SPIRIT REINVENTS WHAT THE EGO INVENTED TO RETURN THE SON OF GOD TO PEACE AND EVENTUALLY TO GOD.

It is the ego that invented scientific psychology, just as it is the ego that invented the universe. The ego is the son of God that is sleeping and dreaming through a false self; he has the power of God and can invent things, including inventing the universe and inventing psychology, psychiatry, and science.

The ego invents science and psychology not to destroy the ego and its world but to use them to maintain the ego and the egos' world.

The Holy Spirit does not destroy what the son of God in his madness invents; he reinvents them; he uses the egos' world, egos psychology, and science to help make the ego sane and awaken the ego's awareness that he is the sons of God and return him to peace.

The ego, the sleeping son of God, is very rational; given its rationality, it has invented ego secular psychology. It wants to understand the ego but use that understanding to maintain the ego in existence in the egos' world; it does not want to end the reign of the ego; the ego does not want to give the son of God peace and joy; it wants to continue the world of mutual attacks and defenses we live in.

The Holy Spirit takes ego science and psychology and remakes them to give egos peace. In spiritual psychology, the psychology of the ego is reinterpreted, remade but not destroyed.

Spiritual psychology does not posit new psychology or new science. The Holy Spirit reinterprets all ego psychology and ego science but does not invent new psychology and new science.

Spiritual psychology reinterprets all psychiatric clinical states. Let us consider a few of them (all of them will be reinterpreted in a regular 30-page paper).

Delusion disorder stems from the desire to be the most powerful ego to mask a powerless and inferior-feeling ego. The Holy Spirit reinterprets that to say that the ego itself is the problem and that the ego needs to be given up if the son of God dreaming as the ego is to return to peace and awaken from the dream.

The ego is rebellion against the real self. The real self is unified self; the ego rebels against union and wants a separated self. That rebellion ends when the son of God accepts unified self, not just improved separated ego-self as psychology wants to do.

In schizophrenia, the ego has bizarre delusions and hallucinations; these disturb the ego-mind and the ego wants them to end. The Holy Spirit wants the son of God to give up the ego entirely so that he does not dream during the day or night through hallucinations of a big self.

Ego psychology sees fear and anxiety as a response to threat to the ego. True. The Holy Spirit sees fear and anxiety as a response to unified spirit's threat to the ego; the ego perceives unified spirit, God as a danger to its continued existence as a separated self. Holy Spirit asks the son of God to give up the ego, return home, and do not perceive his real self, unified self, as a danger to his existence for his real existence is in God.

Anger: Ego psychology sees anger as a response to perceived threat to big ego and urges the ego to shrink itself to normal ego so as to not be prone to anger temper tantrums. The Holy Spirit agrees and recommends having no ego at all so as to not feel threat, to begin with.

Fear and anger protect the ego; the ego does not need to be protected but to be let go.

Mania emanates from the desire to make ego important and famous; spiritual psychology says let the ego go for it is unreal and does not need to be made famous and important.

Secular psychology sees depression as a loss of interest in the activities of this world by the ego. The Holy Spirit says true—now, do not have interests in the activities of this world, let the ego and its world go, and experience the new world reinterpreted, remade by the Holy Spirit, the world of light form, the egos' world purified by forgiveness, and eventually let go of all wishes for separated self and return to unified world.

Personality disorders: The ego understands the various personality disorders as resulting from the desire for big egos and tries to make the egos in them pleasant, but the Holy Spirit says do not wish for the ego to begin with; in which case, you would not wish for a big ego or a small ego and would not make egos pleasant; the Holy Spirit has already remade the ego into a happy ego in egoless Christ in the world of light forms.

The Holy Spirit, the higher self, does not destroy ego psychology and the ego but remakes them, reinvents them, so that the son of God now approximates his real self in unified self and lives peacefully. What the son of God made to dream unhappy, separated dreams, the Holy Spirit remakes to enable him to still dream but dream happy dreams.

The ego made ego science to understand the egos' world the son of God made in his dream. Fine. That understanding retains and maintains the world.

The Holy Spirit remakes the ego science and tells the ego that the world you are studying does not exist; let it go and awaken to the real world, happy dream, a pleasant dream; since the ego does not want to do so, the Holy Spirit helps the ego put the product of science to helping all egos live well.

Science attempts to make the ego powerful but the Holy spirit attempts to eliminate the ego so as to give the son of God peace and joy, and bring him close to his true self in heaven, unified self, and when he wants to, he gives up the ego entirely and return to heaven as the prodigal son returned to God.

Post Script:

These notes, to be expanded into a full-length paper, gave me a eureka moment feeling for I suddenly understood the purpose and meaning of spiritual psychology as taught by the Holy Spirit, Jesus Christ, and Helen Schucman in *A Course in Miracles*. I am sending the notes to Dr. Robert Rosenthal, vice president of the Foundation for Inner Peace (the publishers of *A Course in Miracles*).

> MEN SEEK ATTENTION THROUGH THEIR EGOS; THEY SAY, LOOK AT US, ARE WE NOT IMPORTANT MEN; THEY ARE READY TO KILL TO MAKE THEIR EGOS SEEM IMPORTANT AND POWERFUL.

> WOMEN SEEK ATTENTION THROUGH THEIR BODIES; THEY MAKE THEIR BODIES LOOK BEAUTIFUL TO GET OTHER PEOPLE TO ADMIRE THEM AND IN SO DOING, SEEK TO MAKE THEIR BODIES REAL.

> EGOS AND BODIES ARE NOT REAL AND CANNOT BE REAL; THEY DO NOT EVEN EXIST; THEY ARE DREAM FIGURES THAT WE ARE TRYING TO MAKE TO SEEM REAL AND PERMANENT.

> THE REAL IS PERMANENT. OUR SOULS ARE PERMANENT AND REAL.

> THE REAL DOES NOT SEEK ATTENTION; ONLY THE UNREAL SEEKS ATTENTION; BODIES AND EGOS ARE UNREAL HENCE SEEK ATTENTION.

Men seek attention for their egos; they say, look at our egos, we are very important egos; they will kill to get other people to see their egos as important and powerful; they amass power and wealth to make their egos seem powerful.

Women seek attention for their bodies; they say, look at our bodies, are they not admirable? Pay attention to them. In so far, those women seek wealth and power by making their bodies seem admirable; they place expensive pieces of jewelry (made from sand) on their bodies to make them seem important and admired.

Attention-seeking people try to make bodies and egos real. Ego and bodies are not real and cannot be real. Because they are not real, they seek attention.

The real does not seek attention; it is quiet. Our souls are real, and as such, are permanent, self-assured, and do not seek attention; it does not care what you and people say about it for it knows that it is forever.

The ego and body seek attention and want you to affirm its permanency but it is not permanent and eternal; it is always changing, getting old, and dying.

Only the permanent, eternal, and changeless is real; that which is not permanent, body and ego, is not real.

What I said above pretty much summarizes people's existence on earth. I can stand on my head and say it over and over again until I go blue on my face and people will not learn and live it. Why?

To accept and live is to stop their ego games and dances and exit from this bale of tears called planet earth. They do not like to leave the earth; they came to like it.

They like it and give themselves dream pain, fear, anxiety, anger, depression, paranoia, and mania in the process; all are their choices but they blame other people for the things they do to themselves.

They blame other people in an attempt to keep doing what they are doing and not take responsibility for their actions and change them.

Africans blame white people for selling their people so as to not feel guilty; because they do not take responsibility for their wrongs, they keep making them; today, they engage in the most amazing corruption known to man; their leaders are thieves.

All these are due to the refusal to take ownership of their wrongs so as to stop making them. See a blamer and know that he will keep doing what he did that he blames other people for doing, such as selling people and being corrupt.

PURSUING THE BIG IDEAL SELF IS NOT A REASON TO LIVE; LIVING SHOULD BE BEING.

Egoism and delusion ask you to pursue goals outside you as a reason for living. You do and live in pain, fear, anxiety, anger, depression, paranoia, and mania.

Heaven is being; doing nothing and we decided to do something as a condition for living, hence give ourselves madness. Now, we have to return to being, as in doing nothing outside you, attaining no self outside you, and being the self you already are, the self-God created you as, that you denied, and instead, tried to attain a self that must be big, and creator of the world, that you gave to you.

It is now time to feel sorry for you and stop wishing to be anything outside you and pursuing any grandiose, deluded goals that gave you pain and simply be in peace.

Doing nothing, being, is the only reason to live, not the egoistic reasons you gave you, and believe that is reason for you to live.

The ego and its goals are lies we collectively accept as true and must now be let go and we live for no reason.

You do not stay alive to pursue madness, the ego, no matter what you do, you cannot become for it is not you.

Just be who you are, no picture and image of you; be the life in you.

- The idea of just being is actually the summary of Eastern religions: Hinduism, Jainism, Buddhism, Taoism, and Zen.

EGO-LESSNESS IS WHAT A COURSE IN MIRACLES MEANS—A LIFE GUIDED BY THE HOLY SPIRIT.

In ego-lessness, one is still in ego and body but is now guided by the Holy Spirit; one is still in the dream but having holy relationships hence a happy dream; it begins on earth and proceeds to the world of light forms, the real world, the gate of heaven, the bridge between earth and heaven, forms and formlessness.

If you entirely let go of the ego and have no ego, as can be attained in meditations, you would exit this world of forms or the world of light forms and would be in formless unified spirit, heaven.

MY PAULIAN ROLE IN MARKETING A COURSE IN MIRACLES

What I have done with my writing is not to say anything new that *A Course in Miracles* did not say but to translate the book from spiritual poetry to prose so that ordinary people can understand it. The book is obviously the best spiritual psychology on earth today.

I am kind of like Paul; Paul took the parabolic utterances of Jesus, meant for his fellow Jews, to the larger gentile world and in the process, established what folks now call Christianity.

I took the poetry of Helen Schucman that mostly makes sense to her highly educated Jewish psychologists and psychiatrists (I doubt that any African can actually understand the book) to the larger world by translating it to readable simple prose.

Each of us does what he can do best. I write in simple English, although I understand the English language probably better than anyone else (I have written a book on English grammar that is used in many countries). My skill for putting complex ideas into simple readable prose is needed to translate convoluted Jewish poetry to readable English. In the process, of course, I propagated my own more physics-based spiritual psychotherapy.

YOU ARE GROWN UP WHEN YOU KNOW THAT YOUR OPINION DOES NOT MATTER TO OTHER PERSONS BUT CAN GET YOU INTO TROUBLE WITH PEOPLE.

You are a child if you believe that your opinions sway other people's decision-making. The fact is that your opinion is irrelevant to people; they will do whatever they want to do; and you, too, is that way; you do what you want to do regardless of other people's opinions and efforts to sway you to their line of thinking.

People's opinions reflect their self-interests; other people have different self-interests and will pursue them regardless of your opinion that articulates your self-interest.

Therefore, the most realistic and mature thing to do is to keep quiet when folks ask your opinion; just say nothing. Let them do whatever they want to do and take their consequences. That is the nature of being human.

You are an adult when you stop proffering empty opinions that your children, spouse, or friends do not listen to and if they get the negative consequences to their decisions, they turn around and say that you made them do what they did.

People are always looking for scapegoats to blame, to sacrifice for their decisions that did not pan out well for them; do not make you their scapegoat by offering opinions, good or bad to people.

Immature people tend to think that they are powerful if they get other people to listen to their opinions. You do not need that deluded sense of power for you have no power over anyone or over yourself for that matter.

WHERE IS SPIRIT, SELF, MIND? NOWHERE... ALL ARE MERE CONCEPTS.

The universe always has ideas, if you like, the universe always thinks. The universe is a whole with infinite units, parts. Each part may take any ideas that passed through the universe, call it its own, and pursue it.

You take an idea and associate it with your self-concept (your self is a concept not real), defend those ideas, and call them your ideas. No, they are not your personal ideas.

The universe thinks through us, through animals, trees, planets, stars, through everything. Each of us sees ideas pass through his so-called mind and he takes personal responsibility for the ideas that pass his mind that he thinks are his ideas. No, they are not his ideas, but he has the option of deciding which ideas to dwell on or not; either way, the ideas belong to the universe, not to him.

In God, eternity, the idea of separation and thought of being greater than God came out of nowhere and the sons of God pursued it. The thought is not theirs but if they pursue it, then they take the consequences of doing so; they should have just let go of the ideas as they let go of many other ideas. They took the idea of being greater than their father, parts being more than the whole, seriously, went to sleep, and pursue it in dreams, our universe, and suffer birth and death, all because they took a passing idea seriously.

Let ideas pass through your mind and do not attach yourself to them. This is one of the discoveries of the greatest human thinker, Gautama Buddha. Sit quietly in meditation, see ideas race through your mind, and ignore them all and you attain internal silence and escape to formless, unified self and experience its bliss and eternity.

THE SELF-CONCEPT IS FICTION.

An idea of separated self passes through your mind—you take it and see it as your self-concept, and defend it. The self-concept is a mirage, an illusion. There is no such thing as yourself or other selves; those are a mere mirage.

If you take an idea as real, since it is not real, you have to defend it and in defending it make it seem real for you; you defend your self-concept, aka personality, a lie, an illusion, and defending it makes it real for you.

Only the unreal needs defense to seem real; the ego is unreal and must be defended to seem real to its believer, you; if you do not defend your ego, it does not exist for you.

The real needs no defense to seem real. The real in you is the part of the universe in you, in anthropomorphic terms, the son of God in you—that you are eternal, permanent, and changeless.

Do not defend any idea and it keeps going through the universe for other people to take, defend, and suffer psychological pain of their making from the mistake of taking ownership of an idea that is not theirs in origin.

The universe originates all ideas, infinite ideas, and there are infinite universes; each universe is an idea pursued by parts of the universe, sons of God.

THERE IS NO GOD, SON OF GOD, HOLY SPIRIT, AND EGO.

There is no such thing as God, son of God, Holy Spirit, and ego; all those are concepts and all concepts are illusions.

If you like, you could see the four concepts as levels of yourself; God is the highest level of your unified self; son of God is the next highest level, a unit of unified self, God; the Holy Spirit is third, God in the temporal universe of space, time, and matter; the ego is the lowest part of you, the you in the temporal universe trying to adapt to it.

What is real is that thoughts are going through the universe and the universe owns them not one.

THE MOST ABSURD THING PEOPLE DO IS TO FEEL GUILT.

The most stupid thing to do is to have a friend or marry out of a sense of guilt; guilt implies ego, the ego playing nice guy; you must not feel guilty for anything that happens in the world for people generally take the consequences of their thinking and behavior.

People separate from God in pursuit of ego power and experience illusory birth in body, diseases, and death. There is no escape from the consequences of our choices. Everything people do has consequences for them, so do not feel guilty when they receive the negative consequences of their actions.

A BASIC LAW OF THE UNIVERSE IS THAT WE ARE
FREE AND THAT WE CAN CHOOSE TO DO WHATEVER
WE WANT AND TAKE THE CONSEQUENCES OF OUR
CHOICE. UNFORTUNATELY, WHAT WE CHOOSE ALSO
HAS CONSEQUENCES FOR THOSE AROUND US.

The universe offers us perfect freedom with the provision that we must take the consequences of our choices, decisions; there is no escape from this reality.

Mr. Donald Trump, reacting to the election of a black man as the president of the USA, decided to appeal to racist whites who are angry that black folks even live at all, what more, participate in America's politics. He got elected on the basis of angry white men who want to stick it to nonwhites. Good for him.

He and his angry white mob must pay the price of operating in a hateful manner. Their empire of evil will eventually have its rendezvous with history but Trump's hatred is hastening it.

Trump is irrelevant; the relevant point is that all our actions have consequences for us so we had better think long and hard before we do whatever we want to do.

Only choices made out of love for all humanity produce positive consequences for all people. Choose with love, not hate.

- Thank me for giving you these Buddhist gems of wisdom that can make your life peaceful and happy.
- In Hindu categories, I am a Jnana yogi, a thinker; as such, my thoughts appeal to only one percent of mankind, for only one percent of mankind does think at all. The rest of the people are worshippers of non-existent Gods called Bhakti Yogi, or lovers called Tantra Yogi, or doers called karma Yogi, or experimenters called Raja Yogi. I expect only one out of hundred persons to understand what I am talking about; if my ideas are not for you, please do not contort your mind to understand them, pass them over and go to where you belong.

WHAT DO YOU DO WHEN YOU ARE EGOLESS?

I have demonstrated without doubt the problems from having a big ego. If you pursue the ego, you have psychological pain, fear, anxiety, depression, paranoia, and mania (or any other mental disorder) as correlates. You may try to keep your ego, avoid people, and in social avoidance, nurse a big ego that is not ever disputed in society, in the presence of other people; avoidant people avoid people to keep their egos and in the process, do not do anything useful in society and fail.

Having a grandiose ego leads to not doing well at school. The student with a big ego is afraid to make mistakes for making mistakes makes him feel powerless and small; to avoid making mistakes and failing, he drops out of school. We call them opposition defiant kids.

A big ego simply has to be shrunk to the most minimal level; the ego can possibly be retained in the individual and he still lives on earth; that is why they call psychologists and psychiatrists shrinks.

If you totally eliminate your ego, you are no longer in body for the wish for the ego produced body to protect it, and produced the world of space, time, and matter. If you do not have a wish for the ego, you give up the desire for separation (separation produced ego), you leave the world of space, time, and matter and return to the awareness of being an undifferentiated part of life, God-realization, being part of a formless life, peace, and joy.

As long as you do not want to exit planet earth, space, time, and matter yet, you can retain some of the ego but shrink it, purify it. When the ego is totally purified and is at its best, it is like what *A Course in Miracles* called the Christ, the son of God who, while still separated from his father, has reduced his wish for separation to a minimum and now use what is left of his ego to love his real self, love other people's real selves, and live in relative peace and happiness. Such a person is no longer prone to fear, anxiety, anger, depression, paranoia, and mania; he is now, as it were, at the gate of heaven, close to God, close to no ego-self, but has not yet allowed his entire ego to vanish so that he is back to living in no ego heaven, in unified state, in God.

Such a person occasionally sees himself and other people in light forms for he has more or less returned to love, overlooks people doing bad things in egos, and tries his best to correct their hurtful egoism but is very careful for we see other egos with our egos and in trying to correct other egos, we are really correcting our egos, so we might as well figure out a way not to be in ego before we attempt to correct other egos, hence *A Courses in Miracles* says—do not correct other people's behaviors from your ego but let the Holy Spirit do it.

But the Holy Spirit is not outside you; he is your higher, egoless self, so what it really means is only try to correct people's behaviors from a forgiving and loving place.

Okay, so you have shrunk your ego to the most minimum, how then do you live on earth? The earth is still a place where folks exchange goods and services; you still have to have a job skill that produces something that other people desire and sell it to them to make a living.

In this light, what am I now producing and selling to other people that they desire? What do I produce from a non-ego point of view?

I cannot possibly go back to trying to produce ego goods or work in ego work settings, such as teaching at a university, for that is an ego setting. What is a non-ego setting that I can work in daily? It does not exist in the extant world so I have to establish one, a place where secular and spiritual psychologies are taught, as I call it.

THE EGO DOES THINGS AND THE HOLY SPIRIT REDOES THEM.

THE EGO INVENTS SCIENTIFIC PSYCHOLOGY
AND THE HOLY SPIRIT REINVENTS IT.

EGO INVENTS TO MAINTAIN THE EGO; HOLY SPIRIT
REINVENTS WHAT THE EGO INVENTED TO RETURN THE
SON OF GOD TO PEACE AND EVENTUALLY TO GOD.

It is the ego that invented scientific psychology, just as it is the ego that invented the universe. The ego is the son of God that is sleeping and dreaming through a false self; he has the power of God and can invent things, including inventing the universe and inventing psychology, psychiatry, and science.

The ego invents science and psychology not to destroy the ego and its world but to use them to maintain the ego and the egos' world.

The Holy Spirit does not destroy what the son of God in his madness invents; he reinvents them; he uses the egos' world and egos psychology and science to help make the ego sane and awaken the ego's awareness that he is the son of God and return him to peace.

The ego, the sleeping son of God, is very rational; given its rationality, it invented ego secular psychology. It wants to understand the ego but use that understanding to maintain the ego in existence in the egos' world; it does not want to end the reign of the ego; the ego does not want to give the son of God peace and joy; it wants to continue the world of mutual attacks and defenses we live in.

The Holy Spirit takes ego science and psychology and remakes them to give egos peace. In spiritual psychology, the psychology of the ego is reinterpreted, remade but not destroyed.

Spiritual psychology does not posit new psychology or new science. The Holy Spirit reinterprets all ego psychology and ego science but does not invent new psychology and new science.

Spiritual psychology reinterprets all psychiatric clinical states. Let us consider a few of them (all of them have been reinterpreted in my several books and articles).

Delusion Disorder

Delusion disorder stems from the desire to be the most powerful ego to mask a powerless and inferior-feeling ego. The Holy Spirit reinterprets that to say that the ego itself is the problem and that the ego needs to be given up if the son of God dreaming as the ego is to return to peace and awaken from the dream.

The ego is rebellion against the real self. The real self is unified self; the ego rebels against union and wants a separated self. That rebellion ends when the son of God accepts unified self, not just improved separated ego-self as psychology wants to do.

Schizophrenia

In Schizophrenia, the ego has bizarre delusions and hallucinations; these disturb the ego-mind and the ego wants them to end. The Holy Spirit wants the son of God to give up the ego entirely so that he does not dream during the day or night through hallucinations of a big self.

Anxiety

Ego psychology sees fear and anxiety as response to threat to the ego. True. The Holy Spirit sees fear and anxiety as response to unified spirit's threat to the ego; the ego perceives unified spirit, God, as a danger to its continued existence as a separated self. The Holy Spirit asks the son of God to give up the ego, return home, and to not perceive his real self, unified self, as a danger to his existence for his real existence is in God.

Anger

Ego psychology sees anger as a response to perceived threat to big ego and urges the ego to shrink itself to normal ego so as to not be prone to anger temper tantrums. The Holy Spirit agrees and recommends having no ego at all so as to not feel threat, to begin with.

Fear and anger protect the ego; the ego does not need to be protected but to be let go.

Mania

Mania emanates from the desire to make ego important and famous; spiritual psychology says let ego go for it is unreal and does not need to be made famous and important.

Depression

Secular psychology sees depression as a loss of interest in the activities of this world by the ego. The Holy Spirit says true and tells the depressed person to not have interests in the activities of this world, to let the ego and its world go, and experience the new world reinterpreted, remade by the Holy Spirit, the world of light forms, the egos' world purified by forgiveness, and eventually let go of all wishes for separated self and return to unified world.

Personality Disorders

The ego understands the various personality disorders, such as paranoid, schizoid, schizotypal, histrionic, narcissistic, borderline, antisocial, avoidant, dependent, obsessive-compulsive, and passive-aggressive, as resulting from the desire for big egos and tries to make the egos in them pleasant but the Holy Spirit says do not wish for the ego, to begin with; in which case, you would not wish for a big ego or a small ego and would not make egos pleasant; the Holy Spirit has already remade the ego into a happy ego in egoless Christ in the world of light forms.

TRANSFORMATION OF SECULAR PSYCHOLOGY TO SPIRITUAL PSYCHOLOGY

The Holy Spirit, the higher self, does not destroy ego psychology and the ego but remakes them, reinvents them, so that the son of God now approximates his real self in unified self and lives peacefully. What the son of God made to dream unhappy, separated dreams, the Holy Spirit remakes to enable him to still dream but dream happy dreams.

FROM SECULAR SCIENCE TO SPIRITUAL SCIENCE

The ego made ego science to understand the egos' world the son of God made in his dream. Fine. That understanding retains and maintains the egos' world.

The Holy Spirit remakes ego science and tells the ego that the world you are studying does not exist; let it go and awaken to the real world, happy dream, a pleasant dream.

However, since the ego does not want to do so, the Holy Spirit helps the ego put the product of science to helping all egos live well.

Science attempts to make the ego powerful but the Holy spirit attempts to eliminate the ego so as to give the son of God peace and joy, and bring him close to his true self in heaven, unified self, and when he wants to, he gives up the ego entirely and return to heaven as the prodigal son returned to his father God.

Post Script:

People who do what I do generally have a successful book that articulates their philosophy, a book many folks have read and thus, come to him for further exposure to his ideas. Instead of having one well-publicized book containing my entire philosophy, I scattered my worldviews in my many books. I am going to find a way to summarize my thoughts in one book of maybe two hundred pages so that it is readily available to the public.

I DOUBT THAT MAN CAN HAVE REAL WORTH OUTSIDE GOD.

Charles:

Thanks for the above excerpt from Blaise Pascal. Years ago, I tried reading his Pensées and could not make head or tail of it. I gave up. Generally, when writing does not make sense to me, I do not sweat it but leave it alone. I had read about Pascal's spiritual experience which he described as being in a place where it seemed to him, that he was inside a kind of fire (he wrote in the 1500s, even before Rene Descartes, before the discovery of electricity so he was probably describing what we would today call an electrically lite room). Well, it convinced him that he was in the abode of God. As noted, I did not understand him. What you represented that he said here makes perfect sense to me.

On my own, I came to the conclusion that without God, human beings must feel worthless, powerless, and insignificant. As I look at myself, I am a body. I do not deceive myself. I know that my body will die and decay. I was a boy in Biafra. When the Biafrans cleared Owerri, my father and I went to Owerri. We trekked through Emmi and Egbu and entered Douglas road Owerri. As we trekked, we saw dead soldiers on both sides of the road. They were in various states of decay. That was my first sight of dead and decaying human bodies, smelling worse than feces.

Well, that experience stayed with me. As a result, I have never had any illusions about the human body. The human body is flesh that will die and decay. My body will die and decay. If all I am is my body, then I am nothing, period.

Since I have an inner sense that I am something important, what is it, if my body is not it? That was the beginning of my exploration of religions; beginning with Early Christians, I studied Paul's epistles, Origen, Tertullian, and Manicheanism (Gnosticism). I read the early Christian theologians such as Augustine's City of God and Confessions, Saint Ambrose, Saint Athanasius's (his writing influenced the decisions at the council of Nicias in 325 AD where the Catholic Creed that Catholics chant at high masses was composed as the article of faith), Meister

Eckhart, to Thomas Aquinas, Erasmus, then the protestant theologians and Catholic mystics, such as Saint John of the Cross, Teresa of Avila, to more contemporary theologians.

Unsatisfied, I delved into Hinduism, Buddhism, Jainism, Taoism, and Zen. In time, I did my own thinking. I reached the conclusion that without God, man is nothing.

I am a mental health professional and had worked at psychiatric hospitals and know a thing or two about mental disorders. I concluded that most mental disorders originate when folks try to derive worth by ego means.

I have written extensively on this subject. From delusion disorder to mania, depression, to schizophrenia, all are attempts to seem to have worth outside of God. The anxiety disorders, personality disorders, and addiction to drugs are all derived from seeking worth outside God.

Consider narcissistic Donald Trump; he tries to give his self-worth outside God hence his obsessive-compulsive seeking of admiration and sense of specialness from folks, which is what narcissism is.

Well, I have written thousands of pages on the causal factors in mental disorders. I am convinced that until human beings return to God, not primitive conceptions of God, but real God, which, in my opinion, Jesus Christ represents at its best, they cannot have worth; in Pascal's language, they must feel wretched.

I have actually grown to look forward to the vignettes that you post, such as this one from Pascal talking about the human wretchedness without attachment to God; God is our only source of worth. Thanks for sharing with us these uplifting gems of knowledge and wisdom.

RELIGIONS DO NOT PREDICT WHAT IS GOING TO HAPPEN IN THE NEXT MINUTE, DAY, WEEK, AND THE FUTURE. DOES THAT MEAN THAT THEY ARE MERE POETRY AND NOT TO BE TAKEN SERIOUSLY?

DOES SCIENCE PREDICT THE FUTURE?

The coronavirus has literally shot down the world's economy; folks are told to self-quarantine, to stay at home, and when outside, to maintain social distancing and wear facemasks. Thousands are dying from the virus.

None of the religions and their numerous ministers predicted the coming of this pandemic. None of them has predicted how it would end; none of the pastors who normally claim the ability to heal anyone has healed any person with the Covid-19 issue.

We rely on medical researchers to come up with a vaccine to cure the pandemic. We do not expect religions to come up with a cure. Indeed, the churches, including Saint Peters Basilica at the Vatican and the Muslim Rock in Mecca are shuttered up because they cannot prevent the church goers from contracting the virus and dying.

Does this mean that religions are powerless to heal anyone, that they are false promises of God's ability to perform miracles, signs, and wonders?

If so, how would the pandemic affect religions? Would it kill them off and usher in the age of atheism and agnosticism? I do not know.

What I do know is that science is the answer for us. The study of physics, chemistry, biology, geology, astrophysics, and their applied forms is mankind's best hope. Science struggles to understand nature as it is but at present, despite wild claims by juvenile scientists, science does not predict the future nor has it understood more than one percent of phenomena. Consider that it does not know anything about dark energy and dark matter, which constitute 96% of the universe; of the 4% of the visible universe it has, more or less, studied, it has not understood one percent of it.

The physical sciences study the physical phenomenon, not the soul. Human beings are probably more than their bodies; they seem to have spirits in them. How do we understand this real aspect of us?

I have made efforts in that area but must note that so far, no spiritual psychology and secular psychology has shown it useful in healing people's physical issues. All the claims by new-age so-called healers are as good as the claims by the priests of traditional religions.

We simply have to keep plugging away until we figure out a way to connect to what I call unified spirit and in doing so, learn how to heal our psychological and physical issues.

We cannot give up on spirituality for to do so is to say that we are only egos and bodies and if that is the case, we are nothing and might as well not exist at all.

If all we are are mere animals with a built-in desire to live hence struggle for survival and then age and die and that is our end, what is the point in living at all? It is only if there is something in us that transcends our egos and bodies can we be said to have existential worth and life be said to be meaningful and purposeful.

I have a hunch that there is a spiritual part of us, an eternal, permanent, and changeless aspect of us. I have not yet figured it out but intend to do so, sooner or later.

I am an agnostic searching for God (Gnostics believe that they have experienced God hence know for sure that God's existence is real; atheists believe that there is no God; theists believe that there is God but have not experienced him; I must experience God to accept his existence as real.)

YOU KNOW THAT YOU ARE IN YOUR REAL SELF WHEN THERE ARE NO EGO THOUGHTS IN YOUR HEAD.

I have talked a lot about the real self and the ideal self. So, how does one know that one is in one's real self?

You cannot be in your real self and be on earth. If you are in your real self, you are part of unified spirit and are not aware of this earth, not aware of your body, space, and time.

While in unified spirit, you and all of us on earth made a decision to separate from that real self and are now dreaming that you are a self that you see as in body, walking around in space and time. At present, you identified with the separated ego-self in body. You believe that you are one with your body. You are dreaming that you are a separated self in body; while in the dream, you can approximate your bodiless self but will not be it.

When you are in your approximate real self in the dream world, earth, you feel calm, peaceful, and happy; you feel as if there are no ego thoughts in your head; you feel that you are not your body; in fact, you are less aware of your body.

On the other hand, if you are pursuing your ideal self, you have rejected your calm, real self, and posited an imaginary idealized self that you believe that if you attain it and behave from it, you are a very important, powerful, and all-knowing intelligent self and also feel like all people would acknowledge you as that powerful self.

When you are in the ideal self, if other people acknowledge that ideal, powerful self, you feel nice, and if they do not, you feel angry at them. When you are in the ideal, false self, you easily feel fear, anxiety, anger, depression, paranoia, mania, and other mental disturbances.

When you are in your real self, unified self, you are healthy; when you are in your approximate real self, you are somewhat healthy, as healthy as a human being can be and still see himself in body, space, and time (you are what folks call a normal person, whereas when you are in ideal self, you are what folks call a neurotic and know no peace of mind or body).

The pursuit of the ideal self, which is what we came to earth to do, is literally an attack on your real self. You literally want your real self to be killed to allow you to be a different self, the self you made.

God created your real self as part of him, but you want to kill God and your real self and become the different self you made. The pursuit of the ideal is self-attack.

To seek ideal self is not to love one's real self (and you cannot love your real self without loving God and other selves for they are all unified as one self in spirit hence Jesus said love your God, yourself, and your neighbors; in my kind of language, love the whole and its parts).

If you are a neurotic, like I was, you have never loved your real self, not even once in your life. Because you did not love you, you could not love God and love other people; a neurotic is attacking his real self, attacking other selves, and attacking God; the neurotic is at war with his real self and other peoples' real selves (a war his real self, other peoples' real selves, and God ignore and let him knock his ego-self out and then return to his real self).

When you are in your real self, you do only work that you can do and that interests you. For example, I can do intellectual work. I cannot do physical work. If I tried to do physical, hard work, my fragile body feels pained and if I persist, I feel angry at whoever I think made me do it, say, my parents or my spouse when I felt a need to work for the family).

But other people did not cause my bodily pain, nor did they know that I was in pain, so it was not really their fault that I felt overtaxed doing physical work. My physical pain was, if you like, caused by nature (I inherited Cytochrome C Oxidase deficiency, Spondylolysis, and Mitral Valve Prolapse).

All I had to do and learned to do is not do any work that overtaxed my body; I would just quit such jobs even if they paid a lot of money.

My father said that he lasted all of two days working in a coal mine and quit because his fragile body could not take that hard work; at college, I tried to work in a factory and quit the second day because I could not stand on my feet for eight-hour shifts; the pain on my body was intolerable.

Life on earth is withdrawal from love, from one's real self, for the real self is love (love is in union of all selves as one self). On earth, we behave without love, we attack love, and give ourselves pain.

We keep not loving ourselves until we have had enough pain and begin asking questions as to why we do so and at that point, turn our attention to the study of spirituality and . . .

I was going to say psychology until I remembered what American Psychology is. American Psychology is useless. Americans have not produced realistic psychology; this is because they refuse to look inward and know who they are; in so far that you will find a semblance of psychology in America, it is introduced by foreigners, such as Karen Horney's psychoanalysis and Alfred Adler's psychoanalysis (Helen Schucman's spiritual psychology, *A Course in Miracles*, is probably the only good psychology that America's soil has produced).

Albert Ellis and Aaron Beck's cognitive behavior psychotherapy approximates real psychology but is not it.

Listen; do not pay attention to any white American that calls himself a psychologist or psychiatrist for they are folks who have fled from their real selves and take their society's instruments of making them mad, capitalism and the social structures around it, as real. Americans, from childhood, are browbeaten by an insane political and economic system to be afraid of talking about the truth but to always tell lies.

Consider that America is an oligarchy where a few rich folks and their errand boys in the legislature rule but Americans talk as if they have democracy. They hold phony elections where the Republican Party tries its best to prevent most black people and poor white people from voting so that the rich win and yet, the system's academic hacks, political scientists, talk about American democracy.

Americans are good at science (especially technology) that studies things but not people; they are afraid of knowing who people are, for if they did, they would have social justice, not the unjust society they have that marginalize minority persons and abuse poor white folks.

In our extant world, the only just political system is social democracy and the only just economic system is mixed capitalist and socialist economies (where society pays for all people's health care and education through university).

CONCLUSION

It is when you decide to pursue an ideal self, which is separated from other selves, that you disturb your peace and feel fearful, anxious, angry, depressed, paranoid, and manic.

When you decide to live from your real self, which is the same as living from love, you know peace of mind and body.

In unified spirit, there is still thinking, but quiet thinking, not the frenetic thinking we do on earth. Our earthly thinking is thinking based on separated selves, ego-based thinking; they are false thinking that produced our false world of space and time. In reality, there is no space, time, and matter; all selves are in one God-self.

God and eternity are beyond the scope of this essay. If you want to glean eternity, try stopping all ego-based thinking, do meditation, and see what happens when you attain no self-state and know peace

A PERSON'S PERSONALITY ENCOMPASSES THE TOTALITY OF HIMSELF.

The individual's personality represents the totality of his biological and social self. This is so because the personality was formed when the child's whole body adapted to his physical and social world. He does not adapt in half but with all he has, his total bodily and social experience. He formed his behavior pattern, which is what personality is, with his total self. Everything in his body adapted to his world for him to survive.

Because personality represents everything in a person, it is difficult to change that person by merely changing certain aspects of him; his total self, his total behavior repertoire, must change for his personality to change.

You cannot retain a bit of the old personality and become changed; you must change all aspects of you to change you. This reality means that it is difficult to change the human personality despite folks' efforts to do so.

So, can the individual ever be changed? Theoretically, it is possible. For him to change, he must now see himself as not his body and not the separating ego-self that manifested in body and formed his personality. He must now see himself as a different self, say, see himself as the Christ self or the Buddha self, and not as the body, and use the new self-concept, still conceptual hence not real (the real self is part of God and his son, it is beyond concepts) to live on earth.

For example, because of the problems my body had in adapting to the physical environment, I had to approach things with hesitancy, test them to make sure that they would not harm me. Thus, I developed self-doubt and aspects of obsessive-compulsive and avoidant personalities. I must repeat things to make sure that they are okay for me. Now, as an adult, I know that I do not have to engage in obsessive behavior but I still do it automatically. For example, after typing this material, I will save it. But the chances are that I may click the save icon twice to make sure that I have saved it; I type fast and do not have to look at the keyboard to type but when I am typing serious stuff, I automatically look at the keyboard to make sure that I typed the material correctly; I often check and recheck to make sure that my door is locked when I leave home; these behaviors show lack of self-confidence.

Obsessive-compulsive personality, avoidant personality, and dependent personality are characterized by anxiety, fear. They are the group C of the personality disorders. Psychoanalysts consider them anxiety neurosis. They are found in varying degrees in so-called normal persons.

In case you want to know what obsessive-compulsive personality and avoidant personality is, I attach a more descriptive picture of them from psych-central below. Both, like all personality types, were necessary adaptation of a certain type of inherited body to the human environment and both can be understood and technically changed in the individual.

However, I have not seen any human being who completely changed his entire personality type unless he embraced a spirituality that tells him that he is not body and ego and he believes it and no longer identifies with his body and ego and instead, identify with the spiritualized self and behave as such.

That spiritualized self, such as the Christ self or the Buddha self, is still not real, for it is still in form, hence an illusion; the real self is formless and is part of all selves, unified as one self, called the union of God and his son as one holy self, one unified self. Very few people attain this level of evolution while still on earth that we might as well not talk about it.

THE WORLD IS ORGANIZED AROUND THE EGO AND YOU WANT TO GET OUT OF THE EGO AND STILL SUCCEED IN EGOLAND?

The universe of space, time, and matter is a universe produced by the son of God in his sleep and dream of separation hence organized along ego lines. Its premise is that all persons are separated and each is looking after his self-interests and will hurt other people in pursuit of his self-interests; therefore, they must have government and laws based on crime and punishment.

People are free, and in their freedom, can harm other people; therefore, you must punish the guilty. Science, technology, and business are also organized along ego lines.

A Course in Miracles wants to transcend the ego and its divisive world and return you to unified heaven. Its philosophy does not enable you to adapt to the exigencies of this world. If you follow its parameters, you must fail in this world.

However, it gives folks a ray of hope by saying that if they live from the Holy Spirit, their higher self, not their ego lower self, whatever they need to support their body and what is left of their egos would be given to them, made available to them. Does this happen? I have not seen it happen.

Therefore, a realistic person must cope with the exigencies of the egos' world as it is if he wants to make it in this world; develop your talent and compete for the world's rewards; the world rewards the best competitors; therefore, deal with people as if they can screw you, for some will, and live by law and order and punish criminals.

MY CHILDHOOD ANGER AND TEMPER TANTRUMS WERE CAUSED BY THE FACT THAT I WAS PERPETUALLY IN PAIN.

No adult knew about my physical pains; when they asked me to go do what other children do, such as go to the farm with them, I refused to do so and felt angry at them. How dare they have me work when they could not help me reduce the pain I felt?

I did not want anyone to tell me what to do because no one helped me overcome my pain. Western psychology could not help me banish my pain either, hence, I dismissed it as rubbish.

My body reacts to all kinds of things with extra sensitivity, such as feeling faint in a centrally airconditioned office, not being able to work there; feeling dizzy around paint, even food, and electronic equipment that produce a bad smell in my mouth; all those led to my developing a sense of threat to my life hence anger at a world that did not help me overcome them.

MY EX-WIFE DID NOT UNDERSTAND ME.

To make extra money, right after graduate school, in the 1980s, I worked at a 7/11 store in the evenings and had to stand on my feet the whole time (by the cash register). Pain sensations shot from my legs to all parts of my body and after two days, I quit. I inherited serious medical issues: Cytochrome C Oxidase Deficiency, Spondylolysis, and Mitral Valve prolapse.

Because I quit, I could not make the extra money I had wanted to make to supplement my then meager income.

My ex-wife saw my quitting that job and concluded that I did not want to make the income we needed. She had no time to understand my life and its pains. She was focused on the money I brought to the family and when it was not enough, felt disappointed and wanted out.

She had absolutely no understanding of me, nor did I tell her what troubled me for I did not think that she could understand me; her life was focused on her religion; without her religion, she probably would have been depressed.

I am not saying that she was an evil person and that I am Jesus Christ himself. I have my own issues. For example, I was detached. In trying to deal with my physical over-arousal issues, I tend to keep to myself and not socialize a lot. I am not physically demonstrative of love toward people. I tend to overanalyze human issues instead of providing emotional support to people. Sometimes, merely listening to folks and holding their hands is all that they need to feel joined to one, hence feel happy. I did not do that

Be that as it may, no one can say that I am overtly a bad person so I was really surprised when a friend of my wife told me that she complained that I quit a job when we needed that money. I often worked a full-time job and a part-time job to make ends meet so no one can accuse me of being lazy; thus, I was hurt and dismissed her as lacking understanding of my issues; thereafter, I really wished her gone from my life; if we did not have children, I would have simply left her without regret.

The salient point here is that married folks often do not understand each other; they do not have the faintest awareness of each other's issues, particularly medical and psychological issues; they dwell on the superficial aspects of human relationships. This is actually why many marriages end, lack of understanding of each other's pains.

One may attribute this lack of mutual understanding to the spouse's immaturity. Still, human beings have the capacity to understand each other if they want to. Well, my spouse did not understand me and I looked for a way to get out of that marriage and when it ended, I felt relieved.

I resolved that I was not going to marry another woman who does not understand me. I felt at that point that most women were immature and could not understand a man and I did not want anything to do with them. I would prefer to be single than to marry a person who has no clue what my issues are or see them as excuses for me not making the kind of money she felt she needed to live well with. Who needs women if they are so immature and self-centered? I used to ask.

But, as they say, you cannot live without women and you cannot live with them. It is a bummer.

Actually, there are mature and understanding women out there; you just have to find them. I am not talking about such rare human beings here; I am talking about my past experience with a particular woman.

THE LOGIC OF FORGIVENESS IS THAT OTHER PEOPLE ARE YOU AND YOU DID TO YOU THE EVIL YOU SEE PEOPLE DO TO YOU AND DID THE GOOD YOU SEE PEOPLE DO TO YOU; FORGIVE AND GIVE YOU PEACE, BE HATEFUL AND ANGRY, AND YOU DISTURB YOUR PEACE.

DREAM
MAY 1, 2020
5:30 PM

In this dream, I was at a laundry mat and placed a previous user's washed laundry on the table. I came back later and somebody had placed my laundry in the gutters inside the laundry room by the walls. I was angry, took the laundry I saw on the table, placed them in the same gutters as I retrieved my own clothes, and woke up.

This dream showed me behaving tit for tat; that is, not forgiving whoever supposedly messed with me. It shows that I am not a forgiving person; I want to punish evil persons; I am egotistical and when my ego is insulted, my injured vanity wants to punish, even kill the person who belittled my ego; that is, despite reading about forgiving folks, I still do not forgive them. For example, I want racists and thieves to be punished, killed.

But if I am responsible for all the behaviors I saw in my dream if I projected out all the people in my dream and did what all of them did, I was the person who placed my laundry in the gutters, so I was really angry at myself.

The logic of forgiveness is that you did what the person who harmed you did to you; you also did what the person who helped you did to you; you are the racist who discriminated against you, so you are not doing him harm by forgiving him; if you punish the racist, you punish you since you projected him out.

The egos' world is based on separation, on the premise that those you see around you are not you and did to you evil things against your wishes so you feel angry at them and punish them; the logic of forgiveness is that you are all the people you see in your world and did what all of them did in you, son of God's dream, so forgiving them is forgiving you; being angry at them is being angry at you, making life miserable for you.

Last evening, I wrote an essay that showed that I was still angry at my ex-wife for judging me on the basis of the income that I made; I saw her as having no understanding; I never forgave her because I did not accept that she and I are one; I saw what she did to me, which, as the egos' world judges things, is not good, as what another person did to me and justified anger at her.

But if I saw her as me projected out, then what she did to me, good or bad I did to me, and if I punish her, I punish me, make life miserable for me, and if I forgive her, I forgive me and give me relative peace (not the total peace of perfect union; I am still in separation hence cannot have perfect peace).

My friend, Dr. O, does not forgive racists; he wants to punish them, he wants blacks under his leadership to take over the rulership of the world and stick it to those who stuck it to blacks. His gospel is the gospel of the ego, bearing grievances and seeking vengeance, seeing whites as not him, and wanting to punish them to make his ego seem powerful. This is not the gospel of Jesus that sees other people as himself hence forgive them to forgive himself to return to union with them and know peace.

The lesson in the dream of forgiveness instead of the dream of vengeance we currently have is that other people are us, or are parts of us, that we separated from them and projected them out in our dream of separation, and made them do bad or good things (which in truth, we did to us through them) and that we must forgive them to forgive us what we did to us through seeming other people.

Black people enslaved and discriminated against themselves through seeming other persons called whites in their dream of separation.

Forgiving other people's apparent evils to one is forgiving one's apparent evils to oneself and since it is a dream evil that one, others have not done.

What my ex-wife did to me, as the egos' world sees these things, was evil; consider her using the racist's legal system to take most of my money. She did what she did apparently based on her ego's belief that she was not loved and was used. Well, being angry at her is being angry at me; forgiving her is forgiving me; if I forgive her, I forgive me and know peace and joy in the dream of self-attack that is denied and made to seem like other people attacked one.

DISCUSSION

The philosophy embedded in this write-up is for me to understand and live; it is not for other people to understand and live for there are no other people; other people are me denied and projected out in my dream of separation from my entire self; a dream in which I divided me into infinite selves and through some of them, attacked me, hence dream of self-attack, and now dream of self-forgiveness.

Therefore, I should not expect other people to understand this essay for other people are me; the goal is for me to understand it and forgive other people hence forgive me, live in peace and joy, and model it to so-called other people, those parts of me I still separate from and through them, do bad things to me.

I was furious at my father's brothers for not giving me a penny when I came to the USA; I never forgave them and wanted nothing to do with them; I am truly an unforgiving man.

Now I must become a forgiving man for my father's brothers are me and their lack of help for me is my lack of help for me so I forgive them to forgive me.

I am actually the person who gave me the body issues that made me angry at people and the world for not understanding and helping me (other people do not even understand the pain my body gave to me).

The Igbos that I encountered at Nigerian Internet forums were me causing me trouble. From my ego perspective, they are useless idiots since Igbos do not help each other and instead use each other (no Igbo man has given me a penny in my entire life hence to me, they are less than human beings, they are refuse; if you ask whether I have given them money, the answer is yes). I asked, how dare these monkeys, these subhuman beings who would only use me if they could say something bad about me? To me, they were less than animals and if I could, I would have killed them.

But looked at from the idea of oneness, the insulting and useless Igbos are all parts of my one unified self that I separated from and projected them into my dream of self-attack and through them, attacked me and I wanted to kill them. The goal is to see their behavior as my behavior and forgive them and overlook my nightmarish dream.

CONCLUSION

My dream, life on earth, called for all people to do bad things to me and they did as I asked them to do. It is all my script, play, and drama and people enacting parts it called on them to enact for me; the goal is for me to forgive them hence forgive me, become God-realized, return to peace, and give the world, that is, give my entire self, my peace.

There is God. God extended himself to a son. That son of God extended himself to other sons of God. Eventually, there are infinite sons of God. All the infinite sons of God are one with each other and with God; they are literally one shared self and one shared mind.

Whatever any son of God wants to do, other sons of God play parts for him and he plays parts in what they want to do.

I wanted a dream of self-attack and other sons of God played parts in that dream and attacked me. Each of them is having his own specific dream and I and other sons of God play necessary parts for him to have his dream.

The idea is to accept that one dreamed through all people and did to one what all people did to one and as such, forgive them to forgive oneself and know peace.

15

I am teaching a different philosophy, a different way to live in this world. In this world, we are all separated egos and see our self-interests as different from other people's self-interests. In this world, we believe that what we do to other people, we did not do to ourselves. I am teaching that other people and us are literally one shared self and what we do to them, we effectively did to us. This worldview may be too strange for some people to even entertain it at this time. If that is the case with you, please move on. Don't sweat it if it does not make sense to you. People on earth are at different levels in their evolution. We left our unified spirit home in God and like the prodigal son, went on a journey to nowhere since everywhere we go to is in God. Some people are not yet ready to return home. My writings are for those who are itching for the homeward-bound journey. If you are still outward bound, keep going until you learn that you are on a journey without distance (*A Course in Miracles* lovely poetic term) for you are always in God, and while in him, dream that you are apart from him.

WHY DO YOU AND I ATTACK US THROUGH OTHER PERSONS?

The world came into being in a Big Bang. That was a moment when the sons of God attacked each other to push each other away from each other. God immediately brought them back and reassembled them into a physical unity: the separated particles of light, photons unified into electrons and quarks. Quarks unified into protons and neutrons. Neutrons and protons unified into nuclei. Years later, nuclei captured electrons to form atoms. Atoms unified with other atoms to form molecules. Molecules unified to form (stars are formed from clouds of hydrogen that gravity pushed inward until hydrogen united to form helium and ignition starts), planets, plants, and animals.

For our present purpose, the Big Bang is our mutual self-attacks. During the Big Bang, I attacked me through you and you attacked you through me and other people. Our self-attacks through other people is still going on in our lives to the present; I am still attacking me today through you and you are still attacking you through me.

We will keep doing so until we forgive each other's past attacks and no longer attack ourselves in the present and in doing so, return to the awareness of our eternal union with each other, hence know peace and joy, again.

People came to earth to experience a mutual attack. See a person, see what is happening to him—he seems a victim that other people are attacking but he is the one attacking himself through other people, for other people are parts of his unified self that he separated from by attacking them and they separated from him by attacking him to attack themselves but thinking that by attacking other people, they are not attacking themselves.

White people attack black folks and think that they are not attacking themselves, but they are attacking themselves since they are unified with black folks. For one thing, those black folks they attacked will, if not now, in the future, defend themselves and since the best defense is offense, attack white folks.

Racist whites seeing black folks as not themselves attack them, enslave them, discriminate against them, and believe that they are sucking it to other people when the truth is, they are sucking it to themselves. This is literal, not figurative; they are weakening themselves. Their bodies are literally attacked and they become sick from attacking black folks.

Go look at them and you see that their bodies are filled with medications. The typical middle-aged to older white folks are on up to ten or more medications; this is because they have so wreaked their bodies with their attacks on black folks that are attacks on themselves.

Their country, the USA, is literally attacking itself by having people attack each other. The country will, sooner or later, be composed of weak people that an external, vigorous enemy will push slightly and it collapses. That is how oppressive empires decline and fall.

My ex-wife became a literal she-devil; she used the law to attack me in every which way she could. At some point, I realized that she is attacking herself. I watched as the all-powerful attacker who courts and judges lived to enable her to destroy me weakened her body.

Anger literally weakens your body. She became ill and died from her weakened body, a disease that she gave to herself for she wanted to experience that form of self-attack and died from it.

Please note that I am not blaming my ex-wife; she danced the ego dance her own way. I dance my own ego dance my own way. I attracted her into my life to viciously attack me and I to attack her.

No human being is innocent; we came here and live here through mutual attacks. I am not a victim and you are not a victim of other folk's attacks on you. I am not blaming us but just stating the phenomenon as I see it.

If you want to kill another person, you will end up killing yourself. She wanted to kill me and ended up killing herself.

Of course, she merely destroyed her body for her soul is eternal. She will return to this world and keep trying until she learns that forgiveness is love and she would then forgive those she believed wronged her and in so doing, forgive herself the wrong she did to herself through other people's wrongs to her. Thereafter, she would stop attacking her body, her body would become healthy and turn into light body, she would proceed to the world of light bodies, and thereafter, return to formless unified spirit, aka heaven.

In this world, we are attacking each other, meaning that we are attacking ourselves through other people and they are attacking themselves through us. Each attack has consequences for people. If you attack me, you have attacked you that are the consequences you get.

The wages of sin is death. Attack to kill a person and attack to kill you, and you will be killed. Attack people and they will attack you, and both of you will live at war and conflict and know no peace.

You have a choice: stop attacking other people, hence stop attacking you. You do so when you forgive those you see attack you. By not attacking other people in self-defense, you are not attacking yourself and are not weakening your body.

Black people weaken themselves by counterattacking racists; racists attack themselves by attacking black folks; if black folks in self-defense counterattack racists, they attack black folks, hence weaken themselves.

If this race madness continues unabated, there will be a race war and the so-called races mutually destroy themselves and their country would cease existing.

Members of either race can choose to stop the mutual attack by forgiving the attackers. White people attacked me when they denied me jobs. As the world sees it, I am mentally superior to 99% of white folks (I have an IQ of over 140 and a doctorate degree). Yet these mediocre folks will see me as they see black folks and discriminate against me.

Of course, discrimination made me angry. But in time, I learned that the racists were attacking themselves by attacking me and discriminating against themselves by discriminating against me. I realized that they are weakening themselves and in time, will die off. There will be a mass dying off of racists but they do not know it.

I decided to choose forgiveness. By not counterattacking racists, I stopped attacking me and weakening me. I allowed them to attack me, hence they attack, weaken themselves, and die off.

I too will seem to die but merely transition to living in a body of light and from there, transition to living in formless unified spirit self; they, racists, too, will get there but after they have given themselves loads of pain from attacking people instead of loving them.

DISCUSSION

Please don't go sentimental on me here; those you and racists attacked wanted to experience attack, for nothing can happen to the sons of God that they do not want to experience. We all came here to experience attack, set it up for other people to attack us, and we attack them. We are experiencing what we came to experience, war on ourselves.

This is because of the insanity of seeking superiority made possible by separation from other people. We can stop the insanity by stopping our mutual attacks.

Other people are not likely going to stop attacking you. You start the ball rolling by not attacking them (hence not attacking you) and forgiving them when they attack you.

CONCLUSION

In forgiving those you see attack you; you forgive you your self-attack through seeming other people. In forgiving them, you live from the Holy Spirit, from the Christ self. In so doing, you give you peace and joy.

You, by example, teach other people to stop attacking people and forgive those who attacked them to forgive their self-attacks.

When we forgive ourselves, we live in a happy dream, a semi peaceful world and thereafter, transit to the formless, unified world of God, our home, and know perfect peace and joy, bliss.

IT IS DIFFICULT TO ERADICATE OVERLEARNED EGO BEHAVIOR PATTERNS.

DREAM
MAY 2, 2020
10 AM

In this dream, I was arguing with a Nigerian. Suddenly, he balled his fists and came at me to hit me. I do not like to be hit so I went at him with not only my hands but legs, kicking him, with the intention of killing him, and woke up.

The dream says that I still believe in solving attack with attack. I still defend myself when I am attacked or about to be attacked. I do not forgive and walk away.

If you are defensive or defended, you are attacked, but if you are defenseless, you are not attacked. People generally do not attack those who are defenseless.

The defenseless are like children; forces above them protect them, not harm them. But you can say that the powerful do impose and control the powerless and defenseless; true, but the fact is that by being defensive, one acknowledges others' attack and by not defending oneself, one does not acknowledge other folks' attack on one.

Those we see as powerless may be filled with aggressive thoughts; for example, pre-colonial Africans seemed powerless when they were colonized by Europeans but they were, in fact, as aggressive to one another as other human beings are, so they were not defenseless.

Defenselessness is a spiritual quality found in only spiritualized persons, mystics.

If one is defenseless, one tends to be calm and happy. I would like to evolve to a defenseless state; right now, I am still capable of defending myself with great violence if attacked.

When I was at elementary school, Ladi Lak, Randall Road, Apapa, Lagos, I was a quiet boy and mostly kept to myself. I spent lots of money at school; for example, during recess, I would go to the Kingsway store near our school and buy all kinds of European foods. Other kids, especially Igbo boys, we called them wild boys, would try to waylay me. On two occasions, a bunch of them attacked me and tried to take my money; I fought back like a wounded tiger; other kids thereafter called me tiger.

I can be ferocious when I am attacked and am defending myself. In my ego, unconscious or subconscious mind is the programming to defend myself; the Osujis were their peoples' traditional priests and warriors; indeed, if you dared raise your voice at my great grandfather and grandfather, Njoku and Osuji, your head probably would be cut off; I was told to never allow any boy to bully me; I have overlearned aggressiveness and defensiveness; the opposite quality of forgiveness apparently is not having effect on that overlearned propensity of ego defensiveness.

I would like to be like a dove: gentle and peaceful.

ONE MUST STOP THINKING THAT A GRANDIOSE GOAL WOULD GIVE ONE'S LIFE MEANING.

A western psychologist is not grandiose to the point of wanting to change his clients to become different persons. If he can get a person to stop smoking, that is enough achievement for him. He does not want to posit spiritual psychology to get the people to follow him if he cannot prove it as true.

So why would I want to change people, get them to accept spiritual psychology that I do not know is true or not? Grandiose ego state.

In reality, no one can change people or prove the existence of God; so, one must accept minor goals and work to achieve them and stop questing after grandiose egos to give one's life grandiose meaning for that is not going to happen.

It is good enough to build an institute to train people to become leaders. It is not necessary to think that one must be pursuing grandiose, deluded goals to give one's life deluded important existence. People are animals and that is good enough for scientists.

Understanding the human body and physical phenomena is good enough for the scientist to give his life realistic purpose and meaning

I HAVE BEEN FRUSTRATED ALL MY LIFE
HENCE ANGRY ALL MY LIFE.

DREAM
MAY 3, 2020
8:30 AM

I was at a departmental store, Fred Meyer, with my two children, one 12, the other 9. The twelve-year-old immediately left our company and disappeared into the store. After a while, I began looking for her and could not find her. I was frustrated, thinking of any number of things that could happen to her. I then yelled at the 9-year-old when he too seemed out of my sight and he ran into a bunch of clothes being displayed. I got him out and we were now outside the store. I was riding my bicycle and he was standing behind me. We got to a street and I said that we are now too far away from the store and we turned back to the store and he saw his sister by the picture framers' section. We all left the store and I woke up.

In this dream, I was frustrated by the missing child. The frustration and tendency to anger are in a long-standing pattern.

Anger is primarily caused by frustration. One becomes frustrated when one seeks a goal and does not get it. All my life I had a goal of physical health but from childhood, my body was prone to irritation, hypersensitivity, pain, and other issues. When the sun is up, my entire body becomes irritated.

I actually quit my first teaching job at one of California's state universities to move to a cooler climate. I live in Alaska because cold is good for my body; my body gets over-aroused in hot climates.

Anyway, the point at hand is that I could not use my mind to wish my bodily irritations away so I became frustrated. Unable to get what I wish, physical health, I was frustrated and angry during my childhood.

Later events built on the childhood pattern of frustration and anger. For example, living in racist America meant not getting the type of job I wanted and that too led to frustration and anger. I had a wife that would have preferred not to work and disposed me to struggle for money, and that too led to frustration and anger. (Her father was a very successful orthopedic surgeon and provided well for his family so that his wife did not have to work; she did not expect to work.)

My life was a series of frustrations and anger. The good thing is that one can learn from one's life to improve one's life. I did an excruciating analysis of why I am prone to anger and rooted the causation to my medical issues in childhood and my inability to meet the grandiose goals I had set for myself in childhood.

I can remember at age eight telling myself that I must obtain a Ph. D. in early adulthood. I did that in my twenties. I gave myself big goals that are generally difficult to attain and fear of not attaining those goals gave me anxiety.

The point is that my lifestyle was prone to frustration and anger, some caused by medical issues and others by psychological issues such as the inability to attain my grandiose goals. In the end, I learned from all these issues and doubt that I am still prone to frustration and unnecessary anger. I now have a tendency not to sweat a lot of things.

Even death does not faze me; as I see it, if I die right now, that is fine with me. Is there life after death? When I entered this world, I did not know what I was entering into so I will find out what happens when I die; thus, there is no point in worrying about it.

I have a metaphysics; that is conceptual; all concepts, regardless of their profundity, are not true. The truth is that I am agnostic and do not know whether God and heaven exist or not and do not really care whether they exist or not. Oblivion and finitude after death are perfectly welcome to me.

The lesson in this apparent self-preoccupied analysis of my dreams and sharing them with folks is that they too should get to know who they are and get a handle on how they express their emotions and learn to be calm and peaceful.

THERE ARE ONLY TWO EMOTIONS: LOVE AND FEAR.

DREAM
MAY 4, 2020
8:30 AM

In this dream, I parked my Volkswagen car (the bug was my first car when I was at college) on a street close to Saint Mary's Catholic Church, went into the church, came out, and saw Adaem Ejuka, my mother's senior sister walking toward me; she appeared to be smoking cigarette, weird I said (she did not smoke in real life). She came close and pointed behind me and in the far-off distance was a bunch of white folks and she said that they may be beating up black folks and that we should walk away. I looked for my car to ferry us away, could not find it, so we walked down the street and she said that we ought to seek refuge in the houses nearby. She entered a house, I walked on, then saw a young woman and asked her if I could hide in the house. She is standing in front of me and said that if I walk to the backyard, there is a hut for me to hide in the woods. I did walk into the woods and saw a small shade, hut, and a bunch of elephants by a pool of water and woke up.

At around 4 AM, I had used the bathroom and thought about calling my doctor for an elective surgery that was postponed due to coronavirus lockdown. That kind of generated some worry and fear in me. I said I got to do what I got to do so that I may return to Alaska and take care of some business there. I read for a while, went back to sleep, and had the above dream.

The dream clearly shows that there were worry and fear in my mind; this dream was obviously based on fear, shown as fear of a white mob attacking me.

A Course in Miracles said that there are only two emotions: love and fear. Apparently, fear could manifest as worry, which I had, or as anger and other emotions.

On the other hand, if you have love, you do not have these negative emotions.

EVERY PERSON ACTS OUT OF HIS OR HER CHARACTER; YOU RESPOND TO OTHER PEOPLE FROM YOUR OWN CHARACTER AND AS SUCH, ARE NOT OBJECTIVE IN YOUR PERCEPTION AND RESPONSE TO PEOPLE.

In the language of *A Course in Miracles*:

WE JUDGE OTHER PEOPLE'S EGO BEHAVIORS WITH OUR OWN EGO PERCEPTION AND CANNOT BE OBJECTIVE; WE SHOULD LEAVE JUDGMENT TO THE HOLY SPIRIT WHO JUDGES WITHOUT BIAS.

We live in a perceptual world. This is so because we do not know what the truth is. Perception does not reveal the truth. We see with our limited information; we do not see the whole situation. We see with our egos' past learning, which is not total learning. Therefore, no perception, regardless of how refined it is, is objective.

Your ego perception of other egos' behaviors is not objective, is biased in your favor. Your ego tells you that you are right and that other people are wrong.

If you desire objectivity, leave it to the Holy Spirit who knows the past, present, and future of mankind on earth and has complete information on the world to judge what you see for you. His judgment approximates knowledge (knowledge exists only in heaven, in God); the Holy Spirit's interpretation of events transcends perception. Thus, you should not judge; instead, you should keep quiet and ask the Holy Spirit to tell you what to do.

Since I do not hear him, that is, the Holy Spirit, voice of God, I am supposed to just forgive the wrongs I see in the world for they are done in dreams and what is done in dreams are not real.

I OBSERVE EVENTS AND DO NOTHING IN RESPONSE TO WHAT I OBSERVED.

In the past, I had youthful enthusiasm and quickly judged situations as not right and intervened. These days, I observe how I react to what I see other people do. In the past, I would get angry if they did what my ego judged as hurtful. Now, I merely observe how I feel and do nothing.

I do not hear the Holy Spirit telling me what to do.

I work on my character and leave people to do what they do out of their character and not disturb my emotions by trying to correct them.

My past attempts at correcting people's mostly anti-social behaviors were based on fear; these days, I act out of love; love understands and tolerates even the behavior of insane people. For example, most Nigerian leaders are sociopaths, psychopaths, and anti-social personality-disordered folks; they are thieves in political offices. They used to make me angry but no more. They are acting out of their thieving characters and Nigerians who tolerate them are acting out of their fearful characters.

When Africans overcome the fears and cowardice that dispose them to tolerate thugs ruling them, they would rise up and fight for social and economic justice; until then, it is a waste of time talking about the incredible situation whereby a country is ruled by thieves.

I refuse to disturb my emotions just because I see folks who seem to live to be thieves and specialize in corruption; I do not have a magic wand to change them.

HOW DOES THE HUMAN BRAIN PRODUCE DREAMS?

Recently, I decided to write down my dreams and analyze their meaning. Dream analysis is not exactly new. Sigmund Freud, Alfred Adler, Carl Jung, and other psychoanalysts used to ask their patients to bring their dreams to therapy sessions and the analyst analyzed them. There are books out there purporting to explain the meaning of dreams. Of course, all those books, like psychoanalysis itself, are mostly speculations.

There is nothing wrong with speculations.

When we do not understand something, we speculate about it. If we have certainty, we would not engage in conjectures.

I am not here talking about dreams themselves. What I would like feedback from folks is how our brains or minds produce dreams.

I am one of those persons who have vivid dreams. I lay down on my bed, go to sleep, and I am immediately in a dream. In the dream, I see a world that looks like my day world; in the dream, I see people and me doing what we do during our day world. On a typical night, one dream leads to another. On a typical night, I have several dreams but don't remember all of them. Those I remember I write down and try to figure out what they mean. I have no illusion that my analysis is true. I do not know what my dreams mean.

Those psychologists who interpret rapid eye movements, REM, as indicative of dreaming, tell us that animals too dream when they sleep. Do animals dream? Have they told you about their dreams? You are making unwarranted inferences from REM research, my friend.

For me to know what dreams mean, I must first understand how my brain produces dreams. I have taken tons of courses on the human brain. But those did not help me understand how my brain and thinking produce dreams.

My question is: how does the human brain produce dreams?

The neurons (brain cells) in our brains communicate through neurotransmitters (serotonin, dopamine, acetylcholine, GABA, Endorphin, norepinephrine) and certain electrical ions (such as potassium ion, magnesium ion, calcium ion, and so on).

Messages are transmitted from one neuron to another at their synapses through the actions of neurotransmitters and neurochemicals. What it boils down to is that electro-chemical changes (at the synapses of neurons) play roles in message transmission from neuron to neuron.

Electrons play roles in message transmission (both in the central nervous system and peripheral nervous system).

Electrons travel very fast but not as fast as light (light travels at 186, 282 miles per second). Electrons have negligible matter so they cannot travel at the speed of photons that are not matter.

Do we dream with electrons? Do we dream with light? Do we dream with neurotransmitters? Do we dream with neurochemicals? I do not understand how we dream.

If you understand how we dream, I would like to hear from you. I just want to know how our sleeping brains can recreate a world that seems as real as our day world and we live in it and do the things we do in our day world. And when we wake up from our dreams, we realize that that world was not real, did not exist, and was a mere fiction in our brains.

This raises the question: if our individual brains can produce a world for us to dream in at night, what makes us think that our day world is not also produced by our collective brains?

Mind is not a thing; mind is a name for our thinking, so, you can say that our thinking at night produces our nightly dreams and that our collective thinking during the day produces our day world and that both nightly dreams and day world are both dreams, both illusions, and do not exist in reality!

Speculation is allowed where we do not understand what is going on. Please speculate on how our brains and thinking produce our dreams.

Even scientific theories begin with speculations. I read a biography of Albert Einstein where he said that he came by his theory of special and general relativity from a dream he had when he was twelve years old, a dream that stuck with him, and he kept thinking about it and at the age of 26, in 1905, he finally used it to write his theory of special relativity, which was expanded in 1916 to the theory of general relativity.

In the dream, he was at the top of a hill looking down at a meadow, a kind of valley where cattle were grazing grass. From the top of the hill was a barbed wire about ten feet high. The barbed wire ran from the top of the hill to the meadows below.

No cow or person could step across the ten feet wire. But at the meadow, he saw that the wire was less high, about a foot tall, and cows could easily step across it, but they were not stepping across it. He wondered why cows at the meadow were not crossing the low wires.

He could not understand it until much later when he realized that the ten feet high wire at the top of the hill at the bottom of the hill seemed like a foot high that cows could easily step over.

How did a ten feet high wire become one foot at the bottom of the hill? He thought about it, over and over, again, trying to understand the phenomenon of illusions. Finally, he got it.

If you have not read his theory of special and general relativity, please do. I am not going to explain it here, nor can it be explained in a two-page essay.

There is an element of illusion in our perception. The nature of whatever we see depends on the angle we look at it. So, if perception does not yield the truth, what exactly is the truth, anyway?

Do you know what the truth is? How do you know that you even exist? Rene Descartes' cogito ergo sum: I think, therefore I exist.

How do you know that you think? Something else could be thinking through what you call you. Is there even a you or are you a matrix-like figure in some computer programmer's program doing what he programmed you to do?

Abstract thinking is the joy of philosophers like me.

Let me return to dreams in our heads at night when we sleep. How do our brains and thinking produce our dreams (and if the day world is also a dream, produce it)?

George Berkeley touched on this subject and said that the world is in the mind of God, solipsism. English/Scottish empiricists like David Hume dismissed him as an idiot.

When Dr. Johnson heard that Bishop Berkeley said that the world is a dream in our minds, or more precisely, in the mind of God, his sidekick, Boswell, reported that he stuck his toes on a rock and felt pain and said that that is the answer for the Irish Bishop. That is to say that in the day world, he feels pain from things hurting his body, which presumably he does not feel in his dreams.

He was wrong; in dreams, when we hit rocks, we also feel pain, so by his logic, our dreams are also real.

Please remember that Berkeley wrote voluminously on optics, light, so he was a real scientist. That is, he operated under the scientific method and based his conclusions on observation of phenomena.

Let us get back to you. How does your brain, mind, or thinking produce your dreams at night? I welcome your speculations or scientific explanation of the dream phenomenon.

Post Script:

This evening, before writing this essay, I ran the ideas by my friend, Dr. James Agazie, a professor of mathematics. He laughed at me. I asked him why he is laughing at me. He said that I am a funny guy. How can an African struggling to have one good meal a day, especially during these days when he is prevented from working by the coronavirus lockdown, think about such absurd things as dreams? I told him that I understand his perspective; his reasoning presumably is why hungry African writers do not produce abstract writings but mostly produce concrete writing that does not appeal to folks like me.

NOTHING THAT WE DO ON EARTH MAKES SENSE AND THEY CANNOT BE MADE TO MAKE SENSE; LIVING WITH THIS REALITY IS THE GREATEST LIBERATING INFORMATION ON EARTH.

There is nothing that we do on earth that makes sense; everything that we do in society or that society does through its political and economic institutions are mere noise, pure noise, and meaningless noise. They are noise that seem important. Consider that the judicial system, for example, in great fanfare, sends people to prisons or kills them. It says that it protects people in doing so. Okay, but the people it allegedly protects will, sooner or later, die and decay to dust.

If you change our behaviors, hence our earth, we would no longer be here; even what is said to be done in the world of light forms still do not make sense; only being in nothingness, heaven, makes sense.

Therefore, we must tolerate what people do on earth for we know them all to be totally pointless, meaningless, and purposeless and not even a bit of them can be improved.

The world cannot be improved; it is like the anus; no matter how much soap you use in washing it, it would still smell like feces.

The world is feces that we are trying to make to seem important; it isn't going to be important for we shall die and decay and return to light which returns to nothingness, aka spirit; only nothingness that is unified spirit makes sense.

The entire little ego dances people engage in are designed to make their nonexistent and unimportant ego seem important; they are saying: see me, I am rich and socially powerful, therefore, I am an important ego.

It is silliness designed to cover the essential unimportance of life in ego and body.

Normal folks do not see through the valuelessness of being on earth but neurotics see through ego masks of importance but make the mistake of trying to make it seem important or kill themselves.

If you kill yourself, you have not rejected the pointlessness of life on earth and will return to earth to try again until you get it right.

The depressed neurotic makes the mistake of not realizing that there is an important aspect to life, life outside body, the do-nothing being in heaven.

You should not kill yourself to go back to heaven; you do not return to heaven by suicide but by being on earth. You use your mind to reject the earth, then see your body disappear, and experience yourself in formless heaven, eternity, and perfect peace and joy.

The right approach is the realization that being ego in body is worthless and that it cannot be improved by changing the world and achieving things in it; one should smile at the foolishness that is our behaviors and not moralize about them for even if you bring about the desired moral ends, they are still an exercise in meaninglessness.

All we do on earth is vanity upon vanity, the biblical writer of Ecclesiastes (Solomon) correctly said.

The light world is also an exercise in meaninglessness except that it is peaceful and folks know that they are doing nothing important; they are just having a happy dream, still a crazy dream, that separation, space, time, and matter can be possible.

An enlightened person laughs hilariously at people doing what they consider important, such as seeking high social status, money, and power because he knows that they are doing worthless things.

Live peacefully, model peace and joy from doing nothing, sell it in books, speeches, and workshops, and make loads of money from doing so.

You are showing people how to live in peace and joy, and as such, are selling to them, giving to them the only important thing on earth—truth.

The person propagating the truth that the earth is pointless and that there is meaningful formless heaven deserves to have trillions of dollars for he sells the only thing that matter, getting out of the pointless universe by returning to meaningful formless heaven, aka state of oneness.

Post Script:

Read Jean-Paul Sartre's *Being and Nothingness*. In this book, he attempted to provide a positive philosophy to his otherwise depressing existentialism. Sartre came close to saying what I said here. What I articulated here is the mystic's philosophy, a philosophy that sees this world as rubbish and knows that there is a meaningful world in unified spirit, heaven.

YOU CANNOT SEPARATE FROM YOURSELF.

You cannot separate from yourself. While being in you, unified spirit self, you projected a self into body living in space and time and the body of that self made it feel pain and the projector develops an ego-personality that he now thinks is who he is and pursues the ego goals of seeming powerful and rich to make it seem important.

But he is not the ego. The real self is the son of God, a spirit outside body, space, and time. This is the mystic's view.

IF YOU CHOOSE YOUR EXPERIENCES, REINCARNATION AND KARMA IS NECESSARY

According to *A Course in Miracles,* we choose whatever happens to us to experience it; in that light, we chose our birth and where we are born, our parents, our bodies, and everything. This requires us to have lived elsewhere to be able to choose to be born on earth.

It means that reincarnation is necessary; one must have lived on earth to be able to choose to return to earth.

It also requires some kind of karma, choosing to be born in certain circumstances to do what enables one to learn about what one needs to do and to return to the awareness of oneness, aka God and his heaven.

SCIENCE AND ACCIDENTS

Alternatively, is sciences' chance and accident true? According to science, everything happens to us by chance and accident. This is simple. There is no elaborate theology to justify accidents because we could see things happen to us that are not of our choosing. But is it true?

AGNOSTICISM IS DECISION NOT TO DECIDE.

Agnosticism is the desire not to choose and commit to a cause of living, to fence sit. Both atheism and theism have made choices, usually done from incomplete information on whether there is God or not, but both empower their adherents whereas agnostics are depowered and are wishy-washy.

ADDICTION IS A CHOICE NOT TO LOVE.

Addiction is a choice not to love real people but to live to stimulate one's body and ego; to make one's body and ego real is not to love one's real self.

The addict does not love herself, her children, or other people. Men who are addicted to sex and pornography do not love members of their families. Those addicted to alcohol and drugs are total egotists and since the ego is the opposite of love, cannot love.

RELIGION AS MERE POETRY

J saw religion as poetry and repeated her religion's poetry all her life but did not live a life of love, did not make friends with African women, and treated me like shit, all showing that she does not have love, hence was an unhappy person; she lived a miserable life that pretended to be happy.

The goal of life on earth is to avoid love and since that is not possible, to have special love relations that worship ego and body.

WHY DO WE FORGET OUR DREAMS WHEN WE WAKE UP IN THE MORNING?

The dream world has its logic and pattern which is not the logic and pattern of the day world. In dreams, things shift dramatically; you can be in one place and shift to another place quickly and there is no causal relationship between the two places. Therefore, you cannot live in the day world as you live in the dream world. We have to forget the dream world so as to be able to live in the day world.

WE HAVE TO FORGET THE BEFORE-EARTH WORLD TO BE ABLE TO LIVE ON EARTH.

By the same token, when we come to earth, we have to forget the logic of the world we came from, a world where merely thinking about a place and you are there, pretty much like the dream world, except that in the dream world, you are not consciously aware that you wish something, think something, and it happens, whereas in the before-earth world, you are consciously aware that your wishes or thoughts produce where you are and what you experience, so you cannot have that mindset in our earthly world.

ON EARTH, OUR WISHES ALSO PRODUCE THE WORLD WE EXPERIENCE BUT DO NOT KNOW IT

On earth, our thinking, wishes, or mind also produces the place we are and experience but we are not conscious of the correlation; if we were, we would be in the world before life on earth. We came to earth to forget that our wishes and thinking produce the world we see and experience.

YOU MUST HAVE BODY TO THINK, HAVE A MIND, SO THE BODY PRECEDES THINKING, HENCE TREATING THE BODY IS MORE IMPORTANT THAN TREATING THE THINKING, MIND; WE GIVE MENTALLY ILL PEOPLE MEDICATIONS TO HEAL THEIR BODIES SO AS TO HEAL THEIR THINKING, MINDS.

You must have a body to think, so if your body is sick, we have to heal your body, for, without body, you do not think. Ego thinking is based on being in body. However, in heaven, you do not need body to think, that is a different kind of thinking, unified thinking.

WHAT MAKES FOR SUCCESS IN THIS WORLD?

My undergraduate education was really good. I enjoyed the classes that I was taking. But during my graduate school, I had seen through America; I saw America as a bloody racist and exploitative society, a place where nothing said is true. I wanted nothing to do with America.

I would pick up social science journals and they bore me for the writers were merely playing games, not writing the truth. So, what is the truth?

I essentially checked out from schooling. I could have dropped out to go find out what the truth is for me but I hung in there mostly killing time.

Well, since graduate school, nothing I see in the world makes sense to me. The world seems like a pile of rubbish that I have to endure. I sought escape from the world and escaped into fantasies; I would use my mind to imagine how society could be redesigned and people behave lovingly to produce what Aldous Huxley called a brave new world. But those are mere ideation, not real world.

I was depressed by the nature of the real world and lived in fantasy. I had some addictions, addictions to coffee, food, and for a while, to sex. Sex was ridiculous but merely thinking about it or pursuing it tended to offer me escape from the stupid world I saw all around me.

So, what kind of world would give me hope? What kind of world would energize me to work hard for it? I explored religions.

New age religions are the abode of white women escaping from what their men had done with traditional Catholic and Protestant religions. They escape into talking about whatever they wish they get. They are using religion to serve their narcissism.

I am searching for the truth.

I explored western philosophy and psychology; Western philosophy is a made-up jumble of words. Western psychology is too superficial to be taken seriously.

So, what is the way out for me? I cannot possibly return to what is called the African religion. What I am doing is to come up with a religion or thought system that makes sense to me and live it. It is syncretic; it takes from *A Course in Miracles*, *Conversations with God*, and Eastern religions and synthesize them into what makes sense to me.

I must do what makes sense to me or do nothing at all.

To be successful, I must have clarity of vision, know what I am looking for, throw myself one hundred percent to doing it, and do it 24/7, for my life and joy depend on it. If one does so in a realistic line of work, one will succeed, whatever success is.

THE SOUL'S WISH FOR ITS BODY TO DIE

Conversations with God, CWG, says that sometimes, the individual's soul, although eternal, prefers that a particular body it lives in die and essentially instructs his mind (thinking) and body to stop the struggle to live in body and mind (ego). The body dies and the soul manifests in other bodies.

(Most Africans believe in reincarnation. When my mother's oldest children, a boy and daughter, died, she said that she prefers to die and reincarnate in a different situation where her children did not die before her.)

Neale Donald Walsh considered himself a failure in everything he tried and had wished for death before he embarked on writing his *Conversations with God*, a book that has made him fabulously rich.

I myself in assessing my life, concluded that I failed my ex-wife, I did not provide her with the luxurious life she craved for, and did not provide adequately for my children; I did not give them sufficient financial legacy. I hate to see them struggling for money. Thus, I concluded that it is better that I died rather than hang around to see my children suffer.

Actually, I am not afraid of death and would die now if all that life offers me is poverty.

I used to say the same thing about my parents. Since they did not help me with my college education, I used to say that they are living for nothing and are better off dead. I did not see it as my function to support them since they did not support me. I would ask: what are they living for if they do not support their children?

By the same token, I see Igbos and Africans as better off dead since they do not help each other. I would say, what are Igbos and Africans living for? Just to be alive and pretend to be big men? Take them out of my space; they are better off dead rather than live to merely seek their ego bigmanism. To me, Africans are shit, literally, and I had no use for them.

These days, however, I realize that letting go of my pursuit of the grandiose ego returns me to God's egoless grandeur as the son of God; as the son of God, I have access to the abundance of this world. I am entitled to grandeur, not grandiosity. I actually have more money these days than I have ever had before. How? I simply expect the universe, God, to provide for me for I am a part of it and deserve to live well.

Hopefully, I will provide my children with sufficient financial legacy. Why not, selling my eighty books is enough to make them wealthy.

NO GOD MEANS NO ONESELF.

If there is no God, it means that there are no you, at the spiritual level; you are now a mere animal. Doubt of God is self-doubt; if God does not exist, you do not exist.

Society enacts elaborate thinking and behaviors that enable us to see God in a false manner; society is designed to make us forget God so that we may wade through its veils to experience God.

GOD CAN ONLY KNOW THAT HE EXISTS THROUGH HIS SONS.

Without his sons, God would not know that he exists; without other people, we would not know that we exist; other people are our reference point that enables us to compare ourselves to them and from that, know who we are.

WHAT IS IT IN US THAT DO THE CONCEPTUALIZING?

Human beings are concept-making animals. We say things like whole, God, sons of God, parts of the whole; these are concepts. Who is doing the conceptualizing? Scientists say that it is an accidental universe that in 13.8 billion years, produced a concept-making animal. Really?

Religionists say that there is God in us that thinks through us. I am not going to resolve this philosophical issue here.

GOD KNOWS; GOD HAS TO EXPERIENCE WHAT HE KNOWS IN THE PHYSICAL UNIVERSE; BEING, GOD, IN THE PHYSICAL UNIVERSE, REALIZES THAT HE IS GOD AND IS GOD-REALIZED, IS NOW IN BEING, AND RETURNS TO LOVE.

One God divided himself into infinite selves and from them, experience himself, and know himself; each of us is supposed to do the same.

A POTPOURRI OF EASTERN RELIGIOUS CONCEPTS EXPLAINED

In chapter five of the book, the man talked about a bunch of Hindu terms. Nothing new was added or learned by me, for I already have knowledge of Hinduism, Buddhism, and Taoism.

WHERE GOD IS, WE ARE.

CWG said that wherever we are, we are in God and in heaven for God and heaven is everywhere. Everywhere you are, you are in God/heaven, so to say that you are returning to heaven is a misnomer.

What is proper to say is that while we are in heaven, we covered our eyes, engaged in separated thinking, instead of unified thinking, and do not see the heaven that we already are in.

Now, we have to remove the mask, remove the veil, know that we are already in heaven, and experience heaven where we always are.

All we need to do is stop ego-based thinking and return to unified thinking, love for all, to return to the awareness of heaven.

Heaven is not outside us, not a place we return to; it is a state of mind, a pattern of thinking; we rediscover when we stop thinking through the ego wishes for separated existence and self-interests.

IS RENUNCIATION OF THE WORLD NECESSARY TO HAVE GOD-REALIZATION?

CWG talked about the Eastern concept of renunciation, letting go of the things of this world. That would seem like doing a lot. But if you understand that the things of this world are nothing, you let them go and do not miss them.

Take food, for example; if you eat, you are going to poop. If you do not want to poop, then you do not eat, and if you do not eat, food has no attraction for you.

The same goes for sex, wealth, power, fame, and other silly things that hold people hostage and bondage; they are nothing to the enlightened man who knows that he is part of eternal spirit and does not need earthly things to make him seem important.

RELATIONSHIPS

Chapter 8 of the book, *Conversations with God*, is devoted to relationships. It is easily the best in the book. It reads like something written by a sophisticated marriage therapist. It examined relationships as white Americans understand them and offered helpful insight for all married white Americans.

In our lives, we live in groups. There is no such thing as a human being who lives alone. A child needs his parents or other people to survive. Therefore, each of us learns to relate to other people. In fact, what we call ourselves cannot exist without other people.

What one knows about oneself is relative to what one knows about other people. The human self is comparative; it is compared to other selves. Without other people, one cannot exist.

I exist because other people exist; if other people do not exist, I cannot exist for I need them to physically exist and to psychologically exist.

I cannot think or engage in any kind of mental activity unless there are other people who stimulated me to do so.

Other people complete me and I complete other people; without other people, I am incomplete and without me, they are incomplete.

God is not complete without his sons and his sons are not complete without him; you cannot conceptualize God without his sons and the sons of God without God; the whole must have parts to exist and the parts must have a whole to exist.

Because we need each other to feel complete, we go about seeking each other's approval and acceptance. If other people accept one, one feels important and if one does not, one feels unimportant. Much of our social dances are rooted in our efforts to seem important in each other's eyes. In primitive societies, anthropologists tell us, people actually die if they are rejected by the members of their band. The greatest fear of primitive man is rejection by his people. And, of course, society manipulated that fact and threatens to reject the individual if he does not behave as he is told to behave.

To be told to leave the group was a curse greater than death itself; in the more primitive parts of Africa, people still fear social rejection, as if it matters whether other people accept you or reject you; they do not feed you or keep you alive, so what difference does it make to you if they rejected you? An adult in our contemporary world should say, to hell with what other people think of him, I am going to do only what I deem is the right thing and not bother with social acceptance or rejection.

Now the question is, why do we need to seem important at all? It is here that most marriage therapists and therapists, in general, miss the boat. Here is why we seek importance.

Upon birth in the human body, one becomes aware that body is nothing. Body is literally nothing. It is a bundle of 64 elements (mostly carbon, hydrogen, oxygen, and nitrogen) held together by chemical bonds. In time, they will die and decay. If all we are are our bodies, we are literally worthless.

If you cremate a human body, it is not worth a penny; it is useless, except as fertilizer for plants. In body, we are nothing.

Aware that in body and ego separated self we are nothing, we seek to give ourselves a sense of importance, being something, by getting the approval of other people.

If other people tell me that I am important, I feel important and if not, I feel unimportant. But other people are also egos and bodies hence not important so their approval does not make me important, not really, only illusorily.

Other people, nothings, cannot make me important and I cannot make other people important. In egos and bodies, we are not important, we are nothing.

But there is something in us that wants to feel important. At the lowest level, it is the ego. Above the ego is our higher self. Our highest self is rooted in God (unified spirit self).

In God, we are grandeur itself. In God, we are magnificent. But we separated from God and now live in ego and body and feel the opposite of God, opposite of grandeur, and seek ego grandiosity which we cannot get, for the ego and its body is eternally nonexistent and is nothing.

If then you desire good relationships with other people, first tell you that as part of God, you have grandeur. Other people are also parts of God, and as such, have grandeur. But they may not know it.

You should not seek ego grandiosity; other people's approval of you, if based on the ego, would not make you feel important.

Affirm your internal grandeur. In accepting your rootedness in God and affirming your grandeur, you relate to other people from that grandeur to the grandeur in them, from completeness in God to completeness in another son of God.

Here, you do not wish to change anyone for you know that in God, people are perfect and important but in ego, are nothing. You let people be who they are in body and ego and not have the illusion that they have worth in ego and body or that you have worth in ego and body.

When you affirm the God in you, then you can affirm the God in other people, hence your mutual worth in God, and overlook our egos and bodies.

However, if the truth is told, the fact is that the universe exists to let human beings seem to have worth in their egos and bodies; we pursue the illusion of worth in body. We do everything we do to provide for our egos and bodies because we think that they have worth. We eat, take medications, live in houses, wear clothes, everything, to make our bodies and egos seem important. That is the tragedy of being human: seeking worth in ego and body in a place where it cannot be obtained.

Seek and not get what you seek is the philosophy of the ego. Human beings are forever frustrated because they seek worth in the worthless, egos and bodies.

Yet, human beings do not want to let go of the ego and its things; they think that to let go of the ego and its things is a great sacrifice and they do not want to make that sacrifice. The ego and its world are nothing, so sacrifice of nothing is not a great sacrifice. If you know that the ego and world is nothing, you gently let them go without a sense of sacrifice.

If at all there is sacrifice, it is not seeking the things of God, what gives us peace and joy. Fortunately, you cannot sacrifice the things of God for whereas you can close your eyes to them, eventually, you will open your eyes and see them; they do not go anywhere even you we do not look for them. The things of God are eternal and cannot be lost, although temporarily, we can ignore them and live in pain.

The only type of relationship that gives us a semblance of worth is one rooted in God. *A Course in Miracles* calls this type of relationships, holy relationships, as opposed to the ego's special relationships where two or more egos try telling themselves that they have worth via admiring their bodies and egos that are living at the illusion level.

You cannot get worth in ego and body so seeking it, there is the illusion of the ego. Yet, people mostly seek special love relationships, those who affirm their egos' and bodies' worth, and when they stop doing so, the relationship ends and they go seek other egos to worship their egos and bodies and the dance of special relationships continues.

Neale Donald Walsh's God said some useful things about relationships but I decided to go beyond what he said and say it as it is: if you want a good interpersonal relationship, affirm the God in you and in other people; respect your real self, not the ego-self, and respect the real self in other people.

Our real selves are the sons of God, who is spirit, not body; although they are temporarily dreaming that they are ego and body (ego and body are our substitute, replacement selves).

As for what you and folks do with bodies, they cannot be holy; in fact, since ego, body, and the world of space, time, and matter are illusions, dreams, what we do with our bodies have not been done and should be overlooked. They are neither good nor bad for what is done in dreams have not been done in spiritual reality, has no value, and cannot be said to be good or bad.

The type of relationships I sketched here, holy relationships, where we affirm the God in us, is rare, and very few persons attain them. What most people have are special love relationships, where egos and bodies relate to each other and try to make their egos and bodies seem important and since they cannot be important, such relationships end in frustration, resentment, and anger, and if in marriage, in divorce.

Marriage counselors, which is what Neale Walsh's God was playing, try to make special love relationships tolerable, but they cannot make them satisfactory, for in them, people relate to each other from false ego and body selves; those who have denied their real selves, unified spirit, must be angry at themselves and direct their anger at each other.

Special love relationships are the abode of frustration, anger, fear, anxiety, depression, paranoia, mania, and schizophrenia for in them, people deny their real selves and try relating to each other from false self to false self, mask to mask.

We approximate heaven's communion in holy relationships, not the ego-substitute special love relationships.

In heaven, we are not in body and do not live in space, time, and matter hence have total relationship where one person gives all of himself to others and others give all of themselves to him. This can only take place in formless spirit, not in ego and body.

In heavenly relationships, we have peace and joy; in holy relationships, we have approximate peace, and in special love relationships, we have conflict and wars.

Therapists try to reduce the conflicts in our special love and special hate relationships but do not eliminate them.

KARMA AND REINCARNATION

Conversations with God accept reincarnation. Neale Donald Walsh was told that he has reincarnated 648 times on earth; in some lifetimes, he was a king, queen, or philosopher, sage, fool, rich, or poor, man or woman.

The book accepts the Eastern notion of karma. In karma, it is said that our behaviors have consequences, samsara, that we must receive, either in this lifetime or in others. Those with mostly loving lifestyles in the past and in the present are born into the priestly class, the Brahmins, who show the world how to live loving life (upon birth, Igbos deemed me their high priest of Amadioha and I have lived as one all my life, stating the truth, and caring less what you say of it).

Are reincarnation and karma true or false? The evaluation of those concepts would take me into science; I do not want to go there here. Suffice it to say that to science, accidents, chance, and randomness determines our fate and the fate of the universe. Is chance true? It seems true but is it really true? That is a subject for another occasion.

CONCLUSION

The book contains many interesting views that Neale Donald Walsh attributed to God. Some of them are profound whereas many are pedestrian.

It is not necessary to review all the topics his God expressed opinions on. I hope that the above notes stimulate the reader to go read the book and form his own opinion.

To me, the book is a kind of summary of ideas on God that Americans have been forming since their encounter with Eastern religions in the nineteenth century—*Transcendentalism* (Thomas Emerson, Henry Thoreau), Mary Baker Eddy and her *Christian Science*, Myrtle Fillmore and her *Unity Church*, Ernest Holmes and his *Church of Religious Science*, and Helen Schucman and her *A Course in Miracles*.

Ideas from many sources, occidental and oriental, that Neale Donald Walsh had gleaned from his wide reading found their ways into his book and the ideas are attributed to God.

Why not to God? We are all the creation of God and are like our creator so what we say is what God says.

DREAM
MAY 10, 2020
1:50 PM

I was lying on my bed reading a book, *Conversations with God*, and savoring the classical music coming out of the radio by my bed. Apparently, I dozed off to a short sleep (short because I was aware that I was not sleeping at 1:30 PM that is twenty minutes from the time that I woke up).

In this dream, I heard classical music, specifically Beethoven's ninth symphony coming from somewhere. I was intrigued and went to investigate where it is coming from. It was coming from a room where some African classical musicians were playing. Somebody pointed out one of the musicians as Abraham M and I looked and there he was playing on a violin my favorite Beethoven piece and I woke up and behold, that piece was playing on the radio in my room.

I wrote down the dream and began thinking about what it means. My girlfriend walked into the room and I told her about it and told her that ordinarily, Abraham M was an African chap that I consider totally unwashed. I told my girlfriend how surprised I was to have what seems to me a dumb man playing my best classical piece in my dream and asked her what she thinks is the meaning of the dream.

There are two issues going on here. My mind or brain took a piece of music playing on the radio in my room and piped it into my dream; how did it do that? The second issue is that it made an African that symbolizes unwashed status play the music, an incredible scenario.

In the second scenario, my mind is telling me that even those I consider unwashed can do what I consider the epitome of Western civilization, play classical music. That is, Africans can do anything the white man does if they put their minds to it.

The first part of the dream, about my brain picking up music that was playing in my room, is a bit more difficult to understand.

A couple of years ago, I fell asleep while lying on my couch. In my dream, I heard General Carter being introduced to some African dignitaries as the new commander of the US military in Africa. I was listening to General Carter's remarks when I woke up. Lo and behold, on the television, General Carter was making a speech. Since I was sleeping, somehow, my brain picked up his speech while I was sleeping, the question is: how does the human brain do that? I do not know.

The issue that I am pondering right now is how an African I consider uneducated is playing my beloved classical music.

My girlfriend gave me an interpretation that is exactly like mine and added that I should never look down on anyone. I agreed that that is the message of the dream: love and respect all people regardless of their station in life. The lesson I came to learn and practice in this life is to love and respect all human beings. Anything that is not love is not worthy behavior. Love makes the lover and the loved happy and live peacefully.

ANESTHESIA AND THE HUMAN MIND

Recently, I had surgeries that required me to be placed under general anesthesia. Under anesthesia, one is oblivious of what is going on in one's body; doctors operate on one's body, cut it up, and you could also burn it up and there would be no reaction on one's part. For all intents and purposes, one's body is dead to one; one's hitherto body is no longer one's body and it might as well be dead and buried and one would not know.

Thereafter, the timed anesthesia wears off at the appropriate time and one regains consciousness of being part of one's body. How do you explain this?

Where is one when one's body is under anesthesia? Is one outside one's body and the body could not respond to the effort of one's mind to think or operate through the body? Does this mean that mind is outside body?

Alternatively, body produces mind and when body is numbed with drugs, one's mind is also numbed, hence the lack of awareness of what is going on in one's body during surgery.

SPIRITUAL HEALINGS THAT IGNORE MEDICAL HEALING OF SICK BODIES DO NOT HEAL THE MIND, THAT IS, CHANGE FOLKS' THINKING.

A Course in Miracles, Conversations with God, and other spiritual books do not heal people because they completely ignored the role of biology in our lives.

Our bodies and their states affect our thinking. You could say that the human body is like a car and a driver is apart from it but the state of the car decides how well the driver drives. Therefore, to heal the mind operating in body, one must heal the body.

Medicine focuses on body, not mind.

I believe that to heal the mind, one's psychological issues, we must also heal the body, for the state of the body affects how one's mind works.

The reason why talks based on psychotherapy and books on spirituality like *A Course in Miracles* and *Conversations with God* do not heal people is that they ignore fifty percent of the problem, the human body.

Helen Schucman talked about the mind but ignored her body and died from bodily diseases; the same goes for other spiritual healers.

My addition to spirituality discourse is the requirement for folks to understand their bodies and address their issues medically while also talking about their mental issues.

Heal body and mind (to heal mind is to change how mind thinks, think differently, from separated thinking to unified, love-based thinking) to obtain spiritual healing.

SOCIETY AND ITS INSTITUTIONS AND LAWS EXIST TO ENABLE PEOPLE TO PRETEND IMPORTANCE.

Society, its institutions, and laws exist to enable people, nothing, animals, to pretend that they are important in their eyes and in each other's eyes. Society is a milieu that enables those who are nothing to strut around as if they have worth and importance. Society protects people's pretense of value, worth, significance, and importance.

People only have worth in God but separated from it and manifest as animals, hence have no worth, but since they are used to having worth in unified spirit, they now pretend worth in ego and bodies, both of which do not exist, and then have society and its laws to protect them.

Society and special love relationships are means of maintaining the ego and body and making them, nothingness, seem important.

If you disobey the laws of society that protect, that is, make nothingness into false something, society sees you as not validating its pretense and kills you.

White society enacted laws that protected white folks' sense of worth in their eyes, hence no longer animals, and laws that enabled them to pretend that they are better than black animals; if any black person violated those laws, he is arrested, jailed, or even killed.

You can understand the laws of society as a joke but you cannot violate them for you make people feel like they are nothing, you expose their mass pretense.

The best that you could do is drop out of the mutual pretense society and return to the awareness of unified spirit, God. That is what masters, enlightened people, do, take themselves out of social pretended importance and return to real worth, in God, and leave other people to keep on pretending worth in nothingness, ego and body, until they are ready to return to real worth, in formless spirit, God and heaven.

Enlightened persons do not moralize against peoples' pretended worth because they know that it is what people came to earth to do and that only a few persons in a millennia see through the worthlessness of life in ego and body, and for a while, try to make it worthwhile and then all doors to the kingdom of the ego is closed to them. They finally separate from ego and body and return to God in illumination. Such persons cannot return to making it in the egos' world of nothingness. I, for example, cannot make it in the egos' world.

Such persons do not die for they know that bodies do not exist, are dream things; they just awaken from the dream and continue living in spirit; all people are also in spirit but forget it to live as ego and body.

ACCORDING TO CONVERSATIONS WITH GOD, GOD IS KNOWLEDGE AND CREATED THIS WORLD TO EXPERIENCE HIS KNOWLEDGE OF HIMSELF, SO GOD IS EXPERIENCING HIMSELF IN FLESH, IN SHIT, WHAT A GOD!

Flesh is shit; God experiencing himself in body is experiencing himself in shit. What a way to experiencing himself, rolling in shit, in feces. What a powerful God.

Perhaps, it is true for he wants to be in shit and see if he would remember that he is God despite living in shit.

JANIS DID NOT RESPECT ME, OR HERSELF; SHE DID NOT DO ANYTHING TO HELP ME BUT EXPECTED ME TO SUPPORT HER AND WHEN SHE FELT THAT SUPPORT LACKING, SHE LEFT; SHE WAS TRULY A WEAK CHARACTER

Janis did not respect me at all; she did not do anything to support me but expected me to support her and when that support was absent, she left. She was a weak woman. And that was who she was and could not have been different.

J WANTED TO CHANGE THE WORLD THROUGH HER RELIGION.

She wanted to have an effect on the world, change people, and make them loving and united through her religion. Her religion was not a good religion despite talking about the unity of mankind.

Hinduism is an Indian religion just as Judaism is a Jews' religion; Buddhism is an Asian religion. And Christianity, despite its roots in Palestine, is now a European religion.

OSUJISM IS THE ONLY UNIVERSAL RELIGION.

A guy told me that Osujism is a universal religion. This is because it takes from all other religions and science to synthesize a world religion that appeals to all people. It is the replacement religion for all mankind.

> NOTHINGNESS MEANS A DIFFERENT WORLD, A
> DIMENSION THAT WE DO NOT UNDERSTAND IN OUR
> THREE-DIMENSIONAL WORLD; THE BIG BANG CAME OUT
> OF A DIFFERENT WORLD, NOT OUT OF NOTHING.

The Big Bang came from a different dimension, a different world that we do not know in this world. That world created the world of three-dimension; its light spread into darkness to form matter. Nothingness does not mean nothing but something we do not understand.

Light does not come from darkness but from light; from light in a different world, we do not understand. Religionists call that unknown world heaven and see light as coming from God.

> HUMAN BEINGS ARE DRIVEN TO LIVE AT ALL COSTS;
> IT IS A POWERFUL URGE TO SURVIVE AT ALL COSTS
> AND IN EVERY CIRCUMSTANCE AND FEAR DEATH.

Human beings have a powerful urge to live at all costs; they are born with it; when it goes, they commit suicide.

Because of that urge to live, other people can threaten them and make them slaves and they fear death and live as slaves. Black and white Americans are different kinds of slaves.

White Americans, despite the noise of freedom, are ruled by powerful oligarchs and they tolerate them. They are given the second amendment to carry guns and that kind of makes them feel powerful when in fact, they live in abject fear and are ruled by those who use that fear to control them, their oligarchs.

> THINKING IS DONE THROUGH LIGHT AND ELECTRONS.

Stay calm and listen to your brain think. Thinking is done with light and information is stored in electrons. When you are thinking, there is electrical movement in your brain, which can be seen with electric machines that take pictures of light activities in your brain or any part of your body. If you are not thinking, those machines do not see light movement in your brain. When you think intensely, your brain is hot from electrical activities.

My brain's electrical system, my body's overcharged electrical activity, and the irritation they gave me made me conclude that my body is not good hence I hated my body and human bodies in general and especially bodies that look like my body, black bodies. Hitherto, I tended to overvalue white bodies but no more. The only thing that I now value is knowledge, science.

I HAVE A NEED TO SEE MY BODY, IGBOS, NIGERIANS, AND AFRICANS AS NO GOOD. THIS IS ROOTED IN SEEING ME AS NO GOOD DUE TO OVERCHARGED BODY.

I have a need to see those close to me, beginning with Igbos to Nigerians, Africans, and black people as no good; this is because I see myself as no good.

My first impression of Igbos is to see them as no good and criticize them. That is, I see me as no good and criticize myself. I often deny that self-criticism and project it to Igbos.

The new goal is to like me, like those who are like me, accept all people's human imperfection, and leave it at that.

I DO NOT THINK THAT THIS WORLD CAN EVER BE FAIR BUT A FEW THINGS NEED TO BE DONE TO MAKE IT TOLERABLE— PUBLICLY PAID EDUCATION AND HEALTH INSURANCE FOR ALL

I do not think that this world would ever be a fair place. There will always be the rich and poor, the powerful and weak. But we can make the world tolerable by giving all people publicly paid education at all levels and publicly paid health insurance. Do those and I am willing to tolerate America as it is and close my nose at her racism.

ARTISTS MAKE OUR MEANINGLESS LIVES BEAUTIFUL.

My choice of music is classical music. It has been so since I was a child. Please do not ask me why this is so. I simply love classical music. I have been known to go to Germany and Austria to go enjoy classical music festivals (Mozart, Beethoven, Wagner etc.). Well, all I listen to is classical music.

This morning, at 9 AM, my partner told me to take our car to Jiffy Lube to have the oil changed and rotate the four tires. Her grandchildren, ten and eleven-year-old, came along with me. They changed the choice of music station on the car's radio, from classical station to their kind of music, which happens to be . . . what the name is for this type of music, anyway, let us call it hip hop, whatever. I had no choice but to listen to this type of music for the two hours we were driving to and from the mechanic's shop.

As I listened to this music, instead of trying to tune it out as noise, which was my habit, somehow, I paid attention to it. Seeing the two girls having fun from the music got me to thinking that this type of music actually appeals to some people.

I will not bore you with the long chain of thinking that went through my mind in two hours; instead, I will summarize my thoughts for you.

Long ago, I concluded that our lives in body, ego, space, and time are totally meaningless, purposeless, and pointless. I see the human body as something that will die, decay, and smell like feces so I do not take it seriously. To me, my body and your body is nothing.

This approach to my body and life, in general, did not start yesterday. It began at about age six when I began elementary school. I have always felt that life in body is pointless. And don't talk to me about me being a depressed person; if at all I have depression, it is that life in body and on earth depresses me; I call it existential depression and have written volumes on it.

Boethius (524 AD) wrote the *Consolation of Philosophy*. Philosophy is the best therapy there is, not the superficial stuff dished out by psychologists that merely mask folks' real issues, living pointless lives and pretending that their lives are meaningful.

Like my philosophical mentor, Arthur Schopenhauer (*World as Will and Idea*), I believe that the universe made a mistake in producing animals who can cogitate and think. It was better we were like cattle, and are mindless and merely grazed grass. Why think, why bother trying to understand the universe and then die and be eaten by worms?

(Stephen Hawkins of Black Hole fame, at one point, asked: why did the universe bother existing at all if it is a meaningless universe, and science suggests that it is meaningless?)

By age nine, I began using my imagination to come up with what would seem a semblance of a better life in body and on earth. I became an idealist like Plato (Socrates).

An idealist is a person who sees his bodily and ego-self and the world as meaningless and uses his imagination to recreate them into people and world that make sense to him. He then uses his idealized self and world as a standard with which to compare actual people and find them not good enough. Thus, he is a critical person for nothing normal folks do is good enough for him.

Unbeknown to him, normal folks actually enjoy this world and enjoy what they are doing. Normal folks do not find this world meaningless. In fact, they believe that their world is meaningful. They enjoy their body, food, sex, and pursuit of social worth. They work very hard to attain whatever their society deems achievement, such as money, position, and so on. To them, what they are doing is meaningful and satisfactory.

To the teenage me, what normal folks were doing is pointless. Why seek to be a very important person in society when you are going to die? I used to muse. Mine was the life of a philosopher.

Since age fourteen, I have taken refuge in philosophy. Reading and talking Plato, Aristotle, Descartes, Pascal, Leibnitz, Kant, Hegel, Schopenhauer, Nietzsche, Feuerbach, James, Bergson, David Hume (the racist who believed that black people are not capable of thinking), George Berkeley, Nicolo Machiavelli, Thomas Hobbes, John Locke, Jean Jacques Rousseau, and Voltaire were my daily company.

What normal folks do in society did not make any sense to me and I escaped from them into the world of thinking and writing.

So, this morning, I am listening to my partner's grandchildren enjoying what ordinarily I would have dismissed as noise. I suddenly had an insight, a eureka moment, a kind of epiphany.

The insight is that artists (musicians, painters, sculptors, writers, architects) are folks who at the deep level understand the meaninglessness of existence on earth and resolved to provide people with works of art that make them forget their pointless existence and give their drudgery some beauty. Artists make our unbearable lives beautiful.

In the USA, African Americans dominate the popular music scene. They really control the pop culture world. They give Americans beautiful music and that music enables Americans, especially white folks who, to me, are no more than worker bees who must work to provide for the welfare of the queen bee, the oligarchs that rule America. Musicians and other artists make living beautiful for the worker bees called Americans.

Without music and arts in general, what would make an American's life tolerable would be work, work, and work, then die and be forgotten in a week after he is dead.

Igbos, Nigerians, and Africans work hard and struggle to acquire the accoutrement of social prestige. They want to be seen as big men in their world. But then, they die and a week after their death, no one remembers them.

Here is a quick quiz for you: who were the rich and important men in Alaigbo and Nigeria a hundred years ago, a thousand years ago? They are forgotten and might as well not have existed, but as long as they seemed to exist, pursuing prestige and social importance gave their meaningless existence a semblance of meaning.

What a man says about other people is what he says about himself; in effect, I do not want to die and be forgotten, hence it bothers me that folks are forgotten when they die. I desire eternity, permanency, and changelessness. Why do I have those desires? I will not do some metaphysics here.

Long ago, I learned to tolerate the normal person: I see him as a person preoccupied with activities that he must be involved with obsessive-compulsively, for if he did not do so, he would realize his pointless existence, and perhaps, commit suicide. To prevent him from killing himself, I decided that one ought to not tell the worker bees of this world that they are wasting their time working meaningless jobs.

If they were smart, they would do what thinkers do, read books and ponder ideas. Thinking and writing are the joy of the philosopher, not material things. Real thinkers generally do not care for money and other paraphernalia of social significance. They ponder the origin and nature of human beings, the universe, from Big Bang to the present and how it would end.

In sum, this morning, watching two American children enjoy their hip-hop music, or whatever the hell such music is called, made me realize the important role of the artist in society.

Artists make our lives seem beautiful. Listening to music or walking through the Louvre in Paris and admiring beautiful paintings give people a sense that their lives are beautiful.

We must therefore pay for art and the humanities; we must fund creative people for they make our lives beautiful.

As for philosophers, nature is parsimonious with thinkers for it makes in every millennium only a few real philosophers and makes the other people worker bees. That is the way it is and should be. It is not an accident.

Be who you are and don't ever regret being you or wish that you are like the worker bees and their pointless acquisition of useless material things that die with them. Continue seeking joy from thinking, for it's the best type of life there is.

A COURSE IN MIRACLES SAYS THAT WE CAUSE ALL OUR PHYSICAL AND PSYCHOLOGICAL ILLNESSES BY SEPARATING FROM GOD AND WE HEAL THEM WHEN WE RETURN TO GOD, AKA LOVE, UNIFIED STATE.

What are health and wholeness? To be healthy is to be one with all creation and its creator. If one is one with God and his creation, feels joined to them, one is whole, healthy. By that definition, to be sick is to be separated from God and his other creation. One is sick if one feels separated from God and his creation, if one feels individuated.

What is healing for the sick? Since to be sick is to be separated from God and his creation, healing (salvation, redemption, deliverance) is to return to union with God and his creation. To be healed is to accept union with God and all creation. To be healed is to no longer wish separation from God and all creation, and know that one is eternally unified with God and his creation.

To be sick is to separate from oneness; to be healed is to return to oneness. God is also called union and love. Sickness is separation from love, union; healing is return to love and union.

If one returns one's mind to union, love, God, and his creation, one's mind is healed and one's body is also healed.

A sick body is a sick mind that does not want to know that illness is in the mind; a mind that separates from God projects its mental illness to its body and makes it seem ill.

We use physical illnesses to maintain our wished-for separation from God, remain unloving, become preoccupied with our sick bodies, and ignore where the sickness is, an unloving mind.

To be separated from God and other people is to be in ego; to be in ego state is to be sick; healing is to let go of the ego-mind and return to the unified mind, aka Christ mind.

Now that the mind has returned to oneness with God and is healed, then one is no longer projecting illness to one's body and one's body is now healthy. A healed mind, a joined mind, results in a healed body.

As long as you separate your mind from God, retain the ego, your body will be sick and you concentrate on your physical illness and try to heal it whereas healing begins in the mind when you return your mind to God, love.

Love God, you, and all people, and you have returned to love hence is healed, and your body cannot be sick. But as long as you refuse to love God and people, as long as you are separated from God and people, you are sick in the mind, and that sickness in the mind is projected to the body and body is made to be sick and one concentrates on trying to heal one's body, goes to medical doctors etc. trying to heal the body whereas what heals one is to love God and his creation and that heals one's body.

If one returns to semblance of perfect love (heaven is perfect love), one's body will be perfectly healthy. One uses one's healthy body to love and help people learn to love and when one has had enough of life in body, one simply uses one's mind to transform one's body to light body and continues living in light body forever and ever until one seeks to return to the awareness of living in formless self, bodiless, light, or dense state, aka God and heaven.

We on earth cause our physical illness by choosing to separate from God and his son, our real self, and live in separated state, in ego. When we see ourselves as one with God and all people and love all we are now in holy relationships, approximate love, union while one is still in form, and from there, gate of heaven, happy dream, one lets go of whatever is left of the wish for separation and returns to the awareness that one is one formless self with God.

Healing requires one to stop defending separation (ego and body) while pretending to love. Love requires total defenselessness of the ego and being in union, unified started.

The form of the physical illness one has is self-chosen. The initial illness is separation from God and manifesting in body but in body, one chooses the type of physical illness one desires with one's mind. If you have cancer, heart attack, stroke, and other diseases, your mind that insists on separation, on living from ego and its lovelessness, chose it. When you return to union, love, your specific type of physical disorder is healed.

You heal your physical illness by love.

FORGIVENESS RETURNS US TO LOVE HENCE HEALS US.

On earth, other people do bad things to you and you do bad things to people; love therefore requires you to forgive those who wronged you so that your wronging other people is forgiven you. To forgive others means to forgive you; not forgiving others means not forgiving you.

Forgiveness overlooks the world of egos and bodies for it sees them as a dream and what is done in dreams have not been done, so it overlooks the world to return to the awareness of perfect love in God.

If you do not forgive those who wronged you, you do not forgive your wronging other people, hence you remain sick and may die from that physical illness.

Your choice not to forgive, to bear grievances, and seek vengeance and revenge for wrongs done to you is what gives you illnesses and kill you; thereafter, you return to body, ego, separation, space, and time and keep returning to them, reincarnation, until you forgive, love all, and live in a healthy body and thereafter, transit to light body and from there, transit to formless God, aka heaven.

A Course in Miracles teaches that we are the parts of God, the sons of God. In God, we have knowledge of our oneness with all, that is, we know love; but we decided to experience separation, the opposite of union, opposite of love, and manifested in body. In body, we forgot our real self, unified self, and formulated a replacement, substitute ego-self, the separated ego-self. The ego offers us the opportunity to experience the opposite of love, union.

WE CHOOSE WHATEVER WE EXPERIENCE ON EARTH.

The book says that we choose whatever we are experiencing on earth for there is no way that the son of God can experience what he does not want to experience.

If you are physically sick, you chose it; if you are discriminated against, you chose it; whatever situation you are in, which your ego wants you to blame other people for and see you as a victim of the world, you chose it.

You experience what you want to experience and from the experience of lack of love, separation, ego, you learn that love, union, is better and return to love by no longer wanting to be ego and defending ego and separation.

In this brief essay, I have pretty much said all that *A Course in Miracles* teaches on sickness; do I practice it? If I did practice it, I would not be physically sick and seek medical intervention. The goal is to practice it, live in a healthy body, and thereafter, return to perfect love.

Finally, is what the book teaching true or false? I leave that to you to decide for yourself. To me, it seems true.

Post Script:

This week, I read Neale Donald Walsh's *Conversations with God*, book one. Neale had read *A Course in Miracles* before his conversations with God. If you read CWG, you see traces of *A Course in Miracles*, albeit put in simple prose. CWG also says that we choose our physical and mental disorders and choose when we heal them.

THERE ARE NO ACCIDENTS IN LIFE; THINGS ARE THE WAY THEY ARE AND ARE SUPPOSED TO BE.

America's screwed state is how it is supposed to be; America had to be formed by Europeans; Africans had to be enslaved, and natives' lands had to be taken over; all these formed a crazy ego-based, conflict-ridden society.

Nigeria is as it should be, a nation of thieves.

I had to have big ego and struggle to overcome it.

These factors made me ready to teach people ego-lessness, that is, love-based living.

If you take away one photon, particle, atom, or one thing that was done to evolve the universe from Big Bang to the present, you would not have this particular universe, maybe another one. Everything that has happened in the universe had to happen to produce us, you.

Everything that happened in your life and my life, awful as they seemed to be, had to happen to produce us. There are no accidents in the universe or in one's life.

Ozodi Thomas Osuji, Ph.D.

FEAR FROM BIG EGO; DESIRE TO IMPROVE EGO AND ELIMINATE GOD

I made a choice to have a big ego hence live in total fear and from it, try to come up with an improved son of God that is not connected to other sons of God, hence to God, improved individual selves. I lived in total fear because I wanted to kill the son of God, my real self, and have a different improved ego-self. I must now let the improved ego-self die and return inward to regain awareness of my real self, unified self.

MY EGO IS VERY FRAGILE AND EASILY FEELS SLIGHTED AND ANGRY.

Yesterday, in the hospital, to take a test I was told to go into a hall and sit down. A lady comes and calls people's names and takes them to go do the test. Since I had not given my name to her or anyone, I did not know whether my name would be called or not so I asked her if she is going to call my name and she asked: "Did I call your name?" and I felt slighted and angry.

ONE MUST DO WHAT SEEMS TO ONE USEFUL FOR SOCIETY TO BE ALIVE REGARDLESS OF WHETHER OTHER PERSONS BELIEVE THAT WHAT ONE IS DOING IS GOOD OR NOT.

Kofi Acheampong does his sons and daughters of Africa, SADA, thing because he believes that it is necessary to unify all Africans in Africa and in the diaspora and that gives his life meaning and purpose and reason to live long.

CIVIL RIGHTS ACTIVISTS FILLED WITH ANGER AND HATRED SELDOM LIVE LONG; ONLY FORGIVENESS AND CORRECTION OF EVIL ENABLE PEOPLE TO LIVE PEACEFULLY AND LIVE LONG.

My heroes: Martin Luther King, Malcolm X, Stockley Carmichael, Eldridge Cleaver, Hughie Newton, Walter Rodney, Bobby Wright (he wrote the *Psychopathic Racial Personality*), Ivan Van Serbia (he wrote *They Came Before Columbus*; the book was written from ego fighting mood), and Steve Biko who fought against racism. They were understandably angry at their white oppressors; they had rage in their lives; that anger and rage tore them apart and produced all sorts of weak organs in their bodies and they died young.

If you want to live peacefully and long, then have love in your mind.

In a world where bad people do bad things to you, then have forgiveness for them and work to correct their evil.

Forgiveness and working to correct evil are what enable folks to live long and peacefully. If you have anger and do not forgive wrongs done to you, bear grievances and seek vengeance and revenge, you wear down your body and die from heart attack, stroke, diabetes, and other diseases induced by an unforgiving mind.

J died from a disease that her unforgiving mind gave her. My frequent digestive and constipation problems are due to my egoism and my ego's refusal to forgive those who wronged me, hence forgive me my own wrongs to others and live in relative peace and joy.

I am not saying that we should condone evil; it is fear that condones evil; if you are egoless hence have no fear of harm and death, you work to remove evil in society; you fight racism, discrimination, and other injustice issues.

Our world is a place of opposites, good and bad, light and darkness, life and death; there are good people and there are bad people; you must struggle to correct bad people and not tolerate them.

It was just for civil rights leaders to have struggled against American racism and worked for social and economic justice; where some of them made a mistake were to hate the racist. They should have seen racists as unhappy people and forgave their evils while working to correct them, hence shows them how to live peaceful lives.

NO EGO IS CALM.

If one has no ego, one is calm all the time. One has no fear, anxiety, anger, depression, paranoia, and mania (for all those result from pursuing the ego). If you let go of the ego and do not seek it or defend it, you simply live as part of life. Since life is eternal, you are eternal; eventually, you move from life in body to life in light body and thereafter, return to life in formless unified spirit, aka heaven.

LEADERSHIP IS HAVING A VISION, GOAL, AND USING PEOPLE AND MONEY TO ACHIEVE IT; SO, WHAT VISION AM I PURSUING?

Leaders have visions, goals of where they want to go, and use men, material, and money to achieve them. If I am a leader, what visions, goals, objectives, or purposes have I posited and using men and money to achieve them on an ongoing basis?

My goal is to reduce my ego and help people to reduce their egos. People with reduced ego live peacefully and help teach other people how to reduce their egos and live peacefully.

If you are totally egoless, you will not have individuality and if you do not have individuality, separation, you are not in the world of space, time, and matter, the separated world; you are out of here and is in the formless unified world of God, our real self. One lives from unified self, Christ self, lives from love.

The most that you can do and still be on earth, space, and time is to reduce your ego and put it to serving social interest so that you know some relative peace and joy.

PERSONALITY IS THE INDIVIDUAL'S PARTICULAR MANNER, CHOICE OF NOT LOVING GOD AND HIS SONS, A MEANS OF SEPARATION.

The human personality (and the body and society that were used to form it) is self-chosen. It is the individual's chosen manner of separating from God and other sons of God, a choice of how to separate from God.

But since it is impossible to separate from the whole and still be alive, personality, aka ego, is a means to seem separated from God while also seeming connected to him and other people.

Each person has a specific pattern of not loving other people and being individuated.

When I say that the individual chose his personality, his body and ego, let me quickly clarify that the individual does not choose alone; he chooses with all of us; what he chose we helped him choose, hence all of us receive the consequences of his behaviors, for we helped choose his behavior pattern, his personality for him.

Generally, we are not aware at the conscious level of what we are doing with our personalities, so it is pointless blaming people for what they do with their personalities since they do not understand what they are doing at the conscious level; although at the subconscious level, they know exactly what they are doing; we all came to this world to separate from eternal union with God and all his sons, from our real self; we are here on earth to live as the opposite of our real self, unified self, love.

We are on earth not to love each other while pretending to do so through special love relationships (where one protects one's individuality and try to use it to love other individuals; this is ego-based love; real love is spirit-based love).

J chose not to love specific individuals, not to love a man, while seeming to love all people through her phony religion that talks about human unity while members screw people.

J made a choice not to love a specific man, but instead, to relate to all people, men and women, via bantering with them as long as she does not get close to a man and become attached to him; she is afraid of connection, afraid of love and oneness for that, she believes, and destroys her separated self. As a result of her choice to be separated, her mind is sick.

All sickness is in the mind, the choice to separate from love, from God and his sons. That sickness is thereafter disguised by being projected to body and body made sick so that one concentrates on one's medical problem and not concentrate on trying to heal the sickness where it is at, mind; healing means jettisoning separation and embracing oneness with God and his sons.

All sickness lies in the decision to separate from God and people. We hide that sickness by making our bodies sick.

I made a choice not to love God and other people's real selves and my real self, hence have a sick mind, and hide that sickness by making my body pained and having stomach problems.

This choice was made before I was born on earth and has been so from day one of my life. Every person's choice, one's pattern of not loving, one's means of separating from one's real self, other people's real selves, and from God, is there from the moment of one's birth on earth.

The people on earth first constructed the earth and human bodies; each person from pure unified spirit, God, chooses how to experience his desired opposite of his real self, opposite of love, how to be an ego separated self in a dream, and dived into a specific body and society and experience the world as he does it. There are no accidents in our lives.

We can, however, understand our personalities, how they were formed with our bodies and societies and our specific spirit's choice to be in them, decide to let go of our personalities, give up the wish for separated self, relapse back into formless unified self (enlightenment, illumination), and return to peace and joy.

This is the only way to change personality, not the superficial stuff written by ego-based psychotherapists.

Please do not blame you or other people when you observe their specific patterns of avoiding love while seeming to love (which *A Course in Miracles* calls special love relationships), relationships based on ego; what you need to do is have understanding and first change your own pattern of relating to you and other people; regain awareness of your real self, son of God, remember God, overlook other people's ego identifications and ego relationships, and love the son of God in them, the divinity in them.

Love the divine self in you and in other people; you know when you did so by having peace and joy in yourself and seeing peace and joy in those you love.

In a dream, one's thinking produces a world that seems real.

Could one's mind not also be producing the day world?

In one's dream at night, one's thinking produces a world that looks like one's day world and peoples it with people doing what folks do in one's day world. In effect, one mind produced a world, using the people in one's day world to do what one wants done to achieve one's dream goal.

Could it not also be the case that one's day world is produced by one's mind, using people to enact roles that enable one to accomplish the goals one wants to accomplish in one's day world? In other words, one schedules the world in such a manner that one accomplishes whatever one wants to accomplish in one's life and therefore, one is responsible for what one experiences and for what happens to one.

One attracted other people and events into one's day and night dreams to do what one wants them to do in the dream script that one wrote.

The world may not exist apart from our dreams; we write the script, now, and populate it, now, and enact it along as we write the script, play, or dramas.

That is, the universe begins and ends with our collective dreaming, collective consciousness, that produced it (while thinking about it).

MISSION STATEMENT

The center for egoless living is an organization dedicated to enabling people to live less egoistic life hence live peacefully and happily.

It uses what we learned about leadership to establish a vision of a world where people live less egoistically hence more peacefully and happily; the center is a school; it will be established everywhere in the world and teach people about the nature of the separated ego-self and unified spirit self and help them live less egoistically. That is its mission.

If one entirely lets go of one's ego separated self, one is back to the awareness of one's real self, the son of God, who is one with God and who thinks with God and God thinks through him; one is no longer in form, but is formless; one is not in space, time, and matter, that is, not in the world of illusion.

Since one has experienced ego, one understands the ego as an illusion, knows about the ego, also knows God, and can intervene in the egos' world, one then is the Christ self.

The Christ self has experienced heaven's oneness but is not in formless heaven but in the world of light forms, still in form but form of light and from there, help people in the world of dense forms, on earth. He is now a spirit guide for those still on earth.

He is what Buddhists call Bodhisattva—people who have experienced oneness, nirvana, and could remain there but chose to be in the intermediate astral world and from there, help those in the lower egos' world, our world.

Those who are too egoistic need to reduce to ego-lessness, not eliminate their ego entirely, for to eliminate it is to be out of this world but if reduced, one still lives in this world but does so peacefully and happily, with less fear, anxiety, anger, depression, paranoia, and other mental disturbances.

There are people who appear less egoistic but are very wicked egos; they are single-minded in their evil behaviors; whereas big egos act narcissistically, small egos kill people; people need to reduce their ego and make it ego of forgiveness and ego of love.

DREAM
3:30 PM
MAY 17, 2020

In this dream, I was sitting in front of a tabletop computer typing when the national warning signal comes on saying that they will announce impending danger soon, for folks to be on alert. Suddenly, the computer screen went wavy and I suspected something major and got up from my seat, ready to run out of the building, and it is now Saint Michael's church, Umuohiagu, and I was sitting and typing in front of the altar. I got up and walked toward the door and woke up.

This dream tells me that something scared me; it is normal ego response to fear. However, because I was sitting in front of the altar, it means that whatever danger coming at me will not harm me.

THE AMERICAN MIND IS CHARMED BY HIS POLITICAL SYSTEM INTO SEEKING MATERIAL THINGS INCESSANTLY, NOT THINKING ABOUT WAYS OF LIVING PEACEFULLY AND LOVINGLY

Each human civilization charms its people to seeing phenomena in a specific way but not in the many other ways that things can be seen. A civilization changes or collapses when its people begin to see the world differently—when the scale covering their eyes falls out.

Americans from childhood are socialized to be little capitalists, to incessantly seek material things. They work hard to acquire all kinds of toys, toys that they use for a day or two and throw away and to eat, eat, and eat until they grow fat and die from heart attacks, strokes, and diabetes. They cannot relax, take it easy, consider that social democracy is actually a better form of capitalism, and read, love, and get along with people.

When you talk to Americans about other ways of living, they do not hear you. Eventually, the scale before their eyes will fall off and they see what some of us see, the value of mixed economy and social democracy; in the meantime, they live as slaves, they are enslaved to their way of living.

What I said about Americans apply to other civilizations. If you are an African, say, Igbo, you see the world through the prism of Igbo culture, and to you, that makes sense, but unknown to you, other people see you as myopic; it might help you to consider how other people see the world and incorporate them to how you see the world.

If you expand your horizon, you are called cosmopolitan and urbane; if you keep seeing the world only through the parameters of your culture, you are called parochial, particularistic, and not universalistic in your approach to phenomena.

THE EGO IS A FALSE SELF THAT WE MADE FOR OURSELVES TO AVOID LIVING AS OUR REAL SELF; IT MUST BE GIVEN UP FOR US TO BECOME AWARE OF OUR REAL SELF, SON OF GOD.

The ego is the separated self that one, with the help of other people, made and with which one replaced the unified spirit self that God created one as.

One must give up the ego to return to the awareness of the unified self that God created one as. As long as one is in ego and its material body, one lives in the world of space, time, and matter in self-forgetfulness, illusions. You can keep the ego for as long as you like but eventually, you will realize that it is not your real self, realize that your real self is not in form, not in body, but in formless spirit and return to it by giving up the ego.

The ego gives us pain and suffering. It is false and must be defended to seem real in our awareness. When we are tired of pain and suffering and tired of being defensive, defense of a false self that does not exist, then we give our egos up and become aware of the unified self, the sons of God in us that are always there for us to acknowledge them by jettisoning the ego.

WOMEN TRADITIONALLY DERIVE A SENSE OF POWER FROM TELLING THEIR CHILDREN AND OR GRANDCHILDREN WHAT TO DO; DON'T TAKE THAT POWER AWAY FROM THEM UNTIL YOU PERMIT THEM FULL PARTICIPATION IN RUNNING SOCIETY AND FROM SO DOING, DERIVE POWER AS MEN DO.

Lately, I have been observing a woman tell her children what to do. On the other hand, I have no desire to tell the children what to do. In so far that I have needed to tell anyone what to do, it is my fellow men in the adult society. I want to participate in how the society I live in is governed and resent it if other people do things without consulting me.

From this observation, I came to the realization that we all, as egos, have need to tell other people what to do. Men tend to do so by telling other men what to do or by participating in the governing of their society. Women tend to derive that ego power from socializing children, making sure that they learn the norms of their society and punishing them when they misbehave.

Until we give women equal opportunity to participate in governing society, and we must do so, they probably will keep supervising children as they currently do.

Women are the repository of each society's culture and transmit it to their children; without women, there can be no civilized human society, so we must appreciate what they do for all of us, transform us from little savages to law-abiding human beings.

PERSONALITY, NORMAL OR ABNORMAL, IS A MEANS OF HIDING FROM ONE'S REAL SELF, GOD AND HIS SON, AND DEFENDING THE SUBSTITUTE SELF ONE MADE TO USE IN HIDING FROM ONE'S REAL SELF.

One's real self is the son of God, a part of God, a part in the whole; the part is like the whole but cannot ever be the entire whole for the whole has many parts and is larger than the sum of the parts for it contains all the parts.

One did not like to be a small part of the whole and wanted to be larger than the whole, larger than God, an impossibility. So, one invented a false self that seems powerful and larger, more powerful than God and other people and pretend to be it, hide that big self from other people and instead, present a let-us-get-along-equal self to other people.

The ego is made and used to hide the wish for one to be more powerful than the entire universe, and anything that makes one seem not that powerful makes one feel slighted; thus, one becomes angry, fearful, and anxious.

All mental disorders, such as anxiety disorder, personality disorders, and depression, paranoia, delusion, mania, schizophrenia, and alcohol and drug addictions are invented to hide the desired all-powerful self, the self that is more powerful than the whole self, more powerful than God and all his creation.

Give up the desire to be more powerful than the whole self, God, and other people and accept sameness and equality and personality is transformed, healed, used to join all people, and becomes normal. One is only healthy when one no longer needs to live in ego and body and return to unified spirit.

When you meet a person, enter a situation, or see an event or encounter, the world does not project your interpretation of what they mean to them; keep quiet; if you really accept that your opinions and interpretations are false and keep quiet, the Holy Spirit, your higher self, will tell you how to relate to what you see, which is to love all people and be fearless, for you are eternal and nothing can harm your eternal soul.

If you continue along the path of not coloring the world with your interpretations and relating to your opinions of what reality is but not reality itself, someday, you would see the entire world disappear and you experience formless, oneness, spiritual light.

And from that experience, you know that only God, unified spirit self, which you are a part of, exists, and that the rest is the ego and its complicated world of space, time, and matter, the world of chaos and noise.

But before you experience God, enlightened, and illuminated to your real self, you must first have faith in God, for you left God by having faith in the ego, illusions, and must first have counter faith in God before you experience what you have—faith in God (you had faith in the ego and see you as the ego and its world; you must now have faith in God, love to experience God; faith precedes experience).

God and his world are very simple: eternal, permanent, and changeless, peaceful and joyful.

> I DO NOT RELATE TO PEOPLE AS THEY ARE BUT AS I INTERPRET THEM TO BE; I DO NOT RELATE TO THE WORLD AS IT IS BUT AS I INTERPRET IT AND SPECULATE THAT IT IS; THUS, I RELATE TO MY OPINION OF REALITY, NOT REALITY; WHAT REALITY IS, I DO NOT KNOW.

I see people, things, events, the world; I do not know who and what they are. I have perception of them, I have interpretation of what they are, and I have speculations of what I think that they are. I then relate to them as if they are my perception, interpretation, and conjectures.

In doing this, I have made two mistakes; first, I took the formless world of God that can only be experienced, put them in pictures, and placed them in space, time, and matter so that I can perceive them; reality is not perceived but known; the second mistake is to have interpretations of what they are and mean and then relate to my interpretations, not to the pictures I see.

I relate to my opinions of people and the world but not to actual people and the world. I relate to reality that I made not reality as it is. What reality is, I do not know.

I want to know what reality, people, events, and the world are. I have to stop projecting my interpretations to people, events, and the world, stay quiet, and let my higher self, the holy self, tell me what they, and how to relate to them, or transcend the world, return to God, and relate to truth, not interpretations of things.

All my perceptions, interpretations, and speculations are shaped by fear. The Holy Spirit sees people and the world without fear and shows me them as they are in the world, still illusory but more approximating the truth.

One can think, speak, and behave from ego; that is, the false self and false interpretation of things; from the Holy Spirit; from true interpretations of things and people, but still false because he is still relating to pictures; reality is not in pictures, but falsity that gives one peace; or from God, when one reverts to no separated self.

In God, one is formless and not aware of one's earthly body and does not know that body exists; one's body is gone but one can later take on another bodily form that looks like one's old body or any other body to relate to those still in body and return to formless unified spirit.

THE DELUDED PERSON BELIEVES IN HIS DELUSIONS AS TRUE HENCE IS PSYCHOTIC.

The deluded person believes his delusions, his ego, to be real and behaves as if his fictions are real; he is no longer in social reality and must escape from society to defend his false, grandiose ego-self.

The neurotic or person with personality disorder knows that he is not his wished big ego but desires it and does not want to let it go, hence still feels easily slighted, but he is fairly normal.

An example of a deluded person is Nebo Adele. He is no longer aware that everything he says is false but believes his lies that gratify his grandiose ego to be the truth. He ran away from the truth to go defend a false big self and that big self's interpretations of the world of pictures that the sons of God in their ego state made.

Post Script:

I personalized this essay to make it realistic; where I said I, please replace it with you, for you are probably also coloring the world with your false interpretations of it and seeing a world that you made, a false world, and relating to your false picture of the world. Now, keep quiet and ask God or his Holy Spirit to tell you what the truth is; stay silent until you sense what is the truth but do not jump to what your flippant ego tells you is the truth; the ego speaks first and the Holy Spirit speaks second, to correct what the spurious ego said or did (*A Course in Miracles* says).

I FAILED ME, MY CHILDREN, AND EX-WIFE.

I identified with a big ego, defend it, did not get into the world, compete in something, and succeed in it. My ego makes noise of being big—that it is always right and other egos are always wrong—but I did not make a good living for my ex-wife and children and now they are each taking care of themselves.

I need to give up the ego, change, and live from refined ego, normal person; or live from the Holy Spirit-directed self or from God directly.

If I change, I change the trajectory of my life, from failure to success, for God that created the sons of God, who later invented this world, has enough power to give one the abundance one needs to live here on earth.

Just give up the ego and then see what happens; the least one gets is fearlessness, peace, and joy.

GOD CANNOT HAVE CONSCIOUSNESS UNLESS
HE HAS OTHER GODS, SONS; IT TAKES TWO OR
MORE PEOPLE TO HAVE CONSCIOUSNESS; SO, GOD
AND HIS SONS ARE THE SAME AND EQUAL.

God must have a son to be a father and the son of God must have a father to be a son of God; more importantly, God requires another self to have consciousness; it took the sons of God for God to have consciousness, so God and his sons are coequal and the same. Nevertheless, God is the whole and the sons are the parts. The whole is larger than the sum of the parts for it contains them; God is larger than you, a son of God.

GOD AND HIS SONS DESIRED EXPERIENCE IN MATTER, SPACE, AND TIME; EXPERIENCE IS STORED IN MEMORY; EXPERIENCE AND ITS MEMORY THEN MAINTAIN THE WORLD.

IF EXPERIENCE IS MOSTLY UNPLEASANT, ONE FEELS ANGRY AND SEEKS REVENGE; ONE MUST NOW FORGIVE THAT EXPERIENCE, OVERLOOK THE EXPERIENCE AND ITS WORLD TO RETURN TO THE AWARENESS OF GOD.

The sons of God, one shared self, experienced separation in matter, space, and time; they hurt each other and feel angry (even siblings sometimes hurt each other and feel angry at each other).

As long as they store the experience of mutual hurts in their memory, they feel a need for grievance, anger, but if they overlook the experience, memory, forgive it, they overlook the world and the experience they had in it and return to awareness of unity, God.

To forgive is to overlook the wrongs done on earth, to change our memories from hurt to gratitude, transcend the earth, and return to God, to joy and bliss where separated folks will no longer hurt each other.

EGO GAMES ARE AN EFFORT TO MAINTAIN SEPARATION HENCE AVOID LOVE AND GIVE ONESELF AND OTHER SELVES PAIN AND SUFFERING; IT IS NOT FUNNY TO GIVE ONESELF AND OTHERS PAIN AND SUFFERING JUST BECAUSE YOU WANT TO PRETEND TO BE SEPARATE AND POWERFUL; THE EGO DOES NOT EXIST, SO STOP ITS GAMES, RETURN TO UNION, AND KNOW PEACE AND JOY.

Ego games are not amusing for they keep one in pain and suffering and one then gives lack of peace and suffering to those close to one. One must stop playing ego, pretending importance games, and return to peace and joy.

FORGIVENESS IS RELEASE FROM EGO AND BODY AND RETURN TO JOY.

When you forgive other people, you release them from pain and suffering and release yourself from pain and suffering. If you do not forgive, you keep yourself and people in pain and suffering.

BODY IS THE SAME AS NATURE AND AS SUCH, HAS
NO PAIN AND SUFFERING; YOU CAN BURN IT AND IT
FEELS NOTHING BUT THE MOMENT YOU BREATHE
CONSCIOUSNESS INTO IT, IT FEELS PAIN AND FEAR.

Our bodies are composed of atoms and elements and those are in the stars that burn twenty-four seven and in rocks and they do not feel pain and suffering. But when you give them consciousness, in animals and human beings, they begin to feel pain. If you remove that consciousness, as in death, the body feels nothing.

It is consciousness that makes matter and body feel pain. Consciousness must be apart from body to have that effect on body—body that by itself does not have consciousness of pain and suffering.

SELF-CONSCIOUSNESS IS CONSCIOUSNESS OF ONESELF
AS A BODY, A PAINED BODY, AND THAT BEGINS
THE DREAM LIFE OF ONESELF AS BODY; REMOVE
CONSCIOUSNESS FROM BODY AND BODY IS LIKE A LOG
OF DRIED WOOD AND ROCK, AND FEELS NOTHING.

A COURSE IN MIRACLES WANTS TO CHANGE OUR
PERCEPTION, FROM EGO-BASED PERCEPTION TO HOLY
SPIRIT-BASED PERCEPTION, BOTH ILLUSIONS BUT ONE
APPROXIMATES THE NON-PERCEPTUAL WORLD OF GOD.

In formless unified God, there is no perception for there is no other person to see. In our world of separation, we have perception.

In this world, we have ego perception that sees others as not part of oneself hence one can harm them.

In Holy Spirit-purified perception, one sees other people as part of one, loves, and forgives our mutual wrongs to return to some peace and when perception ends, return to oneness, the non-perceptual world of God.

THE WORLD IS A DREAM ALRIGHT BUT THOSE IN IT TAKE IT AS REAL AND AS SUCH, DO FEEL PAINED WHEN ATTACKED AND THEREFORE, THEY SHOULD NOT BE ATTACKED.

The world is a dream and what is done in it has not been done and does not matter and those in it should feel nothing. But those in the world, dream, take it as real; they see themselves as their egos and bodies, and believe that their egos and bodies are real, hence do feel pained when harmed.

Therefore, they defend their bodies if you attack them and defend their egos if you attack them but enlightened persons who know that the world does not exist do not feel pain when you attack them, for they are no longer identified with body. There are just a few enlightened persons in the world at any point in time; the rest of the people see themselves as their egos and bodies.

Do not attack anyone; if you do, unless he forgives you, you are not released; you are held a prisoner in this world, live in pain, and suffer.

(If you forgive a person, you release him from the karmic law that he must suffer for his injuring other people bodily or psychologically.)

THERE IS A CREATIVE FORCE IN US. THAT CREATIVE FORCE IN US IS THE SONS OF GOD. WE CREATE OUR FALSE EGO REALITY

There is a creative force inside us; we are creators; we co-create our personalities and the world around us. The creator in us use our inherited bodies and societies to create our personalities and the world we experience; each person with the aid of his body and other people created his unique personality, his unique manner of dealing with other people, and manner of hiding from his real self, unified spirit self, God.

The ego personality we created is false hence is deluded because we believe in what is not true as true. Because it is not real, we must perpetually defend it to make it seem real to us.

If the world is a dream, hence false, we then created a false, mad world. The ego-self and its world are the creations of a madman; the sleeping sons of God created a false separated and deluded self and world; we created a mad world.

A Course in Miracles eschewed the term creator but called us inventors; it says that we invented our false ego selves; what difference does it make whether we invented or created a mad self and mad world?

Artists are said to be creative whereas engineers are said to be inventive; both invent temporary things that do not last forever.

The book said that God created us, the real sons of God; what God created lasts forever; it called the spirit in us spirit but the original draft of the book used soul; the original draft probably used the word creative and the editors leave the term creative to God and his son in wake heaven, but says that we miscreate in our dream state.

The Holy Spirit, the book says, reinvents the false world we made to a semblance of a real-world and remakes our false egos to Christ, a loving and forgiving self.

We can use the term creative for what we do on earth.

We create our personalities and our realities, albeit false realities, as new age religionists say.

WHO IS A TERRORIST?
WE ALL ARE TERRORISTS.

Terrorism inheres in using force, terror (arousing intense fear that makes a person cower and beg for his life) that threatens to harm or kill somebody if he does not do what you ask him to do. We all do so at some level.

Slave masters use force and threat of harm and death to intimidate slaves into being slaves against their wishes; Slave catchers and sellers use force to intimidate those they catch and sell as slaves; thus, the slave seller (Africans), buyer and user (whites and Arabs) are terrorists.

White Americans who had slaves were terrorists. Africans who caught and sold their people were terrorists. Africa's ruling thugs are terrorists. Kidnappers and criminals who rob at gun points are terrorists.

THE OPPOSITE OF TERRORISTS ARE THOSE WHO INFLUENCE PEOPLE WITH LOVE AND FORGIVENESS

Jesus Christ used love and forgiveness to influence people to return to love, to God, and therefore is not a terrorist; love is the opposite of terrorism.

Love is the opposite of fear.
Love is of God; fear is of the ego.

NOTHINGNESS

In the beginning is nothing (there is no such thing as beginning but in our present mode of speaking, we assume a beginning, so let us say so). There was absolute nothingness. That nothingness is neither this nor that but exactly what its name says nothing. There was nothing.

However, it was nothing that can become whatever it wants to become. It is nothing that has become all that we see in our physical universe of space, time, and matter.

The real universe is composed of nothing, literally, not figuratively. As such, we human beings are literally nothing (you are probably already scared for the whole business of being a human being is a futile effort to be something important, significant, superior, and powerful to counteract nothingness). We are nothing.

Properly put, we are part of the giant nothingness that is the real universe. The universe is one nothingness that at the same time is infinite nothingness, for the moment you say one, you have implied two, three, until infinity.

The universe, that is, nothingness and its parts, we (in our nothing state) want to become something. It is impossible for nothing to become something, but nothingness has the apparent ability to seem to become something, albeit illusory something.

Thus, 13.8 billion years ago, nothingness produced light. That light shattered into particles of light called photons. The photons immediately recombined into matter, such as quarks and electrons (and their opposites as anti-matter—matter and anti-matter attacked each other, annihilated each other, and returned to light, radiation, but some matter remained to continue our matter-based universe).

Quarks combined into protons and neutrons. The early universe was then composed of electrons, protons, and neutrons. Protons and neutrons combined to form nuclei. Thus, now we have nuclei, electrons, and photons (this is called the state of plasma). The universe remained this way for almost half a million years.

The universe expanded at a speed greater than the speed of light; light travels at 186, 282 miles per second. This greater than speed of light velocity is called inflation; it prevented the early universe from collapsing back on itself and thus, ending the incipient universe from coming into existence.

Thereafter, nuclei captured electrons, and atoms of hydrogen and helium were formed. The universe is now a sea of hydrogen and helium and remained so for millions of years.

Thereafter, space occurred in the sea of hydrogen and clumps of hydrogen separated from each other. Gravity acted on each clump of hydrogen and pressure and high temperature led each clump, in its core, to ignite, fuse into helium.

The fusion of helium from hydrogen is what a star is. A star is a clump of hydrogen in which core pressure and high temperature lead to the fusion of four atoms of hydrogen into one helium atom. This process is called nucleosynthesis.

There are now trillions and trillions of stars. The stars are separated into galaxies. Each galaxy is composed of, at least, 200 billion stars; there are, at least, 200 billion galaxies.

It takes light 100, 000 years, to travel from one end to the other of our Milky Way galaxy, and millions of years from our nearest galaxy, Andromeda, to us. Some of the stars whose light we see at night are long exploded in supernova.

The early stars were huge in size and occasionally explode in supernova. When a star has almost exhausted its hydrogen, it begins to fuse helium to other elements until it reaches iron and explodes. During the explosion, enormous heat is generated and all other elements beyond iron are formed. There are about 92 elements in nature (scientists have synthesized another twenty elements).

Planet earth and its star, the sun, was formed from exploded huge stars about five billion years ago. Our sun has enough hydrogen to keep fusing helium for the next five billion years; thereafter, it would have less hydrogen and start fusing helium to other elements and thereafter, grow in size and explode in supernova. The sun will thus die, along with the earth and its other planets (Mercury, Venus, Earth, Mars, Jupiter, Saturn, Uranus, Neptune, Plato), and the comets and asteroids that circle the sun.

On planet earth, the ninety-two elements in nature gathered in a pool of water and heat produced by lightning that kept striking the water until it fused the 64 elements that are found in biological organisms (carbon, hydrogen, oxygen, nitrogen, potassium, magnesium, sodium, iron, zinc, calcium, copper, and so on) to form the basis for cell life in animals and plants and thus, began biological evolution.

Single-celled organisms, such as amoeba, were formed and those combined to multicellular organisms and in time, evolved to animals like human beings.

In time, the entire stars in the universe will explode in supernova and shatter into the elements that composed them. A few trillion years from today, all the stars, planets, people, animals, and trees would have decayed back to the elements that composed them. The elements would decompose to electrons, protons, and neutrons and all those would decompose to light. This is called the Big Chill.

Thus, the universe that began in light returns to light. Light in turn would decompose to the nothingness from which it came.

A universe that currently seems to be something solid will decay to nothingness; hence, the universe is nothingness.

In the meantime, the universe produced seeming solids, things including us. Some of the things it produced were imbued with the desire to fear demise. People, animals, and other sensate things fear death. We all fear death.

But our bodies must die and return to nothingness despite our fear of death.

We are given the desire to seek to become important, significant, powerful, and superior to each other.

I completed secondary school in 1973. At the end of that year, my fellow students disappeared to the end of the world. I disappeared to the USA the following year. Occasionally, I run into a former schoolmate but beyond that, I have no idea where they are.

What happened is that all of us were imbued with the desire to become something important and significant. That desire for personal worth manifested itself in the desire for education so we went to universities. After undergraduate education, then graduate education; in my case, to the doctorate degree. And thereafter, we sought jobs that would make us seem important.

To be human is to be cursed with the desire to seem important and that is what all of us are doing. As long as we have the desire for significance, we are human; we seek worth based on separated ego and body and suffer psychological pains.

We are nothing seeking something and in the process, suffer.

OTHER FOLKS' EVIL BEHAVIORS ENABLE ONE TO LEARN AND CHANGE AND ACCEPT ONE'S REAL SELF.

All our evil behaviors are rooted in our desire to be important. Whites want to be superior to blacks. Igbos do not want to be important but assume their total superiority to all people, white folks included. It is desire for superiority and importance that keeps us suffering and living in pain.

If you take away the desire for importance, worth, and power, you recognize our utter nothingness. The world keeps marching on with people seeking worth and value and some being totally evil in so seeking.

Adolf Hitler wanted to seem superior to other people and in pursuit of that chimera, killed over fifty million people (then he died and his body decayed and smelled like shit).

Since we are nothing, nobody was actually killed. Hitler killed fifty million people in the dream that separation from our real self, nothingness, is possible, but in truth, killed no one.

You can return to the awareness of your nothingness by relating to evil souls, seeing them strive to seem important, and out of it, do evil. You allow them to do their evil to you, such as put you down and you learn that you were never up, and as such, could not be put down by the deluded creature trying to degrade you to seem upgraded himself; like all of us, he is absolutely nothing.

DISCUSSION

What would happen if one accepted that one is nothing? Go find out.

I look at myself in the mirror and told me that I am nothing, that my body is nothing (matter does not exist, it seems to have temporary existence), that what I call myself, the ego, separated self, is a mere mental and social construct; something in me, the conceptualizer, conceptualized the ego-self and defended it, otherwise, the ego does not exist independent of my desire for it to exist.

If I stop desiring the ego and its body, they literally do not exist; they disappear from my awareness and from the universe. So, I reminded myself that I am not my body, not my ego, that I do not exist, that what exists in the universe is the conceptualizing force in the universe, and that conceptualizer is not my body or ego, it is nothing. I accepted the fact that I do not exist.

I accepted that I am nothing and stopped wishing to be something important, for what does not exist cannot be important.

What happens when one accepts one's nothingness is that one feels perfect sense of peace and joy, bliss (I have written about enlightenment in other places); the goal here is to state the simple fact that I do not exist, that you do not exist, that only nothingness exists, and what that nothingness is cannot be explained in words for it transcends words.

CONCLUSION

If what I said here does not make sense to you, please accept that temporary reality for you, for you cannot run until you learned to walk.

People are at different stages in their evolution. Some are now capable of accepting their nothingness whereas many still want to believe that they have worth in their nonexistent egos and bodies and defend those.

When you are ready to accept reality, you will do so but until then, be where you are at. Live in illusions that matter, space, and time, your body, ego, and world is real.

We are here on earth to first deny our truth of nothingness and construct the chimera that we are something important and when we have tortured ourselves long enough trying to live in illusions, we begin striving to know the truth, look for it, find it, and know peace and joy.

EVERY RELATIONSHIP OFFERS ONE AN OPPORTUNITY TO LEARN ABOUT ONESELF AND CHANGE.

Every situation can teach you about your real self. If you have a tendency to jealousy and have a girlfriend that wants to talk to all men, you could feel jealous and walk away from her or stay and accept that you do not have control over her behavior and cannot decide who she relates to or not; that cures you of your jealousy and a false sense of control over her; you have no control over you or another person. Thus, having a girlfriend that spends all day at Facebook talking to all manner of people, irritating as it is, is designed to enable one to deal with one's tendency to jealousy.

ONE FEARLESS LEADER CHANGES THE WORLD.

One leader does change history. People are afraid of death hence stand by as evil is done. Whites and blacks stood by as a racist white police officer, Derick Chauvin, on May 25, 2020, in Minneapolis, Minnesota, USA who kneeled on the neck of George Floyd, a black man, and choked him to death. Not one of the onlookers went and dragged the Neanderthal, the psychopath in police uniform, away from him. They were afraid of being shot to death by the other three police goons standing by.

But if there was a man without fear of death, he would have jumped in, dragged the pathetic scumbag of a police officer away, and perhaps, got shot to death; he would have joined the pantheons of the heroes of mankind. His behavior would have taught folks to intervene and do well and not allow fear to deter them from doing well.

Peoples' fear of harm and death leads them to tolerate evil. America will change when people, black and white, start standing up for the good and stop tolerating evil behaviors out of fear.

Terrorist police officers such as Derick Chauvin control people through fear; these cowards do not understand that love is what they should use to influence people, not brutal force; they keep using terrorism to intimidate folks to obeying their idiot society's unjust laws.

CREATIVE DEPRESSION IN ARTISTS

Artists, especially singers, are often depressed and out of their depression, seek ways to give people lovely melodies that make our depressing lives tolerable. Because they are depressed, they tend to self-destroy with drugs.

Fela Kuti was depressed and medicated himself with nicotine and marijuana. Yet, there is nothing any of us can do about their depression, for it is part of their creativity, what I call creative depression.

DREAM
MAY 27, 2020
5:30 AM

In this dream, I saw governor Wike of Rivers state in Nigeria with a cane, and with it, walking along a line asking people to stay on the line and keep six feet apart from each other and people obeyed him. I do not know what they stood on the line for but those who got to the end of the line got their business taken care of and went to their cars and drove away. I admired the orderliness of the whole process and woke up.

Before going to sleep, I was pondering that Wike is the only real leader in all of Igbo land and wished he is the leader of all Igbos and shaped them up.

In our dreams, our mind takes what we are thinking about during the day to produce dreams for us.

UNDERSTANDING AND COPING WITH THE BLACK AMERICAN WOMAN

Both men and women are vain but they manifest their vanity differently. Generally, men posit ideas on what constitutes social accomplishment, pursue them, and when they believe that they have attained them, they feel socially seen by other men as important and they feel important. If they do not attain what their society considers important benchmarks of accomplishment, men tend to feel unimportant, like they are failures. Power, money, and prestige are some of the things that men seek.

Women, on the other hand, were prevented by men from seeking social, political power, and prestige and thus, tend to use other ways to attain their desire for ego importance. In the extant world, we all can see that most women tend to gratify their vanity by seeking men and women to see their bodies as beautiful and object of desire.

If a woman is physically beautiful and most men desire her body, she tends to feel as if she has social worth. Those women who are plain, ugly, or are not desired by men and women tend to feel undesired and generally have less social and personal worth.

What I just said about men and women applies across the board regardless of race. White women, black women, and Asian women all seek admiration of their bodies as a condition for their sense of social importance; men seek worth through wealth, social, and political accomplishments.

In North America (USA and Canada), generally, white flesh is deemed preferable to black flesh. White women are deemed more beautiful and desirable by the male society. In effect, black women are deemed less desirable.

To seem desirable, black women do their best to seem to meet the attributes of white women, such as straighten their hair, bleach their skins, and so on; most black women want to look like white women (while doing so, of course, they deny what they are doing).

Black men, by and large, tend to admire black women with straight hair, not the wooly hair that they have naturally. In the ghettos of North America, fair-complexioned black women tend to have better opportunities attracting black male attention than strictly black-skinned women. A fair-complexioned black woman is more likely to be married than a dark-complexioned black woman. Indeed, black men tend to want their children fair-complexioned.

(I have made a lot of general statements, stereotypes; in every general situation are exceptions.)

In North America (and up to a point in Africa and elsewhere), black women's vanity was attacked by America's preference of white color to black color. Black women are angry at being diminished in social worth; each of them deals with that social diminishment in her own way. In fact, how a black woman handles the issue of color largely determines her character.

Some black women are so angry at what they believe that white society did to them that they could easily kill black men they see hanging out with white women (their enemies).

Within the group, darker colored black women resent light-skinned black women; the rivalry between these women is thick.

If you are a black man in America, you must understand the angst of the black woman and handle it gently; you must thread gently or the sisters would bite off your head.

Certainly, if you are seen hanging out with white women, you might as well forget all kinds of social rewards. Barack Obama, a person of mixed race, hence fair-complexioned, married a strictly Negro, dark-complexioned black woman. He is loved by black women for doing so for he makes them seem to have value and worth in their men's eyes.

They say that hell has no fury like a woman scorned. White America and the contemporary world ruled by white values scorned black women, and black women are furious, albeit suppressed rage.

I was married to a white woman and know from experience the level of animosity black women extended to me. Nevertheless, I did not quite understand the degree of this hatred until yesterday.

On Facebook, I have this elderly black woman friend (she is 81-years-old). She posts stuff on Facebook that I do not like but by and large, I keep quiet about them.

Three days ago, she posted stuff on the white cop killing a black man, George Floyd, in Minneapolis, Minnesota, USA. I responded to her write-up with a simple question.

"I said one understands that there are many black youth gangs, such as Bloods and Crips, so how come those do not go after white folks who kill black folks, such as Tyrone Martin and now George Floyd, how come they only kill their fellow black folks?"

Monday, May 25, was Memorial Day, and we all expected a blood bath in South Chicago, South Los Angeles, South Boston, North East Washington DC, etc. as black youth gangs murder each other as if they are at battlefields. Since they apparently enjoy killing folks, why not direct their killing to those who kill blacks? I see George Zimmerman still at Fox News justifying killing a black boy, but I do not see black street warriors doing to him what he did to their younger brother. Why this anomaly? That was my question.

The elderly black women in question went ballistic telling me that in Nigeria, Boko Haram kill Igbos and other non-Muslim Nigerians, that Nigerian politicians are essentially thugs using their goon squads to kill people so as to stay in power, and that black on black killing is not restricted to North America.

Her observation is defensive of her ego that felt attacked by my question yet she is correct; so, I did not respond to her rather lengthy verbal vituperative response. I let it pass.

She did not answer my question but merely restated it in a different form: why do black folks kill black folks but not their obvious oppressors, white folks? She is obviously uncomfortable with the possible answer to that question: black folks are cowards!

Yesterday, May 29, 2020, the same woman posted on Facebook a video by some young black man urging blacks not to do anything in response to the killing at Minneapolis that such action was a waste of time. The man said that what would follow is the usual charade of setting up commissions of inquiry, finding that there is racism in America and that no one would try to solve the problem. The young man asked his followers to give up on America. and instead, return to Africa; he told them to go buy lands in Africa and make a new beginning in a place where they are accepted, respected, and not the target of white supremacists.

I decided to ask a question. My question was: "Is this man's solution, return to Africa, not an escapist solution, which is not a solution? Black Americans helped build America so why should they abandon America and return to Africa? If anyone needs to leave America, it is white folks; they should return to Europe."

Later in the day, the black lady in question wrote many paragraphs of diatribe against my person. She called me every name one hears folks called in the ghettos. I am supposed to be a self-hating Uncle Tom who fled Africa and instead, live in the USA. What the hell am I doing in the USA? I am supposed to hate and loath my black skin (and she has her hair conked, never mind). I am supposed to be sick because I see some good in America.

America is totally evil, she said. She said that she had read some of my writing in which I tried to see some good in white folks and reminded me that I was once married to a white woman (how did she know about that? Apparently, these people do personal research on folks they see at Facebook).

The lady went on and on talking about me that I wondered whether she lost her mind. If she was in my presence, I would have evaluated her for possible Bipolar Affective Disorder, who probably was in the manic phase of that mood disorder, hence her florid, word salad, and other senseless utterances. I would have recommended that she be given anti-mania and anti-psychotic medications (a good dose of Lithium or Depakote and Haldol, Zyprexa, or Risperdal would calm down her worked-up body).

I am not in a position to do anything about her agitated outburst. Instead, I pondered whatever I did that could have triggered her meltdown and possible psychotic decompensation.

I asked questions that made it seem like she is a contributor to her fate and not the total victim that she would like to think that she is.

Here are facts. Black folks kill each other and blame it on white folks. As we talk, they are killing each other in Africa and blame it on whites, colonialism and neo-colonialism; in North America, their inner-city domains are battlefields and they blame it on white folks who brought drugs into the hood.

Listen up, I see the role played by white folks, but how about the role played by black folks? Why are your kids taking drugs? Can kids be raised not to take drug? I do not even know what drugs look like because neither of my parents smoked or did drugs.

No one in his right mind would minimize the effect of racism and slavery in the life of black folks. Be that as it may, blacks play some roles in their dreadful situation. They must take personal responsibility for what they do and correct those and not just blame all the woes of their lives on white folks.

Apparently, my questions led this elderly black woman to experience cognitive dissonance. She felt cognitive conflict. All her life, she had easy thinking, blaming whatever is wrong in her life and in the lives of black folks on white folks. I urged her to look at the role she and black folks play in their fate.

Did she do her best to prevent her children from doing drugs, stealing, and becoming jailbirds? Or was she busy doing what Franklyn Frazier (see his *Negro Middle Class*) called the black middle-class neurosis where black folks wear expensive clothes, drive fancy cars, and masquerade around as important persons while contributing nothing of value to middle-class America, and worse, not spending money to train their children, then blaming their subsequent failures on white folks.

In *Black Skin and White Mask*, Franz Fanon talked about Negroes pretending to like their black skins while doing everything to seem like they have white skins.

In the *Autobiography of Malcolm X*, Malcolm talked about how he was black and proud while straightening his hair for it to look like white hair.

James Brown yelled I am black and proud while conking his hair. This mama claiming to be black and proud conks her hair!

Society plays roles in our behaviors but the little we have control over, we must manipulate. The elderly lady in question probably felt that I blamed her for the dreadful fate of black Americans and simply dumped her frustrations on me.

Everything that she said about me does not apply to me. She does not know me from Adam. She saw something in her, weak character, denied it, and projected it to me. She wanted me to take responsibility for her obvious infantile emotional status.

She has an external locus of authority, that is, sees external persons and events as determining her life as opposed to those with an internal locus of authority who believe that they are in charge of what happens to them in life.

Developmentally, she is about eight-years-old; emotionally, she is not an adult at all. Educationally, she is stock at about sixth-grade education and does not reason like someone with even secondary school education (her vocabulary and grammar, I must say are good; she wrote in complete sentences, not Ebonics stuff).

I took her verbal abuse calmly but made a note to try to understand why she felt a need to literally assault me with her wicked mouth (she could kill for a woman who said what she said to me is probably a potential killer; she probably has been in and out of prisons, perhaps even killed a person).

This woman probably has an antisocial personality disorder (rule out sociopath or psychopath); she probably does not feel guilt or remorse from stepping on other people's feet, or from taking what does not belong to her.

I suspect that she is a criminal; certainly, her thinking and behavior showed criminal thinking pattern—always blaming other people, for one's woes sets them up to be attacked, even killed, to make one feel that one is not responsible for one's horrible fate.

She is a coward, a talker, not a doer; if she took her gospel of return to Africa seriously, she would have returned to Africa instead of living in Ohio while asking other people to return to Africa.

Actually, she does not have to return to Africa and abandon America; the entire world belongs to all humanity and one has a right to live wherever one wants to live.

I have a right to live in Africa, Europe, Asia, and America. You cannot tell me not to do so and if you do, you are merely acting like a predatory, territorial animal demarcating your territory with arms; only fear would lead me to cede an inch of this world to you; courage requires me to tell you that the entire world belongs to all of us and so let us share it and make the most of it.

This verbally abusive woman needs psychiatric emergency intervention but it is rather too late to recommend psychotherapy for her, so let us do the next best thing that we can do: learn from her stunted and arrested emotional development.

WHY DO BLACK PEOPLE IN THE USA AND AFRICA KILL EACH OTHER AND NOT THEIR WHITE OPPRESSORS?

White Europeans enslaved Africans, colonized them, and at the moment, through neocolonialism, rule and make a mess of Africa. Whereas all of Africa's problems are not due to the evil machinations of Europe, a large portion of them are.

In North America, white folks rule the roost and Africans are shunted into inner-city ghettos where their lives are circumscribed by what white folks want them to do and if they step out of line, they are shot at and often jailed or killed by the white occupation police in their ghettos.

Having acknowledged the role of the metropolis in the periphery, one asks the question: why don't black folks in Africa and in America fight their white oppressors? Instead, they take out their frustration and anger at their fellow black folks.

The answer is that they are afraid of their white oppressors. They think that if they act out, that since their white oppressors are mostly psychopaths, who do not hesitate in killing people and in fact, enjoy killing people that they would kill them (see Bobby Wright's the *Psychopathic Racial Personality*)? To avoid being killed as blacks in Africa and as slaves in America, they go along with their white oppressors and instead, displace their anger at their fellow blacks.

They say if a boss abuses a worker and the worker is afraid of being fired from his job, he does not fight his boss, go home to displace his anger at his wife and family members, and abuse them. Displacement of anger is one of the twelve ego defense mechanisms. The rest are repression, suppression, denial, displacement, projection, rationalization, fantasy, avoidance, pride, shame, guilt, fear, anger, minimizing, reaction-formation, sublimation, etc.; look them up.

Black folks in Africa and the Americas do not fight their oppressors, white folks, because they are afraid of being killed; they are cowards. They kill those who cannot fight back, their fellow black folks.

In Africa, they tolerate the thugs that pretend to rule them instead of mobilizing, going out there, fighting them, and if needs be, get killed, and those left alive live as free men.

The tree of liberty is watered with patriots' blood. Get up, fight your oppressor, and do not kill your fellow black is the message.

Black men who do not fight their real oppressors have self-contempt and easily channel their self-loathing to their fellow black folks.

The elderly black woman who dumped her anger at me feels self-loathing because all her life, she tolerated white folks fucking black women, sending their children to jails, generally abusing them, and did nothing to stop the abuse. She projected her self-loathing to me.

In Eldridge Cleaver's book, *Soul on Ice*, she is Lazarus, is dead, and needs to be resurrected by somebody, herself.

DISCUSSION

One fully understands black women's angst from being seen as not as good as women of other colors. One is also adult enough to realize that color does not make a person.

All human beings are the same and coequal. There is absolutely no difference between blacks, whites, and Asians. Because they are all the same, only social conventions prevent them from socializing and intermarrying.

It was racism that restricted marriage to one's so-called race. As those social conventions fall, people will marry whoever they get along with and can live with. Race will no longer be a consideration in marriage.

You cannot because your men marry folks from other races and that makes you less desirable, then dictate that your men should not marry folks from other races. That desire on your part is dictatorial; no one made you a decider of who marries whom.

You only have the right to choose who you marry but cannot choose for other people. Grow up, deal with reality, and do not tell other people who to marry.

Talking about contributions to the black race, take a look at black men who made seminal contributions to the race's struggle for racial equality; they include Olaudah Equiano, Richard Wright, and Franz Fanon. They were married to white women!

One is not advocating interracial marriage or opposing it but merely stating that some persons married to folks from outside their race made seminal contributions to their race.

In the world of arts, think about Alexander Duma, Beethoven, and Pushkin; they were all persons of mixed white and black race; no one has contributed to their fields more than they did.

Listen, marry who you want to, have the courage to marry, and stop being a coward; you cannot change reality and make it what you want it to be; accommodate reality and flow with the wind; don't only take refuge in your so-called race while trying to prevent those who have the courage to step outside their so-called race.

There is only one human race, homo-sapiens; deal with that reality and stop shaking your weak hands at the sun.

CONCLUSION

I wondered where a pathetic elderly woman got the idea that I loathe myself. I got it. In some of my writings, I made it crystal clear that the real self is not the ego and its body but spirit; I noted that enlightened persons, such as Buddha and Jesus Christ, rejected their egos and bodies and accentuated their spirits.

Spirit is not in form; it transcends body and ego. This dense woman probably read into that philosophical stance her crazy belief that I hate myself.

In her, Americans are judged only by their bodies and egos; the typical American identifies only with his body and ego, is narcissistic but does not transcend those, and seeks spiritual aspects of our being.

Self-realization means rejection of one's body and ego and accepting one's spirit real self. This benighted woman saw my saying that I reject the physical aspect of me as my rejection of my black body.

Of course, I reject black and white body and ego and accept myself only as a spiritual being. I am not at the mere animal status of evolution where she sees her body as all she is and her ego, her enslaver as whom she is.

If only women realize the joy of transcending the ego and body and living at the spiritual level. Unbeknown to them, the human body to some people is filthy, something that revolts them, and they only desire spiritual things.

This woman is too low evolutionally to be bothered with but is only useful in that she gives one the opportunity to understand the mind of stunted human beings operating at an animal level of evolution, Americans.

17

THE LIFTING OF THE VEIL

Recently, I had an elective surgery. I checked into the hospital. I was assigned a room. The surgeon came to my room and told me exactly what he was going to operate on and that it would take about two to three hours to do it. Thereafter, the anesthetic doctor came into my room and explained what he is going to do, inject something into the IV by my bedside and place a mask over my nose and that I would be out for the duration of the surgery. A cardiologist came into the room and told me that my body's potassium level is low so he gave me some intravenous potassium before the surgery.

At exactly 1:30 PM, a hospital aide rolled my bed to the surgery room. In the room, there were several doctors and nurses. They placed me on the surgery table and the anesthetic doctor did what he said that he was going to do and I was out. I took a look at the clock on the wall before he placed a mask over my nose and it was almost 2 PM.

When I woke up in the post-operation area, it was five minutes after 5 PM. A nurse came in and told me that as the anesthesia wears out, I would begin experiencing pain. She showed me a little button for me to press whenever I wanted some relief from pain.

I was rolled back into my hotel suite-like room. The door was closed and I was alone. Thereafter, a nurse came in and introduced herself as my nurse and told me to press a certain button whenever I wanted to talk to her or have her come into my room. She, again, told me what to do if I am in pain. I asked her what is initiated by me pressing the little button. She said that it activated the morphine bottle; she pointed to where it is hanging, to release a drop into my IV and that that would reduce my pain. I tried it once and as I had expected, the morphine almost stopped my heart and made my eyes itch so I decided that it is better to tolerate the pain than risk my heart stopping. Thus, I did not use the morphine.

The next time that the nurse came into my room, she said that she had noticed that I had not used the morphine medication and I told her why. She looked for a doctor and one was found and he recommended that I be given liquid Ibuprofen and two tablets of Tylenol every six hours; he said that that would help reduce the pain.

Throughout the evening and night, my mind drifted from this world to other worlds. At one point, I was looking at a world filled with tennis-ball-sized golden orbs of light and the ambiance looked like an evening during a summer. My mind would drift from that lovely and calming sight to another world where it looked like a dark night on earth with stars dotting the sky.

An interesting thing would happen. One of the golden orbs would turn into a human face and gravitate to the starry night world. I wondered why occasionally, one of the tennis-sized balls turned into a human face and subsequently migrated to the starry night situation.

Without really thinking about it, an idea entered my mind. The first situation with tennis-sized balls was near heaven, the gate of heaven (heaven itself is formless), and that once in a while, one of those balls became a human being and migrated to the physical universe, the starry place. This may or may not be true.

I was fully aware that whatever chemicals the doctors poured into my body during the surgery, it was probably clouding my thinking, giving me the imaginary worlds that I was looking at.

In pain, our minds take refuge in fantasy, so maybe the alternating pictures I was looking at are fantasies.

My mind shifted between these two worlds; the beautiful summer evening filled with tennis balls-sized golden orbs to the starry night.

I asked: why doesn't the tennis ball-sized orbs of golden light fall to the bottom of the globe? Why are they in space? What holds them there: gravity, electromagnetic force, strong or weak nuclear force?

By the third day, I noticed that my mind was no longer seeing the two worlds that my head seemed clear of all the chemicals they had poured into my body during the surgery. My head seemed to operate normally.

The thinker in me kicked in and I began processing the whole surgery situation. When I was under anesthesia, I did not know anything about our world for three hours. I did not feel any pain as the surgeons cut up my stomach, where the surgery was done. How come I did not feel pain? How come I did not know anything during those three hours of surgery? Where was I?

Do I have a mind, a self apart from my body that left and went somewhere while the surgeons operated on my body?

Alternatively, is the human mind epiphenomenal, a product of the dance of atoms, especially electrons and light in the brain? If this is true, then if we die, we cease existing.

Is mind apart from body? This is a question that I have grappled with all my life. The events on the surgery table would seem to say that mind is a throw-up of body and not independent of body, hence atheism is the only logical philosophy.

On the other hand, I have had what folks call spiritual experiences. I have seen my dense body disappear and now see me in light form and in a place of light forms; I have occasionally jolted myself back to this world for I would find myself talking to what folks call ascended masters, such as Jesus and others. I would be sitting on my couch, my attention would shift, and I would be in a place where I am talking to a master and we are strolling along a quiet lane, then there would be sound in the room and I would become aware of the room as where I am.

Please, please, do not tell me that in such situations, I was having visual hallucinations. You do not want to get into the subjects of psychology and psychiatry for those is my cup of tea. I know the difference between hallucination (visual, auditory, tactile, olfactory, and so on) and reality, whatever reality is; I know what delusion is.

I have had so many of what folks call spiritual experiences and it is not funny at all. Because of those experiences, I could not quite embrace atheism but resigned me to agnosticism, not theism or atheism; I am a doubter.

MULTIVERSE

What is going on, really? I believe that there are infinite universes; Hugh Everett's 1958 doctoral dissertation at Princeton University posited the many worlds' interpretation of quantum mechanics; our three-dimensional universe is one of many worlds, each with its own laws of physics. They are all where we are, but we tend to be only aware of the one we identify with.

Currently, those of us on earth identify with the three-dimensional universe and are not aware of others. Occasionally, folks like me shift our attention to other universes. How we do it we do not know.

I believe that when we came to earth, we consciously agreed to close the veil, block awareness of other universes, and concentrate on the exigencies of our current universe.

For some of us, occasionally, the veil is lifted and we have a glimpse into other universes, albeit momentarily.

If you have not had a lifting of the veil and found yourself in another universe, there is simply no way you can understand what I am talking about. If you have not suddenly seen you playing with my friend, Immanuel ben Joseph, go right ahead and keep calling him your master. To me, he is just a friend.

GUARDIANS

Each of us has friends in other universes. Those friends guide us in our current universe. I have had ideas that I believe could only have entered my head through the auspices of other forces.

CONCLUSION

In this piece, I wanted to observe that there is such a thing as the lifting of the veil. Please do not ask me to explain how it works because I do not understand how it works.

Other philosophers have had the same lifting of the veil. My philosophical mentor, Arthur Schopenhauer, 1788–1860 (see his major work, *The World as Will and Idea*), before he finally died, had what folks now call near-death experience. He went to a place where all he did on earth was in a book (what Hindus call Akashic record), realized that there were no accidents to his life on earth, and that all things that happened to him were part of a script that he and all of us wrote for him to dramatize.

You, on earth, are dramatizing your own play.

Peace.

Today, June 1, 2020, is a new beginning for me. I have examined life in every which way one could and wrote about what I found. From now on, I will simply live what I have found to be the truth. The time for mere introspection and talking is now over; it is now time for action.

Here is my finding. Love is the highest good in life; therefore, I live love, and not merely talk about love; I have found the ego as a separating device for keeping the false self alive; it is an instrument for giving me and people pain. I have chosen not to give me and people pain so I relinquish the ego and will not defend the ego in my life.

In all situations, I ask: what would love have me do? Love asks me to care for me and all people so I dedicate my life to caring for all people, me included. I will help all people as much as I can, emotionally and financially.

MY BODY ONLY HAS A TEMPORARY EXISTENCE.

I look at my body. What I see are 64 elements (mostly carbon, hydrogen, oxygen, nitrogen, potassium, magnesium, iron, copper, calcium, zinc, and so on) held together by chemical bonds. My body is one giant molecule composed of 64 elements.

Each of those elements is composed of particles of electrons, protons, and neutrons. Those particles are composed of quarks and photons.

In effect, where I see my body are really photons, light, swirling. If I have the right microscope, what I would see in my body is swirling photons.

If I look further, I would see nothing for matter and energy came from nothing. Nothingness, that which is not in form, is of God.

We came from God and cannot understand God while we are in ego, body state. In the meantime, I let go of my attachment to the ego and body for both are false; my real self is nothing; if you like, I am spirit as is everyone. Spirit cannot be understood in ego terms.

In the meantime, whereas my body is nothing and does not really exist, yet the entire universe exists and was formed to produce the illusion of my body, your body, give it problems for me to struggle to make it survive, and in doing so, make it seem real. The universe exists to make my nonexistent ego and body seem to exist. I let go of my desire for the physical universe, ego, and body.

LISTENING TO CLASSICAL MUSIC MAKES ME PROUD TO BE A MEMBER OF THE HUMAN RACE.

Life to me is pointless, meaningless, and purposeless but listening to classical music makes me feel that at least, there is one thing that is elevating in people, music. Science, that is, physics, astrophysics, geology, and biology is also elevating.

THE MEANING OF MOTHER AND MERCEDES BENZ IN MY DREAM

In this dream, my mother was driving a Mercedes Benz car and I was sitting on the passenger side beside her. She stopped at Walmart store to go buy something and left me in the car. She was taking too long to return back to the car. I got out to stretch my legs and noticed that the wheel and tire on the passenger side of the front wheel are bent. I asked a passerby to go into the store and tell mother what happened. She came out and took one look at the bent wheel, said not a word, and instead, joined other young ladies and they walked off to where I did not know.

The meaning is that she gave me a luxurious car, my body (my body contains the highest level of human intelligence), but a body with problems (the fallen off wheel). She is telling me that she has done her best and that it is now time for me to fix my body, the car, by myself and stop waiting for her to do things for me.

I used to be a spoilt boy, a pampered boy who expected his mother to do everything for him or he felt angry. She is saying that it is now time for me to solve my problems; she has lived up to the contract she and I had before coming to this world, for her to be my mother and for her to give me a good body with medical issues and now the contract requires me to fix my body and live fully.

My recent trip to a hospital is part of my effort to fix my stomach problems so as to live fully. I wish the lady goodbye for now. I am a big boy and can take good care of myself. Our mother-child relationship is now over.

FOR GOD TO KNOW BLISS, HE MUST ALSO KNOW PAIN.

To experience joy and pleasure, one must know pain and displeasure. One must know the opposite of the effect one is experiencing.

Neale Donald Walsh's God, in his *Conversations with God* series, said that God created his opposite to be able to experience his opposite. He is unified and he created separation to know separated existence.

This explanation is of course mere rationalization for we do not know anything about God and why he does what he does, or even whether he exists or not.

WHAT IS THE MEANING OF AKATA?

I have always heard Nigerians and other West Africans refer to their black American girlfriends as akata. Akata in Nigerian language means fighter. The implication is that black American women are fighters—that for the littlest thing, they would fight you and threaten to bite off your head. I had no occasion to be exposed to black American women fighting me so I let sleeping dogs lie and did not investigate the phenomenon.

However, recently, in a span of three days, two black American women literally fought me. I asked a question and one took off from it and wrote a book on what she believes is wrong with me. What came out of that woman's mouth would make my mother ashamed to be a woman. Mother would insist that her mouth be washed with soap. How could she say such nasty things about a stranger she met on Facebook and has no clue that he is?

Two days later, I forwarded a post in which a medical examiner said that drugs and alcohol were found in the body of George Floyd, the black guy murdered by racist police in broad daylight in Minneapolis, Minnesota USA. I do not know whether it is true or not that he had drugs in him. Three different medical examiners have provided three different views on Mr. Floyd's death.

Out of curiosity, I wanted to know how old Floyd is and understand that he is 46-years-old. I asked: why is a 46-year-old man doing drugs?

Oh, I understand all the usual explanations on how life is very stressful for blacks in America and they need to use drugs to calm down. I get it but one expects that to be the behavior of those under age twenty-five, college kids, not for a forty-something-year-old man.

Drugs and other negative lifestyles do kill people; they contribute to death caused by other medical issues.

Black males' life span in the USA is about 64; it is about 78 for white males and 86 for white females. Folks do not need to shorten their lives by doing drugs. You can figure out other ways to cope with stress, such as running, walking, playing tennis, swimming, and riding your bicycle, and of course, eating well, particularly staying away from red meat.

Well, another black woman took off and gave me her tongue. She began by asking me if at all I can read. I was shocked that a person could ask me that question. She proceeded to say that I have written a ragged book and is a clown (since I did not tell her about book writing, where did she get that information?).

I do not know this woman from Eve and had never seen her even once on Facebook and yet, she felt a need to talk to me in the manner she did. So, I asked, is this how black American women talk? Is this why they call them fighters, akata?

The crazy akata who was calling a stranger putdown names probably has a paranoid personality, attacked me, and set me up to counterattack her, and then she would see herself as a victim attacked by men, not realizing that she brought the attack on herself by attacking folks. What do you do? I simply blocked her. And that was not enough for her. She went on and on abusing me some more, even sending me private messages in which she abused me; what a rabid dog, I told me and moved on.

The first woman probably had a mental and emotional meltdown; she probably suffered psychotic decompensation and was in a manic (bipolar affective disorder) phase of her mental disorder. She has a grandiosely deluded self-concept, a false sense of worth, and my question made her feel diminished, and she went off on me like a rocket talking gibberish about herself that she projected to me.

Can a man live with these two wild women? I know that I cannot. No wonder their men abandon them and they essentially raise their children by themselves. Their mouths are poisonous. They are wild things and are not fit for marriage. It is best if one walks away from them.

No one deserves to be verbally abused by immature women, especially if done on a regular basis, as that would be the case in a relationship.

These wild women give their men high blood pressure, heart attacks, strokes, and other diseases that dispose them to die young. I do not want them in my personal space. A man should prefer to be single than live in proximity with wild akatas.

Post Script:

This essay made over-generalization, stereotypes of people; clearly, in every situation, there are exceptions to the general rule. There must be calm, loving, and respectful black women out there

WOMEN ARE PRONE TO DEPRESSION BECAUSE THEY OVERVALUE THEIR BODIES.

To be depressed is to feel that life is no longer worth living, to lose interests in the activities of daily living, to have no desire to go to work, school, play, groom the self, or do anything at all but wanting to be left alone as one vegetates on one's bed. Some depressed persons reach a point where they want to kill themselves and some do, in fact, kill themselves.

These days, psychiatrists attribute the origin of depression to biochemical imbalances in the brain, low serotonin in the brain; the anti-depressant medications (such as Prozac, Paxil, Zoloft, etc.) are mostly serotonin reuptake blockers that enable the neurotransmitter to accumulate in the brain, hence give people a feeling of wellbeing.

Obviously, our bodies play roles in our mental and emotional status but I doubt that unbalanced neurochemicals are the only cause of mental disorders, such as depression, anxiety, mania, or schizophrenia. There got to be other causal factors in the etiology of mental disorders; below, I explore one such cause.

Women are more likely to be depressed than men. Why?

Women are poetic and metaphoric. For example, they find it difficult to apply the correct anatomical name to their sexual organs. They would rather not call having sex having sex but use grand terms like making love.

They say that men have sex and women make love. This is because women are aware of the nothingness of their bodies and are disgusted by them but instead of accepting that reality, clothes it in metaphors that make the body and its activities seem elevated. Thus, they are making love which puts sex at the level of God, if God is love, except that God's love transcends physicality, body.

Women, in effect, flee from their physical reality, and instead, live at the metaphorical level, the poetic level where what is animalistic, sex, is now equated with the divine.

If you tell a woman, let us have sex, she would feel demeaned but instead, want you to wax poetic by saying let us make love.

Women flee from human-animal reality and live at the false, sham, and phony poetic level where nonsense is made to seem like a big deal. They take their bodies as important. To say let us have sex makes a woman's vanity think that her importance is devalued.

Even prostitutes have to be paid money, for money makes their bodies and sex seems important in their eyes.

Ordinary housewives want you to buy them roses, beautiful clothes, jewelry, and other things they place on their bodies to make their bodies seem valuable in their eyes, anything, but to accept animality is women's goal.

Women become depressed if, for some reason, those around them do not collude with them and overvalue their bodies and sex.

They temporarily cure their depression by leaving men who do not place them on a pedestal and run to men who do so and nowadays, to other women who value their sexual organs and their bodies.

Women are easily depressed and deluded because they value that which has no value, the human body, and when worth is taken away from those, they feel depressed.

To heal them of their depression, they must be taught to accept their bodies as nothing, as not important; that is kind of difficult to do for they must value their bodies to value their children's bodies. Nevertheless, they have to place the human body in proper perspective if their mental disorders are to be healed.

If you accept that your ego and body is nothing, has no worth, and live as such, you cannot have any kind of mental disorders.

Mental and personality disorders emanate from people's desires to make their egos and bodies, nothingness, seem important. Folks must devalue their bodies (which are nothing) and value their spirits (which are something important).

Post Script:

What I presented is heuristic; a mere hypothesis that needs to be proved or disproved.

WHAT IS MY VISION, GOAL?

Leaders posit visions, goals to which they dedicate their lives, goals they want to accomplish on an ongoing basis. They establish organizations as means for accomplishing their visions, goals, and objectives.

If I am a leader, then what is my vision? What goal am I trying to accomplish? I want to understand and get rid of the ego.

However, if you get rid of the ego, yours and other peoples', the universe of space, time, and matter end for you and people for the universe exists to enable people to pursue their ego separated selves and their ego goals. Crazy as those goals are, but that is what the universe exists for, so if you end the ego, you end the universe.

You can understand the ego, yours and other peoples', and improve your ego and show other people how to improve their egos but you cannot improve their egos for them, for each of them came here and made his ego separated self-concept with the aid of all of us and only he with the aid of all of us can improve his ego.

Each child uses the configuration of his inherited body and social experience to form his ego-self-concept, and as such, is unique; you cannot understand another person fully.

Only the individual can understand his ego and do what he has to do to change it, improve it; you cannot do it for him for you do not understand his body and social experience that led to the formation of his ego-personality.

The ego is voluntarily chosen and given up, not forced. The goal is for me to establish an organization through which I teach people about their ego (psychology, psychiatry, neuroscience, metaphysics) and how to improve them but not eliminate them.

On earth, people cannot attain perfection, for perfection they already are in God, in spirit outside body, but in body, they undertook to be imperfect and struggle to become perfect in body and when they accomplish that goal, their existence in body ends.

Perfection lies only in spirit, in heaven, not in body, on earth.

Your ego asks you to look out for words, see imperfect egos, talk about them, and worry about changing them. You cannot change other people; you can only change your own ego, up to a point, not completely, for if you totally improve your ego and become perfect, you are out of this world and enter heaven, to oneness, God.

In heaven, oneness, you feel bored with perfection and seek its opposite, imperfection, invent another physical universe, enter it to seem imperfect, work your way to perfection, then leave the universe and return to the spiritual universe of perfection, stay there for a while, and leave to go experience imperfection.

Life is a continual effort by perfection, your soul, to experience imperfection and then return to perfection.

I establish the center for ego-lessness, not center for no ego, for no ego means return to awareness of unified spirit self, heaven, oneness, God; you can choose to do so at any time but in the meantime, our goal on earth is to shrink our egos and make them less painful so that we live peaceful and happy lives, devoting our time to the study of physics, chemistry, biology, astrophysics, geology, and the other fun subjects taught by science.

All human beings are the same and coequal. At root, they are spirit, part of unified spirit, aka God. They left unified spirit, which is characterized by sameness and equality, to go experience inequality in body, space, and time. They all pursue becoming powerful egos.

What differentiates people is their pursuit of ego separated selves. Some people seek to become more powerful egos than others.

I am an Igbo (Nigerian, African). Please do not ask me how it came to be but the observable fact is that each Igbo, man and woman, feels special; he feels that he and his people are the best human beings there are. He feels superior to other people, including white folks.

The worst thing that you can say to an Igbo is to ask him to be non-Igbo. Simply put, these people are egotistical beyond belief. Each of them wants you to see him as a very important, significant, and powerful person. He works hard to attain the accoutrements of social prestige, masquerades around as a very important person, and wants you to see him as the coxcomb he wants to be seen as.

In Alfred Adler's psychoanalytical terms, they are mostly neurotics seeking phantom superiority over other people and in the process, living in tremendous psychological pain.

I do not intend to enable them to get rid of their grandiose egos but instead, to redirect their egos, to put their egos to ego of service; I want to enable them to use their egos to love all people.

If Africans, who are raw egos, learn to use their egos to serve the public good, I doubt that any other human group can outcompete them in any fields of human endeavor.

Don't get rid of your ego, for if you do, you leave this world; redirect it to becoming ego of love and service for all humanity. That is my goal.

If you choose to completely let go of your ego, you relapse to peace, joy, and the bliss of heaven, oneness, get bored, and thereafter, return to our egoistic world to suffer some more and then return to love, heaven, and the pattern is repeated over and over, again.

THE DESIRE TO CHANGE PEOPLE IS GRANDIOSE, IRRATIONAL.

The desire to change other people is grandiose, unrealistic, and unattainable; one human being does not have the power to change other people, not even himself. It is actually a bizarre wish for if you think about it, you do not know enough about yourself and other people and you cannot change what you do not understand. At best, you can struggle to change yourself and show people how to do so for themselves.

Even after they have done their best, people will remain imperfect for perfection is only possible in spirit, not in matter, body, and ego.

Igbos, for example, will remain egotists that boast about their powerless power, but we can become bemused by their claims of having power that they do not have.

THE EGO, SPACE, TIME, AND MATTER ARE SAID TO BE UNREAL AND DO NOT EXIST EXCEPT AS ILLUSIONS; WHAT THEN EXISTS, UNIFIED STATE, HAVE YOU SEEN THOSE.

Oriental religions and philosophies, such as Hinduism, Buddhism, Taoism, and Zen tell us that the ego separated self-concept and its world of space, time, and matter are illusions and do not, in fact, exist, or seem to exist as illusions but in fact, do not exist.

We are told that what exists is unified state, unified spirit self, aka God. Okay. Have you experienced unified spirit self? If you have not experienced it, how do you know that it exists? You are taking the word of mystics who claim to have experienced it as true. Shouldn't you only accept what you have firsthand knowledge of as the truth?

I am saying that those into spirituality accept their supposed truths on belief; hence, spirituality is accepted on faith as religion is.

The good of science is that folks accept only what they can observe, verify, and prove to exist. As for me, if an idea is not verified or experienced, it remains heuristic, not a proven fact.

The idea of oneness, the opposite of separation, seems true but heuristic until I have experienced it. You can stand on your head and say that something is the truth but until I experience it, I will not accept it. That is why I am agnostic; I have been so all my life.

I leave belief to theists and atheists, those who have no facts but believe in something to be true and behave accordingly.

WHY DO THE OTHER RACES OF MANKIND NOT CONSIDER BLACK PEOPLE HUMAN BEINGS?

(Thank you, Ejike Osuji, for your contributions to this essay.)

Would you use your two knees, carrying the full weight of your 190 pounds, to kneel on a dog's neck, a cat's neck, or on any other animal's neck?

If you contemplated doing so, something in you would tell you that you would cut off air going into the animal's body and choke him to death. Moreover, you would know that you are going to cause the animal pain and such behavior is considered cruel. Thus, rational human beings would not kneel on an animal's neck.

Now, picture a full-grown white man, Derick Chauvin, a policeman at Minneapolis, Minnesota, USA, kneeling on the neck of a black man, George Floyd. He had his hands in his pockets and looked like he had no concern in the world.

The black man complained that he could not breathe and the white man tuned him out and choked him to death. Apparently, he wanted to kill him, for something in him would have told him that he was going to kill him. Apparently, his victim's death did not concern him; to him, the black man is not even an animal for he did to him what even five-year-old children would not do to their pet animals.

The picture you just saw is exactly what white folks do to black folks. They are always kneeling on the necks of black folks and do so as if they are not aware of the pain they are causing them, or are aware of the pain and do not care and want black folks to suffer and die from asphyxiation.

This is the situation of black folks all over the world. The inevitable conclusion is that white folks do not consider black folks to be even animals and want to kill all of them; they want all black folks dead.

If you are a black man and applied for a job, the white man doing the hiring essentially feels irritated that you dared apply for the job and the moment you are out of his office, he forgets you and does not take you seriously; he may tell himself that you are not intelligent and not qualified; Derick Chauvin is apparently qualified to be a police officer.

What white folks do to black folks is done to black folks by other races. East Indians from India do not even see black folks as human beings. Chinese do not see black folks as human beings. Indeed, Native Americans do not see black folks as human beings. Those are very vicious toward black folks and discriminate against them more than racist whites do.

My question is this: why are black folks not considered human beings by other races of mankind and are subjected to cruel and unusual treatment, cruelty not meted out to other races (white folks do not treat Asians as they treat blacks and Asians do not treat other people as cruel as they treat black folks}; why are black folks hated and treated with disdain and killed as if they are not even as good as mosquitoes? Why?

And if you are black, please do not become emotional here. Africans hate themselves. In Nigeria, for example, Fulanis and their herdsmen kill other Nigerians with impunity and it is as if they killed no one. These primitive Fulanis actually believe that they have a right to kill other Nigerians and take over their lands; apparently, their Arabian Muslim God, Allah, gave them the right to engage in ethnic cleansing of non-Fulanis.

Other African groups kill other African groups. In the 1960s, Hausas and Yorubas killed 3.5 million Igbos and it was like they did nothing wrong. In 1994, in Rwanda, Hutus killed over a million Tutsis.

Intra-ethnic group killing is rife in Africa; this reminds you of black kids in the ghettos of North America killing each other without regard for their dignity.

Black folks are seen as not having worth; no one respects them and they do not respect themselves.

And this whole bizarre situation did not begin today. Historically, non- Africans did not take black folks and Africans seriously.

Consider. The Egyptian civilization was in North Africa, by the River Nile. River Nile has its source in Lake Victoria, in Kenya. It apparently did not occur to the Egyptians to navigate the river to its source, in which case, they would have penetrated into interior Africa five thousand years ago and spread their civilization to Africans. Instead, they related to other Middle Eastern people and ignored Africa and Africans.

Greeks explored their Mediterranean world. Alexander the Great conquered Egypt around 300 BC. Greeks had powerful navigation powers and it did not occur to them to navigate the Nile and get to its source, in which case, they would have encountered Africans in interior Africa (never mind about the idea of mosquitoes keeping them out; there are more mosquitoes in Europe and North America than in Africa).

The Romans, 2, 300 hundred years ago, defeated Carthage in North Africa and began building their Mediterranean and European empire. They had ships that navigated the Mediterranean Sea and yet, they did not try to navigate the Nile and get to its source, hence encounter Africans.

Beginning around 1460 AD, the Portuguese navigated the coasts of West Africa. They rounded the African coast, West and East, around 1490 AD. They established trading posts along the coast of Africa but did not enter into interior Africa. If their reason for not entering Africa is climate, well, Brazil, where they settled around 1500, is as hot as West Africa and have the same ambiance.

The Spanish, Dutch, English, and French did what the Portuguese did, navigate the coasts of Africa and establish posts from where they bought slaves but did not enter into interior Africa until the mid-1800s.

So, why did folks not enter Africa long ago and related to Africans? I ask this question for if folks had related to Africans for thousands of years, they would have, at least, see them as animals and not kneel on their necks and choke them to death.

What exactly is going on between the rest of the world and Africans? I do not know but want to know. In this essay, I will provide some speculations.

I should say that this essay is based on my conversation with my junior brother, Ejike Kingsley Osuji. He provided the metaphysical view on which the essay ended.

AFRICANS ARE SUPPOSED TO BE UNINTELLIGENT.

Some say that the reason why other groups consider Africans less than animals is because Africans are not intelligent.

Are white folks intelligent? Is Derick Chauvin intelligent and if he is intelligent, would he have done what he did? He is not intelligent. White folks are not intelligent.

Let me give it to you straight: I have not seen a white person that I consider intelligent, not even a little bit. And this is the case with most members of my ethnic group, Igbos.

Igbos consider white folks inferior people. In the 1960s, while at elementary school, I spent two years with my grandfather, Osuji-Njoku in his village. He would look at a white man, usually British, and say to me, Ozodi, my boy, that man is not intelligent at all; he is not even as smart as a dog. I would ask him why? He would say that he does not know the difference between human beings and animals. I asked him the difference and he said that human beings are those creatures that love.

To love and respect people is the sign of intelligence, my grandfather said. He said that white folks do not love, do not respect people, and believe that with guns, they can conquer the world. He would then say: pay attention because, sooner or later, the entirety of mankind would consign white folks to garbage cans, for they are not human beings.

To grandfather, white folks are less than animals in spiritual evolution and he would rather talk to me, an eight-year-old boy, than to adult white folks.

He said that he learns nothing from talking to those fools, as he called white folks. Now, we can dismiss what grandfather said for it is subjective; I cited it to make the point that contrary to white folks' apparent belief that black folks are not intelligent, Africans do not consider white folks as intelligent.

CONTEMPORARY AFRICANS' INABILITY TO GOVERN THEMSELVES RIGHT

A reason often cited by white racists to prove their belief that Africans are unintelligent is Africans' apparent inability to govern themselves right.

Most extant African countries are poorly governed. Except, perhaps, Rwanda under Paul Kagame; no African country can be said to be properly ruled.

Yet, what these countries need to do is simple. Africans inherited their countries from Europeans. Those are artificial countries. What they need to do is reconfigure the countries.

Each ethnic group ought to be made a state, given semi-independence, govern itself, and then have the central government take care of foreign affairs and military affairs. In time, this political arrangement would be transformed into an African federation with about five hundred states, each state a tribe, and all of them with a central government, kind of like the USA.

I have, at several places, delineated what needs to be done to govern Africa properly; I am flabbergasted that no African country is really properly governed.

WHY DID ANCIENT CIVILIZATIONS BYPASS AFRICA?

My junior brother, Ejike Osuji, tells me that there was a reason why ancient civilizations skipped Africa. Nature and nature's God probably wanted it to be so. God designed world civilizations to be the way they were and for them to bypass Africa and Africans.

It is probably because to God, Africans are the most mature of his children. Whereas all people are the same and coequal, spiritually speaking, Africans are closer to God than other people. How so?

Africans understand that love is all that matters in our lives. God is love; to love is to be closer to God; to love is to be spiritually powerful whereas to clubber folks with clubs, as white folks do, is to be an animal, a Neanderthal.

Nature preserved Africans and protected them from the civilizations of other groups so that eventually, Africans would civilize other groups.

Africans will civilize Europeans, Indians, Chinese, and Americans. By this, it meant that Africans will teach these other people love, for they do not know what love is.

When you think about it, who is better qualified to teach love than those who were degraded and dehumanized and yet love people, Africans?

I agree with this conclusion; think about it and make of it what you like. Actually, if I am honest with you, if you are non-African, I would tell you that I do not care for your opinion. I see it as my mission to civilize non-Africans.

THE MISEDUCATION OF AFRICANS

I have asked why contemporary Africans seem unable to govern themselves right. I believe that one of the reasons why Africans are making a royal mess of self-governance is because they were given western education.

In line with Carter Woodson (1933, *The Mis-Education of the Negro*, New York: Amazon Books) I believe that Western education is a waste of time for Africans.

Africans have to throw away their western education, assume that they are not educated, and then reeducate themselves.

This is easy to do in light of the fact that despite all that Western education, white folks still do not see Africans as educated.

Consider me. I have a basket full of degrees, including a doctorate from the University of California. Do you then think that I would be able to obtain a job with this education? Of course, not. To clearly unintelligent white employers, I am still a nigger.

I threw away my western education and embarked on reeducating myself. I am now self-educated and have no allegiance to any western educational institution; my ten years at Western universities were a total waste of my time.

Those currently ruling Africa are miseducated and confused and do not know what to do to solve Africa's problems. They have to be reeducated, given education that serves them right, and only Africans can give them such education.

I have been at work writing books and articles trying to come up with what constitutes proper education for Africans. I have written 82 books and hundreds of articles. You can begin your proper education by perusing some of my books.

CONCLUSION

Ever since I began living in North America, I have pondered why the other races reserve cruel treatment for black folks. They treat Africans worse than they treat their pet animals. This behavior does not make sense to me.

At some point, I regarded all white folks as evil, as not human beings, as a plague to be done away with. I had no use for their idea of civilization.

Over time, I came to the realization that there are metaphysical issues going on here. In this essay, I speculate that nature and nature's God kept Africans behind so that they would eventually civilize human beings.

To be civilized is to love. Africans, as I know them to be, are the most loving people on earth. Their function is to teach the rest of the world how to love hence civilizes them.

Of course, Africans must do science and technology, too.

If you are an African, please do what I do: while retaining your African capacity to love and care for people, be up-to-date with physics, chemistry, biology, astrophysics, geology, and the other physical sciences and their applied forms.

HELEN SCHUCMAN WROTE ETERNAL VERITY IN POETIC FORM; IT IS FOR ME TO WRITE IT IN PHYSICS FORM.

JESUS WROTE IN POETRY VIA HELEN; JESUS WROTE IN PHYSICS FORM VIA OZODI.

Now, I get my role, as Jesus himself told me in a vision. The book, *A Course in Miracles*, was written by a woman and is mostly for women; women enjoy poetry and refined language so the book was written in a poetic and refined language.

Men speak in the language of science, physics, chemistry, and biology; I am a man and my job is to rewrite the same eternal verities articulated in *A Course in Miracles* in men's language, physics, so that men would understand it without spending thirty years trying to understand what its poetic figures of speech mean.

WE, THROUGH THE UNIVERSE, PUT OUT A SHOW FOR US TO SEE.

The universe, us, puts out a great show for us to see. Nothing exists but the universe makes it seem like something exists; our bodies, space, and time were all designed to make us feel like we are experiencing something, seeing something where nothing exists. These things were used to put out a great show for us to see, to like it, or be angry at it.

TO JUDGE IS TO ASSUME THAT THINGS EXIST; IF NOTHING EXISTS, TO JUDGE IS TO BE FOOLISH.

To judge what we see—space, time, matter, bodies, and sex as good or bad—is stupid for you are judging what does not exist, what people use to play separation that does not exist and play union in body; sex gives them a semblance of pleasure when what they need is to let go of ego and body and they lapse back into God and experience total bliss; leave them to have their substitute pleasure in body.

THERE IS NO UNIVERSE AND NOTHING IS HAPPENING.

There is no universe and nothing is happening. Therefore, keep quiet for there is nothing to say about anything for nothing exists.

WOMEN USE APPRECIATION OF THEIR BODIES AND EGOS TO JOIN TO PEOPLE, TO OBTAIN PSEUDO CONNECTION, UNION.

Women identify with body and want their bodies to be appreciated, then give them appreciation in body until they return to spirit and have total sense of connection in it.

If you do not appreciate women, they feel unconnected to you, disconnected, and their egos go mad and they can kill you; they will leave and do crazy things; marry the next man on the street that appreciates them (JAI took Frank for she felt totally unappreciated by me, hence totally alone, not unified with me at ego body level).

MEN SEEK CONNECTION THROUGH POWER AND WEALTH.

Men seek connection to other men by achieving things, amassing wealth and power; they believe that if they are wealthy and powerful, other men would respect them and that respect translates to connection with them, hence return to a sense of union with them.

As in the case of women, this is substitute union, of course; real union is in spirit and you do not have to do anything to have it.

You are always in spiritual union with all creation and its creator, God; you do not have to do anything to earn union, for you are always in union, God. Hence, the truism that you do not have to earn salvation; all you need to be saved is to let go of your identification with ego and body; that is, you undo what you did to separate from God and you know that you are always already in God.

As long as you are attached to ego, body, space, and time, you are separated from God, albeit illusorily. Let go of separation and its means and you experience unified spirit and know that you are always in God.

SEEING WITH LOVE AND LIGHT

The universe of space, time, and matter literally does not exist. But we want it to exist so we see it. We are hallucinating when we see people and things in bodies. The choice we now have is to see the world with love and light or to separate from people and hate them.

To see with love means to see in light; in love, you see you and all things connected, you have unified seeing, and see the world in light forms, still hallucinatory and fictional but a purified one, that gives us some peace and joy; this is salvation from the hallucination of seeing a world that does not exist.

LOVE, LIGHT, AND FORGIVENESS

I see a separated world; a separated world does not exist and cannot exist; only a joined world exists; therefore, I am seeing what does not exist when I see a separated world.

Seeing a world that does not exist makes me angry. The Holy Spirit takes that separated world and shows how it is, in fact, joined, hence healed, purified, unified, and no longer makes us angry and is now in light form.

Both the separated dense world and the separated light world do not exist; only the formless world of God exists and in it, we are peaceful and happy, live in bliss.

SEEING SEPARATED THINGS IS DELUSION AND HALLUCINATION.

I am in this body; this body lies on a bed; I type on a computer; this is a separated world and does not exist; I do not exist in body and do not lie on a bed or type on a computer. I am insane for seeing these separated things.

There is no me in body, no other people in bodies; therefore, no one is doing any of the things I see people do on earth; for example, no one is having sex; to have sex is the ego's attempt to unify at the substitute, replacement level, that is, first accepting space, time, matter, and body, making body real, and using body to join other bodies in sex; we cannot use body to join for body does not exist.

The Holy Spirit takes our separated bodies and things and makes them into light bodies; in light bodies, we feel peaceful and happy and no longer need pleasure derived from body.

GOD USES LOVE AND LIGHT BUT TRANSCENDS THEM.

God is beyond anything that we can conceptualize or see with our physical eyes; God's thinking is beyond our ego thinking; in God, which we always are in, we think with his mind, but that is not the thinking we have on earth.

God has a different notion of light; it is the light inside us; God has a different kind of love, the love inside us; physical light and our earthly love are special situations and are not love and light as God knows them to be.

So, when folks say that God is love and light, they are correct provided that they do not mean the light we know on earth for our earthly light is related to matter, form, and does not exist, is an illusion.

VISION IS MADE FROM THE LIGHT OF THE HOLY SPIRIT INSIDE US, NOT PHYSICAL LIGHT.

Vision, the world made from God's light, is not made of this world's physical light but the light inside us.

If you have not had vision, you cannot understand what it is. Not that I expect you to understand it. Here is an example of vision: I am sitting in my room. I close my eyes. I am now with Jesus Christ, talking to him. Both he and I are in light forms, in a world where all things are like they are on earth but are in light forms; you could see through peoples' seeming solid bodies for they are made of light. Vision, which is what I just described, is seen in the light; in God's light.

In case you want to argue with this old agnostic, try letting go of your attachment to your ego and body; see all people as one with you, love, and forgive them and then sit quietly and tell yourself that the seemingly real world of matter, space, and time are illusions and tune them out. If you love and forgive all, you will experience the world of light forms, aka vision.

FORMLESS UNIFIED SPIRIT STATE, AKA HEAVEN

If you continue on the part of love and forgiveness, one day, the entire physical universe disappears for you and you experience yourself as part of God, as the one shared son of God who is one with God.

Please do not try to understand what union with God means with your current ego-mind, for you cannot. You have to tune out the ego's mind and be egoless and God's mind dawns on you. After that unified experience, you laugh at atheists, theists, and agnostics for you know for sure that only formless God and his unified son exist; all else are apparitions, illusions, hallucinations, and delusions.

CONCLUSION

This world is not real; it is an illusion. But we do believe that it is real. In that case, let us make it a happy illusion.

You and I must fight Trump and his psychopathic crowd until we transform America and the world into a fairly loving place, a place where all children are given publicly paid education through universities and all people are given publicly paid health insurance; we must seek rational ways to combine the productivity of capitalism with the caring philosophy called socialism.

Please do not ignore the injustices of this world by telling yourself that you are religious or spiritual; to do so is defeatist, is to escape from this world's reality.

We must beautify our world, albeit illusory, and from it, gravitate to the gate of heaven, aka the world of light forms and over time, return to the awareness of heaven, formless unified state, where we always are and while there, dream that we are in a world of separated people and things.

Ozodi Thomas Osuji, Ph.D.

FROM EGO-BASED PSYCHOTHERAPY TO SPIRIT-BASED PSYCHOTHERAPY

The term psychotherapy means any effort to change the processes of the mind, to change the individual's pattern of thinking, from one manner to another.

Psychotherapists are usually psychologists and psychiatrists.

There are many forms of psychotherapy, from Sigmund Freud's psychoanalysis to Alfred Adler's psychoanalysis, Carl Jung's psychoanalysis, Skinner's behavior modification, Albert Ellis and Aaron Beck's cognitive behavior therapy, R.D Laing's existential psychotherapy, Abraham Maslow's humanistic psychotherapy, and many, many others.

You learn about all those psychotherapies at graduate school. You are supposed to apply to your clients which one they are amenable to or which one you believe that would suit them; for example, if they are hyper-rational, cognitive behavior therapy probably would suit them; if they are philosophical, existentialism that takes from Jean-Paul Sartre, Albert Camus, Karl Jasper, Heidegger, and others that confront the meaninglessness of our lives on earth would be useful; whereas if they are not intellectual, mere supportive therapy, hand-holding, would suit them best; most therapists are eclectic, that is, choose those therapies that would apply to their clients and use them in talking to them.

Typical therapy is one hour a week, for about a year or more. Therapy costs money, up to $200 to $500 an hour; as a result, many poor people, especially black folks, cannot afford it and use alcohol, drugs, and sex to cope with the stressors of their lives in America; if they are court-mandated, say, for anger management, they do group therapy; those are cheaper, about $35 per session (usually for two hours on a weekday evening), a week, for a year.

People who believe that their pattern of thinking troubles them go to psychotherapists to help them change their pattern of thinking.

The typical client for psychotherapy has, at least, a college degree; people with less education tend not to have the intellectual ability to process their pattern of thinking.

Generally, clients believe that there is something wrong with their patterns of thinking, believe that their mind is weak, and expect the psychotherapist to make their minds stronger.

For example, the client may say that he has low self-esteem and self-confidence and wants the therapist to help him develop positive self-esteem and social confidence and believe that to do so, he should have a strong ego-self.

Naïve therapists often try to make their minds stronger. If they do, they actually compound the patient's issues, for now, his wrongful pattern of thinking is made stronger and he suffers more psychological pain than he did before he went to therapy.

Consider college female students. They are told by their teachers in sociology and women's studies departments that all men are their enemies, are benefiting from patriarchy, and therefore, must be persecuted, pulled down. Women's studies departments teach these impressionable kids that men are abusers and make them angry at men. They take assertiveness training classes and become aggressive (normally, women tend to have a passive-aggressive style of communication). Now, they are confrontative with men. They were told that they have historically been men's victims; they see themselves as victims and see men as victimizers.

(As an aside, let me say that both men and women are victims of each other; never mind; I am not here to correct the immature and juvenile ideas that masquerade as good ideas at women's studies departments.)

Naturally, men run from confrontational and paranoid women, for the typical man does not see how he oppresses women. In his mind, he is a slave who works hard to make a decent living for his wife and children and does not see himself as an oppressor of women, so to be told that he is an oppressor puts him off and he avoids vociferous feminists.

Feisty feminists generally end up single, lesbians, and in old age, are at assisted living homes and old folks' homes, lonely and abandoned.

Listen, we need to change the pattern of male and female relationships and make them equalitarian and mutually respectful of each other; one is not denying that in the past, men had more power than women; this got to change, but we must go about it in a friendly manner not by telling men that they are all abusive oppressors.

In the meantime, neophyte therapists help their clients to develop strong egos. Because the client is now inflexible and stronger in his pattern of thinking, he experiences more psychological pain.

He is sent to psychiatrists for medicinal intervention. If his issue is anxiety, he is given any of the anti-anxiety medications; if it is depression, he is given any of the anti-depression medications (if it is mania, schizophrenia, and delusion disorder, he is given medications right from the get-go for those usually are not treated with talk-based therapy but with antipsychotic medications).

In time, if the patient is frustrated enough, he seeks other forms of psychotherapy. If he tries spirit-based psychotherapy, he is told that his issues emanate from ego, big or small, and that it does not need to be made stronger but weakened, even eliminated, if he is to be healed from psychological pain.

I worked as a secular-scientific therapist for over twenty years before I gradually recognized that people are spiritual beings having physical experience; thereafter, I trained myself on spiritual matters; I read up on the religions of mankind, such as Hinduism, Buddhism, Taoism, Zen, Gnosticism, African and Native American religions, and then reviewed my inherited Christianity, traditional, new-thought religions and new age Christianity; building on those, I formulated spiritual psychotherapy that may be applied to clients who so desire it.

Spiritual psychotherapy means letting go of one's ego, big or small. This generally entails decompensating one's ego and instead of recompensating it, making it strong but asking what Christians call the Holy Spirit, or if you like, one's higher self to now help one think properly.

The Holy Spirit is a fancy name for thinking that is driven by love and forgiveness for all people. If you love you, love all people, and forgive all those who wronged you, you are being guided by the Holy Spirit and will immediately experience less psychological pain.

Spiritual psychotherapy is an attempt to eliminate the individual's ego and make him egoless so that his higher self, his loving and forgiving self, called the Holy Spirit by Christians, think through him. Such thinking makes one feel peaceful and joyous.

Spiritual psychotherapy enables one to return to love; it is the only therapy that heals people (to heal is to join what was separated from; to heal is to return to union with God and all his creation).

God is love; we separated from love, from God, to go hate ourselves and each other in the false world of separated selves, space, time, and matter. When we return to God, that is, to union with all and love for all, we are healed.

I am not going to even try offering details of spiritual therapy beyond saying that it entails returning to love, to forgiveness and God. You can peruse some of my books and articles to have a glimpse of spirit-directed therapy.

The rational thing to do is to combine spiritual psychotherapy with secular psychotherapy and where necessary, with medications. Human beings, in their present state, are made of bodies, minds, and spirit and all three aspects of them have to be addressed in psychotherapy.

Ultimately, we are only spirit. If you return to the awareness of only spirit, you will not see this world or see it only when you want to do so; you are now an illuminatus; you are illuminated to your light self, your real self; you are now in God's love and light; illuminated persons include Buddha, Jesus, and a few other enlightened persons.

EGO-BASED LEADERSHIP VERSUS LOVE-BASED LEADERSHIP

The ego is the wish to live as a separated self in body; that wish generated fear in people, fear of harm and death. All people, animals, are prone to fear. Those who live in fear can be controlled by those who threaten to harm, jail, or kill them.

Ego leaders have goals (power), threaten to kill those who live in fear, and do kill them if they do not do as told to do. Ego-based leadership is fear-based leadership. This is the type of leadership that mankind has known throughout its existence.

Love is the desire to unite with all people and things; in love, there is less fear and in total love, there is no fear, for one is now in union with all things and there is nowhere for union to go but to exist.

Love-based leadership is not based on fear but on love, on doing things that serve social interests. This type of leadership has not been tried on earth; it is for me to bring it about.

AMERICAN LEADERS ARE EGO- AND FEAR-BASED NOT LOVE-BASED.

American leaders are ego- and fear-based leaders; they use terror to intimidate most Americans, terrorize them, and cow them into accepting a corrupt psychopathological goal of oppressing the people. American conservative leaders will kill you in a jiffy if you stand on their way to acquiring power to screw the people, make money, and live like bloated animals.

My goal is to gradually transform American ego- and fear-based leaders to love- and courage-based leaders that do the right things.

YOU TRAIN YOURSELF TO BE EGOLESS AND LIVE PEACEFULLY AND JOYOUSLY BUT YOU CANNOT MAKE OTHER PEOPLE TO BE EGOLESS AND JOYOUS.

You can study the ego, understand it and its correlation with fear and psychological pain, and let your ego go, become egoless, and live peacefully and joyously.

You can establish an organization to help train other people to be egoless and loving but you cannot make other people be egoless and loving for they came to the world to be egos and to not love but you can choose to be egoless and loving and live in peace.

In ego-lessness, you can live like the Japanese samurai, fearless, and can become an awesome warrior. The samurai and kamikaze have no desire to live as fear-based ego but to dedicate his life to serving a noble goal, nationalism.

AMERICAN JUDGES ARE TOTALLY SPINELESS, FEAR-BASED COWARDS.

Members of the US Supreme Court are cowards hiding under the law. They enforce laws that oppress the people.

American legislators, bureaucrats, and the president are all ego-based, hence fearful cowards masquerading as powerful people.

AMERICAN POLICEMEN ARE TOTAL COWARDS PRETENDING TO BE POWERFUL FOLKS.

American police are fearful people. Derick Chauvin, the murderer of George Floyd, was the picture of an egotist, a psychopath; the psychopath seems lacking in fear but lives at an animal fear level where fear is unconscious in him and he kills without qualms.

AMERICAN ACADEMIA IS THE ABODE OF COWARDS.

American college professors live in total fear, afraid of being fired from their cowardly jobs. The professors are living dead persons. Through them, their oppressive system oppresses not only minority persons but all Americans.

I HAVE A DESIRE FOR TOTAL FREEDOM AND POWER.

When I was at graduate school, at the University of California, I took a class from a professor who teaches political psychology. He liked me for he bought books and gave them to me as gifts. At the end of each quarter, the professors you took classes from write their observations of you, and those are placed in your file. This man wrote that I have a will to power and do not like anyone to tell me what to do. He observed that if that will is properly directed, I would make a powerful leader but if not, I could become a dictator. Keep an eye on him, he concluded.

The man said what I already knew about me. From the day I began elementary school at age six, I have resented anyone telling me what to do, and this included my teachers at school. I have desire for total freedom; that is, I have desire for powerful ego. My ego does not like anyone to tell it what to do and feels angry if other egos tell it what to do.

I quickly assess who has power and do not like him to tell me what to do. I enter organizations, know who has power in them, and resent my powerlessness in them.

In graduate school, I entertained the idea of working for the united nations but realized that they obey the powerful nations like the USA and USSR; the leaders of the superpowers rule those in international organizations through their power of the purse and I did not want to be told what to do by these leaders; I did not want to become the errand boy of the superpowers so I did not pursue that line of work.

The fact is that from childhood, I want to be free and do my thing and must have my own organization where I am in charge and do my thing. I must exercise leadership by setting up an organization to do what I know is good, be egoless and teach people to live egoless lives, and not worry about whether they achieve the goal or not; what matters is for me to live egoless life, hence live in peace and joy.

It would be silly denial for me to deny that I want to have power to live without other egos telling me what to do; it simply makes me angry if another man born of woman tries telling me what to do.

I am the ultimate alpha male and must be in charge. There is nothing wrong with that state of being; the universe produced me to be that way.

Why should I allow other men, ego fools, to tell me what to do when what I want to do is good for humanity?

I have total contempt for extant leaders; Trump and Buhari, to me, are idiots and I do not have to listen to them; they can only be my servants, not the other way around.

GOD AND HIS SONS HAVE POWER.

The son of God has the power to invent and invented the physical universe; he has awesome power, for a power that invented this universe must be truly powerful.

God is powerful; he creates everlasting beings, such as his sons, not the temporal universe his sons invent to play with until they awaken to the fact that they are one with God

WHITE FOLKS LIVE IN EGO, HENCE ARE FEARFUL AND ARE EASILY CONTROLLED BY THEIR PSYCHOPATHIC LEADERS.

White folks live in ego hence in fear; they are cowards and lack the courage to do the right thing; they kill out of their ego-based desire to control other people so as to live out their fantasy of being powerful egos.

WHITE POLICEMEN ARE TOTALLY POWERLESS PRETENDING TO BE POWERFUL.

White policemen are totally egoistic; they kill black folks to seem to have power when in fact, they are mere security guards guarding the properties of the rich; they are animals, not even human beings yet.

Black Africans, like white folks, also live in ego, hence in fear; those do not even have the animal courage to challenge their mostly thuggish leaders and demand economic and social justice; they are living like slaves, self-assigned second class situation; all they need do is have less ego and willingness to die fighting for social justice and they obtain a good society.

ARTISTS TEND TO OBTAIN FAME, DIE OFF, AND ARE HEARD OF NO MORE.

Artists, that is, writers, painters, sculptors, musicians, etc. tend to obtain fame early in life. Chinua Achebe obtained fame with one book, *Things Fall Apart*, at age 28. But artists lack political power and are on the fringe of society and cannot change society. They are being themselves.

It takes volcanic forces of nature like me to change society politically, or philosophically and religiously.

LEADERSHIP PRINCIPLES CAN BE PUT TO POSITIVE OR TO NEGATIVE GOALS.

If you understand the attributes of leadership, such as setting goals, visions, and mobilizing people and money to attain them, you can put those principles to positive or negative goals.

Adolf Hitler understood leadership and used it for negative goals; Mother Theresa understood leadership and put it to positive goals. Inner-city gangs have leaders who use other people to sell drugs and kill people. White racists understand leadership and use it to pursue goals that harm and kill black folks.

The universe is impersonal and does not care what you put knowledge to.

DOES METAPHYSICS PUT THE CART BEFORE THE HORSE?

In the empirical world, we observe that the state of the body determines one's thinking, one's mind. If your body is sick, you are in pain and think of ways to survive and do what enables your body to survive. You know for sure that your body affects your thinking, your mind.

Metaphysics tells us that it is thinking (in spirit) that determines the existence of body, its sickness or health; that body is neutral and reflects one's thinking. There is no evidence showing that thinking, mind, determines body's health or lack of it beyond peripheral aspects of our being. If you are born blind, your thinking did not determine it, at least not your thinking in this lifetime; and as far as we know, this lifetime is the only life we know about; all others are conjectures.

FORGIVE PEOPLE'S BRUTALITIES TO EXPERIENCE SALVATION.

On Monday, May 25, 2020, in Minneapolis, Minnesota, USA the entire world witnessed American police brutality on camera. A policeman, Derick Chauvin, placed his knees on the neck of a black man, George Floyd, in his custody; the black man said that he could not breathe and the white policemen ignored him and chocked him to death. The policeman murdered the black man.

How did that make me, a black man, feel? I felt anger. My ego wanted to shoot the policeman, to kill him, to teach him not to abuse and kill black persons. But I was nowhere near him, and even if I was near him, there were three other policemen, with guns who would be willing to shoot me to death if I tried to interfere with police officers in their line of duty to kill black persons. They are white policemen told to maintain the evil empire called the USA.

My ego told me to bear grievances against the white race that authorize white policemen to murder black men in broad daylight. I seek vengeance and revenge but know that at the moment, I do not have the ability to fight back and hope for the day that black folks would have the power to tear down this house of evil and brutality called the USA and replace it with a loving empire (whatever that is).

I decided to analyze Derick Chauvin, the police officer who cavalierly murdered a black man. Was he really a courageous person? Was he fearless?

Would a fearless and courageous person kneel on the neck of a man lying face down? If he was courageous, he would know that the handcuffed man is powerless to harm him and would not take on the pose he gave to the world, a conscienceless killing of an armless black man.

The policeman is clearly a psychopath. On the surface, he appears fearless but like all antisocial personality disordered persons, he is really driven by fear except that that fear is unconscious in him.

Derick Chauvin and the other three police officers standing by as a man is murdered do not really have real power. They live in fear. Who lives in fear?

THE EGO LIVES IN FEAR, HENCE IN HELL.

It is the ego that lives in fear. The ego is each of us human beings who live in body and is acutely aware that he could be harmed and killed. To be an animal and human being is to be conscious of harm and death hence to live in fear. The ego, all of us, lives in fear.

We as egos seek ways to protect our vulnerable bodies and selves. We defend ourselves psychologically with the various ego defense mechanisms (repression, suppression, denial, displacement, projection, rationalization, minimizing, fantasy, sublimation, reaction-formation, pride, shame, guilt, fear, anger, and so on); we defend our bodies with food, clothes, medications, and houses that shade us from the vagaries of inclement environment.

Everything we do on earth is motivated by our efforts to defend our fragile egos and bodies. We live in fear.

Those who live in fear live in hell.

The white policemen who killed George Floyd are egos; they live in fear, hence live in hell.

George Floyd was an ego separated self in body; he, too, was aware that he lived in a precarious body and could be killed, hence defended himself. He lived in fear, hence lived in hell.

All human beings live in fear and thus, live in hell.

The police and those they serve, the political rulers of this world, live in ego and fear. The American president, Donald Trump, lives in total fear although he talks tough; point a gun at him and his ego panics and he runs and pees and poos in his pants.

The members of the US Congress, the justices of the US Supreme Court and the bureaucrats who implement the laws made by the oligarchic rulers of America to protect themselves, are egos, live in fear, and thus, live in hell.

What I said about Americans apply to all other people. All the rulers of Africa, Europe, Asia, and their people are egos and live in fear, hence live in hell. To be a human being is to live as an ego hence live in fear and in hell.

The white policeman killing George Floyd lives in ego hence in fear; I, Ozodi Osuji, is an ego hence live in fear and hell. My ego wants to protect me by killing the white policeman killing a person who looks like me.

THE LOGIC OF FORGIVENESS

Given that we live in egos and fear and are in hell, what is the most appropriate response to our brutalities? How should I respond to Derick Chauvin? My ego says kill the motherfucking scumbag. The logic of the ego is killing those who kill folks.

Another part of me, my higher self, tells me to forgive him.

Really, I say, forgive the man who just killed a man? Does forgiving a murderer not mean giving him permission to kill some more? If you saw a rapist and did not kill him, are you not giving him permission to rape other people? If you saw a thief stealing something and forgive him, overlook his criminal act, have you not approved what he did?

Forgiveness has a different logic than my ego's logic. If I forgive the murderous policeman, the rapist, and the thief, what I did is say that he is an ego and lives in fear, in hell, and that I ought to help him rather than compound his hellish existence by punishing him.

Look at white Americans—they live in hell, afraid, packing guns, thinking that guns would protect them from those they abused; they eat like pigs, eating and growing fat, and dying from heart attacks, strokes, and diabetes; these people are in a hell of their own making. What should one do to those in hell, punish them or liberate them?

Since I am like white Americans and do the evils I see them do, if I forgive them, I am really forgiving me. If I overlooked their evil behaviors, I overlook my own evil behaviors.

But would forgiving racists not enable them to keep on being racists and oppressing black folks? Shouldn't we push them and give freedom to those they oppress? This is the logic of my ego, hence oppressed people, all over the world, arm themselves and try using force to liberate themselves from their oppressors.

The logic of the ego is what is done in our world. It is the ego's solution to abuse.

On the other hand, what would be the benefit to me if I forgive the police oppressor? Here is a shock for you. If I forgive him, I forgive me for he is me projected out. I did what he did and he did what I do.

We are in a nightmarish dream and in our dreams, mutually project what we see as each other in bodies, walking in space, time, and matter.

The moment I forgive the oppressing white race, I forgive me. At that very moment, something happens to me. I would see me in a light form and see those I forgive in light forms. This is literal not figurative.

Do you want proof? Look at a person who did you wrong and instead of defending you by attacking him, forgive him. At that moment, you are saved from the world of the ego and its body, from living in hell. You would see you and the person you forgive in light form.

SALVATION TAKES YOU TO THE WORLD OF LIGHT FORMS.

There is another world, a world of light forms, it is our world remade in light forms. It is what Christians call new Israel, new Jerusalem, new world, and new man (written about in Revelations or Apocalypse in the Bible). It is our present brutal world purified, forgiven, made loving; in that world, there is no attack and killing; it is a world where the lion lies with the lamb friendly and peacefully; in that world, there is no sickness and death.

This is the saved world. It is a world at the gate of heaven but not yet heaven. It is not heaven because we still see things in forms, albeit in light forms.

In heaven, there are no forms and all things are unified as a formless one shared self with one shared mind.

In salvation, you escape from our brutal world and live in the world of light forms. You are now in peace and joy, at the gate of heaven, from which you talk forgiveness and love to those still in the nightmarish hell called planet earth.

The ego part of me tells me that even if that is true, I to go to the world of light forms and leave other people in the world of dense forms; our world is escapist and defeatist but my ego asks me to stay here and fight to bring about social democracy, mixed economy, a world where all people are given publicly paid education, at all levels, and publicly paid health care for all people.

Escaping from our present world does not change this world. So, one leaves our world and now lives in the world of light forms but in our dream of self-attack, people are still abusing people, white supremacists are still packing guns and killing black folks, and thuggish African leaders are still looting their people's wealth and killing those who oppose them.

My ego tells me that I am a coward by giving me salvation and leaving my brothers to still live in hell; abandoning our world does not seem like a courageous thing to do; ego courage suggests that I stay here and fight to improve the world for all of us.

WE EXPERIENCE ONLY WHAT WE WANT TO EXPERIENCE.

Ego courage assumes that people are victims. We are not victims. Each of us is a son of God and is in God and while in God, is sleeping and dreaming that he is in a world of people, space, and time; he peoples his dream with the people he sees in his world.

Everything that happens to him on earth is part of his dream; his thinking and mind is in cahoots with all of our thinking and minds produced his world and what happens to him.

The police officer and his apparent victim are doing what they came to do—one to abuse and the other to be abused; they alternate roles in different lifetimes.

There are no accidents; there is no way something can happen to any of us without us wanting to experience it.

The world is our collective dream; we dream the world; as dreamers, we produce the world we see, what happens to us. We experience whatever we experience on earth by our choice.

This does not mean that we ought to be allowed to be abused and murdered because it is our choice to experience those horrors; we must intervene to improve our world. Nevertheless, if we are abusers or abused, we chose it.

While in the dream, we can recognize that being the abuser and abused is based on our false, substitute selves, our ego replacement selves housed in bodies; to awaken from the dream, we must recognize our real selves, the formless sons of God.

AS A BLACK MAN, MY EGO FEELS HUMILIATED BY WHITE MEN AND I SEEK TO MAKE MY EGO STRONGER TO BE ABLE TO FIGHT BACK.

As a black man watching white policemen murdering black folks, I feel outraged. My ego feels humiliated and is in a murderous mood. I want to murder the next white policeman I see, to get even. Revenge is of the ego. To the ego, revenge is the sweetest thing on earth; it means that it is powerful.

Over time, I learned that when I feel belittled, humiliated, and seeking vengeance, I am acting in the ego. My ego never, ever attains a sense of power.

My ego always feels humiliated and yells at those who humiliate and that does not change anything for me; I am still a weak ego that other people can easily humiliate.

FORGIVENESS IS SALVATION.

As long as I live as an ego, other egos can humiliate me and I can humiliate other egos. But if I choose forgiveness, I live from a different self, the higher self, the Christ self, the self in light form, and no one can humiliate that different me.

My true strength lies in me forgiving my humiliators so as to live as Christ. Being in Christ is having true strength. Is this mere fantasy or the truth?

If in doubt, look at white Americans. They have guns and walk around armed to the teeth. Are they strong? They live in ego and live in fear, hence live in hell; they are weak despite their entire amour!

THE PSYCHOPATHIC, SADISTIC EGO, AND THE MASOCHISTIC EGO

One of the lessons I learned from living in the USA is that the typical white man is a psychopath; he enjoys harming, enslaving, and giving black folks pain. That is the role his ego plays; he is the psychopathic ego.

The psychopath feels weak and wants to seem strong. He hates weak people. Black people and Africans are weak and white psychopaths hate them and want to punish them for they represent what white psychopaths do not want to be, weak persons.

In this light, if black folks and Africans want white folks to stop abusing them, they just have to become strong. That means developing Africa. If Africa is developed, white folks would no longer see Africans as weak rubbish to be abused.

Hitherto, Asians were weak and white folks used to have no regard for them. Asia is now developed and the white man no longer looks down on Asians. Little North Korea's dictator, Kim Jon Un, tells the big USA and its clownish president, Donald Trump, to shut the hell up or else, he nukes them. Strength gets the attention of the white man, and since he respects strength, he respects Asians.

When Nigeria is industrialized and has formidable military weapons, white folks would no longer fuck them, as they currently do.

YOU HAVE TO SHUT OUT OUR EGOS' WORLD TO SEE THE WORLD OF LIGHT FORMS; TO EXPERIENCE THE FORMLESS WORLD OF GOD, YOU HAVE TO TRANSCEND THE EGO'S AND CHRIST'S WORLD.

At night, we sleep. In sleep, we tune out our day world and dream. In our dreams, we see a different world, our day world put to a different purpose.

You cannot see your nightly dream world and the day world at the same time.

By the same token, you cannot see our world and the world of light forms at the same time. You have to consciously tune out our day world to have a vision, that is, see the world of light forms.

The objective of meditation is to tune out our egos and the egos' world so as to see the Christ's light world; you cannot see the light world and our world at the same time; it is either one or the other but not both at the same time.

If you want to experience God's formless world, you have to tune out the ego's dream world and Christ's dream world.

DISCUSSION

This essay in no way says that oppressors should be tolerated. People live in bodies. People who live in bodies do feel pain when you attack them. George Floyd lived in body and did feel pain when Derick Chauvin knelt on his neck. Chauvin knew that he was giving another human being pain.

What you do to other people will be done to you until the people you did harm to decide to forgive you. Mr. Chauvin will be judged with the laws of the ego.

The laws of the ego are the laws of extant human beings' demand that he be punished and he must be punished. He had no business going about killing people.

Those who punish people who offend them will remain in the egos' world and will be punished by those they offended. This is the nature of our world.

Oppress people and you will be oppressed. White folks who go about oppressing black people will, sooner or later, be oppressed by black people. This is the nature of our world. You do not get away from this law, karma; that is why great empires decline and fall; those they oppressed tear them down.

That being said, if you, on the individual level, want to exit from this world, you must forgive those who harmed or even killed you. That is what Jesus Christ demonstrated at Calvary.

If you recall, Jesus was crucified and he asked his father to forgive those who murdered him because they know not what they were doing; they did not know that he is immortal and cannot be killed; they were in ego and believed that all egos can be killed. His real self is the immortal Christ, the son of God who is one with God.

Jesus' entire gospel was teaching forgiveness. In the Sermon on the Mount, he asked folks to turn the other cheek when one side is slapped.

He told a parable that when a man is going to pray and remembers that his neighbor wronged him, he must first go home and forgive the neighbor before worshipping God. God hears all our prayers and knows what we ask for but insist that we forgive those who wronged us, as he has forgiven us our trespasses.

In the only prayer he taught his apostles, our Lord's prayer, he told them to forgive those who wronged them if they want their father to forgive them.

And they brought a woman caught in adultery to him and asked him if they should obey the laws of Moses, the Old Testament, the laws of the ego, and stone her to death. He said: let those who have not sinned be the first to stone her. All are sinners and we must forgive each other.

Simply stated, Jesus and his Holy Spirit taught forgiveness as the path to returning to love, God. If you are seeking salvation, that is, if you want to leave planet earth and first return to the world of light forms and ultimately to formless God, you must forgive those who wronged you.

I made the choice to forgive all because I have chosen salvation. You have to make that choice when you are ready. No other person can make that choice for you.

If you are still identified with ego and its body, you have not chosen salvation and will resist those who attacked you, take fight to oppressors, and that is the nature of life in egos.

If you want to live in ego and mitigate its suffering, then do unto others as you want them to do to you, love them and do not oppress them, as Jesus said. That way, we have relative peace and happiness on earth, not the perfect peace of heaven and God.

CONCLUSION

I wrote this essay for me, not necessarily for other persons; I wrote what I want to learn. If you are not yet ready to return to God, this essay may seem like gibberish to you.

I recommend that you read Helen Schucman's *A Course in Miracles*. What she said in poetry I said in prose.

18

FORGIVENESS IS SALVATION

(See if you can understand the essay below; if not, don't worry about it; it may not be your time yet to be saved; we are all on a journey, separation from God and return to God, and are at different stages of that journey; some are closer to animals whereas some are closer to spirit; some are about to awaken from the dream of self-forgetfulness and know that they are the sons of God, whereas others want to sleep and dream some more that they are what they are not, egos in bodies.)

Forgiveness is rooted in the understanding that the world is a dream and what is done in it has not been done since a dream is not real. Thus, you overlook what other people did to you, for they did it in a dream and have not done it in reality. In so doing, you overlook the seeming evil you did to other people for you did so in the dream and have not done it in reality; you forgive dreams, not reality.

The egos' world is nothing and nothing has been done in it so you overlook it; you pass through the world without taking it seriously; you make only one judgment—that the world is a dream, nothing, and overlook all of it.

DESIRE, WISHES, AND BELIEFS PRODUCED THE EMPIRICAL UNIVERSE.

The world came into being via our wishes and beliefs. Originally, we were pure formless spirits; we were, and still, are in one spirit, in God.

We wished to separate from God and from each other and go create a physical world of forms that we can see. Thus, we invented the world of energy, matter, space, and time, began the physical universe, and now seem to be living in it.

We valued the world we made thinking that it has worth and importance, hence created an elaborate ego that wants to seem significant in the world.

SACRIFICING NOTHING IS SACRIFICING NOTHING.

All of the physical universes are nothing, is a dream; giving up a dream is not sacrificing what has worth but sacrificing nothing; but the mind that made the ego and its world, the sleeping son of God, values the world it made.

In valuing it, he keeps himself in chains, in fear and hell. He did this to himself by desiring the valueless that he had believed has value.

We bestow value and worth on the ego and its world to make them desirable and thus, live in prison and chains.

We must now recognize that the physical universe we made has no value and worth, is meaningless and purposeless, except the fantasy meaning and purpose we gave it, and then stop doing so.

THE WORLD OF LIGHT FORMS IS REMADE FROM OUR WORLD OF DARKNESS.

When you let go of this world, you see the world that the Holy Spirit already made with which to replace this world. So, sacrificing this world would not leave you empty-handed. You would see the world of light forms, our present world purified by forgiveness, by overlooking it and not desiring it.

In the world of light forms, things approximate heaven, for they are eternal and permanent but still in space and time.

From the world of light forms, one returns to the formless, timeless, and spaceless world of God where all know each other as one and do not need words to communicate; on earth, this is experienced during the Holy Instant when the egos' world is tuned out, forgiven, and God gives one his unified and holy self to experience.

THE TEACHERS OF GOD

If after you have experienced the world of light forms and the world of formlessness you return to the awareness of living in body, space, and time, you now know that they are dreams and do not defend them; you do not defend your ego for it is not you. You are ego defenseless, for defense assumes that the ego is real; but what needs defense to seem real is not real.

You are now saved and can save other people in the sense of telling them the truth that only unified spirit exists and for them not to take the unreal dream seriously.

You are now part of the saviors of the world, such as Buddha and Jesus Christ; you are now a teacher of God, a Bodhisattva.

AFRICANS AND WHITE FOLKS ARE AT THE LOWER STEPS OF THE EGO AND ONLY WISH FOR EGO THINGS THAT THEY STORE WORTH ON.

The typical Igbo (my ethnic group), Yoruba, Hausa, Nigerian, African, Black American, and European desires big ego and ego things; he values his ego and body, thinks that they have worth, and desires them; these people are willing to sell their people to get money and material things to make their egos and bodies seem to have worth.

They decorate their bodies with elaborate clothes and jewelry and when they die, want to be buried with gold and such. To them, the ego and body are worthwhile.

Those who seek ego things are closer to animals than to Christ; Christ is the most developed human being before we return to formless heaven.

Africans and Europeans are closer to animals than human beings; Asians tend to be closer to real human beings because they pursue spirituality the right way, by recognizing that the ego and body are not who they are and they seek formless unified self in Samadhi, Nirvana, and Satori.

GIVEN MY PRIOR IDENTIFICATION WITH A POWERFUL EGO, I AM IN A POSITION TO TEACH THE WORLD TO LET GO OF ITS PURSUIT OF EGOS.

Who is best able to teach people spiritual reality but a person who hitherto wanted to make his ego and body important and paid the price of fear and anxiety? I over-identified with the ego and gave me both physical and psychological pain.

My grandfather (Osuji), father (Johnson), and I (Ozodi) pursued important egos and were ready to punish those who belittled us. Now, I know that we are an exaggeration of the ego and that the ego, big or small, is mankind's main problem.

The ego is the separated self we invented and with which we replaced our real self, the unified son of God. We have one problem, separation, and one solution, return to unified state.

The ego is a veil preventing us from seeing Christ, light formed us; we must thus jettison the ego to live from Christ self, light self.

THERE ARE NO ACCIDENTS; WHATEVER HAPPENS TO US IS WHAT OUR EGOS MADE AND THE HOLY SPIRIT USES THEM TO REDIRECT US TO PERFORM OUR FUNCTIONS.

I desired total egotism, a big, powerful ego. That ego butted heads with the white world that relegates black folks to menial jobs. Since I see myself as superior to all white folks, it follows that I could not accept the white world. I flunked out of the white world. I did not desire what the white world offered me. They pushed me out and I pushed me out of their world (which I considered decadent).

My ego felt badly treated by white folks and sees me as a victim. I am no one's victim; I experienced what my ego set up.

My higher self, the Holy Spirit, uses my big ego and racism in America to redirect me, to teach me my real function.

My real function is forgiveness; that is, my function is to overlook my ego, black folks' egos, white folks' egos, and accept my real self in space, time, and matter, the Christ self in light form.

Having accepted that Holy Spirit-directed self, I live in peace and joy and become a teacher of God. I then teach white folks and Africans who had hitherto seemed to reject me and who I rejected what they need to do to be saved, jettison their egos.

I HAVE NOW FOUND MY VOCATION, FUNCTION.

I had a difficult time settling on a vocation and put all my energies, twenty-four-seven, one hundred percent, into doing it and succeeding in it. I could have been an ego psychologist or political scientist but those areas where I had training were not good enough for me so I flunked out of them, or were pushed out of them by racists (both racist and I did what I asked us to do to me).

I have now found my vocation, my function, and role in life: my vocation is to let go of my big ego, live in peace, and teach other people how to let go of their egos and live in peace; in peace, we build a new self and a new world, the new Owerri (new Jerusalem) and new man.

I set up an organization, center for egoless living, to teach us how to live from the egoless, Christ self, and in so doing, bring about a peaceful world.

CHANGING YOUR MIND MEANS CHANGING YOUR PATTERN OF THINKING.

I have now changed my mind, that is, changed my pattern of thinking, from ego-based thinking to Christ and Holy Spirit, that is, forgiveness-based thinking; I now overlook the ego and its world and think from the Holy Spirit, Christ, my real self; I now live in peace and joy, not the war, the self-attack, and split self (two selves, son of God and ego) I lived in when I tried to live as an ego-self.

PURE REASON DOES NOT TELL US WHAT IS THE TRUTH; SCIENCE UNDERSTANDS THE TRUTH OF MATTER, SPACE, AND TIME BUT NOT OUR THINKING, MINDS, AND SPIRIT

Pure reason does not tell us the truth of who we are; reason could be used to pursue fantasies as Adolf Hitler did.

Science only understands matter, space, and time but not the thinker. Science does not understand us, our thinking, but understands the products of our thinking, the material universe.

We must return to God, at first taken on faith and later experienced, to know who we are. We are the unified sons of God who share one self and one pattern of thinking, one mind with God.

MY INABILITY TO SETTLE ON A VOCATION WAS MY EGO REFUSING TO DO ITS FUNCTION OF LETTING GO OF THE EGO.

I was unable to settle on a profession, be a psychologist or political scientist; I kept waffling and not been fully committed to either profession. I see the utility and shortcoming of either profession: psychology studies, the peripheral aspects of the mind, but refuses to go deep to understand the mind; political scientists are essentially glorified reporters for political actors, describing their activities instead of seeking the ideal realistic human polity and insisting on it; either profession disappointed me and I fence sat and could not commit to either fully.

This was my ego refusing to commit to something. The good part of it is that what it refused to commit to is not worth coming to, for either profession is moribund, cowardly, and refused to do what is expected of it.

I did not waste my time by not committing to either. The goal was for me to understand them, understand the world, decide what the truth is, and commit to it.

The truth is that we are egotists, must reduce our egos, and if possible, eliminate them and become love serving ego separated selves and from there, journey to unified self in God.

DON'T MORALIZE ABOUT PEOPLE NOT BEING PERFECT.

In the meantime, I must stay silent and not speak about other people, about who they are and what they are doing—right or wrong. They are by the logic of their bodies and social experiences and cannot be the fearless giants I had expected them to be. People are being their biosocial selves, doing their bests but cannot do better as I had expected them to do.

People are essentially animals and it is for me to show them what their real self, Christ-actualizing self, is like.

By keeping quiet, not criticizing people, and instead of doing what I know is right, I actually get people around me to do the right things more than I did when I spent most of my time criticizing them, pointing out what they did wrong and showing how imperfect they are.

Leave people alone and simply do what you believe is right, which is to live in an egoless way, not moralizing about the ego and what it does wrong; the ego is a dream self and cannot do right or wrong.

One must be amused by the ego and its bodies pretending to be important, significant; egos are mere fantasy selves, dream selves that do not exist.

People's real selves, the sons of God, are in God where they are always perfect; their dream selves are merely living out the script, play, drama their egos collectively wrote.

Ignore the ego and its dreams and love the dreamer, the unified son of God, and in doing so, live in peace and joy. Tune out the egos' world, people in bodies dancing their ego dances for importance, for those are futile; egos will die and disappear from existence.

What is eternal does not change; people's real selves, sons of God (and Christ in the world of light forms, the midway between heaven and earth), are perfect and as such, do not need me to improve them.

WE MADE DREAM FIGURES AND WANT TO MAKE THEM SEEM IMPORTANT.

You can come to understand human nature by observing yourself in an objective and dispassionate manner. Through self-observation, you can come to know a lot about you and since all people are like yourself, you know about other people.

My self-observation tells me that in ego and body, I am nothing, literally, not figuratively. This awareness is always in my mind but I reject it and want to become somebody important.

Everything that I do is to make me seem important in my eyes and in other people's eyes. I want all people to see me as important.

If other people overtly or covertly say or do something that tells me that I am not important, I feel angry at them; in anger, I may kill them.

This is actually rational behavior because my ego is aware that people tend to harm or kill those they see as unimportant so if people see me as unimportant, they can disrespect and kill me, so my ego says kill them before they kill you.

In an extant society, we see some people as more important than others; actually, some people want to be seen as more important than others.

White folks would like black folks to see them as more important than black folks; they actually want black folks to see white folks as more important than black folks; they want black folks to accept white folks abusing and murdering black folks.

Stop right there and think about it. What jumps at you?

Even ordinary animals do not allow you to kill them without putting up a fight. The fact that white folks want black folks to allow themselves to be killed by white folks means that we are dealing with insanity here. White folks are really insane, deluded.

Racism is a mental disorder; it is part of delusion disorder, belief in what is not true and acting on it as if it is true.

You are deluded if you see yourself as better than other people; the truth is that all people are the same and coequal.

White policemen, usually morons in intelligence, believe that they have a right to kill black folks whom they see as unimportant; they feel surprised that black people do not want them to kill them. These murderous white police officers are obviously psychotic in their belief that one human being has a right to kill others.

No one has a right to kill others, but that is not the subject at hand; the present subject is human desire for worth, importance, significance, and fear of being seen as unimportant.

It is my ego and body that wants all people to see me as important. A higher part of me, my spirit self, knows that it is important regardless of how other people see it.

As sons of God, all of us have grandeur and magnificence. But we denied that grand self and currently identify with ego and body and want to make ego seem important.

The ego and body do not exist; they are dream figures and nothing we do can ever make them seem important, for nothingness cannot be important.

Where you see you and other people is nobody; what you are looking at is a mirage, a dream figure, an illusion that you want to make to seem real; you invest your dream figure and other people's dream figures with worth and significance.

Each mass of flesh and bone wants to be seen as important, worthwhile, and valued.

If you give people's egos and bodies worth, you make them seem to exist; after all, all they do on earth is a futile effort to obtain worth for their egos and bodies: food, clothes, jewelry, houses, mansions to protect bodies, cars to carry bodies, and what does not exist from place to place.

Since flesh and ego do not exist but want to exist, if you take away worth from a person, you have literally attacked and tried to kill that person and he will fight back and take away worth from your ego and want to kill your ego and body.

I saw Igbos dancing for ego and body worth, put them down, and they felt like I wanted them dead, hence attacked my own ego and body with the intention of killing it.

I saw my ex-wife dressing herself up to seem to have worth in ego and body and did not affirm her ego's worth, so she felt like I attacked and devalued her ego.

At the spirit level, all of us have eternal life and grandeur (because we have grandeur in spirit, we seek it for the ego and body we made) and nothing we do to each other detracts from our grandeur in spirit; it is at the ego level that we can seem to devalue each other.

Hitler killed fifty million egos and bodies; white folks desecrate millions of black egos and bodies to make their own nonexistent egos and bodies seem real and important.

My ex-wife left to go seek ego and body worth from other men. In effect, I contributed to her death by not affirming her ego's worth.

One is seeking ego worth by talking all the time to people on the internet; one is seeking attention and affirmation of one's ego; I must affirm people's egos as much as I can while knowing that in spirit, they have perfect worth (we know that in spirit, we are all of worth but came to the dream to make our egos and bodies seem to have worth, so give ego worth to people but do not seek it for yourself).

If you do not seek to make your ego and body significant, you would not ask other people to see them as significant and it would not bother you whether they do so or not. You would live in peace, calmly. You would feel a part of life and life is a mystery, for it produced this universe; a force that produced this universe, albeit a silly universe, is powerful.

You would go about doing what you believe is useful to you and mankind; for example, I believe that it is useful for mankind to understand that much of their civilization and drive is rooted in their drive to seem significant because they feel insignificant as they are.

PEOPLE ARE NOTHING SO SEEKING THEIR ATTENTION IS SEEKING NOTHING'S ATTENTION AND EVEN IF THEY GAVE IT, YOU WOULD STILL FEEL LIKE NOTHING.

People as egos and bodies are nothing; you as ego and body are nothing; you feel that if you obtained attention from other people, they would wash away your nothingness and make you feel like you are something important. But since they are nothing, even if they give you attention, you would still not feel like you have worth; thus, it is useless seeking other people's attention.

Yet, egos are enslaved to seeking other people's attention thinking that people's conferment of worth on them would wash away their sense of nothingness and make them seem to have worth.

All of society is dedicated to people seeking each other's attention and worth but not getting it, for nothingness cannot give nothingness worth.

WORTH IS ONLY DERIVED FROM GOD.

Worth is only derived from God and that worth is given freely; you do not have to seek God's attention and worth; all you have to do is remove your ego and stop seeking ego worth on ego terms and have an empty mind; that is, do not think in ego terms and you have God's worth that is already in you and you denied it while seeking futile external worth.

Tune people out; do not seek their attention; go inward and see the grandeur that you already have inside you as the son of God.

You denied your eternal worth in unified state, invented a false separated self and it feels incomplete, and seeks ego- and body-based worth from other egos and bodies that it would not get.

The curse of the ego is that it must seek ego worth from other egos and not get it.

THE IRONY OF RACISM

If you take away worth from other people, you take away worth from yourself; white racists take away worth from black people; would you say that they have worth? They have fantasy worth and build a deluded civilization bound to collapse at any time; theirs is a house built on sand.

LIVE WHAT YOU BELIEVE IS TRUE AND NOT JUST TALK ABOUT IT.

If you believe that something is true, then live it. If you believe that the pursuit of ego and body worth, aka superiority, is the source of your psychological suffering, then don't just talk about it, live it; stop seeking worth and significance and live equality hence peacefully.

Your calmness is now unrattled; in the past, when other people did what seems to detract from your ego and body worth, you counterattacked them; now you are quiet regardless of what other people say to you.

A healthy person lives the truth as he sees it; he leaves other people to talk about their mostly deluded ideas on the nature of reality and live in fear, anxiety, anger, depression, mania, delusion, and other mental disorders.

Your peace and happiness in this turbulent world are an advertisement for the truth; the truth is that we are the sons of God, parts of unified spirit self; in that state of formless union with the creator and his creation, we are peaceful, happy, and eternal.

FROM THE EGO TO THE CHRIST TO THE SON OF GOD AND GOD

There is one God. God is a father. A father must have sons to be a father. God has sons. To have sons, God must be creative; God is creative and is forever creating his sons.

The sons of God are like their father, are creative, and are forever creating their own sons, all of whom share one self with God.

In eternity, aka heaven, God created his sons. God and his sons share one self. They are one self and one thinking, aka mind.

Where God ends and his sons begin is nowhere. There is no space and gap between God and his sons. God is in his sons and his sons are in him and in each other. They live in a formless state where there is no separation between them.

They literally share one self and there is no need to see each other for there is no each other (even on earth where there seem separation, where you see the sons of God, you see God for God is in each of his sons; God is in you, in me, in a dog, a mosquito, trees, and in everything).

Our true identity is the formless sons of God who are one with God and each other.

God and his sons are always thinking; creation is done through thinking; the idea of becoming more powerful than God entered the thinking, minds, of the sons of God.

How can they accomplish this thought since they are one with God and each other? It is impossible to be more powerful than God and your brothers.

Since this idea cannot be accomplished in (spiritual) reality, we sought to accomplish it in fantasy, in dreams.

As it were, we made ourselves go to sleep (Hinduism says that we cast Maya, spell, on ourselves to forget our true self, Atman who is one with God, and now see ourselves as Ahankara, separated egos) and in our sleep dream.

The physical universe is our dream. We have been dreaming for however long our physical universe existed.

Physics says that our physical universe began 13.8 billion years ago and has been expanding since then. We have been dreaming for fourteen billion years.

(In heaven, God, there is no space, time, and matter, so when we talk about the age of the universe, we are talking about the egos' world.)

During those fourteen billion years, we use our thinking, mind, to invent light particles, photons, and used those to invent electrons and quarks and combined quarks into protons and neutrons and combined those into nuclei and later, combined nuclei with electrons to form atoms.

The initial atoms were hydrogen, helium, and lithium (please take physics and chemistry if you ever want to follow my writing, okay). The universe then was a sea of hydrogen, helium, and lithium. We thereafter separated this sea of atoms into clumps.

We invented gravity (we also invented the other three forces of nature: electromagnetism, strong and weak nuclear forces) and had gravity act on each clump of hydrogen atoms and in its core, hydrogen fused to helium and light were produced. Thus, a star is born.

A star is a clump of hydrogen in whose core four atoms of hydrogen fuse into one atom of helium. The light and heat produced by this fusion (called nucleosynthesis) walk their way from the core of the star until they escape at the surface as the light we see as starlight.

The initial stars were very massive in size and in a few million years, exhausted their hydrogen and began fusing other elements. When the fusion process reaches iron, the star blows up in supernova, and in the superheat that accompanies the supernova elements beyond iron, is fused.

In the extant universe are 92 elements, plus the ones that scientists form in laboratories. The different elements are atoms with different numbers of protons and electrons. For example, hydrogen has one proton, one electron—some of its isotopes have neutrons; helium has two electrons, two protons, and two neutrons; carbon has six electrons, six protons, and six neutrons; oxygen has eight electrons, eight protons, and eight neutrons; uranium, the heaviest element, has 92 protons, 146 neutrons, and 92 electrons.

Exploded stars have their inner cores collapse into either blackhole (which are so dense that not even light can escape from their event horizons) or neuron star that spin at incredible rates. When medium-sized stars like our sun explode, their inner cores become red dwarfs, shine for a while and die, and become rocks in space.

Our sun came into being four and half billion years ago, from the debris of exploded supersized stars, and has enough hydrogen to keep fusing hydrogen into helium for another five billion years. In about two billion years, it will begin running out of hydrogen, begin fusing other elements and expand, incorporate its planets, and explode (the planets orbiting our sun are Mercury, Venus, Earth, Mars, Jupiter, Saturn, Uranus, Neptune, and Pluto; plus the asteroids and comets circling it).

The universe has trillions of stars; these stars are grouped into galaxies; each galaxy has over 200 billion stars, and there are over 200 billion galaxies.

The galaxies are expanding away from each other. In trillions of years, there would be too much space between galaxies and stars so that they become cold and decay.

All-stars will decay to their constituent elements; the elements would decay to their constituent protons, neutrons, and electrons. Those particles would decay to photons. Thus, the universe that began in hot light ends in cold light (Big Chill).

GOD CREATED THE SPIRITUAL UNIVERSE; THE SONS OF GOD MADE THE PHYSICAL UNIVERSE.

It is us, the sons of God who formed the physical universe and around some stars, formed planets. On planet earth, the 92 elements gathered to form the hot land.

Over time, water was brought to earth by comets; water cooled the superhot earth. The earth's surface is covered with 70% water.

BIOLOGICAL ORGANISMS

In the waters, 64 elements, especially carbon, hydrogen, oxygen, nitrogen, potassium, magnesium, iron, copper, calcium, and so on combined to form biological organisms. Our bodies are made of sixty-four elements.

We evolved our bodies from single-celled organisms to many-celled organisms until we reached homo sapiens. The human body, other animals' bodies, and plants are made from the same elements.

THE SEPARATED SELF, THE EGO, AND ITS SPECIAL LOVE RELATIONSHIPS

We, the separating sons of God, seem to have entered bodies and conceptualized separated self-concepts for each of us. Each of us, working with all of us, and the entire physical universe, constructed his self-concept.

The separated self-concept, the ego, is constructed with our bodies and other people, society. The ego is the son of God in his dream state.

THE EGO IS VERY POWERFUL.

Please do not minimize the ego for it represents the thinking, mind of the sons of God. Thinking, minds that invented our physical universe with its stars, galaxies, planets, animals, trees, and all in the perceptual universe, is very powerful. The ego is very powerful.

You must carefully study the ego, that is, your human pattern of thinking (in both scientific and spiritual psychology) and then undertake to let it go but do not deny its power in your life.

And do not abuse other egos; if you put other egos down, given that the ego seeks power, egos will kill you. Always respect the ego even when you are trying to get rid of it; it can turn the table on you at any time.

On May 25, 2020, a white policeman, Derick Chauvin, killed a black man, George Floyd; my God, I reverted to my ego and was in the mood to kill any and all white persons I see around me. The ego bears grievances and seeks vengeance and revenge for every humiliation it feels in the hands of other egos.

If you want peace, do not insult other egos; always treat the ego respectfully, as if it has worth (in reality, it is a dream self and has no worth).

The actual son of God is unified with God but the ego is seemingly separated from God and all his brothers.

BODY WAS MADE AS A MEANS OF SEPARATION.

We made our bodies fragile and vulnerable so that they are easily hurt and destroyed by other sons of God. This was done deliberately, to make separation possible.

When I see you, I know that you have the capacity to destroy my body, and you know that I have the capacity to destroy your body.

We expect each person we see to destroy our bodies. As such, we fear each other (body and fear are means of separation). We relate to each other gingerly, afraid that each person, animal, and tree we see could destroy our bodies.

In a split second, we decide that other people could harm us and we run away from them to go retain our wished-for separated ego selves in bodies, to keep our special selves (special self is separated self).

SPECIAL LOVE RELATIONSHIPS

We form associations where we are afraid to give of ourselves completely to each other, for we are afraid that other people could destroy our wished-for separated ego selves. Thus, in our human relationships, there is always an escape route built into them, the desire to leave and go live separately.

We formed what Helen Schucman, in her book on spiritual psychology, *A Course in Miracles*, aptly called special love relationships.

Specialness is the individual's wish to be more powerful than God, the desire that led to separation from God and other sons of God.

We have special love relationships based on our mutual undertaking to unite but keep the option of separation whenever we so desire. Thus, upon the slightest problem in our human relationships, we run from our relationships and go form different ones, always ones that enable us to keep our specialness, our desire to be individuated.

The ego is the son of God that is now individuated, separated from his father and brothers, houses himself in body, and lives in space, time, and matter. He is us on earth.

UNIFIED SPIRIT SELF, AKA GOD

In God, we share one self and one thinking and cannot be separated from each other. When we went to sleep and now dream that we are separated from God and each other, God could no longer be heard by his separated sons.

KNOWLEDGE VERSUS PERCEPTION

In God, we are unified and know each other completely. On earth we, as it were, tune out God and hear only our ego voices. The world is a place of separation, space, and time.

Where there is separation, we see each other; hence, the world is a world of perception. Perception means that you are separated from the thing or person you are seeing.

In perception, you can see a person but cannot know him. I can see you but cannot know who you are and you can see me and cannot know who I am. We each live in our cocoons.

Knowledge is only possible in unified state, in God, heaven.

THE HOLY SPIRIT

God decided to give his sons the ability to hear him. He created the Holy Spirit and through him, communicates to his separated sons. And through him, his separated sons on earth can speak to God.

The Holy Spirit is the communication channel, the link between God and his separated sons. God, every minute of the day, speaks to you through his Holy Spirit and you speak to God through the Holy Spirit.

The Holy Spirit is the bridge between God and his separated sons; he is the voice of God, the voice for love, the voice for union whereas the ego is the voice for separation, the voice for hate and war.

I am talking as if the Holy Spirit is a person apart from us; he is not a person; he is a part of you and me. In our thinking, minds are three patterns: holistic/unified thinking, aka the thinking of God and his sons; ego thinking, that is, thinking that wishes separated self and different interests; and Holy Spirit or Christ-directed thinking that knows that you are eternally a part of God and all people and you love all people.

God the Father (transcendent God, God in heaven), God the Son (us in the temporal universe), and God the Holy Spirit are one self; one self acts in three aspects.

The ego is the dream self-projected out by the sons of God. The ego and its dream world are not real and do not exist but seem to exist.

If you follow my writing and give what it says a try, love and forgive all, you will begin seeing yourself and people in light forms, eventually experience our material universe disappear from your awareness, you experience formless unified spirit self, and in it, feel at home, peaceful and happy; the prodigal son in you, the ego, would finally return home to his father and brothers.

You can, of course, deny the truth and keep on pretending to be a Christian, praying to Jesus Christ to give you this or that material thing.

Listen, Jesus is not your lord; he is your brother who found a way to return to God; you can see him right now in his light form, his glorified form; I am showing you how to do what Jesus did; please stop pretending that you are a Christian.

A true Christian loves and forgives all sons of God and like the good Samaritan, serves our mutual needs.

WE DELIBERATELY MADE OUR BODIES FRAGILE TO ENABLE US TO FEEL PAIN, HENCE JUSTIFY SEPARATION FROM EACH OTHER.

When we separated from God, we housed ourselves in fragile bodies made from matter. Our fragile and vulnerable bodies were deliberately designed to enable us to separate from God and each other. You can harm and destroy my body and I can do the same to you; you can give my body pain and I can give your body pain; anticipating you causing me pain, I avoid you and you do the same to me.

LIGHT BODIES, THE CHRIST

God, through the Holy Spirit, remade our bodies that we made with dense matter into light bodies, bodies that do not hide our thinking, our minds.

The body in light form is called the Christ body. The Christ is the ego remade into light body. In light selves, we understand what each of us is thinking about without speech.

(If you have ever had an out-of-body experience or near-death experience, you have seen yourself in body of light and seen other selves, animals, trees, everything in our world in light forms and in that state, do not open your mouth to talk but know what every person around you is thinking and respond to their thinking and they respond to your thinking.)

In light form, we are still in our earthly body-like state except that the bodies are made of light and are transparent; they are no longer used to hide from God and from each other.

The Christ self is our egos transformed to light selves so that we can now communicate openly to God and to each other.

Christ is the ego that has understood that it is one with God and all other sons of God and is no longer wishing to separate from them.

Christ is still living in the illusion of having form, albeit purified body, living in the illusion of space and time but now uses those to love other sons of God in bodies, hence he approximates how his father created him, unified with God and all selves.

Whereas the ego thinks of his separated self-interests, the Christ thinks of his unified and collective interests.

White Americans and Igbos (and other human beings) are separated egos; they are capitalists; they are deluded sons of God who think that they have different self-interests; they are insane.

The Christ is any of these misguided Americans and Igbos and all human beings who now knows that he is one with God and all people and while on earth, works for our social interests.

On earth, the Christ is a socialist; the capitalist is the epitome of the ego. Christ is the purified ego with a purified body—from body of flesh to body of light.

Ego is an illusion that does not exist in God. Christ is also an illusion that does not exist in God, for Christ is still living in the world of forms and separated states but Christ easily communicates with God. The Christ is the ego saved.

God does not destroy what his son made in his madness, his desire to separate from him, but instead, use it to show him how to relate to him and his other sons with it. In Christ, we use our egos and bodies to love each other.

In salvation, your body is transformed to light form; you are now Christ; Christ and you now live in a world of light forms, a forgiven world, a world where you have overlooked your dense body and other people's dense bodies and know that they are dream figures and what they do is dream activities and what is done in dreams have not been done in reality, so you overlook their bodies and earthly activities; you know that you are one shared self with all people; you love all people.

Despite our dreams of harming people, we remain as God created us: innocent, guiltless, sinless, and holy.

CHRIST, HOLY RELATIONSHIPS, THE WORLD OF LIGHT FORMS

The saved ego-self is the Christ self, a self in light form, a self whose relationships have been transformed from special love to holy relationships.

In holy relationships, you know that you are one with all people. On earth, you do what serves our collective interest; you work for publicly paid education at all levels, work for publicly paid health insurance for all people, and generally help the poor for you see them as parts of you.

If you attain Christ status while still on earth, when you die, you live in the world of light forms, variously called gate of heaven, happy dreams, purgatory.

If while on earth you completely forgive people, you do not have to die to leave the earth; you can transition from dense body to light body and live in the world of light forms. Only a few persons like Jesus have done so.

FROM GRANDIOSE EGOS TO CHRIST

On earth, we live in egos and bodies. We misunderstand egos and bodies. For example, right from my birth, I have seen all people as idiots and as inferior to me.

By age ten, I saw all Igbos, Nigerians, Africans, and white folks as animals rather than human beings. I have never seen people as like me; to me, people are garbage. How could they steal, rape, and kill people? Those thoughts seldom enter my thinking, mind.

Over time, I recognized that most people live at a lower level of evolution whereas there are advanced souls like Gautama Buddha and Jesus Christ.

In my youth, I saw people as total ego identified; I wanted to escape from my ego and body; I used my thinking to formulate ideal self and ideal world (neurotic self and neurotic world, fantasy world).

I rejected people in bodies and desecrated them; I called people monkeys and apes and wanted nothing to do with them.

I avoided people because to me, they are animals. In time, I learned that what I rejected are people's egos and their bodies but that there are inner selves in them in light forms, Christ selves. Those light selves began to interest me and I explored religion, such as Hinduism, Buddhism, Taoism, and Gnosticism.

I learned to overlook people's dense bodies and egos. In doing so, I occasionally see people in light bodies (as Christ selves; this is called having Christ vision). I also occasionally see myself in light form.

I overlook peoples' dense bodies and egos and their ego acts and focus on the forgiving selves in them, the Christ selves in them.

Ultimately, I know that in God, we are all one shared formless unified self.

DISCUSSION

I hope that I have described what constitutes the son of God, our real selves; the Christ self, our purified ego selves; and our egos, our separated, animal selves.

The ego and Christ are illusions but the Christ is a purified illusion who still is living in the illusory temporal universe but because he has remembered that he is joined to God and all creation, he loves all creation and thus lives in peace and joy.

Whereas the ego lives in fear, anxiety, anger, depression, paranoia, mania, and schizophrenia, Christ is healthy, still, and strong.

Transform your ego to Christ self and become a strong self, a self you will increasingly see in light form and a self that occasionally disappears from the world of perception, enters the formless world of oneness, and knows itself as one self with God and all creation.

God and his unified sons cannot be described in words, for whereas they understand words, they communicate instantaneously, each relating to others' thinking; this is kind of like what happens with entangled particles and their non-local communication.

CONCLUSION

If you overlook your ego, other people's egos, and the seeming evils we do in egos and love people, you become the Christ.

If your name is Thomas, you are now the Christ. Under the direction of the Holy Spirit, Christ is a teacher of God. He does what I did in this essay.

From Christ, you remember your true identity as the formless son of God who is one with God. You return home and live in peace and joy.

We, the sons of God, made this matter-based universe. We made the ego separated self-concepts and the Holy Spirit remade them to Christ light selves; we made special love relationships to seem united but hide from each other and the Holy Spirit remade them to holy relationships so that we can use them to relate to each other. We made the world of matter and the Holy Spirit remade it to the world of light forms.

Post Script:

As I typed the last word in this essay (I did not look up during the two hours it took me to type this essay this morning), my classical radio station began playing one of the best pieces by Franz Joseph Haydn, and I automatically said: thank you God for this beautiful music. Man is a spiritual being; only spiritual beings could give us classical music.

Europeans, especially Germans, gave us classical music. A race that produced Bach, Mozart, Beethoven, Handel, Haydn, Wagner, and other classical musicians must be the sons of God. Therefore, much as my ego urges me to hate white folks for abusing black folks, I cannot do so. They gave me my only source of joy in life, classical music and science.

FROM THE EGO PERSPECTIVE, A COURSE IN MIRACLES IS AN ESCAPIST PHILOSOPHY.

Before you accept a philosophy, you ought to know what its premise is. *A Course in Miracles* wants you to negate this world, escape from this world, and return to a better world; first, to the world of light forms and eventually, to the formless world of God, aka heaven.

A Course in Miracles presents this world as coming into being because of our act of rebellion; it says that we are the sons of God who rebelled against their father. They did not like that their father has more power than they; he created them and they did not create him or create themselves; they wished him dead so that they would take over his creatorship throne and go create themselves and the universe.

They had already been created and could not create themselves. Since they could not do away with God and his universe, they went to sleep and in their sleep, invented another world, one where they invented space, time, and matter, used matter to make bodies for themselves, and now seem to have created themselves by inventing separated self-concepts for themselves, as opposed to the unified self-God created them as.

They are the prodigal son who went on a journey to a far country to live his own life (in imaginary dream country for they are in the meantime inside their father as parts of him and cannot separate from him).

In the dream world, we invented separated ego selves in bodies and defend those. We give ourselves pain and suffering. We desire the temporary ego-self and its world thinking that it is worthwhile but in fact, it has no worth; only the permanent has worth; nothing in our world has eternity so they are all worthless. Ultimately, we will die and the ego wants us to go straight to hell for disobeying our father.

Christians call separation our original sin, the act of disobeying God for which we must die or become saved by relinquishing the world we made and return to God.

A Course in Miracles is the religion of Gnosticism re-presented in psychoanalytic language. If you recall, in Gnosticism, the angel Lucifer resented God as his creator and boss and organized rebellion against

God and the angel Michael organized a force to defend God; both fought and Lucifer was defeated and chased out of heaven and came to earth to establish his own kingdom of darkness.

To Gnosticism, the world is darkness and heaven is light. Gnosticism wants us to jettison the world of darkness via having no ego and return to the world of egoless heaven, the world of light.

The Gnostic story of Lucifer is sometimes presented differently; the rebelling God is sometimes called Demiurge; indeed, some call the Jewish God, Yahweh the rebellious God.

As we all can ascertain from reading the Old Testament part of the Bible, Yahweh is very immature and proud; he punishes or kills you if you do not totally obey his childish and arrogant commands and respect him; he cast Lot's wife into a bag of salt for merely looking at a burning city of Gomorrah, hence is a false God, Gnosticism says.

The Persian thinker, Mani, established the first universal Gnostic religion; his followers were called Manicheans. Many pre-Christian Greeks were Gnostics.

Some of the disciples of Jesus, even Jesus himself were Gnostics (the Jesus' story of the prodigal son, leaving and returning to God, is a classic Gnostic story). See the Gnostic gospels of Thomas, Judas, and Mary Magdalen.

Saint Augustine, the bishop of Hippo, in North Africa, the guy who wrote the *City of God and Confessions* was first a Manichean Gnostic before rejecting it and accepting the views of Athanasios; Athanasios' views informed the council of Nicaea in 325 AD, hence underpin the Catholic Church's theology.

A Course in Miracles said that when the sons of God, in pursuit of their desire for self-creation, separated from God and invented our present universe, God created the Holy Spirit and through him, recreated the universe his sons made.

Thus, there are now three selves in one God: God the Father, God the Son (us), and God the Holy Spirit, all three are parts of God and are parts of each of us.

The Holy Spirit, that is, God in the temporal universe, reinvented our world of dense matter into a world of light forms.

The Holy Spirit wants us to negate the world we made of dense matter. The Holy Spirit wants us to replace the ego-self we made for ourselves with the Christ self he made for us.

Christ is the son of God in light form (the real son of God does not have form; but we made ourselves have bodily forms).

The Holy Spirit does not want you to value anything in the ego and its world of darkness. So, let go of the ego and its world and come to the light world.

The light world is still in space and time, is still like our world, but it has been purified by forgiveness and returned to near love, hence is eternal.

HOLY RELATIONSHIP, BASED ON CHRIST, TO REPLACE OUR PRESENT SPECIAL LOVE RELATIONSHIPS BASED ON EGOS

In the light world, we have holy relationships; these are relationships where we see ourselves as unified, as one shared self, hence love each other; holy relationships are used by the Holy Spirit to replace the special love relationships we have in the egos' world.

In special love relationships, each of us sees himself as a separated self and pursues his self-interests but sometimes, cooperates with other persons for their mutual good or separate from other persons when they do not serve his self-interests.

Special love relationship is capitalist people's relationship, whereas holy relationship is socialist people's social relationships.

The goal is to replace our present ego-self-concept in body with Christ self in light form. From light self, we thereafter return to the awareness of our true self, the formless son of God who is one with God and all creation. Thus ultimately, we return to heaven; we return home and end the journey away from our father, one's real self.

The egos journey is a journey without distance and a journey to nowhere, for wherever the son of God goes, he goes in God, for God is everywhere (we merely dream that we are in the world of space, time, and matter, the physical universe; in fact, we are always in God's unified and formless universe).

EGO-LESSNESS GIVES US PEACE AND JOY.

From my personal experience, I know that it is true that if you have ego and defend it, you will suffer psychological pain, and in the end, die. Twenty-five hundred years ago, Gautama Buddha recognized the same truth.

If you do not defend the ego, you feel like you have no self and live peacefully; if you have no ego to defend, you live without fear, anxiety, anger, depression, mania, delusion (of being a big ego-self that you are not), and schizophrenia. This much is true for it can be proved as true psychologically; that is, science can prove that with less ego, you are not mentally ill, not a paranoid defending a false, grandiose self.

NIGERIA IS IN A MESS BECAUSE NIGERIANS WANT TO BECOME BIG, IMPORTANT EGOS.

Most Nigerians identify with big ego selves, defend them, and that gives them the quality that folks see in them: being infantile.

Frederick Lugard, upon seeing Igbos, said that they are infantile, that they identify with false, big selves, and seek to become them and in so doing, sell their people into slavery to get the money with which to buy the accoutrement of bigness.

Lugard was correct in his assessment of the immaturity of Nigerians. I reached that same conclusion while at college before I read Lugard's autobiography, *The Dual Mandate*, in British Tropical Africa.

My assessment of Nigerians is that they are very childish; I actually do not believe that Nigerians can govern themselves right; I see them always making a royal mess of governance because they find it difficult to transcend their big egos and work for the public good. That is why I dedicate my life to helping shrink the Africans' inflated, swollen egos to normal levels so that they can work for social interests, hence produce well-governed societies.

THE UNPROVEN ASPECT OF A COURSE IN MIRACLES

What is not proven is whether the new self, Christ, and new world, variously called gate of heaven, real world, world of light forms, happy dreams, invented by the Holy Spirit to replace our world, is true or is a mere wished-for world, a fantasy.

We do not know that heaven exists.

There is no doubt in my mind that *A Course in Miracles* wants us to escape from our world of matter, a world of suffering, and return to heaven and world of light forms. We do not know for sure that heaven (the formless unified world of God) and purgatory (world of light forms) exist.

Is the book, therefore, selling a hill of beans to us? I do not know. I am agnostic.

What is evident from its pages is that it wants us to leave our present world; it says that desiring it gives us pain.

Gautama Buddha said the same thing; he, too, asks us to jettison the ego and its world, for they give us suffering, and come to the light world and ultimately to the formless unified world, in Nirvana.

Gnosticism was probably borrowed from Buddhism; Alexander the Great and his Greek soldiers got to India around 300 BC. Thereafter, Persians and Greeks learned from Hinduism and Buddhism and gave them Greek colorations in Gnosticism.

CONCLUSION

Understand a philosophy and then decide for yourself whether you want it or not. *A Course in Miracles* teaches escape from the phenomenal world; that is a fact. Decide whether that is what you want to do.

As for me, I would like to be on earth, study science, and use science to understand matter, space, and time and develop technologies to make living on earth beautiful; thereafter, I die and leave it at that.

In the meantime, I jettison the ego; I do not defend the ego for in desiring and defending the ego, I give me fear, anxiety, anger, and mental disorders; I do not want those. I want to live in peace.

Post Script:

Today, I leave Arizona and return to Alaska. I have been away from my beloved Anchorage for five months. I will put my Alaska house in order, edit the two manuscripts, one 350 pages, the other 180 pages, both of which I completed while in Arizona, and mail them out for publication.

From July and so forth, I become an itinerant traveler, traveling all over the world giving workshops on all kinds of subjects.

19

I PERSECUTE MYSELF. NOTHING OUTSIDE ME CAN HURT ME FOR NOTHING IS OUTSIDE ME

Nothing outside me can happen to me unless my mind produced it for there is nothing outside me; it is my mind, thinking, that produced the people and the world I see as outside me.

Nothing outside me can persecute me. I persecute myself; my thinking produced the images of what seem like external, other people persecuting me, doing something to me against my wishes.

I persecute myself with nightmarish dreams of unseen things attacking me; unseen things represent my idea of ghosts, ghosts attacking me, and there are no ghosts except the ones my mind made up to scare me.

I persecute myself during day life by seeming racist discriminators; racists represent my thinking. My fear-based thinking produced those seeming external bad events.

I persecute me and I also save me; my salvation is the product of my corrected thinking; my persecution is the product of my ego- and fear-based thinking.

I produced everything that seems to have happened to me. I projected the world and peopled it with people who seem to do good or bad things to me.

There is no world outside me. The world I see as outside me is my thinking projected out. The external world is the mirror of my thinking.

There is no world outside me. The seemingly external world I see is inside me, that is, is produced by my thinking; outside my thinking, there is no external world, no heaven or hell.

I do everything, good or bad, to me. And the same applies to all people; each of us produced his world with his thinking; we collectively produced what we call the physical universe we live in with our thinking; we do affect each other for we share one self, in heaven and on earth. In fact, we are one self.

You have to accept this philosophy or keep thinking that you are the victim of other people, that you are innocent, and other bad people harm you. There are no other people; all people share one self, the unified son of God who is infinite in numbers.

What one part of that unified son of God thinks and does affect all other parts; this is why you must only have loving thoughts toward all people, for that way, you see other people do loving things to you.

There is no way a son of God, you and I, can be hurt or experience what he does not want to experience, for his mind produced the world he sees.

If you want to experience peace and joy, then love you and all people and forgive those who seem to harm you (you seem to harm yourself through them). Love, and you know peace and joy.

This is the reality of our lives but our egos want us to see ourselves as victims that other people harm.

In the past, Africans captured and sold their people to Arabs and Europeans; in the present, they steal from their people instead of working their little asses off for their people's good, then complain that they are poor, and blame it on Europeans; it is self-evident that they are responsible for their fallen house.

WHEN GODS AND HUMAN BEINGS AGREE

Yesterday, I got done reading Neale Donald Walsh's *Conversations with God*, book two. I found everything he attributed to what his God responded to his questions what I have written about in my countless essays and other writings.

His God's metaphysic is that there is God and he manifests in each of us and that what we do is what God does, is him experiencing himself, albeit egoistically with the goal of remembering that he is God and God is love, hence for us to love one another. It's what I have said in several essays and did not attribute that self-evident conclusion to God.

I know that all matter is formed from light energy, and ultimately, will be reduced back to light energy; our bodies and everything in the universe is disguised light.

During the Big Bang, 13.8 billion years ago, out of nowhere, a point of light came out, exploded, and formed infinite photons, particles of light; those particles formed electrons and quarks and quarks formed protons and neutrons; protons and neutrons combined to form nuclei and over time, the expanding universe of nuclei and electrons combined; nuclei captured electrons to form atoms, hydrogen, and helium, and those formed the early universe. In time, the subsequent cloud of hydrogen experienced space, and each clump was acted on by gravity and in its core, ignition occurred; that is, pressure and high temperature led hydrogen to form helium. In many articles, I elaborated on the nature of nucleosynthesis, the origin of stars, how stars work, age, and explode in supernova and how the expanding universe will end in all stars and planets exploding and returning to photons and those light energy returns to the spiritual energy, spiritual light, from whence they came. Simply put, all things in our world are formed from light energy.

I speculated that light energy came from spiritual light. That hypothesis is not yet proved; it remains a mere belief on my part.

COG's God, for example, wants a one-world government that coordinates the activities of the nations of the world; the world government acting as a kind of central government in a federation with each present national state a constituent state in it, kind of like the United States of the World (USW).

His God wants a government that makes sure that the poor is helped through some social programs and that the capitalist tendency to reward only the rich is obscene. There is no reason why Jeff Bezos of Amazon should have one hundred and forty billion dollars while some Americans make less than forty thousand dollars a year, cannot really live well on that paltry income, and do not have health care.

His God wants health care publicly paid for all people and education publicly paid at all levels for all people. Simply put, his God wants what I want. Both of us agree on the need for a mixed capitalist, socialist economy, and social democracy, kind of like what they have in the Scandinavian countries today, as the way for all mankind to do.

My question is this: what happens when the gods agree with human beings? Does that make what they agree on true?

Jesus of the Bible was clearly a socialist who asked his followers to share their wealth, see his parable of the Good Samaritan, but perverted Christianity wants folks not to care for the poor. There is no such thing as a true Christian church in the contemporary world.

My question is this: what happens when one's political economy is the political economy of a so-called God?

It means that one should simply go ahead and live what makes sense to one. I must live what makes sense to me, what I independently reached as correct approach to life regardless of what other people or God says about it.

One should not seek the validation of other men or God to do what is right, for what is right can be independently ascertained. What is the truth?

The truth is that love is the highest good in our lives; so, love you and love all people and the rest is noise.

I will begin reading *Conversations with God*, book three, sometime this weekend. I hope that this time, it tells me what I do not already know. If it says something new, I will write about it but if not, I will not waste my time writing about it.

AFRICANS, LIKE ALL PEOPLE, EXPERIENCE ONLY WHAT THEY WANT TO EXPERIENCE!

Here is my philosophy: we, the sons of God, experience only what we want to experience, good or bad. It is only if we experience what we want to experience can it be said that the universe is just and that there is a just God.

If it were possible for each of us to experience what he does not want to experience, then the universe is not just and God is not just.

If what I do not like to experience can happen to me against my wishes, the universe is not just and God is not just.

An unjust universe should not exist (see Arthur Schopenhauer's *The World as Will and Idea*); an unjust God must not exist and if he exists, he must be killed (see Frederick Nietzsche's *Thus Spoke Zarathustra*).

It is only if I experience what I want to experience, even if I am not conscious of it, that the universe and its God can be said to be just.

Please take your time to ponder what I just said; chew on it for however long you want to. If it does not make sense to you, then reject it. It makes sense to me and I accept it.

I accept that I experience only what I want to experience, regardless of whether I am consciously aware of wanting to experience it or not. I take ownership of all my experiences.

I also believe that you are responsible for all your experiences.

The difference between us is that I do not blame other people for what happens to me whereas those who believe that what they do not want to experience happen to them against their wishes, blame those they believe did bad things to them.

The ego (our earthly selves) likes to see itself as innocent and see other people as guilty (it projects its guilt feeling for doing this to itself, separating from God and from his true identity as the son of God and causing itself pain and suffering to other persons). The ego does awful things to itself and then blames other people for its suffering.

The ego sees problems in itself but instead of solving them, it wants every person around it to change but not itself. It believes that if other people change and do the right things, that it would live well.

Well, other people do not change and do the right things for the ego; so, it lives its crummy life.

The lesson here is that the world is not going to change for you to live well. Only you have to change for you to live well.

The external world is the outward projection of your and my thinking; the world you see reflects your and our thinking; your thoughts and our thoughts and beliefs produced the world we see.

Since the external world reflects your and my thinking, how is it going to change unless you and all of us change our thinking, our minds?

The world you see cannot change unless you change your thinking; different thinking on your part will produce a different world for you to see but until you have changed your thinking (mind is a euphemism for our thinking, the universe is a thinking universe; there is no concrete and tangible thing called mind existing independent of our thinking).

I am an African; specifically, I am an Igbo. I have traveled all over Western Europe and live in North America. I can tell you that as an African, I am treated differently from the way white folks and Asians are treated.

Whenever I am crossing a border in a western European country, the immigration officers ask me humiliating questions, such as where are you going to stay? Do you have enough money? Normally, I do not respond to their questions for they do not ask white travelers similar questions; they just stamp their passports and let them pass through but the moment they see a black man, they feel that you are a poor man who has come to seek economic refuge in Europe and feel that they must ascertain your monetary status before they let you in.

I am an American citizen and travel with an American passport; I know my rights and if you select me out and ask me racist questions, I do not respond to you. My silence tells you that you have no right to ask those questions and you get it and hand my passport back to me and I am on my way.

I have traveled with Nigerians who travel with Nigerian passports. At border crossings in Europe, they are insulted, mightily. They have to answer all sorts of degrading questions. It does not matter if they are so-called ministers in Nigeria; they are still treated as if they are niggers. The brothers swallow their pride and answer the insulting questions they are asked so as to be allowed in. In some instances, they are not even allowed into some countries. They are perceived as potential thieves coming to rob white folks and kept out.

The world these days associates Nigerians with corruption and the famous 419 scams. Young Nigerians use the internet to scam Americans and Europeans. The line is always the same.

The scammer tells you that he is the son of the president of Nigeria or a Nigerian prince. His father has billions of dollars in Nigeria. He wants to send some of that money to Europe or North America. He asks you to give to him your bank account and he would put that money into your account. If you are dumb enough to fall for his criminal ploy and give him your bank account, he would withdraw all the money in your bank account within minutes and disappear.

Nigerians also scam folks' credit cards. These days, they tell old white ladies that they want to marry them and if those fall for it, they ask for their bank accounts so as to put millions of dollars into them. If those give them their bank accounts, they clean them out.

Some may use the ladies to come to the West and after the two-year probationary period is over and their permanent residency is now permanent, they disappear from the women's lives; they move to other states.

The rate at which Nigerians engage in criminal activity is mind-boggling. If only they put their ingenuity to doing the right things, Nigerians would have been developed.

Most Nigerians are cowards; only cowards steal; courageous people do not steal; courageous people fight for good governance in their country and if necessary, die fighting for it.

Did I hear you say that Nigerians should fight for a clean government in Nigeria? They will not. Like cowards, they are afraid of being killed by the thugs that rule them. The thugs in Nigerian government steal all their people's money; instead of trying to bring about economic and social justice in Nigeria, Nigerian cowards endure their shitty fate and then screw unsuspecting foreigners.

We can generalize and say that most Nigerians are cowards and you had better be cautious when relating to them, for they would scam you in a jiffy and not feel moral qualms; they have no sense of guilt or remorse; they are lacking in social conscience.

The world has a pretty good idea of who Nigerians are and generally treat them as if they are criminals (this, of course, is an overgeneralization; there are decent Nigerians; the human mind is prone to making stereotypes of people; you, too, do make generalizations, don't you; let us not nitpick here; we are all, sometimes, illogical thinkers).

In the white man's world, Africans are considered not intelligent and are the last hired and first fired. They are seldom given responsible positions for folks expect them to steal. Put a Nigerian in your accounting department and he cooks the books and steals your money.

Non-Africans do not respect Africans and Africans know it. But Africans want non-Africans to change and begin respecting them while they, Africans, do not want to change; they want to keep doing what they do, being thieves in governments, and want the rest of the world to change and respect them.

Well, that is not going to happen. The rest of the world would continue seeing Africa, in Donald Trump's colorful language, as a shithole.

Trump believes that Africans are so unintelligent that he does not want them to come to the USA; instead, he wants the whitest of the whites, Scandinavians (Norwegians, Dane, and Swede), to come live in the USA.

Instead of changing, Africans keep being their old corrupt selves and instead, want the rest of the world to change and respect them.

In the past, Africans used to roam around in their continent capturing and selling their people to Arabs and later to Europeans; in the present, their leaders are practically all thieves; instead of correcting these odious behaviors, they want other people to respect them while they remain as they are, lacking in integrity.

The Africa house has collapsed and instead of rebuilding it and in doing so, gain the world's respect, Africans want the rest of the world to respect them despite having corrupt and backward countries.

Africans having made a royal mess of their continent quickly blame the white man for their problems; they know how to talk the politics of neocolonialism and tell you that Europe, the metropolis, the center, steals from the periphery, Africa, and that accounts for their poverty.

Asians used to blame Europeans for their poverty; they have changed their thinking and are now no longer blaming Europeans; they have rolled up their sleeves and developed Asia; most Asian countries are now on par with Europe (GDP speaking).

Africans are still where they were in the 1960s, poor. Blaming others may make you feel good but does not improve your life.

The worse part of the ridiculousness of Africans is that they bought liberal anthropologists' idea of cultural relativism. The idea is that all cultures are good.

The culture that sent a man to the moon is the same as the culture that worships the moon as a God. Thus, primitive Africans keep doing their primitive things that made it possible for a handful of Europeans to colonize them, thinking that they would obtain different results

They say that the definition of insanity is doing the same thing and expecting different results.

It took less than a battalion of British troops, one thousand soldiers, to conquer all of Nigeria. Stop right there and let that sink into your mind. The British easily conquered Nigeria because Nigeria lacked modern science and technology (our ancestors fought the British, their machine, and maxim guns with bows and arrows!).

Common sense would tell Nigerians to embrace science and technology so that no foreigners would easily defeat them. No, they dance around in their primitive cultures and insist that the West embrace the rubbish of multiculturalism.

The culture of Berkeley (University of California), the culture of Westwood (UCLA), the culture of Palo Alto (Stanford), the Culture of Pasadena (Caltech), the culture of Cambridge, Massachusetts (Harvard), the culture of New Heaven (Yale), the culture of Oxford and Cambridge is superior to the culture of my hometown, Owerri.

Around these great universities of the world, you find teenagers talking abstract physics, astrophysics, chemistry, and biology but at Owerri, you find young people talking rubbish about cults, about how to use talisman to become rich.

Elsewhere, I wrote about scientific culture as a replacement culture for African cultures. I do not like African cultures because they are pre-scientific and preliterate and made it easy for us to be defeated by white folks.

Scientific culture is predicated on the scientific method; here, every human behavior is based on observation, and only the verifiable are embraced; logical positivism and empiricism is the philosophy of science.

DISCUSSION

Over time, it gradually dawned on me that I experience only what I want to experience. Nothing that I do not like to experience ever happens to me and if it did, I experience it in my own way.

The world we see as outside us is the product of our individual and collective thinking. I do think; you do think; our mutual thinking produced the world we see.

We do affect each other with our thinking and behaviors. Therefore, we had better improve our thoughts so as to produce a positive world.

Please note that science and technology are based on our thinking. It is our thinking that enables us to observe how nature works and design technologies to adapt to it.

If you are experiencing a negative world, please know that it reflects your negative thinking. You may deny this fact all you want but the fact is that you experience only what your thinking produced.

Africans experience a negative world because their thinking is mostly negative: how to steal, not how to love and work for our collective social interests.

In the USA, there is racism. Racism is the belief by white folks that they are superior to black folks. They treat black folks as if they are not human beings, as if they are animals who ought to exist to be their slaves and servants but not their equals.

Due to racism, employers do not hire black folks for good jobs. White policemen, who are mostly anti-social personality disordered, sociopaths, and psychopaths, enjoy beating up and killing black folks and do not feel that they did wrong in killing blacks.

At the moment, we are talking about the psychopath called Derick Chauvin kneeling on the neck of a black man (who worked in the same night club that Chauvin works at as a security guard) and killed him; George Floyd was murdered in broad daylight.

This kind of thing happens all the time in the USA. White police came into being during slavery times; their jobs were to keep blacks as slaves and kill them if they stepped out of line.

White judges exist to punish black folks, put them in jails and prisons. The fate of the black man in the contemporary world is crummy.

The black man knows that all the other races, such as whites, Arabs, Asians, and Native Americans consider him an inferior being hence want to treat him as garbage.

I know how white folks see me; they see me as inferior to them. I am not in the business of denial and deluding me with what is not true as true; I deal with reality as I see it.

The question is: what am I doing about it? I am an ego. As an ego, I want white folks to change and treat me better while I remain as I am that makes them see me as worthy of disrespect. I do not want to change so that other people would treat me differently.

If black folks study science and technology and modernize Africa, as Asians have done, white folks, Asians, and Arabs would respect them. But, no, African politicians see public offices as from where they steal and do not care for their people. Africa is thief land. The people are so corrupt that it is not funny.

So, you remain shiftless Nigerian politicians and want the rest of the world to respect you, eh? They will not respect you; human beings respect those who do the right things.

In as much as Africans do not do the right things that would get the people to respect them and they keep doing the wrong things and people keep disrespecting them, there is only one logical conclusion left for us: Africans want to be disrespected by the rest of the world.

Africans, in effect, are experiencing what they want to experience: universal contempt. All humanity sees Africans as shit, literally.

Yet, Africans do shitty things that dispose other people to see them as shit. Thus, logically speaking, Africans want to be disrespected.

Being thieves and wanting to be respected is not logical. If you are a thief, people will not respect you and should not respect you.

If Africans want to be respected, they just have to start doing the right things, such as governing Africa well.

I can just see some Africans saying that I am blaming the victim, not the victimizer, white folks. You are free to take that posture. How has it helped you, if I may ask?

You blame white folks for your shitty house, make their liberals feel guilty and out of guilt, they give you some economic aid and you steal it instead of using it to develop your country.

In the meantime, your lack of development makes white conservatives like Donald Trump to see you as unintelligent and only fit to serve them.

CONCLUSION

What I presented in this essay is a philosophy, my philosophy; I live it. Consider it; but if you prefer to see yourself as a victim to whom other people do bad things and you suffer and blame them, keep doing so.

We are thinkers; the world we experience reflects our thinking. We are the parts of a thinking universe (sons of God. God is the thinking universe; he is not a person).

Our thoughts produced this universe and when we change our thinking, we produce a different universe.

Argue with me all you like; the fact is that you are the one who produces the shitty world that you live in—Africa; blame white folks all you want and you would still live in the cesspool called Africa.

You stop living in shit when you think correctly, when you love yourself, love your people, and do science and technology, that serves the public good.

Please become realistic and do what Asians did. Asians, such as the Chinese and Japanese used to have elaborated native clothing. They have mostly given those up and are now found in Western business suits for those are more conducive to the world of science and technology they want to live in.

Nigerians must discard the agbada they wear for those are more appropriate for Arab Middle Ages society, not for the modern industrial and scientific world.

Now, go ahead and tell me that I hate me and that I hate Africa and like to be white-like. I have heard that nonsense from many Africans.

Do you know what self-love is? Do you know what it means to have positive self-esteem? If you like you, you must love those around you, and in Alfred Adler's psychological categories, serve social interests and work for the people.

You cannot remain a self-centered neurotic while talking jazz about someone else having low self-esteem and hating himself.

Please stop projecting what you see in you, dislike of Africa, and deny it, to those who insist on stating the truth as they see it, and if that means saying that Africans are backward, they say it.

I eschew political correctness and say it as I see it, not what would please African egos and make them seem perfect while they do imperfect things, such as stealing from their people and not working hard to develop Africa.

Whereas I do not want to dwell on Europeans and other groups, let me just say that like Africans, they are experiencing what they want to experience. Whatever you see them experience is what they want to experience.

If white folks are abusive and oppressive of Africans, that is what they want to experience for there is no way that they can experience what they do not want to experience.

Like Africans they, too, are taking the negative consequences of their lack of love-based thinking and behaviors: their hate-based civilization is on its last legs before it collapses and Asians take over the ruling of the world.

Africans' turn to rule the world is in the future when they have put their house in order; we are talking hundreds of years in the future.

PS: The philosophy expressed in this essay is similar to Dr. Helen Schucman's philosophy in *A Course in Miracles*.

CHRISTIAN LEADERSHIP AND MANAGEMENT MANIFESTO

INTRODUCTION

Two thousand years ago, a man called Jesus appeared in Israel. He had experienced God and shared his experience with the people around him. Not one of them understood what he was telling them. Instead, they taught ego gospels in place of the Christ gospel he taught them.

That message got to Europe and was totally distorted and called Catholicism and Christianity. There has never been a true Christian church in Europe or anywhere else in the world.

Professor Helen Schucman, a clinical psychologist and poet, rendered the true teaching of Jesus Christ in poetic form in her book on spiritual psychology, *A Course in Miracles*. She correctly articulated the teaching of Jesus Christ. However, her writing was done in Shakespearean verse and is difficult for folks to understand. I have understood the message of the Holy Spirit and Jesus Christ. With the help of other persons, we form an organization dedicated to teaching and learning about the Christ self.

We form Christ based-organizations, Christian organizations led by Christ-like people. We teach Christian leadership and management styles, not the egoistic leadership and management styles found in the extant world.

Each of us has a self, in heaven and on earth. One always has a self. If one has no self, the universe would not exist for one. Rene Descartes said, cogito ergo sum. Properly understood, he is saying that without the self, the universe does not exist. Who is to know about the universe if there is no self? An unknown universe does not exist.

In heaven, unified spirit, each of us has a self. That spirit self knows itself to be one with the infinite selves created by God. That heavenly self knows itself to be the same and coequal with all selves.

The heavenly formless unified selves subsequently desired to have ego separated selves. Please listen. The difference between the self of heaven and the self of the ego is that the self of heaven is unified with all selves and is not proud and arrogant; the self of the ego is the self that wishes for specialness, pride, vanity, and separation.

The ego is a symbol of arrogance, specialness, pride, and separation. The ego is the opposite of the humbled and unified spirit selves of heaven.

The special ego-self seems to have separated from God and invented the world of space, time, and matter we seem to be living in. That world is not real. It does not exist. It is a dream that seems to exist for the children of God seeking specialness and separation.

It does not exist but that is the self and its world we find ourselves in. God takes his children where they think that they are. He teaches them how to return to the awareness of their true selves, Christ selves.

The Holy Spirit is the agent for that teaching. Jesus listened completely to the Holy Spirit; he learned the lesson of the Holy Spirit, gave up thinking and behaving from the ego, and now lives through the Holy Spirit (whole spirit, meaning God, for God is the whole and we, his, sons are his parts).

The Hindu mystic, Ramana Maharshi, understood the message of the Holy Spirit clearly. He distinguished between the unified self of God (the I of God); the self of the son of God (the I of the sons of God, aka Atman); and the self of the ego (the I of the ego separated self). His whole message is to get Hindus to jettison the self of the ego and return to the self of the Son of God (Atman, Christ), and in so doing, experience the unified self of God and its peace and joy, bliss.

We continue the message of the Holy Spirit and Christ through our Christian organizations and Christian leadership and management styles.

The Christian leader leads from the Christ in him; that is, he is egoless. He does not think or behave from ego but from the Holy Spirit; in real terms, this means that he does whatever he does to serve the public good. He does not just talk about it, talk is easy, but lives it.

The Christian leader and manager model Christ living. In his presence, you feel his lack of ego and his peace and joy.

LEADERS BRIEFLY DEFINED

In the simplest terms, leaders are persons who see a problem in their world and want to solve it. They may try solving it individually or with other persons.

Generally, most problems can only be solved by many people working together. Thus, you need human organizations to solve problems.

Leaders organize people; they bring people together to solve problems. They must have good interpersonal relationship skills to be able to put together teams aimed at solving a problem.

Problems are solved not only with people's efforts but with other resources, such as money and equipment.

For example, if you perceive the issue of illiteracy in your community, you know that it takes people and money to solve it. You have to get the teachers to teach the students. You have to obtain the money with which you pay the teachers. You have to build schools where students are taught. You need classroom equipment such as teachers' desks, students' chairs and desks; you need chalkboards and books for the students; you need a school library or reading room; you need information technology, such as personal computers. There are many things needed to have a full functioning school in place.

Leaders are people who see a problem, study it, and come up with plans on how to solve it. They gather people and the capital necessary for solving the identified problem.

Leaders coordinate and monitor the activities of those solving the perceived problem and make sure that all of them work toward attaining their set goals.

Leaders must be good at gathering human resources and capital for their projects. Where and how you obtain the funds needed to achieve the goals and objectives of the organization is part of the functions of leaders.

Leaders are problem-solvers; they are people who see a problem and are self-motivated to solve it (they don't wait for other persons to tell them to solve the identified problem) with human beings and materials.

CHRISTIANITY SUMMARIZED

Let us begin by saying that Jesus did not call himself Christ. Some people at Antioch, Syria, during the first century of our common era, saw how the followers of Jesus lived their lives, serving each other's needs, and concluded that their leader must be truly the anointed son of God. Christ is the anointed son of God.

Jesus taught in parables. In the parable of the Good Samaritan, he described what he expects his followers' behaviors to be like. That parable essentially defines a Christian's behavior. A Christian loves and cares for his fellow human beings.

The Parable of the Good Samaritan: Luke 10: 25–37 ESV (English Standard Version)

[25] And behold, a lawyer stood up to put him to the test, saying, "Teacher, what shall I do to inherit eternal life?" [26] He said to him, "What is written in the Law? How do you read it?" [27] And he answered, "You shall love the Lord your God with all your heart and with all your soul and with all your strength and with your entire mind, and your neighbor as yourself." [28] And he said to him, "You have answered correctly; do this, and you will live."

[29] But he, desiring to justify himself, said to Jesus, "And who is my neighbor?" [30] Jesus replied, "A man was going down from Jerusalem to Jericho, and he fell among robbers, who stripped him and beat him and departed, leaving him half dead. [31] Now by chance a priest was going down that road, and when he saw him he passed by on the other side. [32] So likewise a Levite, when he came to the place and saw him, passed by on the other side. [33] But a Samaritan, as he journeyed, came to where he was, and when he saw him, he had compassion. [34] He went to him and bound up his wounds, pouring on oil and wine. Then he set him on his own animal and brought him to an inn and took care of him. [35] And the next day he took out two denarii[a] and gave them to the innkeeper, saying,

'Take care of him, and whatever more you spend, I will repay you when I come back.' ³⁶ Which of these three, do you think, proved to be a neighbor to the man who fell among the robbers?" ³⁷ He said, "The one who showed him mercy." And Jesus said to him, "You go, and do likewise."

To be a Christian is to follow the path of the anointed son of God. One must, therefore, understand who the anointed son of God is.

At the beginning of his ministry, Jesus called himself the son of man; later, he called himself the son of God. From the moment he called himself the son of God, his behavior changed. He no longer thought and behaved like an ordinary human being. He now thought and behaved like a human being led by the Holy Spirit. In effect, a son of man behaves like ordinary human beings; a son of God, while on earth, is led by the Holy Spirit. The Holy Spirit asks those he leads to forgive and love all people.

Jesus was led by the Holy Spirit for a while but when eventually he merged his human self with God, he became the Christ and did what the Holy Spirit did for those still living as human beings.

Christ is the human being who lives as the son of God and as his father created him, not as the ego separated self he made for himself.

The ego separated self is the old man, the man born on earth. That old man, the old human self, mostly looks after his self-interests and grudgingly cooperates with other people to serve their mutual interests.

When the old self dies, a new self is born in one; the new-self lives as Christ, the son of God who is as God created him, and thinks and behaves as God does, that is, loves all creation and its creator. The new self, the Christ self, a Christian, now lives to serve all selves in a new world, a world led by Christ.

He now lives in what traditional Christians, interpreting Revelation of John, expect to be called new Jerusalem or new Israel; a world ruled by Christ, not by the ego-self.

Romans 6:4–6 New International Versions (NIV)

"⁴ We were therefore buried with him through baptism into death in order that, just as Christ was raised from the dead through the glory of the Father, we too may live a new life.

⁵ For if we have been united with him in a death like his, we will certainly also be united with him in a resurrection like his. ⁶ For we know that our old self was crucified with him so that the body ruled by sin might be done away with, [a] that we should no longer be slaves to sin."

Revelation 21:19-21 New International Version (NIV)

"¹⁹ The foundations of the city walls were decorated with every kind of precious stone. The first foundation was jasper, the second sapphire, the third agate, the fourth emerald, ²⁰ the fifth onyx, the sixth ruby, the seventh chrysotile, the eighth beryl, the ninth topaz, the tenth turquoise, the eleventh jacinth, and the twelfth amethyst.[a] ²¹ The twelve gates were twelve pearls, each gate made of a single pearl. The great street of the city was of gold, as pure as transparent glass."

Traditional Christians believe that the new self and new world would come into being when this world ends. They expect Jesus to come down from heaven to rule the saved people who now live in the new world (also called new Jerusalem or new Israel).

The old self lived in the city of man; the new-self lives in the city of God.

The new self begins any day when one decides to give one's life to Christ; that is, the day one decides to live as Christ, as exemplified by Jesus.

If one voluntarily allows one's old, separated ego-self to die and the Christ self to be born in one, Christ has come a second time into one's life.

Christ was first born in one when God created one, when God extended himself to his son. One then lived in union with God (in heaven).

Christ died in one when one decided to separate from God and go live as a separated self. Christ died when the prodigal son left his father to go on a journal to a faraway land.

The Parable of the Prodigal Son (Luke 15: 11–32, ESV)

¹¹ And he said, "There was a man who had two sons. ¹² And the younger of them said to his father, 'Father, give me the share of property that is coming to me.' And he divided his property between them. ¹³ Not many days later, the younger son gathered all he had and took a journey into a far country, and there he squandered his property in reckless living. ¹⁴ And when he had spent everything, a severe famine arose in that country, and he began to be in need. ¹⁵ So he went and hired himself out to[a] one of the citizens of that country, who sent him into his fields to feed pigs. ¹⁶ And he was longing to be fed with the pods that the pigs ate, and no one gave him anything.

¹⁷ "But when he came to himself, he said, 'How many of my father's hired servants have more than enough bread, but I perish here with hunger! ¹⁸ I will arise and go to my father, and I will say to him, "Father, I

have sinned against heaven and before you. ¹⁹ I am no longer worthy to be called your son. Treat me as one of your hired servants.'" ²⁰ And he arose and came to his father. But while he was still a long way off, his father saw him and felt compassion, and ran and embraced him and kissed him. ²¹ And the son said to him, 'Father, I have sinned against heaven and before you. I am no longer worthy to be called your son.'[b] ²² But the father said to his servants,[c] 'Bring quickly the best robe, and put it on him, and put a ring on his hand, and shoes on his feet. ²³ And bring the fattened calf and kill it, and let us eat and celebrate. ²⁴ For this my son was dead, and is alive again; he was lost, and is found.' And they began to celebrate.

²⁵ "Now his older son was in the field, and as he came and drew near to the house, he heard music and dancing. ²⁶ And he called one of the servants and asked what these things meant. ²⁷ And he said to him, 'Your brother has come, and your father has killed the fattened calf, because he has received him back safe and sound.' ²⁸ But he was angry and refused to go in. His father came out and entreated him, ²⁹ but he answered his father, 'Look, these many years I have served you, and I never disobeyed your command, yet you never gave me a young goat, that I might celebrate with my friends. ³⁰ But when this son of yours came, who has devoured your property with prostitutes, you killed the fattened calf for him!' ³¹ And he said to him, 'Son, you are always with me, and all that is mine is yours. ³² It was fitting to celebrate and be glad, for this your brother was dead, and is alive; he was lost, and is found.'"

The prodigal son finally judged the old self and the old world as not good and constructed a new self for him self, a new self living in a new world, a world where we serve each other's needs. Thus, the second coming of Christ and the day of last judgment happens for each of us when we accept Christ as our real self; it does not happen in a day in the future for all of us at the same time.

THE LAST JUDGMENT AND THE SECOND COMING OF CHRIST

Jesus and his apostles spoke of the coming of a final judgment in Matt. 25:31–46; Rom. 2:5–10; 2Cor. 5:10. 2Tim. 4:1; 1Pet. 4:5; Rev. 20:11–14.

Jesus made several references to a future time when Christ comes to judge the people of the earth. * For example, Matthew 25:31–33 says:

"When the Son of man [Jesus Christ] *comes* in his glory, and all the angels with him, then he will sit down on his glorious throne. All the nations will be gathered before him, and he will separate people one from another, just as a shepherd separates the sheep from the goats. And he will put the sheep on his right hand, but the goats on his left."

This time of judgment will be part of a "great tribulation" unlike anything in human history. That tribulation will culminate in the war of Armageddon. (Matthew 24:21; Revelation 16:16) Christ's enemies, described in his illustration as goats, "will undergo the judicial punishment of everlasting destruction." (2 Thessalonians 1:9; Revelation 19:11, 15) In contrast, his faithful servants, the sheep, will have the prospect of "everlasting life."—Matthew 25:46.

Jesus said: "Concerning that day and hour nobody knows." (Matthew 24:36, 42; 25:13) However, he did describe a visible, composite "sign" that would identify the period leading up to his coming.—Matthew 24:3, 7–14; Luke 21:10, 11."

LEAVING GOD

To be on planet earth, each of us left his status as the son of God. In heaven, we are all the sons of God. As sons of God, we are one with God and each other. There is no space and time between God and his sons. God and his sons are unified as one shared self and one shared mind. There is no space and gap between God and any of his sons.

God is in his sons and his sons are in God and in each other; where God ends and his son and sons begin is nowhere. God and his infinite sons shared one unified spirit self. They begin and end nowhere.

God and his sons are formless; that is, they are not in matter, space, and time; they are intangible pure intelligence that cannot be touched. They are everywhere. Where God ends and his sons begin is nowhere; they are in each other.

To be in each other, they must be formless, the same, and equal. The only difference between God and his sons is that he created them and they did not create him or create themselves.

God created each son by extending his already existing self into the son of God. All of God is now in his son. God gave his son his creative power so that each son of God also extends the God in him and himself to other sons of God. That way, creation begins in God and extends to infinity. Creation is always taking place. There is no end to creation by God and his sons.

God is one force that extends to each of his sons and gives his sons his creative power so that each son of God extends to other sons of God.

Creation begins in God and extends outward forever; there is no time when creation is not taking place.

GOD AS SPIRITUAL LIGHT AND EACH OF HIS SONS A PARTICLES OF THAT LIGHT

Although God is not in physical form and cannot be imaged, for the sake of understanding, we can visualize God as one wave of spiritual light that begins nowhere and ends nowhere. That wave of light has infinite particles of light in it.

Wave and particles are the same; they share one self. In their eternally joined state and unity, they are harmonious and in peace and happiness, in bliss.

SPECIALNESS: THE DESIRE TO REPLACE GOD AS CREATOR OF THE UNIVERSE

The following story of the origin of the physical universe is taken from Helen Schucman's book, *A Course in Miracles*. It is a mythology but essentially states the truth that cannot be expressed in words.

This myth of creation and separation says that at some time, a time that has not occurred, the sons of God decided to separate from their father and from each other.

The motivation for this wish for separation is the sons' wish to seem special. By that is meant each son's wish to create his father, create his bothers, and create himself.

The sons of God, in effect, wanted to chase their father away from his creatorship throne and sit on it; they wanted to replace God as the creator of the universe.

God's universe is the universe of spirit; it is a union of joined spirits, a universe of perfect equality and sameness.

Each son of God is like other sons of God; his thinking is open to other sons of God to know what he is thinking. There was no hiding of one's thinking from other sons of God and from God.

Then the sons of God had the desire to seem special and separated from their father and from each other. In reality, the parts cannot separate from the whole; the sons of God cannot separate from their father and from each other because their father is in them and they are in their father and in each other.

Separation from the whole is impossible; if it were possible, the parts and the whole, sons of God and their father, would cease existing.

Existence is only possible because of the eternal union of the parts and the whole, the sons of God and their father.

Wherever the sons of God are is their father; wherever they go, they go with their father in them. There is no journey that the sons of God will undertake without taking their father with them. Thus, the journey to planet earth is a journey without distance for the sons of God while on earth are still in God; they brought God with them to earth (God is now hidden from their awareness; this is because they are now sleeping and not awake).

Unable to separate from their father and go seem superior to him and to each other, as it were, the sons of God cast a magical spell (Hinduism calls it Maya) on themselves, and seem to have gone to sleep.

In their sleep, they dream that they have separated from their father and from each other.

They cannot separate from their father; they merely sleep and dream and in their dream, see themselves as separated from their father; they see themselves as on planet earth. They can awaken from that sleep-dream and know that even when they thought that they were on earth, they were in God, in unified spirit state, in heaven.

THE BIG BANG 13.8 BILLION YEARS AGO/ORIGIN OF SEPARATION FROM THE WHOLE

To make separation seem possible, in their sleep-dream state, they invented a universe that opposes the unified universe of God.

God's universe is a universe of bodiless and formless spirits that are in each other.

The sons of God invented the universe of space, time, and matter. In the story of the Big Bang that supposedly took place 13.8 billion years ago, the sons of God invented physical light and transformed that light to electrons and quarks; they transformed quarks to protons and neutrons.

They also invented anti-electrons, anti-quarks, anti-protons, and anti-neutrons; collectively, they invented matter and anti-matter.

Matter and anti-matter were supposed to be the same in quantity and when they attacked each other, ought to have annihilated each other and returned the universe to radiation, hot light. Instead, there was more matter than anti-matter so that when the attack occurred, some matter remained to continue our matter-based universe.

The incipient universe expanded at what Allan Goth called inflationary speed, speed greater than the speed of light); light's speed is 182, 282 miles per second. That inflationary speed prevented the early universe from collapsing back to itself and aborting the universe.

Apparently, something planned for the existence of matter-based universe was at work right from the beginning of the universe and through the universe's evolution to the present; if you think about it, as Stephen Hawkins said, the universe ought to not exist.

The series of seeming accidents that made the existence of the universe possible is called anthropoid accidents.

The inventors of the universe (sons of God) unified protons and neutrons to form nuclei (and hold them together with the strong nuclear force).

Over time, they had electrons circle nuclei. Thus, they formed atoms. When nuclei captured electrons and formed atoms, light was liberated from the initial plasma universe. That light, now called Cosmic, Background Microwave radiation, was seen in 1965 by Robert Wilson and Arno Penzias.

It was from this microwave radiation that George Gamow's hypothesis that the universe began in an explosion was verified. Prior to Gamow, George Lemaitre had also speculated that the universe began in one place, what he called the cosmic egg. Alexander Friedmann and Edwin Hubble, in the 1920s, posited that the universe is expanding.

The initial atoms or elements were mostly hydrogen and helium.

The sons of God used the atoms they invented, especially the lightest atoms (hydrogen and helium) to invent stars.

NUCLEOSYNTHESIS

As the universe expanded, the ocean of hydrogen that was everywhere separated into clumps. Each clump was acted on by gravity; that is, pressured inward; in its center, hydrogen fused to helium and star is born. This process of fusing hydrogen to helium, initially discovered by Fred Hoyle, is called nucleosynthesis.

Stars are oceans of hydrogen that gravity acts on and pushes inward and in their cores, pressure and heat lead to ignition; that is, fusion occurs; hydrogen fuses to helium and generates heat and light.

That light gradually travels from the core of stars, reaches the surface, and escapes as the light we identify as coming from stars.

The initial stars were massive in size. Those massive stars did not live long; they quickly exhausted their hydrogen and began fusing other elements.

When the nucleosynthesis process reaches iron, the stars enlarge, become very hot, and explodes in supernova.

SUPERNOVA, NEBULA, BLACK HOLES, NEUTRON STARS

Some of the cores of exploded huge stars collapse to form black holes; a black hole exists where not even light can escape from its event horizon.

Some star cores collapse and crush all elements to neutrons to form neutron stars; neutron stars spin at incredible rate.

There are many types of stars, including binary stars, red giants, white dwarf stars, quasars, pulsars, and so on.

Stars group themselves into galaxies. Today, there are an estimated 200 billion galaxies; each galaxy is estimated to contain, at least, 200 billion stars.

Around some stars are planets, asteroids, and comets. On an insignificant star system, solar, at the tail end of a spiral galaxy, Milky Way, where it is neither too hot nor too cold, the goldilocks section, biological life sprang up.

SUPERNOVA AND FORMATION OF ELEMENTS BEYOND IRON

In the heat of supernova explosion, all other elements on chemistry's periodic table, beyond iron, are formed.

There are 92 naturally occurring elements in the universe, from the lightest, hydrogen, to the heaviest, uranium (scientists have formed about twenty elements; those quickly decay).

THE ELEMENTS

An element is distinguished from others by the number of electrons, protons, and neutrons in it. In hydrogen, for example, is one electron and one proton (isotopes of hydrogen have one or two neutrons); in helium are two electrons, two protons, and two neutrons; in carbon are six protons, six neutrons, and six electrons; in oxygen are eight protons, eight neutrons, and eight electrons; you go down the periodic table until you reach the heaviest element, uranium, with 92 electrons, ninety-two protons, and one hundred and forty-six neutrons.

Most elements have isotopes, meaning that they may have more neutrons than protons.

NEBULA; STARDUST

The elements spilled out during supernova form nebulae (stardust). In time, that stardust aggregates into medium-sized stars, planets, asteroids, and comets.

Our sun, solar, and its nine planets, asteroids, and comets (Mercury, Venus, Earth, Mars, Jupiter, Saturn, Uranus, Neptune, Pluto) were formed four and half billion years ago from exploded massive stars.

COMETS BROUGHT WATER TO EARTH.

On planet earth, water was brought by comets; the initially hot earth was cooled by that water. The earth's surface is now covered by 70% water.

Water is composed of two atoms of hydrogen and one atom of oxygen.

EVOLUTION OF BIOLOGICAL LIVES ON PLANET EARTH

In the waters on earth, sixty-four elements (primarily carbon, hydrogen, oxygen, nitrogen, copper, calcium, iron, magnesium, zinc, sodium, potassium, magnesium, phosphor, chlorine, and other elements) mixed to form the basis of biological life forms.

Apparently, heat brought by lighting acted on the water containing the sixty-four elements and made them combine to form the basis of biological life (amino acids, fats, and minerals).

Plants and animals formed in the waters on earth. The initial plants and animals were single-celled. They gradually combined to multi-celled plants and animals.

In time, some of the plants and animals left the waters and became land plants and animals. Over time, the animals evolved from single-celled animals to multi-celled animals.

Evolution continued until about two million years ago when bipedal, humanoid animals were formed in East Africa.

Homo sapiens evolved into what we now call human beings. About 100,000 years ago, they began to spread from Africa to the rest of the world. They spread to Europe, Asia, and crossed from Asia to the Americas, and crossed from India to Australia and the Pacific islands. Thus, today, the earth is covered by homo-sapiens. There are billions of them on earth.

So far, we have not been able to discover life on the other planets around our sun or on faraway exoplanets.

GOVERNMENTS

Human animals live in groups; they are social beings. Since they live in groups, their behaviors affect each other, for good or bad. To reduce their harmful effects on each other, Thomas Hobbes (in his 1651 book, *Leviathan*), rationalizes, that they formed governments.

Governments are mandated by the people to make laws that protect all the people in a human polity.

WORK ORGANIZATIONS

People have different skills. Each of them is good at doing certain things and not others. They therefore produced different goods and services.

Initially, they bartered their goods and services and eventually devised monetary means for exchanging goods and services.

A sells to B what he produces and B sells to A what he produces. That way, they meet their mutual needs.

LEADERSHIP AND MANAGEMENT IN LARGE ORGANIZATIONS

In small business activities, folks did not really need the function of specialized managers to coordinate their activities.

In time, small-scale societies gave way to large-scale societies. Cities were formed. In cities, people must come together to do certain things together for their mutual benefit. It is no longer enough for each person to go his separate way and produce simple goods and barter or sell it to other people. Now, they must work together.

When people work together to produce goods or services, they must coordinate their productive behaviors.

Leadership and management come into more pronounced play when large-scale work organizations came into being.

Organizations are aggregations of people that pursue the attainment of stated goals. People come together and coordinate their activities so that their work leads to the achievement of their organizational goals.

Leaders are people who help to set organizational goals and help people to work together, to coordinate their activities so that they do what attains their organizational goals.

Managers may not have helped establish work organizations' goals but they internalize organizational goals and help attain them as if they are their personal goals.

IS LEADERSHIP INHERITED OR LEARNED?

Some say that leadership skills are inherited and others say that they are learned. It is both inherited and learned.

There are those who even as children have more ability to initiate social activities and coordinate the activities of many people to attain group goals.

Some kids would go get a ball and get other kids to play with them. They would assign positions to the players and they play and win or lose.

Other kids learn organizational skills. Let us not quibble about whether leadership and management skills are learned or not; they are both inherited and learned.

DEPARTMENTALIZATION

Our modern world work organizations are huge affairs; those who start work organizations have to coordinate the activities of many persons needed to achieve organizational goals.

Thus, we now have within work organizations, those who specialize in general management (CEOs); those who specialize in getting money for the business organization (finance); those who keep financial records (accountants); those who market what the business produces (marketing and sells); those who produce what the organization produces (productions management); those who hire, train, and fire people (human resources); those who are responsible for the businesses contracts (lawyers); those who are responsible for the relationship of labor and management (labor relations); those who are responsible for information technology (computers, e-commerce); and assorted other workers, such as clerical workers who keep records and technical workers.

The modern business organization is a complex organization where you find many people with different skills working together, all of them coordinated by leaders and managers (managers are specialized leaders in each of the departments of the organization).

If your studies included having a Master of Business Administration, you probably understand how to manage and perhaps lead modern business organizations.

What Christian leadership and management principles add to your basic skills set is that it provides you with a Christian guidepost, a road map on how to lead and manage people with Christ-based ideas.

SEPARATED EGO AND UNIFIED SELF

Jesus was a human being, a separated ego, who while on earth realized that he is really not separated from his father and brothers. He knew that in spirit, they remain unified. They are eternally in unified spirit state. But in their present mental awareness, they seem separated.

Now, they are separated and living in bodies; each of them has the illusion that he should work only for his separated self and its different interests.

How can these separated selves pursuing different interests live and work together? Christian leadership teaches people that whereas it seems that they are separated, in fact, they are unified and have to transcend their separated egos and their self-centered motivations.

People have to see themselves as a collective whole and work for the collective, for organizations, the group of human beings, and the business organization.

Each member of the business organization must be trained to see the organization's goal as his personal goal and work toward its attainment in a selfless manner (if what the organization exists to do does not appeal to him, he does not have to work for that specific work organization, but as long as he undertakes to work for it, he must work selflessly).

The employee must transcend his self-centered tendency to work for the separated self alone. He must now, in Alfred Adler's psychological terms, work for group, social interests.

The worker must work to attain organizational goals; he must be selfless in his work; he must get along with other people; he must quit hiding his ego to go seem special and separated from other workers; he must be open to his fellow workers so that they know what each other is thinking and doing; he must reduce or eliminate his separated ego (reduce his egoism).

In eliminating his ego or no longer defending it, he feels less fear; actually, he may attain a state of fearlessness; if one entirely gives up one's desire for special separated ego-self, one no longer gives in to fear and anger.

Egoless people do not easily give in to anger, depression, paranoia, and other emotional disorders for those arise when folks are working toward ego separated interests, not when they work for unified goals.

THERE IS GOD AND WE ARE HIS SONS.

Christian leadership and management principles accept that there is God and that God is not external to us; he is in us as part of our higher self.

Each of us is a son of God, an extension of God. We cannot use our ego separated minds to understand the nature of unified spirit selves.

Speech and language are designed to help those in the world of separation to communicate with each other.

In God's unified state, all of us know what each of us is thinking for our minds are open to each other; there is no hiding from each other.

OUR NATURE IS LOVE.

Whereas we cannot possibly understand the nature of God with our earthly minds, we can understand that love is the glue that unifies God and his sons together.

God is love. God's sons are love. Love is union. Therefore, if you are in your right mind, you must love yourself and love all people.

THE HOLY SPIRIT AND FORGIVENESS

On earth, since we do harm each other, love entails forgiving those who harmed us. We must, however, attempt to correct each other's harmful behaviors.

Forgiving wrongdoers does not mean allowing folks to murder other folks, or for folks to rape others, or for pedophiles to rape children.

Those who engage in antisocial behaviors must be arrested by the police, tried at courts of law, and punished (sent to jails and prisons).

Nevertheless, we must try as humanely as possible to forgive each other. We must not bear grudges and grievances and seek vengeance and revenge for wrongs done to us.

We must attempt to correct wrongs and then continue loving each other. Christian leadership and management principles require us to live as Jesus did: love one another and do unto one another as we want them to do to us.

Each of us wants to be loved and cared for by other people; we must, therefore, love and care for other people.

Jesus Christ taught his disciples to forgive one another. One of his disciples asked him how many times they should forgive those who wronged them. He said seventy times seventy times, meaning, infinite.

He followed that teaching up with other examples. And they brought a woman caught in adultery to him and asked him what to do to her. He asked for anyone who has not sinned to be the first to throw a stone at the sinful woman. All had sinned and thus, left the woman alone. He told the woman to go home but to sin no more. That is, we must forgive those who wronged us.

Moses taught punishment for sins (hence the Old Testament) but Jesus taught forgiveness of sins (hence the New Testament).

Jesus asked his followers to turn the other cheek to be slapped when one side is slapped. He told them to give their entire clothes to the thief who demands their jacket.

The Adulterous Woman (John 8: 1–11; New American Standard Bible, NASB)

8 But Jesus went to the Mount of Olives. ² Early in the morning He came again into the temple, and all the people were coming to Him; and He sat down and *began* to teach them. ³ The scribes and the Pharisees *brought a woman caught in adultery, and having set her in the center *of the court*, ⁴ they *said to Him, "Teacher, this woman has been caught in adultery, in the very act. ⁵ Now in the Law Moses commanded us to stone such women; what then do You say?" ⁶ They were saying this, testing Him, so that they might have grounds for accusing Him. But Jesus stooped down and with His finger wrote on the ground. ⁷ But when they persisted in asking Him, He straightened up, and said to them, "He who is without sin among you, let him *be the* first to throw a stone at her." ⁸ Again He stooped down and wrote on the ground. ⁹ When they heard it, they *began* to go out one by one, beginning with the older ones, and He was left alone, and the woman, where she was, in the center *of the court*. ¹⁰ Straightening up, Jesus said to her, "Woman, where are they? Did no one condemn you?" ¹¹ She said, "No one, [a]Lord." And Jesus said, "I do not condemn you, either. Go. From now on sin no more."]

The Parable of the Unforgiving Servant (Mathew 18: 21–35, ESV)

21Then Peter came up and said to him, "Lord, how often will my brother sin against me, and I forgive him? As many as seven times?" 22Jesus said to him, "I do not say to you seven times, but seventy-seven times. 23"Therefore the kingdom of heaven may be compared to a king who wished to settle accounts with his servants.ᵍ 24When he began to settle, one was brought to him who owed him ten thousand talents.ʰ 25And since he could not pay, his master ordered him to be sold, with his wife and children and all that he had, and payment to be made. 26So the servantⁱ fell on his knees, imploring him, 'Have patience with me, and I will pay you everything.' 27And out of pity for him, the master of that servant released him and forgave him the debt. 28But when that same servant went out, he found one of his fellow servants who owed him a hundred denarii,ʲ and seizing him, he began to choke him, saying, 'Pay what you owe.' **29**So his fellow servant fell down and pleaded with him, 'Have patience with me, and I will pay you.' **30**He refused and went and put him in prison until he should pay the debt. **31**When his fellow servants saw what had taken place, they were greatly distressed, and they went and reported to their master all that had taken place. **32**Then his master summoned him and said to him, 'You wicked servant! I forgave you all that debt because you pleaded with me. **33**And should not you have had mercy on your fellow servant, as I had mercy on you?' **34**And in anger his master delivered him to the jailers, ᵏ until he should pay all his debt. **35**So also my heavenly Father will do to every one of you, if you do not forgive your brother from your heart."

Eye for Eye (Mathew 5: 38–39, New International Version, NIV)

[38] "You have heard that it was said, 'Eye for eye, and tooth for tooth.'[a] [39] But I tell you, do not resist an evil person. If anyone slaps you on the right cheek, turn to them the other cheek also.

Our Lord's Prayer (Mathew 6: 9–13, NIV)

This, then, is how you should pray: "Our Father in heaven, hallowed be your name,

> **10** your kingdom come, your will be done, on earth as it is in heaven.

> **11** Give us today our daily bread.

> **12** And forgive us our debts, as we also have forgiven our debtors.

> **13** And lead us not into temptation, ᵃbut deliver us from the evil one.ᵇ"

THE MEANING OF OUR LORD'S PRAYER

Jesus taught his disciples only one prayer, Our Lord's Prayer. It goes like this: "God, forgive us our sins because we have forgiven those who sinned against us; give us our daily bread when we forgive those who sinned against us."

This prayer means that God predicates forgiving us when we forgive those who sinned against us. He has already forgiven us and answered all our prayers; he has already given us what we asked for. We can only receive the answers to our prayers already given to us when we forgive those who sinned against us.

Forgive all wrong doers and you see the abundance that God had already given to you, his son. But until you forgive all, you will not see the abundance you are already in.

Abundance is a spiritual term meaning love. We live in the presence of love but do not see it; we see it when we forgive those who wronged us.

God's gifts are love, peace, and joy. It also includes material things if those are helpful for us in doing our work of loving one another.

Jesus showed his disciples what it means to forgive. He went about doing good works but the Jews wanted him dead and accused him with trumped-up charges.

He was arrested while praying in the Garden of Gethsemane. Peter tried to defend him with his sword. He asked Peter to put away his sword, to turn it into plowshare (meanings of farming, producing food) for those who live by the sword die by the sword.

He was arrested and taken to Pontius Pilate and falsely accused; he did not defend his ego and body. He was crucified but instead of being angry and seeking vengeance, he asked his father, God, to forgive those who murdered him because they do not know what they are doing. The man walked his talk.

Father, forgive them because they do not know what they are doing. (Luke 23:34, NIV)

Jesus said, "Father, forgive them, for *they don't know what they are doing.*" And the soldiers gambled for his clothes by throwing dice. And Jesus said, "Father, forgive them, for they know not what they do." And they cast lots to divide his garments.

WE DO NOT KNOW THAT WE ARE SPIRITS BUT THINK THAT WE ARE EGOS, HENCE DEFEND OUR EGOS AND BODIES.

We do not know what we are doing. We think that all we are is bodies that live for a hundred years and die.

If we know who we are, as Jesus did, we would know that we are the eternal sons of God dreaming that we are mortal and living in bodies.

Whereas our bodies could be destroyed, our spirits cannot be destroyed. That which can be destroyed, body, has no worth and value and should not be cherished or defended.

We are in a dream of specialness and separation in which we made bodies seem real in our awareness and when we perceive danger to our bodies and egos, we defend them.

Jesus knew that he is not his body and ego hence did not defend his body and ego when they were attacked and destroyed. In forgiveness, he lived the gospel of the Holy Spirit.

THE HOLY SPIRIT

When we separated from God, God could no longer communicate with us. He created another self, the Holy Spirit, and placed him in our right minds.

The Holy Spirit does not ask us not to separate from God but tells us, when we ask him, that our true self is unified spirit self. He tells us that the world of space, time, and matter, the ego and body, are illusions and do not exist in fact.

They seem to exist because we desire them and defend them. What we desire and defend seem real to us. If the ego and body are not defended, they disappear for they are make-belief reality.

The Holy Spirit, the immanent God in his sons' sleeping minds, teach the dreaming sons of God to overlook their egos, bodies, and the egos' world and in doing so, see the ego, body, and world of space, time, and matter disappear from their awareness and they experience Holy Instant, oneness with God, in unified spirit self.

UNIFIED MIND, RIGHT MIND, AND LEFT MIND; GOD, CHRIST, AND EGO

Our true minds are the unified mind we share with God; the ego-mind tells us to separate from God, adapt to the exigencies of this world, and not forgive those who harmed us; the Holy Spirit, also called Christ, is in our right minds; he asks us to forgive those who wronged us and in doing so, overcome the world, as Jesus did.

THE HOLY TRINITY

In eternity are God and his sons. On earth, in the dream of separation, there now seem three Gods. God the Father (transcendent God); God the Son (us now sleeping and dreaming that we are separated ego selves); God the Holy Spirit, God in the temporal universe.

METAPHORS ARE NOT WHAT THEY REPRESENT.

All three Gods share one self and are one mind. God, son of God, Holy Spirit, and ego are not actual persons; they are metaphors for our patterns of thinking; if we think ego thoughts, we separate from each other; if we think forgiving thoughts, we return to unified living; when we totally give up all wishes for separation, we awaken to our true status as the sons of God. Christ is the sons of God who think from their status as the sons of God, lovingly.

COMPARATIVE RELIGION, HINDUISM, AND BUDDHISM

If you like, you could see the whole thing as Hindus see it. There is only one God, Brahman. Brahman has infinite parts called Atman. God through his parts, Atman, is dreaming that they are separated from each other and from God.

Atman can stop dreaming separated self and awaken to the fact that they are one with Brahman (and experience Samadhi, Buddhist Nirvana, or Zen Satori).

Simply put, according to Oriental religions, one God dreams as his sons and awaken through his Holy Spirit.

One God is doing the dancing of the world. We are God dancing that we are egos; when we overlook our egos, we return to the awareness of our one shared self, God, unified spirit self.

HAPPY DREAM, LIFE IN LIGHT FORMS

While we appear to be on earth, in separation, we can allow the Holy Spirit to guide us. That is, we can use our right minds to overlook what our ego-minds did. In doing so and still living in the illusion of separation, we transform our world into a happy dream.

When we die, we see ourselves in a world that still looks like our earth but there, everything is in light forms and we are in light forms (here, we live in what traditional Christians call the glorified body of Christ, the uncorrupted, non-decaying body of Christ).

From Christ light forms, we transit to the formless world of God and our journey to nowhere ends; separation ends; we awaken to where we always are, in God.

God and heaven are not outside us. It is inside us. We have to go inside to see God and his heaven. We go inside when we love ourselves and love each other and thus, bring the kingdom of God to be on earth (Christ replaces ego).

THE UNIVERSE WILL END IN COLD RADIATION OR WHEN WE AWAKEN FROM THE DREAM.

All talk about God, the story of the beginning of this universe, the mythology of creation, also talks about how the universe would end.

Astrophysics teaches that the universe is expanding (to where?). The trillions of galaxies are expanding away from each other. As the space between galaxies increase, say, the space between our Milky Way Galaxy and our nearest galaxy, Andromeda, the universe becomes colder.

In a very cold universe, stars lose heat and explode to the elements that compose them. The elements decay to the particles that compose them. Protons will be the last to decay.

Ultimately, all particles decay to light. Thus, a universe that began in hot light ends in cold light. This will happen in trillions of years in the future.

But do not despair. Astrophysics dreams that, sooner or later, we shall have the science and technology to travel to other star systems. As our earth dies in five billion years when the sun dies, we hop to other star systems; that way, we keep on migrating from one galaxy to another.

Before all galaxies die, before our universe dies, we would discover wormholes and have the technology to tunnel our way to other universes.

There are infinite universes so we keep on tunneling to them and that way, live forever in ego and body. This is the advice against despair given to us by our favorite friend, the separated self, the ego in body.

The metaphysical way of explaining the end of the universe is to say that what does not exist does not end. It is merely overlooked to end.

Our physical universe does not exist and seems to exist in a dream; it exists because we desire it and because it enables us to dream that we are separated from God and from each other.

Each of us does what he has to do, forgive all of us, to remember his real self as the son of God. When a son of God awakens, he now lives in the world of light forms.

Each of us awakens when we plan to awaken. Ultimately, all of us will awaken and live in the world of light forms, aka gate of heaven, purgatory.

When we are all at the gate of heaven, we give up the desire for specialness, end our separated state, and regain the awareness of our eternal oneness in unified spirit. That is how the universe would end.

The universe ends in peace, joy, and love, not in the cold universe that science speculates to be how the universe would end.

By the way, the ideas of heaven, gate of heaven, world of light forms, happy dreams, are metaphors; they are not places outside us; they reflect our patterns of thinking.

Think lovingly and you are in unified state, in God; be in separation and forgive all who wronged you and you are in the world of light form; do not forgive folks the wrongs they did to you and you are in human flesh, suffering pain, sickness, and death.

All these are illusions, for if you wish and love and forgive all, you would see your body disappear and you do not feel sick or die.

In the here and now, we seem to live in body and need what supports our bodies; we need food, medications, clothes, and means of transportation. These require us to engage in industry, manufacture things, and have work organizations.

EGO VERSUS CHRIST'S POLITICS

In politics, our politics is based on Christ politics which is politics based on love. There is Christ realism, which is politics of love for all humanity. This is our politics, Christ politics or Holy Spirit-directed politics.

This is not naïve, idealistic politics, the seeking of the fantasy of love; no, it is how the Holy Spirit part of our minds construe politics, politics from our right minds, politics from Christ, from love; politics that overlook ego politics and corrects it with love-based politics.

LIVING FROM EGO IS LIVING FROM FEAR; LIVING FROM HOLY SPIRIT BRINGS ONE NEAR LOVE; LIVING FROM LOVE IS LIVING FEARLESSLY.

If you live from your ego, you live in fear. The ego points out to you what could harm or kill you and ask you to take defensive measures.

Your ego imagines all kinds of things that could harm you, such as ghosts killing you (and since there are no ghosts in the day world, your ego in your nightly dreams presents to you ghosts trying to harm you).

In fear, one populates the world with fearful things, avoids them, and lives in isolation from other people.

In fear, you imagine what other people would say or do and respond to them; you are not responding to actual people but to your imaginations of what real people would say or do; you are responding to your projections to other people.

In obedience to your ego, you mostly relate to your ego, not to other people; you avoid other people and not relate to them realistically and do what you need to do to succeed in the egos' world; you fail.

To be an extreme ego is to fail in life.

IN LOVE, GOD, YOU ARE SAFE.

God is love; in love, God, you are safe and do not feel fear. God is fearlessness.

If your thinking and behavior are directed by the Holy Spirit, you are not in God, for if you are in God, you would not need the help of the Holy Spirit.

Christ is your real self; he is formless and unified with God; he is in love and does not feel fear. Right now, you live in ego and body and do feel fear. To live as an ego in body is to live in fear. The ego is the prisoner of fear. Christ is fearless.

Return to Christ to return to living fearlessly hence peacefully and happily.

TO HAVE EVEN A LITTLE EGO IS TO BE IN THE PRISON OF ONE'S MAKING.

If you have even a little bit of ego, you will defend it; you will be conscious of how other people treat it. When you feel that your ego is slighted, albeit it slightly, you feel disrespected and angry. The level of your anger from this minuscular slight is as much as when you are physically attacked.

The ego feels angry at those who slight it or attack it; in anger, the ego defends itself and can attack to kill the person it feels humiliated it. From this situation, you can see that the ego is madness itself. To live in ego is to be insane.

CHOICE TO LIVE FROM EGO OR HOLY SPIRIT/CHRIST: TO SERVE ONLY ONE'S SELF OR TO SERVE THE COMMUNITY?

When you wake up in the morning, you do not know what life is going to throw at you today; you have no way of predicting what today and the future will bring.

The only thing you have control over is how you choose to respond to the present and future events in your life.

You have two choices, to respond from ego (selfish thinking and behavior) or from the Holy Spirit/ Christ (thinking and behavior that serves social interests).

At any point in your life, you are choosing ego or Christ, selfish interests or social interests. If you choose ego, you receive conflict and lack of peace and joy in your life; if you choose to have the Holy Spirit, your right mind, the part of your mind that thinks about what serves our collective good to guide you, you experience peace and happiness. The choice is for you to make.

EGO-LESSNESS MEANS PEACE AND JOY.
EGOFULNESS MEANS CONFLICT AND WAR.

If it were possible to attain no ego in you, and you think and behave from a non-ego, that is, non-self-centered, from no desire to do things that serve only your self-interest at the expense of other people; if it were possible to do only what serves the public good, you would know only peace and joy in you.

But as long as you are on planet earth, you are in ego state; as long as you can see yourself in body and see other people in bodies, you are in ego state; the most you can now do is think and behave from the right part of your mind; metaphorically, this means that you think from the Holy Spirit and the Christ part of your mind; that part of your mind thinks as God thinks; that is, it does what serves the whole instead of the part.

This is the wisdom of Gautama Buddha's no self-approach to people and Alfred Adler's injunction to think and behave from what serves social interest.

That is, if one wants to heal one's neurosis (Adler defines neurosis as self-centeredness and pursuit of a false superior self to mask a false inferior self) and become happy and peaceful.

TO HAVE EGO IS TO BE PRONE TO ADDICTIONS.
YOU CANNOT QUIT ADDICTIVE BEHAVIORS
FROM EGO THINKING AND BEHAVING.

The *Alcohol Anonymous*, AA big book has what it calls the twelve steps to quit addictions. The first step is that one understands that all of one's behaviors were from the ego and that one has now quit doing so and given one's life to a higher power to guide one.

When I first came in contact with that philosophy, I dismissed it as religious razzmatazz for I did not see how a human being who by nature is a separated ego-self can behave as if he is not an ego.

Well, over time, I tried to quit my only addiction, eating too much food. I found that as long as I approached the problem from my ego thinking, I could not quit overeating. I would always rationalize with thoughts like this: we have to eat to live; our bodies need food; if we do not eat, we would not live; starving people die; food tastes good; in heaven, we live in bliss so our nature is to seek bliss, now in body called pleasure.

But when I resolved to not think from the ego but to see things from my right mind, that is, to allow me to be guided by what had hitherto seemed to me an irrational way of thinking, asking God to help me, I found me able to resist addiction.

THE LOGIC OF THE HOLY SPIRIT CANNOT MAKE SENSE TO THE EGO'S LOGIC.

If you allowed the Holy Spirit to guide you, you have denied that you are only ego and body. The logic of the Holy Spirit does not make sense to the logic of the body and ego.

To the ego, that person slapped you and you feel pain and it seems only natural for you to defend yourself by counter slapping him. If you do, you and he remain in ego for you have reinforced the ego in both of you.

The Holy Spirit's logic, the logic of God, does not make sense to the ego's logic. The Holy Spirit's logic presumes that you are not ego and body and that what is done to your ego and body is not done to you. The Holy Spirit's logic says, in effect, you have a spiritual self that is not the body and ego you see with your physical eyes.

These days, I always ask the Holy Spirit, God, to guide me and give him thanks for the good and bad that happens to me (we learn from the bad that happens to us as much as the good that happens to us).

Try it, allow your right mind, the Holy Spirit/Christ, to guide your thinking and behavior and see if you would not live a more peaceful and happy life.

EVERY CHOICE THE INDIVIDUAL MAKES, HE MAKES FOR THE ENTIRE PEOPLE AND UNIVERSE.

Everything that I choose to do affects those immediately close to me and ultimately affects all people. By the same token, every choice another person makes affects not only him and those close to him but all humanity and the universe. This includes choices made by non-human beings. A butterfly flying affects everything in the universe.

If one inherited certain biological issues, one asks: when did I make the choice to have those issues? The fact is that all people who lived in the past, all animals, and all things made that choice for one as one's own choice affects the birth of every child, animal, and thing on earth.

The universe is a system; what one part of it does affect all parts of it. There is no such thing as an individual's choice that does not affect other people and the universe. The universe is one organic whole and what any part of it does affects all parts of it; what one person chooses, he has chosen for all people and the universe.

Within the universal system is individual systems; one's body, for example, is a system; disease in any part of one's body makes all parts of one's body respond to it with disease.

So, you ask: when did I choose to be prone to fear? You chose it when you were born in a specific body that is prone to fear excitation. All people and the universe worked together to make that body possible so all people and the entire universe chose it for you and you chose it for you.

If you prefer to put it in religious metaphors, you can say that you, a son of God, and all other sons of God, chose it for you and you chose whatever happens to other sons of God (sons of God include animals, trees, and everything in the universe, galaxies, stars, planets included for they all work in concert, as one whole, affecting each other).

The entirety of the sons of God, the entire universe, dreams through each individual; there is no such thing as one dreaming alone.

The choice of one son of God made all sons of God, animals, and all things for it affects all of them. So, if you say that you do not know when you made the choice to be who you are, the answer is that all people and you made it for you in the past, as you participated in making choices for all people in the past, present, and future.

What you need to do in the present is to accept that your choices affect all people and things and therefore, make sure that your choices are well-intentioned, are good for all people and all things.

In physics, what I said above is called systems thinking; we live in a general system where everything affects everything else; you affect all people and they affect you.

Why are you poor or rich? It is because of the actions of all people and your own actions. Your parent's actions, your society's action, contributed to your poverty or wealth.

If that is the case, then we must all work for every child's welfare through giving him publicly paid education through university and giving all people publicly paid health insurance. It is stupid to work only for your self-interest and ignore other people's self-interest.

THE ENTIRE UNIVERSE THINKS THROUGH ONE.
THE ENTIRE SONSHIP THINKS THROUGH THE INDIVIDUAL.

The entire universe thinks through each of us: human beings, animals, trees, and everything. Whatever a person does is done by the entire universe.

If one is rational, the universe is rational through one; if one is irrational, the universe is irrational through one; if one is sane, the universe is sane through one; if one is insane, the universe is insane through one; if you are healed, the universe is healed through you.

The universe acts through me, and you. I am therefore the universe and you are the universe. If the universe is the collective sons of God, then we are the collective sons of God acting through one. If the universe is God, then one is God. I am God and you are God and all of us are God.

The idea of individuality, by one's self doing something without others' involvement in it, is balderdash. Lift your hands; wind state permits you to do so; if the wind is strong, you cannot lift your hand. Whatever one does, the entire universe allows one to do it; therefore, it is fantasy to say that the individual by himself can do anything.

In religious language, Jesus said: by myself, I cannot do anything but by the power of my father in me, (meaning the whole universe) I can do anything. True.

CONCLUSION

God takes his sons where they believe that they are at regardless of whether they are there or not. We believe that we are in the universe of space, time, and matter and live in bodies that have needs.

So, let us then figure out a way to organize our social and work organizations so that we are productive and get along with each other.

Christ leadership and management principles train us to lead and manage our social and work organizations, be they families, schools, or work organizations in such a manner that work well as teams doing what contributes to our material abundance, welfare, and social peace.

Humanity has tried secular, scientific leadership and management styles; those have worked up to a point.

Christian leadership and management institute teach an additional angle to leadership and management matters; it teaches leadership and managing people from a Christian perspective.

What constitutes a Christian perspective is difficult to ascertain. We employ the Bible and *A Course in Miracles* to help us to understand what constitutes Christianity and how to use its principles to manage work organizations.

Does it work to lead people from Christ perspective? Until we try it, we shall never know.

21

TOMORROW, I WILL BE BETTER: IS ONE OF THE TRICKS OF THE EGO TO KEEP US UNHAPPY

I do not know about other people; I know about me. One of the driving forces of my life is the hope to do better tomorrow. I was always hoping to do better in the future than I did today. This way, I keep pursuing ideal, grandiose goals that are not attainable in the real world.

I was trying to become a perfect self that will never come into being; the ideal self is unattainable; the goals of the ideal self, which are always grandiose and perfect, are unattainable.

In high school, I used to dream of how to make Africa modernized. My undergraduate years were devoted to figuring out ways to develop Africa.

Later, I studied Africans' individual psychological makeups and realized that they are prescientific in their thinking and behavior; you are going to have to change their pattern of thinking before you can modernize Africa; as they currently are, with the psychologies of primitive people, Africa is not going to be developed in the next five hundred years;

you have to transform Africans' thinking processes, from primitive to scientific, a journey that normally takes five hundred years to accomplish.

The West began its scientific journey in 1543 when Nicolas Copernicus posited that the sun is the center of our solar system; in 1610, Galileo Galilei used his telescope to verify that the sun is indeed the center of the solar system and that its (then known five planets, they are nine) planets orbit around it; those two scientists established the scientific method in the West; Isaac Newton gave science a kickstart with his theory of gravity and the three laws of motion (published in 1687). It has taken the West five hundred years to get to where it is today; Africa, a pre-scientific society will take, at least, five hundred years to get to where the West is today. (The Greeks had science, sort of; they had rational philosophers, such as Plato, Aristotle, Democritus, Pythagoras, and Ptolemy; those were not scientists as we now know what science is.)

Despite my wishes, Africa has a long way to go before it would become like Western Europe and North America: France, Germany, Britain, and the Scandinavian countries, the USA and Canada.

Thus, I realized that I am not going to bring into being my wishes for a modernized Africa but the desire for it is still residual in me.

I learned that the drive to be better, to have a better future, is rooted in a self that rejects what it is today, sees what is not good enough, and wants a better self.

In Karen Horney's psychoanalysis, which built on her neurotic drive to succeed (see her book, *Neurosis and Human Growth*, New York: Norton, 1950) observed that the neurotic child rejects his real self and wants to become an ideal self. He hopes to attain the ideal self. The struggle to become the ideal self leads to fear of being the rejected real self hence the neurotic's free-floating anxiety.

I learned that I am wasting my time by trying to become perfect tomorrow. I am never going to be perfect in ego and body; society is never going to become perfect.

I and all people are already perfect as we are. Our inner selves, the selves that are as God created them, the sons of God, the unified spirit self, are always perfect.

In God, we are perfect but we rejected the self that God created us as, as part of his unified spirit self, and tried to recreate ourselves into separated ego selves and placed our egos into imperfect and vulnerable bodies and those became an excuse to pursue becoming perfect in ego and body.

Ego and body will not ever become perfect; the civilization of the ego will never become perfect. What one needs to do is stop pursuing the ego's externalities, going inside one's self, and accepting one's already perfect spirit self.

When I stopped seeking a neurotic perfect self, I attained inner calm. I am now at peace. To be in peace is to be happy; I am happy.

I have extricated myself from neurotic hold, the neurotic curse, for one to continuously pursue perfection.

God, I was driven by neurotic goals. I did not know peace. I am not from a rich family but was driven in such a mad way that I attended the best universities in the world and had the doctorate degree early (at age thirty, I was already teaching at a university in California).

My ambition was all or nothing (Alfred Adler talked about the neurotic's all or nothing drive to succeed, to become superior). I knew no peace of mind and body when that ambition was in full throttle.

I have given up that neurotic drive for success. I have no need to become something better than I am; I have no need to become a grandiose self. I know me to be part of the universe, part of God and that is good enough for me.

When I used to struggle to succeed, I used to fear being defeated; I would say, I will not allow white racism to defeat me. I did not want racists to win and marginalize me, relegate me to where they relegated black Americans, to doing menial jobs for them.

Later, I realized that I do not have to dance to white folks' standards. What exactly is success? Who defines it—me, white folks, or Africans?

If other people define what constitutes success for you, they have defined you; they are now your master and you are their slave; your goal is now external to you and you are condemned to struggling to become as external others want you to be. You receive fear, anxiety, anger, depression, mania, paranoia, and other mental disturbances from living as other and society-directed person.

Instead, you must define what to you success is and live it. I now define success as being my inner self, the son of God, the self as God created me to be. I do not have any desire to be anything outside me. In just being me, I am in peace.

Interestingly, in peace, I am very productive. On a typical day, I wake up around 5 AM and type, at least, five single-spaced pages in about two hours; that is about 150 pages a month. If this is not being productive, I do not know what is productive. I produce four books a year.

The salient point is that when you are being yourself, you tend to be more productive than when you pursue deluded, grandiose goals that other people and pathological society gave you and you bought into.

THE EGO IS WHAT RELIGIOUS FOLKS CALL SATAN; THE EGO OR DEVIL WANTS YOU TO KEEP STRIVING TO BECOME SUCCESSFUL ON EGO TERMS AND IN SO DOING, NOT KNOW INNER PEACE AND JOY.

The inner self, a part of the universe, in anthropomorphic terms, a son of God, does not strive to become important, it just accepts itself as it is. It lives in peace and in peace, is more productive than the driven life of the ego-identified person (which is most of mankind).

The ego is a false, dream self trying to achieve stuff in its dream world to make its dream self and dream world seem real; they are not real.

Our real self is the son of God; he is spirit, part of God's unified spirit self.

Stop trying to be the ego separated self and accept your true identity, the son of God. However, since you had already made the false, ego-self in body, the Holy Spirit had remade it into a self still in form, now light form (the self in light form is what Christians call Christ self, and Hindus call astral self).

The Holy Spirit is God in the temporal universe. What the Holy Spirit, that is, what God made is permanent, eternal, and changeless. The self in light form that the Holy Spirit remade from our dense selves in matter lives forever and ever.

If you try very hard, you would see your supposed dead parents in light forms; in that state, they and all people, animals, trees, planets, stars, and galaxies exist forever and ever (in the light formed universe, aka the gate of heaven; heaven itself is formless; heaven is pure intelligence that is everywhere, including in us, animals, trees, planets, stars, galaxies, everywhere).

Ozodi Thomas Osuji, Ph.D.

DREAM
JUNE 21, 2020
4 AM

In this dream, I was sitting on a bed and had a sense that my brothers were in the same room with me although I could not see them. Suddenly, I felt two pairs of hands pushing my head, trying to keep me from standing up from the bed. I tried to stand up and the hands kept pushing me to the bed. I tried talking, asking for help and nobody came to help me; my voice was muffled so my brothers in the room could not hear me and therefore could not come to help me. I felt fear, that some person, albeit unseen, was trying to harm me; I forcefully exerted myself to get up and stood up and woke up from the dream.

Here is some background information. I had been away from my apartment for five months. In this same apartment, there used to be weird sounds in my bedroom. I did not hear that sound during the five months that I was away or during the first five days of returning to my apartment, but yesterday, the sounds returned with vengeance; they continued all day long. I dismissed them as rubbish trying to elicit fear in me and decided not to be afraid. Apparently, the renewed sound touched a part of my brain and triggered it to have the dream of an unseen person; a ghost supposedly responsible for the sound in the apartment is pushing me down. That is, an unknown force is oppressing me.

I dismissed the weird sound as the fiction of my imagination but other folks think that there are ghosts in the apartment. I am agnostic and do not consciously believe in ghosts and such stuff.

I will soon get the hell out of this freaking apartment; my apartment living days are nearly over. I lived in an apartment to be by myself and simply read and write (and teach). I did not want to live in a house and have to do all that it takes to maintain a house (when I was married, I lived in a house and did not want to pay the kind of money I used to pay to maintain the goddamned place and thought that an apartment is a kind of break from the struggle to live like the Jones).

This dream showed that I have fear in my mind, in my consciousness, in my thinking; it showed that I believe in an unseen person, ghost, trying to harm me; it showed that my call to be helped when I was in fear did not bring anyone to help me.

The lesson is that only I can help myself. The story of my life is that only me can help me; no other person, not God, not Jesus, is meant to help me; only me can help me; only me can save me from my ego and its fears. My salvation comes from me, giving up my ego, and returning to identification with my real self, son of God, not from other persons.

THE EGO IS A CONCEPT AND CAN BE RECONCEPTUALIZED BY THE CONCEPTUALIZER; THE THINKER THAT THOUGHT THE EGO INTO BEING CAN THINK THE CHRIST INTO BEING.

The term ego, the human personality, is a concept. It can be re-conceptualized by the person who originally conceptualized it in the individual. The conceptualizer of the ego separated self is the sleeping and dreaming son of God.

God is a thinker; through his thinking, he created his sons; God's sons are also thinkers; through their thinking, they invented our ego separated world of space, time, and matter.

Upon birth on earth, something in each of us, the son of God in us, who, while in God, went to sleep and dream that he is separated from God, is individuated, independent, and uses the body and society it is born into to conceptualize an ego separated self for it.

It is the son of God who made the body and society it now finds itself and uses to formulate its ego-self. He is not a victim; he is experiencing the ego-self he wants to experience.

The nature of the body and society, healthy or unhealthy one is born into (which one chose before birth), determines how one's ego-self-concept is conceptualized.

If one has a healthy self-concept, okay, one needs do nothing, but if one has a personality disorder or mental disorder, one should try to re-conceptualize one's ego.

The difficulty is that the ego is conceptualized with one's body and society and as long as one still has one's body and lives in human society, it is difficult to have a totally different ego-self-concept. This is why it is difficult for psychotherapists to help people to change their personality disorders and mental disorders.

ESCAPE TO A DIFFERENT UNIVERSE: THE UNIVERSE OF LIGHT FORMS

Occasionally, an individual, regardless of whether his ego is healthy or unhealthy, somehow escapes from thinking and behaving from his ego-self-concept. This is more likely to happen if the individual is caught up in an accident and escapes from his body, or in near-death experiences (I escaped from my ego and body in near-death experiences).

Here, the individual escapes to a different dimension. In my own case, I escape to the world of light forms, a world that still looks like our present world of space, time, and matter with people, animals, trees, planets, stars, and galaxies in it but they are all made of light. You could look through a person's body for it has no solidity. You could go through walls for your body and walls do not have solidity.

This world I call the world of light forms; Hinduism calls it the astral world; Helen Schucman calls it the gate of heaven, happy dream, real world; she says that it is recreated by the Holy Spirit part of our minds.

Call it what you like. That world is as real as our world. Both, however, are fictional; both are dream worlds. One is better than the other; the world of light forms is the world of dense forms refined.

UNIFIED SPIRIT SELF, GOD, AND HEAVEN

Ultimately, both our dense matter-based world and the world of light forms are let go (often done in meditation) and one attains formless unified spirit, what folks call heaven. In it, one knows oneself to be one with all selves and with God.

GOD, THE CREATOR, IS LIKE HIS CREATION BUT IS NOT HIS CREATION.

In heaven, one still knows that there is a God. We are not God. God created us and we did not create him or ourselves.

The creator, God, is not his creation, although his creation is like him. If you are an artist and create a painting, sculpture, write a book, your artwork represents your thinking and is like you but is not you. You are different from your artwork; by the same token, God, although is like us, he is our creator and is not us.

This point must be grasped for it is the wish to be God that led us to go on this journey of inventing the physical universe. You and I are not God and cannot ever be God. God is our creator, our father.

You must resolve the authorship issue in your mind: you did not author yourself, God authored you; God created you and you did not create you or God.

Let that truth sink into your mind and infuse all your thinking; thereafter, you know peace and joy; but as long as you think that you are so powerful that you created you, other people, and God, you are living in pain, in a hell of your own making.

MULTIVERSE, PARALLEL UNIVERSES

Hugh Everett at Princeton University, in 1958, used his scientific thinking and understanding of quantum mechanics to conclude that during the Big Bang explosion, 13.8 billion years ago, many other universes were created along with our universe. We have not proved the existence of these parallel universes.

I can assure you that many universes exist; this is because I have been in one of them, the universe of light forms. There are infinite universes; each operates with its own physical laws.

For our present purposes, there are three universes: the formless world of God, the light formed world of the Holy Spirit and Christ, and the dense world of God's sons, our present world.

WE ARE THE SONS OF GOD BUT NOT GOD.

Each of us is a creation of God and is like God, formless intelligence. We, as it were, went to sleep and dream our present universe.

In Hindu categories, there is Brahman, God; Brahman has parts, sons of God called Atman; Brahman and Atman share one self.

Atman, us, casts Maya, magical spell on ourselves, and went to sleep. And in our sleep, forget our true selves as Atman and invent new self-concepts for us, called Ahankara, aka ego.

The objective of Hinduism is to enable us to awaken to our true identity as Atman. Meditation and other means are employed to help us go through Moksha and Samadhi and become enlightened to our light forms, first astral selves, be at gate of Brahmaloca and thereafter, disappear into formless Nikalpa Brahmaloca, formless heaven; our true home in God

Upon birth in our present universe, we use our inherited bodies and their health status and our society's laws, to create our self-concepts. We created our self-concepts.

If our self-concepts are problematic, as in those with personality or mental disorders, we can recreate them, for what we conceptualized, with more information, we can re-conceptualize them.

However, in as much as we still live in bodies, bodies and society affect our conceptualizations, our new self-concepts will still take into cognition our bodies and societies.

On earth, we cannot escape the limitations imposed by body and society and still live in this world. In meditation, we can negate our identification with our egos and bodies and temporarily escape to the world of light forms; ultimately, we can escape to the formless world of God, our real home.

We are always in unified spirit state, heaven; from there, we dream that we live in one of the infinite universes that exist. Indeed, we can dream that we are living in many universes at the same time. That subject is beyond our present concern.

WE CAN CHANGE OUR SELF-CONCEPTS.

The individual conceptualized his self-concept. On earth, if he gains more information on how thinking, mind, works, he can change his self-concept, change his personality. However, as long as he lives in the same body and society, those will still affect his new self-concept.

Occasionally, one may escape to a different universe, such as the universe of light forms. In the final analysis, one can escape from all universe of forms and escape to the formless universe, what religious folks call heaven.

Heaven is our real home. We have not and cannot leave heaven. We are always in heaven as part of God and while there, as it were, sleep, forget our real self, and dream that we are on earth or other universes.

When we wake up, first, by stopping at the gate of heaven, and then finally wake up in unified spirit self, we feel at home and in that state are eternal, permanent, and changeless.

Like the prodigal son, we sooner or later leave unified state, again; leave God and his heaven to go experience other separated states, such as our world.

The eternal sons of God keep amusing themselves with experiences in different universes.

THE SELF MUST BE RECONCEPTUALIZED WITH THE HOLY SPIRIT FOR IT TO BE BETTER.

One's original ego-self was conceptualized by the thinking, mind of God's sleeping son in one. That mind wished for separation and power. It is a mind that invented the ego's problems (ego is the dream self, our current selves).

The same mind, thinking pattern that invented a problem, cannot solve it. It takes a different kind of thinking, mind, to solve a problem.

One must now think with a mind that wishes for inclusion in God to be able to come up with a different self. Christians call this type of mind the Holy Spirit mind, thinking that accepts the whole and does not want to separate from the whole, that is, God.

Holy Spirit thinking is still one's thinking but it is done with forgiveness and love and does not feel guilty for separating from one's real self, son of God and God. One is now not driven by fear and guilt. One is calm.

THE CHRIST SELF: THE OPPOSITE OF THE EGO-SELF

When one's thinking is infused with the Holy Spirit and one uses it to re-conceptualize one's ego, one conceptualizes a new self, the Christ self.

The Christ self is still an illusion but it is now a refined illusion. It is in light form; on earth, it is very light. Now, one feels light, as if one is carried along by gentle breezes and one does not have to make strenuous efforts to do anything.

The Christ self is a replacement of the ego-self. The Christ self made by the Holy Spirit, God, is meant by God to replace the ego separated self that the son of God made for himself, a self that caused him pain; the Christ self is meant to give one peace and joy.

THE GRANDIOSE EGO SEEKS A BETTER THAN VERSAILLES' CASTLE TO LIVE IN.

I desired a better self; I also wished for a better everything. Things as they currently are, are not good enough for me.

Houses looked crummy. I wished for perfect houses, and the Versailles' palace came to mind. Why not, a man built the Versailles, so why shouldn't I build one?

During my first year in graduate school, I bought a Euro rail pass and spent summer in Europe; I was all over Europe, sleeping at pensions or hostels; I visited famous places like the Vatican in Rome, the Louvre and Versailles in Paris, London's palaces, and whatever is good looking at Geneva, Venice, Vienna, Munich, Frankfort, Copenhagen, and Stockholm; in short, I visited most Western European capitals; I loved the magnificence of the Versailles and wished to build one of those for me, why not, is King Louis the fourteen better than me?

There is absolutely nothing wrong with me having such a house or having the best car on earth. Cars are built by men and men who have money buy the best cars.

The son of God is entitled to the best cars, houses, everything. The question is what mind, thinking, is he using to get them?

If you use your ego-mind, ego thinking, you will suffer to get the good things of this world. If you use your Holy Spirit thinking, your Christ mind, you get the best things that this world offers and do so effortlessly.

God does not want you to live in poverty. As long as you want to live in body, space, and time, God, through the Holy Spirit, gives you the best of this world.

If you truly love yourself and all people, your body would be transformed into light body and you would not have to die to leave this world.

HOLY SPIRIT AND CHRIST-DIRECTED AMBITION

The question is: who is directing your ambition, your pursuit of goals, ego or Christ? Strive after things with your Holy Spirit mind; desire only what the Holy Spirit, love, and lack of guilt and fear dispose you to desire and desire it for the rest of the world, too.

What is realizable in the egos' world? What is realizable in the Holy Spirit's world, if you cannot do away entirely with the ego then desire what is attainable in the egos' world? What is ego realistic—find out a good or service that people desire and produce it, and sell it to them?

Better still, sell to people what the Holy Spirit knows is good for them and make money from it. Holy Spirit and Christ realistic goods and services mean selling what is good for all people, what serves social interest.

God does not want you to be poor and die poor; poverty is what the ego tells you that you deserve for denying your true self as the son of God.

Now, accept your true identity as the son of God and respect God but do not fear him for he is your father; one should not fear one's father; one should love him; Love God, love you, love all people, and work to correct our screwed-up world by showing people, through your example, how to love one another.

You must tell hateful white Americans that only love for all people, including black people, will make their empire survive and that hate for some of God's children guarantees that their empire built on slavery and hate would collapse and join the other empires built with hate and lack of love.

Summa, Egypt, Persia, Greece, Rome, Britain, the USSR, etc. were once great empires that ruled a chunk of the world but are today no more. America will join them but does not have to do so; she can redirect to love and service for all and last much longer.

Find a specific way, usually what you have aptitude and interest in, to serve the people and see wealth roll into your life. You cannot serve people through aptitudes that you do not have.

I have amazing aptitude in philosophy, psychology, and physics and use those to serve people; you are not me and I am not you; don't envy anyone; figure out what you are good at and use it to contribute to mankind's good.

This universe came into being because the sons of God desired to be special, to be superior to God and to each other. In the process of evolution, each of us has developed special skills. Each of us, over many incarnations on earth, learned certain things. I learned psychology and psychiatry in several incarnations so that even while at elementary school, I could stare at you for a while and tell you whether you are normal or mentally ill.

I literally had accurate diagnoses for my peers who were odd and they turned out to be as I expected them to be; a boy was always laughing as if he won the lotto and I concluded that he is going to have a form of mental disorder where people laugh a lot and he became bipolar affectively disordered, manic in his early twenties; the other boy was always suspicious saying that we, boys, were after his life. I said to me that that boy is going to develop a mental disorder where folks feel like the entire world is persecuting them and at age eighteen, he was diagnosed with schizophrenia, paranoid type.

The point is that each of us has different talents; identify yours and optimize yours; do not wish to be like other persons for you are not other persons; you are you, not me, and I am not you. You cannot do what I do and I cannot do what you do. Remember the parable of talents told by Jesus Christ. Maximize your talent or you waste it.

Finally, I am not teaching the so-called gospel of prosperity that has taken hold of poor African countries. I am teaching a new philosophy, one that asks us to love one another as the sons of love.

God is love; as his sons, we must love all people. Love and see your life improve, now, not tomorrow. Hate and live in the squalor of Africa.

African pastors, like their ancestors that captured and sold their people to Arabs and Europeans, are evil persons. They were given the gospel of love called Christianity. They have bastardized it to mean asking their gullible followers to tithe them so that they become fabulously wealthy while their followers live in the slums of Ajagunle. No, Jesus did not ask you to tithe anyone.

In the parable of the Good Samaritan, Jesus asked all of us to serve the sick and poor, not take from them.

Africans should try doing what serves the public for a change; if they do, they would actually create abundance; they do not have to become wealthy through religious 419 schemes, as their evil pastors do.

22

BECAUSE I DID THIS TO ME, OTHER PEOPLE DESERVE TO LIVE

We can talk about love and forgiveness all we want; the fact is that if other people are responsible for what my life turned out to be, they do not deserve to live or me loving them. If other people are responsible for my pain and suffering, they ought to die, I mean die right now. It would mean that people are evil and evil people do not deserve to live; they are better off dead.

As Arthur Schopenhauer said in his Magnus Opus, *The World as Will and Idea*, the universe ought to not have produced people; it was better that the universe did not produce people; indeed, the universe ought to not exist if the best it could do is produce people who hurt each other.

I do not care for a God that allows his sons to hurt and kill each other; such a God must not exist and if he exists, as Fredrick Nietzsche said, we ought to kill him. We are better off without that kind of God.

The good news is that upon excruciating examination of my life, from about age six to the present, I can honestly say that other people did nothing bad to me. To the extent that something bad was done to me, it was by my inherited problematic body and the trouble it caused me; bad as that is, I learned a lot from it so it is not really bad.

I believe that I chose my rickety body to experience the pain and suffering it caused me and from it, learn about human nature. This is not some kind of new-age idea that we create our realty and that there are no accidents in our lives for we chose all of them; it is a conclusion based on reflection on my life.

I am by nature agnostic; I am not a believer in religions' God; I see no need to fit my thinking to any extant religion, old or new; I only accept what makes sense to me.

Science makes sense to me; however, whereas science does an excellent job explaining matter, space, and time, it is abysmal in explaining consciousness; neuroscientists say that our thinking is the product of electro-chemical dances in our brain. That is not true. There is a will agency in us; I got up this morning and decided to type this essay; something that has an ability to be intentional made that decision; it was not made by the dances of neurons, neurotransmitters, and atoms in my brain.

Listen, I understand the physiology of the brain. We have not understood our thinking and consciousness.

I was born with a body that is extraordinarily sensitive to changes in the environment. When the ambient temperature is hot, my entire body itches. I am sensitive to heat, cold, smell, paints, fragrances (if women have their fragrances on in a room where I am, I must walk out to be able to breathe or I feel dizzy and faint).

Electronic equipment, such as computer, television, and smartphones emit smell that my mouth and nose picks up and it makes my mouth smell awful; if I am in front of a computer for an extended time, the smell makes me dizzy; I cannot watch television for more than a couple of hours before the smell from the television makes me dizzy.

When I drive cars for an extended time, say, for four or more hours, electrical currents from the pedal go to my legs and my legs feel hot and numbed; I have to stop and stamp my feet on the ground several times to return feelings to them.

All kinds of food cause me stomach pain. Other children would eat and go out and play. After eating, I feel stomach pain and feel tired and must go lie down for a couple of hours to recoup some energy.

I was born with certain genetic disorders, including Cytochrome C Oxidase deficiency, Spondylolysis, and Mitral Valve Prolapse.

For our present purposes, what is relevant is that my complicated body causes me unending discomfort.

Connected Lives

My father's body is like my body. My grandfather's body is like my body; my daughter's body is like mine; I inherited my bodily issues and have passed them on to my children.

Clearly, my parents gave me their body types hence contributed to my bodily pain and suffering. Each of us came into this world through the genes of our parents. The chromosomes from one's father and mother combine to produce a fetus and a new human being is born.

We are the physical products of pre-existing other people; other people do affect us. None of us is an island; we are all part of a general system and other parts of that system affect us and we affect them; each of us is always reacting to what happens in other parts of the system.

The stars, galaxies, other planets, space, time, and matter affect how our bodies feel at any point in time.

Indeed, without light energy from the sun, our bodies would not exist. Our bodies are actually congealed light.

Beginning from the Big Bang's light, 13.8 billion years ago, light transformed itself into electrons and quarks; quarks combined into protons and neutrons; protons and neutrons combined into nuclei. Nuclei captured electrons to form atoms.

There are 92 different types of atoms; each type of atom is called an element; an atom's internal configuration differs from other atoms by the number of electrons, protons, and neutrons in it.

Hydrogen, the lightest atom, has one electron and one proton (its isotopes have one or two neutrons); helium has 2 electrons, 2 protons, and 2 neutrons; carbon has 6 electrons, 6 protons, and 6 neutrons; oxygen has 8 electrons, 8 protons, and 8 neutrons; go down chemistry's periodic table and get to the heaviest element, uranium with 92 electrons, 92 protons, and 146 neutrons.

Our bodies are composed of 64 elements, chiefly carbon, hydrogen, oxygen, nitrogen, potassium, magnesium, calcium, iron, zinc, copper, etc.

The arrangement of elements in our bodies affects how our bodies feel. The manner in which the elements are arranged in my body gives me loads of pain I feel.

(I am not here talking biochemistry but let me just observe that Cytochrome C Oxidase deficiency has to do with the electron oxygen transport system in human cells; it would take elaborate chemistry to explain how this enzyme works; moreover, I do not assume that the reader has graduate studies in physics and chemistry so I will skip the explanation about what goes on in the mitochondria, the cell's factory).

I inherited a problematic body that has caused me loads of pain and suffering. If other people did this to me, I want them dead. I will not forgive them.

I know that nobody consciously did any harm to me. Beyond contributing their problematic genes to me, I do not remember my parents abusing me. All I know is that as a child, I felt excruciating pain. I felt weak physically. By the time I began elementary school at age six, I was already wishing that I had a better body. I used to daydream, fantasizing that I had a healthy body like other boys have. That wish progressed to me wishing that I were better than other boys (in my world, boys did not compare themselves to girls).

In Alfred Adler's individual psychological terms (1911, 1964), I felt weak and inferior physically and compensated with desire for a superior body (which transmuted to a superior self).

At elementary school, I was not particularly smart and I wished that I was smarter than the smartest boys in my class.

At secondary school, I was considered smart for I always made good grades in my class. At the university, I was mostly an A student (GPA 3.8).

We are not talking about reality here but my feeling. I felt inferior and weak and reacted with a desire for superiority. As Adler pointed out, the desire for superiority is neurotic. In Adler and Horney's categories, I was a neurotic child.

Neurotic children have aspects of delusional disorder. Delusion disorder inheres in wishes for superiority and belief that one is superior to other people. Deluded persons believe in what is not true as true; they feel totally worthless and restitute with grandiose self-concepts; they believe that they are superior to other people.

As a child, I felt like I was superior to other kids even though many of them did better than I did at school and certainly at sports; I was no good at sports.

I was tense and serious most of the time. That tension emanated from my desire to seem my idealized self-concept; I could not relax, for if I relaxed, I could make mistakes and show myself to be dull.

At age eight, my parents sent me to their village to live with my grandparents. Hitherto, I spoke only Yoruba and Pidgin English; now I was forced to learn Igbo, my ethnic language. I did not do a good job speaking Igbo. I did not know the names of animals, insects, and trees in our Igbo world.

I recall when a bunch of us kids was roaming around in the village's bushes and one of the kids, Hyacinth Nwachukwu, initiated a game of naming every tree, animal, and insect we saw. I did not know their names. Hyacinth composed a song on the spot about my lack of knowledge of things in our Igbo world. He sang:

"Thomas horu Ekweru Nwa Dede kpoya Ngbaradu, Omara kwanna, ogara Ikpuya akpo."

In English, he said that I saw a certain insect and called it the name of another insect that looks like it but is not it; if I had known the difference, would I have made this colossal mistake? In effect, I do not know the names of the insects in our village and by generalization, I do not know anything in the village; I am ignorant of our village's world.

His song was calculated to put me down, to show that I knew little about my world. Given that I was a city boy, how was I supposed to know what African village boys know about their world?

I felt ashamed, degraded, and embarrassed. Whenever I feel degraded, I tend to avoid the degrader, so I left the boys and went home.

I doubled my efforts to do well at school and since the boy who composed the song that made fun of my ignorance is not particularly academically smart, I felt totally better than he.

The point here is that by age eight, I was aware that I felt superior to some children and envied those who seemed superior to me.

In Adlerian psychological categories, I was a neurotic child. I was filled with what Karen Horney called neurotic anxiety. Here, the child rejects his real self, uses his mind to invent an ideal self, and wants to become it.

The ideal self is the self that the boy's significant others, ala Harry Stack Sullivan, would approve. The neurotic child rejects his real self and pursues becoming an imaginary ideal self that he feels his parents, siblings, peers, and society would accept.

The discrepancy between the imperfect real self and the perfect ideal self causes the neurotic child anxiety. He fears becoming his non-ideal self.

All through my childhood, I lived in anxiety; I was afraid to fail and be my real self that I construed to be no good; I wanted to be my desired ideal self (the ideal perfect self is imaginary; there is no such thing as a perfect human being).

Since as the world sees it, I am not particularly dumb, I felt superior to average boys around me. At secondary school, when some of my teachers recognized that I was gifted and told me, my head swelled up. For example, I would read a history book, a book that is supposed to be studied during the six years of education, in a week, and know all about it.

By my second year at secondary school, I was ready to take the school certificate examination but was required to stay on for the required six years, most of it a waste of my time.

Luckily for me, I liked reading novels and read up on English literature, such as the writings of Geoffrey Chaucer, William Shakespeare (I read the complete Shakespeare during my second year at secondary school), Marlowe, John Milton, Alexander Pope, Walter Scot, Dryden, Charles Dickens, Jane Austin, George Elliot, George Orwell, Thomas Hardy, Oliver Goldsmith; you name any English writer of note and I had read most of his novels or plays.

Reading novels was a way of killing time for the subjects they taught in the classes were too simple for me and bored me. I came to the USA a few months after leaving secondary school.

In three years, I had a bachelor's degree, three masters' degrees, and a doctorate degree from the University of California.

I really was not committed to any discipline and therefore, could not put my mind into it and do it to the best of my knowledge and succeed at it.

I was kind of like a dilatant, reading whatever interested me without really devoting me to any particular subject. I certainly could teach physics, chemistry, psychology, philosophy, political science, or business studies but I was not committed to any of them.

You have to devote all your energies to a field to excel at it. In the language of the world, I would be considered mediocre (except that if you called me a mediocre, I would challenge you to a competition and outperform you). Nevertheless, as the world sees it, I am a failure.

In thinking about why I failed, I recognized that other people are not responsible for my failure. I was responsible for my failure. If other people are responsible for my failure, I want them dead. If the world is responsible for my shitty life, I would destroy the world in a second.

The fact is that other people are not responsible for my failure. Other people did not give me my experience.

One day, it dawned on me that I chose whatever I have experienced in my checkered life. I chose my precarious body. I chose a body that would give me the pain and suffering my body gave to me. I made my body weak and vulnerable so that it would dispose me to avoid all kinds of situations that I anticipate would cause me pain (my MMPI personality profile says that I have avoidant personality disorder with the features of obsessive-compulsive, dependent, and paranoid personalities).

Because I have a vulnerable body, I did not obtain a solid sense of social worth. In the boys' world, if you are good at sports, other boys admire you. I was no good at sports so other boys did not admire me.

Indeed, I was seldom selected to play, say, soccer with other boys. I was considered too clumsy to be part of a winning team. I sat mostly on the sidelines watching good soccer players do their thing.

Simply put, I did not obtain social attention, hence a sense of worth through boys' normal physical activities. What Adler would call my inferior body and lack of social worth gave me a sense of inferiority and restitutive desire for superiority.

I am always seeking attention, worth, importance, and significance from other people. Sometimes, they give it to me but I do not feel like I have it.

Later, after I had studied spiritual psychology, especially, Helen Schucman's *A Course in Miracles*, I learned that people are dream figures; people on earth are egos in bodies and those have no worth and significance.

People from whom I sought worth do not have it for they are nothing. Nothingness could not give me a sense of some-thingness. Thus, it was useless seeking worth from other people.

My life on earth, as is yours, is a game. I set it all up (and you set yours up; we collectively set up our collective life on earth). I chose to have a rickety body that made me feel inadequate and fail in physical activities. That failing led my ego to seek success.

If other people do not acknowledge my social worth, I felt angry at them.

Do you know what? I do not remember one instance when a human being, not one boy in my childhood days, told me that I am inferior. If anything, they admired my omnivorous mind. Boys used to say: Tom, your mind is insatiable in its search for knowledge; I wish that I have your mind.

Simply put, no one looked down on me. Yet, I feared being looked down on. Nobody did anything harmful to me. To the extent that I feel inadequate, no other person made me feel so.

I have lived in the USA since I left secondary school. No white schoolmate or work peer has ever told me that I am inferior to him. No white person has come right out and said to me, Ozodi, you are inferior.

White folks make much ado about the shibboleth called IQ. Well, my tested IQ is 148, which is in the top one percent of humanity.

I do not make much of IQ tests; for one thing, white folks, such as Binet and Wechsler designed them. White men have no business testing black folks' intelligence for that reflects master-servant relationships. Nevertheless, some people are more intelligent than others.

Be that as it may, I felt inadequate to Western civilization. I am the one who drew from my painful bodily and social experience the conclusion that I am inferior.

No one else told me that I am inferior; no one else did anything that is hurtful to me. I did it all to myself. Of course, there is racism in the USA but if I had concentrated on one subject, I would have done well.

Indeed, when I tried a bit, I easily shot to the top. I have been the executive director of a few mental health agencies and a professor in a couple of universities. I have written 82 books and tons of articles.

I am responsible for my feelings and psychological state. Biology played a role in my feelings.

As I pointed out in other writings, we are the sons of God. In God, we are perfect and are the same and coequal but we desired to seem different, some better than others.

While still in God, we invented matter, space, and time and now seem to live in bodies. The state of our bodies and social experience affect how we feel.

Body and society were deliberately designed to make us feel inferior or superior to other people. The state of one's body and one's social interaction can make one feel inferior.

Interestingly, I have never felt inferior to any white person; if truth is told, I see white folks as inferior to me (of course, this is neurotic feeling; mental health tells us that we are all the same and equal).

I do not blame any other person for how my life turned out. Whereas my life cannot be considered socially successful, I know that I learned a lot from it. I doubt that there is a human being out there that can beat me in the subjects that I am interested in.

I chose my life so as to be able to learn what I have learned and then share it with the world. If I had a healthy body, I would not be a philosopher; if I was a normal chap, I would not have studied psychology; if I was not curious about how the universe came into being and is put together, I would not have voraciously consumed physics as I did.

My life was set up by me to be exactly the way it was and is. I like it. I may not be rich and may not have given my family wealth, yet I like what I have done with my life. I will not exchange my life for another person's life. I am me and like me.

EACH PERSON IS WHO HE IS AND YOU CANNOT CHANGE HIM.

In 2005, a friend, an English lady, told me about what she called Nigerian Internet forums and told me to join them and share ideas with Nigerians. I did and upon seeing what the folks write, I was shocked. These are university graduates but all they seem to do with themselves is write abusive stuff about each other and their ethnic groups.

Igbos abused Yorubas and Yorubas abused Igbos. I was horrified at what I saw. I decided to teach them a bit of psychology and what constitutes good self-esteem; people with good self-esteem do not put other people down to make them seem important and superior.

I wrote on all aspects of psychology that I thought could help them stop insulting each other. I then progressed to writing on other subjects.

For fifteen years (2005-2020), I tried to help these apparent primitive people become civilized, as I understand civilization to be.

I did not get any of them to change; they are still living in the gutter and while there, abuse each other verbally. The lesson I learned is that one cannot change other people.

I used to share my writings with my daughter. But instead of her becoming more psychological and flexible, she is now a rigid Bible-thumping woman. She quotes from every part of the Bible, especially from the Old Testament, to make whatever point she is making.

I get the feeling that she is using the Bible to make her feel superior to other people. I believe that she wants to seem superior to other people and quotes from the Bible parts of it that make her seem more religious.

She is using the Bible to reinforce her neurotic desire for superiority to other people.

I have a friend, Dr. O; he takes from the bible passages that he says make him the sole representative of God in the present world. The man, in my judgment, has delusion disorder, grandiose type; he is a paranoid prophet. He is not going to change.

The point is that one cannot change other people. One is, therefore, best served to be who one is, and do one's own things and leave other people to do their own things and not worry about their mental disorders.

As I pointed out elsewhere, this world is a delusional place. This is delusional because here, we live with false identities. In truth, we are parts of God's unified spirit self; we seek separated selves, some superior to others.

In God, we are one shared self, same and equal; we came to this world and structured it for some to individually seem superior to others and for some groups to seem superior to others.

Since in spiritual reality we are equal, whoever feels superior to others is deluded, insane. The world is a place we come to be deluded, insane.

In God, there is no perception, there is only knowledge of our oneness but in this world, we invented space, time, and matter and those make it possible for us to see each other.

This is a world of perception where there is nothing to perceive; we are all hallucinating; to be on earth is to be psychotic, to hallucinate and be deluded.

Leave people to be psychotic in their own specific ways. White folks gratify their psychosis by seeing themselves as superior to black folks; black folks, in their own ways, gratify their own mental disorders by fancying themselves superior to white folks.

The world is an all-around mess. Let the mess be and do not worry about it. Don't ever try to change people and make them healthy.

One should just live one's understanding of mental health, which, to me, means love for me and for all people, working for our collective social interests, and being a social democrat, a mixed capitalist, socialist in one's political economy.

THE WORLD IS A DELUSIONAL PLACE
SO LET PEOPLE BE DELUDED.

In eternity, heaven, we are formless unified spirit. We desired separated selves in forms and invented this world and now live in forms.

Forms make for perception, so we perceive each other. Since our true selves are not in forms, we are deluded if we see ourselves in forms and hear voices that are not there. To be on earth is to be deluded and to hallucinate.

We want to be different from each other, some superior to others. Ego and body enable us to seem unequal in body, color, and size.

So, let people do what they came to do, be deluded in their individual ways (by each seeming superior to others or in groups; each group believes itself better than other groups; there are individual delusions and group delusions, (folie à deux).

People will do so until they are ready to return to God, in which case they give up their egos and forms and return to formless unified reality and its sameness and equality. In the meantime, delusion is the motivation for being in this world. To be in this world is to be deluded.

WHAT GOD CREATED LASTS FOREVER; THE LIGHT
BODIES MADE BY THE HOLY SPIRIT LASTS FOREVER.

God created us, sons of God, as part of his eternal formless self. We, the sons of God invented space, time, and matter and now seem to live in forms made of matter.

The Holy Spirit, God in the temporal universe, reinvented our bodies into light forms and our world of space, time, and matter into light forms that last forever; God made them for his sons to play with and what God made lasts forever.

We in light forms will last forever and ever; the world of light forms will last forever and ever. Occasionally, those in light forms return to formless God and in it, rest for a while and then reappear in forms of light, as Jesus does.

Upon the death of your body on earth, you will see you and your parents in light forms and in that state, you and they see each other for as long as you want to do so.

God can never be in form, for he is the formless self that is all selves; if he is in form, then he is separated from his other selves and that would mean that he is insane.

CONCLUSION

In this essay, I wrote my philosophy. In philosophy, you express what makes sense to you. Philosophy is not science.

In the physical sciences, you write what you not only have observed but proved to be true. The scientific method requires us to only posit ideas that are observable, verifiable in a laboratory, and as Karl Popper added, falsifiable. I am a scientist and understand the scientific method. I am also a philosopher.

In philosophy, we do not have proof of what seems rational and true. I do not have empirical proof for my philosophy.

Be that as it may, my experience leads me to believe that we chose our parents and they chose us; we chose our siblings and they chose us; we chose our groups and they chose us; we chose our vocations (having no vocation is a vocation); we experience whatever we want to experience; we chose whatever has happened to us in our lives; we are not the victims of external circumstances; we chose where we live and will live in the future; we chose those we met and will meet in the future.

I have always had what psychologists call internal locus of authority. I have never believed that the external environment, despite my rickety body, controls me. I do think and what my thinking believes is true, I live. I act on my convictions.

If something makes sense to me, I live it regardless of whether the entire world opposes it. In fact, the more I am opposed, the more energy I have to fight the opposition for then, it becomes a battle of wills and I do not like any man born of woman to defeat me; if I am right, I fight to prevail but if I am wrong, I accept guidance from even a child.

I do not blame anyone for my apparent poverty and what folks call failure. I chose to experience poverty and failure.

On the matter of slavery, we are all culprits. Africans roamed around Africa, captured their people, and sold them off to Arabs and later to Europeans. Arabs and Europeans bought Africans and used them as slaves.

Africans, Arabs, and Europeans were all culprit in the iniquitous trafficking in slavery. We are collectively responsible for this sin.

All of us who were not slaves must pay reparation to ex-slaves. African countries must pay African Americans and African Arabs for selling them. Arabs, Western Europeans, and white Americans must make monetary reparation for slavery.

We all must make amends for our sins. You cannot just sell a person or use his labor for free and talk rubbish about how innocent you are.

That being said, I believe that slaves chose to have their slave experience, awful as it was. I know that you could not enslave me. Given my warrior mentality, I would kill you if you tried to enslave me, and of course, your fellow psychopathic slave masters would then kill me.

If slaves fought and were killed, there would be no slavery. But they preferred to live at all costs. It is people's fear of harm and death and God's supposed punishment of them in the afterlife that disposes them to tolerate other people's abuse and oppression.

I have made my metaphysics abundantly clear. We are the sons of God who at all times are in God (God is love, hence in love) but who dream that we are separated from God.

Our goal for seeking separation from God is to invent unequal social relationships where some seem superior to others. We came to earth to seem unequal to each other. The pursuit of social inequality is existential.

For example, I feel superior to all people. I have felt that way all my life. To me, people are mere animals and are beneath me. And this applies to white folks. I have not seen a white person that I did not see as inferior to me. That was just the way it was with me. This is deluded belief for in truth, we are equal.

At the spiritual level, we are the same and equal but on earth, we are all deluded with the false belief in our sense of superiority.

If you want to understand delusion disorder, also called paranoia, please read David Swanson et al.'s *The Paranoid* (1970), David Shapiro's *Autonomy and the Rigid Character* (1972) and *Neurotic Styles* (1965), and William Meissner's *The Paranoid Process* and *Psychotherapy for the Paranoid Process*(1982, 1984). You can also read the relevant sections of the *American Psychiatric Associations Diagnostic and Statistical Manual*, 2013.

We came here to be deluded; to be on earth, we denied our true selves, which are unified spirit, structured a world of matter and bodies, and now seem to live in separated bodies.

The eventual goal is for each of us to become aware of our unified spirit nature and awaken from our identification with ego separated self and its body.

Please do not talk to me about science and its theology of accidents. I do not believe that there are accidents (chance and randomness); we are responsible for what we encounter on earth.

This is my belief; you can stand on your head and talk about accidents until you go blue on your face and you will not persuade me.

To me, it is infantile to believe in accidents, chance, and randomness. Quantum physics' ideas of nonlocal communication of entangled particles, Heisenberg's uncertainty principle, in fact, all of physics convinced me that we the sons of God designed this world.

As I see it, the physical universe is kind of like a matrix. We remain in unified spirit but project ourselves into matter, space, and time, and through those, our double dream figures act as we act on earth.

I am African, a black man. I know that black folks and Africans like to see themselves as victims oppressed by white folks. They like to blame white folks for their poverty.

In the meantime, they are mostly thieves who steal the money they could have used to develop their countries right. They can blame white folks all they like but they are responsible for their shithole continent, as the idiot in the white house, Donald Trump, calls Africa.

This essay is a statement of my philosophy; accept or reject it; that is your prerogative; I am entitled to my beliefs.

One of my friends likes to relate to many men and women without being committed to any of them. She invented a "reality" where she has many friends none of whom is she intimate with; hence, she lives a lonely life. That is her choice; she invented her reality and lives it. She is a son of God and has a right to invent the reality she likes, live it, and take the consequences of her choice.

I came to this world to be free of serious attachments to anyone so that I can live alone and do my own thinking and writing. I invented a reality where I am not bonded to anyone.

My parents parceled me out to go live with their parents so I did not develop strong bonds with them; at age thirteen, I went to a secondary boarding school and later came to the USA where I lived in a college dormitory full of white kids. I did not develop strong bonding with all these people.

In graduate school, I got married to a hyper-religious woman who paid more attention to her religion than to me and that did not bother me for it left me free to read books.

My entire life and its events were designed, by me, for me to be alone and have the freedom to think my thoughts and produce the philosophy I have produced.

23

REMOVE THE OBSTACLES TO LOVE AND YOU EXPERIENCE LOVE/GOD/UNION

In our world, we say that love is earned. When you have to do something to earn love, that is not real love, and we all know it. If I have to earn your love and you have to earn my love, it is clear that neither of us loves each other. Indeed, we do not even know what love is. Love is not earned.

Love is who we are. We placed obstacles to the awareness of love. We are love, always live in love, and cannot not live in love. But while in love, we decided not to be aware of love.

We sleep and dream that we are outside love. The entire dream of separation from God is separation from love.

We desire to experience the opposite of love. Our reality is love and we wanted to experience the opposite of love.

The universe of space, time, and matter was designed to enable us, the sons of God, not to experience love.

Our egos, bodies, and society were designed to enable us not to experience love. Our bodies were attacks on love; they were designed to enable us not to feel part of love, to feel separated from love (love is union with all; bodies enable us to seem separated from other selves and things).

Love is union. In love, we are unified with all beings. In love, all things are joined as one thing. To be joined, things have to be the same, equal, and formless.

In our reality, we are the same, equal, formless, and joined. We are always so and cannot not be so.

While in this state of eternal union with each other, in love with each other, we placed blocks to the awareness of love, awareness of unified self, and now feel that we are not loved. We feel outside love. We live in love and feel outside it.

To return to the awareness of love, we have to remove the blocks we placed to the awareness of love; we have to remove the veil we used to mask the love that we always live in.

The block, the veil, is our wish for separated existence and what we made to make it seem real: space, time, and matter.

Tune out your identification with body, space, time, and matter and you immediately experience the fact that you are always joined to all people at a non-physical level; that is, you are always in love with all existence.

In formless unified state, aka heaven and God, we are always joined and will always be joined. There is nothing that we can do to not be joined. If it were possible for us not to be joined, the universe would not exist; we are always joined hence exist and the universe exists.

We wished to seem separated from the whole (God) and the other parts of that whole (other sons of God). Since in truth we cannot not be joined with all being, we seem to go to sleep and in our sleep, dream that we live in a universe where there is space, time, and matter and we are all separated from other people, animals, trees, and everything else.

What we see with our eyes is separation. Separation seems real. But we are seeing with physical eyes; physical eyes see separation and since separation does not exist, physical eyes see nothing. Indeed, physical eyes do not exist.

Real seeing is seen with spiritual eyes (in the world of light forms). Spiritual eyes see union (there is a fine thread, a line that connects everything; this is kind of like what superstrings theorists talk about).

At the individual level, we want to seem separated from each other and do things that make us seem separated from our real self, the son of God, and from other sons of God.

When we stop doing those things that make us not aware of the love we are in, we experience love, right away, not in the future, for in love, in God, there is no past, present, and future; there is only now in love.

When we remove the obstacles to the awareness of love, we experience love and in it, know ourselves to be eternal, permanent, and changeless and live in peace and joy, in bliss.

EGO, BODY, PERSONALITY, SPACE, AND TIME ARE MEANS OF SEPARATING FROM LOVE.

Each individual has a personality, a pattern of thinking and behaving; his pattern of thinking and behaving is his personality; it is the way he separates from love, from other people, and from God.

When other people come nearer to us, we panic for they are about to destroy our cherished separated ego selves in bodies; we run from them or do what makes us justify separating from them.

I cannot possibly exhaust what each of the seven billion human beings on planet earth today does to separate from other people. Therefore, I will describe how I separate from love and leave it to you to understand how you separate from love, from union, from joined state, from God.

HERE IS HOW I SEPARATE FROM LOVE

My personality is avoidant. The avoidant personality, in common parlance, the shy person, feels that as he is not good enough and that if other people come close to him, they would see that he is no good. He is filled with fear and anxiety from anticipating rejection from other people. To avoid rejection and reduce his anxiety, he avoids people. He keeps to himself.

There is always a biological, medical disorder, a reason that made the shy child feel not physically good hence believe that other children would see him as not good and reject him. In my case, I inherited a hypersensitive body (I have described that elsewhere).

I have always feared rejection by people and kept to myself. Avoidant personality disorder, as is all other personality and mental disorders, as well as so-called normal personality and body, are means of separating from other people and retaining the desired sense of separated self.

When I relate to people, I want them to accept me. If I feel that they would reject me, I withdraw from them. In avoiding them, I retain my grandiose ego and thus, avoid the fact that I am joined to all people; I avoid the awareness of love, awareness of God.

I AM WHAT FOLKS CALL AN IMMATURE PERSON.

In intellect, I do not mind telling you that I have not seen any human being who can match me in philosophy and psychology (even physics). But emotionally, I am immature. I use my immaturities to avoid people and retain my ego-self, my separated self.

I am acutely aware of human nature, yet I do not do what enables me to relate well to people. For example, in relating to women, I know that they are vain. I know that they value their egos and bodies and want you to tell them that their bodies are beautiful. If you have sex with them, they want you to tell them that they are the greatest sex you have had in your life even if you feel that they are not good at sex. You have to praise a woman's appearance and tell her that she is beautiful, that her clothes are great; when she does what women do to their hair, you have to notice them. You simply have to gratify women's egos and their dance of worth in ego and body.

If you want to get along with your wife and women in general, you must praise their ego dances. What do I do? I know what they are doing. I know that their egos, their special selves, want me to acknowledge them for them to seem alive. I know that their egos and special selves are not real, are not their true selves, and are their dream identities. Instead of being amused by them, as I should if I was a true mystic, I, in my mind, say, get the hell out of my sight, you childish egotist.

I do not affirm women's egos and bodies. I avoid them. So, you are a woman and you put on the best makeups in the world, dress in expensive clothes, wear expensive jewelry, and drive a Rolls Royce or whatever your idea of expensive car is; I literally do not acknowledge your presence.

I have actually gone to an office and the boss there, say, a permanent secretary in a Nigerian ministry, is a woman and I treated her as a toy and have no respect for her.

Of course, she notices that I do not respect her ego and body, that I do not admire her painted body (I call the dressed up human body whited sepulcher), and so she tries to make life difficult for me by not doing what I came to her office to get done.

Women can be very petty if you do not, in words or non-verbal means, tell them that they are beautiful; you simply have to satisfy their vanity for them to like you.

Women will do for you what you want done if you see their egos as admirable and their bodies as beautiful. You are reinforcing their ego selves and keeping them in the egos' dream world, where they want to be. Me, I ignore them and they detest me.

I treat men even worse; I do not acknowledge their wealth, social position, and power. Men seek social achievement, wealth, and power believing that those make them important in other men's eyes; they want you to acknowledge their power. I see their dance for power- and ego-based worth as childish and ignores them.

My immature behavior is my attempt to not love other people, my efforts to maintain my desired separation from them.

We, all people, are always joined but in my dream of separation, I want to seem separated from people. My God, since I was a child, I have not acknowledged social classes.

At college, I visited Washington DC. I visited the White House and Ronald Reagan was the president of the USA. I was on the line to get into the house. I saw a friend from the University of California walking by; he said, so, you want to go there, and pointed to the White House. I said to him, no I do not want to go see that garbage called Reagan; I just want to see what the White House looks like.

At college, I was a socialist and detested capitalists; now, I am a mixed economist who accepts both socialism and capitalism and wants to mix them to produce a just society.

My disdain for so-called important capitalists continues. When I visited the Vatican, Buckingham Palace, and anywhere else that so-called important people live in, I kind of think that monkeys live there. To me, those living in those magnificent houses are subhuman beings, not worthy to be close to me. Those people tolerate social injustice and as such, are subhuman beings.

What I was doing is putting those people down. By putting them down, I am separating from them. That way, I maintain my desired separation from other people and live as an individuated ego. I stay away from love, from union with other people.

As noted, in childhood, I was shy; I had an avoidant personality; I desired attention from my significant others. I often pleased folks around me to get their attention. You would think that pleasing people is nice, right? Wrong!

If you please people, you are trying to appeal to their egos so that they may like your ego. Only the ego pleases other egos. Pleasing other people, in effect, is a means of maintaining your ego; the pleaser is making an effort to retain his ego of separation.

Don't please anyone; stick to doing only what you believe is right, which invariably means what loves you and all people.

My immature behaviors were my means of escaping from love, from union, from feeling of being joined to all people and live as a separated person.

I am very aware of my behavior. This is because I came to this world, already beginning to awaken from the dream of self-forgetfulness; I was on the path to salvation.

Most people are in deep sleep, deep dreaming, and have not begun the awakening process. They are not yet aware of what they do to avoid awareness of love.

I mentioned women above. All their dances, wearing beautiful clothes, jewelry, having expensive cars and houses, are efforts to make their egos and bodies seem real in their awareness; their egos and bodies are used to avoid union with other people, avoid love.

Look at what you do; if you are capable of self-observation in an objective manner, write what you observe about you down on paper; they are your means of separating from other people, means of separating from love. That is your own ego dance. It is what keeps you on earth.

Now, consciously decide to know that you are always unified to all people, joined to all people. When you make that decision, then stop doing all the things you hitherto did to separate you from people and affirm your ego-self. Everything you do is designed to keep you away from love.

Consider watching pornography. Given who I am, a thinker, I asked myself why I watched men and women having sex (I did not want to see homosexual scenes for those made me vomit).

So, why did I watch pornography? By watching pornography, I avoided relating to actual women. Pornography is a means of separating from women, a means of avoiding love for women (even at what Helen Schucman, in *A Course in Miracles*, called special love level relationship, pornography does not respect other people's egos and bodies hence does not love peoples' egos and bodies and certainly does not love their spirits).

I am not a moralist; I am not preaching against pornography. I am just observing what we use it to do. As long as people want to avoid loving each other, they will focus on their bodies and sexual organs. Let people who want to do that do it. It is where they are at in evolution.

If you want to return to the awareness of love, you must overlook people's egos and bodies, what they do with their egos and bodies, and focus on their inner selves, their spirit selves, the sons of God in them.

Sex is a dream activity that affirms ego and body as real; as a dream activity, it is nothing; it has not detracted from the love in people.

Love pornographers and ignore what they do with their egos and bodies. They have done nothing good or bad.

Sex, ego, body, and the physical universe are dreams and in truth, do not exist. If you focus on love and overlook folks' bodies and egos and o the universe of space, time, and matter, you will one day have the delightful experience of seeing the physical universe disappear from your awareness and you experience union with all; you literally feel unified with God and all his creation and in it, know that there is no space and gap between you and God and other sons of God.

God is in you and you are in God. Other people are in you and you are in them. All existence shares one self, the self of God, and share one mind, our collective thinking.

WHAT IS LOVE?

What is love? Love means recognizing the son of God in you and in every person you see, in animals, trees, in everything, as unified with you.

Everything is a part of God. Accept that fact. Accept that all creation is unified and joined. See all people as parts of you and you as parts of them.

YOU NEED DO NOTHING TO EXPERIENCE LOVE.

If you accept our eternal union with each other, you do not need to do anything else to experience love.

Love is not what you give to people or what they give to you. We are always already joined, in union, in love with one another.

We invented space, time, matter, ego, and body and use those to mask the love we already live in.

Remove the things we employ to enable us to not experience the love we always live in. Remove the blocks to the awareness of love and you do not need to do anything else to know love.

You must remove your identification with the ego and body, sit back, and relax into the awareness of the love that you always already live in.

You do not need to be running around giving people money, buying things for them to show them that you love them.

Of course, if you have money, by all means, share it with those who do not have money, but that is merely gratifying your egos' sense of importance and their egos' desire to receive things; that is not love.

(This evening, June 22, an old woman that I used to give rides to go shopping knocked at my door and said that she had not seen me in six months and asked where I was; I told her that I was out of state. She said, may I come in and I said yes. She came in and told me that she wants to ask me a favor. I said that I am all ears. She said that she has not been eating well and asked if I could help her out. I said yes. She gave me a list of groceries she wanted to buy and said that she does not have the money to buy them. I accepted the list and told her that I would go buy them for her tomorrow; it is about one hundred dollars. I had her come into my kitchen and take whatever canned foods she wanted. She filled grocery bags. She said that she has not talked to anyone in months and said that she wanted to talk to me. I said that I am willing to listen. After all, I am a psychotherapist and made my living by listening to people. This woman sat there for three hours pouring the story of her life to me, including her trips to psychiatric hospitals for depression. I am not doing clinical work here but if I put on my clinician's hat, I would diagnose her as having major depression with paranoid features; she has loads of fear of people and thinks that they could harm her; I would recommend some of the anti-depressant medications, such as Prozac, Paxil, or Zoloft for her. I said nothing beyond asking leading questions to get her to talk. Well, I listened and finally escorted her to her apartment, promised to go buy the groceries she wanted, and gave her some money, maybe a hundred dollars that I would withdraw from my bank. Am I doing this out of love? No. I simply helped a fellow human being. Whenever I am driving and stop at a stoplight and some ragged-looking person comes to my car's window asking for money, I open my wallet and if there is money in it,

I give whatever money is in it, usually five, ten, or twenty dollars to him or her. At a deep level, we are all joined, in love with one another. Love is not earned but known when we remove our egos. Her list included buying packets of cigarettes for her. I will not buy cigarettes for her, not because of the cost but because I do not approve of anyone smoking, doing drugs, or drinking alcohol. I draw the line there; one should not abuse one's body and mind with these poisons.)

In love, you do nothing; love is not earned. Love is who we are. Remove your ego and body and you instantaneously know that you are in God and in love.

AM I TALKING METAPHYSICAL MUMBO JUMBO?

All these may sound esoteric and metaphysical to you. They are not. Why don't you remove your ego (first transform it to ego of love, which is what Christians call Christ)? Eliminate your ego; do not think or behave from your ego's self-interest.

Do not identify with your body (body that will die and dissolve to elements, elements that will decay to the particles of electrons, protons, and neutrons that compose them, and those decay to light, and light decay to nothingness from whence we conjured them out during the Big Bang explosion).

Do nothing and know love.

Do nothing means do not do ego things. Accept you as part of love, accept all people as parts of love, accept God as love; accept that in love, all things are joined, not physically but with a spiritual thread.

Do so, close your eyes, tune out the physical world, take a deep breath, and see yourself in a world of light forms, and thereafter, experience the formless unified world of God; that is, experience perfect formless love (the type of love that our neurotic friend Saint Paul said passes human understanding).

SICKNESS IS A MEANS OF DEFENDING THE EGO AND BODY.

When one begins to gain awareness that love is who we are and that love means not identifying with ego and body, one fears the death of one's ego and body; one uses one's thinking, mind to make one's body sick.

If one is sick, then one's body seems real to one. One devotes one's time to seek medical remedies for one's sick body.

As long as one concentrates on getting medical help for one's weak and sick body, one would no longer know that thinking, mind, caused one's body's sickness.

Sickness seems like what happens to one against one's wishes, for who consciously wants to be sick? Sickness makes the body seem real like we are determined by our bodies hence by external things in the environment.

We are not determined by our thinking, minds, the ego tells us. Sickness is a defense of the egos' world view that we are victims punished by nature and God, hence makes it seem logical not to pay attention to God.

If you understand all this, you can change your mind, love, and heal your body's sickness. But if you are not yet ready to realize that only the mind determines what happens to you and believe in the efficacy of medications, by all means, go to medical doctors and take the medications they give to you.

You cannot run until you have learned to walk. Understanding spiritual matters takes time; most people are at the lower steps of that understanding and cannot use their thinking mind to heal their apparent sick bodies.

It is our thinking, mind that invents medications so taking medications is indirectly using our minds to heal our bodies; nevertheless, medications, like food, maintain the illusion that body determines mind.

On earth, we need food and medications but enlightened persons in the world of light forms do not need food or medications to live.

DEATH IS A DEFENSE OF EGO, BODY, AND SEPARATION.

When love, that is, union, joining, losing the ego separated self, becomes known to one's mind, one prefers to die. Thus, one dies. All death is suicide.

One prefers to die rather than face the fact that that there is no such thing as death; there is no body, space, and time but the dream death folks go through makes it seem like death is real.

If death is real, then the ego and body are real; God has abandoned his son to death and the ego has won its war with God.

Alas, death is dream death. When you think that you died in body, you merely see yourself in a light body in a world of light forms.

Since you have not learned that there is no such thing as death, you re-manifest in body, again, and give you sickness and death to make ego and body seem real.

You keep playing this game until you accept that you are the immortal son of God who does everything to you to experience what you experience on earth. Thereafter, when you seem to die, you do not reincarnate back to earth (Buddhists call it breaking the wheel of rebirth on earth).

There is no sickness, no death, no separation, no ego and body; only God and his sons exist in a formless unified state.

It is you and all of us that want to experience the opposite of God, opposite of eternity, opposite of love, and give you the games you play on earth of being born in body, being sick, aging, and dying—all false.

If while you are on earth you remember that sickness and death is your game and that there is no death and sickness, you will simply see your body change to light body and you disappear from this world and join the teachers of love, the teachers of God, those who help those still living on earth; they are called spiritual guides or angels; they help us to learn about eternal verities. They put ideas into your mind, perhaps, by directing you to go to lectures or read books that will enlighten you, and if you can handle it and not think that you are hallucinating, going mad, they may actually talk to you directly or show themselves to you in visions (I have seen Jesus Christ in visions ... and he is not my lord, he is just my friend).

Their advanced students of love, teachers of union, and teachers of God while on earth, do what I am doing in this writing.

CONCLUSION

Everything that we do on earth is defense of separated existence. The study of science, technology, and medicine all are efforts to adapt to the world of separation, not transcend it. Eating food, wearing clothes, taking medications, etc. are efforts to make the body survive, hence are defense of what body protects, separated selves.

Since the world does not exist, we are then defending what does not exist that we believe exists. We are defending an illusion; we are defending madness.

Connected Lives

If you do not defend anything in this world, you do yourself a favor, for an undefended world disappears from existence. Stop defending separation and revert to union. When you stop defending separated ego existence and their bodies, you revert to awareness of formless unified self and in it, know peace and joy. When you stop defending your ego and body, separation, you become aware of the love that is everywhere and that you always are a part for you cannot separate from love.

Defenselessness and return to love mean escaping from the physical universe of separated things. If one still wants to live in the physical universe and doesn't want to negate it, then one defends the ego of love, aka Christ self, and experience relative peace, not the perfect peace of formless unified heaven.

EVERYTHING PEOPLE DO ON EARTH IS TO ADAPT TO THE EXIGENCIES OF THE EARTH; THAT IS, TO COPE WITH THE DEMANDS OF THE EGO AND ITS SEPARATED WORLD.

ON THE OTHER HAND, EVERYTHING THAT MY METAPHYSICS TALKS ABOUT IS TELLING PEOPLE TO NOT ADAPT TO EARTH, TO GIVE UP THE EARTH, AND NOT DEFEND THEIR EGOS AND BODIES AND IN SO DOING, EXPERIENCE HEAVEN, UNIFIED SPIRIT STATE, AND RETURN HOME.

SINCE I AM TELLING PEOPLE TO DO WHAT THEY DID NOT COME TO DO ON EARTH, IS IT ANY WONDER THAT THEY DO NOT LISTEN TO ME OR BUY MY IDEAS?

VALUING THE WORLD IS VALUING NOTHING.

ONE MUST HAVE DETACHMENT IN VALUING THE WORTHLESS

If you look at the world and the things in it, what you see is ephemeral and transitory. People are born, age, and die. Houses become old and collapse, even pyramids will, in time, return to sand. All the material things people are proud of, such as expensive cars, etc. in a few years, are sent to the junkyard. Nothing in this world is permanent (except, perhaps, change).

People, especially Americans and Igbos seem oblivious of the nothingness of the material things they struggle to acquire, that they sold or enslaved their fellow human beings to acquire; they acquire worthless stuff that would return to sand.

Therefore, the best approach to life is to be detached from the things of this world. Obviously, we need material things to live on earth but seeking them with attachment is a way of guaranteeing headache for one when they are gone.

Please do not get me wrong; I am not ascetic; I do not urge folks to not strive to have the good things of this world; I want to live well, die, and heard from no more; as long as I am alive in ego and body, I want the best cars, such as Rolls Royce and Lamborghini, the best of anything that human science and technology can produce, and I deserve them!

Seek things in a detached manner because you understand their nothingness. Use them to live well. I do not like poverty. I want to live well and do live well. But I am not attached to any material thing and for that matter, to anything on earth. My philosophy is that the earth is a dream; the things of the earth are dream things. Our lives are the stuff dreams are made of, said the old Bard.

Dream and dream things are not permanent and are not real. Why should I sweat dream and dream things that are here today and are gone tomorrow? When we wake up from this nightmarish dream called life on earth, all that we valued is gone. Therefore, I choose to be detached from the earth and its fantasy things.

Pursuit of wealth and political power should be seen as means to living well in the extant society. We should use political power and wealth to organize society well but not have the illusion that they are worthwhile.

People say that they want to write their names in the sands of history. Great. How many people in your world that lived a hundred years ago or a thousand years ago do you know about? History remembers one in millions of people and even those will be gone as time progresses.

We today remember the great physicists, chemists, and biologists, such as Copernicus, Galileo, Kepler, Huygens, Tyco Brahe, Newton, Dalton, Boyle, Thomas Young, Michael Faraday, Henri Becquerel, Pierre and Marie Currie, J.J. Thompson, Ludwig Boltzmann, Max Plank, Albert Einstein, Ernest Rutherford, Neils Bohr, Warner Heisenberg, Erin Schrodinger, Paul Dirac, Pauli, Broglie, Wheeler, Jenner, Charles Darwin, Mendel, Alexander Flaming, James Watson, Francis Crick, and a few others (see my book that reviewed what the great scientists, psychologists, philosophers, and technologists such as Alexander Graham Bell, Thomas Edison, John Rockefeller, Henry Ford, Steve Jobs, Bill Gates, etc. did or said).

In a few hundred years, these great minds' discoveries would be child's play as science advances to the stratosphere and no one remembers those earlier scientists and their discoveries (we are on the verge of understanding anti-matter, dark matter, dark energy, and multiverse and that will take our science to a whole new level).

Nothing in this world is permanent except change. So, work hard, play hard, and enjoy the world but do not take it seriously. See the world and its activities as a source of mirth, joke for you.

The world must be taken humorously; it is a joke, really. We are the things of dreams; we are here today and gone tomorrow and are forgotten, said the immortal Bard, William Shakespeare. We are like a tale told by a fool, full of sound and fury but signifying nothing; we are like actors on a stage, we strut about, making noise, and then are heard from no more (Macbeth).

Please do not get me wrong; I am not depressed or despondent; I have the temperament of the philosopher. In my youth, I found joy in reading Homer, Plato, Aristotle, Virgil (Aeneid), Marcus Aurelius, Seneca, Cicero, Machiavelli, Leibniz, Rene Descartes, Blaise Pascal, Voltaire, Jean Jacque Rousseau, Kant, Hegel, Schopenhauer, Nietzsche, Feuerbach, William James, Henri Bergman, Thomas Hobbes, John Locke, Adam Smith, our racist friend David Hume (that Scottish boy thought that he was smart and that Africans are dumb; I would have liked to sit with him, talk philosophy and science with him, and put him to shame, show him that Africans are as smart as anyone else), George Berkeley, Jeremy Bentham, and John Stuart Mill.

Philosophy and science are the consolations of thinkers who find the world depressing, said Boethius. As our stoic philosophers such as Zeno said, approach the world with great study and dedication but do not take it seriously; Epicure said, enjoy your life for we are here today and gone tomorrow (see the writings of the Roman stoic cum epicurean thinker, Horace).

If Eastern philosophy, aka religion, is your cup of tea, read Confucius, Lao Tzu, Gautama Buddha, Shankara, Ramanujan, Ramakrishna, Ramana Maharshi, etc. These all say that we should be detached from the things of this world for it is tinsel, mere dream thing.

Remember Buddha's four noble truths: Human life is characterized by suffering; suffering is caused by our desire to live as separated egos in bodies; suffering is eliminated when we give up desiring to be egos; or mitigated when we adopt a detached approach to living on earth.

Buddhist Chinese and Japanese and Asians in general work hard but do not have emotional investment in the products of their hard labor; this is unlike childish white Americans and Igbos who think that they are their material things hence become depressed or commit suicide when shiny objects dim.

I am a laughing philosopher; I do not let this world's ups and downs disturb my emotional equilibrium. Yet, I work as hard as any human being who claims to work hard!

I woke up at 1 AM this morning and typed this stuff in less than one hour; I am going back to sleep!

DEFENSE OF SELF IMAGE, SELF-CONCEPT, AND BODY

Spirit, the son of God is formless; it has mind; in unified spirit self, it has no self-concept as a separated self, and no self-image for a self-image must be predicated on body. So, it invented space, time, and matter and used matter to fashion body for it; it then used his mind to fashion a self-concept as a separated self housed in body, an ego; it made a self-image for that separated self and body enabled it to do so.

Without body, space, and time, it could not have self-image; it would be in heaven's formless state. Now that it has a self-image rooted in body, it made body vulnerable, seeing things as trying to snuff it out, kill it, and became invested in protecting the attacked body. It then defends the body and its self-image. It spends all of its life, every minute of it, defending the body-based self-image.

All of its life on earth is devoted to defense of the self-image which it thinks that if it does not defend its body, it would die and it would go out of existence.

Actually, if it does not defend the self-image, the body does not exist for the body is a dream body.

Stop talking and from now on, do not defend your self-image for it is not you; stop worrying how other self-images see it for other people are not self-images either, you are merely playing games with them to keep yourself in self-image defense, hence limit your God state, God awareness, hence depowering you.

If you do not defend your self-image and body disappears, you have the power of the son of God, total power.

25

TEACHING LEADERSHIP OF ORGANIZATIONS AND NOT LEADING ANYONE IS ABSURD!

I teach other people about organizations and their leadership; they use that information to go start and lead organizations and make money. So, what organization have I started and led with my knowledge of organizations and leadership?

I teach people to eliminate their egos and self-images; have I eliminated my own self-image, self-concept, and ego and known peace, or am I just going to talk about it only?

I am not body; I made my body to see me in body image; I must stop defending body-based self-image.

You are not your self-image that you made; the self-image vanishes when you stop defending the self-image. You have a self, a formless self who is eternal, the son of God; life itself would not die if you do not defend the self-image.

WORRYING ABOUT WHAT OTHER PEOPLE THINK ABOUT YOU KEEPS YOU IN THE EGO.

Do you worry about what other people think of you as a person or your behavior? If the answer is yes, then you are operating from the ego.

The ego is a self-concept with an accompanying self-image that says that one is separated from God and other sons of God.

The separated self feels incomplete (we cannot be complete unless we are rooted in God and the whole). The incomplete ego-feeling person then feels that he is going to become complete if other egos like him, approve him, and accept him.

He devotes much of his thinking and behaviors to try to do what he thinks that other people and society would approve, such as obtain an education, a good job, money, marry (regardless of whether he likes marriage or not), have children (regardless of whether he wants them or not); he generally tries to have social prestige so as to be liked by other people.

He is a slave to what other people would think of him. Other people control him because he must conform to their opinions.

This is a pity for this person does not realize that there are people who do not give a damn about what other people think of them, people who merely do what they themselves think is right and live in peace.

The ego makes itself seem alive by trying to live up to other egos' opinions and in so doing makes other egos seem alive; thus, our collective egos seem alive by conforming to each other's opinions.

In truth, people are the sons of God, are unified, and are not egos. Egos are dream figures housed in bodies that desperately are trying to seem alive. They do not exist.

Egos are like people you see in your dream; when you sleep and dream, they do not exist but seem to exist for as long as you sleep, dream, and take your dream as real.

Life is found only in unified spirit, God. Egos are ghosts, apparitions; they are illusions; you see them with your physical eyes and they seem to exist but in truth, they do not exist.

Where you see people and things are no persons and things. This seems incredible but is true. The person or things you see is composed of the various elements (carbon, hydrogen, oxygen, nitrogen, etc.); those elements are composed of electrons, protons, and neutrons; those particles of the atom are composed of quarks that are composed of photons.

Wherever you see, people are nothing but light that your eyes deceived you into seeing them as solid objects.

Light itself is conjured out of nothingness during the Big Bang. What exists is formless spirit. You are a formless spirit (which is part of God's formless unified spirit).

For our present purposes, do not worry about what other egos, people, think of you for that is a waste of your time. Simply do only what your inner self tells you are right, which, if you are sane, is that you should love yourself, other people, and God (the whole).

IS EGO-LESSNESS POSSIBLE IN THIS WORLD?

Can you become egoless? The physical universe of space, time, and matter is of the ego. The sleeping sons of God projected out space, time, and matter, used matter to construct human bodies, and now seem to be living in bodies, as egos. It all seems real.

If you let go of your ego, you see the universe of space, time, and matter disappear and you experience yourself as part of unified spirit; this is literal not figurative.

But as long as you are on earth, you are in ego and must see space, time, and matter.

Only a few people experience formless unified spirit (in Samadhi, Satori, Nirvana, and what Christians call the mystical union of the son of God and his father).

What is more likely to be attained is to transform your ego of hate to ego of love. When you use your ego and body to love all people, you would occasionally see you and people in light forms.

There is a universe of light forms. This is where the saints are. Only the spiritually advanced people are in light forms; they guide people who are on earth by teaching them the truth.

Those in the world of light forms occasionally disappear into the formless world of God and from there, reappear in the world of light forms and continue teaching those on earth how to find their lost way back to unified spirit.

CONCLUSION

What I said here is said by the mystics of all religions. Please read Evelyn Underhill's *Mysticism*; Richard Maurice Bucke's *Cosmic Consciousness*; and William James' *Varieties of Religious Experience*.

I urge you to pay particular attention to the poems of the Sufi Muslim mystic, Rumi. When I read him, I felt that somebody else experienced what I experience: the literal oneness of all people in the formless unified world of God and the understanding that our present physical universe of space, time, and matter is a literal dream by all of us, the formless sons of God.

The true goal of religion is to figure out a way to awaken from the dream of self-forgetfulness and regain awareness of our true home in unified spirit, in God and his heaven, an experience that convinces one of our immortality, permanency, and changelessness in God; an experience of indescribable peace and joy, pure bliss.

HEARING THE COSMIC BACKGROUND MICROWAVE RADIATION

To kill time, I am currently reading Bill Bryson's book, *A Short History of Nearly Everything*. He is really not saying anything that I do not already know or have not written on. Nevertheless, the way he says what we already know gives me a new slant on old subjects.

If you are into astrophysics, astronomy, and cosmology, you already know that the universe came out of nothing about 13.8 billion years ago. Out of nothing, a photon of light, radiation came out; it grew incredibly hot and exploded and expanded at what George Gamow and Alain Goth called inflationary speed. Within a fraction of a second, it expanded billions and billions of miles (into space that it created, not into a preexisting vacuum).

That light transformed itself to quarks and quarks joined to form protons and neutrons (held together by the strong nuclear force; weak nuclear force makes them decay); light also transformed to electrons; that is to say that light formed matter (and formed the four forces of nature: gravity, electromagnetism, strong and weak nuclear force).

Light also transformed itself into anti-matter. Anti-matter and matter attacked each other and were supposed to have annihilated themselves, and returned to radiation, hence ending the incipient universe.

But, for some reasons, there were more particles of matter than antimatter so that when the mutual attack occurred, some matter survived to continue the evolution of our matter-based universe.

Stephen Weinberg, in his book, the *First Three Minutes*, told us that within three minutes of the universe's existence, protons and neutrons combined to form nuclei of the simplest elements (hydrogen, helium, lithium).

Thereafter, the universe was plasma; that is, it was a sea of unattached nuclei, electron, and photons. It was that way for 400, 000 years.

For some inexplicable reasons, at the 400, 000-year mark, nuclei-captured electrons and atoms (of hydrogen, helium, and lithium; the rest of the elements were formed either inside stars or during supernova when stars die in huge explosions) were formed. This event allowed light, aka radiation, to escape from the hitherto plasma universe.

Those photons, radiation, that escaped are what Arnold Penzias and Robert Wilson accidentally discovered at the Bell Laboratory in New Jersey in 1965 and for which they were given the Nobel Prize in 1978 (Dicke, at Princeton University, who was searching for this radiation, which George Gamow had suggested existed from the Big Bang, ended up not winning the Nobel).

If you turn on your television and happen to have it at a station that you do not receive, you see a wavy and hissy sound on your television screen. What you are seeing is the cosmic background microwave radiation. That is the light that escaped during the era when nuclei captured electrons to form atoms.

The cosmic background microwave radiation is everywhere but we do not see it with our naked eyes; however, we have learned to use it, such as the radiation you use in your microwave oven.

This information is what any student of physics gleans during his first year at college so it is not a big deal. What is a big deal is that this morning, I suddenly realized that the hissy sound that I generally hear in my head when I am calm, what my Hindu Swamis told me is the Om sound that mystics hear before they transcend our world and reach the world of light forms and thereafter the formless world of God, could be part of the cosmic microwave background radiation.

When I was a kid and we drove from Lagos to Owerri, my home town, about five hundred miles away, thereafter, for two days or so, I would hear the sound of the motor of the damn car running in my head. It used to drive me bananas and I would talk to my parents about it and they did not know what the hell I am talking about.

If I was taken to a psychiatrist, he would probably have given it a psychiatric diagnosis. Luckily, I was not exposed to ill-educated psychiatrists (I have supervised many of them and know that their knowledge of physics is abysmal).

How can I prove that this hissy sound is part of the cosmic background microwave radiation? I do not know how.

For now, I posit that the hissy sound could be part of the Cosmic Background Microwave Radiation (radiation is a fancy name for light). My postulation is merely heuristic. If you are a scientist, please think about it, research it, and tell me what you found about it.

THE PARADOX OF MAN: MAN'S PERIOD OF GREATEST PRODUCTIVITY IS OFTEN HIS PERIOD OF GREATEST CRUELTY!

The past five hundred and thirty years, no doubt, has been the greatest era in Western Europe's productivity. During this period, a little landmass that would fit into West Africa conquered the world and gave the world its culture. How did this happen?

In 1453, Muslim Turks finally overran Constantinople (and renamed it Istanbul); they took over what was called the Byzantine Empire (Eastern Roman Empire).

The Muslims prevented the Venetians, Portuguese, and Spanish (the great powers of Europe at this time) from going through the land route to India, China, and Japan (called Silk Road). The Turks made themselves the middlemen and brought the goods of Asians to Europe and sold them at exorbitant prices.

Generally, people want to buy cheap so Europeans began looking for an alternative route to Asia. The Portuguese felt that they could reach India by rounding Africa's West and East coasts; thus, beginning around

1460, they began sending sailors to explore African coasts. Eventually, they got to South Africa in 1488 (they established the Cape of Good Hope, today called Cape Town); Vasco Dagama got to India in 1494.

The Spanish hoped to reach India by going directly into the Atlantic Ocean, going west. Christopher Columbus got to the Caribbean in 1492.

Portugal and Spain, as they say, discovered the Americas, North and South, and reaped a great deal of wealth from the two continents. Portugal and Spain became the greatest economic and political powers in Europe. Gold and agricultural goods poured in from the new world (corn, potatoes, and tobacco, for example).

The Northwestern Europeans got envious and wanted to get into the action. Initially, England encouraged its pirates, called buccaneers (think Francis Drake), to harass Portuguese and Spanish ships laden with goods on the high seas. English men became pirates stealing from the two Iberian countries.

In 1517, Martin Luther broke from the Roman Catholic Church. The Pope sent his Christian armies to go reconquer Germany. Germany was subjected to 100 years of religious wars, during which one-third of its population perished.

In 1532, England, under King Henry the eight, broke from Rome. The Catholic loyalist forces had their eyes set on reconquering England for the Holy Roman Catholic Church. Add the harassment of English buccaneers and Spain gathered an Armada of warships and sent them, in 1588, to go subdue the little pesky England.

Nature intervened, scattered the great Armada, and helped England to win. That victory made the English Navy a force to be reckoned with.

That same year, the British tried to settle in North America at Roanoke Island in North Carolina and failed but in 1607, England managed to establish a colony at Jamestown, Virginia, and its North American empire began.

British North America, let us cut through the chase, includes today's USA and Canada. Imagine that, a little island has a subcontinent all to itself!

The British eventually established colonies in Australia and New Zealand and took South Africa from the Dutch in 1807.

The Portuguese and Spanish established their great empires in Latin America and parts of Africa.

In 1870, Germany was unified by Otto Von Bismarck, demanded its own colonies, and got Tanganyika, South West Africa (Namibia), Togo, Cameroon, and Islands in the Pacific Ocean, such as New Guinea.

Europe was on the roll. The entire world was declared Terra-Cotta, uninhabited by human beings, and Western Europeans gave themselves the permission to take any part of the world.

The Slavic race, such as Russia, moved eastward, took the Turkistan countries and Siberia, got to the Bering Sea, crossed it in 1746, took Alaska and kept on going south, and got to San Francisco, California before the Spanish in Mexico made it known that the West coast of North America belonged to them (they established Catholic missions along the coast; they actually got to Alaska and named some of the cities, such as Valdez; the USA bought Alaska from Russia in 1867).

Western Europeans eventually tried to take the ancient civilizations of India, Japan, China, and other parts of Asia and up to a point, succeeded.

Europeans now ruled the entire world. They exported their institutions and culture to the entire world (I am an African and I am writing in English, meaning that I was culturally and mentally conquered by Europeans).

In 1543, Nicolas Copernicus posited that the Sun is the center of our local solar system. He, in effect, put away Aristotle's and Ptolemy's geocentric worldview where the earth is said to be the center of the universe. He established the heliocentric worldview.

In 1610, Galileo used his improved telescope to prove that, indeed, the Sun is the center of our solar system. Johan Kepler, Christian Huygens, and Tyco Brahe added to the West's nascent astronomy.

In 1687, Isaac Newton (in his book *Principia Mathematica*) discovered the law of gravity and posited the three laws of motion (my friend, you must take basic physics; you must understand mechanics, heat, light, sound, electricity, and quantum mechanics to live in this world or else, you are primitive).

European science was solidly established in the seventeenth century.

(From pure reason's perspective, one would have expected Buddhist China to have originated modern science because the Chinese did not have to deal with the shibboleth of God; they were totally free to think; they did discover many things, including stars, supernova, gun powder, and printing; that science began in primitive Europe with its Christian God and the inquisition, burning whoever did not agree with the gatekeepers of that God, the Catholic Pope and his cardinals, is an amazing thing.)

In the 1600s, some progress was made in the European scientific journey, mostly in France. In the 1700s, John Dalton rediscovered atomic theory (the Greek Democritus talked about the atom as the indivisible part of nature). The atom, Dalton said, is the most indivisible part of matter.

Robert Boyle established chemistry by talking about how gases behave. In the mid-1700s, James Watt invented the steam engine; Stevenson constructed the first train; the industrial revolution began in little old England around 1746.

In 1803, Thomas Young, in the double-slit experiment, showed that particles passing through two holes left interference marks on the paper behind them; this proved that particles are wave in nature.

Newton had observed that particles of light were corpuscles, particles. Quantum mechanics proved that light is both wave and particles; Werner Heisenberg noted in his uncertainty principle that particles behave as the experimenter wants them to behave for him, wave or particles.

The nineteenth-century can be said to be the dawn of science as we now know it. In 1859, Charles Darwin established his theory of evolution. Michael Faraday discovered electricity; James Clark Maxwell wrote his four equations on electromagnetism; at Cambridge University, J.J. Thompson in 1897 discovered the electron.

In France, Henri Becquerel showed that the nucleus of atoms do decay, releasing alpha, beta, and other types of radiation and electrons. Pierre and Marie Curie showed that when nuclear decays, elements transform to other types of elements. Uranium, for example, decays and becomes lead.

In Germany, Rontgen discovered X-ray (which is from the light given off when nuclei of certain elements decay).

At the turn of the twentieth century, Max Plank discovered that light is in quanta, particles. Albert Einstein in 1905 showed that photons, particles, have the capacity to knock off electrons, particles on a hot object. He also wrote about his theory of special relativity (modified to theory of General Relativity in 1916).

In 1911, Ernest Rutherford of New Zealand working at Cambridge discovered the proton (nucleus of atoms, so, the atom is not the final part of matter, after all).

In 1932, Rutherford's student, James Chadwick, discovered the neutron. The atom is now known to be composed of electrons, protons, and neutrons (protons and neutrons are in the nucleus, held together by the strong nuclear force); study your valence.

By the 1920s, quantum physics was established; folks like Louis Broglie, Paul Dirac, Werner Heisenberg, Erin Schrodinger, Ludwig Pauli, Lise Meitner, Otto Hahn, and Max Born made their contributions to quantum physics, also called new physics, different from old or classical physics that studied motion, heat/thermodynamics, light, electricity, sound.

Meitner showed that if the nuclei of an atom are struck with neutrons, it could produce chain reaction that split the nuclei and tremendous energy is released. That was exactly what the Manhattan project led by Robert Oppenheimer accomplished.

In 1945, the first crude nuclear weapons were unleashed on Nagasaki and Hiroshima, Japan and ended the Second World War.

Later in the 1950s, hydrogen bombs were invented (hydrogen bombs are produced through two processes; first, you produce nuclei fission by using neutrons to split the nuclei and the enormous heat released fuses protons and neutrons called nuclei fusion, as takes place inside the core of stars) and that releases deadly radiation.

The West now is the power that dominated the world. Until the end of the twentieth century, there really was no rival to Western power, economy, science, technology, and industry.

The Asians appear to have caught up with the West technologically but not in producing original thinking in theoretical science; by and large, Europe and North America, the Germanic civilization, is still at the top of everything.

Africans are at the bottom of everything. Apparently, Africans satisfy themselves with stealing from their common wealth and do not want to make any contributions to science and technology. Let us forget Africa and move on.

Maybe in a couple of hundred years, Africa will join the human race and start competing in the world of mathematics, science, and technology; at present, they steal and use the money they stole from their people to consume what Europe and Asia produce; and complain about how Europe underdeveloped them. They forget to tell us how in the past they sold their people to Arabs and Europeans and in the present, steal from their people hence stifle modernizing their continent.

WESTERN CRUELTY

What I really want to talk about is that during this most productive era of Western civilization, we also had the West at its cruelest. The West almost killed off Native Americans and what was left of them was packed off to reservations.

The West killed off Tasmanians and relegated the aborigines of Australia to zoos; it tried the same genocide in New Zealand and the Maoris fought valiantly to live. It tried the same pogrom in South Africa, Kenya, and Rhodesia.

The West enslaved Africans in the Americas and used their labor for free to develop the Americas. It colonized Africans and treated them like animals.

As the West was brutalizing the rest of the world, its scientists did not say peen in opposition; they did not complain about their siblings' unprecedented cruelty, but instead, escaped into their laboratories discovering the things that have made the West what it is today.

Scientists left politics and social justice alone, and instead, concentrated on their scientific discoveries. Many scientists don't even know what politics is all about!

I am around college campuses. I go to the science departments and would not hear a word of complaint about how America treats black Americans like shit; instead, the scientists do their work and chase after the Nobel Prize.

In the 1960s, Americans were grappling with racial inequality, fighting for civil rights and fair housing, but that war did not concern scientists; they lived on a different planet, not concerned by the cruelty that their brothers in politics and economics visited on nonwhite folks; cruelty that acquired the resource that made their scientific inquiries possible, thus willy-nilly, they participated in the oppression of non-white persons; they are not innocent human beings at all.

The cruelty of their political and economic brothers does not seem to bother scientists; they do not even talk about it. Their siblings oppress and abuse the rest of the world and the scientists do not say a word about what is going on.

Please do not remind me that I am making generalizations; I know what I am doing; I know that a few scientists complained. I can think of Norm Chomsky at MIT.

In the main, scientists completely tuned out social injustices so as to focus on their science. Like children, they want to get their cherished prize, the Nobel Prize, but do not care how society is run.

At a point, I considered scientists sub-human beings; how could they not care about the oppression of people? I had no use for these monkeys in human form, I used to say.

DISCUSSION

Man is a paradox; his era of great productivity is often also his era of great cruelty. How do we reconcile this paradox? Perhaps we cannot.

I personally wish that there is a way to pay attention to the plight of the poor. I am not a spring chicken; I know that the majority of mankind are average and under any social system, will sink to the middle or bottom of the social order; there is nothing that we can do to change this pathetic situation.

Consider. I got up at 2 AM this morning, lay on my bed, began thinking about the ideas in this essay, went to my computer, and typed them within two hours. This is how my frenetic mind works.

Some people would take months, if not years, to produce the ideas I produce in a few hours. That is just the way it is.

The salient point is that most of mankind is average or unintelligent and will always sink to the bottom of any social totem pole but we can establish a social democracy with a mixed economy and have society provide publicly paid education for all people through university and health insurance for all people and then let the people swim or sink.

There will always be winners and losers in society. Even in heaven, there is God and his sons and God is the boss of the joint, not his sons; his sons can only dream of an imaginary place where they are the head honcho, our world.

I am a realist and accept social inequality but want to mitigate poverty in the masses.

CONCLUSION

The paradox of man is that he is capable of love for his fellow men and at the same time, capable of great cruelty. Imagine Adolf Hitler killing fifty million human beings. Imagine Donald Trump thinking that it is funny to have racism in America.

Yet, human beings produced mother Theresa who devoted her life to saving lives in the slums of Calcutta, India.

In the era when the West was as brutal as brutality can be, its best minds produced the science that I am proud of.

Good and evil seem inherent in man and in human society.

My idealistic nature wished that we only had good in man and his civilization but history teaches me that that probably is not going to happen. What is history but a documentation of man's inhumanity to man? So, I grind my teeth and accept social realism, but do not like it.

Still, we can strive to produce a balance: make life worth living for the masses of humanity.

TALKING ABOUT LEADERSHIP IS DIFFERENT FROM BEING A LEADER.

Chinua Achebe talked about the trouble with Nigeria having a lack of good leaders in the country. Did he then become the solution to the problem he identified? Was he a leader or a mere talker about leadership?

You must stop talking about leadership of society and organizations. You know what leaders do; they posit visions, dreams, goals of what they want done and use people and material to accomplish them. Instead of telling people to do, what leaders do, you must posit a vision and pursue a strategy to achieve it.

Instead of telling other people how to become leaders of Africa, you become a leader in Africa, at least, in one small area of African life.

Posit goals, have strategies on how to accomplish them, and pursue attaining those goals; until you have done so, stop talking about leadership and goals.

ATTAINING EGO-LESSNESS AS LEADERSHIP GOAL

If attaining ego-lessness is my goal, what is that? Have clarity of vision. Then I must give up my ego; I must not defend my ego with anger, fear, guilt, shame, and simply let life live through me.

ONE HEALED PERSON, ONE JOINED PERSON, HEALS THE WORLD, JOINS THE WORLD INTO ONE SELF.

One healed person, that is, one changed person, changed from ego separated self to Christ joined self, heals the world in the sense that he is now joined with all people, not separating from people, and no longer defending his separated ego and the people see him as joined with them.

Since he is not defending ego and is living from joined self, Christ self, people know that he is joined to them and feel peace and joy in his presence or when they think about him; in this sense, he is now a savior of the people, a savior of the world (I am translating Helen's poetry to prose).

HAVE CLARITY OF VISION AND GOALS.

I must ask myself: what is my goal? What am I trying to accomplish? Are that goal and vision realistic and accomplishable in this world?

Don't just talk about it, do it; accomplish it or shut the hell up.

If ego-lessness is my goal, then live egolessly; that is, do not defend my ego; I must live from Christ, live from my inner joined self, loving self; go from Helen's poetry that she did not live to what you believe is true; until you live your conviction, you are merely making noise, as most religious people do.

EGO-LESSNESS IS NOT AN END BUT A MEANS TO LIVE IN PEACE.

One already has an ego or else, one would not live in a separated body in space and time on earth; all that one can do is recognize one's ego, one's pattern of thinking separating thoughts, and stop doing so. To give up one's ego and stop defending one's ego are a means to an end.

The end is to have thinking that gives one fearlessness, angerlessness, and guiltlessness; to have a thinking pattern that gives one peace and joy.

To be egoless is a way of living that one pursues as a career that one truly likes; here, one lives in accord with one's inner self and is not driven by goals meant to please society and that gives one fear and anxiety from fear of failing them.

Writing and living egolessly, that is, defenselessly, is my career. This vocation gives me peace and I give my peace to the world by living peacefully and modeling how to live peacefully to all people, not by merely preaching about living peacefully but being peace (which means being a Christ self, a joined self, not a separated ego-self).

LIVING OUR JOINED SELVES

A Course in Miracles says that if you forgive and love all people, you are saved. You learn that and tell it to other people.

Here are facts. You can stand on your head and talk until you go blue in the face telling people to change and become better and they would not do so.

It does not matter whether other people change and are saved or not; what matters is: are you changed, saved? Do you love, forgive, and live in peace?

Instead of telling other people what to do to be saved, you should concentrate on saving you, changing you, and living a changed life, and if other people like what they see in you, they copy it, but do not waste your time and energy telling people to change; you cannot change other people.

Other people's bodies and social experiences are different from yours; you cannot understand their bodies and social experiences; you can understand your body and experience and learn what you do wrong and change it; do so and don't talk about changing other people.

The ego (separated you) likes to tell the rest of the world, other egos, to change while it does not do what it has to do to change; you have to discipline your mind (that is, your thinking); you have to remove fear and anger from your thinking; you have to love and forgive to live in peace.

YOUR SELF-CONCEPT AND SELF-IMAGE ARE TESTED BY EVENTS OF EVERYDAY LIVING.

Through pure ratiocination, I concluded that I ought to let go of my old self-concept and self-image, aka the ego. In the past, my ego was such that very little things made me angry. In anger, I fight back. I am not known for being a shrinking violet. If you did something that made me feel belittled, I would fight back and I do not care if you are my employer; if you are my employer and said what my ego felt is insulting, I would ask you to take it back and if not, tell you to stuff your job wherever you want to stuff it and quit. I do not tolerate emotional abuse from any human being. I have quit a job that paid almost $100, 000 a year because a white boss treated me as a boy, as they treat African Americans. I am a man, damn it, and you dare not treat me as a boy; fuck you and your job; I am out of here.

This afternoon, around 2 PM, I decided to go to a used bookstore (it also sells other things) and buy some used books. This is in Anchorage, Alaska, my hometown. I drove on Lake Otis Road and as I got near Northern Lights Boulevard, I realized that I got to turn left at the intersection (I have been out of town for six months so things are a bit hazy). I quickly changed lanes and went from the right lane to the far left one so that when the light turned green, I could turn to the left.

I waited for a while and finally, the green arrow was on and I turned to Northern lights Blvd. I was now close to the University of Alaska campus when I noticed that a police car is flashing its green light behind me. I did not think that I did anything wrong, so there was no need for me to be concerned. Nevertheless, I looked in front, behind, and sideways and noticed that I was the only car in several blocks so he must be flashing for me to stop.

I stopped and a white policeman, he is about twenty-eight years old, came to my car's left window. I said nothing; generally, when a white policeman stops me, I do not say anything. I know about Miranda rights. If he steps out of line, I would go to his boss and complain.

He asked for my driver's license and evidence of insurance. I gave him both items. He walked back to his car to check me out.

My mind began speculating about what I could have done wrong and could not come up with one. I probably have the best driving record in the world. I do not remember the last time I had a traffic ticket. I decided not to speculate and simply wait for him to come tell me what I did wrong.

In about ten minutes, he came back, gave me my IDs, and said that at the light, Lake Otis and Northern light Blvd, I turned left from the middle lane. He said that he is not going to give me a traffic ticket and walked back to his car.

Turning from the middle lane was not my recollection; as noted, I had quickly moved to the left lane and then stopped and waited for the light to turn green.

I knew that I did not do what he said I did. I felt messed with by a white boy trying to show me that he has power.

My old self kicked in. I felt like driving straight to the nearest Department of Law Enforcement office on Tudor Road and Boniface

Parkway and filling a report of false police stop. In the past, I would have done so and demand investigation.

I thought about it for a while and decided not to do so. My ego said: do you want to let that silly police boy get away with harassing a black man? What are the reasons for you not to seek to punish him?

It occurred to me that lately, I have been talking about the need to be egoless, hence to not feel fear and anger when environmental stimuli seem to slight my grandiose ego.

I said to myself that here is a perfect challenge, to react as my old warrior ego that wants to punish anyone who slighted me would react or let slights go.

I said to myself: I got to let it go. The feeling of slight is of the ego. You must identify with the ego and feel slighted by other persons' seeming belittling behaviors (what is slighting behavior is not self-evident; it is always an interpretation).

My ego retorted by saying to me, you cannot just let that white boy in a police uniform get away with a lie. He probably wanted to give me a ticket but found out that I have a perfect driving record and probably suspected that I would dispute his ticket and go to court and the judge, on the basis of my clean driving record, would dismiss the ticket, so he decided to seem generous by not giving me a ticket.

This is a speculation on my part; I do not know whether it is true or not. I decided to not react as my old egotistical self that told me to teach this white boy some lesson urged me to react.

I decided to let it go and drove on to the store instead of the police station as I would have done in the past.

The lesson here is that when you decide on a different lifestyle, you will immediately be tested. If you react as you did in the past, your old self won but if you react as your new lifestyle proposes that you react, you positively reinforce it, and if you continue doing so, you make it a habitual behavior pattern.

I decided not to seek vengeance and bear grievance; I decided to forgive that boy who runs around in a police car pretending to be powerful when, in fact, he is a mere security guard for the oligarchs that rule this joint called the USA.

I got to the store and while inside it, felt a new kind of peace in me. I felt like I had behaved as a forgiving person would and felt happy.

If I had behaved in the old way, I would have been furious during the rest of the afternoon.

My old ego does not give up easily. It asked me: did I give in, allow myself to be cowed by that white boy? My ego says yes but the Christ self in me says no.

I simply overlooked the world as it is and behaved as Christ would, love, forgive, and know peace. I like the sense of peace and joy that I feel and will leave it at that.

I am not a black coward who allows white terrorists to use intimidation to terrorize his soul and make him feel fearful and out of fear, do what white folks want him to do.

No man born of woman can intimidate me; I would rather die, right now, than allow another person, black or white, to intimidate me into doing what I do not want to do.

I was not terrorized although the boy may have had that intention (which I do not know). What matters is the peace I felt.

I am not going to spend the rest of the afternoon worrying whether I should have behaved from the ego or from Christ.

In every situation, one has the option of behaving from ego and know war or from Christ and know peace.

I choose peace. The strong choose peace; the weak choose war.

LISTEN TO CHURCH MUSIC AND BEHOLD MAN AT HIS BEST.

The classical music radio station in my neck of the woods, on Sundays, 6-9 AM, provides what it calls sacred music. They are mostly chorales by the giants of western baroque and classical music, folks like Johann Sebastian Bach (and his relatives and children), Handel, Haydn, and the other musicians that if you are a Catholic, Anglican, Presbyterian, and Lutheran you grew up listening to (my parents are Catholic but I attended an Anglican secondary school; I had to listen to Christian music every morning during our church service in our school's chapel).

If you listen to Christian music (and for that matter, any other religion's sacred music), you must suspect that there is a God.

Human beings are at their best when they sing to their supposed creator. I am agnostic but whenever I listen to Bach or Handel, I have a feeling that those men are truly good men trying to reach their creator through their lovely music. I love sacred music.

At age 14, I read Charles Darwin's *Origin of Species* and he put to rest my inner debate; I had been debating in my mind whether there is God or not. I was raised in a Christian household and given my own bible the moment I learned to read, around age six. I read the entire bible several times. Somewhere along the line, I suspected that the bible is a book of fairytales, a mythology, kind of like Homer's Odyssey and Iliad and Virgil's Aeneid (if you attended a good secondary school and took Latin and Greek, you probably had to translate Virgil's Aeneid from Latin to English, as we did at my school); well, I suspected that the stories in the bible were fake but used to teach people moral values.

Like Thomas Jefferson, I convinced myself that Jesus Christ was perhaps the world's best moral teacher but I had no use for his belief in God and life after death.

I saw religion as fit for morons. However, I love Christian music and every Sunday, I dutifully went to church, not to pray to God but to listen to Christian music.

Boy oh boy, listening to Gregorian chants and other sacred music puts me in heaven (by that I mean happy mood).

Simply put, I love Christian music.

Later, I dabbled with Hinduism and Buddhism; I also love those religions' sacred music; somehow, I love everything that has to do with God even though I am agnostic.

Have you ever gone to African Americans' Pentecostal church services and listened to the sisters sing gospel music? My God, you would feel like you are in heaven. I love Christian music.

Have you ever listened to the recordings made by Voyager(s) as it flew by the various planets it flew by? If not, please do (google it). I call it the music of the sphere.

The sound of the planets, especially Earth, Mars, and Jupiter as they orbit around the sun, is lovely. They kind of make me think that there is a divine aspect to our world.

I understand the physics of the universe; it suggests that the physical universe is a product of the concatenation of accidental occurrences beginning with the Big Bang, 13.8 billion years ago.

Be that as it may, certain aspects of our lives, such as sacred music make me suspect that there is God. I have actually had experiences that only mystics have but I am still open to the notion that our universe is meaningless and purposeless.

I agree with scientists and conclude that there is no meaning to our world but listening to sacred music, as I am doing right now, puts me in a heavenly mood (peaceful and happy mood, blissful is the right word).

When something seems good to me, I tend to share it with other people; in that light, may I suggest that you listen to Christian sacred music? It would make you happy.

We need joy in this screwed up world, a world where seeming rational persons support a racist in the White House, a man trying to bring about a race war, another holocaust as his ancestors brought to the world in the last century.

Music enables us to lighten up in a world that makes us feel tense. Artists, who include musicians, make our absurd existence, as my existential mentors (Sartre, Camus, Heidegger, Jasper, Dostoyevsky, Kierkegaard, and Nietzsche) told us.

Now, go listen to Christian music and know pure joy. You do not need alcohol or drugs to find happiness in this apparent upside-down world; sacred music will do it for you!

PARANOID THINKING AND EXCESSIVE USE OF THE EGO DEFENSE MECHANISM OF PROJECTION

Generally, human beings are motivated to find out why things happen as they do; this is the foundation of science. They are even more acutely motivated to understand why bad things happen to them.

If they can understand why bad things happen to them, they are more able to predict the future of their lives hence live with more security.

Human beings with insecurity, say, those born with medical handicaps and those discriminated against as are blacks folks in North America, want to know why awful things happen to them; they want to predict their future so as to have a modicum of security.

They want to know why other people did to them what they did to them; they speculate on why people behaved as they did. No person is a mind reader so their speculations on why people did what they did, do not yield factual results.

If you proceed and take your speculations as the real reasons why people did what they did to you, you are merely attributing your thoughts to other people; you are using the ego defense mechanism of projection.

In projection, you think that this is why folks did what they did, which is your thought, and project it to them, and behave toward them as if, in fact, they did what they did because of the reasons you believed that they did it.

You tell people why they did what they did (this is accusatory behavior). Those people generally feel surprised that you believed that they did what they did because of the reasons you attributed to them. If, for example, you believe that people are hostile and unfriendly toward you, hence did bad things to you and you accuse them of trying to harm you, they would be surprised by your attribution of evil intentions to them.

Now that you have falsely accused them, they may, in fact, do bad things to you. This is called paranoid self-fulfilling prophecy. You see people as unfriendly, behave defensively toward them, and they subsequently behave unfriendly toward you. People thus do what you initially falsely accused them of doing.

The fact is that you do not know why somebody did what he did to you, and he himself probably did not know why he did it.

Your mind, thinking, goes to work trying to understand why he did it. You speculate on why he did what he did. Perhaps, he did it deliberately to hurt you, to damage your reputation, to accomplish this or that objective. You speculate forever why other people do what they do. The fact is that you do not know why they did what they did.

You may go and ask a person why he did what he did to you. He may not know why he did it and even if he tells you why he did it, that may not be the real reason why he did it, he may merely be speculating on why he did it.

What is self-evident is that he did something. You want to understand why he did it. You are not a mind reader and cannot understand why he did it.

You can come up with what seems to you like plausible reasons why he did what he did. You proceed to attribute your reasons why he did it to him and say that that is why he did it. You then behave toward him as if he did it because of your interpretation as to why he did it. What you have just done is project your causal explanation to him and then behave toward him as if your projection is true. Your projection may or may not be true.

Much of our behaviors toward other people are rooted in projection. When we think that we understand why people did what they did, we are engaged in projective thinking. We suspect that they did what they did because of what we think is why we ourselves would have done what we see them do.

The fact is that other people are not you and do things for different reasons, not for your reasons, so your projective identification is still speculative and not true.

So, what is the way out of this conundrum? If you see a person do something, just observe the objective behavior, what he did; ask him why he did it; if he dissembles, assume that you do not know why he did it.

You should keep quiet and not assume that you know why people did what they did, for all your conjectures as to why people did what they did may not be the reason why they did what they did.

On your own, you can never know why people did what they did; you cannot understand other people's motivation on why they did what they did, so just keep quiet.

If you come up with an explanation why people did what they did, project it to them, and act toward them as if indeed they did what they did because of your extrapolation as to why they did it, you may act hostilely toward them when they did not intend to be hostile toward you. You may fear them by believing that they have nefarious intentions to you when they do not have such intentions.

If you overuse projection, you are said to be paranoid. A paranoid person wants to know why people did what they did.

Paranoid persons are generally very insecure and have the belief that people do things with the intention of harming them, even killing them.

They come up with reasons why people did what they did. They do not bother asking the people why they did it and even if they asked and were told reasons why folks did what they did, they would not believe them. They would say that they are being lied to. They are convinced that the people want to cheat them, harm them, and even kill them.

They project their own reasons as to why people did what they did to them and respond to them as if they did what they did because of the paranoid's reasoning.

He may think that a person wants to kill him (his own fears) and defend himself by avoiding that person or by attacking, even killing that person.

In paranoia, we see projection acutely at work. But the same thinking, ego mechanism, is also at work in most people.

Do you know why people do what they do? You don't. If you come up with a reason why they did what you see them do and act on the basis of your reasoning, you have acted like the paranoid character.

White people, for example, have all kinds of weird explanations of why they think that black folks did what they did and act toward black folks on the basis of their causal analysis (projection); black people do the same to white people, project their causal analysis to white folks.

People respond to each other on the basis of their false causal analyses.

Since we cannot know why people did what they did or will do what they will do in the future, the best policy is to keep quiet.

Observe what people did; try to understand it but realize that your explanation of why they did what they did may not be correct; just keep quiet.

Of course, if other persons physically attack you, you have a right to defend yourself. It is the law of nature for those attacked to defend themselves.

If you slap me, without thinking about it, I will defend myself in one of two ways: walk away from you or slap you in self-defense.

DISCUSSION

Let us suppose that you are a black man and applied for a job and the employer is a white person and you did not hear from him or he interviewed you and did not offer you that job. Your immediate explanation probably would be that he did what he did because of racism. That is your conjecture. You do not know why he did not employ you; all your explanations as to why he did not employ you are conjectural, not factual.

You should not bother trying to understand why he did not employ you. Go and work for yourself and not work for white folks. Leave them alone. They have a right not to employ black folks.

The point here is don't waste your time trying to understand why other people did what they did. If you are discriminated against, tell yourself that you were not meant by your higher self to obtain that job, go have your own business, and employ yourself and your fellow black folks. Leave white people alone. They are entitled to be racists. It is not for you to make them non-racists, hence real human beings.

CONCLUSION

There will be fewer misunderstandings, conflicts, and wars in society if we did not assume that we know why people did what they did and simply don't bother with trying to understand why people did what they did and when we do so, know that our explanations are speculations and not the truth.

The individual, in all situations, should just do what he believes is the right thing and not bother with trying to understand why other people did what they did or speculating on that subject; if we collectively did so, society would be more peaceful than it is.

Finally, write below what you think that you heard me say; the chances are that you did not really hear me correctly but will project to me what you think that I said.

27

CLINICAL ISSUES

In my observation, many Igbos tend to be deluded persons so let me expand this essay a bit.

In delusion disorder, one believes what is not true as true. One uses one's thinking to reach a reason why things happen to one or are the way they are, and not know that it is just one's speculation and one believes in it and acts on it.

The deluded person believes what is not true as true and acts on it. His false belief is generally systematized and difficult for him to give up despite contrary facts.

People around him do not believe what he believes to be true. Consider that most Americans, white and black, know that Donald Trump is a racist (whites may keep quiet about his racism because they think that he is serving white folks' interests but black Americans know that he hates them). Now, how do you think that many Igbos see Trump?

Many Igbos looked me in the face and told me that Trump is a godly man, a Christian. For the records, Trump probably has not read the bible, nor does he have the mindfulness to read more than a page at a time; I bet that he has not read the bible; he does not go to church; but when it serves his propaganda interests, he waves a bible, probably upside down.

The man hobnobs with prostitutes and pornographers (remember Stormy Daniels and the many women whose sex organs he said that he grabbed?).

The man is as racist as racists can be but many of our Igbo brothers see him as a Christian and their savior. They think that he is going to give them their Biafra. He has been in office for almost four years and has not given them Biafra. He probably does not know where the map of Nigeria is on a world map. He has signed executive orders banning Igbos (Who are the Nigerians that mostly come to the USA? How many Hausa Fulanis are in the USA?) from coming to the USA.

If Trump had the ability to do so, he would prevent all black folks from coming to the USA and as he said, allow only whites from Norway to come to the USA.

I really shouldn't have to explain that Trump is racist for even a six-year-old boy knows that; that I have to explain it to many Igbos is a wonder; it tells you that those folks are deluded, psychotic; they believe what is not true as true and use their irrational explanations to try convincing you that a racist is a Christian saint.

I know a saint when I see one. I saw Pope John Paul and Mother Theresa and knew that they are saints. They loved all humanity, not just their so-called race.

There are five types of delusion disorder:

Grandiose type, here, the person sees himself as the most important person on earth; he believes that he is superior to other persons (many Igbos believe that they are superior to other Nigerians).

Persecutory type, here, the person believes that those he feels superior persecute him (many Igbos believe that the Nigerians they believe are superior persecute them, that Hausas, Fulanis, and Yorubas persecute them).

Jealous type, here, one accuses one's friend or spouse of cheating on one when he or she is not doing so (in the USA, many Igbos accuse their wives of cheating and routinely kill them).

Somatic type, here, one believes that one has medical issues that one does not have.

Erotomanic type, here, one believes that a famous person loves one when that person does not even know that one exists and even if he does know that one exists, he does not care for one (many Igbos believe that

Trump is famous and powerful and that he cares for them when he does not give a damn about their existence. Trump is not powerful; he is a sick poppy, a pathological narcissist who thinks that the entire world should serve his supposed superior but empty-headed self).

There are other types of unspecified delusion disorder:

PARANOIA

Delusion is the same as paranoia. Paranoia is a Greek word for believing what is not true as true. The paranoid person believes that he is who he is not (he is like all of us, ordinary, but believes that he is a superior person).

He believes that other people are out to get him, kill him, and is defensive; he avoids them or attacks them.

He is guarded and scans his environment looking for danger and often finds what he is looking for.

He is argumentative and wants to win his debates so as to seem superior in his knowledge, even as he is shallow in his fund of knowledge (many Igbos believe that they have superior knowledge but talk to them and you find that their level of knowledge is not even fit for a child of a ten-year-old child).

He accuses other people of doing what they did not do.

He fears being belittled and accuses people of belittling him.

He is suspicious and does not trust other persons; he always suspects that other people want to take advantage of him or harm him and guards himself lest he is exploited.

He is rigid, inflexible, and not spontaneous in his thinking and behaviors; he must think things through lest he makes mistakes, seems small, and other people laugh at him.

He must at all times try to seem grandiose, important, so that other people respect him (to mask his underlying sense of inferiority).

The causal explanation of paranoia is that something made him feel inferior and inadequate and he compensates with a false sense of superiority; instead of working to overcome his sense of inferiority, realistically, he pretends to be superior to his shadows, certainly not to other human beings for it is impossible for one human being to be superior to others.

There are many other paranoid traits; from those described above, you get the idea.

The thing is that such persons appear normal and often have the best jobs in town (some of them are the presidents of their countries; an example is President Richard Nixon of the USA), district attorneys, judges, policemen, immigration officers, and so on. Despite their apparent social success, in the area of their false beliefs, there is nothing that anyone can do to dissuade them from having their false beliefs

Can you persuade an Igbo whose IQ is 70 (hence a mentally retarded person) that he is not superior to Hausas, Fulanis, and Yorubas? He actually wants you to accept the rubbish that one human being can be superior to others; all of us are the same and equal.

Paranoia is rooted in human insecurity. All kinds of things, including medical disorders and social factors, make human beings feel insecure. However, if you love children, they tend to be relatively more secure than those not loved.

The chief ego defense mechanism of paranoia is projection. It is a primitive defense mechanism in that it is found in all people and is accentuated in people when they are weak; if there is a social or natural mishap, such as earthquake or terrorists killing people, we will all suddenly become paranoid, not trusting our neighbors; if you go to nursing homes for the elderly, these old folks feel weak and tend to become more paranoid than they were when they were young and vigorous; now, they cannot protect themselves and use fantasy protection, belief that they are powerful to falsely protect themselves.

Nigeria is ruled by Fulanis; Igbos feel like they cannot protect themselves and use fantasy protection, belief in their imaginary superiority, to falsely protect themselves.

Immigrants in foreign lands, such as non-whites in the USA, tend to feel weak and protect themselves with paranoid defenses.

Minority persons who are often attacked and killed by majority persons, such as black folk who white folk kill as if they have no human dignity, tend to employ paranoid defenses to try to falsely defend themselves; those defenses do not work for white folks still kill black folks when they feel like it; a month ago, we all witnessed a white policeman, Derick Chauvin, murder a black man, George Floyd, in broad daylight, at Minneapolis, Minnesota, by kneeling on his neck and choking him to death; that sort of things happens all the time in supposed Christian America.

The Christianity of the Bible teaches love for all people, not killing of some people, those perceived to be inferior.

Projection includes seeing something in you that society does not approve of and you do not like and you deny that it is in you and projects it to other people. For example, there are white folks who only like to have sex with Asians or blacks; since their society disapproves of it, they deny it and project it to meaning that all black men want to have sex with white women and they resent them and attack them. Listen, there are some black men who like to have sex only with Asians or white women; their percentage is exactly the percentage of white folks who want to have sex with members of other races, maybe three percent. Most black folks want to have sex with members of the opposite sex of their so-called race. Instead of projection, please accept what you see in yourself and do it, provided that you do not harm other persons; consensual sex between adults is okay.

Sigmund Freud in his only book on paranoia, the biography of a German judge, Schreiber, a man who liked to dress as a woman, said that he was homosexual, denied it, and thus, acted like women by wearing women's attire. Freud suggested that paranoia is caused by denied homosexuality. I do not know if Freud is right or wrong. I go with my clinical experience.

There are insecure men who imagine that they are homosexual and since society disapproves of homosexuality, do not like it in them and if you ever called them gay, queer, fagot, dyke, or queen, they would attack you to prove that they are masculine men. Are they members of the queer nation? I do not know.

Please note that the delusion or paranoid disorder that I described here is what we might call non-psychotic delusion and paranoia. In psychotic delusion and paranoia, such as is found in schizophrenia, paranoid type, the delusion is bizarre and also, there is hallucination in one or more of the five senses, such as auditory or visual hallucination; in bipolar affective disorder, mania, and depression, there may be delusion but they are generally making grandiose claims such as a manic chap who lives on handouts telling you that he is the richest man in the world and writes checks for money he does not have. I am not focusing on psychotic delusion in this write-up.

If you are psychotic, please go see a psychiatrist for you need neuroleptic medications; mild delusion does not need medication (anti-anxiety medications may deal with these folks' inordinate fears).

Many Igbos in their total self-hatred identify with white sociopaths, killers headed by Trump that they erroneously believe are powerful persons. See Adorno et al., the *Authoritarian Personality*, to learn why weak people identify with seeming powerful persons.

There are many other ego defense mechanisms, such as repression, suppression, denial, displacement, rationalization, fantasy, reaction-formation, sublimation, pride, guilt, shame, fear, anger, avoidance, and others. I will not bore you further with explanations of these defense mechanisms and paranoia; if you are interested in the subject, read the below books.

28

NOTES IN ARIZONA

While in Arizona, I had two surgeries to take care of, a lifelong problem. All my life, after eating food, I feel drained of energy and have to go lie down for a couple of hours to recoup some energy. I limited my eating to once a day.

The surgeries seem to have taken care of that problem (with the attendant making me eat three meals a day and posing the potential for me to gain weight). The hospital bill was about $180, 000. My outpatient copay was around $5000 (I saw the doctors in their private offices outside the hospital every two weeks). The cost of this treatment is not the issue. The issue is what transpired during the two surgeries.

I am rolled to the operating table. There are about three doctors in the operating room and two nurses. The anesthetic physician told me what he is going to do. He is going to inject some medication into the IV bag, place a mask over my nose, and I will go to sleep and wake up in about three hours, after the surgery. I said okay. He did what he said he was going to do and I was out.

Three or more hours later, I am in the post-operating area, awake. Everything is hazy but my consciousness slowly returns to me. A nurse asked me if I am awake and I said yes. She asked: are you in pain? I said no.

She said that is fine for it would take a couple of hours for the painkillers I was given in the OP room to wear out and the pain comes.

A hospital aid rolled me into my room (a room that kind of looks like a suite in an expensive hotel). I am told to press a certain button if I need a nurse's attention and a certain button if I am in pain and morphine will drop into the IV bag to take care of the pain.

I do not like taking medications; certainly, I do not like taking any painkillers. I told the nurse so and she said that the pain will soon come when the medication they gave me in the operating room wears out. Okay, I said.

In a couple of hours, I was in excruciating pain. I pressed the button and the nurse was in my room and I told her that I am in pain and still do not want the goddamned morphine. I know how addictive those damn things are.

She went out and brought the doctor for the night shift into my room. He listened to me and said okay. Let us try something else. He recommended a high dose of liquid Tylenol to be injected into the IV and another over the counter tablet, a pain killer to be taken orally. I accepted those two alternatives; I was given those every six hours and they reduced but did not eliminate the pain. Five days later, I was discharged from the hospital.

I was told to go to my doctor, Dr. Theodor Haley, perhaps, the best surgeon in the whole world (he and I struck an immediate friendship when he told me where he did his internship, at Providence Hospital, Anchorage, which is beside my school, University of Alaska; we talked about his experience at Alaska) every two weeks for post-op treatment.

Here is the deal: during the three consecutive hours of surgeries, I do not remember what transpired. Generally, when I go to sleep, I immediately dream and do remember some of my dreams. I do not remember dreaming during the surgeries; was I asleep and if so, why didn't I dream?

Simply put, I do not remember whatever happened during the six hours of two surgeries that I had. Where was I?

Is this like death? Do we not remember anything when we die? Does physical death result in finitude, oblivion? That would seem the obvious answer.

I am normally agnostic and do not know whether there is God or life after death or not. For an agnostic, however, I have had more mystical experiences than Hindu so-called saints and God-realized persons.

I have read Ramakrishna, Ramana Maharishi, Vivekananda, Yogi Yogananda's autobiography, and other Hindu so-called holy men.

I had had out of body experiences, and near-death experiences.

In near-death experiences, I found myself in a world of light forms; every person in that world is in light form; it is like our world except that everything in it is in light forms (Hindus call it astral world, gate of heaven, but not heaven).

I have had what Hindus call Samadhi; it is a world that cannot be described in words for it transcends human language; all that I can say about it is that I was what one might call a formless soul in a sea of joined formless souls and an entity that is also formless that we all automatically know as our creator; we know ourselves as his extension, in Christian language, he is God.

We are joined to God and he is joined to us; there is no space and time between us; God is in each of us and each of us is in God; where God ends and each of his sons begins is nowhere and where each of God's sons end and another begins is nowhere; we all share one self and one thinking, one mind (we know what each other is thinking and respond to him instantaneously; this is kind of like what Albert Einstein called spooky action at a distance where two entangled but separated particles respond to each other instantaneously regardless of the distance separating them, indicating that distance and time are illusions).

In that formless place, I felt perfect peace, as opposed to my anxious-driven life; all my earthly life, I have lived in total anxiety, from age three, which was the first time I realized that I have a separated self in body.

Reading somehow calms my mind; I read compulsively to obtain some peace of mind. So, here I am in a place of perfect peace; I felt eternal, permanent, and changeless. The place has no space and time in it. Everything in it happens now. I really cannot explain that experience.

I would love to stay in that unified state but, alas, I am, sooner or later, back to the awareness that I am in my body, in old Ozodiobi Thomas Osuji, the anxious chap.

I am back to my hellish existence on earth, in body and ego. But what can you do? Such is life, so it is back to reading books.

How do I explain the unified experience I had? I know what religionists call such experiences. The skeptical part of my thinking, mind, tells me that I just had a wonderful dream, a dream of the opposite of our lives on earth, in body and ego. It is a dream, not reality, even though while in it, I felt that it is real and our earth seemed the dream.

When I first had a near-death experience, my then-girlfriend, a German psychologist, was in the same room with me; she was fooling around on the computer that is always by the side of my bed, while I lay on my bed.

My mother died a few months ago and her death had depressed me. Anyway, Monika and I were talking when suddenly, I found myself out of my body, at the ceiling; I looked down and saw my body on the bed; I looked up and saw total darkness.

In the midst of that darkness was a point of light, about the size of a pinhead. I was fascinated by it and began moving, flying toward it and as I got closer to it, it became larger and larger until everywhere, there was light.

I noticed that my mother was now holding my hand. She asked me if I want to be with her over there. She reminded me that my children are still young and need to be trained. I said, okay, mom I have to go take care of my children; I was immediately back in my body (in my body, I felt heavy compared to the light I had felt when I was outside my body).

Monika in the meantime thought that I may have had a heart attack and died; for I was no longer responding to her. She had called 911 for help.

I told her what happened and she, an atheist, said, get out of here; you are making it up or had a wonderful dream. Go see a neurologist for you may have a brain tumor that produced such a vivid dream.

The point that I am making is that if I wanted to believe in God, I have had enough so-called spiritual experiences to do so.

Folks talk of Jesus as their savior and do not see him. Sometimes, I go into meditation and I am in the world of light forms and I am with the old boy himself, Immanuel Ben Joseph and we talk like old friends.

At no point did I see Jesus as my savior; he is just a knowledgeable chap who I exchanged ideas with. He is a poet and I am a philosopher and scientist. He talks in his familiar poetic language, in parables and convoluted metaphors, and I translate his metaphors to rational prose.

Sometimes, I try to teach him physics and chemistry, but he is not interested in those subjects; he says that they deal with matter, space, and time and he is not interested in that illusory world. To him, those are part of the illusions of the ego, the attempt to make separated selves seem real.

Each person is different; Jesus is a poet and I am a rationalist and scientist; let us leave it at that.

One would think that my so-called spiritual experiences would make me a religious person. Nope, they don't.

A few minutes after hanging out with the old boy, I am back in my head thinking about my favorite friends (Plato, Aristotle, Leibnitz, Pascal, Kant, Hegel, Schopenhauer, Nietzsche, Feuerbach, Berkeley, Hume, Hobbes, Locke, Rousseau, Descartes, Voltaire, James, Bergson, and others); my mind would thereafter drift to the empiricists, the logical positivists who are always looking for proof of whatever we say is real and I would think about the physical scientists (I wrote a book on the ideas that changed the world in which I reviewed the philosophers and scientists).

Well, this old boy is agnostic and he cannot force himself to be a Gnostic, theist, or atheist. People are who they are and must accept who they are and leave other persons to be who they are.

In light of my total blackout during six hours of surgeries, I ask: is oblivion what awaits us when we die?

Do you want my honest answer? It is that I do not know. Most people actually do not realize how the godliest people are agnostics whereas persons who masquerade around as Christians, Muslims, Hindus, or Buddhists are frauds.

Mother Theresa of India left a diary. In it, she poured her soul out. It turned out that she is like me, a God-obsessed person yet an agnostic. She kept asking her Jesus and God how they could tolerate the painful poverty and suffering in India. It does not make sense, so she accepted Jesus as her moral guide but doubted that there is God or life after she died.

She died in 1997; the world lost a beautiful soul; she was one of the creatures that make folks like me glad to be human beings (look at the idiots who call themselves pastors in Nigeria; they have perverted Christianity to mean stiffing people for money, asking for endless tithes when the actual Jesus and his followers went about helping the needy; well, I have no use for so-called ministers of God, they are the scum of the earth).

Do God and his heaven exist? Frankly, I do not know. However, I hope that they exist. I want God to exist; I want heaven to exist. If they don't exist, then we do our best here on earth and later join the night's train.

I know that the best-lived life is to love me, love all people, forgive those who wronged me, and help correct our mistaken behaviors (I do not condone evil).

Therefore, make my book what you like. What you make of it is your business, not mine. However, if I may express an opinion, I just hope that the book enables you to love all humanity and work for social democracy and mixed economy where we offer all children publicly paid education through university, offer all people publicly paid health insurance, and thereafter, leave people to compete in the capitalist economy.

In the end, I have no proof that God and heaven exist; but I have proof that there is intelligence in the universe; the proof is us.

Intelligence operates in human beings, in stars, plants, animals, and in the planets. Consider our planet earth, the marvelous coordination of its crust, mantle, outer core, and inner core, all needing to be so for the earth to exist and produce biological organisms; consider the levels of the atmosphere that gradually becomes space, all seemingly designed to make a biological life possible.

It does not seem like all these are the products of accidents. Whereas I reject religious mumbo jumbo and mysticism, I hold that there is intelligence operating in this universe.

If folks choose to call that intelligence God, that is fine with me, provided that they do not worship it as if it is a pathological narcissist who needs admiration and praises or else, he kills people.

My God is a God of love. My God is love; we, as the creations of God, are love. Love is good enough for me, and I hope, for all biological organisms.

Post Script:

A friend told me that the reason why I could not remember anything during my anesthetized body, surgery, is because the medications deadened my brain. My brain and body during the surgery for all intents and purposes were dead; my body was now kind of like a log of wood and whatever was done to it, I could not remember. He said that my soul had left my body and was still alive in a different dimension of existence, say, and the world of light forms or even in formless heaven. When the medications given to deaden my body wore off, my soul returned to my body and my brain regained awareness of my consciousness (I could thereafter retrieve information stored in my memory bank).

What this perceptive man said seems to have some merit to it; however, it did not solve the problem of not knowing, for I do not consciously remember being in a different dimension during the surgery. I take his feedback, which seems to make an argument for life after death, with caution.

THIS IS NOW THE BREAKING-OUT MOMENT FOR ME;
THE TIME FOR MERE UNDERSTANDING AND TALKING IS OVER;
IT IS NOW TIME TO THINK AND BEHAVE AS I KNOW TO BE TRUE
EGO IS MEANS OF SEPARATING FROM ONE'S REAL
SELF, THE FORMLESS SON OF GOD, OTHER FORMLESS
SONS OF GOD, AND FROM FORMLESS GOD

The ego (the human personality) is a means of denying one's true self, other people's true selves, and God's true self; our true self is formless unified self.

We individually and collectively made the ego-self-concept and self-image, which body makes it possible to have. Now we emphasize our egos, self-concepts, self-images, and bodies, defend them, and in doing so, retain and maintain them.

EACH PERSON IS A VARIETY OF THE EGO.

Each person is a variety of the ego. Each ego is carefully planned to be as it is; the owner, son of God, working with other sons of God, chose the body that would make the chosen ego type possible; the individual and all of us chose a body, society, family, and historical time when the individual is born, where he is born (say, in America with its racism so that one experiences that racism and create the ego one wants to respond to it; or in Igboland, where folks do not care for each other so that one develops an ego of self-centeredness).

GRANDFATHER OSUJI HAD A DEFIANT EGO.

Grandfather Osuji's type of ego is the ego of defiance; he felt attacked by his senior half-brother, Nzewuloba; he and his mother correctly felt that Nzewuloba wanted him dead so that he takes their land. He developed a defiant personality, a defensive ego from childhood.

He was always trying to prove that he is powerful least he is seen as a push-over and his land taken by his brother and his numerous children.

The white man came to his world and he saw him as trying to be powerful and rule him and he defied him and tried to seem powerful vis a vis white folks.

Of course, his puny ego was not able to defeat the almighty British Empire so the British took over his world; he merely chaffed on the sidelines.

The march of the collective ego civilization is more powerful than the individual's ego; European empires were stronger than primitive African societies; Europeans had to rule Africans and introduce them to the contemporary world, contemporary ego politics.

THE HOLY SPIRIT'S COURAGE IS DIFFERENT FROM EGO COURAGE.

In ego terms, Osuji seemed courageous but in Holy Spirit's terms, he was not courageous. In Holy Spirit's terms, to be courageous is to overlook one's ego and other people's egos and bodies and what is done with them, to forgive; one does not fight other egos for to fight them is to acknowledge their power when the ego is totally powerless.

The ego does not even exist but seems to exist; as long as you are responding to other egos, even if you do so boldly, you are weak.

Every person on earth, in the dream of separation from our real unified self, is a variety of the ego that manifests in a type of body, family, and society to enable it to behave as it does and make it seem that the environment made it do what it does when, in fact, the external environment does not exist; only the son of God exists; he sleeps and projects out the physical world of space, time, and matter and populate it with seeming people in bodies; one interacts with the illusory people and in doing so, make one's separated self-seem real to one.

THE EGO IS A MEANS OF SEPARATING FROM OTHER EGOS WHILE SEEMINGLY JOINED TO THEM.

The ego is a means for separation from other people while pretending to be in fellowship with them; its fellowship is a sham for it wants to be separated from other egos.

The ego is totally self-centered; when you offend it, it lets go of its phony joining with you, fight for its self-interests, and may kill you to gratify its self-interests.

THE HOLY SPIRIT TRANSFORMS EGOS' SHAM FELLOWSHIP TO A HOLY RELATIONSHIP.

The Holy Spirit accepts egos where they are at and uses them in their forms; he gets them to forgive what they do in egos, to overlook what they do in egos, and not desire to do those things.

When they overlook the ego and its pattern of thinking and behaving, they occasionally see themselves in light forms and from that state of salvation, let go the ego in any form, matter or light (for both are false), and experience formless union with all sons of God and God, hence awaken from the sleep of self-denial, self-forgetfulness, and now know themselves to be the son of God, who is one with God.

CONCLUSION

In the meantime, you and every person you see is thinking and behaving as he and all of us chose him to behave.

Do not moralize about your and other peoples' behaviors; you and all people are behaving the way you and they have to behave, given your/their egos, bodies, and societies.

Can you change other people? You cannot change other people. All that you can do is see your and their ego dances, how they deny their truth and use their egos and bodies to avoid relating completely to other people, decide to give up your own ego, be completely your real self, and relate to other people's real selves and God.

When you live from your real self, son of God, who is love, love you and all people and forgive our wrongs, you live in peace and happiness and model it for other egos.

NOTE ON LEADERS

The ego made leaders to coordinate the activities of separated egos in pursuit of their collective ego goals. The Holy Spirit does not destroy what the son of God made in his madness, what he uses to seek separation and have a sham union; he uses leaders to teach egoless living, to teach folks to be Christ, the self that loves and forgives; to build organizations that unify them in time, space, and matter.

GOD AND HIS SON HAVE ALWAYS EXISTED; IF THE SON OF GOD DOES NOT EXIST, GOD DOES NOT EXIST; IF GOD DOES NOT EXIST, HIS SON DOES NOT EXIST.

God is a creator; he is not so until he has created a son. God and his son, in so far that God is a creator, a father, have always co-existed.

God could not exist without his son and his son could not exist without God; both exist eternally.

In Genesis, God talked to someone saying:

> "**26** Then God said, "Let us make mankind in our image, in our likeness, so that they may rule over the fish in the sea and the birds in the sky, over the livestock and all the wild animals, and over all the creatures that move along the ground." **27** So God created mankind in his own image, in the image of God he created them; male and female he created them."
>
> Genesis, Chapter 1:26–27, NIV

In the Gospel according to John, Chapter 1:

> "^{1}In the beginning was the Word, & the Word was with God, and the Word was God.^{2}The same was in the beginning with God.^{23}All things were made by him, and without him was not anything made that was made.^{34}In him was life, and the life was the light of men.^{5}And the light shineth in darkness and the darkness comprehended it not."
>
> Gospel according to John, Chapter 1:1–5. NIV

John 1:1–5, apparently, was referring to Jesus Christ as the son of God who was with God in the beginning and he, the son of God, created the world. God, the whole, created his son and the son created his own sons.

"6There was a man sent from God whose name was John. 7He came as a witness to testify concerning that light, so that through him all might believe. 8He himself was not the light; he came only as a witness to the light.9The true light that gives light to everyone was coming into the world. 10He was in the world, and though the world was made through him, the world did not recognize him. 11He came to that which was his own, but his own did not receive him. 12Yet to all who did receive him, to those who believed in his name, he gave the right to become children of God"

Gospel of John chapter 1:6–12, NIV

The whole produced the part; the whole has parts and the parts have a whole; whole and parts require each other to exist; without one, the other would not exist.

The part of the whole, the son of God, is like God. Like God, the son of God, has creative power. Like God, the son of God does create his own sons.

Creation begins from God and continues forever and ever. God created his son and his son created his own sons who create their own sons, ad infinitum.

Each of us is a son of God. In God, aka unified state, heaven, each of us is creating the sons of God.

There are infinite sons of God but they are simultaneously the one son of God; each one of them symbolizes the son of God.

The sons of God are connected to each other and connected to God; the parts of a whole are connected to each other and to the whole, God. The whole and the parts, the parts and the whole, God and his sons, cannot separate from each other and still survive; separation, if it were possible, leads to the death of God and his sons, whole and parts; they would not exist if separation is possible.

What one son of God did, all of sons of God did; if one son of God does an evil thing, all sons of God did it; if one son of God did a good thing, all sons of God did it.

The sons of God, us, affect each other, both in spirit and in matter, space, and time. Everything in the world of space, time, and matter affect us; if a star explodes somewhere in space, it affects us and we respond to it.

When each of us is saved, that is, overlooks the dream of separation from our real selves and awakens to unified self, he is now a point of light in the darkness that is the egos' world and shines that light to the rest of us who are still sleeping and dreaming that we are separated from each other; he joins the saviors of the world in trying to save all of us.

Each of us must accept that light of knowledge, personally give up the wish for separation, and experience union to be saved.

Union, unified state, is the light to the darkness of separation.

You cannot directly save other people and they cannot directly save you but you can indirectly save them and they can indirectly save you; when you show people how to become saved: forgive, that is, overlook separation and what is done in it.

This means, love you, love the parts, love other people, love other parts, and love the whole, which means love God.

YOUR SELF-CONCEPT DETERMINES HOW YOU CONCEPTUALIZE OTHER PEOPLE AND THE WORLD AND RESPOND TO THEM; THE NEED TO CHANGE YOUR SELF-CONCEPT TO SEE THE WORLD DIFFERENTLY.

There is no such thing as seeing other people and the world objectively; you always see other people and things and the entire universe with your self-concept (self-image, ego).

Upon birth, the child takes his biological and social experience to construct a self-concept for him. His self-concept is realistic to his inherited body and experience in a family. Thereafter, he sees himself, other people and things, and the universe through the construct of self he has (his perceptual lenses).

He responds to other people as he conceptualizes them to be, as he perceives them to be, all influenced by his self-concept.

The self-concept is an assumption one makes of who one is, and subsequently, who other people and things are. Assumption is not the truth.

Because the self-concept and assumptions made on it are false, one must defend one's self-concept to make it seem real to one. It is not real. The individual does not know who his real self is (I am not doing spiritual psychology here; if I am, I would tell us that the real self is a son of God, part of unified spirit self).

If, for example, as a child, the child developed a self-concept that fear being belittled, he will see other people and interpret their actions as meant to belittle him; sometimes, that is the case and at other times, it is not. He will respond to them defensively, behave to seem important so that no one could belittle or humiliate him.

He may act aggressively toward other people to prove to them that he is important or he may withdraw from other people to go protect his desired important self. Both aggressive response and avoidant response are personality disorders, not healthy.

Because the self-concept is conceptual, one can let it go and re-conceptualize it, construct a different self-concept. The new self-concept still must take one's body and social experience into consideration.

If one is black in America, one knows that white folks respond to one as an inferior self just because of one's body; one has certain social experiences and those play roles in one's old or new self-concept.

One can, however, construct a self-concept that does not give a damn about what white folks think about one. Normal black Americans dismiss white folks as fools whose perceptions of them are biased so they do not bother them; they just do what they believe is right in every situation. This is good.

Better still is to have no self-concept, to completely let go of one's self-concept, let go of one's ego. It is possible to let go of one's ego, separated self-concept in body. Very few human beings accomplish this goal. If you let go of your ego-self-concept, you would not be defensive of any self at all; you allow life to live through you and you go through life peacefully and happily.

IF YOU ARE A MISTAKE, THE ENTIRE UNIVERSE IS A MISTAKE.

Your body and upbringing, say, a black in the USA, could give you so much trouble that you construct a self-concept that says that you are a mistake (racist whites actually tell black folks that the universe made a mistake in producing them and justify discriminating or killing them).

Here is the logical deal. If the universe made a mistake in producing you, then it follows that the entire universe is a mistake, and as such, should not exist.

Old-time religions, such as the Catholic and Protestant churches used to tell their members that they were born in sin, are mistaken, must confess their sins, and repent for God to accept them. Thus, Christians run around considering themselves mistakes. If they are mistakes, their creator, God, and the universe is a mistake. Thus, their God and universe should not exist.

No human being is a mistake. There is only one you in the entire universe. The universe produced only one you so you are not a mistake.

Regardless of whether you are a man, woman, black, or child, you are not a mistake; you are a perfect creation of God, must see yourself as perfect, and accept it (I mean your real self, the son of God in you is perfect; your ego-self and your body may have problems, negative self-constructs that you must study; understand and change them so that you behave differently).

If you accept yourself as perfect, you will accept other people as perfect, love all people, and live in peace.

A CASE STUDY

This is a case study of a totally stupid human being. There is this Igbo guy called Nebu Adiele (that is not his real name, of course); he came to the internet with one goal, to shame people. He looks for every opportunity to make people feel bad about themselves; he even investigates their background looking for any skeleton in their closet to splash on the Internet and hope to have shamed them from doing so.

I observed what he is doing and realized that he is psychologically sick. If he was healthy, as a black man, he would know that racism makes all black persons feel bad hence are less productive; he would feel motivated to improve his fellow black folks' self-esteem, not desecrate them.

Why is he invested in shaming and humiliating black folks (if he did that to children from middle-class families, their parents would sue him, clean him up if he has money, or put him in prison for damaging their children's self-esteem; shamed people often commit suicide)?

I deliberately decided to humiliate him. I have psychological tools. I used it to analyze his personality and showed that he is a sociopath with an anti-social personality and paranoid personality. He has a history of stealing from people (that is why he relates to his fellow Nigerians with a fictitious name, he is a freaking coward by doing so). I wrote about his distorted character and dared him to defend himself legally (he claimed to be an attorney, he is not) so that I come to court and ask for a psychological profile to be done on him and put him on psychotropic medications for the rest of his sick life or even send him to prison because of the willful damage he is doing to other people's self-confidence.

The interesting thing is that he is so stupid, to try to shame a psychologist who can actually pressure him to commit suicide.

I am not quite sure why I should feel ashamed of myself. I should feel ashamed of myself that I had the doctorate degree from one of America's top universities in my twenties, at an age that he was probably house servant in Nigeria.

I later re-interpreted the situation as one of those where the universe gives one a person to study and learn from him and in so doing, help other people learn about themselves.

I used the sick poppy to teach the other members of the internet forum about personality and mental disorders. Hopefully, they learned a few things about themselves.

29

THE FIRST TIME THAT I YELLED AT MY FATHER

In my part of the world, Igboland, children do not talk back to their parents; regardless of what the parents said, the children are supposed to tolerate it and keep quiet. I kept quiet when my parents talked. In this sense, I was a typical Igbo child.

One Christmas, I was fourteen years old; I came to our village from my secondary boarding school. I was not aware that my father was in the village. One evening, he and his three brothers were sitting in their compound chatting. It seemed lovely so I sat down to listen to them.

Suddenly, my father began talking about his wife and children in a derogatory manner. None of his brothers talked about their wives and children and certainly did not talk derogatorily about their families. So, I sat there wondering why father was talking about his family members in a rather degrading manner. He degraded my mother no end. He said that I was a lazy boy.

I finally could not contain my anger and called him an idiot; I told him that mother worked around the clock to obtain the money that trained his children at expensive secondary schools and that left to him, we would not even be at secondary schools since he made very little money. I firmly told him to shut up his idiot mouth and respect his wife and children. If he is going to talk about his family members, he ought to talk about them in a positive manner.

I asked him why he said that I was lazy, lazy in relation to what other fourteen-year-old boys in the compound or his village. What makes me lazy, a boy at a boarding school and when he comes home, at Lagos, goes to his mother's restaurant and works there all day long helping out?

I told my father that my mother and her children supported his lazy ass and that he had better shut the fuck up or I would slap him.

All four of them, he and his three brothers, shut up. I got up and left the gathering. From that moment, I had little or no respect for my father and he knew it. I really no longer talked to him.

During my last year at secondary school, I went to the USA Embassy at Lagos, obtained information on American universities, and applied to three universities. I was admitted by all three of them (I had As in my GCE Advance Level). Three months after secondary school, I was in the USA.

It was my mother that was mostly responsible for paying my first year's school fees. Father, however, took credit for what he did not work for.

Mother insisted that all her children go to universities and we did, except one; he was not academically oriented and obtained vocational training.

Over the years, I asked myself why father thought it necessary to desecrate his hardworking wife and children. I came to the following conclusion.

Father had an inadequate personality. His ego wanted his brothers to like him. He put his family members down to get his brothers to like him (but he was stupid enough not to notice that his brothers did not put down their wives and children so as to get his attention).

The man was seeking his brothers' attention and felt that the best way to do so was to put his wife and children down.

I considered his brothers not useful to us. At Lagos, they stayed in our house and my mother fed them until they had their own jobs and thereafter, they did not really extend any help to us. Each of them cared for his family, which is as it should be, but it was my father and mother that was always helping them, but not they to us. I did not particularly care for his brothers.

Over time, I analyzed my father's personality and behaviors. I believe that as a child, he invented a self-concept, an ego that wanted to be number one. At his village school, his peers said that he always wanted to be first in their class. If he did not make it to first, he felt diminished.

After elementary school, he left his village. He went to Enugu; from there, he apprenticed himself to traders. By age sixteen, he was traveling all over West Africa, from Calaba to Accra, Dakar in Senegal, and south as far as Lobito in Angola. He learned many languages and fluently spoke French, Spanish, and Portuguese, plus, our local English, Igbo, and Yoruba.

He was trained as a trader. In time, he settled at Lagos where he lived for the rest of his life. Occasionally, he visited his village at Owerri.

I believe that father invented a grandiose ego that wanted to be number one in everything that he did. He did succeed, relative to his peers; at a point, he bought for his brothers all the modern items that during his time (1940s) were considered symbols of wealth, such as bicycles, fancy clothes; indeed, he got wives for them (in his world, they paid bride prices and he paid for them).

He was always struggling to seem important in his brothers' eyes but they could care less for his opinion of them; as noted, not one of them helped us financially; father helped some boys from his village to go to the USA but none of these people helped us; it was always one-way traffic, from us to them.

I believe that father was neurotic; I mean neurosis in Karen Horney's terms. In childhood, he rejected his real self and used his mind to invent an idealized self. He pursued becoming that ideal self. He drove himself ragged trying to become the ideal self. In the process, he felt enormous anxiety; he feared not becoming an ideal self.

His attempts at pleasing his brothers were due to his desire to get them to approve of his idealized self. In Alfred Adler's psychological categories, father felt inferior and compensated with desire for superiority. He pursued an imaginary sense of superiority all his life. He paid the price of neurosis: having anxiety most of the time, from fear of not becoming his desired superior self.

I do not believe that father has a diagnosable personality disorder or mental disorder but if I am forced to give him one, I would say that he had a combination of avoidant and dependent personality disorders (those are part of the neurotic syndrome).

Like the avoidant personality-disordered person, he wanted other people to like and accept him; he feared that he is not good enough and would be rejected by other people; to avoid rejection, he kept mostly to himself.

At Lagos, he mostly kept to himself; he went to work, came home, ate, drank one beer, and stayed to himself.

He was incredibly smart; therefore, as a child, I and other children sat with him and he talked to us; his mind ranged from one subject to others; he knew a lot; I would say that he had a gifted IQ, over 132.

He was dependent because he did not posit social goals and pursued them with vigor. Given his smarts, I believe that he could have become a leader. He certainly knew more than the politicians of his world that I used to listen to during my childhood in the 1960s.

Father could have done something to improve his world; instead, he adored his leaders, such as Nnamdi Azikiwe. He saw Zik as a God. If you said something negative about Zik, father punished you.

During my college days, I read up on Zik and dismissed him as a third-rate mind and lacking leadership qualities; I read his book on Liberia and his autobiography, *My Odyssey*, and concluded that he was a petty bourgeois who was not actuated by a political ideology; he helped establish Nigerian ideology-free politics.

I liked folks like Kwame Nkrumah, Julius Nyerere, and others who had socialist inclinations (I am a social democrat).

Father was dependent because he did not feel strong enough to fight for what he believed in and instead, wanted other people to fight for him and he followed them.

Again, he did not show any particular personality disorder but had traits of avoidant and dependent personality disorders. He did not have a mental disorder.

My father was a pleaser; he strove to please his siblings, and in the process, was willing to desecrate his family members and in doing so, earned our hatred of him.

Until he died, I really did not have much to do with him beyond perfunctory exchange of greetings. We were courteous to each other but not emotionally bonded with each other. This is sad because he and I are actually similar in mental and personality makeup (my tendency to pleasing other people manifests differently; when I pass homeless folks, I look into my wallet and give them whatever is in it; luckily, I do not have anything beyond a few dollars in my wallet; I use credit cards for most of my financial transactions; this afternoon, I drove to a store, saw a bunch of homeless folks by the door of the store, and gave each of them five dollars).

I should have been closer to my father than I was; I should not have put a distance between us. All that distancing was because I felt that he insulted my mother, me, and my brothers.

I guess that this is why they say we must forgive people for their mistakes. If I had forgiven this amazing man, we would have been friends and helped each other more than we did on our journey through planet earth.

LEADERS HAVE CONFIDENCE IN THEIR BELIEFS AND THOSE INSPIRE PEOPLE TO FOLLOW THEM,

Human beings, in varying degrees, feel weak and lack self-confidence; they lack certainty in their lives. They are always looking out for people who appear to have confidence in themselves and who know what they are doing and where they are going.

Occasionally, they see such persons, they call them leaders, and follow them.

Leaders tend to have exquisite confidence in themselves; they have certainty of purpose; they know where they are going; they have clear goals and visions and inspire people to follow them to go to where they want to go.

People derive confidence by following leaders. Because followers are given a modicum of certainty by following leaders, they are ready and willing to give their monies to their leaders; they support their leaders financially; leaders do not have to work for their daily bread; their followers pay for their upkeep.

People derive a sense of direction from leaders and the sacrifices they make to support them financially are justified.

Ask yourself: do you inspire people to go in a direction, to feel like life is worth living, or are you always criticizing and desecrating people?

Leaders make people feel proud to be alive; critiques make people feel rotten and people abandon them.

Leaders believe in something totally; they have no self-doubt; they have a sense of direction, purpose, and vision; people lacking those qualities follow them.

You cannot fake having leadership qualities if you do not have them. You either have them or you do not have them.

You cannot have leadership qualities in all areas of life. The areas of life that you have leadership skills may not be areas of life that other people have.

The totality of your life, your body, social experience, your physical strength, etc. made you feel strong and have a vision of where you want to go to.

Ordinary leaders are generally tall and athletic; they feel strong and inspire people in their youth.

World transformational leaders go through a life of pain and suffering until they find meaning and purpose in their lives; they then inspire people to follow them in the direction they are going.

Through trial and error, I stumbled on a spiritual direction; actually, the totality of my life led to that direction; in effect, I was born to be a spiritual leader.

I already had a political direction; I am a social democrat; I have always been a social democrat; in class one at secondary school (age thirteen), I read Karl Marx's *Das Capital* and it made sense to me and I declared myself a socialist.

I am totally and unequivocally convinced that my spirituality is true; I live it; I go in the direction it points to; I articulate its truth with amazing clarity; it gives people's lives a sense of direction. (They are tired of the nonsense they called Christianity that Europeans gave to them.)

I am not fake; I believe in what I am doing; those who do not have my absolute confidence in my direction cannot fake it to inspire people.

Africans are lacking in leadership in all areas of their lives; they are lacking political leaders, economic leaders, spiritual leaders, and even artistic and intellectual leaders; what they have are self-centered so-called leaders who are really gangsters, thugs stealing from them.

Africans are crying out for leaders to point to a direction for them to follow. Some people, such as Chinua Achebe and Professor Patrick Lumumba talk about Africans' lack of leaders but they are not the leaders that the people are yearning for.

Nnamdi Kanu has some leadership qualities; he knows that his Igbo people are looking for self-governance and what he calls Biafra could do it for them; however, he is not dedicated enough to the cause; if you said boo, like the big fat coward, Emeka Ojukwu, he would run away.

Leaders do not run from their vocation; nevertheless, because Kanu articulates what many Igbos desire, they follow him; they are willing to go to war for him; they support him with their money.

I point to political direction (social democracy, mixed economy) and spiritual direction (Gnosticism) for folks to follow and they will follow.

WHY MY FATHER HAD A NEED TO BE RESCUED BY OTHER PERSONS

Socrates said that an unexamined life is not worth living.

The saddest aspect of African lives is that Africans seldom examine their lives. They mostly have crummy personalities and do not bother to examine their personalities, understand them, and make necessary changes so as to become better functioning human beings.

And when they try to explain their shiftless lives, they employ the tools of sociology and politics and look for external scapegoats to blame for their crummy lives. They blame white folks for their poverty; as if given all the money in this world that that would improve their lives. A fool and his money soon part ways!

What would improve their lives is the understanding of their medical and psychological makeups and making appropriate improvements to more effectively adapt to their changing environment.

I assume that my father has the same biological makeup as I do. I was born with certain genetic issues (Cytochrome C Oxidase deficiency, Spondylolysis, and Mitral Valve Prolapse). The cumulative effect of these medical disorders is that I feel weak. Feeling weak, I attempted to compensate with the desire to seem strong.

In Alfred Adler's psychoanalytic terms, I was driven to seem superior to other people. Above all, I was motivated to be self-reliant. I do not want anyone to do things for me. In fact, I tend to feel insulted if other people try to do for me what I can do for myself. If you try to help me, I ask you to buzz off and let me do things for myself.

The same issues left my father with the desire to be helped by other people. He wanted other people to rescue him. Feeling weak, he wanted the people around him to rescue him. He was looking for a hero on a white horse to do things for him. He felt unable to do what he needed to do to survive by himself.

He felt overburdened by the act of raising his children and solicited his parents' help in doing so. He sent his first son, Eugene, to go live with his folks in their village. Eugene was eight-years-old when he was sent to the village (the same age that I was sent to the village). Eugene completed his elementary schooling in the village, came back to Lagos, and took one year of what they used to call model school, and then went off to Hussey College Warri, one of the best secondary schools in Nigeria.

Eugene is eight years older than me. When I was sent to go stay with my grandparents, he was at secondary boarding school. Thus, I grew up without much interaction with him. He is my brother only in name.

During the Christmas holidays, when I visited Lagos, I saw Eugene but he had nothing to do with me. Generally, he had his own room; he and his peers socialized. At the end of Christmas, both he and I left Lagos, he to his boarding school, me to my grandparents.

I have always been extremely perceptive, even as a child. I noticed that Eugene seldom talked to his parents. In fact, he did not talk to his father but said hi to our mother and ignored me and my junior brother, Geoffrey. His friends were only those he socialized with. I asked myself why he had nothing to do with his family.

It took me years, after taking classes in psychology, to understand what was going on with him. He was essentially abandoned by his parents and grew up without emotional bonding with them. They were essentially not his parents. They paid his school fees but beyond that, were not related to him.

His schoolmates at Hussey College and other elite secondary schools such as Kings College and Saint Gregory were only those he related to (he began elementary school with them at Lagos Island before his parents sent him to their village so he generally had many of his elementary schoolboys at Kings, as we called that school).

Deep down, Eugene was angry at his parents for parceling him to go live with their folks, 400 miles away, from age eight to age thirteen and thereafter, to a boarding school for another five years. He was emotionally abandoned and had no use for his parents (other than the money they gave to him, and mother gave him loads of money).

I had the same upbringing. At age eight, my mother took me to our village and left me there to be with my grandparents. At that time, I did not even speak Igbo; I spoke only Yoruba. Well, I adapted to the Igbo world, stayed in the village for three years, came back to Lagos to complete elementary school, and went off to a secondary boarding school (Anglican Grammar School, Port Harcourt).

Like my senior brother, I had nothing to do with my parents. I found relationship with my fellow schoolboys. My parents were not emotionally bonded to me and I did not really care that much for them.

After secondary school, I was in the USA living in a college dormitory full of white boys; I learned to cope with them and seldom related to my parents.

The point here is that I did not have a strong emotional attachment to my parents. They were my parents in name only. I had no need to talk to them and actually do not remember ever talking to them about whatever bothered my life.

If I think about it, I actually had it good. At least, I had good education. Many Nigerian children were not even given much education. They were abandoned by their parents.

I read about the Almajiri kids in northern Nigeria. These kids were produced and left to become street kids. Their parents could care less whether they survived or not; they sort of survive by begging for food on the streets and sleeping on the streets.

Many Africans produce children and do not emotionally nurture them; the children grow up emotionally crippled.

I believe that the incredible stealing and corruption going on in Nigeria is mostly due to the fact that most Nigerians were emotionally abandoned by their parents and grew up in emotional pain.

They use alcohol, drugs, and sex to try to reduce their emotional pain but nothing replaces parental nurturing.

I just hope that at some point, Nigerians would start taking emotional care of their children. When they do so, Nigerians would become human beings and stop stealing too much. As they currently are, I expect Nigerians to be thieves and not be able to govern themselves well.

Let me elaborate a bit more on my father (I wrote a 350 pages biography of him). My father's troublesome body disposed him to feel both physically and psychologically weak. Yet, he had to operate in his pathological Igbo culture that accepted folks only when they seem strong, powerful, and accomplishing great things. So, he went to school, got a trade, married, and had children.

He felt like he needed help in taking care of his children. Thus, he farmed his first two children out to his parents to take care of him (mother refused to farm the other two out to be raised by other people for them and insisted on doing so by herself).

After our secondary schooling, father wanted us to go get jobs so as take care of him but our mother insisted that we must go to university. If we had listened to him, we would have started taking care of him right after secondary school. Both Eugene and I ignored him.

Eugene got out of Hussey College, Warri, and made plans to go overseas. If not for the Nigerian civil war, he would have been at the London School of Economics or University of Illinois; both admitted him. As for me, I got out of secondary school and a few months later, went to the USA.

I had no time to take care of a man who did not want to take care of himself, a man who really emotionally abandoned me. As I saw it, if you cannot take care of yourself, you should die. No one should be a burden on other people to take care of him.

At any rate, we took care of father as much as we could (when you retire from work in Nigeria, you do not get pension, and if you do, you may not get paid for years as the thieves in government steal it).

I am very active on the internet. I am known for speaking my mind. I do not mince words. At one point, I examined the Igbo character, found it really troublesome, and wrote about it.

Igbos were always putting Hausas and Fulanis down and those feel angry at them and make life difficult for them; indeed, occasionally kill them. I called on Igbos to respect their neighbors instead of always desecrating them.

Apparently, to get back at me, some Igbo busybodies began talking about my supposed crummy relationship with my parents. They said that I abandoned my father.

Assuming that that is true, it is not true, what business of theirs is it? And who said that I should support my father? Igbo culture? Since when have I been part of Igbo culture? I accept only what I call scientific culture, a culture based on the scientific method.

In my scientific culture, you do not support other people; you help all people to be independent and take care of themselves.

If you decide to marry, and you don't have to do so, and have, say, two children (which should be the optimal number of children a family should have), you train them through university so that they are able to take care of their lives but you do not expect them to take care for you in your old age.

You save money for your old age. Your children are not your pension plan. Better still, you work to have your society initiate a pension plan for all people above the age of seventy, kind of like the US' social security program. Here, working people pay money into a pension fund that the government invests for them and they get it back in their old age.

It is not for children to take care of their parents in old age. You take care of your children for few years and then expect them to support you for, maybe, thirty years of your so-called old age?

As I see it, you ought to die rather than be a burden on your children!

I do not know where the Igbo busybodies got the impression that I did not take care of father, as if I came to the world to take care of him (psychologically, what they were really saying was that I did take care of them, Igbos; they are dependent personalities wishing that independent folks like me take care of them).

Listen, the only thing that I care for is ideas, and producing ideas, not taking care of other people. I help people as much as I can but do not see it as my responsibility to carry them on my back and they break my back. Carry yourself or die; nobody should live to support you, as if you are a child.

In sum, my father had biological and medical reasons that made him feel weak and he felt that he needed to be rescued by other persons.

Nobody exists to rescue any other person; if you live your life expecting other people to rescue you, you are not going to be rescued. You must rescue yourself and not depend on other people to do for you what you ought to be doing for yourself.

It is, however, true that father's medical issues made him feel weak and dependent and needing others' help. I understand his issue.

That is why all lives must be subjected to biological and psychological analysis and understood; for a life that is not studied and understood is a wasted life.

You, the reader, should try to understand your biological and psychological makeup, make adjustments that enable you to live an independent existence, and do not expect other people to carry you on their backs, for if they do so, you break their backs (or they do what they do in Nigeria, steal to get the money to support the many relatives that depend on anyone with a job).

IF GOD DEFENDS AND PROTECTS US, HE HAS ACKNOWLEDGED THE EGO AND ITS SEPARATED WORLD.

If you look at the human condition, it is very difficult to accept religions' thesis that there is a loving father God that protects human beings. Let us see.

If you wish to harm or kill me, you can do so whenever you so desire to; I can also do the same to you. Additionally, natural disasters, such as earthquakes, volcanoes, hurricanes, tsunamis, floods, droughts, diseases caused by bacteria, virus, and fungi kill people (we are right now going through a pandemic caused by the coronavirus, aka Covid-19).

Our lives are very precarious and vulnerable. We all know it and spend most of our time and energy defending our bodies with food, medications, clothes, shelter, and other means for self-protection.

At the psychological level, we are aware that other people could snuff us out, or even enslave us, as Arabs and white folks enslaved black folks and think that it is funny to do so. We employ the various ego defense mechanisms that psychoanalysts wrote about, such as repression, suppression, denial, displacement, projection, rationalization, reaction-formation, sublimation, fantasy, pride, shame, guilt, anger, fear, anger, minimization, projective identification, etc. to defend our ego separated selves.

We are literally defended at all times. No wonder we are both physically and psychologically tense and die young. If we did not have to engage in all these physical and psychological defenses, we probably could live to be 120 years (live to do what, a nihilist might ask).

The various religions of mankind tell us that there is an entity called God and that he protects us. The idea that God protects us is actually laughable.

Sigmund Freud laughed at it in his book, *The Future of an Illusion*. Richard Dawkins laughed at it in his book, *The God Delusion*. Christopher Hutchins laughed at it in his book, *God Is Not Great*.

How can you say that there is a loving God and he does not do anything to stop our pains and sufferings?

Adolf Hitler decides that he loves to kill people and by the time he is stopped by those who want to live, he had been instrumental in the death of over fifty million persons, including 25 million Russians, 6 million

Jews, and an untold number of Africans. No, it is very difficult to accept that there is a loving God who protects humanity.

Voltaire looked at the earthquakes in Chile (?) and made fun of Christians' God in his satire, *Candido*. Pure reason would suggest that scientists are correct in saying that we evolve from the concatenation of the evolving universe. The universe came out of nowhere and evolved energy and matter, and in time, produced biological life forms. We are biological life forms. We are part of nature and are not special.

Nature kills us whenever it wants to do so and we as part of nature kill our kind whenever we want; worse, we come up with weird rationalizations, such as the rationalizations that justify slavery and racism to make life miserable for us.

Simply put, it would seem that we are nothing; our lives have no worth, purpose, and meaning. We are just dust in the wind.

The atheistic explanation of us, on the surface, seems to make sense. However, if one is a scientist and appreciate the little, we know, and the much we still do not know, we do not know ninety-nine percent of the universe (we know nothing of dark energy and dark matter and those two alone constitute 96% of the universe); we have not even begun understanding our bodies (intricate wetware); it is kind of difficult to affirm the atheist's argument for it is based on little or no information.

Atheism and theism (belief in God) seem vacuous. I clung to agnosticism because I accept that I wish that there is life after we die even though I do not know that there is life after we die. I keep my mind open to whatever new information comes my way. I do not need to have a closed mind; I eschew rigid thinking that closes any avenue of investigation.

I went along as an agnostic until friends asked me to read Professor Helen Schucman's book, *A Course in Miracles*. I had difficulty understanding it. Eventually, I think that I understood it. Its arguments concerning the role of God or lack of his role in our suffering seem to make sense to me. Let me briefly summarize the 1, 200 pages book.

The book says that there is God; God is formless intelligence. He is everywhere and everywhere is in him. God is formless spirit that extends to infinite parts; all the parts are in God and he is in them. There is no space or gap between God and his extensions, God and his sons. This is the state of eternity.

God and his unified sons are eternal, permanent, and changeless. God and his sons exist as one unified self with one shared thinking.

God and his sons live in bliss, in perfect peace and happiness, for the unified must live in peace.

The sons of God, the book says, wished to be separated from God and from each other. That is impossible, for, by definition, God and his sons, the whole and its parts are eternally unified.

If separation were possible, God would be incomplete and his sons would be incomplete. An incomplete God is no God; incomplete sons of God are not the sons of God. If separation is possible, God and his sons would not exist.

God and his sons do exist so they must be complete and unified, the book says.

Unable to become separated from God and from each other, the sons of God, as it were, cast a magical spell on their thinking, and engaged in erroneous thinking.

They made themselves go to sleep, and in their sleep, dream that they now live as the opposite of God; they are now separated from God and from each other.

To seem separated from each other and from God, there must be space, time, and matter; so, they invented the universe of space, time, and matter, used matter to invent bodies, and now seem to live in bodies and walk around in space and time.

The book says that they do not live in bodies, space, and time and that space, time, and matter do not exist, those are dream phenomena.

In effect, the me I see on earth do not exist; my earthly self is a dream figure. A dream figure is this Sunday evening typing away at my dream computer. The same applies to you.

The book says that the physical universe does not exist but we want it to exist and make it seem to exist; we are sleeping and dreaming separation from our real self, formless unified self.

By the way, what *A Course in Miracles* says is what Hinduism, Buddhism, Taoism, Zen, and Gnosticism teach. And I have studied those oriental religions, known that Dr. Schucman captured their essence, and placed it in a Christological context; she is, in my opinion, the best spiritual poet the universe has so far produced.

THE HOLY SPIRIT

God tried to communicate to his sons, as he normally does in formless spirit and could no longer reach them; they could no longer hear him for they are sleeping and fancy themselves in a different world.

God senses that there must be a reason why his sons are unable to hear him. They are sleeping and dreaming that they are apart from God, from eternal union of the father and the sons.

God is perfect freedom and does not destroy what his sons made, even if they were made in opposition to God, to eternal unity. So, God did not want to stop his sons from sleeping and dreaming. Instead, he decided to create another self, the Holy Spirit, and placed that new self in the thinking, minds, of his sleeping and dreaming sons.

The Holy Spirit or the God in the sons' dream of self-forgetfulness sees what the sons of God are doing; he sees the cities and countries they formed on earth.

The Holy Spirit decides to make the world invented by the sleeping sons of God lovely. The Holy Spirit reinvented what the sons of God made to separate from God and each other to what they can now use to return to God, love, and forgive each other.

Their bodies made of dense matter are remade in bodies of pure light; their matter-based universe is remade in pure light. Everything in our universe: galaxies, stars, planets, plants, animals, cities, etc. were all remade with light; our dense world has already been reinvented in a world of light form.

You, currently a person in dense body, have another version of yourself in light form. Everything on earth has versions in light forms.

As an aside, this is kind of like Hugh Everett's many worlds' interpretation of quantum mechanics; everything we do on earth is done elsewhere in a different form, in light form, in a more beautiful form; our thoughts here produce our world and those same thoughts produce a different world, produce the world of light forms; and those same thinking produce infinite universes; all of the multiverse coexisting at the same space, time, and matter (different forms of matter).

THE EGO SEPARATED SELF AS REPLACEMENT SELF

In the meantime, we, on earth, in the sleep, have evolved replacement selves. God created us as unified self; now, we have separated ego selves.

On earth, each of us has a separated ego-self. That ego-self lives in body and perceives things as arrayed against it and defends against them.

The ego is not our real self; it is our substitute self; our real self is formless, unified spirit self.

Dr. Helen Schucman, a clinical psychologist, and her Holy Spirit says that if we stop wishing for ego separated selves and its world, love and forgive all people who wronged us, and overlook the earth, we would see ourselves in the Holy Spirit's purified light selves and world.

By the way, there are people who claim to have seen the world of light forms; Hindu saints make that claim all the time and call it the astral, the light world.

THE HOLY TRINITY

So, now we have four selves, one of which is false: God, the son of God and the Holy Spirit; these three are said to share one self and are one self. Christians call these three selves in one self the Holy Trinity.

The fourth self, the ego in body, is said to be unreal, a dream figure, and does not exist but seems to exist in a dream setting.

God the Father, God the Son (us, now dreaming), and God the Holy Spirit are one self and think with one mind. There is no space between them.

One way to understand the concept of triune is to see God as a formless force that operates in his sons and the Holy Spirit; in effect, you, the son of God, are part of that one force; if you stopped trying to take credit for anything, good or bad that you did, you are one God operating in the universe.

In the Gospel of John, Chapter 14, Jesus said exactly the same thing; he said that where you see the son of God, you see God, for God is not apart from his sons; and what the son of God did, God did. In effect, he and God are one. Jews accused him of blasphemy, of claiming to be God, and killed him for it.

Our separated ego selves do not understand the concept of God in three selves; so, let us not bother trying to understand it; as long as we think with our current ego separated minds, we cannot understand union.

In the meantime, we are in the dream of self-attack, the dream of self-forgetfulness. You and I are on earth where we attack each other and natural disasters attack us (we made those natural forces hence attack ourselves through them). We are defensive.

On earth, we feel unsafe. We wish that we are safe (saved, redeemed, delivered, which the book says can only happen if we give up our identification with the ego).

ATTACK AND FORGIVENESS

On earth, I, a black man, see you a white person discriminate against me. I defend myself with the various ego defenses. Other people defend their egos; the one key variable here is that we see ourselves attacked by each other and by nature and defend ourselves.

We wish that we did not have to spend all our time and energies defending ourselves. We wish that God defended us. It is wearying to constantly defend ourselves.

IF GOD DEFENDED US, HE HAS ACKNOWLEDGED SEPARATION AND OUGHT TO HAVE STOPPED IT.

We are God's sons; therefore, if he loved us, he ought to defend us, protect us. Religionists are always asking us to pray to God, asking him to protect and defend us against our human enemies and natural disasters.

A Course in Miracles says that God does not see our world; God transcends our world of space, time, and matter; God is not perceptual for perception accepts the world of separated things.

God does not see me in pain and suffering; therefore, he cannot defend me.

But through his Holy Spirit, God sees my situation and our collective situation. But the Holy Spirit is told not to prevent us from having our dreams of separation.

In this light, the Holy Spirit sees white folks attack black folks, enslave them, discriminate against them, and does nothing to stop it. Instead, he is said to have invented a world of light forms where we do not harm each other, a new world where sheep lie with lions.

Both our world of dense forms and the world of light forms are fictional, dreams, not real; but the world of light forms is a dream that approximates heaven's formless self hence is relatively better than our extant world.

For our present purposes, the God in the temporal universe, the Holy Spirit, does not try to stop bad things from happening to us or prevent us from having diseases and dying in body.

This is because he knows that it is all a dream, that in reality, we remain as God created us, formless unified self and eternal; nothing is happening to us so he overlooks our mutual attacks, our diseases, death, and dying for none of those is taking place in reality but in dreams.

The Holy Spirit asks us to overlook the world of attacks. He asks us to forgive attacks and to not be defensive, for defense makes attack real for one.

If I see you attack me, I am not to defend me, for if I defend me, I have acknowledged that you attacked me and thus acknowledged that I am an ego separated self.

If I overlook your attack, forgive it, I say that you have not attacked me; in forgiving you, I see you and me in the world of light forms, the purified world the Holy Spirit remade from our dark world of matter.

IN OUR WORLD ATTACK AND DEFENSE RULES

All these seem theoretical; indeed, my cynical and skeptical mind tells me that *A Course in Miracles* and its Helen Schucman provided the world with a Mephistophelian rationalization for our painful world; it is an elaborate effort to make us not defend ourselves when we are attacked.

This cynical view is made more credible if one realizes that Dr. Schucman's collaborator in writing the book, Professor Bill Thetford, worked in the Manhattan project that invented the atomic bomb, and also worked for the CIA trying to come up with a means to deceive people more thoroughly.

A Catholic priest who had taken courses in psychology from Dr. Schucman at Columbia University, New York, called *A Course in Miracles* the devil's project to deceive people! When Dr. Schucman died a demented woman, the good priest said, "See, I told you, that woman was possessed by Satan; throw her satanic book away." Ah, that satanic book appeals to some of us!

In the here and now world, I see you attack me and you see me attack you and we defend ourselves.

I know myself as weak and know you as weak. Despite all the grandstanding by white racists as the supermen of the universe, they are about to witness massive attack on them by all the people who, for five hundred years, they did nothing but attack, enslave, and discriminate against.

I do not envy the white man. Europe, Europeans, and white Americans are about to experience karma, the consequences of their hurtful behaviors.

All the people they harmed will come at them, attacking them from every side. The Chinese and Japanese would attack them from one side, the Indians from another side, and Africans from yet another side.

Nuclear weapons would not save them, for the entire world soon will know how to make nuclear weapons (many Africans now understand the physics of nuclear weapons; they are waiting for the right technology to use neutrons to split the nuclei of uranium, break the weak nuclear force, cause chain reaction and release energy to destroy the cities of those who believe that their reason for being on earth is to enslave them and discriminate against them).

DISCUSSION

If God defends us, he acknowledges that our bodies and egos are real, he acknowledges that the world of separation, dreams, is real. He will, therefore, not defend us and will not give us protection for he does not know that our ego separated selves and the world is real.

Only we can defend ourselves in the dream; God and the Holy Spirit cannot defend black folks. Believe it or not, black folks will, sooner or later, defend themselves; they are currently weak and as the weak do, biding their time, hoping to obtain a more efficient means of killing those who killed black people.

Arabs and Europeans who attacked black people must be attacked and defeated, if what we know about egos is true.

The ego bears grievances and seeks vengeance for evil done to it; the ego does not forgive a simple slight it suffered.

Those attacked tend to defend themselves; black folks feel attacked and must defend themselves, but at the moment know that they do not have the right weapons to do so but will gradually obtain those necessary weapons and then unleash such fury on the white race that it was better they were not born in bodies.

CONCLUSION

I conclude this essay by agreeing with sister Helen Schucman, that God does not protect us; he does not defend us because for him to do so is for him to acknowledge this world as real; and if the world is real, there can be no attack and defense in it; if the separated world is real, God cannot exist, for God is unified.

God has nothing to do with us in this world. It is left to us to decide what we do with this world. If we continue attacking each other, God will not defend us but we can defend ourselves.

Empires come and go; they come and enslave some people, then those they enslaved acquire the means to counterattack their attackers and do so, and empires end.

Suma, Egypt, Persia, Greece, Rome, France, Britain, USSR, and other past empires are gone. The current world hegemon, the USA, is on its last leg; it will be attacked and relegated to the trash bin of history.

China and Asians are already poised to take over the world's economy. Africans, too, will take over the ruling of the world; give a few hundred years and Africans take over the ruling of the world.

Human beings and civilization began in Africa and from it, spread to other parts of the world; all things will return to Africa.

In the meantime, God does not defend people on earth so it is a waste of time praying to God to protect us. He will not protect and defend us; only we can defend our dream figures and make them beautiful; only we can make our current nightmarish dream a happy dream.

I have never seen people who have as much death wish, what Sigmund Freud called Thanatos, as white folks. They keep attacking black people without realizing that those they attack would not forget their attacks; when the time is right, the attacked will attack to destroy the attackers.

Yet, what needs to be done to have a peaceful world is simple. Bring about a social democratic society with mixed capitalist and socialist economy; give all people publicly paid education, at all levels, and give all people publicly paid health care and some other things and thereafter, let capitalism allocate goods and services. Adam Smith's *The Wealth of Nations* has a good point: the market allocates goods and services better than communist committees.

Love all people and they will love you back. Do not have the desire to harm anyone and no one will harm you.

Instead of doing the obvious, love all people; as if they are drunk, they keep attacking and harming people and literally begging to be attacked; they spend themselves to bankruptcy trying to acquire military weapons with which they would protect themselves.

When the universal attack on their evil empire begins, their military cannot protect them; they may lob nuclear weapons at other continents and those would lob nuclear weapons at them and destroy them.

Those left alive from the coming conflagration would begin at the beginnings and civilization slowly grows, again.

Actually, it is probably better if human civilization did not exist, if it must exist on the basis of human exploitation of man. My favorite German idealistic philosopher, Arthur Schopenhauer, in his magnus opus, *The World as Will and Idea*, said that the universe probably made a mistake in producing human beings, that given their iniquity, it was better that human beings did not exist. I agree.

However, unlike the pessimistic philosopher, I am optimistic and have not given up on human beings. Somehow, I believe that we can transform human beings into loving creatures. Maybe I am naïve but that is my wish. I balance political realism with political idealism.

30

THE IMPLICATION THAT THE UNIVERSE IS EXPANDING INTO SPACE IT CREATED

According to currently accepted cosmology, out of nowhere, 13.8 billion years ago, a point of light appeared (called singularity for it contains or created everything that now exists in the universe). That light became incredibly hot and exploded. It shattered itself into photons, particles of light.

The particles of light immediately transformed themselves into electrons and quarks. Quarks transformed themselves into neutrons and protons.

The point of light while producing matter (electrons, protons, and neutrons) was also producing anti-matter. Matter and anti-matter were supposed to attack and annihilate each other and return back to radiation, hot light. But for some reasons, the incipient universe apparently created more particles of matter than particles of anti-matter, so that when they attacked each other, some particles of matter remained, along with photons.

Proton and neutron unified into nuclei. So now nuclei, electrons, and photons existed in plasma state. All these were done within three minutes.

In the meantime, the incipient universe was expanding at an incredible speed (called inflation); it expanded billions of miles in a second).

But where was it expanding to? Was there a preexisting vacuum or space that it was expanding into? The answer is no. It created the space it is expanding into. Thus, the big bang created matter, space, and time.

400, 000 years later, nuclei captured electrons and formed the lightest atoms (hydrogen, helium, and lithium). That event released photons, light from the hitherto dense plasma universe (plasma is when nuclei have not captured electrons yet).

The cosmic microwave background radiation observed by Arno Penzias and Robert Wilson in 1965 is from the radiation released at the 400, 000 marks of the universe.

The universe is now an ocean of hydrogen, helium, lithium, and photons. Millions of years later, this gaseous universe was separated into clumps of hydrogen gas.

On each clump, gravity pushed the gas inward and in its core heat and pressure, made hydrogen nuclei fuse into helium atoms (hydrogen has one electron and one proton, its isotopes have neutrons). The formation of helium (two electrons, two protons, and two neutrons) is what a star is; a star is the ignition of light when two hydrogen fuses to helium (a fusion process that Fred Hoyle called nucleosynthesis).

The universe is now composed of space, time, and matter mostly in the form of stars. The early stars were huge in size and millions of years later, exhausted their hydrogen and began fusing other elements and when the fusion process reaches iron (iron is composed of twenty-six electrons, twenty-six protons, and twenty-six neutrons), the star becomes very hot, expands, and explodes in supernova.

During the explosion, all elements beyond iron are formed. The inner core of the exploded massive star collapses inward and forms either neutron stars where all elements are crushed to neutrons and spin millions of time in a second or blackholes where whatever is inside it is so dense that not even light that enters its events horizon can escape.

The stars cluster in galaxies. As of today, there are over 200 galaxies; each galaxy has over 200 stars. Our galaxy is the Milky Way. It takes light 100, 000 years to travel from one end of it to the other traveling at 186, 282 miles per second.

Within galaxies are star systems with their planets. The sun, solar, has nine planets (Mercury, Venus, Earth, Mars, Jupiter, Saturn, Uranus,

Neptune, and Pluto) orbiting it. There are also asteroids comets orbiting the sun.

The various planets have moons orbiting them; the earth has only one moon orbiting it.

Planet earth and the other planets around the sun formed 4.5 billion years ago, from debris from exploded massive stars.

The initial earth was very hot. Millions of years later, heavy elements sunk into the earth's core (the inner core is made of iron; the outer core is made of nickel; the mantle is made of viscous hot rocks, and the surface, crust, is composed mostly of silicon).

The hot earth is said to have cooled from the water that comets brought to earth. Comets are rocks with frozen water on them; they kept hitting the earth and the hot earth thawed their frozen water. Over time, 70% of the earth came to be covered by water.

In the waters on earth, sixty-four elements, mostly carbon, hydrogen, oxygen, nitrogen, potassium, iron, copper, sulfur, magnesium, zinc, and others combined into molecules from which biological organisms formed.

First were single-celled organisms, bacteria, such as amoeba; those added cells to themselves to form multicellular organisms. This process led to the formation of human beings about 100, 000 years ago.

Human beings, apparently, were formed in Africa and from Africa, spread to Europe, Asia, Australia, and finally to the Americas less than 35, 000 years ago.

So far, the earth is the only planet that we know for sure has biological organisms. There are trillions of exoplanets around other stars, so common sense suggests that some of them probably have biological life on them, perhaps formed differently from us. We do not know for sure.

What is obvious is that on a little planet, earth, orbiting a sun, in the goldilocks region of the Milky Way galaxy is biological life.

The universe is expanding into space it created. As it expands, galaxies become more distant from others (our nearest galaxy, Andromeda, is becoming more distant from us; it takes light 2.5 million years to reach us from Andromeda).

In trillions of years to come, the galaxies would be so separated from each other that the stars would become cold, explode, and shatter into the elements in them. The elements in time would decay to the particles in them (electrons, protons, and neutrons), and those in time will decay to quarks which would decay to radiation, cold light.

A universe that began in hot light ends in cold light; this is called the Big Chill, as opposed to an earlier belief that the universe would reverse its expansion and collapse into singularity, Big Crunch, and perhaps start another universe (Rebound).

A MAGICAL UNIVERSE

You will probably agree with me if I say that we are truly living in a magical universe if the above speculations are true. Incredible things happen in this universe that if religionists told us about them, we would dismiss them as talking nonsense.

Consider that the earth travels in space at the speed of 67, 000 miles an hour. That is correct, where you are standing now, though still the same earth, will be 67, 000 in a different part of space in an hour. Do you feel that the earth is moving at all, much more that it is moving at 67, 000 miles per hour? That seems incredible to me.

The solar system itself orbits the Milky Way galaxy at incredible speed and takes millions of years to go around the galaxy.

The galaxies are moving in space at incredible speed. All these seem unbelievable.

The earth sometimes goes through a part of space that has a lot of dust in it and we do not know it because the atmosphere of the earth, the bubble surrounding it, filters the dust. The earth's atmosphere is divided into: **Troposphere, Stratosphere, Mesosphere, Thermosphere, Ionosphere, and Exosphere.**

The earth's various levels of atmosphere shield us from all kinds of dangerous objects from space: asteroids, comets, dust, gases.

However, this is not the subject of this writing.

IT IS INCREDULOUS THAT THE BIG BANG CREATED MATTER, SPACE, AND TIME.

It is incredulous that the big bang created matter, space, and time. We are told that the universe is not expanding into an already existing vacuum but into space it created.

One asks, but what lies at the end of the extant universe? Where is it creating space into? One is given the analogy of the balloon.

Draw the map of the world on a flaccid balloon. Then put air into the balloon. It expands and the countries distance from each other and expand away from where they were when the balloon did not have air inside it. This is simple enough for us to grasp. But we all know that the balloon expands in context, of existing space or vacuum.

If you placed a balloon between two walls, say, three inches apart from each other, and then put air into the balloon, it would expand to the edge of the wall and since it cannot push the wall out to enable it to expand the balloon further, the balloon would burst.

If there is a wall at the edge of our universe, it would have no place to expand to. We are told that there is no wall at the edge of the universe and that the universe's edge is nothing, that it creates the vacuum it is expanding into. This is kind of difficult for me to accept for in our everyday experience, something comes out in a preexisting space, vacuum, but does not create it.

THE MAGIC OF THE UNIVERSE CREATING SPACE, TIME, AND MATTER IS REPLICATED IN OUR DREAMS.

How the universe creates space, time, and matter is not self-evident to me; I have not accepted that thesis. If I were to accept it, I would say that the universe is more magical than the magic of our dreams.

At night, we go to sleep. In our sleep, we dream. In our dreams, we see a universe that looks like our daytime universe. We do all the things we do on earth. Then, we wake up and the dream world of space, time, and matter, people, animals, trees, and everything is gone.

How did our brains produce a dream world that looks like our day world? Nobody really has satisfactorily explained this phenomenon.

Science has the habit of ignoring what its methodological tools are unable to explain. The scientific method doesn't help us understand dreams.

Some silly neuroscientists tell us that the concatenation of electricity in the brain (electrons, neurotransmitters, ions in our brain cells, neurons) produce dreams. Really? This is incredible.

If our brains can produce a seemingly real world in dreams and that world disappears when we wake up in the morning, it is also feasible that our brains produced our day world and when we die, that physical universe of space, time, and matter disappears.

In other words, just as the dream world at night does not exist, the day world does not exist; both are make-belief worlds. Both do not exist.

MY EGO AND BODY DO NOT EXIST.

In that light, I do not exist as a person in body, walking in space and time; I am an apparition, a phantom, a ghost, an illusion that seems to exist but does not exist; I am a dream figure.

The affairs of my life give me the illusion that I exist in body. I feel hunger and eat food (hunger and food make me feel that my body exists and is real); I get sick and take medications (sickness and medications make me feel that my body is real and existing); I do get hurt and feel pain (the feeling of pain makes me feel that my body is real); I do feel pleasure from certain activities (those pleasurable feeling make me feel that my body is real); I do feel like I have a separated ego-self in body, a self housed in a vulnerable body, and defend that precarious body; my sense of physiological vulnerability and the efforts I undertake to survive give me the impression that my body exists and that my ego exists.

But if the universe is magical and does not exist, it follows that my ego, body, and all the activities I undertake to make both seem to exist do not exist. I do not exist; my body does not exist. The universe does not exist. The entire thing is an illusion, a dream that seems existent but is not.

This is what mystics have told us from the beginning of time, is it not? Hinduism, Buddhism, and Gnosticism actually teach that the world is a dream, an illusion that does not exist but that our thinking, minds, contrive to make it seem to exist.

If mystics are correct, where is the mind that contrives to make the universe and the self housed in body seem to exist?

Where is the thinker, the mind that makes this world seem existent? I have not seen another self, mine or others outside this world, so how do I know that another self and people exist outside of this world?

That other world could also be an illusion. Thus, what we have is a series of illusions. Where do these illusions begin and end? Nowhere?

WE MUST DO WHAT ENABLES US TO COPE WITH THE EXIGENCIES OF THIS WORLD.

In the meantime, I see myself living in a world of space, time, and matter; I see myself in a body that needs food, medications, clothes, shelter, and means of transportation to get from place to place. I have to work to get the means of survival. If I do not work and get food, I will die.

Thus, illusion or not, I have to do certain things if I want to live in the illusion, on earth. To the best of my knowledge, I have not seen a person who conjures food or gets his medications, clothes, and shelter out of nowhere. Folks work to survive on earth. They live for at most 120 years and die and their bodies dissolve to the elements that composed them and the elements decay to particles that decay to light.

So far, we know that everything came from light and to return to light, but what exists beyond light is not known to us. That is where we currently stand in our science and philosophy.

Religion gives us entertaining magical tales of heaven and hell and other tales of what exists after we die and we cannot prove those stories as true.

ACCIDENTS DETERMINE EVERYTHING IN THE UNIVERSE.

A purposeless point of light, we are told, by trial and error, produced the universe and produced those who have the ability to study it and understand it, us.

It is difficult to accept this accident produced universe. I do not see how pure accidents could produce what grade school students are taught in physics and chemistry. They are taught that there are three states of matter: solid, liquid, and gas (and plasma). These three states can be transformed from one to the other.

Take a piece of wood, a solid, and burn it; that is, apply heat to the solid and it burns. As it burns, it is transformed into gas (smoke). That gas can be caught and cooled into liquid. Thus, matter here is transformed from solid to gas and to liquid. You can also begin from liquid, cool it into solid (ice for example), boil it, and reduce it to gas.

Matter, whether in solid, gas, or liquid is composed of atoms (there are 92 types of atoms, each called an element). The different elements are combined in compounds to form different substances. Consider water.

Here, two atoms of hydrogen combine with one atom of oxygen to form water (water that can be in liquid), gas (steam), or solid (ice cubes).

The making of compounds requires that the various elements in it exchange their outer electrons; this is done through valence. You can combine many elements into compounds and molecules. All these are done by dumb nature.

The strong nuclear force holds neutrons and protons inside the nuclear (and the weak nuclear force can decay them).

The electromagnetic force holds the electrons to the nuclear (as well as when compounds are formed, the exchanged electrons are held together by the electromagnetic force).

The stars and planets are held to each other by the force of gravity.

Motion is done in predictable ways; an object in motion remains in motion until an equal force stops it. You get matter into motion through heat. If you heat wood and produce gas, heat has made the gas into motion and it moves from a hot place to a cool place.

We can talk about electricity, heat, sound, mechanics, and light; we can talk about quantum mechanics. And all these incredible phenomena are caused by mere accidental occurrences? It seems incredible for that to be so.

Yet we do not have an alternative explanation of phenomena; the religious explanation is magical thinking (but is the scientific explanation not also magical?)

TO FORGIVE DONALD TRUMP AND HIS RACIST SUPPORTERS IS TO MAINTAIN MADNESS, NOT HEAL IT.

Donald Trump is clearly a racist. If you adopt the Jesus Christ notion of forgiving evil persons and overlook what the racist is doing, all you have done is reinforce it and keep it alive.

Therefore, you must not forgive racists; you must do whatever it takes to eradicate their disease of hate from the surface of this world.

To keep their disease alive is to maintain their madness, to keep them in the hellish life of hate that they live in.

To heal sick racists is to correct their illness by teaching them that love is the only sane approach to life and if they refuse to love and persist in hate, you fight and remove them from governments.

They are a plague to the life on earth; they cause people too much emotional and psychological suffering. Therefore, the Jesus Christ notion of forgiveness does not help here for to not heal the mad and forgive it, is to let it exist.

If you forgive racists, you are now part of the problem of racism; you maintain it in existence and let madness exist in mad persons; mad persons need to be healed; to be healed is to love all people regardless of race and gender.

THE HOLY SPIRIT USES YOUR EGO AND BODY TO LOVE OTHER SONS OF GOD IN EGOS AND BODIES.

The sons of God currently placed themselves in bodies and live as the opposite of their real formless selves. They walk around in bodies, each looking after his self-interests, attacking others that seem opposed to his self-interests, and cooperating with those who seem to work with him in protecting his self-interest. They live to protect and defend their egos, to defend that which does not exist but seems to exist in the dream and living in fear of what would happen to their egos and bodies, to nothing.

The Holy Spirit teaches them that egos and bodies do not exist but seem to exist to enable the sons of God to dream that they are separated from each other and from their father. He asks them to use their egos and bodies to love other egos and bodies that love the sleeping sons of God. If they do so, their bodies and egos become lighter, flexible.

If you stop defending your ego and body, you become a light self, floating from place to place without sense of carrying weight.

LEADERS OF A NEW MANKIND

Leaders point to a direction they want to go and want people around them to go with them, a goal, and a vision to be pursued.

Leaders represent the aspiration of the people and the people gladly follow them and support them. Leaders do not have to work for their living; the people they lead gladly pay for their support (we pay for our kings and popes' upkeep; political leaders and religious leaders are fed by the people).

You are a leader if the people you lead are paying for your survival and give their last pennies to you to live well and do your work of leading them.

Biafrans are willing to pay for Nnamdi Kanu's upkeep so he is a leader; he wants to take them to Biafra.

However, my kind of leadership takes people to a new lifestyle, to living egolessly, living like Christ, guided by the Holy Spirit loving and correcting our mistakes, to a new world of love. If people are willing to pay for this type of leaders, then they are leaders (please note that Jews did not want to be led by Jesus Christ type of leaders for they did not help them defeat the Romans who ruled them but instead, talked about escaping from their earthly troubles and fleeing to heaven that may or may not exist; that is, the people may not accept the direction you want to take them to, hence not want to pay for them).

FROM EGO DEFENSE TO NOT DEFENDING THE EGO

I go from defending my ego, defending what does not exist, trying to use defense to make it seem to exist and live in fear, anxiety, depression, and paranoia to living without ego defense, total ego-lessness, and the reward is peace and joy.

From ego to Christ; Christ is the undefended ego that is guided by the Holy Spirit (love and forgiveness) hence floats through life without self-consciousness, fear, and anxiety.

THAT WHICH IS PROTECTED BY FEAR AND EGO DEFENSES CANNOT BE REAL.

The human body is protected and sustained in existence by fear and the activities we engage in in response to fear.

That which is defended and protected by fear cannot be real; it is temporary and not permanent; it lives for one hundred years and dissolves to nothingness.

The human ego-based civilization protected by fear and ego defenses do not last long; sooner or later, it collapses to nothingness.

ONLY SPIRIT IS ETERNAL, PERMANENT, AND CHANGELESS HENCE REAL.

But have you seen a spirit? How do you know that spirit exists? How do you know that spirit is not just conceptualized as the opposite of our earthly fear-based temporary self?

You have made eternity your criterion for reality, so how do you know that spirit is eternal? All you know for sure is that our bodies are not eternal.

YOUR GRANDIOSE GOALS ARE IN RESPONSE TO YOUR NATURE; TRANSFORM THEM INTO REALISTIC GOALS.

I have grandiose goals such as wanting to change myself and make my body ideal (whatever that is), develop Africa, transform society into a social-democratic society where people help each other, give all publicly paid education at all levels, and publicly paid health insurance, etc. These grandiose, unrealistic goals are responses to my rickety body that desires surcease of pain and develops an amazing capacity for visualizing alternative to it.

Anything small and ordinary, such as regular houses, did not appeal to me; instead, I wished for grandiose houses such as the Versailles palace near Paris, why not? A man who called his ass the king of France lived in it and I am a man and can live in such a place, although that man used the people's money to build it and live in it and I do not have access to the people's money to steal to build such a mansion.

Nevertheless, it is okay to have such grand dreams that respond to my need for grand things. But the fact is that in the real world, I am not going to build the versatile palace alone. I must then redirect my grandiose goals, not eliminate them to what is doable within my reality. I still have a magnificent beautiful house, and not just hope to have one in heaven or world of light forms built by the Holy Spirit.

I want lots of money, billions of it, why not? Who said that I must be poor? God, what God; God is my idea, not a reality outside me.

GOD IS MY IDEA.

Whatever I say about God is my idea. It was Helen Schucman's idea about God that wrote *A Course in Miracles*, not an external Jesus, Holy Spirit, or God that did it.

That God of hers did not warn her that she is developing cancer until she discovered it too late and died a bitter woman saying that God used her and dumped her.

She did not realize that what she called God, Holy Spirit, and Jesus is all part of her thinking; she came up with the ideas in her book.

WE PROJECT OUR IDEAS TO GOD.

People project their ideas of God to what they call God; ideas about Jesus to what they call Jesus. It is the entire individual's mind that constructed his ideas about God, heaven, and hell.

The individual's mind is very powerful for a mind that understands this universe is very powerful.

OUR MINDS REMAIN A MYSTERY TO US.

Our minds, thinking, remain a mystery to us; in the meantime, we can use them to do what serves us well on earth without giving our ideas of God to others, as Helen, Jane Roberts, and Neale Donald Walsh did, give their ideas to seeming Gods outside them.

I MUST START A BUSINESS TO MAKE MONEY FROM IT.

I must start a realistic business that I can sell to people and use to make billions and trillions of dollars. When? Now.

PARANOIA IS ROOTED IN ONE'S PROBLEMS, DENIED, NOT UNDERSTOOD, AND THEIR CAUSE PROJECT TO OTHER PEOPLE.

The paranoid feel weak, deny it, and project causality to God, other people, and so on and say that they made him weak. No God or people made him weak.

Paranoia is rooted in search for causality of our problems.

Paranoia is rooted in fear of harm and death and futile seeking of projection.

One must accept one's problems and know that the cause is biological and sociological and solve them without attributing their cause to God, spirits, and other people for those do not exist outside one; one's mind can damn one and can also save one; one's salvation is from one's corrected thinking, not from external God and people.

GOD IS A SEA OF INTELLIGENCE THAT MANIFESTS IN ALL OF US AND THE NATURE OF OUR BODIES, THAT IS, SON OF GOD, FIRST MANIFESTED, DETERMINES HOW HE MANIFESTS IN EACH OF US.

EVERYTHING IS A PART OF GOD, A SON OF GOD; EACH ANIMAL. TREE, ROCKS, STARS, AND PLANETS ARE SONS OF GOD; WE ARE COLLECTIVELY RESPONSIBLE FOR WHAT HAPPENS IN THE UNIVERSE.

Everything in being, people, animals, trees, rocks, planets, stars, and galaxies are parts of the whole, in anthropomorphic terms, sons of God. Each is responsible for what happens to it/him and we are all responsible for what happens to it/us and each other. If only human beings are responsible and animals are not and we can kill them, then it is not fair to them; if killed, they want to be killed to experience death. Each of them has an ego, the wish to live in the world of separation and take the consequences.

In the world of light forms, everything, including stars, trees, animals, rocks, and planets have consciousness.

LEADERS WORK WITH IMPERFECT PEOPLE, IN IMPERFECT ORGANIZATIONS, TO ACHIEVE IMPERFECT GOALS.

Human beings are imperfect. As long as they live in bodies and have separated egos, it is doubtful that they can be perfect. Perfection remains a mere imagination, a wish by people. Yet people have goals that they want to accomplish, goals that serve their imperfect state.

Leaders do not wait until people become perfect before they use them to accomplish imperfect goals. Instead, they use imperfect people and imperfect organizations to accomplish imperfect goals. You use people as they are to do what needs to be done; if you wait until people are perfect or desire perfect goals and perfect organizations before you lead them, you are going to wait forever and do nothing.

You make the most of the hand you are dealt.

Idealistic leaders have idealistic goals and are looking for perfect people and perfect organizations to use in accomplishing those goals and naturally look forever, do nothing, and accomplish no goals.

An idealist sees people as egoistic and wishes that that people were egoless; he wants to accomplish a perfect goal, such as a society where people love each other. He is going to wait forever for people are egos in bodies and are imperfect.

In so far that there have been egoless people, it has been a few such as Jesus Christ. Not everyone in this world is going to behave like Jesus Christ, defenseless of their egos, loving, and forgiving.

Realistic leaders use unloving and unforgiving people to accomplish imperfect goals.

31

A COURSE IN MIRACLES IS CLEARLY A PHILOSOPHY OF ESCAPISM FROM THIS WORLD

A Course in Miracles presents a philosophy on how to escape from this world's realities. There is no proof that where it wants people to escape to is real; that problem is the problem of all religions; the world that religions present is not seen.

Nevertheless, given that this world is painful, full of suffering, and ends in death, it seems that a philosophy that juxtaposes a different world to look forward to is useful to balance the futility of these worlds.

Human beings need some escapist metaphysics given the futility of the egos' world.

> NEBU FANCIED HIMSELF SUPERIOR TO OTHER
> PEOPLE BECAUSE HE BELIEVED THAT HE HAD
> THE COURAGE TO ACCEPT ATHEISM.

Nebo Adele fancied himself superior to other people because he had what it seemed to him the courage to accept nihilism, the philosophy of atheism. Having convinced himself that there is no God and afterlife, he felt that he was superior to folks who accept the fantasy of God and heaven and does not have the courage to accept any God.

He lived anonymously and from it, engaged in antisocial behaviors; he is a thief and desecrates people's characters.

If he was courageous, he would do what he does openly, have folks put a bullet into his freaking head, and feed his body to dogs and hyenas. He really did not have courage.

His courage is the imaginary courage of paranoid persons who think that their false grandiose selves are powerful while their real selves are very cowering, fearful, and hide to live their idiot lives.

The fact is that we do not know whether there are God and life after death or not, so the smart person is agnostic, not theist, atheist, or gnostic. That nebula guy is a total coward pretending to be courageous.

I would have loved to whoop his cowardly nigger ass. Actually, the garbage of a human being taught me a lot about his Igbo tribe.

ENERGY

Energy is that which moves.

MATTER

Matter is that which seems to stand still, not moving.

Actually, energy and matter are the same things looked at from two different perspectives.

The universe is expanding. If it is expanding, then there is no gravity pulling it together. Why? To overcome this problem, physicists posit dark energy and dark matter. Dark energy makes the galaxies expand; dark matter makes galaxies not overexpand away from each other.

PHYSICS IS FULL OF CRAP.

All these are speculative; physics is full of crap.

Look, the universe is eternal; perhaps, at its edges, it spawns new baby universes that expand; thus, there are infinite universes.

There is no beginning for all the universes but for each universe; each universe begins and ends and others continue.

THERE ARE NO BLACKHOLES AND NEUTRON STARS.

There are no blackholes and neutron stars; all those are speculative. Physics is full of speculation that the masses were hoodwinked to accepting as true.

LEADING PEOPLE AWAY FROM INSANITY AND TOWARD SANITY.

Every human group tries to move toward a certain vision it deems good for it. Leaders are human beings who move people in the direction they want to go to.

There is no doubt about it at all. Donald Trump leads people toward madness. His followers are angry folks who are full of hatred for non-white people.

Many white folks see their control of America slipping away from them; they fear that black and Latino folks are, sooner or later, going to become the majority population in their country and thus, lead the country. They resent and fear this potential scenario and want to prevent black and Latino people from coming to the USA.

Since they see black folks and Latinos as inferior and uncivilized people, a people that have not produced great scientists or any of the type of things they admire, they fear that their country would go to the dogs should those people take leadership of the country.

In their thinking, America would become a third world country, kind of like what exists in Latin America and Africa, countries led by corrupt people and going nowhere in world economic and power struggles.

They are motivated to prevent this eventuality by any means necessary. Some of the ways they are using to prevent it are through manipulating voting, such as gerrymandering, voter ID requirements, residency requirements, and saying no to mail-in votes.

In the past, they tried literacy testing, evidence of poll taxes, etc. They did whatever they could to suppress minority persons from voting; to them, "ignorant minority persons" should not vote at all; voting should be only for white folks, and not for poor, ignorant white folks.

These people believe that the end justifies the means; since they do not want their country to go to the dogs, they do not want black and Latino people ruling the USA.

They have a point, you know. Can you show them any African or Latino-led country that is well run, that is not, in Trump's colorful words, a shithole country?

Can you imagine Nigerian politicians ruling the USA? In one year, they would transform the USA into the corruption haven that is Nigeria (perhaps the well-established institutions for good governance may reduce eventually but given that Nigerian politicians are literally thieves, they would not eliminate it).

White folks are running scared!

If you cannot govern your Africa or Latin America well, white Americans have justification to fear that you would do to their country what you did to Africa, Latin America, and non-Western European countries in general.

I get what is driving Trump and his supporters. They believe that reason is on their side and they justify what they are doing.

However, in reality, they are motivated by insanity. Their motivation is insane because it is moving against the inevitable.

The inevitable is that all the peoples of the world will live together; and as members of the same species, they will reproduce and become one brown race.

There is really not much that you can do to prevent this eventuality; you can delay it but you cannot stop it. No amount of wall-building at the southern border would prevent nonwhites from coming to the USA and Europe.

However, such immigration should be slowed until institutions for civilizing them are put in place.

Sanity means accepting reality and making the most of it. Sane motivation requires Americans to do whatever they could to prevent their country from degenerating to African and Latin American levels.

One way to prevent the USA from becoming like Africa and Latin America is to provide publicly paid education to all Americans through university and technical schools and provide publicly paid health insurance for all Americans.

Thereafter, America must encourage a competitive economy where only the individual's skills take him as far as he could go.

Capitalism is the most productive economy, but it has some problems; it tends to yield a few rich and many poor people.

Whereas we must reinforce capitalism, we must ameliorate its side effects by using public funds to do something that helps the poor, such as paying for their education, especially education in science and technology.

I understand what motivates Trump and his base; their motivation is egoistic but human. Human beings are egos; they live separate lives; each of them is motivated by doing what is good for him and perhaps working with a few others to serve their mutual interests but do not concern themselves with all people's interests.

Trump and other extant political leaders of the world are ego-based leaders; they are egoistic leaders serving their ego followers' interests.

I wish that I could say that we ought to have egoless leaders serving egoless people. That is simply not going to happen. People are egos and their leaders are egos; ego leaders like Trump serve their ego followers' interests.

Trump is an ego-based leader serving the ego interests of his ego followers.

What is doable is to produce leaders who serve the cause of sanity, who know what reality is like and do what serves many peoples' interests.

In the case of the USA, leaders must serve all Americans regardless of their race and gender. We need universal leaders who lead people to calmness and peace, not to conflict and war, as Trump and other ego-based leaders do.

Sane leaders must understand that they are egos and know that ego is by definition, driven by conflict; the ego is in opposition to unified self; the ego is rooted in our wish to be separated selves; separated selves serve separated and different interests hence conflict is inevitable in a separation-based society.

Sane leaders are not going to eliminate separation, for separation is the basis of this world, but strive to find a middle ground, to serve many selves hence produce a modicum of peace in a world at war with itself.

To be ego is to be at war with one's real self (one's real self is unified self) and at war with all people; we can reduce that war by figuring out ways to serve most people's ego interests.

What the world now needs is sane leaders leading people to human unity; not insane leaders like Donald Trump leading people to racial conflict and war.

The world now needs political and spiritual leaders who accentuate our human unity, not differences.

YOU LEAD PEOPLE GO TO WHERE THEY WANT TO GO; TRUMP LEADS WHITE FOLKS WHO WANT TO GO ON A RACIST PATH.

You cannot lead people to go to where they do not want to go to. White racists want to go on a journey without blacks; they resent blacks and Trump wants the same thing; he articulates their desire and leads them down that path.

Hitler knew that Germans wanted to go on a journey of feeling superior to other people and he himself wanted to feel the same; he led his Germans on that journey and led them to self-destruction as Trump is leading racists to.

LEADING FROM EGO VERSUS LEADING FROM CHRIST

When you lead from your ego, you lead other egos to substitute unions, egos in sham unions; when you led from Christ, you lead from the desire for unified self and lead people to unity while they are still in form; you lead them to light forms.

Even in the world of light forms, there are still leaders leading people to stay in light forms, to unify.

DREAM
2:30 AM
JULY 7, 2020

In this dream, I visited a friend and he is a night's soil man, Onye Oburushi. To please him, I volunteered to go to his workplace and do what he does. I followed him to his work but could not do what he did, carry other people's shit on my head. I walked away and told him that I could not do it and he carried shit on his head and walked away. I walked to what seemed like a suburb. I saw a Chinese child coming home from school and called to his mother standing on a balcony; I jumped from higher ground to lower ground and woke up.

The meaning of this dream is that no matter how much humility I wish for, I will not be humiliated.

THE EGO INTERPRETS HUMILITY AS HUMILIATION.

The ego takes humility as humiliation. No, humility is accepting God guiding one; if God is all-powerful, he gives one abundant resources.

The ego says that there is no God; it teaches that one must be humiliated to prove that one cares for other people. No, God does not ask you to be humiliated but to be glorified.

ONE SHOULD NOT BE POOR.

Why should I tolerate poverty? Poverty is false humility; poverty is humiliation; if one believed in God and God is abundance, one would know that God would give his sons whatever they ask of him in love, in Christ. True children of God live in material abundance, not poverty. The ego gives its followers poverty; Christ (our real self) and his father, God, give us wealth. If you are poor, you live in ego, not in God.

Africans are totally egoistic, hence live in poverty. When they love all people, hence live in Christ, and work for the good of all people, they would no longer live in poverty.

OTHER PEOPLES' LIVES ARE NOT MORE IMPORTANT THAN ONE'S LIFE AND ONE SHOULD NOT SACRIFICE ONE'S LIFE FOR OTHER PEOPLE'S GOOD.

Other people's lives are not more important than one's life; therefore, there is no reason why one should be sacrificed for other people to live well.

What are other people living for, anyway, just being egos? That is not a good enough reason to sacrifice one's ego to live.

JESUS DID NOT DIE FOR ME TO LIVE BUT TO LIBERATE HIMSELF FROM THE PRISON OF EGO LIVING.

Reason dictates that we all live but ego says that you must die for other people to live, rubbish. Jesus did not die for me to live, that is ego speaking right there.

Jesus died to his ego to live in spirit. He did not sacrifice his self, ego, and body for me, but to live well. Before I went to sleep, I was thinking about following a new vocation where I do not have ego, kind of like the Christ and work in an egoless way.

Working in an egoless way, as Christ, is good for one for it means that one is calm and peaceful; it does not mean that one is a slave to other people as the ego pretends it to be and makes one believe.

ANYTHING YOU DO TO STAY ALIVE IN BODY, SEPARATED SELF IS EGO; HENCE, BUDDHA SAID THAT DESIRE TO BE ALIVE IN BODY ITSELF IS EGO.

Ego defense mechanisms include the wish to stay alive as a separated self in body. No ego includes the wish to not be in body.

That is why Gautama Buddha taught his followers to give up all desire to live as ego separated self so as to live in the bliss of formless unified self.

IN EGO, YOU ARE IN FEAR, ANGER, DEPRESSION, AND PARANOIA AND IN FALSE SELF HENCE IN HEAT; YOU LOOK FOR WAYS TO REDUCE YOUR HEATED BODY AND EGO; DRUGS, ALCOHOL, SEX, AND MEDITATION HELP US REDUCE OUR HOT BODIES.

Since everything you do with ego is done with heat, your mind and body are heated. What is it that you do without doing it in heat, fear, anger, paranoia, or depression?

It is when you live with love. But we already live in formless love, so, this kind of love entails simply letting go of all efforts to be ego and you experience the love that is already inside you; you need do nothing to have it; you always have it, for it is the God in you; you live peacefully and happily.

DOING SOMETHING FROM SELF-CONCEPT AND SELF-IMAGE IS DOING WHAT GIVES ONE HEAT, FEAR, AND ANGER.

You have a self-concept and self-image and behave to conform to them; in doing so, you live in heat, false self, fear, anger, and paranoia.

Whenever you do things to conform to your self-image and self-concept, you experience heat in your body.

Your real self is not a self-concept or self-image; it is formless so you do nothing to conform to it; you are quiet.

I want to go toward love and peace.

I lead people who want love, union, and peace; we go on that path to reawakening to our union in formless state, even though we are still in separated earthly state.

We will, of course, not replicate heaven's perfect peace on earth for heaven is formless whereas earth is in forms. But we can make our earth more peaceful than it is now.

SOMETHING DOES THINKING IN US.

Something does thinking in us; it is the son of God, part of the whole self that does the thinking in us. That part of the whole, son of God, is formless.

THE SELF IN LIGHT FORM IS STILL IN HEAT AND IS NOT REAL; THE REAL SELF IS FORMLESS HENCE IN LOVE AND PEACE.

The improved self that the formless Holy Spirit formed for each of us, the self in light form, is still in light and light does have some heat hence the light-formed self is not totally peaceful and happy.

Only the formless self that is not in light or matter can be totally peaceful and happy.

Light came from the hot big bang and from stars (fusion of hydrogen to helium); light has heat in it and cannot give one total and perfect peace of formless heaven.

Cold light, as in microwave light in our microwave oven, still has heat in it; we use microwave radiation, light to heat up our food.

THE HUMAN BODY ALWAYS IS HOT; BODY TEMPERATURE IS 98.6 DEGREES FAHRENHEIT.

The human body is always in heat for it was formed from heat, heat of the big bang and hot temperature of the stars and light. Inside the body is 98.6 degrees Fahrenheit, almost enough heat to boil water.

So, even if you meditate, you are not going to be totally cold. Even if you die, the atoms in your body generate some heat.

CENTER FOR SCIENCE OF THINKING, CST

Mind is not a person or thing; what exists is self and self thinks through our brains, bodies, hence ego-based thinking.

Mind is not an independent thing that thinks; what is true is that there is a self in us that thinks through our brains. We need to study the science of thinking, not science of mind.

EGO IS A PATTERN OF THINKING THAT WISHES AND SUPPORTS SEPARATED EXISTENCE; CHRIST IS A PATTERN OF THINKING THAT SUPPORTS UNIFIED EXISTENCE.

Both the ego and Christ are patterns of thinking while we are in forms. Ego pattern of thinking wishes separation, and as such, is in body and body is shaped by big bang heat hence is hot.

Christ is a pattern of thinking that wishes union with all hence is less hot but still in light form and has some heat.

Only the son of God that is formless has no heat in him, is totally cold, calm, and peaceful.

I TEACH REMOVING THE EGO TO LIVE IN LOVE AND PEACE.

My profession, vocation, and career are to live from less ego so as to live from Christ; that is, to live from love (union of all selves as one self); love is already inside us and thus, we don't have to attain it but merely remove ego and we live from love and live in peace. Thereafter, we show other people how to reduce their egos and live from love hence in peace.

I must leave egos like Trump and the people of the world alone; they pursue their ego substitute selves and goals and as such, live in conflict.

I live from Christ, love, and peace.

I have found my vocation at last: it is to live from less ego (if I am in form, I am still living in ego, space, time, and matter), live from the union of God, his sons, and the peace they have and model that peace for people without doing anything other than showing how to reduce the ego.

CONSCIOUSNESS, THINKING, AND SPEECH CAN ONLY EXIST
WHERE THERE ARE TWO OR MORE PEOPLE COEXISTING;
GOD THEREFORE MUST HAVE ALWAYS HAD OTHER GODS
IF HE HAS CONSCIOUSNESS, THINKING, AND SPEECH.

If God exists and has consciousness, thinking, and speech, he has other Gods, for there must be two or more of the same kind of agents for there to be consciousness, speech, and thinking.

If only one God exists without similar Gods (sons of God), he cannot have any kind of consciousness.

32

DELUSIONAL THINKING, BEHAVIOR, AND HUMAN GROWTH

In delusional thinking and behavior, something medical or social, makes a child, or an adult, feel utterly weak and not good enough.

He is unable to accept his sense of weakness and inferiority. He denies it. Delusional thinking and behavior emanate from denial of one's underlying sense of utter weakness and inferiority.

One denies what one sees in oneself: not being good enough, posits an imaginary self that is perfect, identifies with that false self-concept, and presents it to other people to accept as who one is (and if it is group delusion, as who one's group is, this is called folie à deux).

One overuses the ego defense mechanism of projection that all human beings use; now, one projects what one sees in one and denies to other people. Having denied that one is weak and inferior, one projects it to other people, sees them as weak and inferior to one, and relates to them as if they are actually weak and inferior.

The deluded person relates to his projections to people but not to people as they are! (Do you relate to people as they are? How are people, do you know?)

One now pretends to be one's desired grandiose, ideal, and perfect self. One no longer deals with one's imperfect reality or any kind of reality at all. One has escaped from reality and lives in fantasy, the world of wishes.

One is no longer solving our earthly problems as they are; one seeks fantasy solutions to our problems.

One wants other people to accept one's false self-concept and false self-image; one compulsively wants to become that false big self-concept and self-image and wants other people to accept it as who one is. If they accept it, one feels fine; if not, one feels sad. Sometimes, one feels angry at people if they do not accept one's false big self.

One is afraid of not being the wished-for big self hence one is full of fear and anxiety from fear of not living up to the false, grandiose self-image.

In the meantime, one is not doing anything realistic in the real world to become the powerful person one wishes to be. One ignores social and political reality.

For example, one ignores the fact that people choose who is their leader or in power in their polity and pretends to have power that one does not have.

One now is living in perpetual fear, anger, paranoia, mania; all those emanates from efforts to seem a false big self. One does not know peace and joy in one's life.

STOP TRYING TO BE A FALSE GRANDIOSE SELF-CONCEPT AND SELF-IMAGE.

If one simply stops desiring any kind of big self-concept and its self-image, one feels peace and joy. *A Course in Miracles* says that having any kind of separated self-concept, big or small, is delusional. It says that our real self is part of one unified life, aka God and his sons, and we currently do not know it and pretend to be big separated selves.

If we give up our desire to be any kind of separated self, do not defend a separated big or small self, we experience ourselves as part of one unified life and in it, feel peaceful and happy.

At any moment we desire separated big or small self in body, we are back to delusional thinking and behaving.

IGBOS' DELUSIONAL THINKING AND BEHAVIOR

Igbos entered the modern world in the late nineteenth century; they entered it with absolutely nothing that modern civilization deems important; they have no writing, no wheel, no schools, no books, no monumental constructions, and no large-scale governments (their governments are limited to their villages).

They see those things in the white man's world and in some of their neighbors' worlds, such as in Edo, Hausa-Fulani, and Yoruba worlds. They feel utterly inferior to those who possess what they lack, civilization.

They compensate by calling those they feel inferior to putdown names. They feel inferior to other Nigerians, deny that feeling, and instead claim to be superior to other Nigerians.

They deny their weakness and inferiority by claiming to be its opposite; they claim to be responsible for other people's accomplishments, such as their absurd claiming to be Jews.

In claiming to be Jews, they take psychotic ownership of Jews' considerable accomplishment in the last four thousand years of their written history.

They even claim to be the original Egyptians hence built the pyramids and that fiction kind of makes them feel like they are a superior people.

In Nigeria, they claim to be responsible for all that is good in it and deny anything bad that they do.

They are very boastful; they are always bragging about their phantom achievements and saying that their neighbors have accomplished nothing.

This tendency to put their neighbors down to make themselves seem elevated irritates their neighbors who then hate, attack, and sometimes kill them.

They are engaged in delusional thinking and behavior, a type of thinking found in people who feel utterly weak and inferior.

Like psychiatrically deluded people all over the world, Igbos want you to collude with them and see them as they want to be seen: a superior and great people.

You can see that they are at the lowest steps in the civilizational ladder (they did not invent writing and wheel, the beginning point of civilization).

Given their efforts to seem who they are not, they make their minds and bodies tense; they live in tremendous physical tension and are full of fear, anxiety, anger, paranoia, and mania.

All they have to do is let go of the wish to be powerful and important selves and they relax and become calm and healthy.

What I said about Igbos is a gross generalization; there are exceptions; there are Igbos who are not denying their underlying inferior feeling selves and pursuing imaginary grandiose selves. In other words, there are some healthy Igbos, just as there are some healthy human beings who accept themselves as they are without any conditions that they must meet before they accept themselves.

ASSUME THAT YOU ARE NOTHING IMPORTANT AND YOU ARE ABLE TO BE HUMOROUS, LAUGH, AND LIVE IN PEACE AND JOY.

To heal delusion disorder, what I call delusional thinking and behaving, is very simple; you must assume that you are nothing and that you are not important. You must accept that you are nothing and worthless, as all human beings are.

Make that assumption and you are no longer seeking to become a grandiose self-concept and self-image and you relax, smell coffee and roses, and live peacefully and happily.

DISCUSSION

What I described above, in degrees, apply to all people; that is actually what it means to be human. Human beings are those creatures that know that they are food for worms, and are nothing special to nature for they will die and rot, but they deny that fact and pursue becoming important and special selves.

In pursuing big self-concepts and self-images, they give themselves unnecessary tension, fear, anxiety, anger, paranoia, and mania (and even schizophrenia; psychosis results from pursuit of false important selves).

To become healthy, human beings must give up all pursuit of false, big self-concepts and self-images and accept that they are nothing; they are just part of life.

CONCLUSION

Life lives in all biological organisms, dies, and what exists after animals die is only speculated on but not apparent.

Religion gives people fantasies of what lies in store for them when they die. Apparently, some people need religions' fantasies to tolerate their apparent meaningless and purposeless existence in what science suggests seems an accidental universe.

Or is the universe determined and has meaning and purpose? That is a subject for other writings.

The cure for delusional thinking and behavior posited above is also the cure for all mental and personality disorders, for all of them inheres in wishful thinking, the desire to be important in a world where they seem unimportant.

Correct thinking and behavior accept our existential nothingness and still do what we enjoy doing and have aptitude for doing regardless of whether there is meaning in our lives or not.

Below is written on a different occasion but is pertinent to deluded thinking and behaving so I will add it to the above essay:

LET GO OF THE DESIRE FOR A BIG SELF.

Who are we human beings? I do not know. What I do know is that I have a separated self-concept and all people have separated self-concepts. Some people have humble separated self-concepts (we call them normal folks) whereas others have false, grandiose self-concepts (and we call them neurotics or psychotics).

Some people have self-concepts that want to be big. They posited their wish for big separated self-concepts in their childhood. Like all people, they use their (big) separated self-concepts to interpret events in their world and to see other people.

No one really see other people and things as they are objectively; we always see people and the world with our self-concepts hence in a biased manner; we do not know what we are seeing; we do not even know whether what we think that we are seeing is actually there or whether we are merely projecting our thoughts to what we think is out there.

Connected Lives

Try this experiment: completely let go of your self-concept, big or small, and have no self-concept at all (this is the purpose of Hindu, Buddhist, and Zen meditation, to have no ego separated self).

If you succeed, what would happen is that you would have no self-consciousness; you would feel that there is life in you and that that life has no shape at all; it is undifferentiated life (we use body and social experience to differentiate life to what we call our self-concepts).

If you let go of your attachment to your separated self-concept and your body, you notice only life existing in you. That life in you could be used to conceptualize another self-concept for you and for other people.

If you let go of your separated self-concept, you have life, what folk's call spirit. If you remove your separated self-concept, your wish for a big self in particular, what happens is that life speaks through you; if you like, spirit speaks through you.

This is why in the old, they used to have some people take some herbal brews, drugs, and have them dance to certain music until they are in a trance, that is, lose their separated self-concepts. When they attain a no separated self-concept, they get in touch with what folks called the spiritual world, what I call undifferentiated self, and from there, they speak as what folks used to call oracles. They can talk about the past, present, and future with some knowingness that boggles our ordinary minds.

I believe that when the deluded person stops thinking from his wish for a big, separated self, his mind, as it were, gets in touch with undifferentiated life, undifferentiated self, and he thinks, talks, and behaves from that higher place in him and folks say that he is in touch with God, that he speaks for God.

When the paranoid, deluded person heals his thinking, and now has a mind that no longer is trying to speak from a grandiose self-concept, he becomes able to talk as the prophets of old did.

When deluded, Igbos stop trying to think and behave from their wished-for big selves. They suddenly begin speaking truth more than you would expect, more than they did when they were trying to shape reality with their wished-for big selves.

Remove your desire for a big self and what folks call spirit talks through you. A healed deluded person, that is, a man who has changed his pattern of thinking and behaving from a false grandiose self-concept to no self, becomes a speaker of truth.

Many healed Igbos speak the truth more than you would believe.

What science teaches us is that the universe is an accidental place; events beginning from the big bang to the present seem the products of accidents.

However, something tells me that there is a spiritual side to human beings. What it is I do not know. Life does not seem just the product of accidents. I believe that there is a spiritual side of us; I cannot prove it.

Each person is moving on a trajectory, moving in a direction, and all that happens to him that seem accidental are really not so; they are shaped by his wished-for ideal, separated self, which in turn were determined in his childhood by the confluence of his inherited body and social experience. There was a reason why things happened to him as they did.

When he removes his wish for a big self and experiences himself as just life living through him, he is healed. In that healed state, he is calm, peaceful, and happy and feels like there is no self in his head. He can actually perform miracles from that no separated big self state.

This is what Jesus did. The man let go of his wished-for big separated self and was no longer thinking from a deluded self but thought and spoke from his real self, which is an undifferentiated self and could then speak like the oracles of old and heal the sick for he is in what folks call God, what I call unified self.

In unified state, one knows that there is one connected life, one joined life, and that love is what joins all life forms into one unified life and one loves all selves and things.

One becomes a teacher of love, who is a teacher of God and a giver of peace and joy to those suffering from their efforts to live as separated big or small selves.

Let go of your self-concept and self-image, big or small; do not do anything from your hitherto sense of self-concept and its self-image. Your brain is emptied of any idea of self; you now have no ego-self.

In a mind, in a thinking emptied of the wish for separated ego-self-concept, one begins to think from one's real self; one now thinks loving, unifying thinking, and one's behaviors serve all people. One is now a healed mind, a healthy person.

Pride in African culture may kill you!

"Culture is the customs, arts, social institutions, and achievements of a particular nation, people, or other social group."—Dictionary.com

Every group of human beings who lived in a specific part of the world did what they had to do to survive in that particular environment or else, they would not have survived.

Culture is the sum of whatever a people did to adapt to their particular environment and survived in it. All cultures are adaptive to certain environments.

In the late nineteenth century and the beginning of the twentieth century, Western anthropologists fanned out in what they called primitive people in Africa, Asia Pacific Islands, and the Americas. They studied the peoples' cultures, their ways of life, and came to understand that though what they are doing is different from what was done in Britain, France, Germany, the USA, and Canada (those are what we mean by the West) that whatever they did enable them to adapt to their world hence must have been the right things for them to do.

Thereafter, these liberal western anthropologists, beginning with Margaret Mead in the 1930s, began talking about cultural relativism, the idea that all cultures are equally good.

In the 1960s, that hazy concept morphed to what is called multiculturalism. The idea is that all cultures are good for they enabled people to survive in their worlds. That truth soon segued to the idea that you can live in London and New York and import the African culture that enabled you to survive in Africa and live it in the West.

This is not true. What your people did in your particular part of the world may not be adaptive in other parts of the world.

I am from Alaigbo and was socialized to Igbo culture. Now, I live in Anchorage, Alaska. The moment you come out of Ted Stevens International Airport at Anchorage, you quickly learn that you need a different culture to survive here. Let us say that you got here in November and the temperature outside the airport is below 20 Degrees Fahrenheit, you will not be able to walk around in the scanty clothes you wore in tropical Africa. If you do, you will be uncomfortable and if you persist within a couple of days, you will die from cold.

If you are rational, from the airport or from your hotel room, you head on to clothing stores and buy appropriate clothes that enable folks to adapt to the harsh cold of Alaska. Gradually, you begin to do what enables you to live in the subarctic world of Alaska or else, you die.

If you do not adapt to your new land, you are like the dodo bird that refused to adapt to its new environment and died off. The point here is that what enabled you to adapt to a particular part of the world may not enable you to adapt to another part of the world.

Sticking to your old culture in a new environment may be the quickest way for you to die. Pride in your people's culture to the point of not changing it to adapt to changed circumstances may kill you.

Environments may remain the same but what it takes to adapt to them may be different. That is to say that you may remain in Africa but the culture needed to adapt to its changed conditions may be different from the old culture of your people.

Your people were subsistence farmers. Before 1900, there were probably fewer than 20 million Nigerians. Those people could survive by practicing subsistence farming. Today, there are, at least, 150 million Nigerians; all these people are trying to survive by living in the same environment that twenty million subsistence farmers survived in 1900.

If the people of today's Nigeria do not change their farming methods to one that produces more food from the same piece of land, they will die off. Their old subsistence farming method would not enable them to survive.

Now, they need mechanized farming and the soil needs to be added fertilizers to yield more food to feed an increasing population.

Your old African farming culture is now not a survival mechanism but a death and dying mechanism. You cannot take pride in it. You must now study agricultural science, which includes physics, chemistry, biology, geology, astronomy and through them develop scientific culture, a culture based on the scientific method if you want to survive in today's world regardless of where you live.

Therefore, rational persons discard aspects of their old cultures and embrace different ones that enable them to survive in their new world or else, they die off.

If they insist on taking pride in their old culture and since it is no longer adaptive to their new world, they would be like the dodo bird and die off and that is their choice so you do not cry for them.

You cannot afford to allow Western white liberals to "play you," tell you that all cultures are equal when your old culture is a highway to your death. You must change your culture if you want to adapt to your new circumstances.

China, Japan, Korea, and other Asian countries have had four thousand years of continuous culture. In terms of the old world, no culture on planet earth was better than the culture of China. That was until the West discovered the scientific method (from the early sixteenth century Nicolas Copernicus, Galileo, Newton, etc.).

In the mid-1700s, England began the industrial revolution, beginning with James Watt using steam to do work. Steam, that is, hot water, was used to drive engines (steam engines) and the factory system came into being.

England became the first industrialized country. In the early 1800s, France, Germany, and the USA became industrialized and joined England in the club of industrialized countries.

Since then, these European countries have led the world in everything.

In the mid-1800s, western countries came to Japan and China and the Japanese and Chinese observed them and called them savages, people who are not worth their attention (the Chinese consider themselves the most civilized people on earth).

The Asians did not realize that the white man came with a new type of culture, machine culture. Before Asians knew what was happening to them, the West carved up Japan and China among themselves and controlled them.

The Chinese finally realized what is happening to them and belatedly tried to understand science and technology. That process was completed by Mao Tse Tung who in the 1960s engineered the Cultural Revolution. He deliberately asked young people to destroy their old Confucian culture (they held China back) and in its place, established the scientific culture.

By the early 2000s, China reached the West in science and technology. As I write, China now is the largest economy in the world.

What China did was to throw away its 4000-year-old culture and accept a new culture that adapts to their new circumstances. The Asians, as we talk, outcompete the white man in what the West began, modern schooling.

Africans, on the other hand, are impressionable; they were played by Western patronizing and condescending liberal anthropologists; they were told the nonsense about how their past cultures are as good as the culture that sent men to the moon.

Africans wear discarded Arab robes (agbada) and call it their national attire. They operate like folks living in the feudal age, not in the twenty-first century.

The few African countries that are making it in the modern world are Ethiopia and Rwanda; both consciously embraced the West and today, their people wear suites whereas shiftless Nigerians wear Arab discarded agbada and are not productive.

Africa cannot become modern and productive unless it changes its culture and embraces scientific culture (not ancient Egyptian culture, as some deluded Africans think is feasible).

Old Egypt did not have science and technology as we know them today; moreover, it is debatable whether ancient Egypt was Negroid in origin; their language certainly was not the same as West African languages but similar to today's Semitic languages.

The only way forward for Africa is for it to become like England both in culture and people's individual behaviors; there is no real alternative to this reality. Your pride in your so-called past culture is not going to feed you and modernize your economy so that it competes with Asians and Europeans.

Cultures are not static but dynamic; influences from other cultures are always diffusing to one's culture. Whether one likes it or not, one is influenced by other people.

Rational and pragmatic people swallow their shame that their people were primitive and learn from those whose cultures embody science and technology and be like them.

You cannot walk into the same river twice; things are always moving forward not backward. Change your culture or die from taking pride in your anachronistic world view.

APPARENTLY, HUMAN BEINGS RECOGNIZE THE TRUTH AT DIFFERENT STAGES IN THEIR LIVES.

Some members of our family apparently did not like some of my choices on the race issue. I am glad that some of them are getting around to seeing the logic of my choice. In a few hundred years, all human beings will be brown for what used to separate people, distance, would be gone and they will interbreed for they are members of one species.

Human beings are truly at different stages in their evolution. I began elementary schooling at age six. At that age, I knew that there is only one human race. I refused to see myself as Igbo, Nigerian, African, and black and simply saw myself as a human being. I saw people from all so-called human races as my siblings.

Other people apparently need elaborate persuasion to accept their human oneness. They apparently are at a lower level of spiritual evolution.

At college, I encountered the Baha'is religion. I read what their founder, Bahaullah, said about how all people are one; he talked about human unity and how we all need to have one language, one government, and intermarry. I asked: what is the big deal about what he said? And I noted that I have known all those since I was a child.

Folks were surprised at my claim for apparently, they were laboring under the illusion that there are differences between the races. What differences are there in the races?

There is absolutely no difference between Blacks, Whites, Asians, and other so-called races. Some of us knew that from the moment we were born and others need education to accept the truth.

Give all children publicly paid education through university and publicly paid health care and they would perform at the same rate regardless of their so-called race. There is only one human race.

We must stop emphasizing what divides us and accentuate what unifies us. In union with all, we know peace and joy, for union is our reality; separation is an illusion.

THE IDEA OF JESUS DYING FOR OUR SALVATION
IS ROOTED IN THE EGO WISHING FOR OTHER
EGOS TO DIE TO MAKE IT SEEM POWERFUL.

Christians have this cute idea that Jesus Christ died for their sins. What sins and what dying? What they are really talking about is the observable fact that the ego, the individual's sense of self, wants other selves to die for it so that it feels powerful; the ego wants to feel that it has gotten another person or persons to die for it so that it lives.

IF JESUS IS ALIVE IN SPIRIT, HOW COME HE HAS NOT
DONE SOMETHING TO STRENGTHEN HIS CHURCH?

The Romans in 70 AD destroyed the Jewish Temple at Jerusalem and the dead Jesus who presumably lived in spirit where he has all power did not stop them. To the present, what passes as the Christian church are human egos trying to make it powerful and the leaders of the church trying to make a living from it.

Folks pray to Jesus for material abundance; he has not made them rich; indeed, he has done nothing to tell them what the true Christian doctrine is and strengthen it.

His church in a few more hundred years would die as science replaces it. The point is that there is no Jesus out there; all that is called Christianity is the dynamics of the human ego pretending to be God.

A Course in Miracles comes along saying that it is from Jesus and Jesus could not heal Helen Schucman of her cancer, or heal Kenneth Warpnick of his cancer, or heal Bill Thetford of his heart attack.

This is because there is no Jesus to heal them.

(Professors Helen Schucman and Bill Thetford were professors of psychology at Columbia University, New York City; Kenneth Warpnick was a clinical psychologist who edited the book, *A Course in Miracles*.)

What is real is that a part of Helen, the part that is in touch with higher intelligence, wrote the book and she was too fearful to call it her book, for that would make her seem grandiose, powerful to know what the truth is; so, she attributed her thoughts to a nonexistent Jesus, a person that people already accept to be powerful and knowledgeable on religious matters.

It does not matter that she attributed her thoughts, probably the best such thoughts produced by the twentieth century, to Jesus for the highest part of us, undifferentiated intelligence, has no personality and whatever personality you attribute to it is your business and it does not mind.

Please note that I am not denying what folks call God, I just call it undifferentiated intelligence (aka unified self). It is beyond each of us to understand.

If you deny that intelligence, you are a fool.

Listen, I get up from sleep in the morning and go to my computer, sit there, and within two hours, type six pages of profound thoughts; where those thoughts came from, I do not know. Carl Jung would say that they came from our human collective unconscious mind (they usually encompass Western philosophy, psychology, and science, all in my unconscious mind).

If I wanted to be cute, I could say that they came from Jesus or God; I say that they come from the highest part of us that we do not understand.

The individual must not take ownership of such thinking but must attribute it to where it came from, undifferentiated thinking.

Jesus was smart in attributing his profound thoughts to what he called his father and not take personal ownership of them, for if one takes such personal ownership, one could become psychotic, deluded. It is better to say that one does not know where such amazing thoughts come from.

I am thinking about the latest discoveries in physics and thereafter, my mind shifts to spirituality; how my mind does it I do not know.

There is a mystery behind our existence; I am not about to deny that mystery; all I can say is that as an agnostic, I do not understand it.

IT IS MY THINKING, MIND, OPERATING FROM UNIVERSAL INTELLIGENCE THAT PRODUCES MY DREAMS AND VISIONS; THERE IS NO EXTERNAL JESUS APPEARING IN MY VISIONS.

My individuated thinking, mind, derives its source in universal thinking. From that source, my thinking produces my dreams and visions and peoples them with the dream figures I see in my dreams, and peoples my visions with Jesus and make him seem apart from me, telling me to go write my own book on spirituality and leave the poetry of Helen Schucman and the Bible alone; the Bible and Helen's spiritual psychology is useful for some people but mine is for a different class of people, the philosophically and scientifically educated.

I had a dream in which my mother essentially told me that she did her best for me and then she walked off with other women.

I thank you mother, Ugoji Theresa Osuji. Only God knows how blessed I feel that you are my mother.

What actually happened is that my higher mind, in my dream, tells me that mother did her best for me and has walked into the mist of time, wherever that is, and for me to bless her and leave her alone.

In other dreams, my higher self tells me that my assessment of my father as an immature man who wants his children to support him is correct; it says that his dependency was due to his problematic body but beyond that, he was a good man; my higher mind tells me to bless my father for his efforts to have all his three children university educated (the fourth one went to a technical school), leave him alone, and move on with my life. I agree.

I thank you father; you did your best for me. Thank you Ohaegbulam Johnson Osuji.

Ozodi Thomas Osuji, Ph.D.

IT IS A MISTAKE TO DISMISS THE MYSTERY OF MAN OR TO BELIEVE IN MYSTICAL EXPLANATIONS OF HIM.

I am by nature a skeptic. I am not motivated to see people's bodies as anything but a bunch of elements held together by chemical bonds, bodies that will die. The chemical bonds decay and the elements separate, go their parted ways, and go reassemble elsewhere in the universe. My natural inclination is to see people as not different from animals, trees, and any other thing in the universe. I am not given to the mysterious.

Having said that, how our brains produce thinking is beyond my grasp. I have tried very hard to grasp it but failed.

However, I am not willing to accept that mere concatenation of atoms wrote Shakespeare's plays, Einstein's equations, and my philosophy. But try as I do, I do not understand it.

I am just going to say that there is a mystery in our lives that I do not understand. When I look at me or other people, I see some mystery that I have not understood. Something tells me that there is a spiritual angle to our lives (by spiritual, I mean non material).

I am not going to give it any specific religious explanation. This is because religion has deceived man more than any other thing people do. If you accept the religious explanation before you know it, you are attributing the events of your daily living to what spirits did to you and such rubbish.

I once moved into an apartment and from the first night, began hearing what seemed like footsteps running by the walls in the bedroom. My girlfriend, Lady Jewells, who moved in with me, heard the footsteps and said that they are probably from ghosts. Other people, too, heard the sound.

I talked to the manager of the apartment about it and she told me that the guy who lived there died about a month before we moved in. I was tempted to attribute the sound to ghosts.

The moment that I attributed the weird sounds to ghost, I began having dreams in which unseen things were attacking me and scaring me.

What you believe to be true happens to you, at least, in your dreams. Believe in ghosts and ghosts appear in your dreams; do not believe in ghosts and there are no ghosts in your dreams, so I choose not to believe in ghosts (the sounds were still there but when I stopped attributing them to ghosts, I no longer had nightmarish dreams).

Yet, there is an unknown aspect of us. We are a mystery to ourselves. So, what should a cynical guy like me do?

I will have an open mind and listen to folks talk about the supernatural but not believe them. If there are spiritual beings, I do not want them to show themselves only to me, for that would be subject to my making it up, but show themselves to many people at the same time, so that we all can confirm their presence.

My hunch is that there is a higher part of us, what I call unified self or undifferentiated intelligence that manifests in our lives and is responsible for what we do at the individual level.

A part of that unified self stores all that human beings do, a kind of universal memory in pictures, and from it, invents dreams for us with people from the past in it.

Carl Jung had a concept called the collective unconscious mind; according to him, all that human beings experienced in the past is stored in the collective unconscious mind and our individual unconscious minds tune into it and extract what Jung called archetypes of behavior and those influence us.

I believe that an unknown part of us is responsible for our individual and collective lives on earth; somehow, it coordinates what happens to each of us, all of us, and society in general. How it does it I have no clue and speculating will not help me much.

I let the unknown be and concern myself with the known and knowable, the part that science can study and understand (but what is it in us that do the studying of science, electrons, photons, or spirit? I do not know).

Each of us is very different. My body, for example, is hypersensitive and picks up smells that other people do not pick up. Consider cellphones, computers, televisions, and other electronic equipment; they produce noxious smell in my mouth and nose so that I have to use electronic devices only when it is absolutely necessary for me to do so.

People are biophysically and biochemically different and you had better believe it before you harm yourself. During my college days, I once tried to work in a factory; the smell in it and the fact that my legs could not stand at a spot for eight hours, it experienced extraordinary pain, so I lasted only two days and quit; other people enjoyed the job!

That is to say that I could not do what other people can easily do and they cannot do what I do very easily. Each of us is unique and you better believe it and not delude yourself with the liberal bugaboo that we are all the same. It may take you a week to read a 400 pages book while it will take me less than a day to do so. Please accept that we are different from each other and don't go about with the fantasy that you can do what all people can do; I cannot do what Albert Einstein did easily (physics and mathematics) and in my area of aptitude and interest (philosophy and psychology), he cannot do what I find easy to do. Such is life; C'est la vie!

THE UNIVERSE CAME OUT OF NOTHING AND NOWHERE PROBABLY MEANS THAT IT CAME FROM WHERE WE DO NOT UNDERSTAND.

Contemporary cosmology says that 13.8 billion years ago, the universe came out of nothing and nowhere. What this probably means is that it came from somewhere we do not understand. That somewhere could be another universe with different laws of physics. The concept of multiverse posits infinite universes each with its own laws of physics. Therefore, our universe may have come from a different universe. I do not know.

IN CHILDHOOD, I WAS OVERSTIMULATED AND AS A CONSEQUENCE DID NOT LEARN TO SPEAK UNTIL AGE FOUR AND WAS A POOR LEARNER AT ELEMENTARY SCHOOL

My parents and other folks around me said that I did not learn how to speak until age four; they said that when I began speaking, I spoke our language well, meaning that I was learning it but did not speak it during those first four years.

My explanation of this problem is that I tend to be conscious of making mistakes and probably did not want to make mistakes hence did not babble the language and learn it as less self-conscious children do. I also believe that a causal factor could be neurological and muscular. There is no doubt in my mind that I had and still have an undetermined nerve and muscle issue. My body was and still is easily aroused, excited. I have extreme hypersensitivity and often muscle twitches; this probably was due to an inherited nerve and muscle problems, such as dystonia, myoclonus, chorea, athetosis, and hemibalismus; I do not know. But that is not what I am talking about here.

What I am talking about here is that my slow learning of language (grammar and any other subject that requires rules such as mathematics) gave me the opportunity to learn them slowly, and eventually, learn them well. This means that in childhood, I was not incorporated into my people's culture but slowly came around to learning it.

If you learn a language, you become incorporated into the culture bearing that language. Because I was not readily incorporated into my people's culture or any culture for that matter, I had to reflect on human cultures, their virtues and problems. I, therefore, saw what needs to be changed in human cultures; I became a change agent.

The world is a dream and since I had a nightmarish dream, I sought a better dream; in the process, I discovered ways to make our dream a happy dream, make our world a loving, peaceful, and happy place.

In effect, my slow learning and dilettantism (bouncing in and out of physics, philosophy, and psychology) enabled me to get to know what needs to be improved in our world.

Every problem is an opportunity to find new pathways to living on earth.

Metaphysically, I can say that my existence did not want me to operate in traditional cultures and disposed me to discover a new culture, what I call scientific culture, a culture based on the scientific method and reason, not belief and faith.

SCIENTIFIC CULTURE AND AFRICANS

In the contemporary world, Africans are at the bottom of most things that human beings do. Indeed, some white racists accuse them of having no relevant culture.

As if to prove that they had cultures, they now cling to what they call their ancient cultures and embrace the concept of multiculturalism.

Some of them go as far as to say that ancient Egypt was African. This would seem to suggest that Africans were capable of having a great civilization. There is usually continuity in change. If Egyptian people were Africans, their language would continue in some form in extant African languages. What seems to be the case is that current Semitic languages seem related to Kemet language.

I believe that one of the reasons why Africans are backward is their nostalgic clinging to what they call their culture. They can get around the conundrum of feeling shame from adapting to European culture by consciously choosing scientific culture, a culture based on the scientific method, on physics, chemistry, biology, geology, and astronomy.

As we talk, young Nigerian college students belong to what they call cults. Here, they even sacrifice human beings to what they call gods hoping that they would improve their lives. There is no evidence that gods exist so their behavior is utterly ignorant and stupid.

Where science seems unable to provide answers, such as the question of whether there is life after death or not, the most rational approach seems agnosticism rather than blind theism or atheism.

Scientific culture is what would move Africa forward. At centers for living from scientific culture, we meet weekly for three hours, teach, and learn how to think and behave from the parameters of science.

SCIENTIFIC CULTURE AND SUPERSTITIOUS THINKING AND BEHAVIOR

Over time, I noticed that I easily attribute causation of what happens to me and around me to supernatural explanations. Such explanations give me fear. There is no evidence that the supernatural exists. Most events in our lives can be explained naturally, that is, scientifically.

Therefore, we establish centers for living from scientific culture; here, phenomena are explained scientifically; our thinking and behavior must be based on the scientific method. This improves our quality of living.

FEAR-BASED THINKING AND FALSE ATTRIBUTION OF CAUSATIONS VERSUS SCIENCE-BASED THINKING

Something out of the ordinary happens around you. Your fear-based thinking tries to understand it. It leads you to attribute the apparent weird event to ghosts, spirits, and gods.

You were led by religions to fear ghosts and God so you feel fear. That fear of ghosts, God, and the unknown paralyzes and immobilizes you.

If you have science-based thinking, you would be led to understand that the event happened for earthly reasons, that there are no spirits and gods and if they exist, whatever we say about them are our thoughts; our thinking created gods; they are not independent of our thinking.

Therefore, do not bedevil yourself with imaginary gods; relax and live in peace.

LIVING FROM REAL SELF IS NOT ESCAPING TO SPIRIT SELF BUT THE REAL SELF ON PLANET EARTH.

Clearly, on planet earth, most people live from false ego selves and need to be taught to live from their real selves and courage to live from those real selves; the real selves are loving selves for they make us live peacefully and happily on earth.

A COURSE IN MIRACLES HIJACKED THE NEED TO LIVE FROM OUR REAL SELVES TO MEAN LIVING FROM OUR SPIRITUAL SELVES WHILE NOT LIVING WELL ON EARTH

Spiritual psychology hijacked the need to live from real self to mean negating the self in body and this world and focusing on spiritual self.

The desire to live from the real self, as articulated by the psychoanalyst, Dr. Karen Horney (see her book, *Neurosis and Human Growth*, New York: Norton, 1950), was hijacked by Dr. Helen Schucman and her spiritual psychology to mean escaping from this world of flesh for flesh is deemed bad and folks are supposed to have a spiritual real self that they must overlook the earth to attain.

In the meantime, people are not living loving lives on earth; they escape into religions' unattainable effort to negate this world and live from an imaginary spirit real self.

There may be a spiritual self, but what it is we do not know. In the here and now world, we must live authentic lives that accept who we are, accept our bodies, and use our bodies to love us and all other people in bodies; we should not waste our time and energy waiting for when we shall only live from spirit; we are always living from spirit even as we live in bodies.

We must teach people to love themselves in their here and now states, in bodies, and then hope for life after they die but not make pursuit of life their primary focus after they die.

We need to have centers across the world where folks are taught to love themselves in the here and now body and not be ashamed of anything to do with their bodies and then hope for life after death.

REBIRTH IN BODY AND IN SPIRIT

Rebirth here on earth means living fully on earth and not escaping to waiting for rebirth in spiritual self; there may, of course, be a spiritual self that folks need to be aware of but the pursuit of that spiritual self should not detract from living authentically and fully on earth.

HUMAN BEINGS ARE CURRENTLY LIVING PHONY LIVES.

In all countries, people are figuratively living dead persons. People are not living fully; their fears lead them to be half alive and half dead persons; they allow their imaginary gods and exploitative religions and governments to use fear to keep them half-dead.

Religions, all of them—Christianity, Islam, Hinduism, Buddhism, and African religions—use fear, guilt, and shame to control people and prevent them from living fully.

Primitive societies use shame to control people, ask them to be ashamed of this or that behavior, behaviors that are perfectly natural.

If you harm or kill other people, governments being the agents of the people have the right to protect people by punishing you, even killing you, as in capital punishment.

A social milieu that provides all people with publicly paid education through university and publicly paid health insurance allows people to love each other and live for as long as it is humanly possible.

As of now, people are living dead persons so if they drop dead at any point in time, it does not really matter, for they are not really alive, anyway!

STOP FIGHTING WITH PEOPLE TRYING TO PROVE TO THEM THAT YOUR PERSPECTIVE IS RIGHT AND THEIRS IS WRONG AND SIMPLY LIVE FROM SCIENCE-BASED PERSPECTIVE.

If you look around you, you will notice that many persons are trying to convince you that their perspective on reality is the truth and that yours is false. This is especially so in the area of religion and politics.

The desire to be right and have other people wrong leads to interpersonal conflicts and wars and causes people loads of unhappiness.

You do not have to be right and other people wrong. Just make sure that your perspective is science-based, and can be shown to be empirical and observable, but do not try to impose your worldview on other people.

This is because not even science is the whole truth; we do not know what the whole truth is despite our best scientific efforts.

WHAT YOU BELIEVE IN MANIFESTS IN YOUR DREAMS; YOU USE IT TO ORGANIZE YOUR DREAMS, HAPPY OR NIGHTMARISH DREAMS.

YOU PROJECT WHAT YOU BELIEVE OUT AS YOUR DREAM.

It is clear that what you believe to be true, you project into your dreams and use it to produce a dream world, pictures that seem real to you.

Your day life is also shaped by what you believe in, except that many people are doing the same thing so you and they coordinate your mutual dreams. Of course, at the conscious level, you do not understand how you and people do this coordination. Computers do it all the time.

To change your life, you have to change your beliefs so as to manifest different things, project out different things. If you desire racist discrimination, you project it out; if not, you do not project it out; you do not attract racists to your life if you do not want to have racist experiences.

IN HAPPY DREAM, YOU KNOW THAT YOUR BODY IS A DREAM FIGURE AND NOT IDENTIFY WITH IT AND NOT DEFEND IT PSYCHOLOGICALLY BUT DEFEND IT PHYSICALLY; OTHERWISE, YOU WOULD NOT BE ALIVE IN BODY

In happy dream, you see your body as not who you are, see it as a dream figure, something your thinking, mind, uses to dream; so you do not psychologically defend it as who you are but defend it with food or else, it would not survive in the dream.

You do not worry about what other people, other dream figures, think of your body and ego; you overlook what other dream figures say about your body and ego and love their inner selves and your inner self.

This way, you have a happy dream, still dreaming but not taking the dream, the world, and what is done in it seriously.

For example, I see what the clown in the American White House, Donald Trump, is doing; he thinks that he is serving his racist base at the expense of black folks. I know that what he is doing is going to hasten the transformation of America to a non-racist society; therefore, I do not lose sleep from his clownish behaviors; he makes me laugh for he is a child playing with fire, a higher part of us uses his fire to build a better America for all Americans.

YOU ARRANGE THINGS TO GIVE YOUR BODY PAIN AND SUFFERING AND ULTIMATELY DIE TO MAKE YOUR BODY SEEM REAL TO YOU; YOU DEFEND YOUR BODY TO MAKE IT SEEM TO EXIST.

The entire physical universe exists to produce your body and cause it pain or pleasure to make you, a part of God, a son of God, to see it as real, as who you are, and defend it.

If you overlook your body and the entire physical universe, it no longer exists for you and you awaken to the dreamer, the person who took threads from the entire universe to make your body seem real, your spirit self.

GOD IS EVIL IF OUR PAINED BODIES ARE REAL.

THE SONS OF GOD ARE HAVING A HAPPY DREAM IF OUR BODIES ARE NOT REAL BUT JUST DREAM FIGURES THAT WE GIVE PAIN AND PLEASURE TO MAKE THEM SEEM REAL

THE THINKING, MIND, THAT CREATED THE EGO AND ITS PROBLEM, THE SLEEPING SON OF GOD, CANNOT SOLVE THE PROBLEM NOR IMPROVE THE WORLD.

WE NEED ANOTHER PATTERN OF THINKING, MIND, TO SOLVE IT, THE THINKING THAT OVERLOOKS THE EGO AND ITS BODY, THE HOLY SPIRIT.

It is the mind of the son of God, his thinking, his wish for separated self in body, and arrangement of the entire universe to make it seem real to him that created our human problem; that mind wants to live in separated ego and cannot solve our human problems.

It takes another mind, a different type of thinking, the thinking and mind of the Holy Spirit that does not cherish separation and ego in bodies and overlooks the world or sees it as a dream, to solve its problems.

The Holy Spirit, thinking, does not value the ego in body; it sees them as nothing, overlooks them, and loves the son of God that is sleeping and inventing the world.

The Holy Spirit or a different way of thinking is what it takes to solve the problems of the world. If you look at the world, the problem with the type of thinking that created it and likes it, you would still have ego thinking and the same problems of the world perhaps in different guises.

Albert Einstein said pretty much what I said here; he said that it takes a different mind to solve our human mind-created problems.

THIS WORLD IS AN AMAZING PLACE; IT REMAINS WHAT YOU SEE IT AS BUT MEANS DIFFERENT THINGS TO DIFFERENT PEOPLE; AND HOW YOU SEE IT MAKES IT HAPPY OR NIGHTMARISH FOR YOU.

The world of perception you see and other people see means different things to different people. If you value, cherish, and defend it, you approach it from the separated self-perspective and will feel frustrated when its ephemeral things disappear, and they are bound to disappear.

If you, on the other hand, see the world as a dream, here today and gone tomorrow, and not take it seriously (look at the world from the perspective of the Holy Spirit), you see the world as a thing of mirth, a play thing to have fun with for a while until you are tired of the game and you leave the world and awaken in your real self, a son of God, a part of God.

The same world has two different perceptions of it; one (ego) makes you feel frustrated; the other (Holy Spirit) makes you relatively peaceful and happy.

AFRICANS LIVE IN NEAR TOTAL DARKNESS, THAT IS, LIVE FROM THE EGO.

Writers employ metaphors to explain the world they see. They employ the metaphors of darkness and light. To live in darkness is to live from the ego, to value the ego and pursue ego things. To live in the light is to transcend the ego and see the egos' world as transitory and ephemeral and while seeking it, not take it seriously so that when it goes as it is bound to do, you do not feel frustrated.

Anyone who has advanced thinking processes, upon visiting Africa or seeing Africans, immediately concludes that they live in darkness (that is, live in raw ego).

Joseph Conrad indeed called Africa the Dark Continent and the Heart of Darkness and I agree with him. Let me explain what I mean by seeing Africans as having hearts of darkness.

Igbos, Nigerians, and other Africans live from raw egos; they look at the world with desire for separated existence and thus, value their egos, bodies, and the things of this world and feel frustrated when those tinsel things flee, as they are bound to sooner or later do. Africans take the egos' world seriously and tend to be disappointed when the transitory things of the world go away.

Even African religions are of the ego variety that takes the world seriously. Africans ask their understanding of God to bless them with material abundance.

They have extremely shallow understanding of Christianity. For example, they see the Holy Spirit as a person outside them and ask him to give them this or that.

The Holy Spirit, like the ego, is a pattern of thinking. Ego and Holy Spirit are not outside us. They are how we choose to think. If we identify with the separated self and seek selfish things, we are thinking from the ego; on the other hand, if we change our pattern of thinking, see the earthly self as a dream figure, see the things of this world as dream things, and still seek them but do so without attachment, in Buddhist terms, see them as play things and not feel disappointed when they flee, as they are bound to flee, we are thinking from the Holy Spirit.

There are three patterns of thinking: God's unified thinking (all of us participate in it, this is creative thinking), the son of God's thinking in unified state (this is also creative, it creates universes); the son of God's separated thinking (this invented our material universe); the Holy Spirit's thinking (this sees the egos' world, gives it a different interpretation and meaning, and uses it to love all people hence attain relative peace, not the perfect peace of unified thinking). All these seeming different types of thinking are done by all of us. God is not outside us but is a pattern of our thinking that sees all of us as one and loves all of us.

When Africans talk about the Holy Spirit, it is like they are talking about a person outside them. The Holy Spirit is a type of thinking that sees the world as a dream, dream it with love and forgiveness to have fun; the ego is also a type of thinking that dreams but takes the dream as real and does not forgive those who offend it.

It is my job to teach Africans and mankind to dream with the Holy Spirit, to have a perception that sees the world as not real hence play with it, not take it seriously, and as a result, have happy dreams.

When folks have corrected their perception, go from ego perception to Holy Spirit perception, and love all people, they experience what they call God. You cannot experience God unless you love you and all people and work for our collective good, even here on earth.

The concept of God is very tricky and must be handled with care. Some deluded persons in ego claim to be God and act as if they are God. They are not God; they are in ego.

It is true, however, to say that God is not a person outside us. God is our highest self, our unified self. If you let go of your desire for ego-separated self and attachment to body, dense or light form of body, you enter your God-self; in that state, you do not know about our egos' world, except through your Holy Spirit that sees the ego and its world as a dream and not take them seriously.

The point here is be careful in seeing yourself as God for although that is technically true, your ego-separated self may start calling itself God and at that point, you are deluded. I know an Igbo doctor in Washington DC who calls himself God but is as egoistic as the ego can be. He is living in total darkness (ego) and has not embraced the light of God (love) but does not know it.

In God, you are not aware of this world; if you are aware of this world, you are not in God's unified state, you are in ego-separated state. I am right now in ego-separated state; otherwise, I would not be able to type this material.

One can be in ego state and think from the Holy Spirit, from love and forgiveness; but if one is in God awareness, one does not see our phenomenal, separated world of space, time, and matter for one is in a different dimension of being, the formless unified state where all selves are one self and there is no such thing as separation, space, time, and matter.

EGO-SEPARATED THINKING; HOLY SPIRIT'S HOLISTIC THINKING; GOD'S UNIFIED THINKING

Ego means separated thinking that serves only the separated self, one; it produces illusions that make one feel separated from other selves, things, and from God and gives one pain and suffering.

Holy Spirit means whole mind; that is, holistic thinking in the world of space, time, and matter; it is thinking from our whole mind while we are still in the world of separated states, our phenomenal world of space, time, and matter. It is a type of thinking that sees all existence on earth as parts of oneself and seeks what is good for all people, what serves social interests, and does the public good. It still produces illusions, for the world of separation is an illusion, but illusion that gives people on earth happy dreams.

God is our unified spirit self; its thinking is holistic, unified; this type of thinking does not see space, time, and matter; it is a type of thinking that we on earth, in the world of separation, are not aware of, but we actually engage in it at our highest level, unified state. Unified thinking, aka God's thinking, is creative; it created the sons of God who while in it creates their own sons. The sons of God in their dreams of separation invent egos and the egos' world of space, time, and matter.

YOU AND GOD ARE ONE BUT YOU ARE NOT GOD.
THE SON OF GOD AND HIS FATHER ARE
ONE BUT HE IS NOT HIS FATHER.
THE DESIRE TO REPLACE HIS FATHER IS
WHAT LED TO SEPARATION.

God is not a person that you can see or touch; he is the formless self, formless intelligence that extended his son, to you and me, his parts. He is in us and all things but we are not him.

We are like him but we are not him. The son is in the father and the father is in him but the son is not his father.

It is desire to replace the father that led the son to go on the journey of separation. Yes, as Jesus said, where you see the son, you see the son, but he also said that the father is greater than the son.

Whereas the father is in the son, he is also in other sons; God is the whole whereas the son is a part of the whole.

You are mentally ill, that is, false thinking, psychotic to claim to be God; you can say that in your formless state, you are like God but you are not God.

You and I do the thinking of the son of God with the thinking capacity of God given to us. We must acknowledge that we are thinking with the mind we share with God but our thinking is not God's thinking.

You do ego thinking when you want to separate from God and do more than God's thinking; and when you do ego thinking, then Holy Spirit asks you to shut up your ego thinking and now listen to God's thinking, or listen to your real self, the son of God's thinking, which in ego you have forgotten.

So, when you say that you are thinking from your highest mind, the mind you share with God that does not make your thinking God's thinking, although it is a good as God's thinking, it is not God thinking.

Dr. O who claims to be God is psychotic; sometimes, he says that he is the representative of God and sometimes, he says that he is God and people should listen to him; all people are parts of God and representatives of God on earth, light (union, love) in the darkness of ego, and separation. No one should listen to his grandiose ego claiming to be God.

God thinks creatively by producing you, his son. The son of God in God thinks creatively by producing other sons of God, for he is thinking with God's mind in him, not with a separated mind.

In ego thinking, the son of God thinks from a separated mind, is still creative but creates the temporary, the false, the universe of space, time, and matter, our world.

The son of God's mind that invented our physical universe is very powerful but not as powerful as the mind of God that creates the permanent universe of spirits.

The Holy Spirit is not creative, it is like the son of God in the dream, ego-mind of the sleeping son of God; he reinvents the illusions of the ego (to Christ) and the illusions of matter, space, and time to the illusions of those in light forms, still illusions, still made but a madness where some truth has entered hence it is relatively peaceful.

EPILOGUE

YOU DO NOT OVERLOOK A MADMAN; YOU TRY TO HEAL HIM.

Germany had a madman, Adolf Hitler, ruling it for twelve years (1933–1945). If Germans had found a way to heal him or remove him from office, he would not have plunged the country into a six-year war that ruined not only the country but all of Europe and the entire world. The man killed an estimated 50 million persons; that could have been prevented if he was not in power.

Therefore, you do not overlook the policies of mad rulers; you seek their correction.

In the USA, we currently have a madman who wants to send black folks back to Africa, prevent Latinos from coming to the country, and generally engages in policies that create an atmosphere of racism.

Under him, racist police feel empowered to abuse minority persons—choke them, such as George Floyd, to death in broad daylight at Minneapolis, Minnesota, USA.

If we take on a sentimental view and say that we forgive the mad man, well, what we have done is empower him to keep doing the evil that he is doing; we would have become perpetrators in his mad social policies. We would have given him permission to do what he does; we would not be innocent!

The onlooker of a crime who did not try to prevent that crime is part of that crime.

Therefore, we should not forgive the man in the White House; we should not overlook the evil that he is doing; we must work to correct his evil policies; we must undo his antisocial policies before he does irreparable damage to the country and the world.

CORRECT BUT DO NOT OVERLOOK EVIL.

Correction of bad social policies and anti-social behaviors in general is the best approach to social living.

The function of the Holy Spirit is not to overlook madness but to heal it. He is created to improve our temporal world. He is not apart from us but is part of our higher selves.

Through his guidance, that is, through love-based thinking, we work to improve our world rather than rationalize evil by saying that we forgive it.

To overlook a man raping a child, that is, forgive him, and not remove him from raping the child, is evil. To overlook thieves and murderers is to become partners in their antisocial behaviors.

We must correct evil behavior; we may not be able to prevent all evil behaviors but those that we are aware of, we must correct.

THE WORLD DOES NOT EXIST; IT'S A DREAM, BUT WE MUST MAKE IT A HAPPY DREAM.

It is true that as *A Course in Miracles* says, the empirical universe is a dream. Where we see the phenomenal world is nothing. There is no physical world. There is no me or you as we see us doing all the things we do on earth.

We remain as God created us, formless unified spirits. However, while we are in unified spirit, in God and his heaven, we dream and see us doing the things we do on earth. In the dream, we do hurt our fellow dream people.

The universe came into being from nowhere, and as such, is nowhere. There is no universe; there is nothing but dreams. There are no me, no you, no us in bodies, space, and time; nevertheless, we want to seem in bodies, space, and time; we do what we do, albeit dreams to seem to be in bodies, space, and time.

If we overlook the world of space, time, and matter and what we do in it, the universe disappears and we awaken to the formless, unified world of God.

Consider. Our bodies are composed of matter; matter is composed of the various elements (different elements are different arrangements of atoms); atoms are composed of particles (electrons, neutrons, and protons) which are composed of quarks and ultimately, are photons of light.

Where we see our bodies and material things are photons of light. Photons that during the Big Bang, 13.8 billion years ago, came out of nowhere and are nowhere; thus, material things do not exist.

Yet, we see material things that do not exist and they seem to exist; we see them because we want to see them and make them seem to exist.

The madman in the White House does not, in fact, exist, but we want to see him seem to exist; we want to see him do the evil things he is doing.

He is giving us nightmarish dreams. We have to correct his political policies and replace them with ones that give us happy dreams.

As long as we want to be on earth, sleep, and dream, it is not right for us to overlook the madman's evil, albeit dream evil; we must correct it.

In the end, there is no physical universe, no computers, tables, us in bodies, but we seem to exist and we might as well make what does not exist but seem to exist lovely.

Scientific evidence tells us that our earth will be around for a couple more billion years before it dies with our sun.

The galaxies are expanding away from each other and in trillions of years, would lose heat and die (Big Chill). We will die with the universe, but not until trillions of years.

As long as we are in the universe, we might as well make it pleasant (when our universe dies, we probably would have the science and technology to tunnel our way to other universes in the multiverse).

It is not right to just overlook behaviors that hurt people, even if they are dream figures and dream behaviors. We should not forgive hurtful behaviors just so we awaken to the perfect peace of God and his heaven.

We are already in that perfect peace of God but as long as we also see ourselves on earth, we must make our temporary abode pleasant.

We must have laws that protect us from our mutual depredations. We must make our world pleasant and not just overlook its evil just because a world's negating, nihilistic theology asks us to do so.

We can walk and chew gum at the same time; we can have both the formless world of God, the world of light forms, and the world of dense matter at the same time, as Hugh Everett told us is existent in his many world's interpretation of quantum physics.

I feel offended by philosophies and religions that ask us to tolerate evil; I am particularly unhappy with myself for not having the courage to let go of such theologies and waste my time on them. Life is very simple: love you, love all people, and leave it at that.

DELUSIONAL THINKING, BEHAVIOR, AND HUMAN GROWTH

In delusional thinking and behavior, something, could be medical or social, makes a child or an adult to feel utterly weak and not good enough.

He is unable to accept his sense of weakness and inferiority. He denies it. Delusional thinking and behavior emanate from denial of one's underlying sense of utter weakness and inferiority.

One denies what one sees in oneself: not being good enough, posits an imaginary self that is perfect, identifies with that false self-concept, and presents it to other people to accept as who one is (and if it is group delusion, as who one's group is, this is called folie à deux).

One overuses the ego defense mechanism of projection that all human beings use; now, one projects what one sees in one and denies to other people. Having denied that one is weak and inferior, one projects it to other people and sees them as weak and inferior to one and relate to them as if they are actually weak and inferior.

The deluded person relates to his projections to people but not to people as they are! (Do you relate to people as they are? How are people, do you know?)

One now pretends to be one's desired grandiose, ideal, and perfect self. One no longer deals with one's imperfect reality or any kind of reality at all. One has escaped from reality and lives in fantasy, the world of wishes.

One is no longer solving our earthly problems as they are; one seeks fantasy solutions to our problems.

One wants other people to accept one's false self-concept and false self-image; one compulsively wants to become that false big self-concept and self-image and wants other people to accept it as who one is. If they accept it, one feels fine; if not, one feels sad. Sometimes, one feels angry at people if they do not accept one's false big self.

One is afraid of not being the wished-for big self hence one is full of fear and anxiety from fear of not living up to the false, grandiose self-image.

In the meantime, one is not doing anything realistic in the real world to become the powerful person one wishes to be. One ignores social and political reality.

For example, one ignores the fact that people choose who is their leader and in power in their polity and pretends to have power that one does not have.

One now is living in perpetual fear, anger, paranoia, or mania; all those emanate from the efforts to seem a false big self. One does not know peace and joy in one's life.

STOP TRYING TO BE A FALSE GRANDIOSE SELF-CONCEPT AND SELF-IMAGE.

If one simply stops desiring any kind of big self-concept and self-image, one feels peace and joy. *A Course in Miracles* says that having any kind of separated self-concept, big or small, is delusional. It says that our real self is part of one unified life, aka God and his sons, and we currently do not know it and pretend to be big separated selves.

If we give up our desire to be any kind of separated self, do not defend a separated big or small self, we experience ourselves as part of one unified life and in it feel peaceful and happy.

At any moment we desire separated big or small self in body, we are back to delusional thinking and behaving.

IGBOS' DELUSIONAL THINKING AND BEHAVIOR

Igbos entered the modern world in the late nineteenth century; they entered it with absolutely nothing that modern civilization deems important; they have no writing, no wheel, no schools, no books, no monumental constructions, and no large-scale governments (their governments are limited to their villages).

They see those things in the white man's world and in some of their neighbors' worlds, such as in Edo, Hausa-Fulani, and Yoruba worlds. They feel utterly inferior to those who possess what they lack, civilization.

They compensate by calling those they feel inferior to putdown names. They feel inferior to other Nigerians, deny that feeling, and instead, claim to be superior to other Nigerians.

They deny their weakness and inferiority by claiming to be its opposite; they claim to be responsible for other people's accomplishments, such as their absurd claiming to be Jews.

In claiming to be Jews, they take psychotic ownership of Jews' considerable accomplishment in the last four thousand years of their written history.

They even claim to be the original Egyptians, hence built the pyramids, and that fiction kind of makes them feel like they are a superior people.

In Nigeria, they claim to be responsible for all that is good in the country and deny anything bad that they do.

They are very boastful; they are always bragging about their phantom achievements and saying that their neighbors have accomplished nothing.

This tendency to put their neighbors down to make themselves seem elevated irritates their neighbors and those hate and sometimes attack to kill them.

They are engaged in delusional thinking and behavior, a type of thinking found in people who feel utterly weak and inferior.

Like psychiatrically deluded people all over the world, Igbos want you to collude with them and see them as they want to be seen: a superior and great people.

You can see that they are at the lowest steps in the civilizational ladder (they did not invent writing and wheel, the beginning point of civilization).

Given their efforts to seem who they are not, they make their minds and bodies tense; they live in tremendous physical tension and are full of fear, anxiety, anger, paranoia, and mania.

All they have to do is let go of the wish to be powerful and important selves and they relax and become calm and healthy.

What I said about Igbos is a gross generalization; there are exceptions; there are Igbos who are not denying their underlying inferior feeling selves and pursuing imaginary grandiose selves. In other words, there are some healthy Igbos, just as there are some healthy human beings who accept themselves as they are without any conditions that they must meet before they accept themselves.

ASSUME THAT YOU ARE NOTHING IMPORTANT AND YOU ARE ABLE TO BE HUMOROUS, LAUGH, AND LIVE IN PEACE AND JOY.

To heal delusion disorder, what I call delusional thinking and behaving, is very simple; you must assume that you are nothing and that you are not important. You must accept that you are nothing and worthless, as all human beings are.

Make that assumption and you are no longer seeking to become a grandiose self-concept and self-image and you relax, smell coffee and roses, and live peacefully and happily.

DISCUSSION

What I described above, in degrees, apply to all people; that is actually what it means to be human. Human beings are those creatures that know that they are food for worms and are nothing special to nature for they will die and rot, but they deny that fact and pursue becoming important and special selves.

In pursuing big self-concepts and self-images, they give themselves unnecessary tension, fear, anxiety, anger, paranoia, and mania (and even schizophrenia; psychosis results from pursuit of false important selves).

To become healthy, human beings must give up all pursuit of false, big self-concepts and self-images and accept that they are nothing; they are just part of life.

CONCLUSION

Life is in all biological organisms and dies, and what exists after animals die is only speculated on but not apparent.

Religion gives people fantasies of what lies in store for them when they die. Apparently, some people need religions' fantasies to tolerate their apparent meaningless and purposeless existence in what science suggests to seem an accidental universe.

Or is the universe determined and has meaning and purpose? That is a subject for other writings.

The cure for delusional thinking and behavior posited above is also the cure for all mental and personality disorders, for all of them inheres in wishful thinking, the desire to be important in a world where they seem unimportant.

Correct thinking and behavior accept our existential nothingness and still do what we enjoy doing and have an aptitude for doing regardless of whether there is meaning in our lives or not.

Below was written on a different occasion but is pertinent to deluded thinking and behaving so I will add it to the above essay.

LET GO OF THE DESIRE FOR A BIG SELF.

Who are we human beings? I do not know. What I do know is that I have a separated self-concept and all people have separated self-concepts. Some people have humble separated self-concepts (we call them normal folks) whereas others have false, grandiose self-concepts (and we call them neurotics or psychotics).

Some people have self-concepts that want to be big. They posited their wish for big separated self-concepts in their childhood. Like all people, they use their (big) separated self-concepts to interpret events in their world and to see other people.

No one really sees other people and things as they are objectively; we always see people and the world with our self-concepts hence in a biased manner; we do not know what we are seeing; we do not even know whether what we think that we are seeing is actually there or whether we are merely projecting our thoughts to what we think are out there.

Try this experiment: completely let go of your self-concept, big or small, and have no self-concept at all (this is the purpose of Hindu, Buddhist, and Zen meditation, to have no ego-separated self).

If you succeed, what would happen is that you would have no self-consciousness; you would feel that there is life in you and that that life has no shape at all, it is undifferentiated life (we use body and social experience to differentiate life to what we call our self-concepts).

If you let go of your attachment to your separated self-concept and your body, you notice only life existing in you. That life in you could be used to conceptualize another self-concept for you and for other people.

If you let go of your separated self-concept, you have life, what folk's call spirit. If you remove your separated self-concept, your wish for a big self in particular, what happens is that life speaks through you; if you like, spirit speaks through you.

This is why in the old, they used to have some people take some herbal brews, drugs, and have them dance to certain music until they are in a trance, that is, lose their separated self-concepts. When they attain separated self-concepts, they get in touch with what folks called the spiritual world, what I call undifferentiated self, and from there, they speak as what folks used to call oracles. They can talk about the past, present, and future with some knowingness that boggles our ordinary minds.

I believe that when the deluded person stops thinking from his wish for a big, separated self, his mind, as it were, gets in touch with undifferentiated life, undifferentiated self, and he thinks, talks, and behaves from that higher place in him and folks say that he is in touch with God, that he speaks for God.

When the paranoid, deluded person heals his thinking and now has a mind that no longer is trying to speak from a grandiose self-concept, he becomes able to talk as the prophets of old did.

When deluded, Igbos stop trying to think and behave from their wished-for big selves. They suddenly begin speaking truth more than you would expect, more than they did when they were trying to shape reality with their wished-for big selves.

Remove your desire for a big self and what folks call spirit talks through you. A healed deluded person, that is, a man who has changed his pattern of thinking and behaving from a false grandiose self-concept to no self, becomes a speaker of truth.

Many healed Igbos speak the truth more than you would believe.

What science teaches us is that the universe is an accidental place; events beginning from the big bang to the present seem the products of accidents.

However, something tells me that there is a spiritual side to human beings. What it is I do not know. Life does not seem just the product of accidents. I believe that there is a spiritual side of us; I cannot prove it.

Each person is moving on a trajectory, moving in a direction, and all that happens to him that seem accidental are really not so; they are shaped by his wished-for ideal, separated self, which in turn, were determined in his childhood by the confluence of his inherited body and social experience. There was a reason why things happened to him as they did.

When he removes his wish for a big self and experiences himself as just life living through him, he is healed. In that healed state, he is calm, peaceful, and happy and feels like there is no self in his head. He can actually perform miracles from that no separated big self state.

This is what Jesus did. The man let go of his wished-for big separated self and was no longer thinking from a deluded self but thought and spoke from his real self, which is an undifferentiated self, and could then speak like the oracles of old and heal the sick for he is in what folks call God, what I call unified self.

In unified state, one knows that there is one connected life, one joined life, and that love is what joins all life forms into one unified life and one loves all selves and things.

One becomes a teacher of love, who is a teacher of God, and a giver of peace and joy to those suffering from their efforts to live as separated big or small selves.

Let go of your self-concept and self-image, big or small; do not do anything from your hitherto sense of self-concept and its self-image. Your brain is emptied of any idea of self; you now have no ego-self.

In a mind, in a thinking emptied of wish for separated ego-self-concept, one begins to think from one's real self; one now thinks loving, unifying thinking, and one's behaviors serve all people. One is now a healed mind, a healthy person

PRIDE IN AFRICAN CULTURE MAY KILL YOU!

"Culture is the customs, arts, social institutions, and achievements of a particular nation, people, or other social group."—Dictionary.com

Every group of human beings who lived in a specific part of the world did what they had to do to survive in that particular environment or else, they would not have survived.

Culture is the sum of whatever a people did to adapt to their particular environment and survived in it. All cultures are adaptive to certain environments.

In the late nineteenth century and the beginning of the twentieth century, Western anthropologists fanned out in what they called primitive people in Africa, Asia Pacific Islands, and the Americas. They studied the peoples' cultures, their ways of life, and came to understand that though what they are doing is different from what was done in Britain, France, Germany, the USA, and Canada (those are what we mean by the West), whatever they did enable them to adapt to their world hence must have been the right things for them to do.

Thereafter, these liberal western anthropologists, beginning with Margaret Mead in the 1930s, began talking about cultural relativism, the idea that all cultures are equally good.

In the 1960s, that hazy concept morphed into what is called multiculturalism. The idea is that all cultures are good for they enabled people to survive in their worlds. That truth soon segued to the idea that you can live in London and New York and import the African culture that enabled you to survive in Africa and live it in the West.

This is not true. What your people did in your particular part of the world may not be adaptive in other parts of the world.

I am from Alaigbo and was socialized to Igbo culture. Now, I live in Anchorage, Alaska. The moment you come out of Ted Stevens International Airport at Anchorage, you quickly learn that you need a different culture to survive here. Let us say that you got here in November and the temperature outside the airport is below 20 degrees Fahrenheit, you will not be able to walk around in the scanty clothes you wore in tropical Africa. If you do, you will be uncomfortable and if you persist, within a couple of days, you will die from cold.

If you are rational, from the airport or from your hotel room, you head on to clothing stores and buy appropriate clothes that enable folks to adapt to the harsh cold of Alaska. Gradually, you begin to do what enables you to live in the subarctic world of Alaska, or else, you die.

If you do not adapt to your new land, you are like the dodo bird that refused to adapt to its new environment and died off. The point here is that what enabled you to adapt to a particular part of the world may not enable you to adapt to another part of the world.

Sticking to your old culture in a new environment may be the quickest way for you to die. Pride in your people's culture to the point of not changing it to adapt to changed circumstances may kill you.

Environments may remain the same but what it takes to adapt to them may be different. That is to say that you may remain in Africa, but the culture needed to adapt to its changed conditions may be different from the old culture of your people.

Your people were subsistence farmers. Before 1900, there were probably fewer than 20 million Nigerians. Those people could survive by practicing subsistence farming. Today, there are, at least, 150 million

Nigerians; all these people are trying to survive by living in the same environment that twenty million subsistence farmers survived in 1900.

If the people of today's Nigeria do not change their farming methods to one that produces more food from the same piece of land, they will die off. Their old subsistence farming method would not enable them to survive.

Now, they need mechanized farming and the soil needs to be added with fertilizers to yield better food to feed an increasing population.

Your old African farming culture is now not a survival mechanism but a death and dying mechanism. You cannot take pride in it. You must now study agricultural science, which includes physics, chemistry, biology, geology, and astronomy, and through them, develop scientific culture, a culture based on the scientific method if you want to survive in today's world regardless of where you live.

Therefore, rational persons discard aspects of their old cultures and embrace different ones that enable them to survive in their new world or else, they die off.

If they insist on taking pride in their old culture and since it is no longer adaptive to their new world, they would be like the dodo bird and die off and that is their choice so you do not cry for them.

You cannot afford to allow Western white liberals to "play you," tell you that all cultures are equal when your old culture is a highway to your death. You must change your culture if you want to adapt to your new circumstances.

China, Japan, Korea, and other Asian countries have had four thousand years of continuous culture. In terms of the old world, no culture on planet earth was better than the culture of China. That was until the West discovered the scientific method (from the early sixteenth century—Nicolas Copernicus, Galileo, Newton, etc.).

In the mid-1700s, England began the industrial revolution, beginning with James Watt using steam to do work. Steam, that is, hot water was used to drive engines (steam engines) and the factory system came into being.

England became the first industrialized country. In the early 1800s, France, Germany, and the USA became industrialized and joined England in the club of industrialized countries.

Since then, these European countries have led the world in everything.

In the mid-1800s, western countries came to Japan and China and the Japanese and Chinese observed them and called them savages, people who are not worth their attention (the Chinese consider themselves the most civilized people on earth).

The Asians did not realize that the white man came with a new type of culture, machine culture. Before Asians knew what was happening to them, the West carved up Japan and China among themselves and controlled them.

The Chinese finally realized what is happening to them and belatedly tried to understand science and technology. That process was completed by Mao Tse Tung who in the 1960s, engineered the Cultural Revolution. He deliberately asked young people to destroy their old Confucian culture (they held China back) and in its place, established the scientific culture.

By the early 2000s, China reached the West in science and technology. As I write, China now is the largest economy in the world.

What China did was to throw away its 4000-year old culture and accept a new culture that adapts to their new circumstances. The Asians, as we talk, outcompete the white man in what the West began, modern schooling.

Africans, on the other hand, are impressionable; they were played by Western patronizing and condescending liberal anthropologists; they were told the nonsense about how their past cultures are as good as the culture that sent men to the moon.

Africans wear discarded Arab robes (agbada) and call it their national attire. They operate like folks living in the feudal age, not in the twenty-first century.

The few African countries that are making it in the modern world are Ethiopia and Rwanda; both consciously embraced the West and today, their people wear suits whereas shiftless Nigerians wear Arab's discarded agbada and are not productive.

Africa cannot become modern and productive unless it changes its culture and embraces scientific culture (not ancient Egyptian culture, as some deluded Africans think is feasible).

Old Egypt did not have science and technology as we know them today; moreover, it is debatable whether ancient Egypt was Negroid in origin; their language certainly was not the same as West African languages but similar to today's Semitic languages.

The only way forward for Africa is for it to become like England both in culture and people's individual behaviors; there is no real alternative to this reality. Your pride in your so-called past culture is not going to feed you and modernize your economy so that it competes with Asians and Europeans.

Cultures are not static but dynamic; influences from other cultures are always diffusing to one's culture. Whether one likes it or not, one is influenced by other people.

Rational and pragmatic people swallow their shame that their people were primitive and learn from those whose cultures embody science and technology and be like them.

You cannot walk into the same river twice; things are always moving forward, not backward. Change your culture or die from taking pride in your anachronistic world view.

APPARENTLY, HUMAN BEINGS RECOGNIZE THE TRUTH AT DIFFERENT STAGES IN THEIR LIVES.

Some members of our family apparently did not like some of my choices on the race issue. I am glad that some of them are getting around to seeing the logic of my choice. In a few hundred years, all human beings will be brown for what used to separate people, distance, would be gone and they will interbreed for they are members of one species.

Human beings are truly at different stages in their evolution. I began elementary schooling at age six. At that age, I knew that there is only one human race. I refused to see me as Igbo, Nigerian, African, and black and simply see myself as a human being. I saw people from all so-called human races as my siblings.

Other people apparently need elaborate persuasion to accept their human oneness. They apparently are at a lower level of spiritual evolution.

At college, I encountered the Baha'is religion. I read what their founder, Bahaullah, said about how all people are one; he talked about human unity and how we all need to have one language, one government, and intermarry. I asked: what is the big deal about what he said? I noted that I have known all those since I was a child.

Folks were surprised at my claim for apparently, they were laboring under the illusion that there are differences between the races. What differences are there in the races?

There is absolutely no difference between Blacks, Whites, Asians, and other so-called races. Some of us knew that from the moment we were born and others need education to accept the truth.

Give all children publicly paid education through university and publicly paid health care and they would perform at the same rate regardless of their so-called race. There is only one human race.

We must stop emphasizing what divides us and accentuate what unifies us—in union with all we know, peace and joy, for union is our reality; separation is an illusion.

Throughout human history, all over the world, it is the youth, ages 20–40, that bring about changes in their society. In youth, people do not yet have a sense of imminent death; they feel indestructible. They are motivated by justice. They strive to bring about a good world in their neck of the woods. If their rulers are corrupt, they demonstrate good governance and if that does not bring about the needed changes, they form revolutionary organizations to fight and die for a better world. In Nigeria, senators and other politicians make over $500, 000 a year and typical Nigerians make $720 a year. This is an outrage that elsewhere in the world would set the youth on fire. Nigerian youths just sit down and accept the thugs and brigands that pretend to rule them but steal from them. They desire to flee to Europe and North America, where they heard that there are good governments (those are now closing their doors to Africans). Some of them take to criminality; they become kidnappers to make money instead of work to bring about a fair government. Some go to social media, such as Facebook, and through 419 schemes, want to rip off white folks. Indeed, some of them will write to older white women and if they get a response, in a week, they are already proposing marriage. It is as if those women do not know why they are doing it, to use them to get work permits in the West, and after the waiting two-year period, disappear from the women. That is, they are not really in love with the women but wanted to use them to escape from Nigeria to the supposed greener pastures of the West. What is preventing Nigerian youth from doing the needful fight for fairness in their country? Fear! They do not want to fight and possibly die for good causes. They want someone else to come and fight to improve their country for them. It does not work that way. Only Nigerians can fight and improve their country. Since they are afraid of harm and death, I decided to write a brief essay on fear. I hope that the below essay on fear would give them understanding of fear and dispose a few of them, the courageous ones, to go to the streets and start fighting for good governance in what Donald Trump called their shithole country. Africans, all over the world, are treated like shit and this does not make them feel angry enough to try to improve their Africa, but instead, they want to crash into the white man's world where they are called niggers. They are contemptible and despicable. The world's perception of them will change when they start fighting and dying for good governance in Africa.

AFRICANS, THEIR FEAR, AND HOW TO TRANSCEND IT

Fear is a physiological and psychological animal response to perceived threat to the animals' life. In fear, the individual's body and psyche alert him to danger to his survival. Maybe there is a lion lurking around, an enemy with a gun somewhere; the individual senses that something from the environment (internal, inside his body, such as illnesses or external, from outside his body) is around and could snuff out his physical life. He is compelled to take measures to protect his existence.

In fear, the individual's body releases certain excitatory neurochemicals, such as norepinephrine, adrenaline, and acetylcholine; those get his body to work at a faster rate. His lungs beat faster, dragging in more oxygen into his body; his heart pumps at a faster rate so that blood takes oxygen and other nutrients released by his body (such as glucose, sugar) to all parts of his body; these nutrients enable his muscles to work harder so that he is more able to fight or run away from the danger to his life.

His nervous system (central and peripheral) works faster sending information to his brain; his brain's memory bank decides whether the individual can fight and defeat the source of danger and if so, he is told to stay and fight back but if not, he is told to flee from the danger. This is the flight or fight response to fear.

These decisions are made in a split second. Without consciously thinking about it, the individual's body prompts him to run away or to stay and fight.

The goal of fear response is for the individual to live. Fear is one of animals' survival mechanisms for it alerts them to danger and forces them to take protective and defensive measures to survive. The goal of fear is the animal's survival. In this sense, fear is our friend because it helps us to survive in body and ego state.

However, everything we do has a cost. The cost of fear is that while it enables us to survive, it also helps us to anticipate danger and be defensive.

The anxious person (anxiety is another name for fear, usually fear, when there is no apparent perceivable external danger) is defensive most of the time. You anticipate threat to your life and your body reacts with fear, aka anxiety, and you defend yourself, fight or flee, as if there is actual threat in your immediate environment (see post-traumatic stress disorder).

In the process, you no longer live calmly and fully. Your body and mind are primed to fight or run away from danger; you are tense and stressed out; your body literally feels hot.

If it were possible for the individual to overcome fear, he would live fully, doing what he wants to do with his life—limited, of course, by what physical laws would not permit (if you wish to fly, you cannot do so since you do not have wings) and what the laws of society do not permit (if you harm other people, their friends would beat you up or kill you or society acts on their behalf, arrest and jail you to protect people from the danger you pose to them).

People do fear other people and society for those could attack and kill them; they also fear the forces of nature for those could kill them (tsunami, tornado, earthquake, volcano, flood, drought, or diseases caused by bacteria, fungi, virus, etc. do kill people).

THE STRANGE FEAR OF GOD

There is fear of God. This is the strangest fear. None of us has seen God. All we do, via our primitive religions, is to assume that there is God, that he is punitive, and that if we disobey him, he would punish us and when we die, he would cast us into eternal hellfire. So, we seek to be on the good side of this unseen God.

Does God exist? The most honest answer is that we do not know; theism and atheism are beliefs.

Another twist to the fear of God is the saying that we actually fear returning to God; it is said that we are sons of God who separated from him, feel that he is angry at us for doing so, and would punish us if we return to him so we fear his presence and do not want to return to him. Fear is seen here as a means of keeping away from God. Fear prevents us from returning to God (awakening to God, our father).

As long as we fear God, we stay away from him. Here, God is construed as so evil that he would punish us if we came to him, so to avoid God's punishment, we stay away from him.

Another perspective is that fear enables us to retain our identification with body and ego and do whatever we have to do to live as separated ego selves in bodies. If we let go of fear, we think that our egos and bodies would die.

We apparently do not want our bodies and egos to die because we fear oblivion and finitude. Or we feel that if we die, we return to God and we do not want to awaken to God.

What exactly is so good about living in a separated ego and body? To live in ego and body, as Gautama Buddha recognized twenty-five hundred years ago, is to live in pain and to suffer. One would think that we would jump and embrace whatever makes us stop living in body and ego. But we want to live in body and ego because we made them; they are our handiwork.

To exit from ego and body is to return to formless unified spirit, God, a world we did not make so we do not want to return to God; to be in ego and body, as it were, makes us feel powerful whereas in God, we feel powerless for God is now in charge of his creations. So goes this Gnostic view of the role of fear in our lives.

GOVERNMENTS ENABLE US TO LIVE IN EGO AND BODY.

Religious speculations aside, what is self-evident is that fear enables us to survive in egos and bodies. Because of our desire to survive in body, we organize society, set up government, and empower it to arrest and punish those who harm us, to send criminals to jails and prisons, and kill murderers and rapists, especially rapists of children.

If you have observed human beings closely, you know that they are fearful creatures. They are afraid of harm and death. They will do anything to avoid harm and death. They fear those human beings who could harm or kill them. These people include criminals, kidnappers, and government.

The folks in government have control over police and military. They could use those to go after you and kill you. So, all over the world, people fear their rulers for those have exclusive control over the means of coercion.

White people fear their leaders and do what they ask them to do or else, they killed them. Asians fear their leaders and do what they ask them to do or else, they are killed. Africans fear their leaders or else, they killed them.

AFRICANS TAKE THE FEAR OF THEIR LEADERS TO A WHOLE NEW LEVEL.

Africans and Nigerians in particular are cowardly; they so much fear being killed by the thugs who rule them that they dare not complain their rulers are brigands carting their revenue from oil for themselves while they live in abject penury. Nigerians are docile and will live under the most egregious circumstances provided that they are allowed to live. If slavery were to be returned today, they would live under slavery to avoid being killed.

WHAT CAN WE DO TO REDUCE OR ELIMINATE FEAR IN NIGERIANS?

It is obvious that unless Nigerians reduce or eliminate their fears, they would continue to live as slaves. The question is: what can we do to get Nigerians and Africans in general to overcome the fear that binds them to live as slaves so that they fight and die for their liberty? What can we do to make you, an African, rise up and fight and if needs be, die fighting for your liberty?

Or must you, Africans, live as slaves?

Nigerians are contemptible and despicable because they tolerate abuse by their thievish leaders. When they overcome the fear that keeps them as slaves, rise up, and fight for good governance though many would die, they would become free.

MY STRUGGLE TO OVERCOME FEAR

I am a human being and have awareness of fear in me. Fear is conscious in my psyche and body. I try to get rid of my fear by not overvaluing my ego and body, by accepting death as my fate and not fearing it.

Do you want to kill me? Do it right now. Until you killed me, I will live my life doing what I believe is the right thing.

The right thing is to love my real self and all people's real selves and work for what serves our social interests.

I borrow from Hinduism and Buddhism and do meditation. In meditation, I relax my body, let go of the tension in my muscles, get rid of my ego and belief that I am body, and simply try to live as part of life. I do not defend my separated life.

This approach to life calms me down. One must do whatever one must do to reduce or eliminate one's fear, anxiety, anger, depression, paranoia, mania, and other mental disturbances that plague mankind.

You, the reader, must do whatever you can to reduce or eliminate your fear and fight for social justice in your world. It is not enough to survive like animals, as Nigerians do. Nigerians live for nothing; that is no way to live.

A man must live for something he finds important and if needs be, fight for it and if necessary, die fighting for it. Liberty and justice are worth fighting and dying for.

DISCUSSION

To overcome fear is not to flee into fantasy of living without fear. People's bodies were designed to pick up dangers to their bodies and send the signal to their brains and they respond with fear. Fantasy is when one uses mere imagination and wishes to try overcoming aspects of our tough life.

The pursuit of ideals and perfection, a world where nothing scares people, for example, is fantasy. There are always threatening stimuli on earth; the objective question is how to cope with them. Some people recommend medications.

Medical doctors do give people with anxiety disorders any anti-anxiety medications (Xanax, Valium, Librium, and so on). They do work temporarily in making sure that excitatory neurotransmitters are covered up with inhibitory neurotransmitters (such as GABA) but they do not provide lasting cure. They are addictive and have side effects. We are not interested in such a cure. We are interested in understanding fear and using our thinking and behaviors to overcome it.

CONCLUSION

If you overcome your fears, you are liberated from what normally holds people down. You would live like what folks called the gods.

The gods are probably the products of our imaginations, our ideas of how we would live if we are not hobbled by fear; we project those ideas to what we call gods.

I doubt that human beings can completely overcome fear and still survive in body. However, it does not hurt to try overcoming fear and living fearlessly, living more fully, and doing what one wants to do with one's life, not restricted by fear of harm, death, other people's disapproval.

Just do what you believe is right that does not harm other people and disregard the fear that tries to prevent you from doing what you believe is right.

WHAT ARE YOU LEADING PEOPLE TO ACCOMPLISH?

Leaders have goals, visions, and dreams of what they want to accomplish and use men and material to accomplish them.

American leaders are generally good in the area of economic activity; they posit products or services that they want to produce, get money, equipment, and workers to produce that product (or service), market it, and make money.

They produce what feeds the world and what makes living in body pleasurable; they are of use to mankind. Mark Zuckerberg, Bill Gates, and Steve Jobs produced computers and software that make living pleasurable. I am right now typing on Bill Gates' word processor.

If I am a leader, I must ask myself: what good or services am I leading men to produce? It is not enough to talk about leadership, one must lead.

Those who cannot do, talk whereas those who can, do. I cannot merely talk about leadership. Suppose that I can do something, what can I lead men to produce that is good for society?

One must desist from talking about other people's poor leadership behaviors for they are meant to show one what one ought to do correctly.

This morning, I wrote a paper on how Nigerian youth are not fighting to take back their country from the criminal looters pretending to rule them; I called them cowards for they allowed fear to prevent them from fighting for social justice.

That is true but what am I doing to improve an area of the human condition? It is not good enough to talk about what other people are not doing right. What am I doing well?

I worry about how fear prevents folks from living fully, preventing them from being leaders. Okay. There is nothing that I can do about their fears. Their fears merely show me my own fear. I am the cowardly Nigerian unable to overcome fear and govern their country correctly.

What am I doing to overcome my own fears so that I would help govern Nigeria and Africa well?

If one must be a leader in teaching people to overcome the fear holding them down, one must first overcome the fear holding one down, live fully and fearlessly, and then model the answer to the problem of fearfulness one is talking about.

As long as one lives in abject fear, one cannot teach other people how to overcome their own fears. A physician first heals himself before he tells other people how to heal themselves, is the idea.

I TALK FROM FEAR, THAT IS FROM EGO; I DO EVERYTHING FROM FEAR, THAT IS FROM EGO; NOW I SHOULD NOT TALK OR DO ANYTHING FROM FEAR AND EGO AND KEEP QUIET.

Whatever I want to give to other people and to the world is what I want to give to me, so give it to me.

Whatever one says about other people is what one wants to learn and improve in one. I see Igbos as seeking importance and power and think and behave from that deluded sense of importance hence have conflicts with people.

What this means is that I have the same problem, I think and behave from a grandiose ego and try to relate to people from a grandiose ego hence have conflicts with people.

I see Igbos as having self-centered leadership style; they are trying to seem important but not serving other people; this is what I see in me; I do not serve people but relate to people from the perspective of seeming important.

I lack leadership skills and Igbos lack leadership skills; it is for me to learn from what I see in Igbos for it is in me and I project it to them (it is also in them).

When I heal myself, no longer see the world from a deluded sense of importance, and serve people, then I model such behaviors for Igbos but not by talking about it.

I become a fully functioning egoless person who models it for all people to emulate and live in the peace I live in.

MY CHARACTER WEAKNESS IS TO SEE FAULTS IN OTHER PEOPLE AND TALK ABOUT THEM INSTEAD OF SEEING MY OWN CHARACTER WEAKNESS AND IMPROVE THEM BEFORE I TALK ABOUT OTHER PEOPLE'S SHORTCOMINGS.

Every person's problems is my problem; their problems are designed for me to see them clearly hence see them clearly in me and solve them in me instead of talking about them in other people (they are what is in me that I projected to other people except that what I see in them is also in them for they are me).

They are there for me to learn and correct my problems and model a healed life, Christ self, for all humanity to emulate and heal themselves; it is not for me to criticize people but to learn from them to improve me and help people improve on what I see in them.

FEARLESS PERSONS LIVE LIKE THE GODS.

If I remove my fears, I would live like what folks call the gods, live limitlessly, and make a load of money from doing so; it is fear that prevents me from making money, living fully, and being a leader.

LEADERS ALLOW THEIR EGOS AND BODIES TO FIGURATIVELY DIE IN PURSUIT OF GOALS THAT SERVE MANKIND WELL AND THEY OBTAIN PEACE AND JOY FROM NOT BEING BURDENED BY DEFENDING THE USELESS EGO.

A leader metaphorically sacrifices his ego and body for the whole self, not in an egoistic sense of dying for the people, but in the sense that he allowed his ego and body to figuratively die in the pursuit of a leadership goal, such as social harmony, love, and unity.

False religious leaders claim to be the son of God or the only representative of God on earth; Bahaullah claimed that and was persecuted for that claim; Dr. O sees himself as God's representative on earth and to avoid the world laughing at him as so-called representative on earth who is poor, he avoids people and in social isolation, he retains his grandiose ego, and pretend that he is the God-man; he is a grandiose, unloving, and unforgiving ego; he does not forgive those he believes slighted his grandiose ego (so is Dr. Duncan, another egoistic black man claiming to be God-realized).

These people are phonies; they were shown to me to make me not be like them, to make me live egoless with Christ-like self, serving all people and bringing peace and joy to the world.

MIND (THINKING) IS FORMLESS ENERGY.

Thinking or mind is a formless universal energy that thinks through human beings, animals, plants, stars, and everything. That energy produces pictures and dreams that seem like solid worlds and seem real.

At night, that mental energy produces our sleep—dreams; during the day, it produces our day world; in other dimensions, it produces other forms of worlds; it also produces the visions that we see when we have visions.

YOU CANNOT SEE THE TWO WORLDS OF LIGHT FORMS AND DARK FORMS AT THE SAME TIME.

You have to shut down one world to see another world. This is what Hindus and Buddhists try to do in their meditation, shut down awareness of our day world so as to see the world of light forms, and ultimately, to experience the formless world of God, formless energy, the producer of worlds.

At night, we sleep and shut down our day world to see the dream world. In visions, mind energy shuts down one's day world and shows one another world, one that still looks like our day world but mind energy uses it to construct a vision to teach one a lesson designed for one.

The world of light forms cannot be seen if one is seeing our current day world of matter, space, and time. Both the worlds of matter and world of light forms seem real to those in them but you cannot see both at the same time; you have to shut down one to see the other; that is how mind energy works.

In my vision of Jesus, my mind energy first invented darkness, then took me to a lit beach where I met the old boy and we talked about my mission on earth; I could not see him in our day world, so our day world had to be shut out and I was shown that vision specifically designed to tell me what my mission during this lifetime is (to write on spiritual matters using insights from science to do so).

Our day world and world of light forms are illusions; they are fictions; they are delusions; they are psychoses where the unified sons of God invent a world of separation to live in, as opposed to their real world, the unified world.

The world of light forms, however, approximates the world of formless unified spirit, aka heaven, more than our current world. Nevertheless, both worlds are not real; they are produced by mind energy. Mind itself is formless energy that thinks and its thinking produces worlds (pictures).

Mind energy is what folks call God and his sons. God is mind energy thinking through all of us (his sons) and producing worlds for us to seem to live in.

Heaven is when mind energy is in its formless state, without pictures of worlds, is not perceptual but knows that it is the one that produces worlds and makes them seem real, hence does not take any of its universes seriously, for any of them can be tuned out.

In my post-surgery daydream, my mind energy produced two worlds and placed them side by side, one composed of golden light orbs (each orb turning into a human face) and the other composed of a starry night, dark environment with stars, points of light in it (our world). My mind energy produced these two worlds and placed them side by side for me to see the difference between our dark world and the beautiful world of golden light orbs.

My mind was a third-party seeing both worlds at the same time (meaning that it is neither of them but produced both of them). My mind energy was trying to decide which one it wants to choose, return to the world of golden light forms (what people call after-death world) or return to our world of darkness with points of light in it, our world.

I chose to return to our world of pain and suffering; I did so because I still have work to do on earth.

CONCLUSION

The point made in this piece is that there is a formless universal mind energy; each of us is a formless unit of that mental energy; with that mental or thinking energy, we produce whatever world we seem to live in, our current world of dark forms or the after-death world of light forms or return to the awareness of formless mind energy, aka heaven.

We cannot see or experience the three worlds at the same time (except when we are trying to choose which one to see and live in, as in my post-operation day dream where I saw a world of golden light orbs in a summer evening like field or a world with a dark background with points of light in it).

The seer of both worlds is the son of God in me (my real self), the dreamer of my worlds. The same applies to each human being, animal, tree, and everything in the universe; we are each the dreamer of the world we see. Our real self, the son of God, is the one doing all these dreams.

When the son of God chooses to awaken from dreams, it no longer sees dreams, worlds, but knows itself to be the unified son of God who is one with God.

RELIGIOUS DELUSION DISORDER AND HOW IT MODELLED FOR ME WHAT NOT TO BE

This write-up is primarily about a friend called Dr. O, an attorney. He found life in body painful and full of suffering; he did not find any profession on earth good enough for him; they all seem too small for him for his ego wants a profession that gives him magical powers with which he banishes his pains and all people's pains and transforms the world to a beautiful fantasy world. There is no such fantasy world.

You reject the world, reject your body, and posit a spiritual body (light body and identify with it). You claim to be God-realized, as Hindus do, but you are still prone to diseases (Dr. O is blind).

To avoid embarrassment, you do not come to the public square and tell people that you are God for folks would say: if you are God and God is very powerful, how come you are blind and poor? So, you stay in your room and while there, hope to one day become pure spirit and surprise the world with it. You have religious delusion.

There may be a spiritual world but its parameters are different from the earth's three-dimensional parameters. If you escape from earth and are in spirit, you do not have the limitations of space, time, and body; you are in light form or in formless heaven.

But the fact is that you are on earth and need food, medications, clothes, shelter, and means to transport you from point A to point B.

In the meantime, you retain your grandiose ego and if anyone slights you a little bit, you feel temper tantrum and drop the phone on him (Dr. O dropped the phone on me whenever I challenged his grandiose claims to be God). He is deluded.

LIVING EGOLESS GIVES ONE PEACE AND JOY.

You take the aspect of spirituality that works on earth. If you do not defend your ego, let go of the wish for a grandiose ego to use as a magic wand with which you conquer the world; let go of fear you live peacefully.

THE HOLY SPIRIT PART OF MY MIND, THE JOINED PART OF MY MIND, SELECTED HELEN SCHUCMAN, DR. O, NEBU, AND IGBOS AND USED THEM TO TEACH ME OF THE NATURE OF DELUSION DISORDER, HENCE GET ME TO LET GO OF MY OWN WISH FOR GRANDIOSE EGO.

The Holy Spirit is not a person outside you; it is the part of your thinking, mind energy that tunes to other minds; it knows those you would learn from to change you.

The Holy Spirit gathers folks like J (who talked religion but does not love), Dr. Helen Schucman (who wrote a wonderful spiritual psychology but did not live it), Dr. O (who has wonderful spiritual insights but did not give up his wish for grandiose ego hence is stuck in ego), Nebu (a deluded character), and Igbos (deluded characters), L (who talks spirituality at the new-age level but not at the level of giving up her attachment to ego and body).

The Holy Spirit gathers these folks and other folks with grandiose egos who were stunted in their growth and presented them to me to learn from and from realizing how their desire for egos warped their growth, made them not live fearlessly and peacefully, have me live egolessly and not seek big ego which means not have fear from seeking big ego and thus, live peacefully.

God, his Holy Spirit, does not abandon any of his sons in his fantasy of having power but uses the people around him to teach him how to liberate himself.

The son of God, me/you, liberates himself; other people do not liberate you; only you can liberate you but all people give you pointers that enable you to liberate you; and you give them pointers that enable them to liberate themselves from the pursuit of big egos, hence live peacefully.

ALL THESE PEOPLE COULD NOT BEHAVE DIFFERENTLY; THEY HAD TO BEHAVE AS THEY DID FOR ME TO LEARN FROM THEM.

One sees other persons behaving as if they are fools and one asks: how come they do not change? They cannot change for they have to behave as they do for one to see them and from their mistakes, learn about one's own mistakes.

As it were, they volunteered to behave as they do for one to learn from them and change, and they cannot change until one changes (and they may not be able to change in this lifetime).

The Holy Spirit in them gathered them around one to enable one to change. They are one's negative teachers, for the lesson, goal, is for one to change, not for them to change.

They are the allegorical John the Baptist baptizing with water before Jesus came to baptize with the Holy Spirit (Jesus Christ brought the Holy Spirit to earth; before him, egos lived, even the old prophets were egotists).

They have many lifetimes on earth to change. I have only this lifetime on earth to change and live egolessly, and that is why these people were gathered for me to learn from them about the pitfalls of grandiose egos.

I must be grateful to them for volunteering to be the obnoxious persons they are. Racists, obnoxious as they are, enable black folks to learn how not to be obnoxious; therefore, the person who discriminated against you and made you angry, showing your big ego, had to be racist for you and black folks to learn not to seek big ego.

The white person who is racist toward you may not be racist toward other black persons because the lesson you have to learn, give up your big ego, is not other person's lesson.

ESTABLISHMENT OF NEW VOCATION AND PROFESSION

If you live egolessly hence peacefully, you can teach people to do so by understanding and letting go of their egos to live peacefully here on earth and give up the fantasy of escaping to ideal spiritual world.

There was a biological weakness, pains that led you to rejecting your body and seek bodiless spiritual self. Since your pained weak body is still there, you accept it and not try to negate it with a fantasy strong body or bodiless self.

There are jobs you can do with a weak body without big ego. You can start a new profession of living egolessly and teaching people to live egolessly hence happily and peacefully.

This is an attained state of being after many years of learning; it is not formed in childhood, for in childhood, one forms the ego of power to adapt to an impersonal world.

We only see the past, not the present.

Helen Schucman, in her book, *A Course in Miracles*, says, over and over again that we do not see anything as it is now but as it was in the past.

She is a poet and wrote in poetic form. Poets and musicians do not explain what they wrote (composed) for they are seldom analytical; they articulate the truth without knowing how they did it (I love classical music; my mother-in-law was a director of a small-town symphony orchestra. I visited her one Christmas and she played Handel's Messiah nonstop during the time I visited. I am philosophical, so I tried to understand what Handel was trying to say in his immortal music celebrating the birth of Christ. I tried talking to my mother-in-law about my understanding of Handel's music. She placed her fingers on her mouth and said, in effect, don't even try it. She meant that neither she nor I can explain classical music or any kind of music for that matter).

Since I think that I see things as they are now, I did not take Helen seriously. Then, I revisited the physics of light and perception.

Light travels at the speed of 186, 282 miles per second. Light strikes an object, say, the table on which my computer is on, and reflects that table's picture to my brain (I will skip explanation of optics here) and my brain interprets what I see as a table.

It took time, albeit a split second, for light to strike the table, take a picture of it, and take it to my brain and it took time for my brain to interpret what I see as a table.

Therefore, what I see as the table right now is the table as it was a moment ago, not as it is at present. I only see the past of the table and everything in the world of perception; perception does not show me the world as it is in the present.

Some of the stars (their light, that is) I see today have been traveling for billions of years before reaching my eyes. Some of those stars are already exploded in supernova and are no longer in existence, yet, I see them as if I am seeing them today.

This means that I do not see things as they are in the present. This begs the question: how are things in the present?

In as much as I respond to what I see, I am responding to the past of what I see, not its present. When you do something and I respond to you, I actually responded to what you did in the past, not present. For all I know, in the present, you may be a loving person while I see your past when you did something that I interpreted as annoying.

A Course in Miracles says that the world we think that we see today is already over and we are seeing a world that is not there. In the present, you are total love but I see you as an enemy, what you were in the past when we attacked each other to separate from each other.

Those with purified eyes, mystics, are said to see people and the world as they are, not quite now but improved, hence lovely. They see with purified vision; they have forgiven our past attacks on each other and now see the loving world the Holy Spirit reinvented to replace the world of attack we invented.

However, both the world of attacks and defense and the Holy Spirit's purified world are illusions for in both, we see things that are not there.

In heaven, we do not see, we know that we are one unified self. There is no space, time, and matter in heaven. In heaven, we live in the eternal now of God, Dr. Schucman said.

Since the past is already gone, when we see it, we see what is not there. We see a past world that is not there; we see nothing when we say that we see the world.

In effect, when we see the world, we are deluded and are hallucinating for we believe what is not there to be there and see what is not there; in the world of perception, we are, therefore, psychotic!

In the meantime, we do not see the near present world of the Holy Spirit (world of light forms, New Jerusalem) nor experience the eternally present God's formless unified world.

Does this view make sense to you?

I know that it is difficult to go from the concrete world we live into the abstract world of pure thinking, but try to think a little bit; the universe gave you mind to think with!

DR. O AND DR. DUNCAN DO NOT LOVE ANYONE.

Dr. O talked to me about how he is a God-realized man. He did so for several months. I listened to him and finally decided to challenge him. I calmly told him that what he is saying does not make sense. He hung up the phone on me. He did not call me for over a year. One of his friends, Dr. Kofi Agyanpong, reconnected us.

He did not remember me and like in the past, kept talking about how he is God's representative on earth, the most advanced person spiritually.

After a couple of months of hearing him talk about this nonsense, I told him that he is not anymore God than any other person on earth. He felt angry at me and hung up on me. It is now four months since that episode.

Every once in a while, I feel like calling him and another part of me says to me, so, you have not had enough of his claptrap that he is God, so I have not called him in four months. I remember that he would call me, say, at 11 PM and talk to me nonstop for four hours until I tell him that I am going to sleep. He would do this every day.

I challenged his claim to be God and he has not forgiven me and has not called me. What does that mean?

It means that he does not love me and does not know what love is. I remember that he abandoned his seven children in this quest for God-realization; I got it, he does not love his children, either.

The only thing that matters to him is to be seen as God. He is deluded.

A deluded person does not love anyone.

Dr. Duncan is another man who claims to know a lot about God until I told him to stop sending to me his daily messages, which he said are from God. Since then, he has not talked to me; I tried vising him and he would not open his door. He, too, does not love me or anyone; what matters to him is to seem enlightened.

The ego is the opposite of love. Religious egos are particularly unloving persons. Political egos like Donald Trump do not love anyone, either. Trump could get millions of Americans to die (from the coronavirus by insisting on folks returning to work and students returning to school) provided that he is president and is powerful.

Whatever one says about other people is really said about one, for when we point two fingers at other people, three fingers point right back at us. What this piece tells me is that in pursuit of God, I do not love people, especially those close to me that need my love; the lesson is to love people and stop thinking that understanding God is more important than love. God is love. The lesson is love people and you have understood God.

WE MUST THEREFORE GIVE UP OUR EGOS; EXCEPT THAT IF YOU TOTALLY GIVE UP YOUR EGO, YOU WOULD NOT SEE OUR EGO-BASED WORLD.

If you totally give up your ego, you would not see our ego-based world, for the world is synonymous with ego; the world of space, time, matter, separation, and ego is the self that adapts to the world of separation and if you have no ego, you will not see the world of separation.

IT SEEMS LIKE MATTER, SPACE AND TIME DETERMINE THE SELF, THINKING, MIND, AND PERSONALITY. BUT MIND, THINKING, EXISTS OUTSIDE MATTER, SPACE, AND TIME.

Everything in our awareness tells us that our bodies, space, and time determined our thinking and perception; to me, it seems that my brain determined my thinking, my mind, and my behavior pattern—*my* personality.

The entire universe exists to make it seem that the material universe determined who we are. Thus, the philosophy of materialism makes sense to us.

Mystics tell us that that is not true. If you happen to have had one of those experiences where you are outside your body but still in space and time, you still think and still feel like you are in body (of light). That is, thinking, mind, seems outside our bodies, space, and time.

A Course in Miracles says that our bodies and the material universe of space, time, and matter do not exist. How can what does not exist determine our thinking? The only thing that exists is mind, thinking.

The son of God, you and I, are thinking and his thinking produces our universe. The universe is the outward projection of our collective thoughts. The universe does not exist apart from our thinking. This is kind of like the idea that we are like simulated persons, different persons, our real selves, the sleeping sons of God, think through us in the world of space, time, and matter. Think of the movie *Matrix*.

THIS IS WHAT A COURSE IN MIRACLES IS TEACHING

There is no world for me to see; the world I see I invented; I give that false separated world the meaning it has for me.

However, since it does not exist, I see a world that does not exist except as in a dream and this makes me upset; I give a meaningless world, a non-existent world, meaning, a meaningless meaning hence feel like a fool.

The Holy Spirit takes the nonexistent, meaningless world and gives it a different interpretation that makes it approximate meaningful heaven. The Holy Spirit forgives it and thus, bring love to bear on it. It is now purified by love. It is now made of light.

Light is still not the truth but approximates the truth. The world of light forms is beautiful to look at but is still not real.

What is real is the non-perceptual unified world of God. Give up the perceptual world, be it the egos' perceptual world of matter or the Holy Spirit's perceptual world of light forms, return to the awareness of the non-perceptual world of God, and in it, feel peace and joy.

THE ONLY PRACTICAL LESSONS I LEARNED FROM A COURSE IN MIRACLES ARE:

It asks me to give up my identification with the separated self-concept, the ego. The ego may still be there but I do not see it as who I am. Who I am is part of life, and what life is, I do not know.

I am not the big ego that I wanted to be. Trying to be a grandiose ego gives me ambitions, what to do to attain the big things a big ego-self requires, concomitant fear of failing, anxiety, pretending that I am important and powerful (paranoid; that is, identification with a person that I am not, delusion), depression, and anger.

If I deny that I am the ego concept, accept that my real self is the conceptualizing self, not its concept, and do not defend a mere concept of me, I tend to have no self-consciousness; I tend not to care for what other people say about me (what me); I tend not to mind folks criticizing me and I tend not to criticize folks; I let folks be and let myself be.

I am not this type or that type of person. I am just a part of life and what the totality of life is, I do not know.

In this non-attachment to ego and non-defensive mode, it is like I am walking on air, carried along by gentle breezes through my days, living quietly and peacefully.

This benefit from *A Course in Miracles* is very good. The other stuff it says, about God, son of God, forgiveness, love, is interesting but I do not know what they are.

EXISTENCE GIVES YOU A PROBLEM TO SOLVE: FOR ME, IT IS TO ELIMINATE MY BIG EGO TO LIVE IN PEACE.

Every person, every group, every nation, every generation is given fights to fight and cannot run away from them and if they try to run from them, they will not grow and move on; they would be brought back to go fight that fight.

A LESSON UNLEARNED IS REPEATED UNTIL LEARNED AND WHEN LEARNED, IS NO LONGER REPEATED.

My fight is to understand the ego separated self-concept, eliminate it in me, and help people to eliminate it in them.

If mankind lives less egotistically, we would produce a more peaceful and happier world.

I tried to run from that task and the more I run, the more I fail, and am redirected to go fight it, remove my big ego to give me peace.

I tried leaving the USA and going to Canada. The USA is where the problem of race that humiliates black folks and makes them angry is magnified and is where I will solve it and find peace.

THE EGO IS LITERALLY MAD.

The ego is a false self; it wants to seem in existence; it easily feels slighted and feels angry and desecrates people it sees as insulting it.

The ego is the opposite of love; it does not love anyone; it seeks not love but attention and admiration for its false dream self; it wants to be told that it is powerful but could care less for folk's happiness.

Therefore, one must overlook the ego and not do anything from its perspective.

WHAT EXPLAINS THE GLAZED LOOK ON THE FACES OF CHRISTIAN PENTECOSTAL WORSHIPPERS?

If you look at Christian Pentecostal worshippers standing up with their hands stretched out in front of them, praising the name of their lord and generally saying nice things about God and Jesus Christ, sometimes, they seem to go into a kind of trance and their faces look blank and glazed as if there are no thoughts in them.

They apparently feel happy in that no thinking mood, for thinking tends to give folks tension. In Hindu and Buddhist meditation, folks try to stop thinking, silence their minds, and attain inner silence, and in that state, look peaceful and happy.

It may well be that the peace and joy seen on the faces of Christian Pentecostal worshippers as they chant praises for their God is what they crave. People want brains that are quiet, without excessive thinking in them. Indeed, people often take drugs, such as tranquilizers to attain peace in their brains and bodies.

IT SEEMS THAT MY MIND LIKES TO LIVE IN CONSTANT STATE OF FEAR; INSTEAD OF DOING SOMETHING TO LIVE WELL, IT PREFERS TO DO WHAT MAKES IT SEEM THREATENED AND THUS, ANTICIPATE DANGER AND LIVE IN FEAR.

My mind makes a mountain of a molehill; it exaggerates small things, builds them into mighty threats, and feels fear. It anticipates threats and danger, feels fear, and is anxious. It is apparent that I seem to like to live in fear and anxiety. Why?

MIXING REALISM AND IDEALISM PRODUCES CONFUSION.

There are clearly ascertainable laws of nature and society; we may call that realism—the way things are; they are often brutal and not pleasant to certain people.

Some people try to circumvent the realistic laws of nature and society by using their minds to wish for idealistic laws, as to how nature ought to be, and how society ought to be.

The idealist obviously cannot change the laws of nature and society, and as such, is wasting his time and energy with his idealism.

Mixing the laws of nature, society, and mere idealism is the greatest source of confusion; it is actually what causes neurosis and psychosis.

The solution is to give up idealism and embrace realism, the laws of science and society, since those are impersonal to live with them or to get out of living with them via spiritual escapism, such as offered by *A Course in Miracles*.

EACH OF US WRITES THE SCRIPT OF HIS LIFE.

A Course in Miracles says that we went to sleep with the desire to separate from God and our unified real self and while in the sleep, write the script of what we dream, as we do at night.

When we go to sleep at night, we do not know what we are going to dream that night but write the script and enact it out in the dream.

All we did in heaven is the desire to separate from God—the day-to-day world is the script that we wrote in the sleep. That is, we are individually responsible for our day world; we write the scripts, plays, and enact them out as we live. The ego-mind writes and enacts the play, life, we see in our lives.

WE NOW NEED A DIFFERENT INTERPRETATION OF THE SCRIPT, WORLD, DREAM, WE HAVE ALREADY ENACTED, THE HOLY SPIRIT'S INTERPRETATION

We have ego interpretations of what happens to us on earth; ego interpretations change minute by minute, day by day, week by week, month by month; we are always changing how we interpret things and respond differently.

CHANGELESS REALITY REQUIRES ONE INTERPRETATION.

Reality is changeless, unified, and formless so all our interpretations do not take us back to reality. The Holy Spirit knows what reality is, sees our world, and has an interpretation that even though it is not the truth, takes us closer to the truth. His interpretation is one. It says that the whole world and our behaviors are dream and that we should overlook all of it, forgive it, not try to keep those aspects of our behaviors and the world that we like, and give up others but for us to forgive all of them, overlook all of them, to see his reinterpreted world of light forms.

THE DREAMLESS WORLD OF GOD

His one interpretation gives us one purpose: return to God, and as long as we still wish to dream, brings us to the gate of heaven, to a happy dream, happy insanity, until we give up all desires for separation, stop sleeping and writing scripts to live in the dream world, and awaken to the dreamless unified world of God. In effect, we stop dreaming with the ego-mind and now dream with the Holy Spirit mind, think and behave with the Holy Spirit's unified purpose, forgiveness.

Dreams can only occur in the world of separation, our world; in unified state, there is no dream hence God's world is a dreamless world.

I WROTE THE SCRIPT OF MY DAY WORLD, I WANTED MY PARENTS AND WHITE FOLKS TO DISCRIMINATE AGAINST ME, PROJECTED THOSE WHO DISCRIMINATE AGAINST ME INTO THE DREAM, HAVE THEM DISCRIMINATE AGAINST ME, AND I BLAME THEM BUT NOW, I MUST OVERLOOK THE EGO SCRIPT, ACCEPT THE HOLY SPIRIT'S SCRIPT, OVERLOOK MY SCRIPT, AND SEE THE LIGHT WORLD.

THOSE PEOPLE ALSO WRITE SCRIPTS THAT REQUIRED THEM TO DISCRIMINATE AGAINST ME FOR THEY AND I SHARE ONE UNIFIED SELF AND DO THINGS FOR EACH OTHER.

While in eternity, unified state, in God, in heaven, I desired separation from all, God, and went to sleep with the intention of separating from my real self, the unified son of God; in the sleep, I write scripts, plays, and enact them out in my dreams on earth for as long as I sleep and dream.

I wanted to be discriminated against and wrote a script where folks discriminate against me and that is what I see and feel angry at people, my parents, siblings, and white folks. It is all my script, my ego dream.

The Holy Spirit asks me to overlook the ego script that I wrote and accept his script of overlooking and forgiving the world I made.

If I forgive those who I see discriminating against me, I see them as Christ and in seeing them as Christ (seeing them not as they see themselves for they still see themselves as egos and see me as ego and do not love themselves or me), I see me as Christ and have a happy dream, not the ego dream of self-attack.

All people wrote their own scripts; in reference to me, their scripts required them to make life difficult for me, to discriminate against me (as my parents did to me), to not love me, and to attack me (as white racist did to me and must do to me).

In them discriminating against me, they alienate me, make me hate them, and then turn around to forgive their script as to forgive my script that required them to attack me (the script required them to discriminate against me and they could not do so; what you see people do to you, they must do so; what your parents, wife, and children did to you, they must do so for your mutual scripts required them to do so); the Holy Spirit used their script of hate for me to save me and them.

DREAM OF FEAR AND LOVELESSNESS AND DREAM OF LOVE

You must forgive others and see them as Christ to see you as Christ; if you are unforgiving and see them as egos, you see you as ego and keep having ego dreams, dreams of fear and lovelessness.

THE END OF FEAR

When you dream with the Holy Spirit, you end fear, for the ego dream gives one fear.

When you dream with the Holy Spirit, you have a happy dream and other people you see as Christ would still be egos and have ego dreams and live in pain, but now, you are a point of light in their dreams of self-hate, as Jesus is a point of light, knowledge of love, for us in the dream of hatred; you model peace and joy for them but cannot directly wake them up; they have to do that by themselves.

OUR SEPARATED WORLD IS AN IMPOSSIBLE WORLD.

At night, I go to sleep. I immediately go to dreamland. My mind, thinking, writes a script and dramatizes it while it is writing it; it does not first write a script and then find actors to play roles called for by the script; no, it writes the script and simultaneously dramatizes it. In my dream, I see myself and other people doing all the things we do in our day world.

While in the dream, it all seems real. I wake up in the morning and it dawns on me that the world I had seen during the night was a dream.

Sometimes, the dream lingers in my mind for a few seconds and then disappears and my mind switches to the reality of my day life.

I ask myself, how does the human mind (and animals; animals also dream; we know this to be so by studying REM, rapid eye movement, that takes place as animals sleep) produce dreams? I read up on it and the explanations provided seem laughable. Some say that dreams are gibberish produced by sleeping minds (gibberish such as me going to an airport, boarding a plane, going to a conference, delivering a paper, and returning home); some say that it is produced by the electrons, light, and neurotransmitters in our brains.

Light in our day world takes pictures of what it strikes on, sends the pictures to our eyes, our eyes send the information to our brains, and our brains interpret what the pictures are and tell us what we see. That in itself is a mysterious event.

How light and electrons produce a world that seems real in our dreams got to be a more mysterious phenomenon. Simply stated, no one has satisfactorily explained the phenomenon of dreams.

Professor Helen Schucman, a clinical psychologist, a poet and spirit medium, wrote an interesting book called *A Course in Miracles* (she attributed its source to the Holy Spirit and Jesus Christ). In it, she said that our day world is also a dream world. She said that in our day world, our minds, just like at night, write scripts and dramatize the script as they are writing them; the writing and enactment of the scripts are simultaneous. Our minds do not first write the script, as playwrights do, select actors, and have them dramatize the script but select actors and dramatize the scripts as they write them.

Religious people say that everything happens in the eternal now of God; past, present, and future all happen in this very moment; the sons of God's minds write a script that contains past, present, and future and dramatize it now, and in it, we see a past, present, and future! This is what happens in our dreams and since that is not our experience in the daytime, we dismiss dreams as gibberish.

That is to say that my day world is a situation where my mind, my unconscious thinking, is writing a script of what my day is like and places people and things into that script and dramatize it for me. The day world is my dream; my mind wrote the script and dramatized it.

I am therefore responsible for what I see as my day world for it reflects my script, my thinking, made into a movie, a video.

The implication of this perspective is world-changing. It means that if I am poor and suffering, if other people discriminate against me, or if white folks do not give me jobs, they are merely enacting a script that my mind (and apparently their own minds, too) wrote. I am not a victim of external circumstances for there are no external circumstances; the seemingly external world I see is the product of my mind and your mind; how we do it remains a mystery, as mysterious as our nightly dreams.

For our present purposes, the lady psychologist says that I produced my world; my world is the outward picturing of my thinking; the world is my script dramatized. I have no one else to blame for my rotten life. I am not a victim of other bad people for they merely acted roles that my script called for and I acted roles for them that their scripts called for.

We, in new-age religious categories, mutually created our day world as we individually created our nightly dream worlds.

The implication that I created my day reality is enormous. It means that I can change my world if I do not like it. But how?

Try as I did, I still see a world where white folks abuse black folks. I do not seem to have the power to change the external world. That would seem to invalidate the notion that it is I who created my reality if I cannot change my day reality.

A part of me tells me that the notion that I created my reality is a cynical ploy by the rulers of society to get me to take responsibility for the world they created and dominate, a world in which black folks are victims. If I accept their maneuver, I feel like I gave me poverty when, in fact, the rulers of society gave it to me.

The philosophy that one created one's world prevents the poor and oppressed from taking action to remove their oppressors, the rulers of society; it perpetuates their poverty and does not liberate them. I can see how the rulers of this world could engineer such belief to get the poor to blame themselves, not their oppressors.

Let us for now assume that the external world I see was created by me and that we all collectively created it; let us accept that our mutual thinking somehow produced our day world. If this is true, therefore, I can change my thinking and change the world; other people, too, can change their thinking and change their world; the collective changes in our thinking would then produce a different world for us.

A Course in Miracles says that the mind that produced our day and night dreams cannot change them. It takes a different type of thinking, a different mind, to change our day and nightly dreams.

It says that we dream with ego-separated minds; it says that we can only change the world if we dream with the Holy Spirit, or Christ mind that seeks union.

It provided ontology, a story of creation to make its argument rational. Originally, we are the sons of God, the parts of one unified self. God is a formless self, a self that extends to infinite selves, all of whom are parts of it. Where God ends and his sons begin is nowhere; where one son of God ends and others begin is nowhere. All sons of God are literally unified; they share one self and one thinking, one mind. We think in tandem, in concert, for there is no space and time between us.

In eternity, where we are right now, there is no matter, space, and time; we are all in each other. God is in us and we are in God and in each other. We are one formless self that has infinite parts, all of them one reality.

In eternity, aka heaven, we think with our one shared mind. However, at a time that has not occurred, since there is no time in God, we decided to separate from God and from each other. There is no time and no space so we could not separate from each other. Where are we separating to go to if we are in each other?

But we are the sons of God and have enormous creative power. Thus, while we remain unified with God and each other, remain as God created us, as one with him, as it were, we closed our spiritual minds, wished separation, and went to sleep and while in sleep, used our sleeping minds to produce a dream world of separated beings, a world of space, time, and matter, used matter to construct our bodies, and now seem to live in bodies that walk around in a world of space, time, and matter.

In the sleep of real self-forgetfulness, we see ourselves as separated selves; the separated self is the ego. The mind of the sleeping sons of God produced our world and produced the ego; the ego is a mere dream figure produced by the son of God and he projected himself to it and makes it seem that he is the ego-separated self.

The ego is the selves we formed in our dreams of separation and project into the dreams. I am over here and you are over there. The I that is over here is my separated self and the you that is over there is the separated you. Our separated egos then interact in the dream world.

Egos are a representation of our wished-for separated selves. We, meaning the unified sons of God, sleep and write scripts and people the scripts with each other, now in bodies, and the things of this world and see them in our world.

Our world is our collective and individual dream. No one in the world is a victim for he is the one that wrote his personal script and peopled it and have them enact his dream and other people do the same and those whose dreams call for them to be close to each other come close to each other and play roles for each other.

In this sense, my dream script called for me to be discriminated against by white people so I place white folks who discriminate against me in my dream and they do what my dream called on them to do. Apparently, white folks have scripts that want to discriminate against black folks and they people their dreams with black folks that they discriminate against. Thus, all of us are collectively enacting what is in our scripts. There are no victims despite the fact that some of us on earth, in the dream, are abused by others (we abuse ourselves through the perceived abusers; the book says that we do change roles; in some lifetimes we are the abusers and in others, we are the abused).

Since I see myself as abused by white folks, how do I change it? Dr. Schucman says that the mind that thinks and projects out the dream world cannot change it. It takes a different mind to change it. Indeed, that mind has already changed it.

Just as the world we see follows a script that has been written and does not exist before the dream, a different part of our minds, the Holy Spirit, follows the ego-mind, and as the ego-mind enacts its world, our day world and our dream world at night, the Holy Spirit, the higher mind, simultaneously writes another script, peoples it, and dramatizes it in a different world, the world of light forms. That is, the ego-mind makes a mistake and the Holy Spirit mind corrects the mistake.

In the dream of the Holy Spirit, the selves we see as ourselves on earth are now in light forms. All the things in our earthly world are in the light world except that they are in light forms. What you see on earth, such as people, animals, trees, mountains, and stars are all in the light world except that they are now in the light forms.

The light world coexists with the egos' dark world. You cannot see the world of light forms and at the same time, see the world of dark forms, our world. It is either you see one or the other (when folks die, they see the world of light forms but do not see our world of dark forms).

In meditation, Hindus and Buddhists claim that they can tune out our present world and see the world of light forms, but that is a very rare happenstance.

The Holy Spirit, the wholly spiritual part of our minds, our holy minds, our unified minds, our whole thinking minds, has already remade the world we currently live in; the remade world is made as we made our present world; both worlds follow scripts that sleepers, sons of God sleeping, write and dramatize.

(Hugh Everett said that the Big Bang that produced our world also produced other worlds. In that light, as our universe is evolving, the universe of light forms is evolving along with it. From Dr. Everett's interpretation of quantum mechanics arose the concept of multiverse.)

There is no time lapse between when we write the script, dramatize it at night, and during the day and when the Holy Spirit writes and dramatizes the script of the world of light forms, they all happen concurrently, simultaneously.

Dr. Schucman tells us that we need do nothing to see the world of light forms. However, we must understand what we need do nothing means. It means that since the world of light forms is already there along with our world, to see it, all we need do is tune out the world of dark forms. She asks us to overlook our present world to see the light forms' world.

She defines forgiveness as choosing to overlook our present world and not try to improve it with our ego-minds, for our ego-minds cannot improve the world of attack and defense it made, but to overlook it, to overcome the world.

She calls the people, us, in the world of light forms Christ for they are now purified and loving, not totally loving as we are in the world of formlessness, heaven. In the world of light forms, we are transparent to each other; we know each other's thoughts and cannot hide from each other.

In the world of light forms, we relatively love each other. That world is relatively peaceful and joyous but does not have the perfect love, peace, and joy of formless unified heaven and instead, approximates it. It is a world at the gate of heaven; it is our world remade for us to enjoy. It is still not real; it is still a dream, a fiction, an insane world, but it so approximates sanity, the unified, holy world of God, that in it, we feel relatively peaceful and happy.

Dr. Schucman says that the way to see the world of light forms is to forgive the person that my ego shows me to have wronged me. The ego shows me a racist hurting me and asks me to bear grievances, seek vengeance, and attack the attacker. If I do, I maintain the egos' world of perpetual attack and defense hence a world lacking peace.

Now, I see you attack me, I see you, a white person, discriminate against me; my ego asks me to be defensive, be angry at you, and fight back, but the Holy Spirit tells me that you did what you did to me in our world of mutual attacks, a dream world; what is done in dreams has not been done; you, the attacker, attacked me in the dream of separation, not in reality. I, therefore, see you as not having attacked me; I overlook your attack on me for what is done in dreams have not been done in reality.

In forgiving you, overlooking your attack, I suddenly see you in light form; I see you as Christ. When I see you with Christ vision, as light, with my forgiving mind, I simultaneously forgive me and see me in light form, as the Christ.

But until I forgive you and see you as Christ, I cannot forgive me and see me as Christ in light form. I must forgive other people to be forgiven by God. I must see you as Christ to see me as Christ.

Christ lives in peace and joy in the world of light forms.

Does forgiving you mean that you would be less racist and hurtful? No. Forgiving you gives me peace and joy but you cannot have peace and joy until you have done what I did, forgive those who attacked and hurt you. You will remain in ego while the forgiving person now knows himself as the Christ. However, the forgiving person is now a point of God's light (knowledge of oneness) in the egos' dream of darkness (darkness is a metaphor for separation).

I forgive you; I am now the Christ; I am in light form. I am a point of light in the ego-separated world of darkness. If you have not forgiven me and the world, you live as an ego. You will still see yourself as in body. But I am now a light-bringer to your world (knowledge of oneness, love) showing you what to do to become aware of yourself in light form.

You are already in light form but will not see it as long as you have not forgiven the world of attack we live in. I show you a touch light, a candlelight pointing to what you need to do to see you in light form. I am now a point of light (a unit of knowledge) in the world of darkness (separation, lack of love) called our ego, separated world.

I have shortened how long it would take you and the rest of the world to realize that you are the Christ by many years, sometimes by thousands of years for without me, light in the dream, knowledge of oneness, you would keep thinking that you are the ego in body, lost in darkness. I have become a savior of the world.

Jesus Christ, by forgiving those who crucified his ego and body, has reduced the time the rest of us would take to realize our light selves, Christ selves, by one thousand years.

All the people who have forgiven the world see themselves in light forms, see themselves as Christ, and are the saviors of the world, bringers of light to the world of darkness.

(To be a point of light, to see me as the light of the world, or to live in the world of darkness are metaphors, not literal light and darkness but metaphors for a person who lives from unified self, who loves all people).

In the meantime, I am still in the world of darkness, the egos' world. What benefit do I get from forgiving racists? I live peacefully and happily. Since I now think with my Christ mind, the Holy Spirit's mind that recognizes our oneness, even those who live in darkness, separation, derive some peace and joy from my presence and when they think about me.

Therefore, they do whatever they can do to help me do my work of being a light in darkness. If I need money to do my work, somehow, those who have money will give it to me without me asking them for money. I will not live in poverty for I am now living from Christ mind.

If the ego-mind could create our world, the Christ mind can recreate it into a beautiful world, a world of abundance, a world where there is no lack, no poverty, and no pain and suffering.

My light body (that is, my loving self) does not know illness for only the body in flesh knows illness. Have I seen anyone on earth who lives in light body, not flesh body, hence is not prone to illness? I have not seen such a person. However, I have momentarily seen people, animals, trees, and myself in light forms (that is, with love and forgiveness).

DISCUSSION
METAPHORS AND REALITY

Although Dr. Helen Schucman claimed to have had no knowledge of Gnosticism, her book, *A Course in Miracles* falls within the spectrum of

Gnostic philosophy and religion. Gnosticism is Hinduism and Buddhism cast in the Greek language.

I studied Oriental religions; what jumped at me when I read *A Course in Miracles* is that it is Hinduism translated into Christological language.

In Hinduism, there is one God, called Brahman; he has infinite parts, each called Atman (God and sons of God, in *A Course in Miracles'* categories); each of us is Atman and is one with God and other Atman.

Atman, that is, son of God, cast Maya, a magical spell on himself that makes us forget our true self, on his unified self, and sleeps and dreams that he is separated from Brahman; in his sleep state, he is called ego, in Sanskrit, Ahankara.

We, Atman, are currently separated from Brahman; Hinduism wants us to awaken to the awareness of our true self, through what it calls God-realization (breaking from moksha, the spell of Maya's illusions; Gautama Buddha did so 2500 years ago).

Gnosticism believes that there is one God and that he is spiritual light, not physical light, and that we are all parts of that God light. Somehow, we separated from God, from light, and now live in the world of darkness. We have to return to the world of light.

We have not really separated from God, light, we merely closed our eyes and do not see the light, God, love, we always live in.

Gnosticism, *A Course in Miracles* included, employs such metaphors as light, light of the world, light in the dream, world of light forms, darkness, Holy Spirit, forgiveness, love. *A Course in Miracles* is a Gnostic religion.

In Gnosticism and *A Course in Miracles*, light is employed to represent knowledge of God; darkness is employed to represent ignorance of God; the world of light forms means a world filled with knowledge of God; a point of light in the world of darkness means a person with knowledge of God in a world that does not know anything about God; ego is separated self; forgiveness is overlooking the separated self and its world of space, time, and matter; Holy Spirit is the part of our minds that overlook the world of separation and what is done in it, for it is seen as a dream; love is employed to mean union of all things in God.

I found it necessary to explicate that *A Course in Miracles* is written in metaphors because some people are not poets and tend to take poetic terms literally. We take religions' poetic representation of God, metaphors, as literal truth.

The fact is that the truth is beyond words; metaphors and figures of speech cannot explain God. No human being, no physicist, can help us to understand where the first light, the light that exploded to become the Big Bang and brought our material world into being came from.

To physics, nothing exists beyond the Big Bang; the Big Bang came from nowhere and from nothing. In our experience, something always precedes what happens now. We may not understand what existed before the Big Bang but that does not mean that nothing existed before it.

A Course in Miracles says that God existed before the Big Bang. The sons of God tried to separate from God during the Big Bang.

But what is God? *A Course in Miracles* says that God is the changeless reality whereas our world is a place of changes. In their unified state, God and his sons are eternal, changeless, permanent, and the same and coequal.

In our world, on the other hand, things change just about every second. What seems like the truth now, in the next second, is no longer the truth.

Our interpretations of what the truth is are forever changing. The Holy Spirit, the part of us rooted in God but sees this world, has one interpretation of all things. It asks us to overlook the world and forgive one another.

Forgiveness is not reality but opens the door to reality. Reality itself is the eternal union of God and his creations as one shared self; love unites them into one self. God is love.

I have had what folks call near-death experience. I saw a world of light forms. In it, people, animals, trees, and stars still look like they do in our world. I could still touch them and they touch me and when people held my hand, it felt like when human beings hold my hand on earth; yet, those people look transparent like they are made of light, not flesh.

Heaven, which I call unified spirit state, is formless; all people in heaven are formless units of one formless self that they all call God; all people in heaven see themselves as units of that unified self. In that state of eternal union, folks feel perfect peace and are happy.

CONCLUSION

Our world of separated beings living in space, time, and matter is an impossible world. It is impossible because despite what seems separation between people, our activities are coordinated as if done by a supercomputer. We affect each other; everything in the universe affects us and we affect them. None of us is really separated from other people and things in the universe although it seems like we are separated from other people and things.

Consider the human body. It seems separated from the sun and other stars. But if you understand physics and chemistry, you know that our bodies are composed of 64 elements, primarily carbon, hydrogen, oxygen, nitrogen, potassium, magnesium, iron, copper, zinc, sodium, phosphor, calcium, chlorine, etc. These elements are different arrangements of the atom.

The atom is composed of electrons, protons, and neutrons. Electrons, protons, and neutrons were formed from quarks and from light.

Everything in our bodies came from light. Our bodies literally are composed of the light we see coming from the sun and stars. If light does not reach planet earth (which it does in 9 minutes, traveling at 186, 282 miles a second), our bodies would not exist.

Our bodies are not separated from the sun and stars for they are of light that came from the stars (and from the Big Bang). We are literally part of everything in the universe for they are all made with light.

We are made of light. We are light that seems separated into different things we see on earth and the physical universe.

But where did physical light come from? Science says that it came from nowhere and nothing. We came from somewhere we do not understand.

We came from God and our present ego-based separated thinking does not understand God's formless unified self.

God and his sons share one self and have unified thinking; they think in concert, in tandem; we also do so on earth but do not know it.

What happens in our nightly dreams, our minds producing a seemingly real world, suggests that our day world is also a dream.

The dreamers are the sons of God who want to separate from their father, God, and from each other.

They cannot separate from God and from each other; they are always in God; while in him, they sleep and dream that they are separated from him.

The world of separation, space, time, and matter seems real but is not real and does not exist, although for now, we must accept that it seems to exist and study it with the scientific method.

I conclude by saying that since my mind produces my nightly dreams, and how it does it I do not know, that it also produces my day world (in concert with other minds), and how it does it I do not know, either.

Since my mind and your mind collectively produce our day world, we affect each other, for good or bad. Whereas, none of us is a victim since we dream of the world collectively; we ought to correct our mistakes and love each other if we want a peaceful dream world.

A Course in Miracles is teaching that the self we see people as, their bodies and personalities, aka egos, are their dream figures, false selves, not their real selves. Their real selves are the sons of God who are sleeping and dreaming that they are the ego selves they project into the dream. We must overlook their wrongs for those are done in dreams and love their real selves. Love the real selves, the Christ selves, and overlook their false ego selves.

In the meantime, people here on earth have physical needs; we must meet those needs unless we want them to die. Therefore, one must care for people's material needs regardless of the fact that the ego and bodies that need care are false.

I love the Christ in people and do whatever I can to meet their ego and material needs. There I stand on this subject.

SOME METAPHORS EXPLAINED

Our world being a dark world means that it does not have the knowledge of oneness in it; it has separated selves in it. Union is light, separation is darkness.

Black Africans were the original people on planet earth and the original separators from God hence dark people. The lighter complexioned people tend to have fewer egos, less wish for separation, and more wish for union, hence light, knowledge in them.

HEAVEN IS DREAMLESS.

This means that in heaven, there is no separation and all are unified; no one has room to spin fictions, lies; whatever is said is true, real, permanent, changeless, and eternal; our world is a dream because everything said and done in it is temporary and disappears with time, is a lie, a fiction, insane, delusion, and hallucination.

ALL MY LIFE, I HAVE LIVED IN FEAR TWENTY-FOUR-SEVEN; LIFE IS NOT WORTH THIS MUCH FEAR SO I AM NO LONGER GOING TO LIVE IN FEAR.

Fear protects my ego's wish to live in body and make sure that I take measures not to die in body and ego. If I have no wish for body and ego, fear would be useless to me.

I therefore give up the wish to be ego, live in body, and will not have fear. I have had enough of fear.

Anambra people seek money twenty-four seven; they must do so to be active and to obtain the means of making them seem important hence alive; ego must feel important to be alive; money and political power make ego seem alive. So, leave Anambra people to seek their money; they cannot stop doing so; if they stopped doing so, they would do other things to keep their egos seem alive,

HOW DOES A COURSE IN MIRACLES HELP PEOPLE ADAPT TO THEIR CURRENT WORLD? IT DOES NOT, ALTHOUGH IT GIVES THEM HOPE IN OTHER WORLDS AND GIVES THEM PEACE.

The current world is a dream, a mistake made by the sons of God. They are trying to adapt to an illusion, a delusion, and a hallucination, to a world of space, time, and matter and bodies and egos that are not there. *A Course in Miracles* through the Holy Spirit knows that the world that the sleeping sons of God are trying to adapt to is not there. He reinterprets their world and shows them a better version of it in Christ vision (dreaming with Christ, Christ dream, as opposed to ego vision, dreaming with the ego, our world) in dream of forgiveness, world of light forms. That world is still a dream but it is better than our ego dream; it is a happy dream; it is not our world.

In our world, we must defend our bodies and egos to survive. Everything we do on earth is effort to make our body, flesh, and ego survive.

Our government protects our egos and bodies until they die. Food, medications, clothes, and shelter all protect our bodies and egos.

A Course in Miracles does not want to defend our egos and bodies. It wants to eliminate fear, anger, depression, and paranoia (delusion that one is the ego-self).

The ego says that you cannot eliminate fear and anger and still be in body, that all you can do is manage your anger, fear, anxiety, self-concept, and self-image; that is, make your ego realistic to the exigencies of the world, but if you eliminate the ego and fear, etc., you leave this world.

To the ego then, *A Course in Miracles* is useless; it does not help one cope with the realities and exigencies of this world, so forget it.

A Course in Miracles provides a means to invalidate this world of ego and body, a means to leave this world; it invalidates all that people do to cope with their egos, bodies, and world, for it sees them as insane, adapting to what is not real.

If you identify with the Holy Spirit, Christ, and ignore the ego and its body, you die to ego and body alright and go to the world of light forms, gate of heaven. But the ego wants to live on earth.

I DID NOT WANT TO ADAPT TO THIS WORLD; I WANT TO RETAIN MY EGO.

My idealism did not want to adapt to the realities of this world; I wanted to escape into mere fantasy, idealistic conceptions, imaginations of how this world that gives me pain ought to be to stop giving me pain. I did not want to return to the world that gives me pain.

All work in this world gives me pain and fatigue so I wanted to leave all of them; throw the baby away with the birth water.

Spiritual idealism as presented by *A Course in Miracles* played into my desire to escape from this painful world. However, the course asks me to leave out my ego and not desire this world as a condition to attain the light world whereas my ego idealism retains my ego and wants to be grandiose ego; kind of like Dr. O who kept his ego and used it to imagine himself as God's representative in this world and if you disagree with him, his ego bares its ugly fangs and shows that it cannot love; he drops you from his mind and no longer knows that you even exist.

WHENEVER I DO A JOB IN OUR WORLD, MY EGO ESCAPES FROM IT INTO EGO IDEALISM.

When I was employed, including top-level jobs (executive director, professor), my mind was not satisfied with them and kept seeking, wishing magically for an idealistic work that does not deal with the exigencies of this world; I was looking for work that banishes the problems of this world with magic wands.

I was engaged in magical thinking and could not adapt to any work specification in this world, for all of them are defending the ego and its bodies and I wanted to escape to a nonphysical world.

I UNDERSTAND LEADERSHIP AND ORGANIZATION; SO, WHAT ARE MY GOALS AND ORGANIZATION FOR ATTAINING THEM?

I understand the nature of leadership and organizations employed in pursuing goals and visions. The problem is what goals and visions am I pursuing?

Am I seeking idealistic, spiritual goals, gnostic goals that are not adaptive to this world hence there are no takers, no people want them, and I have no market for them?

I have written on *A Course in Miracles* for over thirty years but no one has been converted to it for folks understand that it does not help them put food on their tables and ask them to leave this world which they do not want to do.

I write books on seeking idealistic goals and people do not want to buy those books because they are not relevant to their survival on earth.

What is the point of writing such books then? They are exercises in futility.

In my work life, despite writing on spirituality, I am a strict adherent to the scientific method. An idea must be observable, verifiable, and falsifiable for me to pay attention to it. In so far that I have a goal, it is to change society and redirect it to what I call scientific culture, and a world where we use the scientific method to decide what is approved behavior, not some primitive religion and such rubbish.

SCIENTIFIC CULTURE LEADS TO ADAPTING TO THE REALITIES OF THIS WORLD.

Scientific culture is what people do to adapt to their world. It is unscientific to pursue ego or spiritual idealism that takes people away from this world and they are not going to go with me, so they do not want me to lead them to fantasy; they want traditional religions that ask God to help them adapt to the needs of this world.

THE ONLY GOOD OF A COURSE IN MIRACLES AND GNOSTICISM IS THAT IT GIVES PEOPLE HOPE AND PEACE.

A Course in Miracles gives people hope in a world of light forms when they die, and in heaven; if those are not true, it merely gave people false hopes; it does give peace in the here and now for if one forgives, one tends to be less egoistic hence less fearful, angry, paranoid, and more in peace.

YOU CANNOT PRETEND ENTHUSIASM FOR WHAT DOES NOT SPEAK TO YOUR SOUL.

When you are doing a job that is in alignment with your interests and aptitude, you tend to be enthusiastic and passionate.

When I was studying psychology and during the first five years of working as a therapist, I was passionate about the field; when I understood it, understand psychopathology, and the fact that we cannot change anyone to become better, as I was motivated to do, my enthusiasm waned and I looked for something else to do.

A person must be doing what he is enthusiastic and passionate about to really feel alive. At some point, I was enthusiastic about *A Course in Miracles* until my natural agnosticism kicked in; I did not know whether it is true or not, so my enthusiasm was gone.

It did teach me one good lesson, though. If I let go of my desire for a grand ego, I will feel less fearful, anxious, and angry and will not identify with a false ego-self; I will live more in peace.

YOU PERCEIVE OTHER EGOS WITH YOUR OWN EGO.

You see other egos, other people with your ego; thus, you do not see them as they truly are but as your ego perception made them out to be; perception is never true for your perceptual lenses color what you see; what you think that you see is not the truth of what you see. You do not know what you see are!

YOU ALWAYS JUDGE WITH YOUR EGO AND THE EGO HAS LIMITED INFORMATION ON WHAT IT JUDGES.

You judge with your ego; the ego at any point in time has limited information on other people and things; therefore, you cannot judge accurately. Moreover, your judgment is biased by your ego's wishes, whatever they are.

So, do not judge. If you must judge, let your higher self—what *A Course in Miracles* made a person and called the Holy Spirit, the part of your mind that is rooted in God, the whole, that knows the truth of who all of us are, the sons of God, knows that we are sleeping and are dreaming and have taken different selves, separated ego selves in bodies in our dreams and in them do bad things to each other—let him who has information on the past, present, and future of what you judge be the one who judge for you.

The Holy Spirit judges with one criterion, that what it is judging is a dream self, ego, and dream activity that has not occurred and overlooks it, forgive it, and love the dreamer, the sons of God that do the dreaming. It asks us to see the purified self in the sleepers, the Christ selves, still in figures, but relatively loving selves, not the perfect loving selves of the sons of God in their awake self in formless heaven.

The Holy Spirit asks us to work with all egos, dream selves, to correct our dream evils, so as to dream good for each other and have a mutual happy dream before we wake up in our true state: formless, dreamless selves in God's formless unified spirit self, heaven.

SINCE I CANNOT CHANGE OTHER PEOPLE, ALL THAT I AM REQUIRED TO DO IS KNOW THEIR TRUTH, LIVE IT, MODEL IT, TEACH IT, AND LEAVE IT TO PEOPLE TO CHOOSE TO LIVE FROM THEIR TRUTH WHEN THEY ARE READY, WHICH MAY BE IN FUTURE LIFETIMES.

I cannot change other people no matter how I desire to do so. No son of God can dream for other sons of God; all of us chose to enter the dream and have specialized and personalized dreams. You cannot stop other people from having their dreams; they chose bodies and social experiences that enable them to dream as you see them dream, behave.

You cannot prevent people from behaving as you see them behave. All that you can do is understand yourself as an ego, a dream figure, understand that you have a different self, the Christ self in light form, and ultimately have formless self as the son of God who is perfect love.

You behave from your Christ self; that is, overlook what other egos, people, do to see their Christ selves and then work with them to improve their dream selves, egos, and behaviors but you cannot improve them for them.

My job is to talk about behavior from the Christ self, model it, write it, and leave it to other egos to decide when to emulate it or not.

So, what is my profession: what I have just done here, in this piece, I talked about our three levels of selves: ego-separated self, Christ-unifying self, and the formless unified son of God.

CHRISTIAN GNOSTICISM IS A SPIRITUAL SCIENCE ON HOW TO REMEMBER GOD.

Christian Gnosticism (which is Christological rendition of Hinduism and Buddhism) is a spiritual science that shows one how to remember one's true self as part of the whole, as the son of God who is currently dreaming and in his dream, see himself as the separated ego living in space, time, and body; it shows him what to do to remember his true self and awaken in his forgotten real self, son of God who is one with God.

Its lesson is this: you are not the ego-separated self; let go of the ego-separated self and see yourself as the Christ self, your ego now in light form; and, ultimately, let go of all forms and transcend the world of separation, space, and time and awaken in formless, unified son of God and his God.

God and his heaven cannot be expressed in human language for language and speech are designed for communication in our separated ego selves and do not apply to a place where we are one self with one mind.

THE LAWS OF PHYSICAL AND SPIRITUAL SCIENCE

We know that the physical world has its laws; science studies those physical laws; if you want to deal with nature, you have to understand its laws; if not, you can beg nature all you want and it will not hear and respond to you. If you understand medical science, you take good care of your body through it; if you understand the laws of agriculture, you use them to produce food for you but if not, you may pray all you like and die of hunger and starvation.

What we have not yet grasped is that spirit has its own laws that we must study in a dispassionate and objective manner, understand them, and apply them to make our lives more spiritually abundant; if we do not understand those laws, we can beg God all we want and we will live in poverty and die and spirit does not care. Africans, for example, have no clue how spirit works and remain egoistic while praying to what they call God, and of course, do not receive what they pray for and live in abject poverty and die from hunger.

We must, therefore, study spiritual science, understand its laws, and apply them to get the results we desire from spirit; if not, we are wasting our energy and time praying and worshiping God.

Spirit is infinite in numbers but is unified as one spirit. Each spirit is in all other spirits. Love is what holds all spirits together in their eternal union with each other; in union, they are eternal, permanent, and changeless.

To approach spirit, you must do so from love. Forgiveness of the world of separation, space, and time we live in must be done so that your thinking, mind, is not focused on separated selves, egos, if you want to reach the unified spirit.

You must jettison your ego-separated self before you reach the unified world of spirit, for separation and union are opposites and you cannot be in one and talk to the other. If you eliminate your ego-self and approach unified spirit from your higher self, the Holy Spirit, Christ, that knows union as love, you will get what you ask for even in the egos' world, including material abundance.

Hinduism, Buddhism, Taoism, and Gnosticism understand this spiritual law hence encourage people to meditate and in meditation, stop thinking from ego-separated mind and become empty of ego and stay egoless until their higher selves, aka the Holy Spirit, Krishna self, Buddha self, Christ self, becomes clear in their mind.

From Christ, that is, love-based thinking people can get whatever they want. In Christ mind, wish produces immediate results, including what folks call miracles that transcend the laws of nature.

If they give up all wish for separated self in forms, give up the desire for Christ, Buddha, and Krishna self, and extinguish all wishes to live as the opposite of union, they experience themselves as unified with God; in this experience, they know themselves as parts of God, as sons of God, but not the entirety of God.

In God, they create universes; and those who return to earth do whatever they want to do that is within the parameters of love.

We must, therefore, study spiritual science as a replacement of religion and the so-called religious science for those merely study religious rituals that seem to have effect.

The only book in the extant world that best portrays aspects of spiritual science is *A Course in Miracles*; however, it was written in poetic form and what it says is difficult to grasp.

It is my role to rewrite it in prose not poetry so that it is easily understood and thereafter accepted as part of spiritual science. Ultimately, when we operate from spiritual science, we shall produce the kind of results those following the scientific method have produced in the physical sciences.

WHO IS IT IN ME THAT DEFENDS THE BIG SELF? THE SON OF GOD?

Guided by Alfred Adler's individual psychology, I see my desire for a big ego as the compensatory product of my weak body. The big self is a kind of magic wand that I had hoped to use to banish my earthly problems; it is supposed to protect me. But in truth, it became a hindrance.

I had to be constantly defending the wished-for grand self. It does not defend itself. Its inventor defends it. Who is its inventor? My real self is the inventor of the big self.

I was always conscious of the big ego and asked how it would come across in society and if it seemed to not be doing well. Since I do not want it to do badly, I avoided society, people.

My social avoidant behavior is an attempt to defend an imaginary big self. Who is the self who assessed that it would do badly in society and avoided people to go maintain it? This means that there is another self besides the imaginary wished-for big self.

I do not need the big self regardless of whether it was caused by the son of God who went to sleep and dream it or it is the product of my weak body wishing a protector. I will not defend it anymore.

Ozodi Thomas Osuji, Ph.D.

I AM NOT INTERESTED IN MERE ABSTRACTIONS.

EXPLORING SPIRITUAL SCIENCE

I had an excellent undergraduate education. I enjoyed going to classes and reading. Life was pure joy. I sailed through undergraduate education and also picked up two master's degrees from the University of Oregon and then went to the University of California for my doctorate education. Here, I ran into problems.

The professors were totally living in the abstract world. What they said, I suppose, is what they call colleges' academia; their materials were not as relevant to this world as I know it to be.

Additionally, we were required to read academic journals and summarize what we read every week in our seminars (the graduate classes were seminars, that is, the professor sat with about five to ten students around a table and talked as peers on any subject with the professor acting as a facilitator but otherwise, the students were talking as if they are all professionals). The students were the best in the world; most of them came from Harvard, Yale, Oxford, and other topnotch schools; they attended so-called Ivy League schools for undergraduate to get the prestige thing out of the way and then come to the University of California to get real education.

Well, each week, all of us would summarize what we read in academic journals; additionally, each student was assigned a topic to read all there is to read on it and tell the seminar about it, and the students and professor questioned him and he responded as if he is a professor. He was evaluated on how well he did.

The articles in the academic journals drove me nuts; they were exercises in abstractions. They were not telling me anything relevant to the real world (in a seminar on Hegel's philosophy, in which I was required to read the man's phenomenology of mind and present it to the class, I felt like I was reading a psychotic and that I was also psychotic!).

I considered dropping out of graduate school but since I was considered a top-notch student, the professors discouraged that solution. Thus, I plowed through uninteresting graduate education.

My existence required me to seek practical solutions. I had a fierce urgency of now; I was motivated to solve problems, not theorize about them. I was looking for practical solutions not fantasy solutions and talking in a language that the man on the street would not understand a word we were speaking.

To make my studies a bit practical, I registered at the business school and took all the courses for the Master of Business Administration. Those were useful for they were training students to actually go out and manage business organizations and were not escaping from the real world. I got to know a lot about leadership and management (I have taught just about all business classes: finance, accounting, marketing, human resources, contracts, labor, customer care, entrepreneur; I did that teaching at a small college close to me while teaching at my regular college).

I understand leadership. But am I a leader? Leaders have goals and visions that they are passionate about and want to actualize. What goal am I trying to actualize other than write books and articles on leadership? Now, I understand the urban legend that those who cannot do teach. I cannot do and teach.

I like science. The insistence on the scientific method by Francis Bacon in England disposed English men to approach the universe from pure observation, empiricism, and not fly into mere speculations. Test out what you see to make sure it is true. The emphasis on observation, experimentation, verification, and falsification has made little England the world's leader in science and technology.

Lately, I have been engrossed in spirituality. I actually believe that there are other worlds besides our world. But how do I use the scientific method to prove their existence?

There must be a spiritual science that employed the scientific method to demonstrate life after death and existence of God.

Professor Helen Schucman of Columbia University actually believed that her book, *A Course in Miracles* is spiritual psychology and since psychology is a science, that she was positing a science of spirituality; she designed the book as a course to be read and taught as if it is a college course, worked on, and the result is one having spiritual experiences. She has a point.

She wrote in lovely poetic language, was convoluted and hifalutin, and took many pages to say what could be said in a few pages. Her 1,200 pages book could have been written in about five hundred pages of simple prose.

FEAR AND GUILT

This morning, I woke up at 6 AM and was overwhelmed by guilt feeling. The guilt emanated from the fact that I believe that I have not accomplished much with my life. I asked how a guy with the type of education I had have not accomplished much in his life. I felt like a failure in life and began feeling like my life was wasted. I felt enormous guilt.

Thereafter, I realized what Sister Helen Schucman said about guilt. She said that the ego wants the son of God to feel fear and guilt—fear from his belief that he separated from God.

To separate is to attack. We feel like we attacked God's unified world and fragmented it. We fear that God would retaliate against us for destroying his unified world.

We feel guilty because of what we did, destroy the unified world of God in which we felt peaceful and happy, and in its place, invented a divided world where we feel pain and suffering. Each of us is filled with fear and guilt.

She said that we could not separate from God for no power in the universe can separate from God or destroy his unified world, that we are right now in God and while in him, sleep and dream that we live in a separated world of egos, space, time, and matter. We have not separated from God and from each other.

Our world is dream; a dream is not real. God knows that his sons are dreaming and have not destroyed his unified world; he left us to dream but gave us the Holy Spirit to show us how to make our dreams happy dreams until we are ready to awaken to our unified state.

To awaken from the dream of separation is to become aware that we never left heaven and God for a second. Since we are not separated from God, we should not feel fear or guilt for we are still as God created us, one with him; we are ideas in the mind of God; ideas leave not their source. In the state of union with God, we are innocent, guiltless, sinless, holy, and perfect.

To know that we remain perfect, we have to tune out the world of separation, jettison all wishes for separated self, remove our egos, and have egoless empty minds; we must not think with the ego. If we do so, the book says that first, we shall be shown the new world that the Holy Spirit has remade from our dark dreams.

Whatever is good on earth, whatever loving thoughts we have on earth, are translated to a New Jerusalem, a new world, the world of light forms, a beautiful world.

To see that new world, we have to ignore our ego world of attack and defense. We have to forgive each other our attacks for they were done in dreams and have not been done.

I do meditate and have actually experienced the world of light forms. The world of light forms is still a dream, a fiction, still a delusion and hallucination. It is not our home.

Our home is not in forms; it is in God. God and his home in heaven are formless. If you are in the world of forms, our dark forms, or the improved light forms world, you are dreaming. Give up our ego-driven dreaming or the Holy Spirit driven-dreaming and awaken in formless and dreamless God.

So, I got up this morning feeling guilty. I immediately realized that I was in ego state, that the ego wants me to feel guilty like I wasted my life. I refused to give in to that feeling and instead, asked the ego what good it does for me other than give me guilt, fear, and identification with a false grandiose self that I have to defend to make it seem real.

I simply renounced allegiance to the ego and went back to bed. The moment I went to sleep, my mind went from one dream to another. I must have had ten dreams in a space of two hours. After each dream, I woke up and think about it for a few minutes, went back to sleep, and had another dream.

I must say that before I went to sleep last night, around 11:30 PM, I was listening to an audiotape of *A Course in Miracles*; was it probably responsible for the marathon dreams that I had?

Here is one of the dreams:

In this dream, I was in a church, sitting on the third row of pews from the altar. Somebody came along, from the back end of the pews, to make sure that we all practiced social distancing and wore our face masks. The two people sitting close to me left the row and went to sit in the first and second row, thus leaving me the only person on the third row. The law enforcer walked past us. I was then in a farmer's field. I decided to go get some bread and make toast. I went and got bread. I left the bread on a table and went looking for something else. A young white lady came along and made toasts for herself and walked away with her toasts. I saw her walking away and wondered why she did not make some toasts for me given that I got the bread. I thought that she was selfish and began feeling angry at her and woke up.

I immediately realized the lesson of the dream. It is me who attributed the intention of selfishness to the woman and reacted to her as if, in fact, she is selfish. How do I know that she is selfish? Am I a mind reader to know what she is thinking or her intentions?

In our world, it is me who attribute ill intentions to people and react to them as if what I think that they did is in fact what they did.

Attribution of negative motives to people and reacting to them as if they were in fact trying to do bad things to one is part of the paranoid thinking syndrome.

I told me that my attribution of ill motive to the woman in the dream is paranoid thinking and that I should desist from attributing motives, good or bad, to people and simply accept that I do not know why people did what they did.

I reached that interpretation of the dream, went right back to sleep, and had other dreams.

When finally I got up at 9 AM, I began wondering whether our day world is like our nightly dream world. In my dream, obviously, it is me who projects to all the dream figures what they do. I am the one doing what the persons in my dream do. I think through all the dream persons in my dream.

Could it also be the case, as *A Course in Miracles* said, that I think and behave through all the people in my day world? Could all the people in my world be merely enacting my thoughts? Could the world be an external mirror of my thinking?

I am very poor at mathematics. In some of my dreams, I am teaching students calculus. I wake up, go get a calculus textbook, and see that what I was teaching the students is actual calculus. In other words, there is a part of me that understands mathematics but not the part that I see as me during my day life.

Could it be that one me projects out all the people doing what I see them do during the day world? Could it be that there is a part of me, the son of God in me, that know it all and operate through all the people I see in my world but choose to limit myself to doing a few things? I don't know.

These sorts of things need to be explored. We must stop sweeping lessons from dreams under the rug and study them to find out whether there is a spiritual part of us that does all the things we see done in our world. This is why we need schools where spiritual science is studied.

Perhaps, I should start a school where spiritual science is studied. Why not? I have a good command of scientific psychology, physics, Hinduism, Buddhism, and Gnosticism, so why not apply them to the study of spirituality?

Maybe my destiny is to study spiritual science. Maybe that was why I was a dilettante, going from one subject to another, to know a lot about our world and synthesize my encyclopedic knowledge in a new discipline.

CRUCIFIXION AND ANGER

According to *A Course in Miracles*, I crucified myself by separating from God and his other sons and now seeing myself living in body, space, and time, suffering. (See ACIM chapter 6; the observations in this writeup are based on that chapter but might as well be from the whole book, for each chapter essentially makes the same point, albeit differently).

To separate from God and his other sons, I had to attack them to push them away from me. Other sons of God, to separate from God, had to also attack God and other sons of God. In effect, the sons of God attacked God and each other. They separated from reality and are now living in the world of dreams, in illusions.

In the world of dreams, I see other people attacking me, doing bad things to me. I forget that I also attack other sons of God and attack me through them in my effort to separate from them, the whole.

I see racist white folks discriminating against me, that is, attacking me. What happened here is that I attacked God, attacked me, attacked other sons of God, deny my attack on them, and say that only they attacked me, did bad things to me, discriminated against me, and enslaved me. I project my self-attack to them and now see them attack me.

Seeing other people attack me, do bad things to me, I feel angry at them; I call them racist and fight with them. I justify my anger and attack them.

To be in the egos' world is to see other people attack one and one feels angry at them; one forgets that one attacked them and God; in attacking God and his sons, one also attacked one for we are all one. One denies that one attacked one but see only others attack on one and do not see one's attacks on other people and on oneself. One accuses other people of hurting one and forget that it is one who initiated self-hurt by separating from God.

One wants to seem separated from God and other people. God is union; one wants to live as the opposite of union, separated existence. One wants to shatter God's unified, formless spirit world and replace it with one's world of space, time, and matter. One houses oneself in matter, body, and that makes it seem real that one is separated from God and all people.

Thereafter, one feels like one attacked God and other people and feel like they would retaliate and attack one and one lives in fear.

One feels guilty for separating from God. One feels like God would punish one for separating from him. One denies one's guilt and projects it to other people. Since one expects God to attack and punish one for shattering his unified world, one says that it is not one who separated from God but other people and ask God to punish them. Without waiting for God to punish other people, the alleged guilty one tries to punish them on behalf of God by attacking them. Attack on other people is a futile effort to give one's guilt away, give it to other people to prevent God from punishing one.

Yet one retains the source of guilt, desiring separation. The only way to avoid fear and guilt feeling is to know that one did not separate from God.

When we went to sleep and in our sleep seemed separated from God, God created the Holy Spirit and placed him in our minds, our thinking to help convince us that separation is impossible, that we remain as he created us, unified with him and with each other; we are therefore not guilty; we remain innocent and perfect despite whatever we do in the dream of separation, for the dream, separation has not occurred.

The Holy Spirit interprets what is going on in our dream world from many angles. First, he knows that we have not separated from God hence no one has attacked God, other people, and himself. We remain as God created us, unified with God, and all of us hence are always guiltless, innocent, holy, and perfect.

However, in the dream, we see our mutual attacks; that to us means that we have separated from God and each other (which is what we desire; we want to make separation real.)

In the dream, we see other people attacking us and feel angry at them. The Holy Spirit provides another interpretation of these perceived attacks on us.

Other people's attacks on me are done in a dream and what is done in a dream has not been done so they have not attacked me and I have not attacked me and God for I did not separate from God.

I and people remain innocent and perfect. The Holy Spirit urges me to overlook the dream, overlook the attack I see come my way, to forgive the seeming attackers, and in doing so, know that they are innocent and perfect, that I am innocent and perfect. This changed interpretation of the dream gives all of us peace.

But this is not how my ego wants to see it; it wants to see the attack as real. If the attack and separation are real, then I have attacked God and my brothers and fear their retaliation. I live in fear of God's punishment and other people's attacks on me. I feel guilty for attacking and destroying God's unified world. The ego wants me to feel fearful and guilty for my supposed sins.

Fear and guilt feeling is a clever device to make separation and attack seem real in my mind hence justify my anger at perceived attackers, at me, and attack them.

The ego sees what we do on earth as real. It says that slavery was real, discrimination is real, and asks us to feel angry at perceived abusers and to counter-abuse them. We do so and live at war with each other.

We give ourselves physical sickness to punish us in lieu of God punishing us for our sin and guilt from separation.

The Holy Spirit, in effect, tells us that to live in ego and body is to crucify ourselves collectively and individually, to live in pain and sickness, and to justify anger at those we think crucified us, other people, and anger at God for not rescuing us.

The Holy Spirit knows that we could not separate from God, that we dream separation; even that is impossible, so we have not even dreamed separation; the physical universe that seems real to us is a fiction that we want to seem real but is not real.

The universe of space, time, and matter and our bodies do not exist. Nobody has harmed us. The white man who discriminated against me by denying me jobs has not done so; the Holy Spirit tells me to overlook my ego's interpretation of him as hurting me and instead, see him as God sees him, innocent, guiltless, and perfect.

In this light, I must see Donald Trump, despite his seeming racist dance, as perfect and love him. In doing so, my ego tells me that I am doing him a favor but the Holy Spirit says that I am actually doing him and me a favor, for what I see him do I projected to him.

I am the one who seems to have attacked me through Trump. In forgiving him, I forgive myself my own sense of guilt for attacking him and me.

Forgiveness of the other person is a condition for self-forgiveness. When I forgive the other, I forgive me. In forging us, I see us in a changed form, as Christ, in purified form, in light form.

The purified son of God in light form is still a fiction but it is better than seeing him in body. Any perception at all is false for perception is false.

We are always as God created us, formless parts of God. If we see ourselves as in body of matter or light form, we have separated from how God created us. Since we are in the perpetual universe, then change your perception and see other people as perfect to see you as perfect and in doing so, have happy dream and thereafter, give up perception and know that the physical world does not exist, know you to be always in God as part of his formless unified self.

When I give up desiring form, matter or light, transcend perception, I awaken in formless unified spirit self and stop crucifying myself and projecting what I did to me, self-crucifixion to others and making them seem to have crucified me; there is no one crucifying anyone.

Those seeming racist who denied me jobs in their racist world actually did me a favor; through the Holy Spirit in them and me, I was redirected to stop seeking work in the egos' world, stop seeking self-crucifixion, and go do work that awakens me, first changing my perception from ego to Christ and then rising above perception to knowledge of our oneness.

In effect, the racist who discriminated against me is my savior for he redirected me to salvation, to go doing what awakens me from ego. I should, therefore, be grateful to him.

But since he did not discriminate against me, there is no need to forgive him or forgive me or be grateful to him; I just wake up and laugh at the elaborate ego game I and my brothers enacted to seem separated from God and our real selves.

CAN WE SEE WITHOUT THE PAST? NO. BUT WE CAN SEE WITH A FORGIVEN PAST.

We see with our past learning. Our past colors what we see in the present. Light takes pictures of objects and sends them to our eyes and our eyes send them to our brains where the objects are interpreted in light of our past learning. It takes our brains time, albeit brief, to do that interpretation, hence it shows us the past of the object it is interpreting.

Thus, even when we see something right now, we saw it as it was in the past (maybe a second ago but not as it is now). Simply stated, we do not see things in their present state but in their past state. Because we see only the past of things and see with our own past learnings, we cannot see the present; we are hopelessly confused as to what we are seeing.

The Holy Spirit who lives in the eternal present of God and also knows that we see things in the past takes our past and purifies it by forgiving it. If we forgive what other people did to wrong us in the past, do not have grievances, vengeance, and revenge, we tend to see people differently.

Forgiveness purifies our seeing and makes us see people better, closer to their present but not their present, for all perception, ego or Holy Spirit, is done with the past.

The difference between ego perception and Holy Spirit perception is that Holy Spirit perception purifies the past, forgives it.

Without the past at all, we cannot see. Without the past in our world, there is no present and future. That is the nature of our world's perception.

We see what is not there in the present.

Without perception, we shall see nothing at all. Without perception, we return to the state of knowing, which is only possible in God's unified state where things are not divided into parts and placed in space, time, and matter to be seen. In God, there is no perception but only knowing.

FORGIVENESS AND HOLY INSTANT

At any moment, one can decide not to see anything with the past; the result is that one cannot see at all. One is now in a state of no perception.

If in addition one had forgiven the past, forgiven those who wronged one, hence forgiven oneself, one experiences the present as it is, that is, as it is in unified state, aka heaven. This is called the Holy Instant, an instant in which we do not have perception, do not see with egos eyes or Holy spirit's eyes; here, we do not bring our past to color, to distort the present; but know things as they are in heaven, unified spirit, oneness, an experience of total knowing and knowledge of peace, joy, and the fact that we are at the spirit level—eternal, permanent, and changeless.

In the Holy Instant (what Hinduism calls Samadhi and Buddhism calls Nirvana, God-realization), one experiences the eternal formless union of all beings as one being and knows that God and his sons are real.

Experience of Holy Instant gives one conviction that God is real. It is not experienced from ego mentation but when the ego is completely tuned out and one stops trying to understand things through the ego.

You cannot understand anything with the ego. This is because there is nothing to understand and there is no ego. If you know that there is nothing to understand, no material universe of space, time, and matter to see and understand, and no you as separated ego-self to understand, then you experience the real you, the son of God who is one with God and all beings in the Holy Instant.

In the Holy Instant, you return to knowledge, and transcend perception. In the Holy Instant, the egos' dreams are overlooked to know God's eternal present, now.

In God, there is no past, present, and future as is the case in our egos' world.

THE STORY OF THE PRODIGAL SON REINTERPRETED

It is funny how one goes about one's life thinking that one understands things until suddenly, one realizes that one has understood nothing. I had assumed that I understood the story of the prodigal son until last night when I realized that I had not understood it.

In the past, I imagined the story in two ways. One, literally, a son who left his father, made mistakes, recognized his mistakes, came back, and was forgiven. Thereafter, I imagined that the story means our leaving a literal God and coming to earth and while on earth, realize our mistake in separating from our father and return to him.

Last night, I recognized that the story merely symbolizes our states of mind; the story is not taking place outside our thinking, minds; it symbolizes our thinking at any point in time.

At the moment, we think that we are apart from God. Here, the prodigal son, us, has left his father, and brothers; he has left his real self, unified spirit self.

Then, we think that we made mistakes, ask for forgiveness, and begin returning to God. Thereafter, we think that God has forgiven us and welcomed us back in heaven.

Put differently, we live in ego-separated state, we forgive the ego and its separation, and return to union, which is light; we forgive those who harmed us; forgiveness is purified thinking and finally, we think holistically, return to God, and experience God, holiness.

That is to say that the prodigal son did not go away from his father, God, for there is nowhere he goes that God is not there already. It is a going and coming in God, a pattern of thinking; not thinking from one's real unified self, and return to thinking from one's unified self, hence have peace and joy.

GOD EXISTS BUT HE IS NOT OUTSIDE US.

The ego likes debating whether God exists or not. We thinkers, I am a thinker, a philosopher, like to use all kinds of arguments to prove or disprove the existence of God. All those arguments eventually fail.

The only way to know that God exists is to shut down the ego and not think from ego categories at all for ego means divided self. You cannot know God by thinking with a divided mind. You stop thinking altogether, shut up your ego, and stay quiet.

In the stillness of your mind, you experience oneness and know that God is all that exists. God is not outside us; he is inside us and is us.

God is at the center of our being; we are his parts. You do not go outside you to find who you are; you go inside you, that is, you stop searching outside you and keep quiet and the real you, son of God that is always part of God, dawns on your awareness. But as long as you are looking for God all over the place, you will not find him.

UNIFIED SPIRIT, LIGHT, MATTER, OUR BODIES

There is unified spirit, aka God; we are parts of it, sons of God. We wished for separation and specialness. We used our God thinking, mind, to project out physical light.

We used that physical light to form electrons, quarks, neutrons, protons; and combined those to form atoms and matter, space, and time.

In time, we formed our bodies and now seem to be living inside bodies.

Physical light, matter, space, and time do not exist; we do not live in bodies. We have not lived in bodies for a second.

We have not separated from God for that is impossible. Separation, the universe of space, time, and matter, are mere dreams in our sleeping minds. But we believe them to be real and defend them and what we defend seems real to us, thus they seem real to us.

MATERIALIZATION AND DEMATERIALIZATION

If we take away belief in our bodies, we can dematerialize and return to the awareness of ourselves as light forms and ultimately become aware that we are formless spirit who is part of a larger spirit called God.

These things are done by folks who have understood reality but to those in egos, they seem magical. Jesus Christ would materialize where his apostles are and thereafter leave them and is in a different dimension, the world of light forms and sometimes, in formless God. He would then return back to them in form.

These behaviors are done by God-realized persons. Babaji in India did it (see the autobiography of a Yogi).

WAS THERE AN ACTUAL JESUS CHRIST?

If this world is a dream in the minds of the sleeping sons of God, the question is this: was there an actual Jesus?

There was no actual Jesus. But in our dreams of separation, there was a dream figure that folks called Jesus. That dream figure did what folks wrote in the four gospels that he did. He was not an actual person but a son of God that entered our dreams as the Jesus character.

Therefore, folks must stop looking for his bones in Israel for he was not buried there. He simply used his God mind to dematerialize his body to light form and then to formless son of God where he is in God.

The story of Jesus is meant to illustrate the son of God who left his father, is crucified; we are crucified when we live in ego and body, who resurrected; we are resurrected, born again a second time as the son of

God, the second coming of Christ into our lives; this occurs when we are aware of our sonship when we know ourselves as the Christ and who awoke in his sonship in God.

The story symbolizes separation from the whole mind and return to the whole mind, return to God, our real self.

We have states of mind. In God or eternity, we are unified mind; thereafter, we wished separated mind, separated thinking, and that placed us in a dream, on earth, a world of space, time, and matter. Here, we are crucified, for to live as an ego in body is to flee from one's real self, live in pain, and suffer.

A person who denies his real self, son of God, and lives as a false ego-self is self-crucified. We resurrect from our self-crucifixion and know ourselves as Christ, unified sons of God.

In so far that we still want to see ourselves in form, we see ourselves in purified body, bodies of light, for we no longer have evil thoughts; we no longer harm other people and no longer harm ourselves; we only have loving thoughts and that makes our bodies light forms.

We are now enlightened. We are now the points of light in the egos' dream of darkness, dream of separation, dream of real self-forgetfulness; we have remembered our real selves and are now teaching others who have forgotten their real selves who they are; metaphorically, we now bring light to the dream of darkness.

That is, we bring knowledge of our true selves to those who have forgotten their real selves as I did in this piece. I am a bringer of light to a world in darkness.

I CANNOT ANALYZE ANYTHING BECAUSE THERE IS NOTHING TO ANALYZE.

All my life I strove to understand my personality and body and other people's personalities and bodies. Then, I realized that no matter how much I tried, I have not understood myself and other people.

Did Sigmund Freud, Alfred Adler, and Carl Jung understand other people? They did not even understand themselves so how could they have understood other people? Thus, I give up trying to understand me and people.

It occurred to me that the me and people I am trying to understand are their egos and bodies. Egos and bodies do not exist. Moreover, I am using my ego that does not exist to try to understand other egos that do not understand. This is madness. The ego is madness, literally!

I cannot analyze people and things because there is nothing to analyze. There is nothing to understand for the things I see do not exist; perception is an illusion. We can know.

To know people, we have to quit trying to understand their egos and bodies. We have to stay quiet with no ego categories in our minds. The Holy Spirit would show us people as Christ, that is, purified egos, loving selves in light forms, and thereafter, heaven opens its gate and we know all people as sons of God, who are unified with God.

True knowledge is gained when we quit trying to understand the world with our egos.

THE EGO AND BODY ARE ONE; BOTH ARE ILLUSIONS AND GO TOGETHER; IF YOU LET ONE GO, THE OTHER GOES.

There is a spirit self-called the son of God. Spirit self thinking has a mind. It thinks in a unified manner in unified self for it is part of all other spirits.

The son of God wants to think independently and can only do so in the illusion of space, time, and matter. So, it went to sleep and in its dream, evolved space, time, and matter, entered body, and used body to make thinking separately possible.

Body and ego thinking go hand in hand. When you give up one, you give up the other for they are both illusions. If you stop identifying with body, you stop identifying with ego. Give up ego and you give up body and return to the awareness of unified thinking outside body.

If you let go of ego and body, you can rematerialize in any kind of body, especially light body; you need to do the work you want to do and return to formless unified self.

THE SELF-CONCEPT AND THE SELF-IMAGE ARE ROOTED IN BODY AND SOCIAL EXPERIENCE.

The self-concept and the self-image are formed in childhood; it is influenced by one's inherited body and social experience. It is designed to help one cope with life in body and society, space and time. But instead of helping one, one now spends most of one's energy and time defending it; the helper is now helped so it is useless.

One uses its false illusory self and its standards to evaluate one's actual body performance and make life miserable for one, trying to meet its impossible illusory perfect standard. One is neurotic or psychotic. The mad man is trying to become what is impossible to become perfect ego and body.

One must let it go of the self-concept for it shield one from having another knowledge, makes one behave inflexibly trying being it. Since it is formed from body and social experience, when the self-concept and self-image are let go, one now thinks and behaves from light self or from formless unified self.

IF YOU DO NOT USE YOUR PAST TO JUDGE ANYTHING, YOU ARE SAYING THAT YOUR PAST AND THE WORLD IS A DREAM AND DO NOT MATTER; YOU ARE NEGATING THE WORLD. YOU MUST NEGATE THE EGOS' WORLD TO EXPERIENCE THE WORLD OF GOD; A COURSE IN MIRACLES NEGATES OUR WORLD AND ITS HISTORY TO GIVE US PEACE FOR THE WORLD IS NOT WORTH A DIME.

A Course in Miracles teaches that the past does not exist and to the extent that it existed, it was a mistake, seeing with the ego; the world must be overlooked, forgiven, and not used to judge the present for it colors the present and distorts it.

You must overlook the past to experience the eternal now of God, Holy Instant; this negation of the world actually is good for the world; people included are not worth a penny. The world is shit, literally.

IF YOUR BOOK HAS NOT BENEFITED YOU, HOW CAN IT BENEFIT OTHER PEOPLE?

You write a book and want to publish it. Has it benefited you? How? If it is useful to you, then it will be useful to other people and they would logically shell out $30 to buy it. But if the book is no good to you, has not helped you one bit, how can it help other people and why should they buy it?

This is simple logical question. Does the book *Connected Lives* help me, help me negate the world, and do people want to negate their world?

It has one utility: it enables people not to take the world seriously, for the world is an illusion, so it gives people peace.

WHILE I WAS IN SURGERY, I HAD NO DREAMS OR AWARENESS OF BEING ALIVE.

In surgery, even though I was under general anesthesia, I still had the wish for living in ego and body. If I had given up the wish to live in ego and body, I would have died. Because I still had the wish for living as ego and body, I could not escape from this world and see the world of light forms or go to formless unified spirit.

To experience those, you must give up the wish to be on earth altogether. In an accident, although ultimately it is one's choice and one was almost killed, one is in near death, one could have escaped from one's body and experience near-death experience, leave one's body, and see the world of light forms. To experience formless heaven, you have to give up the desire to live in ego and body altogether.

EXISTENTIALISM, LIKE A COURSE IN MIRACLES, TEACHES THAT THIS WORLD IS MEANINGLESS AND GIVES SOLACE IN WORK BUT NOT HEAVEN. A COURSE IN MIRACLES GIVES SOLACE IN LIFE AFTER DEATH.

Existentialism reached the conclusion that this world is pointless, purposeless, and meaningless. It seeks solace in discovering what line of work that one enjoys doing and escaping into it but otherwise, is atheistic.

A Course in Miracles sees a meaningless world, an illusion, and a dream world but provides meaning in negating this world and escaping into unified spirit. Whether what it offers is true or not remains to be demonstrated. It is Gnostic; it believes that through its path, we can reach God. It is not godless atheism like Existentialism.

PERSONALITY, PERSONA, IS MASK OVER THE FORMLESS SPIRIT SELF.

The term personality is derived from Latin, persona, that is, mask. The idea is that each of us has a persona, a mask he wears over his real self, a mask he must wear to operate in society. So, who is behind the mask of personality?

From our birth, we learn our people's culture, its ways of how to operate within its parameters. As adults, our minds have an overlay of culture which society gave to us in childhood; with culture and our inherited bodies, we form our personalities.

Body and culture determine personality, aka ego; both body and culture are passing illusions; they are here today, are changed tomorrow, and gone tomorrow when we die (our cultures do die; African cultures are in the process of dying; in two hundred years, what is today called African cultures would all be dead; they would be replaced with new cultures, those that synthesizes African, European, American, Arab, and Chinese cultures).

This being the case, therefore, you should be mindful that you are fighting a losing battle when you fight to protect your culture, protect an illusion that will disappear into the mist of time in the future.

In fact, most extant African languages will be out of existence in five hundred years. Thousands of languages have in the past died; your language is not an exception to the impermanency of human existence.

The thing to do is to find out who is behind one's personality, one's persona, behind the necessary mask, body, and culture we have.

Behind the mask of personality, ego is the eternal self, the son of God, unified spirit.

YOU MUST AFFIRM: I AM NOT MY EGO, BODY, AND PERSONALITY; I AM SPIRIT.

You must say: I am not my body, culture, and separated ego-self. I should not be conscious of those for they are ephemeral. I am a spirit that I may not know. Spirit is eternal and does not defend itself; it is the transitory that defends itself; that is, defends body, ego, and personality.

Overlook your ego, body, and personality and try to experience your real self, which is formless spirit. This is really all that *A Course in Miracles* is teaching: overlook ego, body, and the world and find out who you are; you cannot find it out as long as you are attached to ego and body and defend it.

This is also what Hinduism, Buddhism, and Gnosticism are teaching. These three great religions cannot all be wrong.

LAWYERS ARE MOSTLY SOCIOPATHS; THEY ARE LIARS; THESE SOCIOPATHS RULE AMERICA AND THE WORLD.

Today, in the morning, I got up, went to the living room, and turned on the TV and Bill Barr, the US Attorney General, was answering questions before the House Judiciary Committee. I could see that all he was saying were lies, deftly protecting Trump. He is a practiced liar. Now, I know why I could not be a lawyer. I cannot live by telling lies. Life is not worth that to me.

While at graduate school and finding my field of studies not my calling, I registered at a Law school. I tried going to law school and my mind could not take what they were teaching there. They teach people how to operate according to the artificial social constructs called law, rules that maintain an artificial construct called ego society; none of which has anything to do with truth, justice, and right or wrong, but with how society plays the game of crime and punishment and sharing the wealth of the land.

My mind wanted to transcend that game and seek the truth. My mind was seeking ideals; initially, it found some solace in teaching social sciences and business studies; my mind still could not resign itself to the extant world.

The rulers of the world are at home in the world of darkness; they are happy egos and bodies; that is where they are at in evolution, space, and time.

People like me seek spirituality and if spirit does not exist, they are losers.

I am now somewhat retired from formal academia. I establish centers for spiritual science; here, I study spiritual science; spirituality is studied with the scientific method.

However, to attain awareness of God and one's real self as a part of God, as the son of God, one must transcend the scientific method, ego, matter, space, and time, for those were designed to study matter and energy (both illusions).